Huber and Headrick's

HANDWRITING IDENTIFICATION

Facts and Fundamentals

AF832798

Huber and Headrick's

HANDWRITING IDENTIFICATION

Facts and Fundamentals

Heidi H. Harralson • Larry S. Miller

CRC Press
Taylor & Francis Group
Boca Raton London New York

CRC Press is an imprint of the
Taylor & Francis Group, an **informa** business

CRC Press
Taylor & Francis Group
6000 Broken Sound Parkway NW, Suite 300
Boca Raton, FL 33487-2742

First issued in paperback 2020

© 2018 by Taylor & Francis Group, LLC
CRC Press is an imprint of Taylor & Francis Group, an Informa business

No claim to original U.S. Government works

ISBN-13: 978-1-4987-5130-8 (hbk)
ISBN-13: 978-0-367-77825-5 (pbk)

This book contains information obtained from authentic and highly regarded sources. Reasonable efforts have been made to publish reliable data and information, but the author and publisher cannot assume responsibility for the validity of all materials or the consequences of their use. The authors and publishers have attempted to trace the copyright holders of all material reproduced in this publication and apologize to copyright holders if permission to publish in this form has not been obtained. If any copyright material has not been acknowledged please write and let us know so we may rectify in any future reprint.

Except as permitted under U.S. Copyright Law, no part of this book may be reprinted, reproduced, transmitted, or utilized in any form by any electronic, mechanical, or other means, now known or hereafter invented, including photocopying, microfilming, and recording, or in any information storage or retrieval system, without written permission from the publishers.

For permission to photocopy or use material electronically from this work, please access www.copyright.com (http://www.copyright.com/) or contact the Copyright Clearance Center, Inc. (CCC), 222 Rosewood Drive, Danvers, MA 01923, 978-750-8400. CCC is a not-for-profit organization that provides licenses and registration for a variety of users. For organizations that have been granted a photocopy license by the CCC, a separate system of payment has been arranged.

Trademark Notice: Product or corporate names may be trademarks or registered trademarks, and are used only for identification and explanation without intent to infringe.

Library of Congress Cataloging-in-Publication Data

Names: Harralson, Heidi H., author. | Miller, Larry, 1953 August 26- author.
Title: Huber and Headrick's handwriting identification : facts and
fundamentals / by Heidi H. Harralson and Larry S. Miller.
Other titles: Handwriting identification
Description: Second edition. | Boca Raton : CRC Press, [2018] | Includes
bibliographical references and index.
Identifiers: LCCN 2017020188| ISBN 9781498751308 (hardback : alk. paper) |
ISBN 9781315152462 (ebook)
Subjects: LCSH: Writing--Identification. | Graphology. | Forensic sciences.
Classification: LCC HV8074 .H77 2018 | DDC 363.25/65--dc23
LC record available at https://lccn.loc.gov/2017020188

Visit the Taylor & Francis Web site at
http://www.taylorandfrancis.com

and the CRC Press Web site at
http://www.crcpress.com

To a notable researcher, forensic pioneer,
esteemed colleague, and friend …

Dr. Bryan Found
1962–2016

Contents

Preface

In 1999, Tom Headrick wrote in his Foreword to *Handwriting Identification: Facts and Fundamentals* "may I be so presumptuous as to describe this contribution as the Foreword to the First Edition of a progeny that will be followed by many succeeding and constantly improving revisions." This is probably the wish of any author of an academic textbook who knows that their scientific field is constantly shifting and evolving. Unfortunately, Roy Huber and Tom Headrick did not revise their seminal work—a work that has been extensively relied upon by the scientific document examination community for nearly 20 years. No other book has surpassed Huber and Headrick's text with its thorough and investigative assessment of handwriting identification. This book was published during a transitional time period in the scientific development of handwriting identification, which saw a critical review and assessment of the field and resulted in court rulings that placed limits on the "science" of handwriting identification. Even as working professional document examiners, Huber and Headrick were nonetheless courageous in their efforts to investigate and question the science behind handwriting identification principles.

Some of the changes in this new edition include some practical revisions. As we incorporated new material and revised Huber and Headrick's text, we realized that we could not maintain their first person stance as it would inevitably cause the reader to wonder who the "we" referred to and would be potentially misleading as to original authorship.

We have maintained a substantial portion of the original text written by Huber and Headrick and were especially cautious in ensuring that many of their original references were maintained. Although many of the references are dated and more recent research has since been published in peer-reviewed journals, we thought it was important to maintain the older references even from meetings and other less formal sources as it provides source material on which handwriting principles are based and, probably more importantly, Huber and Headrick gathered into one source, rare and difficult to find sources that are not readily available in other books. While many of the references refer to proceedings and lectures, they still provide important background showing the development of handwriting identification science through the years. We have supplemented these sources, where relevant, with recent published studies in the handwriting sciences. We have focused on materials that are published in widely known, peer-reviewed publications such as the *Journal of Forensic Sciences*, *Forensic Science International*, and *Science and Justice*. To a lesser extent, we have also referenced materials from the journals or publications from professional organizations such as the *American Society of Questioned Document Examiners*, *Association of Forensic Document Examiners*, *National Association of Document Examiners*, and the proceedings from both the *International Graphonomics Society* and the *American Academy of Forensic Sciences*. Where relevant, especially with respect to electronic processes and computerized technology, we have also relied on other technical publications. We have stressed the use of references from peer-reviewed journals with high rankings so as to establish the scientific credibility of handwriting identification to the fullest extent possible.

To the over 600 references maintained from the first edition, we have incorporated nearly 200 additional references. The new references primarily serve to update the extensive research carried out and the revised methods developed in the field of handwriting examination since the book's first edition in 1999.

One of the primary contributions to this new edition includes the addition of illustrations. College students using this book as a text for class work frequently comment that it would be helpful in their learning to see more illustrations. Handwriting examination is, indeed, a highly visual process, so we have supplemented the text with over 100 illustrations.

Huber and Headrick voiced their concern about the scientific limitations in handwriting identification in their original work. Many of their questions and concerns have been addressed placing handwriting identification as a viable science in forensics. This is the reason why we decided to revise their section headings from questions into descriptive titles. Many of the questions have been answered, and it is now easier to teach the discipline to new students in the field.

We have maintained as much of the original language written by Huber and Headrick as possible for several reasons. Even though some of their approach may seem dated, it provides a basic framework and historical background for handwriting identification. Their description of the 21 elements of handwriting has been relied upon in groundbreaking studies in the field. It is not to say that other measurements or elements are not relied upon, but to the extent possible we retained the 21 elements, which we consider the heart of the book, in the original state with minor revision.

We consider this revision a work in progress. Handwriting examination methodology is in transition, and the time for revising and updating Huber and Headrick's 21 elements and other components of this book is the task of the next edition. We, along with Tom Headrick, hope that this second edition marks the beginning of several successive and constantly improving revisions.

Heidi H. Harralson, MA
East Tennessee State University

Larry S. Miller, PhD
East Tennessee State University

Acknowledgments

We wish to extend our appreciation to several colleagues who have assisted us with this second edition.

The conversion of the citations and references to APA would not have been possible without the considerable assistance from the librarians at the Sherrod Library at ETSU (East Tennessee State University). We want to thank Patricia Russell Van Zandt, Celia Szarejko, Joanna Anderson, Kathy Campbell, Alison Lampley, Katy Libby, and Jennifer Young for the many hours spent converting hundreds of citations. We also want to extend appreciation to students at ETSU for providing suggestions for text revisions.

We thank Dr. Hans-Leo Teulings at NeuroScript, Professor Martin Jarvis at Charles Darwin University, Cina Wong, Kaleigh Brown, and Johndennis Govert for their assistance in specific areas of the text.

We appreciate Dr. Bryan Found (Victoria Police Forensic Services Department) and Dr. Carolyne Bird (Forensic Science South Australia) for recently publishing a revised version of the *Forensic Handwriting Method* (2016) and making it available to all handwriting examiners. The method was cited multiple times in this second edition. We acknowledge the large volume of research carried out by Dr. Found, Dr. Rogers, and their students and colleagues over the years. Their research (and indeed the research work of many others) was cited extensively and helped make a second edition of this text meaningful as their work was a significant contribution toward the scientific advancement of forensic handwriting examination.

Finally, we wish to thank Tricia Clapp at Mostly Books for her ideas about revising this text and helping to make this second edition possible.

Authors of the First Edition

Roy A. Huber was trained in the examination of questioned documents in the Crime Detection Laboratories of the RCMP (Royal Canadian Mounted Police) from 1949 to 1951. He testified as an expert witness in six provinces of Canada, and in the United States. He authored, or coauthored with Mr. Headrick, 16 published articles and 11 unpublished articles on the subject of questioned document examination, expert evidence, and on science as applied to document examination. He conducted a private practice in the examination of questioned documents from 1976 to 1996, most of which was shared with Mr. Headrick.

He graduated from Carleton University in 1959 with a bachelor of science degree, majoring in chemistry, statistics, and psychology, 10 years after he entered the field of questioned documents. He served for 35 years (1940–1975) as a uniformed member of the RCMP, the last 26 years of which were spent in the Crime Detection Laboratories. He retired from the RCMP in 1975, with the rank of assistant commissioner, as director of the Laboratory and Identification Services.

In 1958, Mr. Huber established and organized the Central Bureau for Counterfeits under the RCMP. In 1961, he was appointed as the RCMP representative on the Bank of Canada special committee to redesign Canadian currency. Mr. Huber served as special advisor on security in printing to the Canadian Bank Note Company, printers of currency, stocks, bonds, passports, licenses, and negotiable instruments, from 1975 to 1986.

In 1960, at the invitation of the Canada Council, Mr. Huber lectured at the Stratford Festival Theatre on Shakespeare's handwriting, at the first Shakespeare seminar held under the auspices of the universities of Canada.

Mr. Huber was editor of the *Canadian Society of Forensic Science Journal* from 1976 to 1981. He was president of the Canadian Society of Forensic Science (1967–1968), a fellow of the American Academy of Forensic Sciences, a diplomate of the American Board of Forensic Document Examiners, and a former board director (1978–1983). He was president of the American Society of Questioned Document Examiners (1996–1998).

Alfred M. Headrick attended primary and secondary schools in Brooks, Alberta, receiving the Governor General's Medal for academic achievement. He received a BSc (cum laude) with a major in physics from Mount Allison University in Sackville, New Brunswick.

Prior to entering private practice as an examiner of questioned documents in 1985, he served 35 years in the RCMP, 32 years of which were spent in the field of document examination and in the administration of the Crime Detection Laboratories. In 1984, he retired from the position of director of laboratories, holding the rank of assistant commissioner. During his time as a document examiner, 1954–1967, he testified as an expert witness in courts in all provinces east of Manitoba and in the state of New York.

Mr. Headrick held the positions of auditor, editor, and president of the Canadian Society of Forensic Science. He held the position of vice-chairman of the Operations Research Committee of the Canadian Association of Chiefs of Police and was a life member of that association. He was a member of the American Society of Questioned Document Examiners.

Authors of the Second Edition

Heidi H. Harralson has practiced forensic document examination professionally since 1997. She has been court-qualified in the United States and in Mexico and has worked on cases throughout the United States and internationally. She has testified in state and federal courts and is the managing partner of Spectrum Forensic International, LLC, a full-time handwriting and document examination practice. She is a court-qualified and board-certified forensic document examiner.

She has authored two books: *Developments in Handwriting and Signature Identification in the Digital Age* (2013) and *Forensic Handwriting Examination of Motor Disorders and Forgery: Research and Applications* (2008). She is the coauthor of a chapter on evidential documents in *Crime Scene Investigation* (2013). She has lectured extensively to professional organizations and universities on the handwriting sciences internationally and published original research in peer-reviewed journals on forensic handwriting and document examination topics. Her research work has focused on electronic signatures, handwriting and neuromotor disorders, handwriting on works of art, development of training courses, and other topics in the handwriting sciences.

Ms. Harralson has been consulted by attorneys, and public and private clients internationally. She is a board-certified diplomate through the Board of Forensic Document Examiners and the NADE (National Association of Document Examiners). She was president of NADE (2013–2017) and has served NADE in other capacities as vice president and certification chair.

She holds a bachelor of science in the behavioral sciences, a master of arts in handwriting science and forensic document examination, and a forensic crime scene technician certificate. In 1999, she assisted Dr. Larry Miller in developing courses for a graduate certificate degree in Forensic Document Examination at ETSU. Currently, she is an affiliate professor at ETSU where she teaches graduate courses in forensic document examination.

Larry S. Miller is a court-qualified, board-certified forensic document examiner. He is a distinguished professor and chair of the Department of Criminal Justice and Criminology at ETSU. He received his bachelor of science from ETSU in 1974, a master of science from Eastern Kentucky University in 1977, and his PhD in health and safety with collaterals in forensic anthropology and criminology from the University of Tennessee in 1981.

He began his career as a crime scene investigator and photographer with the Sullivan County (TN) Sheriff's Department. He worked as a patrolman with the Kentucky State Police and became chief administrative deputy with the Washington County (TN) Sheriff's Office. After receiving his MS degree, he was employed as an assistant professor and director of the Tennessee Regional Crime Laboratory at Walters State Community College in Morristown (TN). It was during his tenure at the crime laboratory that he was trained as a forensic document examiner. In 1984, he became employed with ETSU in Johnson City.

Dr. Miller has been with ETSU since 1984 and normally teaches courses in the areas of law enforcement, forensic science, and forensic document examination. He developed the graduate program in Forensic Document Examination and created a laboratory at ETSU to examine questioned documents submitted by state and local law enforcement agencies in Tennessee.

Dr. Miller's primary research interests are in police studies and forensic science, and he has served as a member of the board of the National Forensic Academy. He has also held offices with several organizations including the NADE (National Association of Document Examiners), the AFDE (Association of Forensic Document Examiners), and the BFDE (Board of Forensic Document Examiners). He served as a member of the group on Human Factors in Handwriting Identification with the National Institute of Science and Technology (US Department of Commerce) helping to develop standards for forensic document examinations. He has authored or coauthored 15 textbooks and numerous articles in criminal justice publications.

Introduction: The World of Documents

Documents are evidence of our compliance with society's requirements, and of the terms and conditions of our interaction with our clients, customers, and neighbors. They are the record of past actions and future intentions, the message bearers of our civilization, and as personifying as a fingerprint or as anonymous as a grain of sand.

As our dependence upon documents grows, so does our reliance on their integrity. As documents acquire new values and serve new purposes, it is understandable that they are frequently the instruments of fraudulent manipulation, the targets of counterfeiting, or the means of concealing incriminating truths. Changes in the world of documents has its ramifications upon the field of forensic document examination, placing new demands upon skill and new taxes on knowledge.

Time has had its effects upon handwriting as well, its status in the school curriculum, and its role in business and social intercourse. Electronic technology has usurped much of the function of handwriting in the business world. Penmanship is no longer assiduously taught nor extolled as a principal goal for the aspiring student. The old triumvirate has become "reading, recording, and texting." Handwriting is taught with less aesthetic and more functional consideration. Consequently, it receives greater latitude in method and yields wider variation in the end product. Accordingly, the approach to handwriting identification must be modified.

With this text, a course is charted for the discipline that begins with a scientific perspective. Forensic document examination deals with physical evidence and physical evidence cannot lie. Only its interpretation can err, and only the failure to find it or the disinclination to hear its testimony can deprive it of its value.

Chapter 1

History of Forensic Document Examination

1.1 HANDWRITING IDENTIFICATION AND THE JUDICIAL PROCESS

The examination of disputed handwriting may well be the progenitor of forensic science. Certainly it is one of those rare disciplines to have been born as a forensic necessity, rather than as a discipline established first in its own right for other reasons, and later harnessed for forensic tasks. Historical references indicate that the practice of forgery and related frauds involving documents evolved almost as early as the development of writing. In the days of the Roman Empire, the law provided for the acceptance of expert testimony based on documents. It was not until centuries later that such testimony was admitted in English-speaking courts.

1.1.1 Documents and the Rules of Evidence

The relevancy of documents in civil and criminal litigation is largely dependent on their authorship or origin. Numerous ways have evolved to attest to the truthfulness of a writing. Before the origin of the signature, the application of a wax seal served to authenticate the document. The wax seal bonded the ends of a ribbon of fabric which fed through a slit in the paper and was embossed with a personal motif. Later, signatures served the purpose, but additionally, the legal process has tended to also require the signatures of witnesses to the signing.

There have always been situations where unsigned or anonymous writings on documents were potentially important, for example, personal notebooks in which relevant or incriminating information was recorded. The provision of proof regarding the authorship of such documents has long been an issue.

Historically, circumstantial evidence was the vehicle by which authorship was established for many cases. This was used in the absence of witnesses to the act of writing. For many years, courts debated as to what evidence was acceptable. Certainly, the inclination was to seek proof that was independent of the document's circumstances. As early as the nineteenth century, Wigmore (1896) commented that the idea of handwriting expertise was novel.

In the course of developing an acceptable standard of proof, many related issues surfaced. Should triers of fact (judge or jury) be permitted to compare writings for themselves? If so, what writings could be used as standards? The answer to the first question became affirmative, provided some kind of corroborative evidence was supplied. Corroboration was then sought through the testimony of a *recognition witness*—someone acquainted with the alleged writer's handwriting. Recognition witnesses then became the means by which writing standards were authenticated and tendered as evidence. The extent of the acquaintance with a person's writing and the manner in which it was acquired were without precise boundaries and the evidence offered proved to be unreliable.

Any person having observed another person write, even once or years before, was permitted to testify regarding the authenticity of a writing. Despite the inherent weaknesses in this evidence, shreds of the policy continue to prevail regarding the proof of writing standards. Requirements were then placed upon the standards. They must have some relevance to the matter in dispute and could not simply represent a given person's writing practices.

The case of *Goodtitle d. Revett v. Braham* (1792) is said to be the first in English-speaking courts in which specially qualified witnesses were proffered. These witnesses would testify solely from direct comparison between standards and disputed writing rather than from recognition. Their special qualifications were acquired from experience as inspectors of franks. They checked the authenticity of the signatures of MPs and others on mail that was dispatched pursuant to the franking privilege. On that occasion, Lord Kenyon admitted the testimony of two inspectors, on the authority of *Folkes v. Chadd* (1782) in which Lord Mansfield admitted the expert testimony of an engineer.

The next year the same evidence was refused by the same judge, Lord Kenyon. Not until Massachusetts admitted testimony regarding the comparison of disputed documents with writing standards in 1835 (*Moody v. Rowell*), and England passed the *Common Law Procedure Act* in 1854, did the practice become more consistent.

1.1.2 Prior to 1900

By the year 1672, Europeans such as Jacques Raveneau had written on the subject of handwriting identification (Buquet 1981). In the 1800s, the La Ronciere case, the Dreyfuss letters, and the La Boussiniere will, all testified to the endeavor to resolve major issues on the strength of writing examination in that part of the world.

In the North America, Albert S. Osborn (1929) is credited with launching handwriting identification as a distinct discipline at the turn of the twentieth century. Furthermore, he broadened its scope to include typewriting, ink, and paper examinations under the wider umbrella of document examination. Others of his era, such as Hagan (1894), Frazer (1901), Ames (1900), and Lee and Abbey (1922) made their contributions in published form. Osborn's works (1922, 1929, 1946), however, are still deemed to be the accepted texts of the specialty, although they were not written expressly for that purpose.

While Osborn's success in gaining acceptance for handwriting identification was achieved largely through his writings, lectures, and testimony, there is no doubt that he derived much assistance from his friendship and association with John H. Wigmore, the eminent authority on American evidence law. Wigmore et al. (1940) held a great personal interest in forensic science and recognized its potential in the court's search for truth. The claim for document examination as a forensic science can be traced to the oracles of Wigmore (1896), some of which were expressed or quoted in the writings of Osborn just after the turn of the twentieth century.

In Canada, provision was made for handwriting examination evidence in the *Common Law Procedure Act* of 1854 of England and that those authorities were broadened under the *British Criminal Procedure Act* of 1865. Remarkably, the Act applied only to civil proceedings. Some courts expressed a preference for expert testimony over lay witness identification of handwriting as early as the 1860s (*Reid v. Warner*, 1867). The *Common Law Procedure Act* and the *Criminal Procedure Act* were superseded by the *Canada Evidence Act* of 1868 that, with some modification, has continued to provide for the admission of expert testimony respecting handwriting—but respecting handwriting only—for the last 150 years. Authority for the presentation of evidence by the document examiner in areas of his and/or her work, other than handwriting, must be sought in case and common law.

The reason for giving handwriting evidence special attention in the *Canada Evidence Act* of 1868 illustrates that handwriting experts were probably the first of the forensic experts to make their contribution to the judicial system. In the absence of precedents, special provision had to be made for their admission. Certainly, the *Canada Evidence Act* of 1868, one of the many early statutes passed after confederation in 1867 when Canada became independent of British rule, merely adopted the provisions of a similar statute on the law books of England from 1856. That being the case, the real reason why handwriting evidence is segregated under the law from other forms of forensic expertise must lie in the history of British law.

1.1.3 The Twentieth Century: The First 40 Years

Notwithstanding the legislation governing its admission into the courts and into a growing volume of judicial decisions, not all members of the legal profession readily accepted the testimony of the expert witness at the turn of the twentieth century. The disparaging manner in which older law literature has referred to their contributions suggests that the vanguard of the profession of forensic scientists left something to be desired in qualification, motivation, or attitude. Wellman (1913) remarked that "expert witnesses become so warped in their judgment ... that, even when conscientiously disposed, they are incapable of expressing a candid opinion" (p. 73). Wellman found that experts were shrewd and cunning. Occasionally, the pages of law books dripped with sarcasm from such statements as, "He swears scientifically does the expert" (Wrottesley 1910). Harris (1911) made a classic statement: "You will be amazed at the elaboration of the system for finding out nothing, which has been invented by science" (p. 140).

For writing identification, such skepticism, indeed hostility, is alleged to have stemmed from the often disputed rationale that underlay the admissibility of handwriting expert testimony. Undoubtedly, admission was granted simply on the grounds that experts could not be worse than recognition witnesses (*Moody v. Rowell* 1835).

While legislation resolved the question of admissibility, opponents continued to argue against handwriting identification on the grounds of weight. Per *Mutual Benefit Life Ins. Co. v. Brown* (1878): "All doubts respecting the competency of the opinion of experts in handwriting based upon mere comparison, as evidence, have been removed by statute, but it still must be esteemed proof of low degree."

A reasonably complete account of the legal history of handwriting identification, as developed and recorded in case law in the United States, may be found in an article by Risinger et al. (1989). Although the article has been criticized for its language, its objective, and for a number of errors and omissions, it presents the beginning of a serious critique of forensic handwriting examination. This in turn led to a reaction of the criticism aimed at the field through published research and standards.

For the most part, the early examiners in North America were sincere, well-intentioned individuals. Despite little training, they had one thing in common: a small collection of the books of Osborn (1929, 1946) and his contemporaries Hagan (1894), Quirke (1930), Ames (1900), and Frazer (1901).

Examiners came from diverse disciplines: bankers, lithographers, engravers, court clerks, and police officers. The greatest number of them was teachers of penmanship and business college instructors. Obviously, it was felt that those who taught penmanship and the preparation of written records were better qualified to discriminate between the writing of different persons. This was because, at a time of strict adherence to copybook styles, there was great similarity in the writing of many people. Furthermore, teachers were able to appreciate the capabilities of the average individual in altering or modifying writing habits.

A second and smaller group included bankers, court clerks, and police officials that developed an interest in document examination, probably as a result of their exposure or involvement in criminal cases. The need for the talents of the document examiner was evident and the availability of such experts was limited.

Initially, document examiners were self-trained. Historically, they did not have educational backgrounds in science and few were called upon in forensic cases more than a few times a year. Certainly, document examination offered few opportunities for full-time employment in North America until the opening of the federal, state, and provincial police laboratories in 1937 and later.

If and when the successful solution of a civil or criminal case demanded it, more than one document examiner would be engaged to examine the evidence. Often, the second examiner would be Albert S. Osborn. Such were the circumstances in the trial of Bruno Richard Hauptmann for the kidnapping and murder of the son of Charles Lindberg, the famous aviator, in 1934. Osborn and seven other examiners testified based on the handwriting of a number of ransom notes, and in so doing, established the legitimacy of writing identification in the eyes of the public. On such occasions, examiners would share experiences, learn from one another, and develop their competence. Osborn was a teacher, a stimulus, and an encouragement to those who were less practiced. Out of these unstructured beginnings, the profession of the document examiner slowly emerged.

Undoubtedly, the growth and development of the profession was not too different in Canada from that of the United States. In North America, police or government forensic laboratories established standards for the work, formalized their own training curriculum, and pursued limited programs of research to assemble much-needed knowledge. However, these institutions were few in number and all had very modest resources.

1.1.4 1940 to 1975

The development of the manual typewriter, the advent of the ball point pen, the introduction of the electric typewriter, and the evolution of the electronic age significantly affected document examination. They profoundly changed the means by which society communicated and recorded its information. The profession of teachers of handwriting diminished. Penmanship was at one time tenaciously taught and diligently practiced. It is, however, no longer extolled as an important student achievement. Writing enjoys greater latitude in learning methods and wider variation in the end product. Whereas the objective in years past was to ensure legibility for the benefit of others, the goal now seems to be to provide a convenient process for note taking, with readability chiefly for the writer. Communications and records are matters for machines; therefore, the approach to writing identification has had to be modified significantly.

The forensic science services that have developed since 1940 have established document examination laboratories in most of the major cities across the land. All are administered by the government authorities responsible, directly or indirectly, for law enforcement in the area. For the most part, the services have been available free of charge to law enforcement agencies at all levels.

1.1.5 1975 till Present

Since the 1980s, the widespread use of computer and digital technology has changed the field of document and handwriting examination in two fundamental ways: (1) the analysis of computerized or electronic documents, and (2) the computerized or digital equipment that document examiners use in analysis. Cases involving the analysis of typewritten documents are now rare and older document examination textbooks and training that focus on typewriting seem outdated. However, it is a reality in casework that older documents come into question and the knowledge of how older documents were produced is an important area of study that can lead to specialization. The George W. Bush letters regarding his service in the Air National Guard (purportedly typewritten in the early 1970s) serve as a popular example as to why document examiners need training in both old and modern writing machines.

The typewriter has been gradually replaced in both offices and the home by computers, printers, and scanners. In the forensic examination of handwriting, the shift to digital technology has required the implementation of software and techniques to analyze handwriting on digital or digitized documents. Document examiners also use digital techniques to photograph evidence and create demonstrative exhibits. The trend to maintain only digital records has resulted in fewer available original documents for examination and a widespread increase in the analysis of digital files. This requires the training and knowledge of document examiners who have an understanding as to how digitization affects handwriting and how documents can be manipulated by splicing handwriting images (i.e., a signature) from a source document onto a manufactured document. Manipulated documents can be created so skillfully with simple office equipment that it sometimes requires scientific instrumentation to detect whether a signature is produced with a real ink pen or is the product of a color printer. In order to maintain current knowledge with rapidly changing technology, professional document examination organizations that provide certification to their members require periodic continuing education.

Regarding trends in training and education, historically there was no university program of study offering courses or training available in North America to those wishing to enter the discipline. In the government sector, an apprenticeship-style training has been promulgated. Per ASTM (American Society for Testing and Materials) Standard E2388, Standard Guide for Minimum Training Requirements for Forensic Document Examiners, the recommended training is 2 years full-time. In a broad sense, the ASTM training standard was used as a guideline to determine the training qualification of an expert document examiner. In the private sector, various schools and courses in document examination have been established, but there has been a lack of standardization of training requirements.

With the increasing popularity of forensic crime shows, a demand for forensic coursework in universities helped to establish three university programs in North America. Oklahoma State University developed a graduate-level forensic program which allows a specialization in forensic document examination. In 2009, East Tennessee State University initiated a graduate certificate program in document examination. In keeping with the ASTM requirements, both university programs require a minimum undergraduate degree as a prerequisite for acceptance into the program. Other universities and colleges sponsor document examination courses within forensic and criminal justice programs at undergraduate and graduate levels, but they are typically one course or one semester in length and constitute an introduction to document examination. One exception is a certificate in forensic document analysis offered by the University of Baltimore, which promotes a four-course undergraduate program.

Standardization in training, certification, and methodology has been a theme in both the public and private sectors of document examination. In 2000, the FSAB (Forensic Specialties Accreditation Board) established accreditation for the forensic science disciplines with support from the National Institute of Justice and the American Academy of Forensic Sciences. FSAB accredits boards in forensic disciplines including forensic document examination. Currently, the National Institute of Standards and Technology (NIST) is developing a formal recommendation that certifying bodies should be accredited to ISO/IEC 17024. ISO is the International Organization for Standardization and it publishes a standard regarding general requirements for bodies operating certifications of persons (2012).

With continued interest and awareness of the scientific underpinnings of forensic disciplines, there has been increased intervention on the part of government-sponsored agencies to create greater oversight and accountability in the forensic sciences. In 2009, the NAS (National Academy of Sciences) published its report on *Strengthening Forensic Science in the United States: A Path Forward.*

In its assessment of questioned document examination, the committee stated: "The scientific basis for handwriting comparisons needs to be strengthened ... although there has been only limited research to quantify the reliability and replicability of the practices used by trained document examiners, the committee agrees that there may be some value in handwriting analysis" (pp. 5–30). Almost as an answer to the criticism aimed at forensic handwriting examination, a 2012 court ruling originating in the District of Columbia Court of Appeals challenged forensic handwriting examination using criticisms taken from the NAS report. In *Pettus v. US*, the appellant's argument was based upon the NAS report's criticism that forensic pattern-based disciplines are not scientific and do not meet the requirements for scientific admissibility. The appellate court agreed with the original trial court's decision that handwriting identification did indeed meet the *Frye* test for admissibility. The court further reasoned that appellant's presentation of the criticism from the NAS report "exaggerates the measured conclusions and recommendations of the Report to read them as a rejection of the scientific basis for all pattern-matching analysis, including handwriting identification" (p. 27). Rather, the court found that the NAS report does not recommend a rejection of handwriting identification, but instead cautions courts to insist on reliability of forensic methods. Overall, the appellate court found that the NAS report did not specify a reason for rejecting handwriting identification noting that the NAS report's review of handwriting identification was brief. The court concluded that the methodology behind handwriting identification is well-established and accepted in the forensic community.

The NIST (National Institute of Standards and Technology 2015) has sponsored conferences involving error analysis and mitigation, which also included handwriting identification. In 2013, NIST sponsored a conference dedicated to the forensic challenges associated with handwriting identification, specifically measurement and quantitative analysis. NIST continues to take an active role in developing standards for the forensic sciences and there are presently several committees developing standards for the forensic sciences within NIST. In 2013, the ASTM document and handwriting examination standards were replaced by the SWGDOC (Scientific Working Group for Document Examiners) standards. The standards are virtually the same, but the revision process of the standards will be carried out via SWGDOC instead of ASTM in the future until NIST formally publishes new standards.

1.2 DEFINING DOCUMENT EXAMINATION

Document examination is the discipline that seeks to determine the history of a document by technical or scientific processes. From the viewpoint of its application to civil and criminal litigation—its forensic function—forensic document examination is the study of physical evidence, and physical evidence cannot lie. Only its interpretation can err. Only the failure to find it, or to hear its true testimony can deprive it of its value.

Forensic document examination may entail the study of a complete instrument of communication, or of some element of it: the writing, lettering, or printing; the ink, the graphite, the paper, or its surface contour. It may also entail the study of the dimensions of any of its attributes. Document examination may seek information about the origin of the document or evidence of the chronology of the events that subsequently occurred. Notwithstanding the many elements of the document that testify to its history, the handwriting it bears is the element most frequently in dispute.

Questioned handwriting and hand lettering, however, may be inscribed on walls, woodwork, or on any other physical object of any size, perhaps using paint instead of ink, and broad markers, brushes, or spray cans instead of the customary writing instruments. The message may be threatening, offensive, obscene, libelous, annoying, or incriminating, and the identity of the author may be essential to establishing liability or culpability. Understandably, the document examiner will be called upon to apply his or her skills to identify the author of the inscription, although the medium (e.g., a lavatory wall or a concrete bridge) does not fall within the common definition of a document. While these occasions are infrequent, document examination and, in particular, handwriting identification, should be thought of in this broader context.

Both ASTM and SWGDOC provide a standard description of the scope of the work related to forensic document examination. This scope tends to deal with a document in the more limited sense. The standard description also makes reference to the qualifications of practitioners, although few specifics are provided except by inference. It does, however, clearly separate forensic handwriting examination from calligraphy, engrossing, and graphology.

1.2.1 The Purpose of Document Examination

The examination of a document is conducted to determine:

- Origin—where did the document come from?
- Production source—what person or machine produced it?
- Production process—how was it made?
- Inscription—what has faded or been obliterated?
- Chastity—what changes, if any, have been made to it?
- Integrity—is it genuine or false?
- Legitimacy—is it an original or a reproduction, and if so, what generation?

The reason for seeking this information through a technical process is to shed light on events in the history of the document that have occurred prior to its arrival in court. This will enable the court to confirm assumptions that may otherwise be made. It will also allow the court to review the correspondence between the technical testimony of the document and the oral testimony of witnesses.

Notwithstanding the breadth of scope of questioned document examination, in practice, most examiners find that a large percentage of their work involves the study of handwriting or handwritten signatures. If some areas of criminal work tend to provide a somewhat different variety of tasks, certainly the private examiner finds that he or she is more constantly engrossed with handwriting. For these reasons, handwriting is deserving of the examiner's most comprehensive attention.

Chapter 2

The Development of Handwriting

2.1 THE MECHANICS OF HANDWRITING

Handwriting is an acquired skill and clearly one that is a complex perceptual-motor task, sometimes referred to as a neuromuscular task. Skilled writing movements are so commonplace that one is inclined to overlook their complexity. Without exaggeration, however, writing is one of the most advanced achievements of the human hand.

The hand is an extremely complex and delicate mechanism, containing some 27 bones controlled by more than 40 muscles. Most of the muscles are situated in the lower arm and connect to the fingers by an intricate set of tendons. Their ability in manipulating a writing instrument is precisely coordinated by a timing system under a neural control of movements of the arm, the hand, and the fingers. The precise ordering and timing of the movements determines the structure of the pattern that is recorded by the pen or pencil.

Writing is a continuous or flowing task, not one of discrete or separated actions. There are apparent interruptions at word boundaries, but in many cases the pen movement may be continuous and uninterrupted, although not recorded as an inked line. A feature of skilled performance, and certainly of handwriting, is that it involves the smooth execution of a structured sequence of coordinated movements in which each movement occurs at its proper time and place in the sequence (Thomassen and Teulings 1983). The particular pattern of these movements constitutes the habitual aspects of writing that are peculiar to each individual. The fact that, with practice and skill, the execution of writing habits becomes more automatic, renders the writing process less subject to conscious control.

2.2 HANDWRITING RESEARCH

Much has been studied and written about handwriting and many studies pursued the correlation of writing features with various medical and mental conditions. Considerable research work has involved the pedagogy of handwriting and remedial approaches to improve its quality in the writing of children.

Historically, many surveys or studies have involved the correlation of handwriting with psychology or behavior. Allport et al. (1933) reviewed and worked with experimental studies on expressive movement in handwriting. McNeil and Blum (1952) examined methodology in handwriting correlated with psychology. Fluckiger et al. (1961) reviewed the experimental research in handwriting and behavior from 1933 to 1960. Herrick (1960b) produced the most comprehensive bibliography on handwriting studies (from 1890 to 1960) that listed

1,754 papers, books, and articles. Unfortunately, up to that point, few of the studies were rigorous and experimental and most were described as suggesting hypotheses rather than testing them.

With respect to handwriting and pedagogy, Herrick and Okada (1963) suggested the various directions that research, respecting the teaching of handwriting, might pursue in the 1960s. Later Askov et al. (1970) reviewed the research of that decade to assess the progress made along the lines suggested. They expressed some disappointment, commenting that handwriting instruction tended to follow accepted practices rather than basing its practices on research findings. A decade later, Peck et al. (1980) reviewed progress and reported finding some encouraging signs. They mentioned the promising trend in experimentation on the handwriting of learning-disabled children. Their comments are of particular interest to handwriting examiners today as they mentioned that in an age of technical communication, handwriting is still relevant as a mode of personal expression.

Huber (1983) endeavored to stimulate interest in the published literature on handwriting among document examiners and added 200 titles dated between the years 1958 and 1983 to Herrick's survey of 1960. Baier et al. (1987) surveyed the material produced relating to document examination from 1873 and cataloged 5,871 monographs, articles, books, and papers, a substantial portion of which deal with handwriting.

A trend toward more rigorous experimental investigation became apparent in the 1960s and 1970s (Herrick 1963). The *International Workshop on the Motor Aspects of Handwriting* in 1982 brought together research scientists from the disciplines of experimental psychology, bioengineering, neurology, and education, and gave birth to a new discipline of graphonomics.

With the advent of graphonomics and its scientific rigor, research is endeavoring to study and understand the development of handwriting as a perceptual-motor skill. Graphonomics has and continues to seek the structures and processes operating at different stages of handwriting, and the factors involved in their modification or change. Thomassen et al. (1983) reported that handwriting is a complex type of motor behavior. The greatest difficulty in writing letters is not in the execution of their particular strokes but in the execution of complex combinations of strokes in ever-changing contexts. The practiced writer does not simply follow a given trace to produce the required movements. Research has shown that the writer retrieves the necessary information from abstract motor memory. Handwriting involves a continuously proceeding output process that intrinsically intertwines the retrieval process, a buffer storage, and a monitoring action. Thus, the brain works much like a computer (Teulings 1996).

The representation of motor acts in memory appears to be nonmuscle specific. Hence, writing follows similar patterns whether executed with an instrument in the hand, held by the foot, or in the mouth. The integrated sequence of movements is a hierarchical process. A combination of letters or a word may be executed as a unit. Thus, the execution of movement sequences appears to be far more independent of the monitoring of a feedback system than was once believed.

As Thomassen and Teulings (1983) have elucidated in some detail, there are at least three different theories of how a skilled performance such as handwriting is achieved, and the role that feedback plays in it. The open-loop theory was described by Keele (1968); the closed-loop theory was developed by Adams (1976). A form of central motor program theory was proposed by Schmidt (1975, 1976) under the name of schema theory. Plamondon and Maarse (1989) evaluated research on biomechanical motor models of handwriting and found that velocity-controlled models best represented natural handwriting.

Caligiuri and Mohammed (2012) summarized decades of motor control research, reviewing the models most relevant to handwriting which included (1) hierarchical models,

(2) cost minimization models, and (3) the equilibrium point model. While all three models accurately describe motor control with respect to handwriting, cost minimization models seem to model the factors associated with simulation in handwriting most effectively. Cost minimization models describe the motor program in terms of movement, and research associated with these models has been based on velocity profiles. Within cost minimization models, other models such as minimum jerk, the isochrony principle, and the two-thirds power law have been developed to explain movement in handwriting. Applying the motor control theory of the isochrony principle, Caligiuri et al. (2012) examined online handwriting features to determine whether simulated signatures adhere to isochrony kinematics. Results demonstrated that simulated signatures do not adhere to the isochrony principle which showed how motor control theories are useful in supporting the scientific basis of forensic handwriting examination.

To write satisfactorily requires the ability to distinguish visually between graphic forms of letters and other characters and to judge their correctness. Learning to write requires the ability to distinguish between the feedback provided by the senses associated with correct and incorrect movements. Modifying or controlling the movement of the writing instrument is also required.

Writing is described as a tool-using skill. Connolly and Elliott (1972) have distinguished seven types of grip for tools, five of which they classify as power grips (as in holding an ice pick or screwdriver), and two that they classify as precision grips (as in grasping a pencil or a pen). The grip employed with a writing instrument may facilitate or inhibit certain types of strokes. The course of development in writing is a gradual improvement in control, especially of the more precise finger movements. This is reflected by a reduction in the size of writing and by a reduction in the number and extent of superfluous movements.

In the development of writing there are both qualitative and quantitative changes. Of the variables that can be more precisely measured, speed is probably the simplest overall measure of proficiency one can use. An increase in speed of writing as a function of increasing age has been described by Cormeau et al. (1970). The rate at which the speed of writing increases is greatest between the ages of 7 and 9 years. It tapers off to 13 years, when there is little further increase

As mentioned previously, writing is a culture-bound activity, not only insofar as language and its orthography, but also in many motor aspects that are greatly influenced by culture and education. This is sometimes overlooked. Writing is spelling, as well as a perceptual-motor task; two quite different educational problems occurring coincidentally, that beg to be tackled at the same time. Teaching the motor preliminaries of writing involves the introduction of cultural standards such as regularity and neatness, the introduction of cultural biases such as slant, counterclockwise rotations, and left to right transport. It also involves the introduction of various constraints such as posture, grasp, and handedness. In different cultures these standards, biases, and constraints may differ, producing different effects in the writing of their subjects.

In the development of writing or drawing, certain biases or rules have evolved for large numbers of the population. There are directional preferences of which writers are not always conscious. These preferences prompt the writer, almost invariably, to execute vertical lines from the top down and horizontal lines from the left to the right. When these rules are broken, the handwriting examiner looks for reasons to explain them, such as the IHP (inverted hand position) in left-handed writers. It may also explain why there are many writers that tend to omit the upstroke in letters such as the "i," "t," "h," or "l," and commence the structure with simply a vertical stroke—from the top down (Rhodes 1978).

With growth in age and development in handwriting, there is increased conformity to the rules, but the strength of one rule may decline while another increases, as Goodnow and Levine (1973) observed.

2.3 ORIGINS OF THE ALPHABET

The fabulous faculty of writing has prompted many to impute its origin to the gods. Assyrian, Chinese, Egyptian, Indian, and Scandinavian deities have all been credited with bestowing on mankind the knowledge of writing (Figure 2.1). In 1750, Champion opined that the invention of letters was derived from Adam.

Whether of divine origin or not, writing is nevertheless considered one of mankind's most important inventions. Coulmas (1989) claims that writing is the most important system invented on the planet and while civilization is not necessarily the product of writing, it is a

Figure 2.1 Thoth, Egyptian god of writing, holding a reed pen (Luxor Temple, Egypt).

tool shaping civilization. Daniels and Bright (1990) purports that "humankind is defined by language; but civilization is defined by writing" (p. 1).

The development of writing is complex because it is, in part, culture-dependent, and cultures differ with locales and undergo constant change. The evidence of this dependence is manifest in class, system, or national characteristics which are of particular interest in the forensic examination of handwriting. In order to identify individualizing features in writing, an examiner must take into consideration the class characteristics of the writing system. A review of the historical development of writing is a broad introduction to understanding class characteristics culturally.

Neolithic man began written communication as long as 20,000 years ago, when he graphically represented objects and ideas in drawings on cave walls that are now referred to as iconographs (Diringer 1968; Diringer and Freeman 1953). After these came the first pictographs or picture stories when action was added to the drawings of animals (Figures 2.2 and 2.3). To these were added figures of man, and the complexity of the depicted events gradually increased to become what were called ideographs or picture symbols.

Ideographs were simpler drawings, such as stick figures, yet more difficult to interpret. Then, iconographic symbols were combined with ideographs to provide more information. Particular combinations expressed ideas. For example, the moon symbol and slashes might represent the lunar month (Diringer 1968; Ogg 1959). The origin of the first systematic method for written communication is uncertain, but the evidence found in artifacts suggests that such a system began sometime after 3500 BC.

In the initial development of writing in any culture, the symbols used represent objects rather than the spoken words. The linguistic elements followed. The phonetic use of symbols to

Figure 2.2 Aboriginal cave painting.

Figure 2.3 Petroglyphs carved in stone (Signal Hill, AZ).

represent syllables of words probably commenced with the endeavors to write foreign names, which conveyed no meaning other than identification. From this, syllabic usage spread into everyday words.

The earliest known forms of Egyptian hieroglyphics exhibited elements of a syllabic system. In fact, they exhibited elements of the final step from syllabic writing to true alphabetic writing in which symbols represented speech sounds and not just syllables (Humphreys 1855).

Early writings took on several forms. The Sumerians produced a cuneiform system that dates back to 3200 BC and is perhaps the oldest writing system. Not to underestimate the importance of cuneiform or its use in recording information, Coulmas (1989) stated that "microchips are merely a technical improvement over clay tablets" (p. 9). Later cuneiform underwent transition to ideographic and syllabic form (Diringer 1968). With the introduction of clay as a writing substrate, symbols were simplified and straight-line wedge shapes, made with a broad-tipped stylus, replacing round lines. Hence, the name *cuneiform* was coined to mean wedge-shaped. In today's digital age, it is interesting to note the return of writing with a stylus on a tablet albeit a digital tablet instead of a clay tablet (Figure 2.4).

Cuneiform was adopted by many Semitic tribes and evolved in different versions under the Acadians, Assyrians, Babylonians, Elamites, Hittites, and Kassites. The combination of ideographs and phonetic forms produced polyphones (symbols with more than one syllabic value), homophones (different symbols with the same phonetic value), and developed a need for determinatives to identify a word as being ideographic or phonetic, and/or its phonetic form. Phonetic symbols also served to sort ideograms with multiple meanings.

Various kinds of cuneiform writing survived throughout Egypt, Asia Minor, and Greece for over 2,000 years. The Persians adapted a mode of it for their use about 600 BC and then simplified

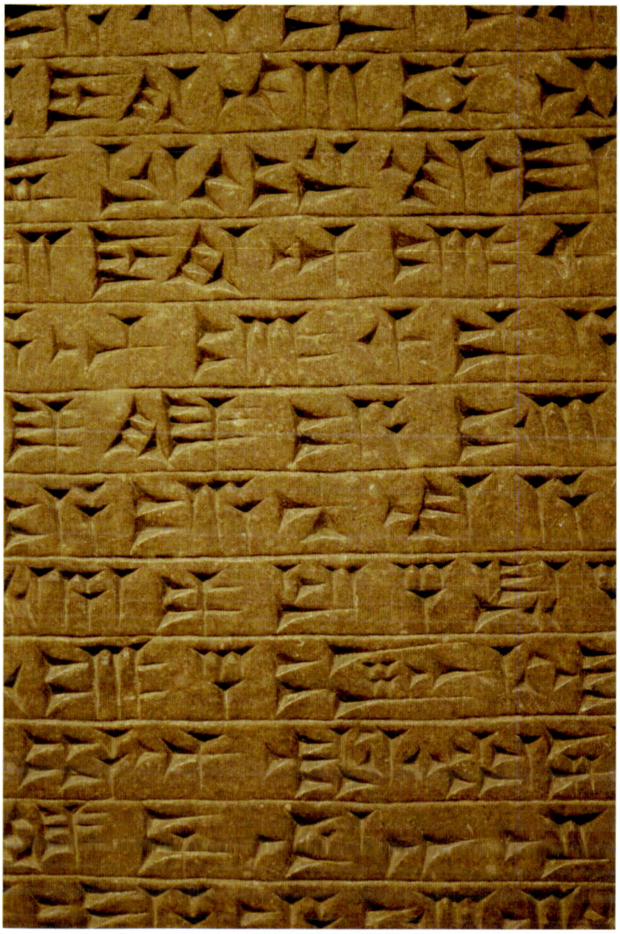

Figure 2.4 Cuneiform clay tablet in the British Museum. (By Matt Neale from the United Kingdom [CC BY 2.0 (http://creativecommons.org/licenses/by/2.0)]. Courtesy of Wikimedia Commons.)

it to about 40 signs, which may have been the beginning of a true alphabet. Cuneiform began its demise around 500 BC. Although priests and astronomers continued to use it at the beginning of the Christian era, there is no record of it beyond 75 AD.

Egyptian writing developed three different styles of symbol systems hieroglyphic, hieratic, and demotic, each using the same combination of characters but in a different written form. Egyptian scripts were essentially national, living and dying only in Egypt. Egypt's hieroglyphics achieved early advancement over other systems, combining ideographs, syllabic forms, and even single letter symbols as well as determinatives. Despite its early growth and advance in development, it did not turn into an alphabetic form. Hieroglyphics, which prevailed until after 500 AD, were preferred for royal and religious inscriptions (Humphreys 1855).

The introduction of the reed pen and papyrus around 2000 BC encouraged the development of hieratic writing that employed simpler forms to depict the same figures. As a result of its speed of execution, arising from the simplicity of some forms, hieratic became the choice for business and private documents.

A highly cursive form of hieratic, called demotic, developed about 700 BC, but since it used the same system as hieroglyphics (ideograms, phonograms, and determinatives), it did not turn into a true alphabetic system. Demotic symbols, however, were so cursive, and execution so much simpler, that it replaced hieratic and hieroglyphic styles, leaving them to religious and traditional transcriptions. The demotic system spread into general use in Egyptian writing, achieving the level of importance of hieroglyphics or Greek. Indeed, the Sumerian and this Egyptian system were probably the most influential on subsequent developments. Champollion's translation of the Rosetta Stone, discovered in 1799, provided the clue to deciphering Egyptian hieroglyphs as three written languages appeared on the stone: Egyptian hieroglyphic, demotic, and ancient Greek (Figure 2.5).

The Cretan civilization, the Elamitic civilization, the Indus Valley civilization, and the Hittite civilization each developed their particular version of Babylonian cuneiform. This was later replaced by more cursive or pictographic systems.

The Chinese writing system has been in continuous, uninterrupted use for over 3,000 years making it unique among writing systems due to its longevity (Coulmas 1989). The Chinese system is markedly different from the Western alphabet and although it has been classically referred to as ideographic or logographic, Coulmas argues that Chinese is more accurately described as a morpheme-syllable writing system. The earliest Chinese pictographic forms were found on oracle bones dating around 1200 BC. However, Ronan and Needham (1978) suggest that writing may have occurred on other more perishable items such as bamboo that have not survived. Over thousands of years, Chinese characters or logograms have increased to number over 50,000, but only 2,000–3,000 hanzi (Chinese characters) are in regular use. In learning to write Chinese characters, the order of the strokes are standardized and precise, and the number of strokes in a character is used to determine its placement in a Chinese dictionary. Traditionally, Chinese is written in columns and is read from right to left. Writing on bamboo as a medium explains why the traditional Chinese writing is written vertically.

Figure 2.5 The Rosetta Stone depicting three different written languages: hieroglyphic, demotic, and Greek.

For Japanese writing, Coulmas (1989) stated that it is regarded as the "most intricate and complicated system ever used by a sizeable population" (p. 122). Although initially derived from Chinese, Japanese writing evolved into a far more complex system. Similar to Chinese, it also consists of over 50,000 kanji (Japanese characters) with a few thousand in standard use. Japanese utilizes syllabic kana which is divided into two syllabaries referred to as hiragana (informal) and katakana (formal) (Robinson 1995). In modern times, there have been controversial proposals to reform and simplify the Japanese system due to the increased use of technology.

Brush calligraphy originated in China and is a stylized, artistic approach to letter forms that focuses on dynamic, continuous movement rather than rigid forms. The letters or images are formed with a brush onto the medium. Brush calligraphy is considered both a practice and an art (Figure 2.6).

2.3.1 The First Alphabet

The Phoenicians, the merchants of the Mediterranean from 1200 to 900 BC, are credited with the spread of the first alphabetic system through their travels from Palestine to Gibraltar (Ogg 1959). Diringer (1968) reported that the first true alphabet surfaced between Egypt and Mesopotamia in the years 1730 to 1580 BC, perhaps in the Sinai Peninsula (1600 BC) where Hebrew-Egyptian script was used to write a Hebrew-Semitic language. The language needed only the development of basic linguistic sounds rather than syllables (Mercer 1959). Diringer contended that Canaanites (i.e., Phoenicians) combined Egyptian and Semitic systems, eliminating everything but the fundamental sounds. As Palestine's culture was highly developed, and an active international trading center situated between the two great cultures of Egypt and Mesopotamia, it is a likely location for the origin of the alphabet.

Figure 2.6 Chinese brush calligraphy. (Joe Mabel [CC BY-SA 3.0 (http://creativecommons.org/licenses/by-sa/3.0)]. Courtesy of Wikimedia Commons.)

The first alphabet was largely a northern Semitic development. The north Semitic true alphabet can be traced to Byblos, Phoenicia about 1100 BC, but may have begun in Gebal, Phoenicia, 200 years before (Irwin 1967; Mercer 1959). While the sounds of the alphabet remained stable, its physical appearances changed significantly. There were three styles of the early script:

1. Phoenician script proper, with Cyprian, Sardinian, and Carthaginian varieties
2. Libyan and Iberian scripts that evolved from the Carthaginian
3. Aramaic script that developed as an offshoot about 1000 BC

Because of the Aramaeans' control of the Damascus area and the retention of the system to the time of the birth of Christ, the Aramaic style acquired some importance for Western civilizations. Another system of note derived from the Aramaean was Arabic. The spread of Islamic with the Arabic alphabet eventually displaced the Aramaic language. A South Semitic alphabet also developed independently with many derivatives.

The Greeks derived and developed their own alphabet from the Phoenician system, introducing vowels to accommodate the Greek language. Other consonants not used in Greek were dropped, resulting in the formation of the Greek alphabet. Evidence of this derivation can be found in the letter names (Fairbank 1955). The names of the letters of the Phoenician alphabet were representative of tangible objects or animals, for example, *aleph* (ox), *beth* (house), *gimel* (camel), *daleth* (door), but the names of Greek letters have no other significance than as names of letters, for example, *alpha, beta, gamma, delta.* In the tenth to fifth centuries BC, there were changes in the methods of writing, particularly in its direction. Those methods went through stages: first right to left, then alternating with each line (sometimes called plowing style or boustrophedon), and finally left to right. By 350 BC, the writing in all Greek states was standardized and Athens had adopted a fixed form for Greek letters (Diringer 1968).

To facilitate the freehand execution of forms, the Ionic Greek alphabet was modified by the scribes. The writing of capitals with ink on papyrus and vellum provided a slight rounding effect that became known as the Greek uncials.

Two classes of writing evolved—calligraphy, which used book-hand forms, and tachygraphy, which used document-hand forms. The former sought clarity, precision, regularity, and beauty and was used to transcribe literature of importance. The latter sought speed and efficiency, and was the style for work documents. Calligraphy maintained a fairly stable design of uncials that became known as book-hand cursive. Tachygraphy allowed changing cursive forms to alter the appearance of the letters. After 250 BC, rounder forms permitted ligatures to link letters and gave writing more speed. The trend continued until the seventh or eighth century AD when a new design of handwritten Greek emerged called minuscule. Some previous uncial forms combined with it and a formal minuscule evolved between 1000 and 1400 AD. The forms of letters in this system do not differ significantly from modern Greek printing.

A derivation of the Greek alphabet was that of the Etruscans in northern Italy, who, around 800 BC, combined Semitic and Greek letters to create their own alphabet. Its final form remained in use from 400 BC until displaced by the Latin alphabet of the Roman Empire in the first century AD. Another derivation of the Greek was the Messapian alphabet, which is thought to date from 800 BC when its people lived in Italy.

The last link between ancient and modern alphabets is the Roman alphabet. Before the Roman Empire peaked, Italy was dominated by the Etruscans in the north and the Messapii in the south, both of whom used alphabets garnered from the Greeks. Consequently, in about 70 to 0 BC, when a script was selected for adaptation to the Latin language, the Romans understandably chose a Greek derived design. The first Latin alphabet consisted of 21 Greek letters from the Etruscan alphabet (Humphreys 1855).

After 600 years of changes and additions to accommodate differences in pronunciation, the Roman alphabet was established. When the Romans conquered Greece in the first century BC, two more Greek symbols ("Y" and "Z") were added. The medieval addition of three more modifications of existing Latin letters ("U," "W," and "J") brought the total to the current 26 letters.

The Romans also developed new forms for the letters, the first of which was called lapidary capitals. The Romans introduced graceful, rounded curves, and tapered stroke endings.

A finishing line, called a serif, across the end of some strokes became popular in stone inscriptions during the first century.

As the use of pen and parchment increased, square capitals, or book capitals that were slightly rounded forms of the lapidary styles evolved. These more freehand formations provided a written rather than a drawn characteristic. At the same time, a second design emerged that sacrificed small details in favor of speed. Serifs became a last turn of the pen rather than a separate stroke. Pen lifts were avoided when possible. The resulting, somewhat casual design, became known as rustic capitals.

The execution of these styles with a broad, flat-tipped pen held at an acute angle to the line of writing, gave the strokes of the letters varying thicknesses. For the square capitals, vertical strokes tended to be broader than the horizontal strokes, but for the rustic capitals, the converse was the case. Both forms were majuscule, that is, the entirety of the letters could be contained between two parallel, horizontal lines. This is roughly equivalent to the meaning of the words *capital letter* today. Rustic capitals, popular for literary works until 600 AD, appeared thereafter only in titles until their demise in the twelfth century.

The everyday Roman writing, used for business during the first century AD, was called cursive capitals. Made with a sharp pointed instrument and fewer pen lifts, the writing line was more uniform in width and connected. Some letters of the style became "minuscule," that is, containing strokes that extended above or below the main body of the letter (e.g., "h" or "g"). This is not precisely the meaning that the word currently carries.

Tannenbaum (1930) reported that Julius Caesar wrote in old Roman cursive, of which there are very few specimens in existence. It is of great historical importance and helps to explain the origin of modern scripts. Several of minuscular letters are traceable to the forms of Roman cursive script found on wax tablets (libelli), discovered at the site of Pompeii in 1875. When this script was formalized, it became the ordinary diplomatic hand of Italy and France until about the ninth century.

The development of writing styles is somewhat obscure in the second, third, and fourth centuries AD, although it became evident that in this interim two new book hands and a new business hand came into use. The older book hand, the Roman uncial, used the broad-tipped pen, but after 500 AD, the pen tip was turned to an angle more parallel to the line of writing. Most of the forms were majuscule, but a few were minuscule. The newer of the book hands, called semiuncials, was written with a parallel pen tip. It was almost entirely of cursive origin and minuscule form (Thompson 1893).

The uncial system fared well until the seventh century AD. After 800 AD it was restricted to titles and disappeared in the twelfth century. The semiuncial system had a more limited use in common literature and died about 1000 AD.

The fourth century saw the introduction of the new business hand called cursive minuscules. It employed a pointed pen like the cursive capitals but utilized minuscule forms like the semiuncials, with a high frequency of connecting ligatures. Their importance in later developments should not be underestimated. They were the basis for the eighth century Carolingian minuscules that dominated Europe for 700 years. The Gothic cursives of the thirteenth to fifteenth centuries that also evolved, yielded to a revival of the pure Carolingian minuscules.

Development in writing systems was encouraged by development in writing materials, all geared to produce speed and efficiency. The domination of Rome produced vellum and the quill pen, but after Rome's decline and the loss of a centralized influence, a new influence surfaced—nationality. From then until today, national characteristics became the major factor in writing styles (Diringer and Freeman 1953; Humphreys 1855; Ogg 1959).

Cursive minuscules were the basis for many national business hands. Uncials and semiuncials were perpetuated in religious texts. An Italian semicursive minuscule of the seventh to ninth centuries was one of the first predominant national styles. From it sprang other national styles such as Lombardic minuscule (tenth to eleventh centuries), Beneventan (eighth to thirteenth centuries) and a pre-Carolingian book hand of northern Italy.

There were numerous other national styles: Merovingian script (sixth to eighth century, France), Visigothic script (seventh to ninth century, Spain), and Germanic pre-Carolingian (eighth to ninth century, central Western Europe). The most important of the new developments were the Insular or Anglo-Irish hands developed by the church, as were most writing systems of the Middle Ages. Of these there were two groups, the Irish hands and the Anglo-Saxon semiuncial. The former is generally attributed to St. Patrick and Irish missionaries, who, using Latin hands, spent countless hours copying Biblical texts. In the struggle for beauty and clarity, new forms of these letter styles surfaced.

The seventh to eighth century Anglo-Saxon hands, a more orderly derivation of the earlier Irish, were employed for Latin until about 940 AD and continued in use for Anglo-Saxon literature. During their time, three new letters were introduced for the sounds of "w," "th," and "dh," but only the "w" survived (Diringer 1968).

Around 800 AD, Charlemagne of France and his Holy Roman Empire became the major centralized influence in Western Europe after the fall of Rome. He learned that many errors had been made in the Biblical texts copied over the previous decades and proposed to correct them. In 781 AD, he persuaded Alcuin of York, a foremost Biblical scholar, to undertake the revision and rewriting of all the church literature. At a school set up in Tours, at the Abbey of St. Martin, Alcuin provided special training for scribes. He introduced a minuscule letter style designed from a combination and modification of the Anglo-Saxon script, Irish semiuncial script, and other early Germanic Carolingian scripts. The emphasis was on simplicity and clarity. Letters were joined for speed in writing, but not at the expense of clarity. The use of some punctuation and of capitals for titles was standardized.

By about 850 AD, the Carolingian developed by Alcuin replaced most of the national hands of Europe, and for 300 years was virtually the only book hand of Western Europe. By the tenth century, however, the Carolingian style had experienced various national modifications. German Carolingian became conservative, the Italian version became a round book hand and eventually the Italian Gothic. English Carolingian and that of northern France was beautiful and regular, and served as the base for German Gothic (Gard 1937; Ogg 1959). The business hands of Western Europe of the ninth to the twelfth centuries were almost exclusively Carolingian. There were national and personal variations, but all became increasingly connected.

During the twelfth and thirteenth centuries a number of factors influenced the development of writing styles. There was an increase in the level of literacy. The use and development of alphabetic systems had become established. Literacy was no longer exclusive to the Church. Changes in alphabets dealt less with basic concepts and more with the design of forms. Styles for artistic purposes were born. The shortage of writing materials could not meet the demand for written works and, consequently, writing was compressed into less space which necessitated some style alterations. Perhaps the greatest factor influencing changes in letter designs was the advancement of printing and the invention of moveable type.

As a result of these factors, German Gothic rose to prominence during the thirteenth and fourteenth centuries. Its narrow angular letters allowed for words to be compacted. As a book hand, it was popular with the scribes who had taken over much of the copying task from the churches. The business of this era also approached this sharp, angular style in the form of Gothic cursive minuscule, but it took longer to exhibit the broad lines of book hand Gothic. Gothic became the first widely used printing design to be spread by the emerging printing industry (Gard 1937; Ogg 1959).

Gothic letter styles, like the Carolingian, experienced national variations and had replaced most of the previous national Carolingian styles by 1300 AD. Gothic, in one form or another, became the major hand of Europe (Diringer 1968; Ogg 1959). Italy was an exception. Though much of Italy used a Gothic cursive, by about 1350 AD that style's illegibility and lack of aesthetic appeal prompted the development of new styles.

The new styles were an attempt by some to revive a simple form of the Carolingian minuscule (Tannenbaum 1930). The first of these, a new book hand, was the product of Poggio Bracciolini who introduced a new humanistic round hand in Florence. This began to replace Gothic as the standard type for books by 1500 AD.

A comparable humanistic cursive was originated by Niccolo Niccoli, an official scribe of the Vatican, which helped to popularize the style. This cursive style, thinner in line and greater in ligature connections than Bracciolini's, was adapted to typeface by Aldus Manatius in Venice in 1501. Originally called Aldinian, it soon became known as italics and, as a running hand, became the standard for writing in most of Europe (Humphreys 1855; Ogg 1959). Cancellaresca, an important variety of italics, became the style of the manual of handwriting *La Operina*, printed in 1522 by Lodovico Arrighi.

From this point on, the progress of printing and the development of paper manufacture forced scribes and their book hands to yield to printers and their typeface designs. From the German Gothic and Italian fonts, numerous national styles emerged: some transient, some enduring, some ornate, and some extremely simple (Thompson 1893).

At the same time, the role of business and personal handwriting also experienced change. The art began growing beyond its restraints. Writing masters, whose primary employment was teaching writing, began to develop individual systems and styles in an effort to compete with each other. The upper class, who wrote at their leisure, developed their own personal styles according to whim or fashion. Although, generally variations of the Gothic and/or Italian hands, the disregard for calligraphic rules often produced designs that defied classification.

One of the more significant variations of the Gothic cursive minuscule to emerge was called the secretarie hand in England, around 1550 AD (Dawson and Kennedy-Skipton 1966; Tannenbaum 1930). Derivations of this design were used by many other countries as well. In France and Spain, the varieties of Ronde that surfaced were based on the secretarie hand, with some influence from the humanistic cursive. Kurrentschrift, a variety of Gothic cursive that was the everyday hand in Germany until after World War II, was based on the secretarie hand and the Gothic cursive hand of Holland (Tannenbaum 1930).

A lighter, more cursive style of the aforementioned cancellaresca became the basis for a manual printed by C.A. Hercolani in 1574. His use of copper plates for printing, instead of wood blocks, allowed more delicate lines for the ascenders and descenders of the letter forms. Between 1680 and 1700, Colonel John Ayres of London worked on merging the cancellaresca hand and the secretarie hand. He introduced a slant to the right and gave delicate loops to the ascenders and descenders. The new vogue formed the basis for many of today's styles. Ayers' variation of what had previously been called testaggiata became known as copperplate, of which there were two designs: round hand—a bold business hand—and Italian, a delicate ladies' hand. By the beginning of the nineteenth century, the English hand was in general use in England, France, Spain, and Italy. In 1809, Joseph Carstairs introduced a system in England that required the movement of the whole forearm, not just the fingers. Many of the current systems are modeled after the Carstairs system (Dougherty 1917).

2.3.2 Recent Writing Systems

In North America, the early colonists used designs that generally relied on the same hybrids of the italic and secretarie hands, as in Britain. Later, derivatives of the German kurrent hand appeared as the style of the Pennsylvania Dutch. In 1791 in Boston, John Jenkins published one of the first American copybooks, which was based on a contemporary English round hand (Nash 1959). After about 1830, a variation of the Carstairs system developed called Spencerian. This was the first major system native to the United States and was later imitated in Britain. Several current United States styles (Zaner-Bloser, Palmer, and others) used the wide swinging style of Spencerian as their basis, but replaced the contrasting thick and thin strokes with lines of more uniform thickness.

In 1913, largely due to a mistake at a London teachers' conference, printing or manuscript writing, called printscript, was introduced (Fairbank 1970). This style found use in the United States as an introductory form for children learning to write. It became a final system of its own in some schools.

In North America today, there are a number of commercial handwriting styles that have been advocated by major companies and school districts. The emphasis for most writing systems is to teach speed and legibility. The student is exposed to one of these copybook designs, but the emphasis on clear and efficient execution soon acquiesces to the idiosyncrasies or individuality of the pupil's own needs, as long as they do not interfere with legibility. The need that causes these minor deviations from the copybook examples is generally the same need that brought the alphabet to its present form—the need to simplify the physical motion required to execute the letter designs.

2.4 HISTORY OF HANDWRITING INSTRUCTION

Probably the earliest culture that possessed formal schools of writing was that of ancient Egypt. Private schools and private tutors taught primarily children of the nobility, as the ability to read and write was a necessary complement to their social status. Working class children who showed some signs of intelligence were sent to district schools where they were taught to read and write by older pedagogues. Trade schools were available to teach job skills to the young (Gilbert 1966). Those who were educated in district schools might become apprentices in scribe offices; after years of training they could enter the profession of a scribe, a highly regarded position. Scribes escaped the physical torment that the working class normally received. They could become notaries, writing letters and contracts for the illiterate, or even achieve a position in administration, or in the house of a wealthy person.

Students memorized the names of designs of the written symbols and were given samples to copy. The copies were corrected and returned to the students who continued to practice until they mastered the art (Bowen 1972). These methods were used for the teaching of the hieratic or demotic forms of Egyptian writing. Hieroglyphic inscriptions, that were matters of drawing and carving rather than writing, were also taught, but their use was generally restricted to the priestly or royal classes for official works (Figure 2.7).

Figure 2.7 Egyptian scribes.

Greece was the next major culture to display an educational system comparable to the Egyptians. While the elements of physical education were the focus of the Spartan civilization, Athens concentrated on education in the areas of language and thought. One of the first subjects taught to any student, in the three major areas of language and grammar, mathematics, and gymnastics, were letters. Earliest teachings in Athens (700 to 650 BC) were likely limited to professional schools for priests and poets. These scribal schools were limited to the wealthy and operated within a system of individual tuition (Beck 1964; Smith 1955). Solon, an early Greek lawmaker in the early sixth century BC, made the learning of letter forms compulsory. The financial contribution of the parents determined the rate and extent of education for the student.

With the expansion of Greek trading, a wider need for reading and writing developed, particularly among the merchants, for the keeping of records and accounts. The teaching of other subjects was eventually combined with the teaching of letters. By the end of the fifth century BC, a knowledge of all letters became the minimum level of education.

In school, students, who were generally boys 7 years of age, were required to memorize the names of each of the letters, learn the appearance of the letter forms, and how to spell certain syllables. The syllables grew in complexity and eventually were combined to form words. The students learned to produce letters with a stylus on tablets of wax, following a light outline prepared by the schoolmaster. When familiar with the movements necessary to generate the letter forms, the student was given a sample of good penmanship to emulate and was required to practice repeatedly, like the requirements of present day copybooks. Speed and quality were encouraged (Bowen 1972; Cole 1950).

When the Romans conquered Greece and eventually adopted much of the Greek culture, they assumed many of the educational methods for writing as well. Reading and writing in Rome became much more commonplace than in any previous culture. Literacy was now within reach of the common man, owing to the affordable cost and availability of reading and writing materials.

With the decline of Rome and the onset of the medieval age, the churches became the only stronghold for formal education (Bowen 1972). The ability to read and write was, almost exclusively, a feature of the church schools. Learning received no encouragement and was of little use, except in the church. Even among the clergy, it was by no means universal (Williams 1903).

Prior to 800 AD, the ability to write, outside of the clergy, was limited and existed almost exclusively within the upper class or their scribes. Even then, contracts and the like were often made verbally for want of scribes. The clergy discouraged education outside of church dogma; the warfare of the nobles did not require it, and the masses were ignorant of it.

A bright spot in education during the Dark Ages occurred during the reign of Charlemagne. His work and that of Alcuin, whom Charlemagne recruited around 800 AD, saved much of the world's literature and the art of writing. Not until the late twelfth century, however, after the chaos of the Middle Ages, was order restored. Political stability became established. The emphasis on chivalry encouraged a higher moral standard and increased manners, courtesy, and literary taste. Among the nobilities emerged a desire and use for the ability to read and write.

Municipalities emerged from the confusion of the feudal system. In more secure surroundings, industry and trade increased and brought a need for improved education. By the thirteenth and fourteenth centuries, the magistracy of many cities established schools to teach the basics: reading, writing, and reckoning. Although teaching was still taught in Latin, the church opened its writing schools to some laymen.

From the fourteenth to sixteenth centuries, education experienced a renaissance, as did most other aspects of culture; yet in all these years of development and growth, writing was still being taught in much the same way it had been taught 2,000 years earlier (Cole 1950). The only major differences were in the designs of letters (national hands replaced hieratic or Greek majuscules) and in writing materials (ink, quill pens, and parchment instead of wax tablets and papyrus). Although great strides were made by the educators of the Renaissance in the instruction of the arts and sciences, handwriting was still taught by the tracing and copying method.

The first writing manual entitled *La Operina* was printed in Italy by Lodovico Arrighi in 1522 (Fairbank 1970). While providing little in new teaching methods, it introduced the prospective writer to two basic strokes to begin any letter, and then introduced the letters in groups of physical similarity. It was, in fact, the first formalized copybook.

The end of the sixteenth century saw the development and rise of the modern current hand, replacing the previous disjointed cursive writing. Instruction in handwriting began to vary, but primarily by style of letter design rather than method of teaching. Consequently, an educated Englishman, for example, would be master of two hands—an indigenous running secretarie hand and an italic. From this evolved the writing master, each with his own preference in copybooks, or possibly with his own, more or less unique, copybook.

One of the first copybooks used on this continent was published in London, in 1570, by John de Beauchesne and John Baildor. This endeavor, entitled *A Booke Containing Divers Sortes of Hands, as well as the French Secretarie with the Italian, Roman, Chancelry, and Court Hands*, illustrated 37 diverse styles, including such extravagances as secretarie, written in reverse to be read using a mirror (Nash 1959). About a dozen different copybooks were printed during early colonial times.

The earliest record of the teaching of writing in America was by William Brewster in the early part of the seventeenth century. He was the only member of the Mayflower Pilgrims with a university education. Accordingly, he was given responsibility for the education of the Plymouth children. He taught them an Italian script that he learned at Cambridge, by the outmoded methods of tracing and copying. The Massachusetts Bay colonies were taught similar practices.

The major problem for the schoolmasters in teaching handwriting was to bridge the gap between the handwriting of their forefathers that exhibited variations and hybrids of the italic and Gothic hands, and the Roman letters being used in printing fonts.

A hybrid called new mixed current, speedy Italian, or Italian Bastarde was the next major copybook style to emerge. The copybooks of Gianfrancesco Cresci and Lucas Materat spread the usage of this style throughout Britain and the colonies, with the assistance of the publishing efforts of Edward Cocker. Again, this publication championed a new letter style but no new teaching procedures.

By the middle of the seventeenth century, the italic form became the form of choice. Secretarie had all but disappeared and Gothic was maintained for decorative purposes only. Instruction was conducted by writing specialists called writing masters, who gave lessons in public or private. They taught students how to sit, how to position the paper, and how to hold and move the pen. They demonstrated the strokes of letters, the designs of letters themselves, and eventually, words and sentences. The master would set the copy in the student's book by writing an example for that lesson at the top of the page, which the student was required to copy repeatedly as well as he could.

The acquisition of the skill was held in sufficiently high esteem to foster separate schools for the art of writing. Boston had one public writing school by 1684. By 1720, it had two grammar schools and three writing schools. The maintenance of materials and the setting of copy, however, generally made such demands on the writing master's time that it precluded any great measure of individual attention, especially in public schools. The development and spread of ruled paper, steel pens, printed copybooks, and tax-supported schools, however, soon helped alleviate some of the problems.

With the spread of printed copybooks, new teaching ideas emerged, and the first self-help writing manuals appeared. The earliest copybook published in America was printed in Philadelphia by Franklin and Hall in 1748. It was called *The American Instructor* or *Young Man's Best Companion*. An earlier edition, by George Fisher, was well known in England. The first truly American copybook offered was Isaiah Thomas's *The Writing Scholar's Assistant*, published at Worcester in 1785. It was aimed principally at those wanting to develop a useful round hand. In 1668, in London, one of the earliest attempts at a systemized method of teaching writing was published by Edward Cocker and called *England's Penman*. This book broke the letters down into strokes between turns or breaks. These strokes were practiced separately first and then combined into whole letters. In 1714, John Clark authored a book that advocated another system. Clark pointed out that the round hand forms were composed of the oval and the straight line, and that "l," "o," "n," and "j" were the fundamental letters.

The most original handwriting teaching system to appear, however, was that by John Jenkins, which emphasized the idea of principal strokes, not full letters, and no strokes between turns and breaks. In *The Art of Writing*, published in Boston in 1791, Jenkins offered a system of six strokes that could be combined in various orientations and combinations to create almost all of the alphabet (Jenkins 1813). This was the core of his system and the highlight of its originality. Jenkins would drill his students on the execution of these principal strokes, then on the combination of them into letter forms. In the teaching of handwriting, this systemization marked one of the first truly original and significant changes in over 2,000 years. Offshoots of the Jenkins system appeared later, including Henry Dean's *Analytical Guide to the Art of Penmanship* (1804) and Allison Wrifford's *A New Plan of Writing Copies* (1810).

The next substantial change in the teaching of writing occurred in 1809 with the development of the flowing forearm style by Joseph Carstairs (Dougherty 1917). In this system, writing was not just the movement of the hand or fingers but was taught primarily as a movement of the whole arm. This movement took precedent over letter forms. Among the claims for the system were the freedom from writer's cramp, and an effortless, tireless writing. In the teaching of this method, the fingers were first taped into position around the pen, and the basic strokes and letter designs were practiced. Once the strokes and designs were mastered, the hand was freed to allow the better execution of details. It was advertised as being possible to learn in 20 one-hour lessons, if the pupil practiced 6 to 12 hours per day.

In the United States, the foremost advocate of the Carstairian system was Benjamin Franklin Foster. His work, *Practical Penmanship Being a Development of the Carstairian System*, published in Albany, NY in 1830, was a significant influence in both the United States and Britain. He recommended the instruction of fundamental movements (arm, forearm, and hand) separately first, and then their combination into the writing movement. During the 1850s, however, Foster switched his allegiance from Carstairs to the system of Henry Dean, a Jenkins disciple.

The 1820s and 1830s saw an increase in the emphasis on legibility and efficiency. The increased importance of writing for strictly business affairs made perseverance and speed more desirable qualities. There was a greater emphasis on "mercantile" penmanship, sometimes referred to as the *scientific*, *practical*, *business*, or *commercial* hands. Exploitation began to be exhibited in this field with advertisements by schools claiming to teach business writing in as little as one day (Nash 1969). The exception to the emphasis on legibility and efficiency in the business hands was that made for ladies' writing and for ornamental writing, but these writings were also taught by the copybook system.

The 1840s introduced a new emphasis and a new term: muscular movement. This system emphasized forearm movement. The arm rested on the muscle pad below (i.e., distal to) the elbow. Its use was continued through the 1850s and has even influenced many modern systems. In the late 1840s, Platt Rogers Spencer, a self-taught writing master, proposed a flowing swing to what was primarily a Fosterian system and thus introduced the first Spencerian system, which he had been designing and developing since 1820 (Nash 1969). Assisted by Victor M. Rice, Superintendent of Public Instruction for New York State, the Spencerian system gained widespread popularity, and became the basis for many of America's present systems.

Spencerian was the major handwriting system taught in the United States until about 1890 (Figure 2.8). The course of instruction began with the introduction of the student to the letter designs and names. As they memorized the names, the students also became familiar with the designs by tracing over large copies of the letters with their finger. The first skills taught were fundamental strokes and movements for the pen. The letters, except for the flourished capitals which required a free arm, were taught to be executed with a free forearm movement while resting the arm on the edge of the desk. When the fundamental strokes were mastered, the students were required to copy the letter forms in the copybooks. To aid the learning writer, horizontal guidelines (like a musical staff) and vertical sloping lines were sometimes printed on the practice paper.

Starting in about 1890 and lasting for about 10 years, a new system sprang up across the country—vertical writing. It was said by proponents of the vertical writing system that slanted writing, with its complex forms and flourishes, induced the pupil to sit crooked and to crane his neck. The simple design and non-slanted style of the vertical system were claimed to assuage the bad posture and poor eyesight caused by the slanted systems. After a few years of use these claims were found to be totally false, and the vertical system was dropped almost as quickly as it had been accepted.

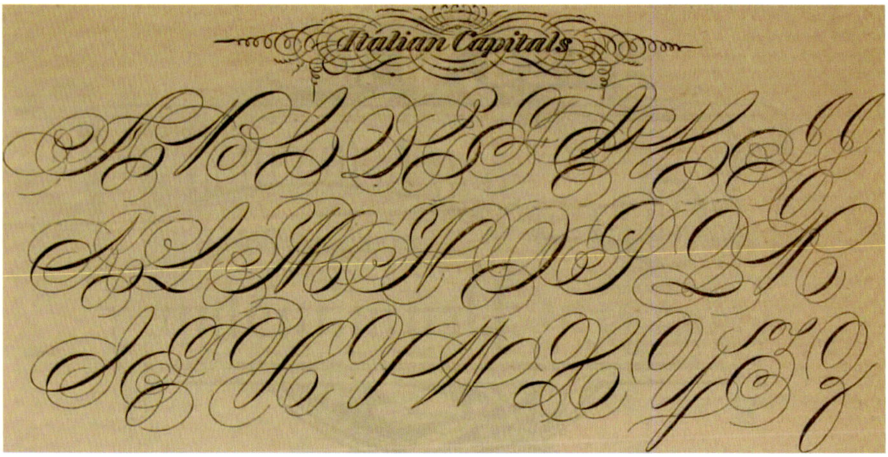

Figure 2.8 Spencerian style handwriting.

Shortly after 1900, most schools returned to teaching a kind of slanted or semislanted writing, frequently Spencerian, with or without a supplementary vertical system. The continued emphasis on speed in business writing, however, reestablished an old and familiar problem. The elegant flowing forms of the Spencerian system, although somewhat simpler than before, could be gracefully formed only when drawn. Under the pressure of the speed required in business writing, they tended to be somewhat distorted and difficult to read and write. This led to the last major profound development in cursive handwriting systems of the twentieth century—the Palmer system.

A.N. Palmer had been trained in writing at the G.A. Gaskell Business College that taught a Spencerian-type system. In about 1880, after teaching penmanship at a business college, he entered the business world. Thereupon, Palmer encountered for himself the problems of speed and legibility. Dissatisfied, Palmer went back to the teaching world with an idea for a new and better business handwriting system. Although based largely on Spencerian, he designed a hand in which the flourishes and shading were quite moderate. He emphasized a free lateral motion of the muscular movement, but reduced excess arm movement in the vertical direction. He implemented finger extensions for lengthened stems and loops. After a period of testing, the Palmer Business Hand was adopted by New York City in 1905 and soon spread across the country.

Herrick et al. (1960) conducted a study of 19 commercial systems of handwriting instruction that represented over 95% of the systems in use in the United States at that time. These systems generally reflected common agreement on methods and objectives. Almost all employed a systematic introduction and practice of the letter forms, and employed some drawing experience to lead into writing tasks. There was only some variation in the order of systematic introduction to the various letters.

Herrick's study found that writing was taught as a tool for communication, not as an end in itself. Motivation for performance was provided by linking the handwriting task with work in other subjects. Legibility and speed were found to be emphasized, with little stress on letter quality beyond simple legibility. The parts of the letters were introduced at a basic level and practiced so that the student could recognize similarities in letter forms. Tracing and copying were still the most commonly found practice methods employed.

Herrick noted that the greatest dissimilarity in the systems occurred in the designs of the cursive forms of capital letters. There were as many as 10 designs for the same letter (e.g., "F" and "R"); for the most part, however, the differences were minor.

Since Herrick's study, a number of additional systems have been recognized in the United States and Canada. In 1965, Beacom (1965) cataloged 10 systems not mentioned by Herrick. Towson (1975) identified additional systems that were extensively used in Canada. Purtell (1980) described eight novel differences among writing systems. Nevertheless, a great deal of information has been obtained in the fields of learning and skill acquisition, particularly of handwriting skills. It is this new knowledge that has engulfed the field of handwriting instruction for most of the twentieth century, and promises to bring about the next significant changes in teaching methods in the twenty-first century.

Huber and Headrick cataloged publishers of handwriting systems that were in use or existed up to the 1990s (see Appendix A). While samples were not obtained in their survey for all of the systems, it was observed that differences between many of them were minor. They noted that the number of persons that may have been exposed to or taught any one of the systems was unknown and impossible to determine. Further, the possibility of positively identifying the particular system behind the writing of any individual of North American origin is problematic.

2.5 HANDWRITING TRAINING IN THE DIGITAL AGE

With the onset of the twenty-first century, some of the handwriting systems identified by Huber and Headrick have been retired or are in limited use. While there are still several handwriting systems currently published and in active use, there are a few that are more widely used (e.g., Zaner-Bloser, Palmer, D'Nealian). The compilation of handwriting systems in Appendix A has been updated to include new systems such as *Handwriting Without Tears* and *New American Cursive*. Other new systems are variations of Zaner-Bloser and Palmer and are directed primarily toward private or home-based schools. The training program *Handwriting Without Tears* (2016) has seen widespread use among millions of grade school students. Developed by an occupational therapist, Jan Olsen, the system advertises easy-to-learn and easy-to-teach methods. Studies on the effectiveness of the *Handwriting Without Tears* program have helped to increase awareness concerning the importance of handwriting skills in the developing brain of grade school children (LeBrun et al. 2012; McBride et al. 2009). Among the teaching methods promoted by newer systems include digital or keyboarding skills that engage students to form letters on touch pads or touch screens in order to bridge the gap between handwriting and computerized tools.

Increased keyboard use and texting has undoubtedly led to a progressive decline in the teaching of handwriting with many citing its irrelevance in a digital age. Indeed, the media has been reporting its decline and death with the added commentary that limited handwriting training and practice has produced immature writing styles prevalent among generations born after 1980 (Suddath 2009). It has been common for school-age children to receive limited training and practice in cursive handwriting resulting in an increase in printing style or combinations of cursive and print. The absence of handwriting training in the Common Core State Standards Initiative adopted among most states in the United States in 2010 contributed to the decline of handwriting training in public schools. Many private, charter, and home-based schools have continued to incorporate handwriting training in their curriculums.

Although handwriting training was not mandated in the Common Core Standards, studies have repeatedly reported on its benefits to grade school children. Two white papers summarized the importance of handwriting training among school children while also addressing the reasons for decline in handwriting (AHAF 2016; Saperstein Associates 2012). These white papers cite over 80 studies reporting on the positive effects of handwriting training among grade school children. Research regarding the positive effects of handwriting training and public campaigns for cursive have produced a resurgence and demand for the return of handwriting training in public schools. Several states in the United States have adopted bills or have modified their state's core standards to allow the return of handwriting training. The decline in cursive handwriting has not been limited to the United States and is indeed a global reaction to the increase in technology-based communication. Other countries have reported on the decline of cursive handwriting and there has been similar campaigning in those countries requesting its return to public education. In Italy, the Campaign for the Enhancement of Handwriting is a call for the preservation of handwriting training because, according to the campaign, handwriting is a heritage of mankind.

From a forensic identification perspective, the main point in understanding the development of handwriting and the influences of handwriting copybook systems primarily involves the identification of class characteristics or characteristics common to a large number of writers. Cha et al. (2006) reported on handwriting copybook style identification as a method in filtering out the class characteristics in which the writer was trained in order to isolate the individual characteristics that lead to identification.

Srihari et al. (2016) carried out a study on the development of handwriting individuality in grade school children (grades 2–4). Not surprisingly, they found that individuality increases as the child develops handwriting skills. Differences from copybook were especially observed in the writing of students in grades 3–4. Naturally, the usefulness of examining what can be observed in a graphically immature writer is important as cases involving threatening notes and graffiti in schools are frequently analyzed by document examiners.

Understanding the levels of graphic maturity is also important in differentiating between child and adult writing. In forensic cases, this necessity mostly occurs in cases when adults may imitate a child's writing (e.g., imitating letters, drawings, or journal entries) or a child imitates an adult's writing (e.g., parental or teacher notes in school). In the 1920s, Saudek discussed the importance of assessing a writer's graphic maturity level before conducting handwriting examinations for forensic identification purposes. He stated that it is difficult to differentiate between lack of graphic maturity and mechanical obstacles, physical disabilities, mental disabilities, lack of knowledge of the language, and other factors. Saudek (1978) advised that "when we are dealing with writers who are not yet completely mature, and above all with children, we must observe certain limitations in judging scripts" (p. 54). Saudek described four levels of graphic maturity that included the stroke, letter, word, and sentence impulse. The first level (stroke impulse) refers to the mastery of the production of the rudimentary stroke, a component of the letter. The fourth level (sentence impulse) describes the mastery of the writer to produce sentences in an uninhibited, fluent manner which suggests that the writer exhibits the ability to write in sentences without having to consciously think about the act of writing.

To some degree, limited copybook training can result in an increase in the development of individualizing characteristics. However, the lack of graphic maturity can also result in increased variability in the handwriting which can make identification more difficult in forensic examinations as pointed out by both Saudek (1978) and Harralson (2013). It is important for handwriting examiners to take into account, as a variable, not only the class characteristic effects of the copybook system but also the level of graphic maturity demonstrated by the writer.

Chapter 3

The Discrimination of Handwriting

3.1 HANDWRITING IDENTIFICATION

There are two fundamental fields of study pertaining to handwriting:

1. The study of handwriting as a neuromuscular activity, its development as a skill, and the effect of various internal and external factors upon it
2. The study of handwriting identification as a discriminatory process

The second uses knowledge acquired through the first but is entirely independent of it. Therefore:

Handwriting identification is a discriminatory process.
Fingerprint identification is a discriminatory process.
Firearms identification is a discriminatory process.
Blood grouping is a discriminatory process.
DNA analysis is a discriminatory process.

Each is a discipline designed to study the respects in which human or material substances are similar or different in their chemical, biochemical, physical, or psychological composition or behavior. Each studies a different kind of evidence to make discriminations. Handwriting identification is a discriminatory process that derives from the comparison of writing habits, and an evaluation of the significance of their similarities or differences. What has been commonly and frequently referred to as characteristics, writing features, or qualities are simply manifestations of the habits formed. They are the discriminating elements of handwriting.

Writing characteristics (i.e., habits) have been commonly described as being of one of two types: class characteristics (the products of prescribed writing systems) and individual characteristics (the particular idiosyncrasies of the individual). Class characteristics were predominant in the writings of the twentieth century when adherence to prescribed writing systems was strongly promoted in educational programs. But the move to electronic communication processes and the concurrent loss of concern for writing excellence has meant that class characteristics are progressively less discernible and identifiable in the inscriptions of present-day writers. Thus, writings have become largely a composition or combination of individual characteristics. It is claimed that they should be more readily discriminated from one another than when copybook was the writing design that everyone attempted to emulate.

Hilton (1982) defined handwriting identification as, for example, the finding of "the same distinctive personal writing characteristics … in both known and unknown writing in sufficient number that the likelihood of accidental coincidence is eliminated" (p. 161). Such definitions invariably contain a rider or condition to the effect that "there are no basic or fundamental differences between the two sets of writing" (p. 161). This, of course, raises the question: what constitutes a fundamental or significant difference? Presumably, it would indicate that two writings, despite other similarities, would not have been executed by the same person. While this topic is discussed further in a later Section 3.8 in this chapter, essentially handwriting identification is a comparison of habits in writing behavior and performance.

3.2 THE PROCESS UNDERLYING IDENTIFICATION

The careful and systematic use of evidence, which is common to the many disciplines of forensic science, is directed toward the identification of an unknown. The process involves three distinct steps or stages, although routines are so well ingrained into the practices of some disciplines that the existence of the three divisions, and the progress through them, often passes unrecognized (Huber and Headrick 1987). The process has been called the Law of ACEs.

3.2.1 Analysis or Discriminating Element Determination

The unknown item and the known items must, by analysis, examination, or study, be reduced to a matter of their discriminating elements. These are the habits of behavior or of performance (i.e., features or characteristics and, in other disciplines, the properties) that serve to differentiate between products or people which may be directly observable, measurable, or otherwise perceptible aspects of the item.

3.2.2 Comparison

The discriminating elements of the unknown, observed, or determined through analysis, examination, or study, must be compared with those known, observed, or recorded of the standard item(s).

3.2.3 Evaluation

Similarities or dissimilarities in discriminating elements will each have a certain value for discrimination purposes, determined by their cause, independence, or likelihood of occurrence. The weight or significance of the similarity or difference of each element must then be considered and the explanation(s) for them proposed.

This process underlies the identification of any matter, person, or thing, by any witness, whether technical, forensic, or not. It is present in the recognition of personal property, familiar objects, friends, or relatives, although its conduct is so automatic that one is seldom aware of its existence. In determining the identity of unfamiliar substances or items, different scientific disciplines study different materials or different aspects of the same material. Thus, the analysis, the examination, or the study differs with the discipline, and sufficient knowledge of the discipline is needed to appreciate what information the analysis, the examination, or the study should seek.

The comparison of elements, attributes, properties, characteristics, or qualities of items is probably within the competence of most literate people to conduct. Whether data is numerical, chemical, physical, or graphical, the comparison is likely to be visual. Where populations of items are larger or data to be considered is extensive, modern technology may assist.

In handwriting examination, discriminating elements must be compared with like discriminating elements. These are elements that are not only covertly similar in form or design, but also rendered under similar circumstances. Handwriting executions are subject to change under the influence of different writing circumstances and conditions (see Chapters 8 and 9). Moreover, any discriminating element of handwriting may be influenced by the particular allographs (letter designs) and/or characters surrounding it. Consequently, comparisons of writing elements must take into consideration the influences of the pen movements (or pencil movements) preceding and succeeding them, or such other circumstances as may be responsible for or expected to produce subtle or gross changes in execution.

The evaluation of the significance of the similarities or differences observed in the comparison is, however, a matter peculiar to the particular discipline. It is the product of proper training and experience. It is the aspect of the process that distinguishes one discipline from another. It is the reason why an individual trained in one discipline is not necessarily competent to make judgments of evidence that may be pertinent to another. It is the essence of the argument as to why graphology and handwriting identification are not synonymous terms.

In the evaluation of handwriting, two properties, if not present, may substantially hinder evaluation: fluency and intricacy of movement. When fluency is absent, the attributes of a signature may exhibit the symptoms of spuriousness. When intricacy is absent, the signature may be deceptively duplicated more easily. Intricacy, in the sense in which it is being used here, is what others have referred to as complexity, with respect to pen movement or signature pattern (Found and Rogers 1996). The importance of these properties of fluency and intricacy arises from the fact that the risk of spuriousness escaping detection in a signature or writing varies inversely with the magnitude in which fluency and intricacy are present. Intricacy in the writing movement is critical to the reliability of the process. Certainly, oversimplification of one's signature pattern reduces it to a series of loops or ovals, or to something that is little more than undulating horizontal lines. This is not uncommon with some writers inclined to stylize their executions. From the viewpoint of security in the signature, however, it provides models that have little in them to complicate the task of duplication.

Intricacy of movement or complexity of pattern is an aspect of writing identification that is seldom mentioned in the classical texts on the subject, but is potentially important. It is a reason why simple tabulations of the frequency of occurrence of the various discriminating elements of a signature cannot be used in probability calculations. They must first be weighted according to their contribution to a signature's self-defense as it is a factor affecting significance. Its absence from the literature may be due to the historic lack of a method that may be employed to measure intricacy or complexity.

It is axiomatic that complexity or intricacy provides evidence in support of genuineness when comparison with standards reveals similarity. It provides evidence in support of spuriousness when comparison with standards reveals difference. In both cases, however, the evidence must be appraised in conjunction with the presence or absence of fluency. It follows that significance in the evaluation of discriminating elements should vary directly with the intricacy or complexity of the element of writing being considered.

There are five components in which a signature, or a writing, may be judged to rate its intricacy or complexity:

1. *The aggregate line length.* Generally speaking, the longer the line, the more complex the design. There are, of course, some stylized signatures that contain lengths of strokes of no purpose.
2. *The number of pronounced directional changes in the line.* When directional changes are angles in the vicinity of 180°, they constitute retraces. When less than 90°, they may

be departures in straight line movement or the commencement of curves. Many, if not most, of the directional changes in a writing will be simply due to allograph design, but the focus should be on those that are not attributable to copybook design.

3. *The number of overwritings.* Overwritings can be misleading as to stroke direction and, thus, confusing as to allograph construction. They may be one of two kinds, retracing or superimposition, and for clarity a distinction should be made between them. A retracing is defined as a line that is situated over another line but is generated by pen motion in the opposite direction. A superimposition is defined as a line that is situated over another line and is generated by pen motion in the same direction. The stem of an "i" and the staff of a "t" when properly written are retracings. The tendency of some European writers to overwrite the bowls of letters in a circular pen motion is a superimposition. Both kinds of overwriting are common in the execution of capital letters in some signatures, although precision in the overwriting is not usually sought.
4. *The continuity of the pen movement.* The interruptions to continuity of the pen are pen lifts that are usually an advantage to the simulator as they provide a legitimate place to pause and consider the next move. However, a pen lift that reflects motion continuity will have a tapered ending and beginning to the pen stroke as the instrument rises from and returns to the paper surface, without a distinct break in its travel (also called a hiatus). This is more difficult for a simulator to duplicate in accurately aligning the elements of the stroke with one another and, at the same time, graduating the deposits of the medium used to generate the stroke.
5. *The repetition of well-segregated, complex pen motions.* Fluent and complex pen motions can be executed with ease, but only when natural and/or practiced. Flawless replication of them is even more dependent on nature and/or practice. Complex pen patterns of the same design that are superimposed upon one another often conceal the evidence of spuriousness that would otherwise be available to consider. The segregation of complex patterns ensures that evidence of genuineness or spuriousness can be judged from the quality of the product.

With the introduction of the complexity theory by Found and Rogers (1996, 1998), quantitatively assessing the complexity of the signature is possible through counting the number of intersections and turning points. Such a method provides an objectively based measure that allows the document examiner to determine whether the evidence is adequate to provide an opinion of authorship. Since the introduction of the complexity theory, other researchers have carried out experiments and further refined the theory. Sita et al. (2002) found that forensic handwriting examiners provide more correct opinions when evaluating highly complex signatures than when evaluating signatures with low complexity. Found and Rogers developed a mathematical formula that could quantitatively rate the complexity level of a signature based on the number of its intersection points and turning points. The theory provides a three-level rating scale that allows the examiner to more definitively assess whether a signature has enough complexity to proffer an opinion. For example, if a signature is consisted of a single loop with three turning points and one intersection, according to the theory and when calculating the formula, the complexity rating for this type of signature is so low that it is advised that the document examiner offer an inconclusive opinion on the signature (Figure 3.1a). This signifies that the examiner does not have enough evidence to form an opinion. A middle level is also calculated that allows document

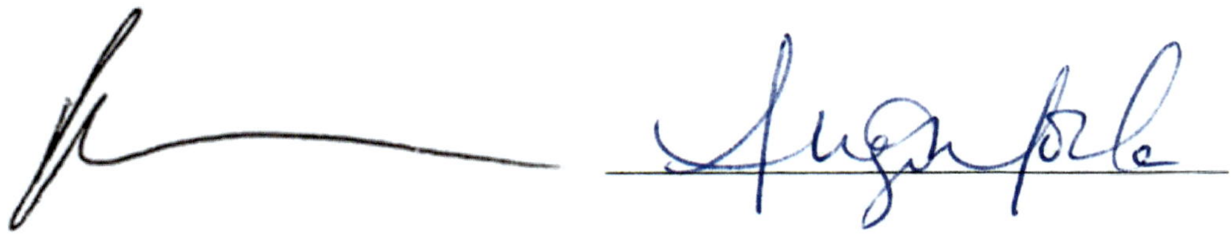

(a) (b)

Figure 3.1 (a) A signature showing little complexity. (b) A signature with a high degree of complexity.

examiners to offer qualified opinions, while a highly complex signature would allow for unqualified opinions or opinions of certainty (Figure 3.1b).

Continued research of the complexity theory supports scientific methodology in the evaluation and comparison of handwriting. In an experimental eye-tracking study, Pepe et al. (2012) found that when examining genuine signatures with a higher degree of complexity, handwriting examiners had longer observation times than signatures with low complexity. In an independent, quantitative study on complexity theory, Alewijnse et al. (2011) supported the use of the model as a less subjective approach to handwriting examination.

The process of identification (the Law of ACEs) is a principle that has been relied upon by document examiners, per Huber, since 1959 and is outlined in recommended standards widely used by document examiners (e.g., ASTM and SWGDOC). The ACE-V (analysis, comparison, evaluation, and verification) method was criticized in the National Academy of Sciences Report (NAS) published in 2009. While the method was not criticized with respect to its use in handwriting examination specifically, it was broadly criticized across forensic disciplines. The NAS report stated its concerns with the method which included its replicability, validity, reliability, standardization, and bias.

An alternative handwriting examination process espoused by Found and Rogers (1999), which was developed by them at LaTrobe University in Melbourne, Australia, and is currently being used by forensic document examiners in Australia, uses a modular approach in handwriting identification. They developed a method flow diagram for handwriting examination that incorporates decision-making about alternative propositions prior to reaching the opinion formation stage(s). The method flow diagram proposes a method of examination to ensure that the examiner carefully evaluates alternative explanations and limitations (e.g., contamination of standards, comparability, altered neurophysiology, altered environmental conditions, and complexity) prior to proposing an authorship opinion. An extensive revision and expansion of the modular method was recently published and includes recommendations in report preparation (Found and Bird 2016).

Hardy and Fagel (1995) in their description of the three phases of the identification process, followed by laboratories in the Netherlands, employ the terms *Analysis of traces or objects*, *Comparison of the analysis results*, and *Determination of the relative individuality of the characteristics*. Slyter (1995) developed specific criteria for formulating levels of opinion based on a methodological and hierarchical analysis of comparison elements. The methodology included careful rating and evaluating limitations in comparison material.

It is questioned as to whether handwriting identification can be refined to a more objective study. Writing is a dynamic aspect of human conduct, undergoing constant but not always discernible change, subject to numerous influences and differing degrees of natural variation. In this ever-changing world, empirical data respecting the writers of today, if it were available, may not be precisely applicable to the writers of tomorrow.

The pursuit of objectivity that Hilton (1995) described as the calculation of a measure of reliability in writing studies is beset by at least three hurdles: (1) natural variations, (2) the unknown interdependence or independence of discriminating elements, and (3) the absence of scales for the measurement or classification of some elements, such as writing quality, fluency or line quality, pen pressure, and some movements. While there has been technological advancement in the quantifiable analysis of handwriting movement, pen pressure, and fluency (to some extent), it is still difficult to examine or measure these elements objectively when examining the static pen trace written on paper. At present, examiners subjectively estimate dynamic movement in a general way. However, research and study into quantifiable measurement using technology that can capture and measure handwriting movement (e.g., NeuroScript MovAlyzeR and OASIS software) can help document examiners visually correlate measurements with the observations made from the static trace. Along these lines, Will (2012) carried out a study showing document examiners' ability to infer relative speed in handwriting samples.

Harrison (1966) seems to share Hilton's views and goes so far as to condemn schemes for "the comparison of writing based on measurement of general features or on some system of scoring points for and against" as being worthless (p. 343). In his view, such schemes will fail to appropriately consider differences, if and when present, that can be vital to the assessment of writings. Nevertheless, the pursuit of objectivity should not be thought entirely futile. It seems so only because, until the arrival of the computer, little thought and endeavor had been applied to a task that appeared formidable.

3.3 HANDWRITING IDENTIFICATION TRAINING

There are four instructional methods that have been employed either discretely or in combination to develop and train handwriting examiners: self-instruction, correspondence courses, apprenticeship programs, and university courses.

Self-instruction was the process, and the only process available, by which most of the practitioners of pre-World War II (1939) learned the business. Many early examiners were accomplished penmen or penmanship teachers. Certainly, as Hilton (1956) pointed out, self-instruction is the most arduous and least reliable learning process over short periods of time.

Correspondence courses have been the means by which some document examiners have received training. Without further instruction or mentorship, this too is an unreliable process of learning handwriting identification and subject to many pitfalls. Historically, there have been differing correspondence courses offering programs that are a few introductory-level lessons in length while others are more comprehensive covering the equivalent of a semester or more of study with assignments, tests, and continued mentoring. There has been no standardization in training through correspondence courses nor do independently sponsored correspondence courses provide valid certification or are part of an accredited learning institution. They offer some training that can meet the recommendations listed in the ASTM or SWGDOC training standard, but, for the most part, the training from correspondence courses should be viewed as a part or component of a document examiner's training.

Historically, there have been few offerings in document examination in colleges or universities, so training has necessarily come from other sources (i.e., self-study, correspondence courses, and apprenticeship/mentorship). More recently, the popularization of forensic science in addition to a demand for standardization and formalization in forensic science training has created a practical need for university courses in the field. To date, there are a few formal graduate-level document examination programs at state universities in North America, all of which are offered as distance learning programs. Additionally, there are courses offered at both undergraduate and graduate levels incorporated into forensic science or criminal justice degree programs that serve as an introduction to the field. There are also noncredit courses in document examination offered at community colleges throughout North America. However, field experience through an apprenticeship or mentorship is still necessary after completion of a formal degree in forensic science specializing in document examination.

Apprenticeship was the process that started practitioners like Ordway Hilton, Donald Doud, Albert S. Osborn, Paul Osborn, Jim Conway, and others in the post-World War II era. It continues to be the process by which many practicing document examiners have been trained. In the apprenticeship system, handwriting identification is learned through programs that invariably have six standard components:

1. A reading component, during which the student is required to read the standard texts of Osborn, Harrison, Hilton, Conway, and others.
2. A writing component, requiring the student to produce essays on prescribed topics, the nucleus of which is found in the texts and in published and unpublished papers of examiners, many of which have been presented at national and international meetings of examiners.
3. A practical component, during which the student is required to conduct examinations of actual or fabricated cases, to render conclusions and write reports, all of which is conducted under the direct supervision and regular review of a competent practitioner.
4. A mock trial component, during which the student is required to present a finding orally, to defend the results obtained, and to demonstrate the ability to express convincingly.
5. An examination or test component, in which the student is required to undergo an examination to measure the scope and depth of understanding and knowledge of the subject.
6. A court introductory component, in which the student gives testimony that is corroborated by the testimony of a mentor or examiner who has examined the same material and reached the same conclusions.

Insofar as apprenticeship programs are concerned, historically the tendency has been to outline a calendar of assignments, headings, or topics that may be as few as 1 or as many as 25 in number. Perhaps, also, this is to identify certain resource material from which the apprentice is expected to extract and assemble information regarding a particular topic that is assigned. In this process, direction is limited, and the apprentice may not know whether the right information has been extracted from the resources until an examination, or test, or written requirement of some kind is imposed.

Furthermore, it is likely to be the case that tutors and their laboratories will possess different libraries of material. The information to be extracted will, therefore, vary from place to place. Without a consolidation or summary of the knowledge of the field, neither the apprentice nor the tutor is aware of what or whether important aspects of the subject are missing.

Almost invariably, these course outlines stipulate a time frame that should be devoted to the topic, which may be a matter of hours, days, or weeks. There is little to indicate whether the time frames correlate with the complexity of the subject or with the extent of the resource material that the candidate is expected to cover. While there is a detailed list of study topics published in ASTM (2005) and SWGDOC (2013a) recommended training standard, there is no indication in the standard to suggest the amount of time that should be spent on each topic, nor is the subject list presented in a way that effectively prioritizes the different study topics.

Without the benefit of much direction, the training enunciated by these programs, on paper, may be little better than a correspondence course, although the time frames and course content may be different due to the accessibility of a tutor and of a library of resource material.

Few training programs conduct closed-book examinations. It is generally thought that the subject is too broad, too varied, or too complex to expect a candidate to convert all that has been written to memory. It is also argued that, for practical reasons, supervised examinations without access to books are more inconvenient to conduct. Whether or not this open-book policy has any bearing on the caliber of the graduate is a moot point. Certainly there are facts and fundamentals of handwriting identification that should be well ingrained in the mind of the student of the discipline to which closed-book examinations might be directed. Furthermore, in the course of giving testimony, there are questions from counsels and courts that are frequently encountered and oral answers will be expected that are clear, comprehensible, and convincing. These answers must be given without reference to a book. Accordingly, they must be learned well in training.

The apprenticeship system of industrial training seems to have originated in the Middle Ages. It was the recognized system of training for all skilled trades in England as early as the thirteenth century. It fell into disuse and was not revived until the era of World War I developed the need for skilled labor. As labor became organized, standards of training and programs of apprenticeship were developed for the evolution of trades and skilled crafts.

Apprenticeship is not a term normally encountered in the professions, although working experience arranged by some academic institutions is sometimes referred to as pupil apprenticeship. The association of apprenticeship with the trades and crafts rather than the professions, the limited involvement of lectures and academic instruction in these fields, and the sparsity of textbooks to facilitate the learning process may betoken the kind and magnitude of the task in the conversion of handwriting identification to a scientific pursuit.

The apprenticeship system of training document examiners has not been without its critics. Leson (1974) maintained that it suffers from a major disadvantage in that without a standardized curriculum there is no guarantee that apprentices are being correctly taught or similarly taught. Without some means of qualifying the instructor and the course, the training process lends itself to the perpetuation of poor training methods. Baxter (1970) went on to say that not only does the period of training vary from individual to individual, but also from the practice of one office or laboratory to another, because it is largely dependent upon the staff, the facilities, and the cases available for training purposes.

Many have written on the subject of the training and qualifications of the document examiner and many of them have itemized a desirable course content, insofar as the topics to be included (Hilton 1956; Cabanne 1965; Mathyer 1965; Caponi and Berardi 1966; Sellers 1966; Purtell 1969; Miller 1972b; Miller 1973; Greenwood 1983; Behrendt 1989; Epstein et al. 1992; Fisher 1992). Some of these papers have covered the selection of candidates and the skills required. None of these papers and presentations that have listed the topics have stated what particular knowledge is intended to be imparted to the apprentice within each area. Several persons have attempted to select and assemble courses from university curricula that might constitute an ideal background program.

Ideally, current students should be trained through university courses to learn scientific method and theory in combination with an apprenticeship/mentorship program in order to obtain the necessary practical experience. The combination of theory and practice adequately addresses the criticisms concerning training raised in the NAS report (2009). The NAS Committee viewed an apprenticeship-type model (widely used in the forensic sciences) as a secondary form of training. Training in a university grounds the student in scientific method and theory which supports the objective, methodological practice of document examination during an apprenticeship. Invariably, in a university setting, the student is exposed to recent research, alternative theories, scientific methods, and different professors, lecturers, and library resources which are not widely available during an apprenticeship.

Students participating in graduate-level programs at a university are not only exposed to academic research but are more likely to engage in new research. While the forensic document examination programs offered at state universities are offered as distance learning programs, the online method allows for wider accessibility to students throughout North America and internationally. Such a method is vital in order to maintain the minimum student enrollment required to keep such programs active.

At Oklahoma State University (OSA) Center for Health Sciences, a master of science degree in forensic science is offered with a specialization in forensic document examination. In addition to core forensic science courses, the specialization includes four courses in forensic document examination including forensic examination of questioned documents, forensic handwriting examination, technical aspects of forensic document examination, and historical aspects of forensic document examination. OSA clearly states on its website that completion of these courses does not result in professional certification as a 2-year mentorship program is required for certification.

The Department of Criminal Justice and Criminology at East Tennessee State University (ETSU) offers a graduate certificate in forensic document examination. Comprised of four courses, or the equivalent of 12 semester hours, the certificate degree typically requires two semesters to complete. The courses include Introduction to Forensic Document Examination, Forensic Handwriting Identification, Forensic Document Analysis, and Forensic Document Practicum. The program does not offer professional certification but recommends that students wanting to work professionally in the field enter into a 2-year mentorship program. The courses can be taken as electives for students enrolled in criminal justice programs at the university.

3.4 CLASS OR SYSTEM CHARACTERISTICS IN WRITING

Definition: Class characteristics are those aspects, elements, or qualities of writing that situate a person within a group of writers or that give a written communication a group identity.

The group of writers or writings in any given class may vary in size from small numbers to continental populations. It may have geographic, religious, national, academic, or political boundaries by which its writing can be related to some recognizable common content. Traditionally, class characteristics in writing have been conceived as limited to national and/or system characteristics, the latter being more often a subdivision of the former. The current concept, however, is much broader, as in the case of European writing or Hispanic writing. Furthermore, the writing systems that these classes represent (and there may be several) are more difficult to define and to discriminate between, if distinguishable at all.

Not too long ago, it was said that national characteristics constituted those class characteristics that serve to differentiate between the collection of systems that are popular in, and peculiar to, different countries. In view of today's constantly changing borders, it may be preferable to say peculiar to different areas of the world. Remarkably enough, where languages and alphabets are similar, if not the same, one finds much similarity in the class characteristics of the writings.

When the quantities of a foreign writing being scrutinized are sufficient, one finds that the national characteristics within a class often give the material a distinctive pictorial countenance ensuing from the collective effect of its common characteristics. The precise causes of its appearance are sometimes difficult to determine because the effects are cumulative rather than particular.

In the traditional sense, class characteristics within a handwriting are those writing habits or features that emanate from the published and/or prescribed method (i.e., system) of writing that has been utilized in the learning process. In the more distant past, they have been of two kinds: (1) unique characteristics or features that serve to distinguish one method or system from another and (2) common characteristics such as slope, spacing, height, proportions, and letter designs that are shared with other systems.

More recent practices have led to greater duplicity in writing systems through the use of optional forms, rendering them more difficult to differentiate from each other. Then too, the liberties allowed in adherence to any prescribed system result in letter forms that may be readable, but not identifiable, with any particular system source. Consequently, the role of class characteristics in the agenda of handwriting identification, because of form differences prescribed and exhibited by different systems, has been greatly diminished if not completely demolished.

There are, of course, within many systems of writing employed on this continent, three distinct styles of writing: cursive, manuscript or script, and block lettering. If the cursive styles have tended to duplicate one another with optional forms, there is an equal amount of duplicity within the script and lettering styles.

Tytell (1991) has gone to some length to summarize and consolidate the definitions that examiners nurse regarding class and individual characteristics. Haywood (1991) devotes time to defining terms presumably for the purpose of determining categories for specialized characteristics.

Found and Rogers (1995) question the orthodox theory that the validity of a document examiner's opinion is based on the ability to distinguish between class and individual characteristics. They maintain that the basics of the "class/individual" theory hinges on the notions of (1) a copybook form, (2) a divergence from the form, and (3) an evaluation of the uniqueness of that divergence derived from the experience of the examiner.

The latitude now allowed in the learning and conduct of writing renders the class/individual theory almost impossible to apply, certainly insofar as signatures are concerned. Harrison (1958b), and then Miller (1972a), reported that it is virtually impossible to correctly identify the system taught. Except for a few elements of some letter forms, most, if not all, discriminating elements of writing on this continent now fall within the old category and definition of individual characteristics.

There are some features that still reflect the attributes of particular writing systems. The structure or design of the capital letters "F," "B," "P," "R," "T," "W," and "Y" exhibits as many system variations as any letter, but the designs and shapes of the lowercase letters "e," "i," "l," "s," and "t" provide little latitude for variation between systems. The majority of class differences are found in the designs and shapes of capital letters. Capital letters, however, constitute a small portion of the writings that come into question (Figure 3.2).

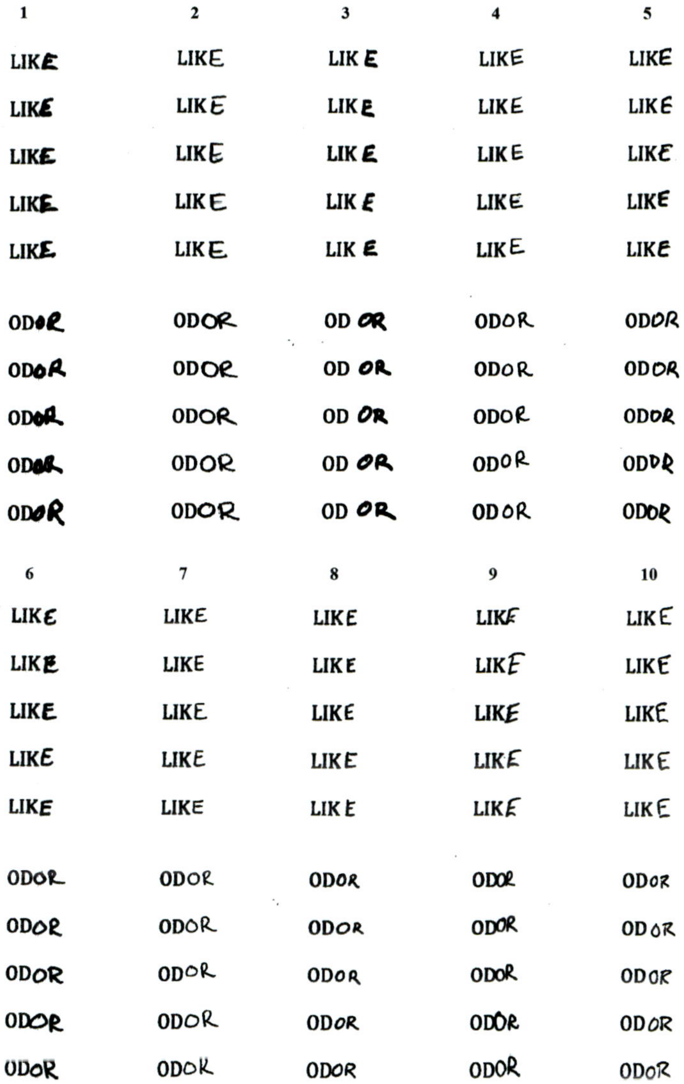

Figure 3.2 Ten individuals were asked to add the handwritten letter "E" to LIKE and "OR" to ODOR. Note that it would be difficult to differentiate these writers based on class characteristics.

Accordingly, except for some general features that may differentiate the writings of different parts of the world, class characteristics are a thing of the past. They are seldom recognizable aspects of today's writings present in copious quantities, and particularly in signatures. The approach to writing examinations must be modified accordingly. The problem respecting system characteristics arises from the task of estimating the significance of these elements of writing if and when appearing. This has always been a problem, even when system features were more exclusively the symbol of a particular writing method. The appropriate data (e.g., the popularity of the system) is no longer of great value. Admittedly, then, system and national attributes have some influence upon populations of people; however, except for a few letters, the influence is indeterminable.

Thus, the class/individual theory is not applicable to many signatures. This is not news or cause to condemn the theory. It is an observation that signature identification, for a number of reasons, must be based frequently on individual characteristics alone. Poor quality extended writing may suffer from the same malady. Notwithstanding the absence of recognizable class, system, or national characteristics within a signature, however, the writing may well be identifiable with a particular individual. There is no practical reason for not doing so. Furthermore, although they may not be numerous or present in many cases, there are still some system and national characteristics that are quite distinctive, which, if present, would provide some evidence of writers originating from the same or different locations.

An interest in class characteristics, however, is precautionary. It is advisable to avoid overestimating or underestimating the value of these features. Despite the lack of precise information and the consequent need to judge any discriminating element conservatively, it is difficult to see where any error in the recognition of a particular class characteristic would significantly alter results. The kinsmen to class characteristics are, of course, individual characteristics defined as those aspects, elements, or qualities of writing that distinguish between members within a group.

3.5 NATIONAL CHARACTERISTICS IN WRITING

Definition: To the extent that writing systems within a country share common features and induce class characteristics in the writing of its people that are different from the products of writing systems of other countries, such features are referred to as national characteristics.

Few document examiners have a large library of books on the writing systems of different countries of the world. Yet, it would seem that a library of some sort is necessary if an examiner is expected to know what the class characteristics are of systems taught in North America and how they differ from other systems taught elsewhere. Although the subtle differences between systems are becoming more obscure because of present teaching practices, there are some more pronounced disparities between regions of the world of which one should be aware.

A number of authors from the US Immigration and Naturalization Service (INS) Lab and the US Postal Inspection Service Labs reported on studies conducted of some 20,000 lettered samples from writers emanating from 77 countries, in an endeavor to provide some empirical data respecting as many as 62 different features of hand lettering, including seven numerals (Berthold and Wootton 1993; Ziegler and Trina 1994; Trizna and Wooton 1995, 1996). The intent of the studies was to determine whether any of these features was peculiar to particular nationalities, or conversely, whether they were notably foreign to a given country.

The preliminary discussion of this research and of the reference material used in the INS collection provides an excellent comment regarding the impact of current immigration policies and practices on American handwriting. To this is added some recent data respecting the population of foreign nationalities and of persons using foreign languages in the United States. The discussion also cites several recognized authors who have expressed themselves on the need for this kind of information (Wooton 1994).

The citations provided in support of the work refer to cursive writings. There is little information as to how or whether lettering or hand printing varies from location to location. Among the 62 features considered, there are some 11 features that exhibited a cursive nature (in the letters "B,"

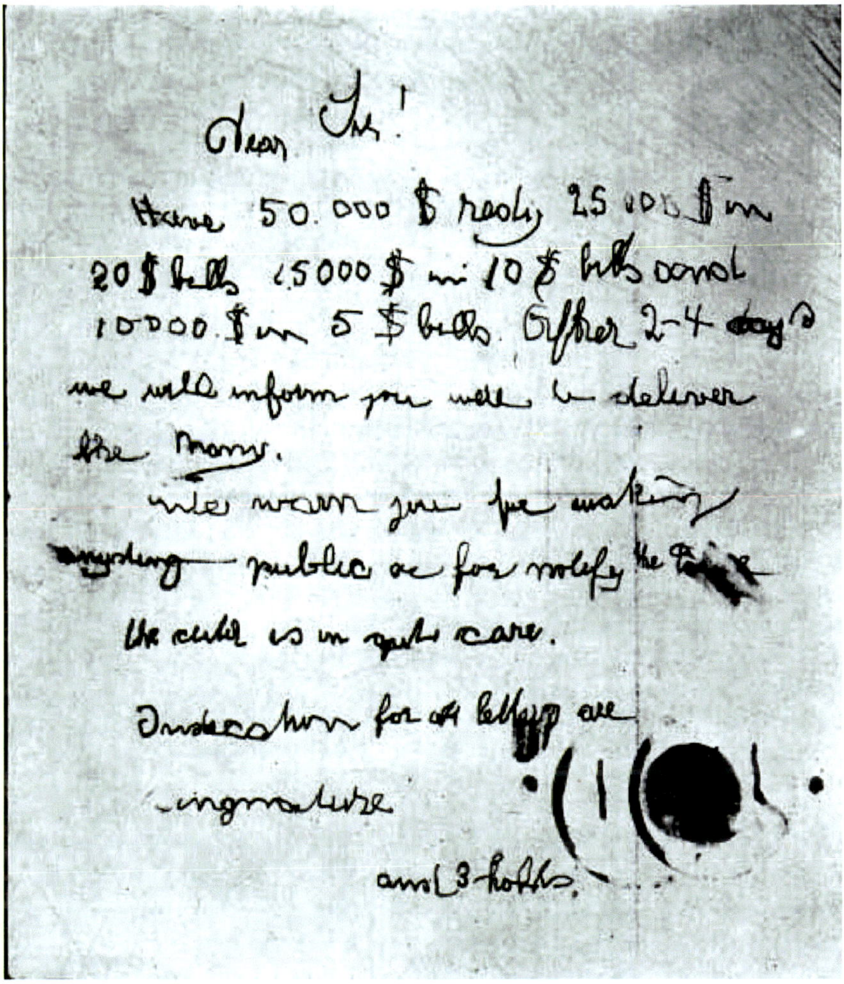

Dear Sir!
Have 50.000 $ redy 25 000 $ in 20 $ bills 15000 $ in 10 $ bills and 10000 $ in 5 $ bills. After 2-4 days we will inform you were to deliver the mony.
We warn you for making anyding public or for notify the police the child is in gut care.
Indication for all letters are singnature and 3 holes.

Figure 3.3 One of the ransom letters attributed to Bruno Hauptmann in the Lindbergh baby kidnapping case. Note the awkward construction of words and letters as well as the German Influence of the writing.

"C," "E," "G," "J," "Q," "R," "T," "V," "Y," and "Z"), and seven numerals (1, 2, 4, 5, 7, 8, 9). These normally fall within the scope of cursive writing styles. Consequently, some useful information is provided that relates to the frequency of occurrence that might be expected of some of these features in the letterings and writings of persons of foreign nationalities (Figure 3.3).

3.6 INDIVIDUAL CHARACTERISTICS IN WRITING

Definition: Individual writing characteristics are those discriminating elements that serve to differentiate between members within any or all groups.

Generally, individual characteristics are thought of as those particular aspects or features of writing that are peculiar to a specific writer (Hilton 1982). In this sense, they possess a character that is infrequently encountered. There are, however, a large number of more commonly encountered elements of writing that may be described as designs, inventions, and developments of a writer that, when considered in combination as a group, give uniqueness to a writing (Osborn 1929). In this sense, it is the composition of the combination that is responsible for the individuality the writing acquires. Although the expression is broadly used and presumably understood, few authors have bothered to define it, perhaps because the need has not been apparent.

Individuality is probably more often exhibited by writers in the execution of the more complex letter forms. Some letters of the alphabet require complex movements of the pen that many writers find somewhat difficult to execute. As a result, copybook or model letter forms are often slightly altered by a writer to a structure or shape more conveniently performed. These modifications, sometimes subtle, sometimes profound, are the individual characteristics of that writer (Figure 3.4a and b).

Because writing must be read, some conformity to copybook design must be furnished, which places limitations on the extent of divergence from accepted forms. The result is that similar individual features may be found in the writing of other persons (Hilton 1983), although a particular group of such features is not likely to be duplicated. It is the group or combination of such features, rather than any specific feature, that serves, ordinarily, to distinguish one writer from another.

Srihari et al. (2002) carried out a widely cited study that established the individuality of handwriting in forensic identification employing an automated system that was originally invented for postal address handwriting recognition. For data collection, samples of representative types of handwritings were used to build a 1,500 sample handwriting database. The data was analyzed for identification of a writer against other writers (identification), as well as for comparing the writing of a document with another writing to verify that it is written by the same person (verification). Results showed that the system had a 98% accuracy rate for identification and a 96% accuracy rate for verification. The high performance of the system's method was based on just a few macro- and microfeatures, but the authors pointed out that such identification or verification could not be determined by a single feature, indicating that handwriting identification and verification is dependent upon a set of features.

Srihari et al.'s (2002) study on the individuality of handwriting was criticized as not representative of handwriting examination because it relied on computational analysis rather than human examiners. It was also criticized for not relying on a more homogenous handwriting sample in its data set. The research was followed by another study by Srihari et al. (2008) on the differentiation of the handwriting of twins, which showed that human examiners outperformed the results obtained from the computer. Durina and Caligiuri (2009) carried out a study on over 50 adults to examine the individuality of a homogenous group of writers. The researchers collected samples from a group of writers who grew up in the same neighborhood, were instructed

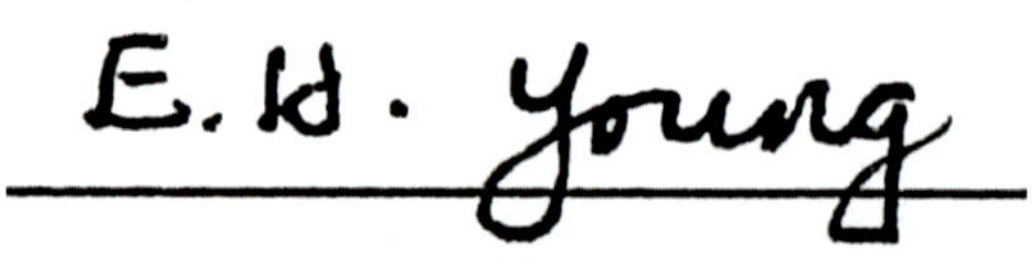

(a)

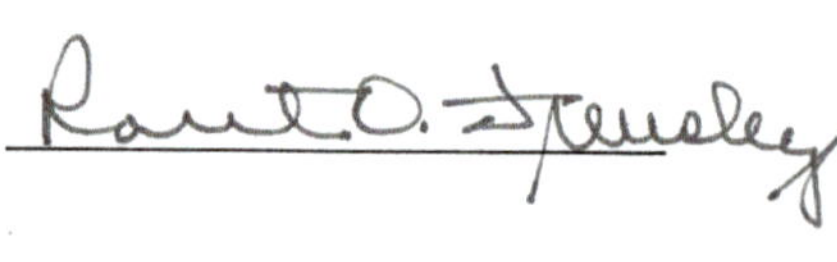

(b)

Figure 3.4 A signature depicting an unusual construction of the (a) capital letter "H" indicating an individual characteristic and (b) capital letter "F" in the last name indicating an individual characteristic.

in the same copybook method by the same teachers, and attended the same school. A group of handwriting examiners evaluated the writers to determine authorship. The results showed that the examiners were able to find features of individuality in the samples that assisted them in differentiating and identifying the writers.

3.7 ACCIDENTALS IN WRITING

There are occurrences in writing that may have little or no plausible explanation. They may be unusual forms, shapes or movements, breaks in the writing line, or even the doubling of some letters or parts of letters. They are more often minor in nature, infrequent, and of insufficient concern to the writer as to warrant attention or correction.

Definition: Accidentals are isolated, brief, or temporary digressions from normal writing practices.

It is seldom that accidentals are noted or observed in writing standards. Rather, it is a designation or label given to an element of a questioned writing that digresses significantly from the normal and natural writing practices observed in the writing standards, and for which there is no other plausible explanation. Its only qualification for receiving the designation seems to be that it is different.

Some examiners have been known to refer to accidental occurrences as accidental characteristics. This is, of course, a self-contradiction, for their occurrence is not likely to be repeated in a similar fashion, and thus, it is not representative or characteristic of any aspect of a writing.

In the section to follow respecting fundamental and significant differences, the general principle advanced by several of the accepted authorities is discussed. The principle is that as few as one difference can offset the weight of a number of similarities in writing examinations and studies. Given the definition for accidentals, one is challenged to resolve the question as to whether a single disparity between questioned and known writings constitutes an accidental in the writing of the same person or a dissimilarity indicative of a disparate writer.

The answer may rest in the opportunities the questioned writing provides for the occurrence to repeat itself. If opportunities are present and the occurrence is not repeated, the occurrence may be considered to be an accidental. If opportunities are present and the occurrence is repeated, it must be considered to be behaving as a writing habit, and thus constitutes a dissimilarity. Obviously, the resolution of the question will hinge largely on the nature and extent of the questioned writing, in which the discrepancy occurs.

If, however, the nature and extent of the questioned writing is limited and opportunities for the occurrence to be repeated are not available, how does the examiner categorize and/or allude to the occurrence? In Chapter 6, the various aspects of writing that are considered and studied in writing examinations are listed and described. These are designated as the discriminating elements of writing that serve the purpose of a writing study whether for or against the identification of a given person with a particular written execution (because their meaning is often imprecise, the use of terms such as *characteristics*, *qualities*, and *features* is avoided whenever possible). Elements of writing that cannot be categorized as to their evidential usefulness are indeterminable elements and remain so until additional writings clarify their character. Such is the destiny of accidentals and/or dissimilarities as long as their true character is in doubt.

3.8 FUNDAMENTAL OR SIGNIFICANT DIFFERENCE IN WRITING

In a world of material things, virtually all things are different, if the examination of them is carried out at an appropriate level of precision. This is particularly so in the comparison of handwritings, for no two samples of the same text, by the same individual, with the same writing instrument, on the same date, and under the same writing and writer conditions will be identical in all respects. Such being the case, the document examiner or handwriting expert is constantly challenged by the same provocative questions: what is a difference and when does it become significant?

Much has been written on the subject of differences, but as McAlexander (1997) points out, little has been provided to clearly establish what a fundamental difference is and what makes a difference significant. None of the widely recognized authorities on handwriting—Osborn (1929), Hilton (1982), Conway (1959), Harrison (1958b), or Ellen (1989)—each of whom has spoken of differences and of the consideration they must be given, has provided definitions of the terms with which examiners might work. Osborn spoke of divergences that extend beyond the range of variation and are not attributed to the writing or writer conditions. He later said that writings by different persons will differ in some of the 27 particulars he lists. He further stated that divergences in two specimens of writing may be found in repeated individual or general characteristics that will be indicative of different writers. None of the other authorities were more precise.

Whiting (1996) lamented the absence of adequate definitions in the literature and the imprecision of those that are offered to properly describe a fundamental difference, the term that is only too often used. While Huber and Headrick agreed with his criticisms, they noted that Whiting did not provide a better definition with which to work.

Differences in writing are of two kinds: *lucid* and *elusive* differences. Lucid differences are those that are markedly distinct in quality or character. They are obvious. Among other things they include differences in allographs (i.e., letter designs), dimensions, slant, or letter construction. Elusive differences are those that are much less pronounced, more subtle, and do not reflect basic changes in design or structure.

There is merit in referring to lucid differences as disparities and in addressing elusive differences as divergences. Lexical definitions of these terms seem to make this selection appropriate. A *disparity* then is a more pronounced difference in writings, while a *divergence* is a less pronounced or more subtle difference. Osborn used the word *divergence* in this fashion.

In Chapter 6, Huber and Headrick list, organize, and describe all of the 21 aspects or attributes of writing that are employed in the identification of handwriting. They speak of and designate these 21 aspects or attributes of writing as being its discriminating elements, an element being defined as anything that is a part of a complex whole. Discriminating elements then are those parts of the complex whole of one's writing that can serve to differentiate between writers.

Huber and Headrick also find that of these 21 discriminating elements, at least 17 may be segregated into one of two prime groups. First, there are seven elements of style, which include arrangement, class of allographs, connections, construction (including design and selection of allographs), dimensions, slant or slope, and spacings. Second, there are 10 elements of execution, which include abbreviations, alignment, commencements and terminations, diacritics and punctuation, embellishments, legibility or writing quality (including letter shapes or forms), line continuity, line quality, pen control, and writing movement.

Elements of style are those aspects of writing that are usually subject to direction in the learning or vocational process. Consequently, they are the aspects that may change with location, change with the school or the teacher, or change with the occupation of the writer. Elements of execution, on the other hand, are those aspects of writing in which personal idiosyncrasies usually develop as a result of personal preferences, personal circumstances, and/or personal skills.

In a review of what has been said about differences, it was found that lucid differences (disparities) occur largely in the elements of style, whereas elusive differences (divergences) occur largely in the elements of execution. It is also apparent that lucid differences occur in those aspects of writing that are more fundamental to the writing process, whereas elusive differences are more personal aspects of the writing.

Disparities, when they occur, are more often attributable to a difference in writers. They are the distinctive and usually observable dissimilarities that emanate from different teachings, different backgrounds, or different practices. They include changes in allographs.

On the other hand, divergences, when they occur, are often the products of variation in the same writer that may be either natural variation or variation due to some special cause. Divergences may also be simply the respects in which two individuals, subject to the same influences, teachings, or backgrounds, may differ from each other in the manner in which they execute a writing movement or manipulate the writing instrument, without actually changing the basic forms or letter structures. They are the subtle mutations observed in the graphs within writers or between writers. It might be said that disparities are differences that discriminate between groups, whereas divergences are differences that discriminate between members of a group.

Fundamental differences then will be disparities, which are dissimilarities that occur with respect to the elements of style, rather than the elements of execution. Accordingly, a proper definition of the term *fundamental difference* should narrow its perspective to the elements of style. In practice, one finds that changes in the elements of style are often accompanied by changes in patterns of execution. To avoid confusion, the assessment of differences should consider first the disparities that may be present in the elements of style. If they exist, they might constitute fundamental differences. If and when there are dissimilarities present in the elements of style, divergences in the elements of execution may be expected and placed in proper perspective as additional evidence of a different writer.

With these interpretations in mind, a usable general meaning for a handwriting difference may be offered as follows:

> **Definition:** In a comparison of questioned and known writings, a difference in a (questioned) writing is (1) a disparity in one of its discriminating elements of style or (2) a divergence in one of its discriminating elements of execution, either of which exceeds the expected range of natural variation for these elements within the writings with which it is being compared. In either case, the difference is otherwise inexplicable.

While this definition tells us what a difference is, it does not suggest why it is. Differences that are found must be studied and considered with respect to possible causes. They may be due to causes that tend to affect the elements of execution, such as writing conditions or other external factors; internal factors such as age, illness, and drugs or medications; and attempt to disguise or deliberately alter normal writing habits. They may, on the other hand, be true differences that are attributable to some fundamental discrepancy emanating from a different writing hand, more often observable in the elements of style.

There are differences then, and there are fundamental differences, that make writings dissimilar from one another. Both must be considered insofar as the aspects of writing in which they are found are concerned. A definition of fundamental difference would be as follows:

> **Definition:** In a comparison of questioned and known writings, a fundamental difference in a (questioned) writing is a disparity in one of its discriminating elements, within the elements of style.

This definition could be qualified with the statement that usually within the elements of form, allow for those few occasions in which there may be special differences in elements of execution. For example, in such features as the location of quotation marks that would normally fall within the category of punctuation however, in some countries, these may be aspects of the system of writing taught.

Now that the reader is better equipped to identify or describe a difference, what then is a significant difference? Significance with respect to similarities, which is the evidence required to facilitate an identification, is determined by the frequency of occurrence of a feature or writing element in the writing of different persons. Significance then is a function of its rarity or uniqueness. It is a circumstance that has a potential for measurement, simply by collecting the empirical data relative to that frequency. There is no empirical data to be collected, however, that provides corresponding information respecting differences. What would an examiner seek to count to measure the importance of a difference? What continuum or scale could be used on which to rank differences? How can then a difference or any difference be classed as significant? Are not all differences of equal significance?

Much of what has been written respecting differences by the recognized authorities on handwriting identification has sung a somewhat similar tune with which most examiners are familiar: that even a single difference can outweigh a number of similarities. Hilton (1982) stated that "it is a basic axiom of identification in document problems that a limited number of basic differences, even in the face of numerous strong similarities, are controlling and accurately establish nonidentity" (p. 10). Hilton goes so far as to say that "a single significant difference between the (known and unknown) specimens is a strong indication of two writers, unless the divergence can be logically accounted for by the facts surrounding the preparation of the specimens" (p. 10). Harrison (1958b) made similar comments:

> The fundamental rule which admits of no exception when handwritings are being compared ... is simple – whatever features two specimens of handwriting may have in common, they cannot be considered to be of common authorship if they display but a single consistent dissimilarity in any feature which is fundamental to the structure of the handwriting, and whose presence is not capable of reasonable explanation. (p. 343)

Harrison reiterated the point:

> The rule that a single consistent dissimilarity, irrespective of the number and nature of the similarities which are demonstrable must exclude any possibility of common authorship may seem harsh, but in practice, it is exceptional for handwritings by different authors to be found to differ in but one material particular. (p. 343)

Conway (1959) expressed the same theme when he wrote:

> A series of fundamental agreements in identifying individualities is requisite to the conclusion that two writings were authored by the same person, whereas a single fundamental difference in an

identifying individuality between two writings precludes the conclusion that they were executed by the same person. (p. 65)

The common thread that these writings seem to exhibit is the importance attributed to a limited number of differences, perhaps only one. In the views of these authors, all and any fundamental difference (i.e., disparity) appears to carry the same weight, the magnitude of which is sufficient to offset the weight of a number of similarities, regardless of their respective importance. Therefore, all differences must be deemed equally important and equally significant. Some differences, however, if not more significant, are at least less disputable as being indicative of production by different writers.

3.9 CONDITIONS CONTRIBUTING TO DIFFERENCES IN WRITING

Osborn (1929) and others previously cited generally agreed that despite numerous similarities in two sets of writings, a conclusion of identity cannot be made if there is one or more differences in fundamental features of the writings. Such statements have prompted the discussion above, in which there was an attempt to define a difference. If there are differences between writings, however, can it be properly concluded that the writings are the products of different writers? Or, is it possible that some apparent differences are not true differences indicative of different authors, but simply variations of the same author resulting from extenuating circumstances?

The simple answer is, of course, "yes." There are a number of extenuating circumstances that could be responsible. McAlexander and Maguire (1991) have suggested a few. They, like most writers on handwriting identification, have commented on the numerous changes in circumstances or conditions that may influence the written product, but few have ventured to say in what particular manners. To some extent this can be explained by the fact that, in the human experience, different factors can influence different people in different fashions. There are, however, some generalities that can be stated.

3.9.1 Adequacy of Standards

In the pursuit of a reasonable explanation for the existence of an apparent difference in the comparison of questioned and known writings, the first consideration must be given to the adequacy of the standards to ensure that the full range of variations of which the writer is capable is represented. Not only must the standards be adequate in quantity, but they must be as contemporaneous as possible with the questioned writing. This is in order that the variables, due to conditions, circumstances, date, development, and maturity, of the writing will be controlled.

The contemporaneousness of the standards is the point most often proffered as the reason for apparent differences occurring in two writings. Because writing is susceptible to internal and external influences, the matching of circumstances between the questioned and known writings is vitally important. It can account for a difference in shape, quality, or particular movements.

3.9.2 Accidental Occurrences

There are occurrences in writing that may have little or no plausible explanation. They may be unusual forms or movements, breaks in the writing line, or even the doubling of some letters or parts of letters. They are more often minor in nature, infrequent, and of insufficient concern to the writer to warrant attention or correction. They are, frequently, completely erratic movements and may reflect a momentary interruption in neuromuscular coordination. Thus, accidental occurrences are best described as brief, temporary digressions from normal writing practices.

3.9.3 Alternative Styles

There are individuals that are said to be versatile writers, that have more than one style of writing, perhaps cursive and script, or cursive and lettering. The second may be prompted by a particular type of occupation such as architecture that requires lettering. On occasion, relapses occur wherein a change will be made in a letter or a word. More often than not, these incidents will be observed in reasonably skillful executions of extended writing. Changes to a second distinctive style are not normally expected in writings but are found in signatures on infrequent occasions, as Hilton illustrated. Other instances have been reported as well, wherein such changes were accomplished. Whiting (1997) describes and illustrates the differences in two styles of writing and signing executed by one individual using two identities. Confirmation that the two identities were, in fact, the same person was provided by a fingerprint comparison.

Without elucidating further on what was meant by *styles* or how they differed, Bohn (1974) reported that the FBI Laboratory (or himself) had frequently encountered cases where a single writer employed very different handwriting styles and cautioned examiners to carefully evaluate whether the observed difference is a fundamental difference.

McCarthy (1988) claimed that it is easier for a poor writer to consistently change letter forms while printing than it is for a highly skilled cursive writer, since habit is not so intrinsically established. For the unskilled person who prints, the act is not fluent but more in the nature of drawing.

3.9.4 Ambidexterity

Some, but not many, individuals—especially among those persons that have converted from sinistrals to dextrals at some point—have the ability to write with either hand with almost equal dexterity. In most respects, the written products are similar. Muscular coordination of the two hands and arms may not be precisely the same, however, and differences in fluency and some movements may be noted.

3.9.5 Carelessness or Negligence

Most writers have occasions when their writing degenerates to a scrawl or scribble due to haste, carelessness, or particularly poor writing circumstances. These executions are usually confined to short notes, addresses, and telephone numbers. Often they are inscribed on small note pads, envelopes, and segments of paper. They frequently contain elements of a person's writing that are unusual or accidental. They may never appear again in another example. They are unreliable indicators of normal writing habits or of a writer's normal range of variation.

3.9.6 Changes in Health Condition of the Writer

Depending on their nature, changes in health may affect the fluency, rather than the designs of writing. The changes can be expected to be temporary, however, and writing facility will likely return with the recovery of health. The deterioration of health generally is another matter and its progress may vary with the individual. Its effect is usually observed in a loss of control and the introduction of more erratic movements. This is one of the aspects that has a bearing on the adequacy of standards.

3.9.7 Changes in Physical Condition of the Writer: Fractures, Fatigue, and Weakness

Fractures of the hand and arm, requiring restraints on mobility that inhibit the grasp of the instrument or the movement of the pen, will, of course, alter the written product. When movement has been restricted for long periods, the full use of the member may not be immediately regained even after restrictions are removed.

Some individuals suffered such serious injury to the writing hand or arm that they were obliged to rely on whatever ability could be developed hastily with the nondominant hand and arm. The quality of the writing is poor in such cases, but depending on the duration of the incapacitation, a measure of skill can be acquired. The differences in the writing should be obvious, of course, but as mentioned elsewhere there are numerous writing habits that will persist in the writing of the nondominant hand.

Studies have also shown that fatigue and weakness have their effects upon the control of the writing instrument and its performance may be altered in unpredictable fashions. These too are aspects that have a bearing on the adequacy of standards.

3.9.8 Changes in the Mental Condition or State of the Writer

As noted elsewhere, schizophrenics and/or persons with multiple personalities can exhibit major changes in their writing on different occasions corresponding to the mental state at the time. These are changes not so much in kind as in quality. A change to a childhood state will be accompanied by a corresponding childlike or immature quality of writing.

3.9.9 Concentration on the Act of Writing

Concentration on the writing act will, of course, render it to be a more conscious process, and consciousness steals from fluency. The action becomes more deliberate and slower. The change will be noted in line quality unless the reason for concentration is due to uncertainty as to the letters or text to be written that may interrupt the writing process more profoundly.

It is said that for some people the nature of a document can have an effect on the writing of signatures applied to it. Certainly wills, mortgages, large contracts, and real estate transactions are significant events in the lives of many persons, and it is understandable that the signing of such documents will be a more conscious act than it is in signing many others. When care is exercised, there can be a greater respect shown for copybook styles.

3.9.10 Disguise or Deliberate Change

Disguise or deliberate change will produce more pronounced results. This will not be an isolated change, however, but will be the kind of modification that tries to exhibit itself throughout the writing. It is frequently suggested as an explanation for differences, but since it is an intentional change it is questionable whether disguise can be defined as an environmental condition.

3.9.11 Drugs or Alcohol

Drugs and/or alcohol can have a marked influence on handwriting. There are several studies on these subjects that have found a number of variances that can occur when a writer is under the influence of drugs or alcohol. Withdrawal effects from intoxication can have as pronounced an effect on handwriting as states of intoxication. Some of the general characteristics that can impact handwriting include errors, lengthening, increase spatial width, expansion, and threading. In some instances, there can be a reverse effect during withdrawal states: contraction and tremor. Additionally, long-term addicts or alcoholics may show less variability in their handwriting when under the influence than those who are nonaddicts and drink less regularly. There may be differing effects on handwriting between alcohol and marijuana use.

3.9.12 Influence of Medications

Like drugs and alcohol, medications can also have a profound influence on handwriting. While medications are prescribed for medical conditions, they are also used recreationally along with nonprescription drugs and alcohol. Certain medications can increase tremor or cause motor movement disturbance, while other medications associated with motor movement diseases are designed to decrease tremor and motor movement disturbances. As an extrinsic influence, medications can cause a temporary or long-term change to handwriting fluency. Medications are typically associated with medical problems and the coexisting influence of the medication with the medical problem's potential influence on handwriting needs to be critically evaluated.

3.9.13 Intentional Change for Later Denial

Although autoforgery is probably a rare occurrence, nevertheless, and notwithstanding the few instances in which a person might be disposed to fabricate an irregular signature of this kind, there are numerous other instances in which a faulty memory coupled with a minor irregularity in the writing may induce an individual to honestly or dishonestly deny its execution. The handwriting examination on these occasions must address the issues of natural variation, accidental occurrence, deliberate modification, and true difference.

3.9.14 Nervous Tension

Severe nervous tension or emotional stress can alter the fluency of handwriting. Time-induced stress caused by deadlines or test taking can cause an increase in right slant and increased elongation and expansion in the writing which detracts from legibility. Other forms of emotional stress can cause tremor, irregularity, contraction, graphic errors, and distortion.

3.9.15 Natural Variations—Beyond Those of Standards

Natural variation is the reason that the adequacy of standards is particularly important. Limited standards may not contain the full range of natural variations peculiar to a given individual simply because some variations are the products of the time, the text, and the circumstances involved in their production. The fewer the standards, the less likely that the handwriting examiner is able to establish a reliable opinion based on comparison material reflecting the writer's natural range of variation.

3.9.16 Writing Conditions—Place or Circumstances

There is wide variation in the circumstances under which legitimate signatures are written and almost equal variation in the results. Recipient signatures for deliveries received are invariably executed in a standing position without adequate support for the writing surface. Furthermore, they are confined to small spaces on forms quite inadequate for the majority of writers. The result is a pronounced change in execution, often so altering the signature that it is beyond a subsequent identification.

Although it is true that these signatures are executed with less care and concern for the final product, the affect that these unusual circumstances may have upon the writing is more severe than that which carelessness and negligence normally generates. Harrison (1958) expounds that "it is not surprising that when specimens of the handwriting of one person written under different conditions are compared, there should be a doubt expressed that one individual was responsible for writing all the scripts, so different do they appear" (p. 297).

Signatures executed at counters may have similar effects. Tables and chairs provide a reasonably consistent set of circumstances for the signing of documents, although there are exceptions to the rule. Counters, however, do not. They vary in height, as do the people attempting to write on them. They are sometimes narrow and restrictive for the writing process. Consequently, the writer's stance with respect to the document is subject to wider variation and the results can be a loss of some quality or control.

Related to this are the situations in which a writer, because of ill health, endeavors to execute a signature when confined to bed. In other situations, an individual may attempt to write or sign a document on his or her knee or lap. For some writers, even the environmental circumstances can have some affect upon the nervous state of the individual and fluency in the writing may suffer.

Writings in moving vehicles of all kinds are remarkably numerous or at least claimed to be so. Depending on the nature of the vehicle, the influence of its motion may be minor or extreme. When extreme the writing may be quite erratic. Whichever it is, the effect will be general and likely apparent throughout the writing rather than localized to one or two elements. While writings in moving vehicles and other extreme circumstances do occur, it is more often a claim made to explain deficiencies or disparities in spurious signatures in an argument for their being genuine.

3.9.17 Writing Instrument

The writing instrument is an intrinsic influence that not only can affect the appearance of the writing externally, but can also affect the way it is written by the writer. A fluid ink pen can change the appearance of the fluency of a writing versus a poorly working ballpoint pen that the writer is using to even overwrite certain sections of writing because the ink is running dry. A writing instrument is more than a pen or pencil held in the hand though. It can refer to a spray paint can used to write graffiti on a wall, a crayon, paintbrush, lipstick on a mirror, the fingertip on a digital tablet, or a knife carving words on the paint of a car.

3.9.18 Writing Position—Including Stance

Writing position (including stance) is an important factor that can cause variation in handwriting. Writing while sitting may have a different slant or size versus writing while standing and writing on a clipboard or on a digital tablet on a countertop. Writing in a hospital bed without hand or arm support is a writing position that is encountered in handwriting casework.

3.9.19 Writing Surface

Unusual writing surfaces (e.g., a concrete wall) may be written on with a pen or pencil, but frequently a spray paint can is used on larger, concrete wall surfaces in cases involving graffiti. Other surfaces, like digital tablets, may have a slick surface or may cause the palm of the hand to stick to the surface while writing. Paper with a high linen content or containing irregular pieces of wood fiber may cause a disturbance in the line quality. Writing with paper on top of uneven or poorly supported surfaces (i.e., the fabric on a sofa arm, the leather on a car seat, or a stucco wall) frequently causes unusual effects in the writing that can be misinterpreted for simulation.

3.9.20 Writing Under Stress

The effects of emotional stress and those of physical stress are differentiated. The emotional or mental state of the writer can have an influence on writing. Especially extreme states of mental or emotional stress can cause extreme tension in the writing, while an overly relaxed state can correspond to a similar carelessness or laxity in the writing. Physical stress in writing is more often described as fatigue. Cases involving fatigue occur when a writer signs several signatures at one sitting and also in cases involving motor disorders (e.g., Parkinson's disease) which induce fatigue states more quickly than in healthy writers.

3.10 ELIMINATION CONCLUSIONS

Handwriting examinations usually have one of three objectives: identification, elimination, or differentiation. Identification is a process that associates writings for a purpose. Elimination segregates writings for a purpose. Differentiation segregates writings for no particular purpose, beyond making the distinction.

Differentiation is a seldom-mentioned process that lies at the root of studies to establish whether or not writings are the products of two or more persons, as they may purport. Marked ballots, testimonials, voter's lists, and other documents are often involved. In these cases, differentiation when achieved usually attests to genuineness. On the other hand, common authorship when established may be a cause to reject a document as invalid, without any necessity to pursue its authorship further. Differentiation is the objective that proves the heterogeneity of writing and the ability of the present processes to demonstrate it. Thus, it is a key to the validity and reliability of handwriting examination.

The term *nonidentity* is often used interchangeably with *elimination*. Differentiation, however, is also a matter of nonidentity. Thus, while elimination may be a matter of nonidentity, nonidentity is not solely a matter of elimination. Accordingly, it is more apt to say that nonidentity is the all-inclusive parent of both elimination and differentiation.

An identification is based on evidence that is quantitatively and qualitatively sufficient to support such a conclusion. The elimination of a writer may be based on what is quantitatively less evidence or on an absence of evidence of identification in the documents at hand. It embraces speculation as to what other documents by the same writer might reveal if they were available. Eliminations are broad and all-inclusive statements that a given writer could not, under any circumstances, have executed a given writing. Identifications are particular and demonstrable. Eliminations are general and speculative.

An important key in the elimination of a writer rests in the contemporaneousness of the standards. Because writing is dynamic and subject to change over periods of time, it is crucial to have within the standards some samples of writing that are contemporaneous with the questioned document.

Because an elimination is such an all-encompassing statement that it has been recommended that the conclusion when expressed should always be qualified. Rather than a bold statement that "K" did not write "Q," it is suggested that the finding should read in words to the effect that "in the writing standards at hand there is no evidence that "K" was the writer of "Q."

There are situations in which unqualified eliminations seem to be justified. An individual cannot be considered a potential author of a writing that exceeds the level of skill of which he or she is capable, provided the standards reliably attest to that level. Nor should an individual be considered for authorship of a writing that contains numerous fundamental disparities in the basic system followed that indicates a difference in national or system attributes, provided the standards are contemporaneous. It is also reasonable to exclude a person as the author of a tracing of his or her own signature, but while tracings usually mitigate against a conclusion of autoforgery, grounds are insufficient to say that it couldn't happen.

It has been implied that the processes of identification and elimination are the same, but only in the sense that the same discriminating elements, sought and appraised in the analysis and comparison, will provide the evidence of sameness or difference in the writing comparisons. The analogy between the two tasks, however, stops there. Although, in practice, the approach to both tasks may be the same, the physical evidence to be considered and its assessment are distinctly different. Identification is an evaluation of similarities, while elimination is an evaluation of differences.

Differences found in writing studies cannot be underestimated. On the other hand, the contention that a single or a few basic differences are controlling and can offset the weight of several similarities may be an overestimation of their role. Although basic differences are frequently considered to constitute adequate grounds for the "elimination of a writer" or a conclusion of "nonidentity," such findings may be more complicated than the simple tabulation of a few disparities between two sets of writings. As Dick (1966) stated, and Dibowski (1975) and Miller (1985) reiterated, a conclusion of elimination may be more difficult, more complex, or have greater risks than that of identification.

More recently, Morris and Richards (2010) reiterated the difficulties with elimination stating that in order for an examiner to research such a conclusion, he or she has to first take into account all variables and circumstances that could produce such a divergent writing. The ASTM (2007) and SWGDOC (2013c) handwriting examination standards specify limiting factors that should be considered when evaluating handwriting. The limitations specified in the standards pertain especially to handwriting samples that show divergence as a result of age, illness, medications, alcohol, writing position, fatigue, use of nondominant hand, disguise, autoforgery, and other factors. The modular method of handwriting examination initially developed by Found and Rogers (1999) and revised by Found and Bird (2016) provides a detailed process that allows an examiner to consider all possible factors that could cause two bodies of writing to diverge in similarity. Proficiency studies reported in the 2016 method have shown that examiners encounter more errors when handling opinions associated with elimination, especially in distinguishing between disguised and simulated signatures. A careful application of these current standards by a trained document examiner should prevent unsupported statements of elimination.

It must be emphasized that the apparent differences in two sets of writings that might be indicative of writings originating from different sources (writers) are seldom found in isolation.

If one is present, a thorough examination will likely reveal others. An isolated difference is more often due to one or more of the circumstances and situations suggested in the previously cited standards.

The position taken by most authorities is that to properly support a conclusion of nonidentity or elimination, differences must be fundamental and repeated. Accordingly, such conclusions can seldom be justified respecting limited textual material as the opportunity for differences to be repeated may not be provided. Disparities in writing can occur for numerous reasons, and the consideration of all of those reasons is what makes eliminations a more complex matter than identifications may be.

When differences are numerous and persistent, and the standards in which they are present are adequate quantitatively and qualitatively, such differences must be entertained as evidence in support of the elimination of the writer. Whether an elimination is definitive or qualified must remain a subjective judgment on the part of the examiner. The benefit to the court, the counsel, or the investigator should be virtually the same in both instances, and the qualified conclusion will avoid indeterminable risks.

Chapter 4

Premises for the Identification of Handwriting

4.1 HANDWRITING IDENTIFICATION AND POINTS OF SIMILARITY

With respect to points of similarity in pattern-based evidence, there is a general misconception that exists respecting fingerprint examination. There is no stipulated number of points of similarity that is statistically supported for the identification of a fingerprint, in existence. The International Association for Identification Standardization Committee conducted a 3-year study and concluded that there was no basis for requiring a predetermined number of friction ridge characteristics in order to establish positive identification (Franck 1996).

There are individual practices of fingerprint technicians, departmental policies, and recommended criteria that call for certain levels of similarity to support positive conclusions—6, 8, 10, 12, or even 14 points, but they are practices, policies, and recommendations. There is no universally accepted or statistically supported number of points of similarity that will serve to discriminate one fingerprint from all others.

In the field of chemistry there are analytical procedures, based on the current knowledge of the chemical composition of compounds that allow an analyst to advance along a program that progressively reduces the number of possible substances that an unknown might be until a single substance remains. There is no point count, however, as the program of analysis varies with the substance being pursued.

Extensive DNA studies have accumulated hordes of information from which the probable occurrence of two persons being the same DNA genotype may be calculated. The levels of probability so calculated are sufficiently low that, for practical purposes, the uniqueness of the genotype is accepted as a certainty.

In fields such as physics, chemistry, and biochemistry, the evidence being sought is thought of as being, for the most part, invariable. Because of its stability, it has been and will continue to be the same for an indeterminate length of time. If it can be found in sufficient quantity it can be identified with known standards, even after long periods. This, however, is not entirely true. The evidence is invariable only if certain conditions are controlled as they usually can be, particularly purity, temperature, and atmospheric pressure. Variables influencing handwriting cannot all be controlled.

The point-count policy, publicly attributed to fingerprint identifications and followed by its technicians, has other inherent errors in it. It implies that each characteristic of the print is of equal significance, so its frequency of occurrence is the same as for any other. This we know is not true for all fingerprint characteristics, but the empirical data has not been broadly studied to determine relative values of significance.

In situations of this kind, science looks closely at the weight to be attached to each of the factors being considered, something that frequencies of occurrence might sustain. Weight, however, is also contingent upon the independence of any factor from any other. Some writing characteristics may be related to the system of writing that was learned. Consequently, some letter designs may exhibit similarities because of a relationship in their background. Point counts, then, are not simple numbers, but are more complex calculations.

The magnitude of the error that a simple point count produces in fingerprint examinations, and the direction in which it may lie is not known. It is assumed, however, that as long as the number of points of similarity is sufficiently large, ample allowance will be made for the inaccuracies that an arbitrary equalization of weights in assessments may generate.

Handwriting is not the same as the subjects of focus in these other fields. It is subject to variation from one occasion to the next and even the range of variations differ with the individual and with the element of writing. Furthermore, writing must be read. It is not free, like DNA, to vary from one subject to another without impairing recognition. It must be reasonably legible in order to be readable. Then too, there are limitations to the manner in which some elements can be varied or changed. How many ways can one write a lowercase, cursive "e" or an "i"? Consequently, for some particular elements of writing, there is greater opportunity for writers to duplicate one another. For this reason, larger combinations of similarities may be required to support conclusions of identity.

Handwriting may never permit precise determinations to be made of the value or significance of any particular writing characteristic or the probability of occurrence level for any combination of characteristics. Nevertheless, approximations are possible that, when used perspicaciously, can be sufficiently reliable for identification purposes.

If then, the analogy to fingerprint identification is not cogent, what analogy can be made to a process that is reasonably reliable and publicly acceptable? In any civil or criminal litigation, the triers of fact take into account various elements of evidence, each having its own significance as a factor in determining the issues of guilt or responsibility. The assignment of significance to each factor is subjective and dependent upon the intelligence, training, and experience of each of the triers of fact, whether they be judge or jury.

The determination that is made is not based on any point count, but it is not less reliable for want of it. Perhaps, having given science and fingerprint identification too much credit for precision, the legal profession has been unaware that its process for reaching conclusions is, in principle, the same as that of the scientist. The court's own criterion for establishing the guilt of a person—beyond a reasonable doubt—discreetly avoids stipulating with certainty or even beyond any doubt (Huber 1972). McElrath and Bearman (1956) stated: "The scientist, too, never proves everything with certainty or beyond a doubt; the best he can hope to say is that he has established a fact beyond a reasonable doubt. The difference between the scientific and the legal situations is that the scientist has learned to calculate the probability of the doubt. This has been the contribution of statistics" (p. 589).

To summarize: (1) There is no minimum point count for fingerprint identification that is supported by statistics and (2) a point count cannot be applied as a primary determination in a matter where the factors being counted vary in their respective significance, without them being appropriately weighted.

4.2 RELEVANT INFORMATION

There are at least two schools of thought on this subject. Some examiners maintain that to ensure impartiality and to avoid influence, one should not have any background information that might suggest a preferred conclusion or a conclusion consistent with that intimated by other evidence. They need know only what writing is questioned and what writings are known or are standards, and perhaps which standards may be doubtful as to their proof (Stangohr 1984).

On the other hand, there are those who argue that because handwriting is subject to the influence of many factors, from failing health, injury, and circumstances to intoxication, sufficient information regarding the writer and the writing occasion is required. This is in order that due allowances may be made for these conditions, if necessary. Only then can true differences be properly discriminated from natural or unnatural variations. The effects of arthritis on the act of writing is an example of a situation in which information about the writer's state of health could be important to the examiner.

The latter position is accompanied by certain risks. It is difficult for the providers of such information, who cannot avoid being prejudiced to some extent, to supply information that is wholly impartial. Conversations normally ensue that may be brief or lengthy during which biased comments are difficult to preclude. If it was convenient to do so, and continuity could be preserved and not be complicated, it might be suggested that a third party, knowledgeable in forensic identification, might be the recipient of material that would be subsequently turned over to the examiner. Necessary and appropriate information might then be solicited from the submitter, and prejudicial statements filtered out of the conversations when relayed to the examiner. Under these arrangements undue influence could be avoided.

Found and Ganas (2013) reported that the Document Examination Unit of the Victoria Police Forensic Services Department implemented modified procedures that manage and essentially filter irrelevant contextual information concerning handwriting examination casework. Bias, contextual information, and its potential influence in forensic casework is covered in more depth in Chapter 10 concerning the cause of errors.

4.3 STATISTICAL INFERENCE IN THE IDENTIFICATION PROCESS

The task of drawing conclusions from data on hand (i.e., a number of standards) about other data (i.e., an unknown) is a matter of statistical inference. Statistical inference, that is, statistical proof, underlies all scientific investigations in some manner and in order to be a scientific pursuit the identification of handwriting must, knowingly or unknowingly, engage statistical proof.

When one brings common sense to bear upon a problem, a mixture of experience and intuition is used. Inferential statistics employ a similar process, substituting data for experience and formulas for intuition. Hence, in practice, statistical methods require us to do, in a more formal and rigorous way, the things that are done, informally, countless times each day.

Whether definitive (i.e., positive) or qualified (i.e., something other than positive), any conclusion of identification derives from statistical inference and is an expression of probability having an arithmetic value somewhere between 0 and 1. In the vocabulary of probability, conclusions of absolute certainty have a value of 1.0 (Bergamini 1963). Matters that are totally improbable, that is to say are impossible, have a value of 0.0. Any other conclusions, which includes all those respecting handwriting, are matters of probability that lie somewhere in-between.

The use by handwriting examiners of statements of probability, commonly referred to as qualified opinions in reports or in testimony, has been debated for some time without a clear-cut decision as to their legitimacy (Hilton 1979; Cole 1980). However, proponents of qualified opinions have not attacked the issue from a legitimate platform of statistical inference (Cole 1962, 1964; Schmitz 1967; Duke 1980). On the other hand, opponents of probability statements have not attempted to review the principles underlying the identification process (Dick 1964; McNally 1978).

Taroni et al. (1998) reported Alphonse Bertillon's (1898) belief that only the application of statistical and correlation analysis to the examination of handwriting could justify the existence of the field. This was the substance of the criticisms of Kirk (1953) more than 50 years later. Osborn (1929) suggested a statistical basis to handwriting examination by the application of the Newcomb rule of probability: "The probability of occurrence together of all the events is equal to the continued product of the probabilities of all the separate events" (p. 226).

Osborn was endeavoring to demonstrate how a combination of similar writing habits in two handwritings would occur with the frequency ratio provided by multiplying together the respective ratios of frequencies of occurrence of each of the habits. Furthermore, if a sufficient number of habits were involved, the frequency ratio of their combined occurrence would be such that they could be possessed by only one person in a given population. Unfortunately, perhaps in his desire to be simplistic, Osborn neglected to qualify the events in his statement of the Newcomb rule as independent events, which is the only condition under which the rule is valid.

Nevertheless, the rule was adapted to constitute the principle of identification, with its application to document examination particularly in mind. Huber (1959) stated: "When any two items possess a combination of similar and independent characteristics, corresponding in relationship to one another, of such number and significance as to preclude the possibility of coincidental occurrence, without inexplicable disparities, it may be concluded that they are the same in nature or are related to a common source" (p. 276). For the application of the principle to be valid in any discipline, some data must be available to demonstrate the independence and the significance of the characteristics of the items that are under study.

A number of papers have been written over the years concerning the application of statistics, particularly the Bayesian theorem, to handwriting examination. The subject is not new, however. An excellent account of earlier attempts to apply the theorem to writing cases, of which Bertillon's was one of the first (1898), is found in the study by Taroni et al. (1998). Bayes theory allows the examiner or the triers of facts to take into account the relevant population of persons that circumstances and other evidence circumscribe in some practical fashion as encompassing the potential authors of a questioned writing. Thus, if a finding is not definitive, that is, it is a qualified opinion, these other factors may provide sufficient information to render the finding more definitive than it is.

Souder (1934) was one of the few and perhaps the first handwriting examiner to employ the likelihood ratio, a progeny of the Bayes theory, to assess the evidence in the identification of writing:

> in handwriting we do not have to push the tests until we get a fraction represented by unity divided by the population of the world. Obviously, the denominator can always be reduced to those who can write and further to those having the capacity to produce the work in question. In a special case, it may be possible to prove that one of three individuals must have produced the document. Our report, even though it shows a mathematical probability of only one in one hundred, would then irresistibly establish the conclusion. (pp. 683–684)

Once rebuffed and rejected, the Bayesian approach now has strong advocates for its use in forensic science. Aitken (1987) wrote that the Bayesian approach is the best measure available for evaluating evidence. Gaudette (1986), without identifying its Bayesian basis, wrote on the evaluation of associative physical evidence. Good (1985), a prolific writer on the topic, referred to Bayesian as the weight of evidence.

Alford (1965), perhaps unwittingly, initiated the use of the Bayes theorem and the likelihood ratio in handwriting casework. On the strength of a paper read at the meeting of the American Academy of Forensic Science by Hilton (1958) and Olkin (1958) explained that the likelihood ratio statistic is the ratio of the probability calculated on the basis of the similarities, under the assumption of identity, to the probability calculated on the basis of dissimilarities, under the assumption of nonidentity. Accordingly, the probability of identity in a population of five persons, on the strength of what Hilton calls the joint probability of three writing features, would be 1/5 to the power of 3, or 1/125. Then the probability of nonidentity would be 4/5 to the power of 3, or 64/125 (approximately 1/2). The ratio of "identity" to "nonidentity" in this case is 1/125 divided by 64/125 and equals 1/64. It is considered to be a measure of the likelihood of "chance coincidence." Hence, the smaller this fraction is, or the larger the denominator relative to a numerator of 1, the less likely is coincidence and the stronger the identification.

The likelihood ratio is a statistical means of testing a calculated value derived from a statistical sample. Relative to handwriting examinations, it is the means of determining whether the probability of identity and the probability of nonidentity are significantly different. In other contexts, the term *odds* is frequently used. To obtain *odds,* invert the likelihood ratio (determined in the previous example to be 1/64), and say that the odds favoring the identification of this subject are 64 to 1 (Evett 1983). Note that it is the likelihood ratio that is inverted to produce the odds not the joint probability of a number of similarities, which in the example was 1/125.

Others have written on the consideration to be given to the question of relevant populations that may strengthen the findings of a writing examination. Kingston's (1989) view was that it was the role of the judge or jury, not the writing examiner, to apply the modification to the handwriting evidence that other evidence may justify. The question arises, however, as to who would be the most competent for the task: the judge, the jury, or the handwriting examiner?

Statistical inference is still an area being researched which is further illustrated in more recent studies. Specifically, Marquis et al. (2011) applied multivariate likelihood ratios to evaluation of the shape of handwritten characters and studied the Bayes factor of assessment of handwriting features. Davis et al. (2012) studied subsampling to estimate the strength of handwriting evidence. Application of likelihood ratios for handwriting evidence was reported by Hepler et al. (2012), Taroni et al. (2012, 2014), and Tang and Srihari (2014).

Needless to say, the problem with establishing statistical probabilities in handwriting identification lies with the lack of meaningful interval or ratio measures of the features of handwriting construction. Obviously, one might establish parametric measures of angle, baseline, and proportions, but these often change with the same writer. In addition, not every examiner agrees on the weight associated with similarities or dissimilarities in writing features. A fundamental dissimilarity for one examiner may be interpreted as a natural variation or accidental movement with another examiner. Perhaps a more reasonable approach to statistical probabilities in handwriting identification is to use nonparametric procedures using nominal and ordinal level measurements. Much like likelihood ratio and Bayesian, nonparametrics (the chi-square distribution) consider the absence or presence of certain features of the handwriting (nominal) and the range of measures from high to low (ordinal). A number of forensic committees, such as those within the NIST (National Institute of Standards and Technology—US Department of Commerce), are currently examining the utility of statistical probabilities and handwriting identification.

Pattern recognition using computer algorithms in fingerprint identification such as IAFIS (integrated automated fingerprint identification system), facial recognition, and handwritten letter forms (CedarFox) have proved to be successful in narrowing down a specimen from a database comparison. But these are only as good as their database allows and may not take into account handwriting simulations and forgeries. Also, humans continue to be better at pattern recognition than machines through an ability to process minute visual constructs (Vida et al. 2016).

4.4 LOGIC AND REASONING UNDERLYING IDENTIFICATION

The argument for the identification of handwriting is an inductive argument. Any argument is inductive if it may be stated as "it is probable that . . ." Such arguments simply claim that its conclusion is reasonable to believe in view of the facts set forth as evidence. Deduction is a matter of recognizing valid logical forms, but induction is a matter of weighing evidence. Although inductive reasoning, unlike deductive reasoning, cannot be reduced to precise rules, there are certain important general principles that must be kept in mind.

Induction is a way of reasoning, as is deduction, yet quite different. Whereas deductive conclusions necessarily follow from their reasons, inductive conclusions are either (1) generalizations or (2) hypotheses. First, suppose a test group tastes a dozen Florida oranges, each of which is sweet. On the basis of this information it may be concluded that all Florida oranges are sweet. The conclusion goes beyond the reasons given. Twelve oranges were offered in evidence but the conclusion is more general than the evidence. It is a generalization.

The second kind of inductive argument leads to a hypothesis. It is the character of scientific investigation. It is not a statement about a class, but about an individual, an event, or a state of affairs. A man named "A" murdered Miss "B" and then shot himself, or "X" wrote the anonymous letter "Q." These are inductive conclusions drawn from evidence. The truth of these statements is not established by direct observation. They are hypotheses. In this kind of inductive argument, there are three elements:

1. A number of facts that are the data of the argument (e.g., "X" exhibits certain writing habits. There is a similarity between the writing habits of "X" and features of the writing "Q." There are no observable differences).
2. A hypothesis: that "X" wrote the anonymous letter "Q."
3. Certain generalizations connect the hypothesis with the facts:
   a. Handwriting is unique to each individual.
   b. Writing is habitual and, therefore, consistent from one execution to the next.
   c. Differences in media or time will not significantly alter writing habits to preclude identification.
   d. Differences between writers are such that, given sufficient writing standards, examiners can discriminate between the products of most writers.
   e. A sufficient number of facts (similarities), in combination, affirms that the hypothesis is acceptable.

As any hypothesis should, this hypothesis derives its persuasiveness from its ability to account for all of the facts. This is the reason why differences or disparities observed in a handwriting comparison must be accounted for before conclusions as to identification can be reached. The underlying principle is clear. Assuming that the generalizations are true, every known fact that can be accounted for by the hypothesis is evidence that the hypothesis is true. While there may be facts that are accounted for by the hypothesis, and that, therefore, constitutes evidence, when it comes to the question whether to believe an inductive conclusion, the problem is more complex.

To begin, any particular fact (e.g., a similarity in a discriminating element in a questioned and known writing) may be an instance of many possible generalizations. For example:

1. In order to be read, any writing will resemble another in some respects.
2. Pupils of the same teacher will write alike.
3. All systems of writing that are taught are similar.

As mentioned earlier, a hypothesis accounts for facts by being connected to them through known generalizations. This is the way lawyers build their cases. It is the way a scientific theory grows and becomes accepted. But, no matter how convincing a hypothesis may be, it is always conceivable that a new discovery will cripple or destroy it. Thus, a hypothesis wears a tentative provisional air. It is accepted and acted upon, but only until a better one comes along (Beardsley 1954).

When there is such strong evidence for a hypothesis (e.g., that "X" wrote the anonymous letter "Q"), that the examiner no longer fears (or hopes for) any further evidence that would be incompatible with it, it is said that the hypothesis has been proved. The practical question is, of course, at what point is the examiner justified regarding the proof of the hypothesis? In handwriting identification terms, that is asking the question how many or what kind of similarities are necessary to prove the hypothesis?

A simple and universal reply cannot be given, for many reasons. Still, there is a key principle that provides a rough estimate of the reliability of a hypothesis. Generally, a fact or a collection of facts can be accounted for by more than one hypothesis. The facts in a writing comparison matter, for example, may be accounted for by either of the hypotheses:

1. "X" wrote the anonymous letter "Q."
2. "X" was taught to write by the same teacher as "Y," that "X" has developed the same writing skill as "Y," that "X" was in the same locale as "Y" at the time "Q" was written, but that "Y" actually wrote the anonymous letter "Q."

Whenever a hypothesis is accepted as true, it is preferred to the alternative hypotheses, which may account for the same facts. Seldom is there one and only one hypothesis. To be reasonable, one must choose the best of a number of hypotheses. This is the root of the problem. How does one determine when one hypothesis is to be preferred to another? What makes it better?

One feature should always be considered when comparing alternative hypotheses to decide which is the more convincing. This is the simplicity of the hypothesis. Other things being equal (a qualification that covers a number of delicate considerations), the simpler of two alternative hypotheses is the preferable one.

Obviously, in the situation suggested above, hypothesis 2 requires one to suppose a longer chain of events than in hypothesis 1. Thus, hypothesis 1 is simpler. Since both may account for the same facts, it is more reasonable to believe 1 than 2. This is not to say with certainty that hypothesis 1 is true. It is an explanation of known facts, it is better than 2, and thus, would be preferred to it. The *principle of simplicity* is an important and helpful consideration that avoids the *fallacy of unnecessary complexity* (Beardsley 1954).

4.5 THE IDENTIFICATION PROCESS AND TRAINING

In the identification process, analysis and evaluation are the two aspects of the process that make formal training necessary, the personal presence of a competent teacher essential, and the accumulation of experience mandatory. One must acquire a knowledge of what to look for in writing and how to assess its significance. It is of even greater importance to those who aspire to become document examiners or handwriting experts to recognize the fact that, because analysis and evaluation varies with the particular case material under examination, neither of these facets of the process can be learned completely from books. Evaluation, particularly, must be learned through training and experience. Sufficient empirical data has not yet been accumulated from which the probability of occurrences of particular writing habits may be calculated. Their significance must be subjectively judged on the strength of the experience of the examiner and his or her tutors. Thus, one's ability to judge the significance of a feature of writing is an element of one's competence that the self-taught novice has difficulty developing.

The trained mind conducts the more thorough and efficient analysis, seeking the more credible evidence, disregarding the trivial, unearthing that of which the lay mind is unaware. In comparisons, experience and familiarity enables one to make far more delicate and precise distinctions. But it is probably in the area of evaluation that knowledge, training, experience, and skill make their greatest contribution. What analysis has found and comparison has revealed, only proper evaluation can make useful.

Once this process of identification is understood and appreciated, progress may be made in identifying matters not within one's normal purview. Thus, problems involving Chinese or Eskimo writing may be intelligently tackled by persons who don't speak the languages. Typewriters may be identified by persons never employed in a typewriter factory. Printing methods may be differentiated by persons never engaged as printers. Counterfeit currency can be identified reliably by document examiners who never made a dollar.

4.6 CRITIQUING HANDWRITING EXPERTISE

The profession of the document examiner, the handwriting examiner, or the handwriting expert has existed in North America for well over a century and undoubtedly longer in Europe. Its practitioners and their labors have been accepted as reliable, and their findings have been considered believable by the judiciary, the courts, and the layman for as many years, notwithstanding the fact that, as with many developing professions, there have been those within it whose services have not been of the highest caliber. The need for these services within the criminal justice and civil litigation systems, the remuneration that seemed warranted, and the absence of a standard to be met, were often the reasons that less qualified individuals were persuaded to become involved, and the process undoubtedly produced some errors.

With the passage of time and the growth of the profession, better methods of training, broader consultation and discussion, and the sharing of knowledge that stems from experience have evolved to furnish greater consistency in methods and more reliability in results. Nevertheless, until recently, an apprenticeship process has tended to underlie the training of neophytes in handwriting identification.

It is not surprising then that the question should be raised as to whether any empirical data exists to support the claim that handwriting specialists possess a handwriting expertise, an expertise that laypersons do not normally acquire. Prior to 1990, there were only a very few studies that examined the reliability of handwriting identification by document examiners, which was reported by Risinger et al. (1989) after what they claimed to have been an exhaustive literature search.

There has been a response from researchers and forensic handwriting examiners as to the criticisms raised by Risinger et al. (1989), Risinger and Saks (1996), Saks and VanderHaar (2005), Risinger (2007), and the NAS report (2009) among others, concerning the reliability of handwriting identification by examiners. Kam et al. (1994), in a study of small samples (seven professionals from a single source, that is, the FBI Laboratories, and 10 nonprofessionals) confuted the null hypothesis suggested by Risinger et al. (1989) that there was no difference between professed handwriting examiners and lay persons in the examination of writing samples. Kaye (1994) commented on the shortcomings of the study and the difficulty in generalizing from the information provided by the limited sample size.

However, reliable and acceptable evidence has been published to dispute Risinger et al.'s disparaging indictments. Studies published in peer-reviewed journals prove the ability of handwriting examiners to distinguish between genuine and simulated handwriting and to match handwriting samples (Kam et al. 1994; Kam et al. 1997; Found et al. 1999; Found et al. 2001b; Kam et al. 2001; Sita et al. 2002; Found and Rogers 2003; Kam and Lin 2003). Compiling the error rates from the published studies, handwriting examiner error rates were in the range of 0.04% to 9.3%. Some of the studies reported that handwriting examiners exhibited more skill than laypersons in performing handwriting identification (layperson error rates were in the range of 26.1% to 42.86%).

The research published thus far has demonstrated handwriting examiner reliability on tasks including both handwriting and signatures, including detection of simulations produced by expert penmen (Dewhurst et al. 2008). Proficiency in evaluating disguised and simulated signatures and/or handwriting was researched by Found and Rogers (2008), Al-Musa Alkahtani et al. (2010), and Bird et al. (2010a, 2010b, 2011, 2012). The nature of handwriting examiner's authorship opinions was evaluated over a 5-year period of blind validation trials (Found and Rogers 2008). Dewhurst et al. (2014) looked at the effects of motivation on the behavior of lay subjects when participating in handwriting trials. The research in this area helps to target problematic areas that can be corrected by training and testing, but also alerts the trier of fact as to the limitations in the field. These studies have helped to define when caution needs to be exercised in expressing handwriting opinions. More research is required and is ongoing with respect to problematic handwriting tasks. Until specific research is conducted on special tasks, and experts are proficiency tested on a wide variety of difficult or special tasks, the *Kumho Tire* ruling that advises expert acceptance based on a review of the "task at hand" is prudent (Risinger 2000).

There may be some examiners that feel that in studies of this kind the handwriting examiner must achieve near perfect results, whereas the lay person should be expected to achieve only the level of chance. This may explain the reluctance of some to submit to such studies and risk a reflection upon their competence and/or on the discipline at large. A properly conducted study, however, designed to confirm or to dispute the allegations of Risinger et al. needs only to reveal a statistically significant difference between the scores of the professionals and of the laypersons to prove the hypothesis that handwriting expertise indeed exists.

Chapter 5

Fundamentals of the Identification Process

5.1 UNDERLYING PROCESSES OF HANDWRITING IDENTIFICATION

Handwriting identification is based on two accepted premises or principles and a corollary to one of them. The first is habituation. Confucius philosophized, eons ago, that men's natures are alike; it is their habits that separate them. People are primarily creatures of habit and writing is a collection of those habits. A habit hierarchy of at least three levels (letter habit, word habit, and phrase habit) are employed according to the degree to which the action process is subjugated to the thought process.

Writing habits are neither instinctive nor hereditary, but are complex processes that are developed gradually. Handwriting, or indeed footwriting, mouthwriting, or typewriting, is a neuromuscular behavior that develops as an acquired perceptual-motor skill. It involves successively higher stages of integration as learning proceeds.

It is a fact that in every language there are certain words, usually short, of frequent occurrence that have only syntactical significance that contribute little to the conveyance of ideas. In the English language such words include:

- Articles: "a," "an," "the"
- Conjunctions: "and," "but," "for," "or"
- Subordinating conjunctions: "if," "that," "as," "than," "when," "where"
- Prepositions: "at," "by," "in," "for," "from," "off," "to," "of," "on," "after," "before," "over," "until," "with"
- Personal pronouns: "I," "you," "he," "she," "it," "they," "we," "them"
- Demonstrative pronouns: "this," "that," "these," "those"
- Relative pronouns: "who," "which," "what," "that"
- Interrogative pronouns: "who," "which," "what"
- Indefinite pronouns: "one," "none," "some," "any," "each," "both"

Because of their frequency of occurrence, their shortness, and their relative insignificance, they exhibit a greater degree of unconscious characterization or individuality than other words may. In accordance with this, it has been claimed that such words, insofar as the mental process of the average penman goes, are not words in the usual sense of the term, but are symbols. They are put on paper not as a successive series of letters, but are executed as single units (Quirke 1930).

In handwriting comparisons, letters, combinations of letters, words, or phrases must be considered according to the degree to which they constitute a collective habit. It is a classic example of synergism in which the whole is more than a sum of its parts. Accordingly, the influence of adjoining letters upon one another will vary according to the role these letters play in words or phrases that have become writing habits as units, rather than as individual letters. Variation in shape and movement can be expected to change in relation to this factor.

Along these lines, two reported studies of the writing of 61 right-handed subjects attempted to measure what was called the AI (Association Index), to describe the degree of association between different features of handwriting (Eldridge et al. 1984, 1985). In this they found higher indices in letters or parts of writing sharing common elements in their design and advocated that they be evaluated collectively, or globally over all letters, rather than as independent factors in a writing examination and study.

The second premise or principle upon which handwriting identification is founded involves the individuality or heterogeneity of writing. Handwriting identification is predicated on the belief that handwriting is unique to the individual. It is axiomatic that any two items of nature may be differentiated, provided the scale of judgment is carried out at a level of sufficient precision. But while there may be no such thing as true identity, the real question for handwriting examiners is whether or not, in writing discrimination, the judgment of the examiner and his or her instrumentation is capable of such precision as to make the necessary distinction. It is not sufficient, and hardly scientific, to argue that because some writings are obviously different, no two writings from different writers can be as coincidentally similar as to be wrongly judged as the product of one person (Huber 1982).

This point was highlighted by Harris (1958) in his account of the similarity he found in signatures or writings of the same names, particularly those consisting of six letters or less. His study also disclosed that some letters provide less variation in shape or design from one writer to the next, and that other, more peculiar letter forms can become popular and appear more often than one might expect. Harris (1980) described the coincidental similarity found in writers of excessively round, bubble writing, the style that enjoys popularity among adolescents.

Münch (1987) reported on the resemblances between the writings of a mother and daughter. The features by which the two writers could be differentiated were subtle and might well have escaped detection in a hasty comparison or one in which the questioned material was textual and limited. A study on twins by Srihari et al. (2008) found that twin handwriting could be differentiated, but there was a slightly higher error rate by both handwriting examiners and an automatic handwriting verification system when differentiating between twin and nontwin handwriting.

These reports do not dispute the hypothesis that handwriting is unique to the individual, and that the written products of different individuals can be differentiated from one another. They simply point out some of the risks involved in working within restrictive parameters in time or material. Discriminations were successfully made, however, they argue for the exercise of caution because of the dangers they demonstrate. At the same time they should not be allowed to rest on the record without some indication of the frequency with which such cases might be encountered. While experientially these cases are rare, there is no empirical data to indicate how rare.

Hilton (1963) made the point that the principle of heterogeneity "pertains to the whole of a person's writing" and cannot be proven or demonstrated on the strength of small samples (p. 110). What is less certain, and at this point the more subjective aspect, is the size of the sample required to allow one to generalize to "the whole of a person's writing."

The heterogeneity of people in respect of the behavior of handwriting is a matter that may never be proven empirically, but will have to be, to some extent, assumed and accepted, much like fingerprints. It is not practical to obtain standards of either writing or fingerprints from the world populations. Fingerprints, however, do have a system of classification that enables the millions of prints recorded so far to be studied for duplicity, and the data is growing daily. Instances of duplicity, if and when such occur, can be tabulated and their frequency of occurrence, together with other information that may have a bearing on duplicity, can be readily compiled. With such information and data, the quality or level of duplication and the impact of duplicity on the reliability of the process can be calculated.

The FBI and the US Secret Service (NIST 2013) maintain automated systems to assist with handwriting-related investigations. The FBI developed the BRNF (bank robbery note file). The database is a digital collection of demand and bank robbery notes and the database searches certain handwriting features (e.g., underlined words, formatting, forms, punctuation, spelling, placement, distortion, overwriting). The system is not designed as a comprehensive handwriting examination system. The FBI also maintains a digital database of anonymous letters, but the system searches the text of the files and not handwriting characteristics. FLASH-ID (forensic language-independent automated system for handwriting identification) is used by the FBI for biometric handwriting examinations. The US Secret Service utilizes an automated handwriting system called FISH (forensic information system for handwriting). The database contains thousands of samples of threatening notes or correspondence and is designed to automate the handwriting examination process through the computerized ability to scan, digitize, measure, store, and compare questioned and known handwriting samples. These database systems contain thousands of samples that can be used for statistical analysis.

Support for the claim of individuality in handwriting and the human ability to perceive it can be established with some confidence by a proper, scientifically-conducted study of the writing products of those persons in whom genetic or external influences are controlled to the extent possible. Pophal and Dunker (1960) demonstrated the highly individualistic character of the movements of the hand in the air in the course of the writing process, by the use of slow motion photography. The studies of Norinder (1946) and Talmadge (1958) on twin differences in writing performance disclosed that slant, minuscule height, supralinear heights, and regularity are not, to any significant degree, genetically determined.

The Dionne quintuplets of Canada provide evidence that the discriminating elements (characteristics) of handwriting are not genetically determined. Being one of the first sets of quintuplets known to survive, responsibility for their welfare was assumed by the government almost within hours of their birth. Under these circumstances, all of the variables respecting the development of their writing habits that could be controlled were, in fact, controlled. They shared the same prepared environment constantly, the same influences which were so restricted as to exclude siblings and parents for nearly 9 years. They shared the same experiences, they ate together, slept together, traveled together, had the same teachers, nurses, food, cooks, clothes, and, until the age of 18, were not permitted to exist for any period of time in isolation from each other. Sample writings exist that were taken during the quintuplets' formative years. While these writings may not be fully representative of their executions after maturity they do demonstrate the individuality of the writings at this age. It is only reasonable to expect that with time, the disparity became more, rather than less, pronounced.

Handwriting studies on twins revealed that document examiners need to use caution when approaching casework as the accidental match of twin writing has a slightly higher error rate than the accidental match of nontwin writing (Srihari et al. 2008). Nonstatistical studies found that some twin handwritings had remarkable global similarity, but that differentiation is still achievable through detailed analysis of microcharacteristics rather than global characteristics (Beacom 1960; Gamble 1980; Boot 1998).

While this may constitute evidence that handwriting habits are not genetically determined, or totally dependent upon environmental influences, the feasibility of any particular group of habits serving to distinguish one writer from all others within a given population is not determinable. It is prudent for the examiner to be alert to these potential limitations and concede to these limitations when examined in court. For example, could there be another writer, whose execution of this quantity of questioned writing, would be so similar to that being studied that such a quantity may be insufficient to permit a reliable discrimination? A step in answering this question was taken by Twibell and Zientek (1995) in a study of the writing of three signatures "John P. Smith" by 130 subjects. Only two writers produced signatures that were deceptively similar, and even they could be discriminated when examined carefully. Whether or not this work contributes significantly to the larger question of the heterogeneity of the writing of the population generally, it does support the cautions of Harris (1958), that care must be exercised in the examination of limited writings with few particularly distinguishing features.

Welch (1996) offered what he considered compelling evidence for the individuality of handwriting in his account of four cases in the United Kingdom. In the first case, Harvey and Mitchell (1973) reported that, on the strength of six writing features, a sample of 1,046 writings was searched to find the writer of a questioned check. A single writer was found that a more complete examination confirmed to be the writer of the check. In the second case, Baxendale and Renshaw (1979) reported that, on the strength of a few single features, a sample of 600,000 writings was reduced to 4,900 for further study. While a few of these aroused sufficient suspicion to warrant obtaining additional writing standards, ultimately, all were eliminated as potential writers of the questioned document. The writer responsible was eventually found in another geographic location by further police investigation.

In an earlier case, again on the strength of an initial study of six writing features, 100,000 writing samples were screened, some of which were duplicates, in an endeavor to identify a particular writer. As in the previously mentioned case, none of the writers were associated with the unknown writing when a full comparison was conducted.

In a fourth case that Welch (1996) describes, 10,000 writers were screened on the strength of five writing features, and any writing exhibiting three or more of these features was selected for further study. Some 1,300 writings had been screened when the writer responsible surfaced in the search. The identification was confirmed by a full examination of the writings, the admission by the suspect and a plea of guilty at the trial.

Shiver (1996) cited a case involving 13 spurious checks passed at two military bases in the United States. Information on the checks suggested that the perpetrator was associated with a particular military unit of nearly 1,000 persons. An examination was conducted of postal locator cards for all personnel of the unit. From a short list of three persons exhibiting some lettering and numeral similarities, one individual was selected and approached for additional request writings, with which a definitive conclusion of identification was reached. The result was confirmed by the admission of the soldier involved.

This case was also offered as argument in support of the contention that writing is unique to the individual. Otherwise, correct discriminations such as this would not be possible. The validity of the argument that any or all of these cases demonstrate the uniqueness of writing is difficult to judge. While identifications and eliminations have been determined by full examinations, it is not known which and how many *discriminating elements* were involved, and whether the same battery of elements would be employed in all cases.

Corollary—the discriminative reliability of the identification process—pertains to the accuracy of judgments made across samples of writing from different persons, including those that are simulations of another person's writing, by whatever process of imitation may have been employed. In one sense, it is a corollary to the principle respecting the uniqueness of writing to the individual. There may be limitations, however, with the capability of the technique that is being employed to discriminate between any two writers. It might be expressed in an interrogatory form: given that no two writings by different persons are identical, are the elements of writing considered in the identification process adequate and reliable grounds for the making of discrete discriminations?

The previously mentioned cases demonstrate large numbers of writings that were successfully sorted and studied in search of the identity of a particular questioned writer. These cases are classic, historic examples of the ability of the process and the examiners using it to differentiate large numbers of writings correctly. The process has been further supported by statistical studies (e.g., Srihari et al. 2002, 2008) that used automated processes to determine the individuality of handwriting.

Huber and Headrick proposed a compilation of 21 elements of writing that are or may be involved in the handwriting examination process (Chapter 6) and believed that these aspects of writing serve to discriminate between any two writers of a given population, and differentiate between the genuine and spurious executions of any single writer. The accuracy of the process of discrimination hinges largely on the heterogeneity of writing. If the process does not discriminate in all cases, some revision or refinement of the 21 elements, or of an examiner's capabilities and facilities, may be required.

The compilation of the 21 handwriting elements that Huber and Headrick developed and originally published in 1999 is based upon the collection of handwritten addresses on envelopes that they received over many years, which provided them with examples of essentially the same textual material from approximately 1,000 different writers. When appropriately considered, these writings, that numbered 2,000 or more in total, provided some empirical support for the hypotheses that: (1) handwriting is sufficiently unique to the individual to permit discrimination between writers, and (2) competent examiners, employing the 21 point criteria (or a better one), are sufficiently capable of discriminating between writers with acceptable low levels of error—to sanction the acceptance of both hypotheses.

The study by Harris (1958), using certain surnames in signatures—*Smith, Shaw, Harris, Dybdahl*, and *Dye*, taken from the Los Angeles County Registrar of Voters—illustrated the deceptive similarity that can be found between writers in certain writing features. The intent of the study was to caution examiners against overevaluating the significance of certain features that were responsible for the pictorial similarity between different writers, especially in the study of short names and single examples. As Harris pointed out, most signatures displayed differences in subtle features that should not be disregarded, as well as similarities in some more striking respects.

On the other hand, Harris (1958) reported on the similarity he found in signatures of the same names, particularly those consisting of six letters or less. His study also disclosed that some letters provide less variation in shape or design from one writer to the next, and that other, somewhat peculiar letter forms can become popular and appear more frequently than might be expected. Accordingly, the discriminative ability of the writing examination process must be considered with regard to the type and quantity of writing to be involved in the study, if valid results are to be obtained. This is further illustrated by a study on complexity theory developed by Sita et al. (2002) which found an increase in errors when there was limited complexity in signatures. Slyter (1995) developed an "elements of comparison" model for use in signature examination that evaluates the quality and quantity of the questioned and comparison material available.

Unfortunately, Harris' (1958) statement that so many of the signatures lacked individuality and looked alike that they were not worth photographing, has been criticized for implying that similarities between substantial numbers of the population do not merit serious consideration by document examiners (*US v. Starzecpyzel* 1995). It may be that Harris' comment regarding the worth of the similarities was with respect to their value as additional illustrations of the substance of the paper. It emphasized the fact that short names, not written as signatures in the customary fashion and comprised certain letters, may afford limited evidence by which writers can be reliably discriminated.

The fact that some writings in small quantities, under certain circumstances, seem similar should not be surprising. As handwriting is a form of communication to be read, writing must conform in some degree to standards of size and design that are recognizable. These standards are provided by copybooks or writing manuals. While individuality modifies the styles of these manuals, it does so within limits, if the writing is to be comprehensible. Furthermore, writing is still subject to some social forces that set penmanship (in terms of quality and consistency) as a desirable attainment. Consequently, small segments of the writings of many persons will afford little evidence by which they can be discriminated. This is particularly because of the fact that the natural variation of any handwriting works against the virtues that discrete measurement might otherwise afford.

Indeed, examination of a writing that consists of habits in number and nature that are less discriminatory, and thereby may be misleading as to their significance, is the reason for consulting adequately trained, competent, and experienced examiners. Examiners advise the courts as to the weight of the conclusions to be drawn from the similarities or differences observed based upon careful, methodological analyses (e.g., ACE-V) that take into account limitations, possible alternatives to propositions, and variables that cause handwriting variation or distortion. What Harris (1958) illustrated is simply one of the situations in which professional evaluation by a qualified handwriting examiner is vital and not likely to be within the competence of the court or jury to judge.

It is useful to reemphasize the argument stated earlier that all conclusions in handwriting identification, indeed in all branches of forensic science, are matters of probability. There is a risk of error in all findings, even when positive conclusions are reached. The intent of the examination process is to minimize that risk to the extent possible and/or to reduce it to a level below which it is impractical to consider. The question, then, as to whether examiners are dealing with a writing where two or more persons may execute handwriting that is very similar, is a question that arises in every case under examination and study.

As long as the limitations imposed by science are taken into adequate consideration by the examiner, experience, case histories, and research have demonstrated that given adequate samples, a careful study, and an appropriate examination, the principle of the uniqueness of handwriting is achievable.

5.2 HOW HANDWRITING IDENTIFICATION DIFFERS FROM RELATED DISCIPLINES

Because it is a member of the family of forensic sciences that is encountered on the investigative scene every day, there is an expectation by some that document examination, and, in particular, handwriting identification, can be as precise and positive in its findings as other branches such as DNA, toxicology, toolmark/firearms identification, or latent prints. Perhaps too, because its focus is on handwriting, many presume that there is considerable correspondence between handwriting identification and graphology. To understand its differences, handwriting identification definitions are reviewed in order to draw comparisons with other related disciplines.

Handwriting is an acquired skill and clearly one that is a complex perceptual-motor task, sometimes referred to as a neuromuscular task. But it is more than just a skill. It is a skilled behavior or performance and one of the most complex neuromotor skills performed. Handwriting identification ensues from a study of habits of behavior.

Historically, handwriting identification has employed particular methods for the analysis of handwriting evidence (e.g., ACE-V) where the analyst endeavors to apply appropriate principles of science and logic in accordance with scientific method. It presupposes the heterogeneity of writing. The method takes into account natural variation of a range, peculiar to the individual, which diminishes according to the level of skill of which the writer is capable. A resolution respecting identity is founded on the presence or absence of a combination of significant and independent similarities and the presence or absence of a number of inexplicable disparities.

The focus of a handwriting examination, which is the physical evidence, is the conscious and deliberate issue of an animate person. In this, it is not unlike two other forensic disciplines, that is, voice identification and linguistics. Notwithstanding the significant differences in the parts of the anatomy involved, these three disciplines pertain to the conscious and at least partially controllable issues of a person. Not surprisingly, it is fairly common for handwriting examiners to receive requests for analyses pertaining to forensic linguistics.

The materials other forensic sciences examine, for example, fire and explosive residues, blood, urine, glass, hair, or paint, are inanimate, or are the involuntary issues of an animate body or person. From the perspective of forensic analysis, the principal difference in the products or issues of animate and inanimate bodies rests in the voluntary control that the body can exercise over its issues. Animate bodies voluntarily control such issues as its communications, its voice, or its grammar, but not the biochemical composition of its blood, urine, or hair. Inanimate bodies, of course, exercise no voluntary control.

In other fields of forensic science such as physics, chemistry, and biochemistry, the evidence being sought, because of its inanimate nature, is considered to be for the most part invariable. Once recovered, because of its stability, it has been and will continue to be the same for an indeterminate period of time, as long as several months or even years. If it can be found in sufficient quantity, it can be identified with today's known standards, even after long periods of time. This, however, is only true if certain conditions are controlled, as they usually can be, particularly purity, temperature, and atmosphere. The variables that influence handwriting cannot all be readily controlled. Time itself constitutes a variable. Consequently, known standards often need to be contemporary in age.

Then too, findings in other scientific studies have a bottom line below which results are not determinable, that is, certain steps in a process must be completed. The findings in writing examinations may vary to a substantial degree, with the quantity and quality of the material submitted for examination.

The phenomena of any two writing dilemmas are never precisely the same. Hence, the evidence available to resolve writing identification questions varies quantitatively and qualitatively. The essences of the analyses are seldom consistent. The essences of other forensic analyses can be compared with remarkable consistency. Thus, handwriting identification differs considerably from other forensic science disciplines.

The principal respect in which handwriting identification differs from graphology is that identification is a comparative process between a questioned sample(s) and a body of comparison material in order to determine or solve authorship questions. Graphology, as the term is understood in the United States, is the study of handwriting for the purposes of personality or behavioral assessment. For example, forensic document examiners evaluate handwriting on anonymous notes in comparison to a suspect's handwriting samples to determine authorship while a graphologist would examine an anonymous note to determine the writer's behavior without comparison to a suspect's writing samples. Handwriting identification frequently requires a number of adequate comparison samples of writing to render a determination. Graphologists may work from limited samples, sometimes from a single sample of handwriting.

It is argued that knowledge of graphology is beneficial in writing examinations for identification purposes, as both fields of endeavor are studying the same elements of writing, albeit with different objectives. The graphologist's objective is to interpret what is observed from the handwriting in terms of personality or behavior. The handwriting examiner's objective is to evaluate what is observed in terms of evidence of authorship. The two tasks, interpretation and evaluation, are based on different premises, and have different requirements. Even the treatment of writing elements that may be studied is different. Graphology tends to treat all elements as independent aspects of writing. Handwriting examination seeks signs of interdependence commonly referred to as "class characteristics," or simply "consistencies," that may alter the evaluation of the elements.

Although both disciplines initially begin an analysis with a detailed examination of handwriting characteristics, the two disciplines vary considerably in the way the information or handwriting data is interpreted: one for identification and the other for behavioral assessment. Thus, the two fields require different training and have different professional standards and ethics, primarily due to the way the handwriting information is interpreted and reported. Because of the different requirements and purposes between the two disciplines, generally, it is unethical and biased for the same examiner to provide a handwriting identification and graphological analysis in the same case or on the same set of handwriting samples.

In certain parts of Europe and other places in the world, the term graphology is defined more literally from its Greek origins (the study of writing) and can refer to handwriting identification examiners. In tracing the origins of graphology in Europe, interest in handwriting as a purveyor of information respecting the writer has probably existed as long as writing has been common to society. In 1622, Camilo Baldi, an Italian scholar and physician, published *Treatise on a Method to Recognize the Nature and Quality of a Writer from his Letters*, a book that is credited with being one of the first to make public an intellectual interest in the subject (Crumbaugh 1986). Johann Caspar Lavater at the University of Zurich is reported to have written and published on similar subjects in the late eighteenth century (Spoerhase 2014), but not until the publication of the works of Abbe Jean Hippolyte Michon of France, in 1872, on *The Practical System of Graphology* was the generic term coined for handwriting analysis.

A disciple of Michon, Crépieux-Jamin (1889, 1892, 1933), because of his interest in the French psychologist Alfred Binet, originator of the first intelligence tests, pursued Michon's studies in handwriting analysis as a technique for testing personality. Since then, interest has been expressed by many writers in many countries, to the point where libraries now offer a wide selection of books on graphology, of an equally wide range of quality. Notwithstanding their range, these books generally represent variants of three major schools of graphology: the trait school, the Gestalt school, and the graphoanalysis system.

The trait school, of which Michon was an early proponent, claims graphic signs (e.g., length, width, or slant of a certain stroke) reflect specific personal traits. The Gestalt school that evolved later and largely in Germany under the influence of Klages (1910), advocated that graphological interpretations must be based on the examination of writing as a whole entity, and not from individual configurations. Klages dealt with "expressive movements" rather than particular graphological elements. The Gestalt approach deviates significantly from the trait school in relying on judgment and intuition of the graphologist. Following Klages, other authors, for example, Dr. Bernard Wittlich and Dr. Klara Roman, attempted to integrate individual graphological traits into the Gestalt picture of the writer (Klimoski and Rafaeli 1983). In 1959, Bunker published a book on *graphoanalysis* as a compromise between the one-to-one sign graphology that typified the French trait school and the broad intuitive Gestalt graphology of the German school.

Graphology is proffered in a variety of applications including behavioral profiling, personnel selection, and aptitude assessment. It should not, however, be confused with the practice of forensic handwriting examination which determines identity from handwriting rather than personality or behavior.

Thus, handwriting identification is different from these other seemingly related disciplines. If the discipline is to serve society properly and appropriately, its differences must be appreciated and respected by examiners, students in training, and those who consult document examiners. Frequently, there is confusion by those who retain or consult document examiners concerning the scope of work, parameters, and limitations of a forensic handwriting examiner.

5.3 DIFFICULTIES AND LIMITATIONS IN HANDWRITING IDENTIFICATION

There are a number of circumstances or conditions that have an effect upon the conclusions which can be drawn in handwriting studies and examinations. These include:

- Qualitative insufficiency (lack of significance) of the habits exhibited by the questioned material, that is, a predominance of letters that provide less opportunity for individualization
- Wide variation in the standards from one writing occasion to the next
- Quantitative insufficiency of the habits that the questioned material contains
- Poor writing skill and the degeneration of letter forms
- Unreliability of reproductions, as a record of writing habits, and of the character of the original document (e.g., consistency of inks and of papers, the sequence of strokes), when examination of the originals is not possible
- Deliberate distortion or disguise of the questioned writing or of the writing standards
- An anomalous condition of the writer or circumstances of writing of the questioned document

5.4 AXIOMS, MAXIMS, PRINCIPLES, AND LAWS OF HANDWRITING EXAMINATION

Discrimination between the terms *axiom*, *maxim*, *principle*, *theorem*, *theory*, and *law* is difficult, and their proper application to the circumstances of writing is not always clearly understood. McCarthy (1978) claimed that the basic axiom of handwriting identification was that no two writings by the same or different persons are identical. At the same time, he argued that heterogeneity **and** natural variation were its fundamentals and further stated that there are no other axioms or corollaries involved in the process affecting handwriting identification.

It must be reiterated that habituation and the heterogeneity of writing are the two principles or premises on which identification is predicated. They are much more than axioms. They are the basis on which other propositions are made, and thus, by definition, they are principles. To these principles is attached a corollary, that given an adequate sample, the discriminatory process employed (the 21 discriminating elements presented in Chapter 6) is capable of making the necessary distinction between any two writers.

Huber and Headrick held a distinctly different view to that of others respecting natural variation. Variation is an attribute of writing that has been observed. It is a reflection of the degree of consistency between or within standards or rather between samples of the discriminating elements present in the standards. As such, it constitutes a condition observed, an attribute of each discriminating element of writing that may be great for some and less for others, rather than a principle as others have asserted. Variations in writing cannot be completely controlled. Hence, they are referred to as natural variations.

Hilton (1963) provided 10 rules and 13 corollaries, thereby introducing these two terms to identify some general truths respecting writing identification that have evolved. To ensure clarity in the use of terms, Huber and Headrick provided the following definitions to assist in sorting and establishing the facts and fundamentals respecting handwriting and handwriting identification:

- Axioms are well established or universally conceded propositions that are self-evident, not requiring demonstration, including some maxims.
- Laws are: (1) particular phenomena deduced from facts, expressible by the statement that it always occurs if certain conditions be present, or (2) the conformity of individual cases to a general rule.
- Maxims are propositions expressing general truths of science or experience.
- Principles are: (1) truths or propositions on which other propositions depend, or (2) assumptions forming the basis of a chain of reasoning.
- Theories are: (1) systems of ideas that account for facts or phenomena, or (2) general principles offered to explain something.
- Theorems are universal or general propositions that are demonstrable.

There are axioms, maxims, and principles, etc. respecting writing, and there are axioms, maxims, and principles, etc. respecting writing identification. With the exception of the two principles and one corollary on which writing identification is predicated, the majority of the other statements that are made respecting writing or writing identification are axioms or maxims according to Huber and Headrick's definitions. Insofar as writing, the following assertions may be made:

1. Writing is an acquired skill that is a complex perceptual-motor task (a fundamental principle).
2. The execution of writing is a voluntary act that follows behavior patterns learned as habits (a fundamental principle).
3. As a complex perceptual-motor task, writing is heterogeneous (a principle).
4. Writing is comprised of major elements, that are more consciously executed and conspicuous, and fine elements that are less consciously executed and inconspicuous (a maxim).
5. With practice, writing becomes automatic (an axiom).
6. With automation, writing becomes more skillful (an axiom).

7. With improvement in skill, writing becomes less variable between executions, although some natural variations are inevitably present (a maxim).
8. Natural variations are the imprecisions with which the habits (discriminating elements) of the writer are executed on repeated occasions (a definition).
9. Natural variation is an attribute of each of the habits (discriminating elements) of an individual's writing. Its range varies with the skill of the writer and the particular allographs (letters) being executed (a maxim).
10. Owing to natural variations, no two writings of the same material by the same person are identical (a maxim).
11. Natural variations in writing diverge with the writer's condition; the writing conditions may diverge with the nature of the document. When conditions are controlled, there is less variation between executions (a maxim).
12. Natural variations in writing are usually less in synchronous writings than in asynchronous writings (a maxim).
13. Handwriting changes progressively over the lifetime of the writer. The change is greater during the earlier and later stages of life, however, the nature and extent of the change is peculiar to the individual (a maxim).
14. Deterioration in writing for any cause affects all of its elements (a maxim).
15. The rate of progression in the deterioration of writing varies with individual circumstances (a maxim).
16. Temporary physical or mental conditions can produce transitory or temporary changes in writing that leave with the departure of the condition (a maxim).
17. A writer cannot ameliorate his maximum writing ability or skill without effort, practice and/or training over a period of time (a principle).
18. Quality in any human endeavor, and particularly in writing, is its own best defense against simulation, forgery, or counterfeiting (a principle).
19. The keys to synchronism versus asynchronism are found in the attributes of consistency and continuity (a principle).

Relative to handwriting identification, the following assertions may be made:

1. Handwriting identification is a study and comparison of habits (a law or definition).
2. Handwriting identification is a process of analysis, comparison, and evaluation (Huber's law of ACEs).
3. What analysis has found and comparison has revealed, only proper evaluation can render useful (a principle).
4. Any conclusion of identification derives from statistical inference and is an expression of probability having an arithmetic value somewhere between 0 and 1 (a law or a principle).
5. The identification of a writer is particular and demonstrable; the elimination (nonidentity) of a writer is general and speculative (a principle).
6. The identification of a writer is a consequence of the evaluation of similarities; the elimination of or differentiation between writers (i.e., nonidentity) is a consequence of the evaluation of differences (a principle).
7. The significance of a discriminating element in a handwriting varies inversely to its frequency of occurrence in similar text material in the writing of different persons (a principle).

8. The elements of writing are reasonably stable from one writing occasion to the next (a principle—the consequence of habituation).
9. No two writings of the same material by different persons are identical (a principle—the consequence of heterogeneity).
10. Age and sex cannot be precisely determined from an examination and study of a writing (a maxim).
11. A simulation of another's writing will resemble it to some extent, depending on the skill of the simulator (a maxim).
12. Intricacy of pen movement or complexity of writing pattern provides evidence in support of genuineness, when comparison with standards reveals similarity; it provides evidence in support of spuriousness, when comparison with standards reveals difference (an axiom).
13. One cannot exclude from one's own writing those discriminating elements of which one is not aware, or include those elements of another's writing of which one is not cognizant (the principle of exclusion and inclusion).
14. It is a greater task to duplicate another's writing habits that are similar to, but discriminable from one's own, because of the difficulty of maintaining subtle or minor changes to one's normal writing habits (the principle of interference).
15. Simulated signatures can rarely be associated with the writing of the simulator (a maxim).
16. Traced signatures can rarely be associated with the writing of the tracer (a maxim).
17. Disguise is the consequence of any deliberate effort to alter the discriminating elements of one's own writing (a definition).
18. Attempts to disguise the less conspicuous features of one's writing for which there are few readily conceived alternatives, are less subject to change and may, therefore, be of greater identification value (a maxim).
19. Attempted disguise produces an inferior quality of writing (a maxim).
20. The level of deception attained by an attempt at disguise will vary with: (1) the skill of the writer, (2) the perceptive ability of the audience, and (3) the nature and amount of writing involved (a maxim).
21. Articles, conjunctions, prepositions, and pronouns in the English language exhibit a greater degree of unconscious characterization or individuality than other less frequently used words (a maxim).
22. In writing identification, the natural variation of discriminating elements mitigates against the virtues that discreet measurement might afford (a maxim).
23. There is no alternative available to examiners other than numbers to define precisely what is meant by *probability, strong probability,* and *very strong probability,* or any similar expression, to indicate the respective levels of certainty that each represents (a maxim).
24. When any two items possess a combination of independent discriminating elements (characteristics) that are similar and/or correspond in their relationships to one another, of such number and significance as to preclude the possibility of their occurrence by pure coincidence, and there are no inexplicable disparities, it may be concluded that they are the same in nature or are related to a common source (the principle of identification).

Chapter 6

Discrimination and Identification of Handwriting

6.1 THE LANGUAGE OF LETTERS

When describing letter designs, there is a tendency to automatically think of the Roman alphabet. Handwriting examiners, however, are frequently involved in the examination of writing in other languages and alphabets in which there is remarkable variety, not confined simply to the formation of characters, but variation also in the number of characters employed. To suit alphabets to their sounds, languages require different numbers of characters or letters. English requires 26, Hebrew and Italian use 22 characters, Arabic employs 28 and Russian, 36. The alphabets of other European languages are equally diverse: Polish, 45; French, 25; Danish, 27; Spanish, 29; Hungarian, 38; and Albanian, 33. Eastern dialects are even more diverse: Tibetan, 35; Telugu, 48; and Japanese, 73.

Under these circumstances, the term *letter* is in some ways an imprecise one. Is the printed (uppercase) "L," the printed (lowercase) "l," and the handwritten (cursive) "*l*" the same letter, or are they different letters? And if they are the same letter, what term is to be used to distinguish between the three designs? Linguists interested in written language use a number of terms that are enjoying a significant degree of widely accepted use within graphonomics and in its research publications.

Ellis (1979) proposed a three-tier system that recognizes the grapheme as the most abstract unit. Hence, the English alphabet comprises 26 graphemes, of which "*l*" is one. In fact, there are more than 26, for there are a number of signs and symbols, such as "$" and "&," that are customarily included with the characters of the alphabet. When writing a word, one has to know the identity and the order of the component graphemes. Spelling processes specify this orthographic structure in terms of graphemes. Thus, a grapheme is the abstract representation of a letter, and a word is spelled as a string of graphemes.

Each grapheme is represented at the next level by a number of allographs, for example, "L," "l," and "*l*." Systems of cursive writing, manuscript, and lettering or printing within a society are found in copybooks, manuals, and printing publications. These prescribe the particular designs of the allographs (and their uppercase or lowercase designs) for each style, to be used in certain positions within a given word. Some systems offer optional allographs for the same grapheme. Thus, in cursive writing there are typically two commonly used designs for the letters "r," "t," and "b," and as many as three designs for the "P," "B," and "R" (Figure 6.1).

Then too, as expounded below, individuals develop their own habits of mixing allographs (cursive, script, and/or lettered) depending upon the position of the grapheme within a word, or upon the allographs that precede or succeed the particular grapheme.

Figure 6.1 Varieties of upper and lowercase letter designs for the letters "T," "P," "R," "p," "r," and "t" suggested in writing manuals.

The third level in the descriptive hierarchy is the actual graph—the pattern of ink on the paper representing, for that writer, a particular allograph. Any given allograph will be produced and perceived, in grossly or minutely different fashions, in the writing of different individuals, or of the same individual on different occasions. These comprise the normal and natural variations between and within writers.

The graph, then (i.e., a written pattern or form) is a writer's rendition of an allograph (i.e., a particular letter or character in cursive, script, or lettered style, in uppercase or lowercase design), respecting a particular grapheme (an abstract entity of a particular alphabet). As Brault and Plamondon (1993) expressed, "for any given word, each letter appears after having gone through three levels of representation: the grapheme (a concept of a letter without a precise form); the allograph (representing a precise type of letter); and the graph (representing the sequence of appropriate movements for the formation of the letter)" (p. 400). There is, of course, a physical and final step that activates the specific muscles, in sequence, required to effectively form the graphs (letters) for the word.

Examiners do not need to abandon the term *letter* when a precise descriptive level is not involved. The system is offered, indeed recommended, for use when clarification of the nature of the character in a process or occurrence is needed. Handwriting examination is a study of graphs that are the writer's graphic representations of a certain set of allographs. Different writers may have different concepts, or choices of the options for the allographs the text of the writing requires. Obviously, an identification of a writing implies that the graphs in the questioned and standard material derive from the same concept or choice of the allographs, comprising the written word.

6.2 DISCRIMINATING ELEMENTS OF HANDWRITING

Numerous aspects of writing become habitual with practice, and execution becomes more automatic as the writing process subjugates itself to the thought process. The individual is more concerned with what is being written than how it is being written. Coincidentally, due in part to the complexity of the writing process, the individual develops his or her own idiosyncrasies in both the shape or form of letters and the fashions in which they are combined, all of which become habitual with practice. All of these habits, considered in combination, constitute the means by which the handwriting of one may be discriminated from that of another, or associated with a writing in dispute.

Similar to fingerprint identification, handwriting identification presupposes that handwriting is unique to the individual. Handwriting examiners have allowed their skill and experience to supply the confidence needed to assume the hypotheses to be true to the extent that, within limited populations, serious errors will not occur. If handwriting is unique, then it is only reasonable to conclude that its individuality lies in the habits that are developed and become fixed to some degree in the writing performance. If individuality was to manifest itself in some more variable aspects of the writing, the potential for and probability of duplication of these features in some other person's writing would increase, and discrimination between individuals would be less likely.

The study of handwriting for identification purposes has innumerable variables for which to account. Perhaps the most pressing problem that Huber and Headrick recognized was the lack of a common terminology to describe or identify writing components, and the lack of a consensus on the factors or aspects of which handwriting is comprised, that serve to distinguish between writers. This was called *conspect reliability* by Klimoski and Rafaeli (1983) in their five-point criteria for the acceptance of a discipline by the scientific community. It was also the concern of a study by Blake (1995) which focused on whether document examiners see and interpret handwriting factors consistently. It was a priority in the six-point criteria suggested to achieve scientific status for handwriting identification (Huber 1995).

In published research from other disciplines, such as graphology and graphonomics, there have been studies on handwriting elements and variables, the research of which can benefit handwriting identification practices. Lewinson (1986) itemized 15 aspects of writing that early graphologists sought to measure. Lorr et al. (1954) measured 16 characteristics. Lemke and Kirchner (1971) claim to have measured 47 handwriting characteristics with a ruler and magnifying glass. Peeples and Retzlaff (1991) selected and studied 25 of these 47 features to determine whether even smaller groups of characteristics might serve to discriminate between writings. It was their finding that the factors of heights, widths, and angles could be used to greatly improve the reliability of handwriting measurement. The IGS (International Graphonomics Society) has published technical abstracts and proceedings about handwriting measurement since 1982. The publications produced by the IGS have improved the reliability of handwriting measurement and revolutionized what is measureable in handwriting to include dynamic movement.

Huber and Headrick's consideration of the matter over a number of years led to the conclusion that there are 21 elements of handwriting examined, as a matter of practice, in the task of identifying or discriminating between handwritings. This is dependent upon how one classifies these elements. Furthermore, it is not surprising that there is considerable correspondence between this list and others, although the terminology and consolidation may differ. The consolidation of terms is probably the principal virtue in the catalog that Huber and Headrick set forth.

Osborn (1929) used the terms elements, qualities, and characteristics of writings without clearly differentiating between them, and others followed his example in their use without clarifying the issue any further. Many examiners use the term *characteristics*, while others use the term *individualities* or the expression *identifying individualities*, as Conway (1959) was inclined to do.

Huber and Headrick chose the term *discriminating elements* as the most appropriate expression to use in reference to the aspects of writings that are involved in their identification or differentiation. The so-called standard texts employ various terms, such as *characteristics*, *qualities*, *features*, and *elements*, and go to some length clarifying the difference between them without attempting to define each of them precisely. On the other hand, the term *discriminating element* lends itself to definition in a particularly simple and understandable form.

> **Definition:** A discriminating element is a relatively discrete element of writing or lettering that varies observably or measurably with its author and may, thereby, contribute reliably to distinguishing between the inscriptions of different persons, or to evidencing the sameness in those of common authors.

There might be some merit in employing a term that is somewhat more or less vernacular that might develop a relationship with handwriting much as the term *symptom* has grown to acquire with respect to medical conditions.

In the Netherlands, Hardy and Fagel (1995) consolidated and delineated the discriminating elements of handwriting in a collection of some 17 points, organized in four categories, that is a program followed by forensic laboratories in the Netherlands. As might be expected, there is some correspondence between their list and the list presented by Huber and Headrick, but there are a number of elements that are found in the present inventory that do not appear in the Netherlands catalog.

In organizing this topic, it helps to segregate the discriminating elements of writing into two principal categories and two others:

1. Elements of style consist of arrangement, connections, construction, design, dimensions, slant or slope, spacing, class, and choice of allograph(s). With the exception, perhaps, of construction, these are the aspects of writing that play a significant role in creating a pictorial, or general or overall effect. Differences in construction, of course, do not necessarily alter the overall effects.
2. Elements of execution consist of abbreviations, alignment, commencements and terminations, diacritics and punctuation, embellishments, line continuity, line quality or fluency (speed), pen control (which includes pen hold, pen position, and pen pressure) writing movement (including angularity), and legibility or writing quality (which includes letter shapes or letter forms for any given allograph).
3. Other elements include consistency or natural variations, and persistency.
4. Lateral expansion and word proportions are also discriminating elements.

Elements of execution are the aspects of writing that are the less obvious, more subtle elements that frequently require the microscope or other technical assistance to fully assess. In large measure, they are the personal idiosyncrasies of writing in which we find the subtle dissimilarities between the writing of one individual and the next.

Thus, without implying their relative importance by the order chosen, it can be stated that writing habits having identification value consist of the following and are appropriately entitled the discriminating elements of handwriting.

6.2.1 Elements of Style

6.2.1.1 Arrangement

Arrangement is a group of habits that are influenced by the writer's artistic ability, sense of proportion, and the instruction received. It may be evident in:

- Placement and balance of text
- Dimensions and uniformity of all four margins
- Interlinear spacing
- Parallelism of lines
- Character, position, and perhaps frequency of interlineations
- Depth of indentions
- Paragraphing
- Use of numerals and symbols in monetary amounts
- Location and nature of headings, salutations, introductions, and conclusions
- Location of signatures, relative to margins, rulings, and constraints
- Style, size, and position of addressing on envelopes

Arrangement can be a matter of considerable importance in the identification of authors of extended writings. Not all aspects of arrangement itemized above will be available to study in every case. The type of document and the extent of the text will determine the factors that might be considered.

Matters of arrangement are taught in many business schools, but the number of graduates from these schools is relatively small. For the most part, people grow into, rather than consciously acquire, arrangement habits. It was Osborn's (1929) view that no other characteristic in handwriting was more indicative of literacy or illiteracy than habits of arrangement.

6.2.1.1.1 Placement and Balance of Text

This aspect of arrangement is closely allied to, if not a product of, the matter of margins. Principally, arrangement refers to the left and right margins of the page giving less attention to the dimensions of the top and bottom margins. To be precise then, marginal dimensions (all four of them) are the cause, placement of a text is the consequence, and balance (in any direction) is a judgment of the result.

Writers that are inclined to dispense with a right margin, are often seen to compress writing to ensure its fit within the edge of the sheet or space available. If compression of many lines of the text occurs, the result is that the text may appear to be imbalanced in that more writing in letters or words is present on the right side of the document than on the left. Balance, however, can be overlooked (Figure 6.2).

6.2.1.1.2 Dimensions and Uniformity of Margins

It is not uncommon for left margins to be pronounced and consistent and for right margins to be completely disregarded. On ruled paper, left margins will be influenced by the location of a

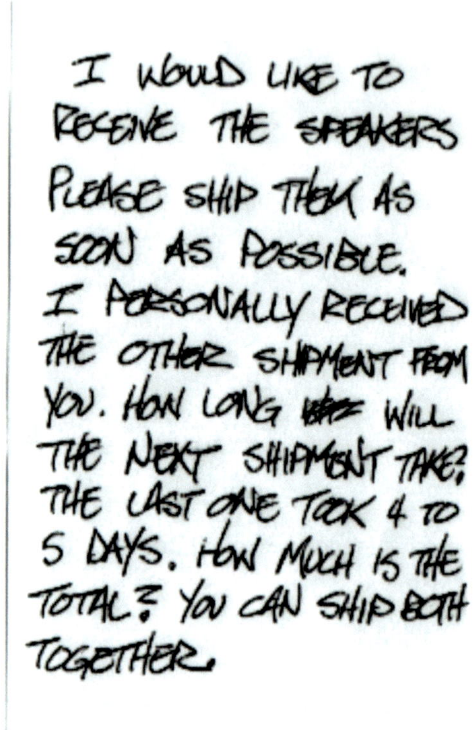
I WOULD LIKE TO
RECEIVE THE SPEAKERS
PLEASE SHIP THEM AS
SOON AS POSSIBLE.
I PERSONALLY RECEIVED
THE OTHER SHIPMENT FROM
YOU. HOW LONG WILL
THE NEXT SHIPMENT TAKE?
THE LAST ONE TOOK 4 TO
5 DAYS. HOW MUCH IS THE
TOTAL? YOU CAN SHIP BOTH
TOGETHER.

Figure 6.2 Example of a narrow, compressed right margin.

vertical rule, if one is present. There are writers that provide substantial margins in every direction, and subsequently, are not adverse to using the space to finish the communication if some space is needed, but not enough to justify another sheet.

Of particular interest in the study of arrangements is the disinclination of the writer to utilize hyphens and to split words out of deference to a particular dimension of margin on the right side of the text. If a right margin of any width has been established, it will be found that many, if not most, writers will violate the margin rather than hyphenate the word.

Another aspect of margins that has been frequently observed is that the top and bottom margins are of a smaller dimension than the side margins. Indeed all four margins may exhibit different dimensions. Unquestionably, margins merit attention and should not be disregarded.

6.2.1.1.3 Interlinear Spacing

Interlinear spacing is usually predetermined by ruled paper. Individual spacing tendencies or habits become apparent only in writing on blank or unruled sheets. Generally speaking, on unruled paper, interlinear spacing for most persons is slightly greater than the approximately 7 to 9 mm in which ruled paper is inscribed. For some whose writing is relatively small, the spacing can be apparently great. For some others whose writing is relatively large, it is not uncommon for the lines to be or seem to be crowded, and for the loops or staffs of infralinear and supralinear letters to intersect (Figure 6.3).

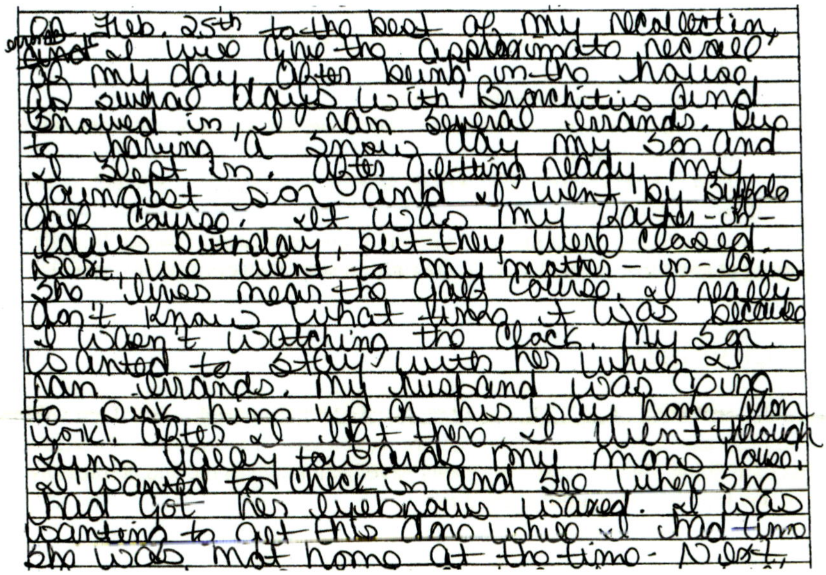

Figure 6.3 Ruled paper writing showing full use of "allowed" space.

6.2.1.1.4 Parallelism of Lines

Parallelism is defined as being the quality or state of being parallel, and on unruled paper, writing lines may not be consistently parallel. The condition being appraised is the overall alignment of each line of writing relative to its imaginary baseline. From the perspective of alignments, all of the line alignments should be viewed in a comprehensive fashion, in order that the cumulative effect of a sequence of lines, if there is one, can be observed, studied, and appreciated. In this respect it will be noted that alignments may decline progressively, and it is not unusual to observe some effort to correct the situation as the writing nears the bottom of the page.

6.2.1.1.5 Character and Position of Interlineations

Interlineations tend to be of two kinds: (1) words or short groups of words inserted into a sentence that alter the context to some extent. This is the short form interlineation; and (2) whole sentences inserted into a document where space is available to inject additional conditions, provisions, or requirements that alter the terms or the context of the document to a significant extent. This is the long form interlineation.

The short form interlineation is usually preceded by the insertion of a caret. A caret is a mark in the shape of a small inverted "v," the name of which was derived from the Latin for something lacking. The size, shape, and position of the caret can vary somewhat with the individual. The principal dispute respecting short form interlineations is whether they are changes made at the time of the creation of the document or sometime after its completion and issue.

The key to the determination of the origin of the short form interlineation lies in its consistency: the consistency in the inks involved, in the writing instrument, and/or in the writer. In this last respect, the nature and execution of the caret should not be overlooked. The study of the points of intersection of writing lines was also recommended by Osborn (1929), but the sequence of the textual writing and the short form interlineation is rarely an issue.

Long form interlineations are not usually accompanied by carets. The intention is to make them appear to be original components of the document. Here again, consistency in the ink, the instrument, and/or the writer will be key to determining whether the material was a later insertion.

Other aspects of the questioned material in suspected long form interlineations, however, must also be considered. If, in fact, it was a later addition to the document, then depending on the amount of text involved and the space available for it, there may be evidence of compression of the writing to render it appropriate for the space. Furthermore, under these circumstances the sequence of the writings of intersecting lines of the questioned material and the text of lines below it, and only below it, may be a factor of considerable significance.

Handwritten interlineations in typewritten text usually eliminate consideration of the consistency of the inks involved, unless there are other handwritten material or signatures on the document with which a comparison may be made.

6.2.1.1.6 Depth of Indentions

The literature has not revealed a source that stipulates what the depth of indentions for paragraphs in extended writings should be. Examples that are provided in penmanship courses range from no indention at all to an indention of half of a line length. The inference to be drawn from instructions that are given is that the writer is at liberty to choose an indention of any length that is pleasing to the eye and conforms to or provides a balance to the text.

Examiners observe examples of both extremes on the scale (none to half a line) with a majority that fall into the group with a dimension between half and one and a half inches. Omissions of an indention seem to be more common in modern writing. When that occurs it is usually accompanied by some increase in the interlinear space immediately above to identify the commencement of a new paragraph.

Obviously, it is an element of writing that can be considered principally in the study of extended writings, such as anonymous letters. Both Osborn (1929) and Harrison (1958b) comment on its usefulness as a discriminating element, but that purpose is served when the depth of the indentions are extreme variations from the norm, in either direction. Admittedly, it is a feature of writing to which persons may not give much thought, and that has a bearing on its usefulness in the study of disguised or anonymous writings.

6.2.1.1.7 Paragraphing

The word *paragraph* was at one time simply the name given to the mark ¶ written in the margin of a manuscript where a unit or subdivision of the text was to begin. The signal currently used for that purpose is to indent the first line, however the pilcrow, the formal name of the mark ¶, is still used in legal literature to mark or identify paragraphs, and is generally employed as a proofreader's mark to indicate a paragraph beginning.

As a signal, then, and an aid in the comprehension of text, think of the indention of the beginning of a paragraph as a kind of punctuation. The rules for the application of that kind of punctuation vary substantially with the nature of the text to be punctuated. Consequently, there is little information as to what would constitute normal paragraphing (i.e., the copybook style), and what practices would be unusual or individual.

Communications that are extended writings, such as are encountered in anonymous letters or disguised writings, are usually classed as expositions. Generally in expositions, a paragraph is defined as a related group of sentences, with or without a summarizing sentence, but the extent to which this rule is consciously followed in personal communications is quite limited. There are some individuals that never paragraph from the beginning to the end, and there are others that tend to make paragraphs out of every sentence.

As with many other elements of writing, greater discriminative value in the examination and study will occur when the writer diverges distinctly from what should be the norm or that which conforms to the above-mentioned definition.

6.2.1.1.8 Use of Numerals and Symbols in Monetary Amounts

Over the years, various endeavors to classify writings have begun with the classification of writing on checks. Prominent in this work were the manner in which numerals were written and how they were used in the inscription of monetary amounts. Horan and Horan (1984) saw fit to include the frequency with which zeros are connected to one another in their study of numerals. They reported that 18% of their population of 700 subjects joined two or more zeros together at the tops. Related to this is the manner in which some individuals employ the "x" or simply the dash in place of the zeros in round figured monetary amounts.

6.2.1.1.9 Location and Nature of Headings, Salutations, Introductions, and Conclusions

There is little that needs to be said on this subject. There are few standards against which the practices of a given writer can be judged. Individual idiosyncrasies frequently appear that are almost self-evident as unusual practices.

6.2.1.1.10 Location of Signatures

There was a time when the signature to a letter was invariably placed below and to the right of center of a text, but that is no longer the case, and signatures may occur in various locations. Their relationships to text, to margins, and to rulings, if any, may all warrant study. The manner in which they occupy a confined space may also be noteworthy.

6.2.1.1.11 Style, Size, and Position of Envelope Addresses

Few people are aware of their habits in respect of arrangements or to appreciate how their habits differ from those of others. Yet their habits may be distinctive as in the extent of indentions at the beginning of lines, the spacing of address lines without the benefit of rulings, and the position of the material relative to the envelope edges.

Harrison (1958b) points out the value in the arrangement of envelope addresses in the study of anonymous letters. As a common act, it becomes quite automatic and is one in which the attention of the writer is directed at legibility rather than arrangement protocol. For this reason writers develop a style for themselves from which they rarely depart.

What must be borne in mind, in the course of obtaining request writings from a possible author, is that in order for the standards to be usable they must be furnished from dictation that is carefully prepared and discretely administered. There must be no external influence insofar as any of the 11 factors of arrangement mentioned previously that the writer might exhibit.

6.2.1.2 Class of Allograph

Style is a term that has been applied rather loosely to apparently different patterns of writing habits executed by individuals under different writing circumstances. For many persons, there seems to be a difference in writing practices between the writing of formal letters and the scribbling of notes. Whether these differences should be identified and described as different styles of writing or whether they are simply alternatives to some gross features, such as slope and lettered capitals that have become the writer's practice in less formal executions or on certain special occasions, is a moot point that only a careful study of adequate writing standards can resolve. They may be simply a brief disregard for care and quality often described as scribbling. Shaneyfelt (1974) commented on the variety of styles of writing exhibited by some individuals in the signatures appearing on FBI fingerprint cards. The writing involved is limited to one or two signatures per card, however, and on the strength of these it is difficult to discriminate normal, natural writing from a short-term or long-term disguise, or from a deliberate modification. Persons in police custody may have good reasons for making at least pictorial changes to their writing.

There are four principle styles or manners in which people using the Roman alphabet endeavor to communicate with the pen. They are, in fact, the four general categories into which all allographs may be segregated (Figure 6.4). Care must be taken that changes in writing quality, due to haste, negligence, or deliberate writer action, are not improperly perceived as changes in writing styles or allographs, which are as follows:

1. Cursive writing, in which letters are connected and are designed according to some commercial system
2. Manuscript or script writing, in which letters are disconnected and are designed similar to upper and lower case printing characters

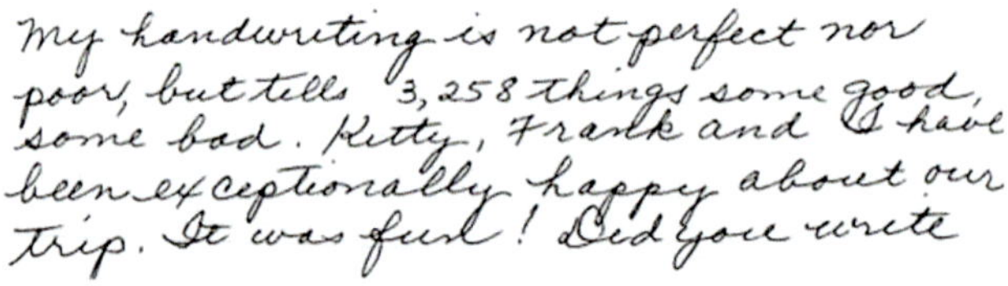

(a)

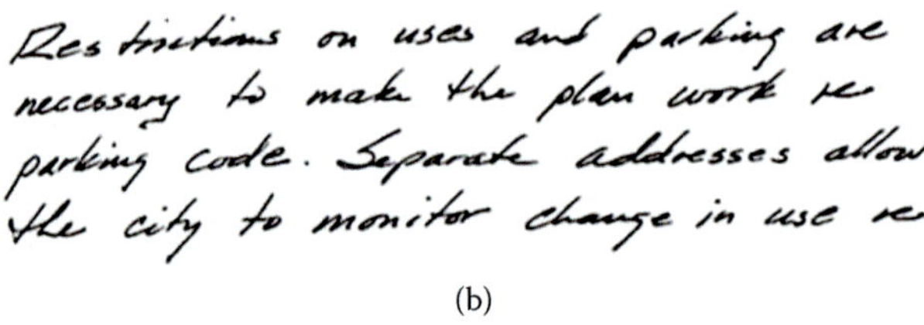

(b)

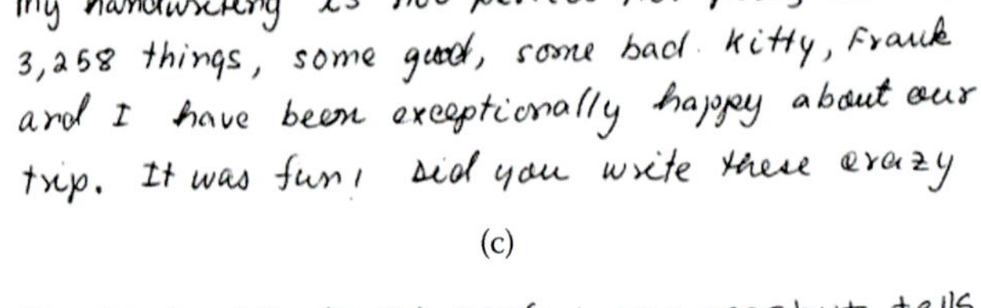

(c)

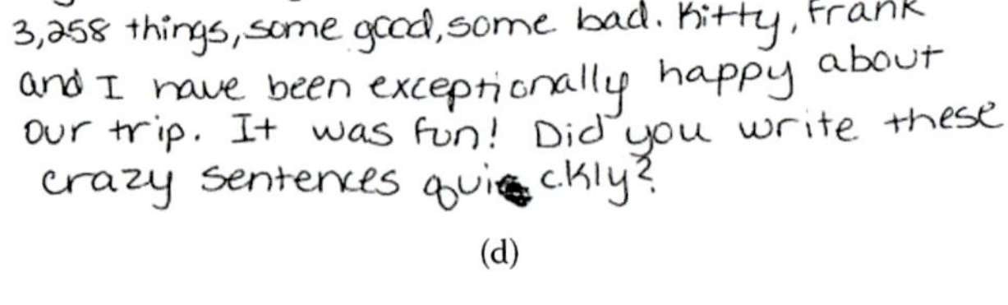

(d)

Figure 6.4 Allograph styles depicting cursive (a), script (b), composite (c), and hand lettering (d).

3. Hand lettering, sometimes referred to as hand printing or block lettering, in which letters are separately structured and more often are designed as upper case printing characters
4. Composites of cursive writing and hand lettering, cursive writing and script, and somewhat rarely hand lettering and script

Osborn (1929) credited England with the origin of manuscript writing, but Marjorie Wise is credited with the development of the first manuscript alphabet for use in the United States in 1921, according to Anthony (1984). Osborn considered it to be a fad that, like most fads, would pass in time. Now, nearly 100 years after its introduction, the manuscript alphabet is still taught and used, although its popularity has waned with the decrease in the mandatory teaching of writing in the public school system.

Producers of commercial cursive writing systems offer a method of manuscript writing for use in early grades of schooling, and some go so far as to recommend its use at each grade level. The American Book Company states: "Manuscript writing is four times easier and 20 percent faster than cursive writing" (Herrick 1960a, p. 32). There is usually a transition point in the school system, however, at which a change from manuscript to cursive writing is arranged. This is frequently at or about grade 3 in elementary school. Historically, there were a few companies that produced commercial systems, and a few school systems that used them, who pursued the pre-World War II policy generally followed in North America in which cursive writing was the sole system advocated. In these circumstances, manuscript writing was reserved for adults with special vocational reasons for adopting a more distinctive and precise manuscript print style, such as architects and engineers.

Anthony (1984) attributes the development of the D'Nealian script writing system to Donal Neal Thurber, who used the letters of his given names to create the acronym. Thurber, a Michigan educator is reported to have begun development in the 1960s in an attempt to ease the learning of writing for the very young and to facilitate the transition to cursive writing later on. Growing out of the Palmer method, simplicity and legibility were the goals in the development of the D'Nealian system. As in other systems developed at the time, slant was not important so long as it was consistent. The publisher, Scott Foresman and Company, claimed that the D'Nealian system (introduced in 1978) was the first new writing system offered since 1931. Starting in the late 1970s, D'Nealian was taught widely in schools and created certain class characteristics that are a part of the system: simplified cursive handwriting and, notably, the uppercase "I" which is written in reverse to the Palmer "I."

Gradually, there has been a decline in the interest to teach cursive in schools especially since the core curriculum in the United States no longer requires the teaching of cursive. This decline has naturally corresponded with an increase in communications technology involving handheld or computerized devices (e.g., use of e-mail and texting on devices). In spite of the decline in teaching cursive writing methods in school, there are a number of new writing systems available on the market. Although the teaching of cursive is not mandatory in public schools in many states in the United States, there are still many teachers who advocate its teaching and ensure that their students complete all their assignments in cursive. Many private and charter schools and homeschool students are also taught cursive handwriting using some of the new methods available that encourage simplicity and ease of learning. Even those who were not taught cursive and use manuscript print sometimes adapt a mixed method style that connects printed letters in a semicursive manner. Typically, the signatures of those who were not taught formal cursive still exhibit strong cursive elements even though the writing frequently exhibits poor fluency.

In spite of the wide variation of handwriting teaching methods and the fluctuation in teaching over the past few decades, many different forms of the same grapheme or symbol are taught in both manuscript and cursive letters and numerals and are similar across systems. Generally, greater variation in shape is found in uppercase cursive letters and numerals, while less variation is found among lowercase cursive letters.

Hand lettering is a style that individuals tend to develop for themselves. Perhaps because the lowercase forms of many print characters do not adapt well to execution by hand (e.g., "a," "e," "f," "d," "r"), there is a preference to use capital letter forms only. It might be argued that this style is simply a limited or modified version of manuscript writing or vice versa.

Where manuscript writing or hand lettering becomes an individual's preferred style, and is used constantly, connections between letters frequently develop as speed of execution is improved. In this process, numerous individual characteristics can evolve. From the standpoint of writing identification, however, the disconnection of letters eliminates several features or writing habits, and evidence that might be utilized is, therefore, diminished.

Some examiners have argued that style characteristics are useless for the identification of a handwriting but allow that they may be indicative of nationality or the writer's country of learning. This then, is to admit that they serve as class characteristics which are very useful evidence in identification, although the weight to be given them must be appropriately modified. They must not, however, be totally disregarded.

6.2.1.3 Connections

1. Intraword, that is, between letters, of particular types, not necessarily related to or arising from the writing system
2. Interword, that is, between words, if, when, and where they occur

The evolution of cursive writing from lettering to facilitate speed and ease led to the introduction of connecting strokes between letters. Harrison (1958b) commented that handwriting was purified by the elimination of connecting strokes. Such a philosophy may have been responsible for the birth of manuscript writing.

Harrison (1958b) writes that in the civil service writing of England the connecting strokes are curved and relatively lengthy, unlike the straight angular connecting strokes of the American business hand. This was because of the abnormal separation of the letters in a word. Osborn (1929) states that the degree of curvature and the slant of connecting strokes is one of the most significant variations in handwriting. Ellen (1989) further describes some of these variations. Lee and Abbey (1922), under the caption of connections, speak of the importance of disconnections as a writing characteristic that in their time, of course, were digressions from the copybook style and were infrequent occurrences. Quirke (1930) placed importance on the forms of connections, categorized them in nine fashions and maintained that they were the progeny of speed, lateral expansion, and spacing. Spacing is, of course, one of the two integral parts of lateral expansion. He asserted, almost as a contradiction of Lee and Abbey, that except in the writing of master penmen, writers do not entirely follow the conventions of copybook connections. Hayes (1987) also dealt with the subject of connecting strokes.

Osborn (1929), Harrison (1958b), and Ellen (1989) all speak of the amount of retracing of the upstroke or lead-in stroke to letters having a bowl or circular component, such as the "a," "c," "d," "g," "o," and "q." All of them consider connecting strokes valuable in the identification process. All of them note that they are frequently overlooked in the simulation of a writing, and all of them comment that the task is more difficult in the examination of writing that is devoid of connecting strokes.

Connections are the unions of two or more letters. In cursive writing they are prescribed, merely by illustration in copybooks, to occur between any two lowercase letters. Some manuals also prescribe, again by illustration only, the connection of certain uppercase to the lowercase letters that follow, but this varies with the design of the uppercase letters that the system advocates. The "boat" letters, "B," "G," and "S" are invariably connected to following letters, but seldom the "I," even in a "boat" configuration. On rare occasions, connections may occur between two uppercase letters or between the characters of block lettering. The Zaner-Bloser Company is known to have offered actual direction as to the manner in which connections should be executed. Many of the more modern cursive writing systems offer improved instructional advice about the direction and connection of individual letters in writing.

Specialists have referred to the upstroke to bowl-type letters as secondary strokes, in that they are not essential to the recognition of the letter. Letters that are not bowl type, but that are loop type, trough type, or arch type, do not have secondary strokes. They commence with an upstroke, described as a primary stroke, necessary for their recognition. Furthermore, according to the copybooks for writing systems, with the exception of the letters "b," "o," "v," and "w" that terminate with a horizontal bar, all other letters terminate with an upstroke that leads directly into the primary or secondary strokes of all other letters. The horizontal bars of the "b," "o," "v," and "w," or "spurs" as Harrison (1958b) calls them, lead directly into modifications of the primary strokes or secondary strokes of the letters that follow, all of which eliminate the necessity for the initial upstroke. The particular modifications of the succeeding letters, or to their initial strokes that bars or spurs may induce, may provide some of the most unique and, therefore, useful discriminating elements of a given writing.

The point of this is that while there are unions of letters, or connections of one kind or another, actually, between lowercase letters, there are no such things as connecting strokes. To use the term *connecting stroke* implies that there is a distinct entity, identifiable as a pen or pencil stroke that occurs between two written characters. What is being referred to as connecting strokes are the many manners in which unions are made between terminal strokes, bars or spurs, and initial strokes, irrespective of whether that initial stroke may be of a primary or secondary nature.

Worth noting is that in simulation of signatures, connections may be particularly important. The simulator may copy the letter designs but overlook a reasonable duplication of the manners in which letters are connected.

Few of the older cursive writing systems prescribed a method for the connection of capital letters to other capital letters. In these relationships one encounters true connecting strokes that are distinct and recognizable entities quite foreign to the design of either letter. As a result, a great deal of individualism can occur in these unions and the consistency of them that is of value in a study of the writing.

Furthermore, it is not too uncommon for a writer to connect words together, and the mere occurrence of these kinds of unions can provide a worthy contribution to the assembly of writing habits of a given individual. Interword connections are not suggested by copybook and, consequently, the pattern of practice in this respect is entirely individual. The practice of connecting words and the consistency in doing so may depend on the letters involved, the words involved, or the writing situation, all or any of which may be difficult to determine particularly if the text material is limited (Figure 6.5).

Thus, interword connections may not appear at first glance to be consistent practices of the writer, except for the fact that they are present. They do not necessarily correlate well with speed. Of some importance to the writing examiner is the fact that in disguised writing they may not always be omitted.

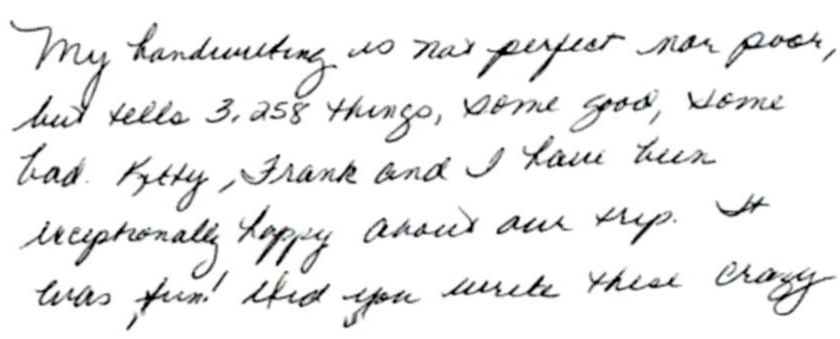

(a)

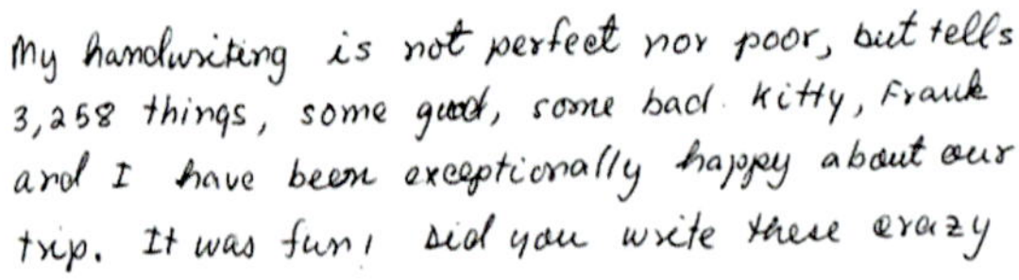

(b)

Figure 6.5 (a) Connected and (b) disconnected writing.

Alternately, of course, the matter of disconnections, that can be of equally great significance as the peculiarities of connections. Because disconnections are seldom, if ever, prescribed in the older writing cursive systems, because they frequently constitute evidence of spuriousness, and because they are often referred to as pen lifts, they warrant separate consideration that might better be dealt with under the caption of line continuity to be discussed (Figure 6.6).

(a)

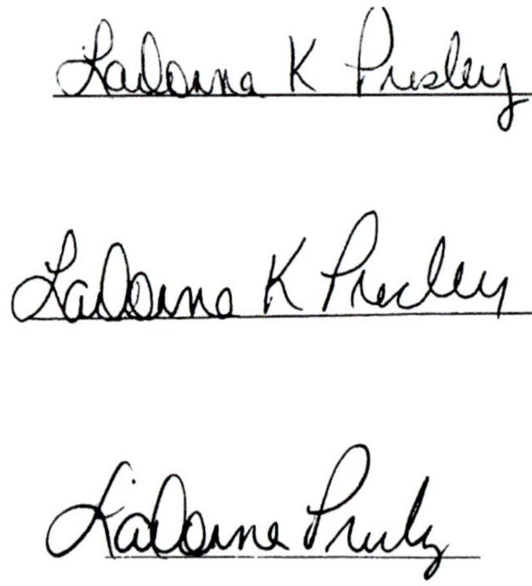

(b)

Figure 6.6 The questioned signature is a forgery (a). Note the disconnected letters compared to the connected letters in the known specimens (b).

6.2.1.4 Design and Construction of Allographs

In this category, factors related to the graphic forms of the particular letters of a writing are included. Elsewhere (class of allograph) there is a discussion regarding style as being either cursive, script, lettering, or mixtures, that are, in fact, four types of allographs for a set of graphemes. In that section, forms of letters are described generally. In this section, there is discussion about some factors that relate to the system learned, some to structure of the character, and some to the patterns or styles selected, including the idiosyncrasies of some writers insofar as the use and misuse of capitalization:

1. Correspondence to foreign/domestic or particular writing systems
2. Number, nature, position, sequence, and direction of strokes in allograph (letter) construction
3. Use of two or more designs for the same allograph

4. Capitalization—divergences from standard practices
5. Allograph (letter) combinations—wherein one allograph's design influences the structure or shape of its neighbor

To facilitate the discussion of the written characters of the alphabet, there are certain general ideas about the Roman hand that are presently described by Tannenbaum's (1930) classification of cursive English writings executed during and after the time of Shakespeare. For him there were four varieties of cursive letters:

- Linear letters are those lowercase letters having no ascending loops or stems, (i.e., not supralinear) or descending loops or stems (i.e., not infralinear), sometimes called minuscules, consisting of "a," "c," "e," "i," "m," "n," "o," "r," "s," "u," "v," "w," and "x." There are no capital letters in this class.
- Supralinear letters are those letters that extend a distance vertically above the linear letters and include "b," "d," "h," "k," "l," and "t." Most capital letters, sometimes called majuscules, are included in this class.
- Infralinear letters are those letters that extend a distance vertically below the baseline of the writing or of the linear letters, and include "g," "j," "p," "q," "y," and "z."
- Double-length letters are those few letters that extend a distance vertically both above and below the linear letters, such as the "f," the "Y," and "Z" and in some systems the lowercase "p."

6.2.1.4.1 Writing Systems

Letter forms (i.e., allographs) are the principal fashions in which systems of writing, advocated by different schools of penmanship, choose to distinguish themselves. Older systems also differed from one another in proportions or relative heights, but dimensions are comparable in most of today's systems.

Letter forms (i.e., allographs) are also the principal means by which nationalities can be broadly discriminated, even today. Numerous other characters or symbols also assist in indicating the part of the world in which a writer developed his writing style. For more information on this topic, see Handwriting Systems Section 8.2.1.

Some rather unusual letter forms and designs (i.e., graphs and/or allographs) have been observed and reported in the literature. Some of these are peculiar to certain occupations (Masson 1990) and some are peculiar to certain populations (see Class Characteristics and National Characteristics Sections 3.4 and 3.5).

6.2.1.4.2 Allograph Construction

Winchester and McCarthy (1971) then later McCarthy and Williams (1987) reported on unorthodox structures of the uppercase cursive letters "J" and "W" among certain students in the southern states of the United States. In these instances the "J" is formed by executing the lower loop first and extending the upstroke from it to form the upper loop in a counterclockwise direction. The "W" is formed by executing a large numeral "3" in lieu of the initial and usually straight downstroke of the letter. This unusual characteristic was seen in use by a limited population several years go, but may not be used anymore.

Daniels (1990) described a very unorthodox structure of the lower case "p" that is without explanation. Normally the "p" is constructed by executing the staff or lower extension element first followed by the forming of a circular bowl in a clockwise direction. In Daniels' example, the bowl has been formed first in a counterclockwise direction that leads into the execution of the staff. When the stroke of the staff returns to the bowl, it proceeds to retrace the lower sector of the bowl, then moves on to connect to the subsequent letter.

Similar to Daniel's discovery, there are numerous unusual structures employed in cursive writing that seem to contradict the teachings of copybooks. The clockwise bowls of the letter "b," and the execution of the bowl after the staff of the letter "d" are two examples. The construction of block or capital letters in the process of hand lettering provides variations that are more frequently encountered. For example, there are as many as four sequences in which the horizontal bars or arms of the letters "E" and "F" may be added. The upper arm of the letter "K" may be either an upstroke or a downstroke. The "M" and "W" may be constructed of a single stroke or as many as four. Even the "O" is sometimes made from two strokes rather than one. Similar variations can be found in numerals, particularly the "4," "5," and "8."

These reported allograph variations from copybook are but a few of the idiosyncratic variations that can occur even after students have been taught a formal cursive or manuscript system. It is not uncommon for allographs to become more simplified by writers after initially learning copybook (Figure 6.7). When handwriting training is not taught or its practice is limited in the classroom, it gives rise to an increase in even more unusual and illogical letter constructions which are present today in modern handwriting and lettering.

6.2.1.4.3 Multiple Designs

Wing (1979) and Wing et al. (1983) endeavored to determine whether the position of the letter or grapheme in a word had any effect upon the allograph selected. Van der Plaats and Van Galen (1991) studied the effect of a preceding letter (i.e., "a" or "o") on the selection of, or consistency in the allograph. These authors point out that problems can arise in studies of allographic choice owing to the somewhat vague distinction that can occur between the allograph and the graph when the range of natural variation is broad. They found that greater variation occurs when the letter is located in the initial position than in the medial or final positions, and that the connection to or terminal stroke from a preceding letter might automatically lead to the selection of a particular allograph or letter design.

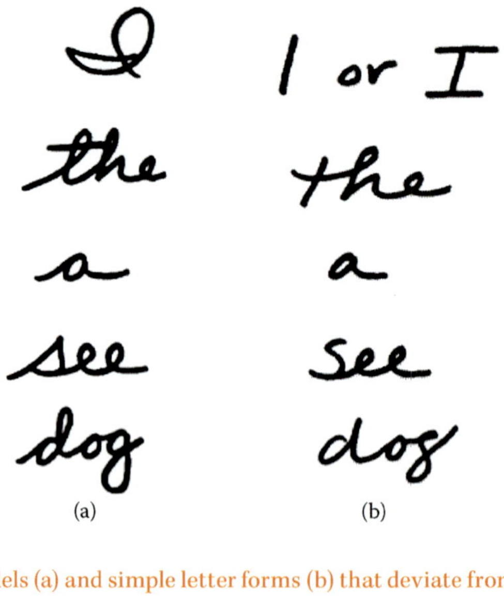

Figure 6.7 Copybook models (a) and simple letter forms (b) that deviate from the model.

6.2.1.4.4 Capitalization

Oddities in capitalization in cursive writing can occur in one of two fashions. Enlarged lowercase letters may be used as capitals, or uppercase letters can be used within words as common alternatives for lowercase letters. Letterings in lowercase styles, rather than block lettering, can produce a mixture of designs the patterns for which, if there are any, may be illogical or may represent a lack of handwriting training.

6.2.1.4.5 Allograph Combinations

Just as positions of a letter within the word (i.e., initial, medial, or terminal) may influence the allograph selected, so also may the nature or structure of its neighboring allographs (letters) exercise some influence upon a character, if not in its shape at least in its size. In such instances, relative sizes can become important discriminators.

Note that, in keeping with lexical and other authorities, the terms *form*, *shape*, and *graph* are used as synonyms. Likewise, the terms *allograph* and *design* are used synonymously. Accordingly, shapes may vary substantially without entailing a change in design (Figure 6.8). This is done to achieve greater lucidity in the language respecting writing. The terms *form* or *letterform* in the broad customary sense are less specific as to whether reference is being made to aspects of the letter design, or to aspects of the shape (or graph) of a letter of a given design.

A letter design or an allograph may have a shape that is quite distinctive for a given writer. The shape will be a product of its dimensions, or the regularity of the curves in the principle strokes with which it is constructed.

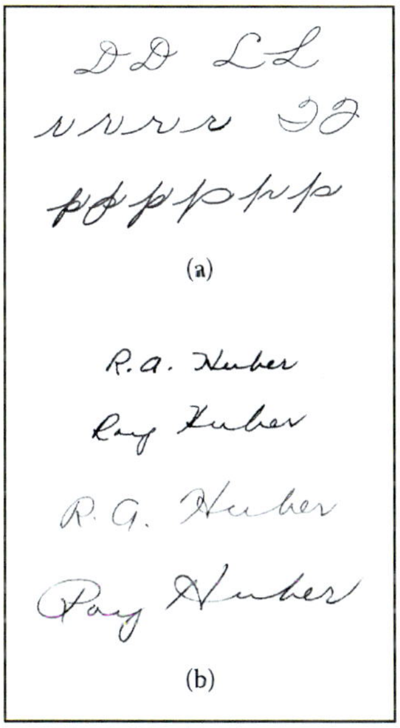

Figure 6.8 An illustration of the variation in shapes of letters that may occur without altering the design of allographs (a). The differences in the signatures in (b), signed by one person, are natural variations of the signature style (see point 18 for a discussion on natural variation).

6.2.1.5 Dimensions

There are a number of expressions that are used to refer to the physical measurements of writing, without an apparent clear distinction between their meanings that can lead to confusion. These include such terms as *proportions*, *relative heights*, *size*, *relative sizes*, and *ratios*. Add to these such terms as *slant*, *slope*, *incline*, and *lateral expansion* resulting in a multitude of expressions without guides as to their particular applications. Different authors and examiners use different terms to refer to the same thing, or the same term to refer to different things. To clarify the situation the principal linear measurements that are involved in the study of writing are separated from the angular measurements, which are discussed later.

Individuals differ in their writing insofar as the vertical dimension and/or horizontal dimension. Copybooks and writing instruction provide general parameters within which the writing should be executed and prescribe certain consistencies that should be observed. Nevertheless, many writers develop their own practices, some of which are quite distinctive and unique. Perhaps a majority of writers, however, will display a degree of similarity in these dimensions.

To clarify, vertical dimensions are measurements or judgments taken or made along a single vertical axis or two or more vertical and parallel axes. Horizontal dimensions are measurements or judgments taken or made along a single horizontal axis. Vertical is understood to mean at an angle of 90° to the baseline of the writing, and horizontal is understood to mean parallel to the baseline of the writing. The baseline of the writing may or may not coincide with ruled lines on the document.

The designs of most letters (with the exception of "M," "m," "N," "n," "W," "w," and perhaps the lowercase "k" and "q") can be considered to have a single vertical axis, that is to say that a single linear rule can provide the measurements of all the essential components in the letter's design (e.g., the length of a loop, the length of a staff, the height of a bowl, the height of an arch, and the depth of a trough). The letters "M," "m," "N," "n," "W," and "w" require two or three separate rules to obtain all the appropriate information.

Furthermore, it should be noted that from the viewpoint of writing identification, there are two aspects of dimensions that are of interest: (1) their absolute measures, and (2) their relative measures. Which of these measures will be important and pursued will depend on the particular writing habit under study.

6.2.1.5.1 Proportions

The term *proportions* is used to describe, insofar as some aspect of size, the relationship of elements of letters to each other, that is, of bowls to staffs (as in the "d," "p," "P," and "R"), of bodies to loops (as in the "z"), of upper loops to lower loops (as in the "f"), of bowls to loops (as in the "b" and "g"), of arches to loops (as in the "h"), of troughs to loops (as in the "y"), of bowls to bowls (as in the "B"), of staffs to arms or legs (as in the "k" and "R"), of upper loops to base elements (as in the "G" or "S"), of upper curve to lower curve (as in the "E"), or simply the relationship of small letters to tall letters.

Osborn (1929) spoke of proportions frequently, in the sense of a class characteristic by which the writing system taught and followed might be identified. He differentiates between systems according to the relationship of short to tall letters as being, for vertical writing (1:2), old round hand (1:2H), Spencerian (1:3), old Spencerian (1:4), and others (1:5). In this fashion, Osborn was using the term respecting the heights of letters relative to one another. In a second and less precise fashion, he speaks of the proportion of parts of a given word. Osborn was dealing with writings executed when penmanship was in vogue and there was greater adherence to copybook standards. When writers varied notably from these proportions, significant individual characteristics developed.

Few of Osborn's contemporaries discuss proportions. Lee and Abbey (1922) mentioned proportions briefly, and like Osborn, for the purpose of making distinctions between the systems of Spencerian and modern vertical writing. They did, however, report on the process of graphometry, developed by Dr. Locard of France in which measurements of letter heights are taken to calculate proportions of letters to each other. Others would refer to this in the term *relative heights*. The results are alleged to provide convincing proof of nonidentity or strong corroborative evidence of identity.

Ellen (1989) speaks of proportions in block lettering in terms of height versus width of particular letters, much as Harrison (1958b) used the term *relative sizes*. He then mentions *proportions of letters within a word* as others would describe *relative heights*. Hilton (1982) speaks of the proportional size of various letters and parts of compound letters, such as "k" and "g," that he says are matters of variation among writers.

Harrison (1958b) uses the term *ratio* almost interchangeably with *proportions* to refer to the relative heights of short letters, such as the "a" and "o" versus the tall letters, such as the "h," "b," and "l." He asserts that, to a great extent, the ratios of letters are maintained despite changes in size, speed, or intent of the writing (normal or disguised). Nevertheless, he holds that a similarity in ratios cannot, alone, be considered a reliable indicator of common authorship, but that a difference in ratios is a safe indicator of different authors.

Relative sizes of letters is a separate topic for Harrison (1958b), wherein he discusses the height versus the width of a letter. Osborn (1929), in his list of points of consideration in the examination of documents, includes proportions of individual letters to each other, and proportions of parts of the same word, without elaborating on the proportions that he had in mind. Accordingly, these are matters of size, and size and relative size should be dealt with separately from proportions as they have distinctly different meanings. Obviously, there is a need for guidelines for the terminology to be used to achieve a measure of consistency and uniformity. Some definitions may help.

Definition: Proportion is the relation to each other of at least two measures along a single axis of a single entity, that is, one letter or character.

Lexical sources define it as the ratio between two quantities of the same kind (e.g., vertical dimensions) and is the relation that one quantity bears to the other, the one being a multiple or part of the other, as in the relation of a part to the whole.

The two quantities are measured along the same axis, so that one quantity is clearly a multiple or part of the other. It should be employed, then, in the sense of the measure of a part relative to another part or to the whole. It would apply to the measurement of one element or component of a letter having two or more components, ("b," "d," "f," "g," "h," "j," "k," "p," "q," "y," "z," "B," "E," "G," "K," "P," "R," "S," "Y," and "Z") relative to its full vertical dimension, or to another component of the same letter (e.g., the two bowls of the "B").

Thus, the height of the arch of the "h" relative to the height of its loop, and the size of the bowl of such letters as the "d," "b," "p," "q," or "g" relative to their ascending or descending stems or loops, are aspects of writing that should be referred to as proportions in accordance with the definition provided above, because the measurement of their components can be made along a single axis.

The relation that the vertical dimensions of the arches of the "m" or "n" have to one another, or that the elevations that the sides of the "u," "w," and "y" might have to each other, cannot be included within our category and definition of proportions. The term should be reserved for measurements that can be made along a single axis in the vertical direction. Obviously, the measurements one would make, insofar as these letters are concerned, would have to be made along two or three parallel axes to ensure accuracy.

It might be argued that the measurement of the arches and sides of these letters along parallel axes should qualify them for inclusion within our definition. Copybook designs, however, almost invariably prescribe that arches and sides of troughed letters should be of equal height. When relationships are considered as a part to the whole, to which our definition pertains, there is a problem in deciding which component of these letters is the part and which is the whole. The more appropriate and less confusing term for such measurements is relative heights.

Finally, proportion should not be applied to the relationship of a letter's vertical dimension to its horizontal dimension (two measures). This may be confusing, since many use this relationship as the basis for judging size.

If an extended amount of writing or a line of writing is to be considered as the single entity, then, as Osborn (1929) did in his time, there is only the measure of the average height of the small

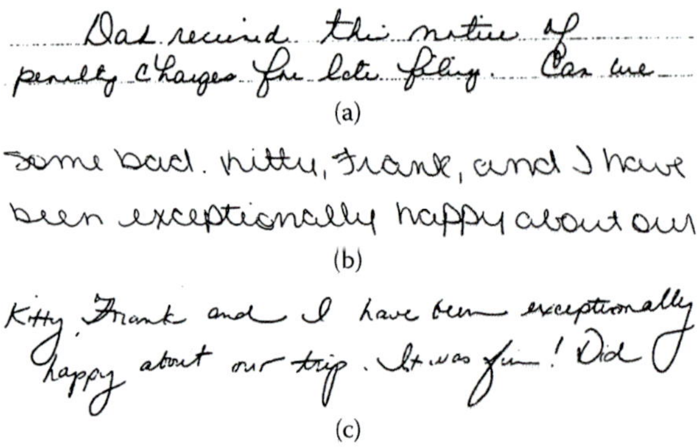

Figure 6.9 Three writings (a-c) showing different proportional height relationships.

letters to the measure of the average height of tall letters that one might consider as a usable factor within the definition of proportion (Figure 6.9). A single, vertical measurement might then establish the proportions of the writing. However, because each of these averages is established on the strength of two or more independent measures of letter heights, it can be argued that relative heights is the more appropriate term to be applied. In either case, however, these measurements are less precise in many writings and the evaluation of similarity or difference must be more judiciously made.

6.2.1.5.2 Relative Heights

Some examiners use the term *relative heights* in reference to those letters in some writings that tend to be oversized for unknown reasons. It has been observed, however, that such letters usually display an increase in their horizontal dimension as well as their height or vertical dimension, the two segments of size. They are, therefore, candidates for consideration under the category of relative sizes. For this discussion, a definition may help.

> **Definition:** Relative heights is the relationship of the measures, along separate axes, of the vertical dimensions (only) of two or more discrete entities or components to each other.

Examples are the height of a "t" relative to the height of an "h" in *the, that,* or *this,* or of the "M" relative to the "rs" in "Mrs." It might be used to refer to the vertical dimensions of the arches of an "m," an "M," or an "n," or "N" relative to each other, or two of any other components of a letter having independent vertical dimensions (the sides of the "u," "w," or "y").

6.2.1.5.3 Absolute Size

The absolute size of writing is an aspect that, like many other writing habits, is of greater value when it exceeds the normal range of writings by being overly large or unusually small. Due to handwriting instruction, and because the spacing of lines provided for writing on printed forms tends to be based on copybook dimensions, many writers tend to develop a size of writing that is similar. Accordingly, that which is unusual will be of much greater significance.

The subject of absolute size of writing is, however, more complex than it appears. Before writing can be judged on size, there needs to be an agreement as to which elements of the writing will be measured or considered. There are several measurements to consider in this regard. For example, measurement of linear letters, supralinear letters, and/or the tops of the tallest supralinear letters to the bottoms of the longest infralinear letters that is from the tops of the "h" or "l" to the bottoms of the "y" or "g." Writings do vary in their proportions of linear letters to the heights of ascenders and the lengths of descenders.

Definition: Absolute size is an approximation of the average heights of the linear letters of a writing, based on the measurements or judgment of their vertical dimensions, presuming that there is sufficient consistency to permit a reasonable approximation to be determined.

This is not to deny that ascenders and descenders have a bearing on size but simply to point out that their vertical dimensions are of greater service in the study of relative heights (and lengths) and proportions. These judgments or measurements, however, are measurements in a single direction, vertically, and there is a question as to what bearing the width of a letter or of the spacing between letters has on the judgment of size?

Osborn (1929) evidently relied on linear letters only, for the application of measuring grids to determine size in writing. His illustrations of the use of the grids, however, were somewhat idealistic in that they made the task appear simple in measuring consistent writings in which all linear letters were of the same height. Both arches of the "m" were of the same height and the central elements of supralinear letters such as the "h," "d," or "b," or of the infralinear letters such as the "g," "j," "q," or "y" were consistent with the size of the linear letters.

In modern handwriting, however, writing is not that consistent and the varying sizes of linear letters and the central components of other letters raises the question of how any scale might be applied to determine reliable and usable estimates of size. Obviously, an arbitrary procedure must be introduced that will vary with the textual material under examination. A particular allograph or allographs must be selected that appear in the text frequently and consistently enough to serve as the base for judgments. Obviously, too, in comparisons with a questioned writing, the same allograph must be selected for analysis.

The absolute size of a writing that is above average is usually reflected in both its vertical and horizontal dimensions. Thus, a larger writing will be taller and wider. On the other hand, a smaller writing that is below average in size is invariably shorter, but may or may not display a similar or corresponding reduction in line length for the same text. This seems due to the fact that smaller writing frequently displays relatively greater lateral expansion (see below).

It should be noted that absolute size is a feature of writing that can be somewhat divergent under varying conditions (Osborn 1929). Harrison (1958b) argued that because handwriting size is controllable by the writer, "it cannot be regarded as an identifying feature of any great value" (p. 312). He does allow that normal and unrestricted writing is of a preferred size for the majority of persons. This seems to be his way of saying that size can be a usable feature when the normality of the writing is not in question. He goes on to say that an increase or decrease in size can be indicative of disguise that seems to contradict his earlier statements, making it a feature of value but for another reason.

Harrison (1958b) claims that fatigue can be responsible for a reduction in size, the omission of letters or of words, or even of groups of words. He maintains that fatigue can be responsible for the tendency of certain letter groups, such as "ing," to become thready or slurred.

Harrison (1958b) also argues that a reduction in size is the usual consequence of an increase in speed in writing. Speed, he says, is determined by the horizontal motion of the writing instrument and that vertical motion is counterproductive and, therefore, diminished as a result.

Greater space or the absence of ruled lines often induces a larger execution. There are occasions when writing must be compressed in order to be accommodated in limited spaces, but as Morton (1980) points out, this reduction is accomplished without fundamental alteration of the writing habits. Hence, there should be caution against crediting divergences in writings to contractions due to space limitations (Burkey 2012).

6.2.1.5.4 Relative Size

Regarding relative sizes of letters, Harrison (1958b) noted that copybook requires that many short letters, such as the somewhat circular structures of the "a," "c," "d," "g," "o," "q," and perhaps the "p" be of equal width, but this is rarely followed. Many writers will exceed or fail to match the normal dimensions of linear letters. He goes on to say that the absolute size of a writing varies with circumstances, but that this does not affect relative sizes. However, constancy in relative sizes of the letters is lost when the writer is experiencing either mental or physical stress.

Of considerable assistance in cursive handwriting studies is the relative sizes of letters or of elements of letters. Herein, one finds greater variation from one writer to another as well as within the writing of the same individual. Some writers will vary the size of a letter with the position it occupies in a word or with the particular letters with which it is combined. In other cases, certain letters will be persistently large or small regardless of location.

It is to be noted that block lettering is not immune to variation in the relative sizes of letters. In practiced hands that prefer or need to use lettering, significant size relationships can be observed in the executions of many persons.

There are many cursive writers that vary the size of a letter. Sometimes the variation is related to its position within a word, or with respect to another particular letter. Some tend to enlarge letters that are the first in a word, for no special reason. Not infrequently, the lower case letter "r" will be found enlarged, especially when it is the first letter in the word. The study of the relative sizes of letters within a writing must take these practices, if they exist, into account to ensure that comparisons with questioned writings are valid comparisons.

Furthermore, to avoid some confusion, the examination must isolate the study of relative sizes of letters from studies of relative heights of letters that was defined and discussed above.

> **Definition:** Relative size is the judgment of one letter against itself in other locations, or against the apparent standard size for other letters within the writing, whereas relative height is the judgment of the vertical dimension of a particular letter against the vertical dimensions of other particular letters.

Relative size implies a two-dimensional consideration of the letter, that is, its height and width, both of which tend to increase or decrease correspondingly when the given letter varies from others in being enlarged or diminished.

So far, there has been a discussion about *relative sizes* and *relative heights* of letters in writing almost exclusively with respect to lowercase letters, and their components relative to one another. In so doing, there has been a focus on the relationships of linear letters to infralinear and supralinear letters, that is, those with ascenders and descenders. It is noted, however, that many other relationships occur in writing that have a bearing on writing identification.

There are height relationships of specific letters with respect to other specific letters, according to their positions in a word or regardless of their location. There are height and size relationships of uppercase letters to lowercase letters, of letters to numerals, and of numerals to other numerals, all of which can be peculiar to the individual writer and, therefore, of assistance in his or her identification. For the most part, all of these judgments will be made on the vertical dimension of the characters, with the exception perhaps of the numeral zero ("0") that is often found to be diminished in both height and width relative to other numerals.

6.2.1.5.5 Lateral Expansion

There is another linear dimension that is variable between the writings of different individuals that is referred to as lateral expansion. It is the product of letter formations, letter sizes, and the spacing between letters and words. Because interletter and interword spacing is the greatest contributor to variation in lateral expansion between writers, it seems more appropriate to discuss it further as a topic under the category of spacing.

6.2.1.6 Slant or Slope

1. Of the writing in general
2. Of letters or parts of letters in particular

Hilton (1982) defines slant in writing as "the angle or inclination of the axes of letters relative to the baseline" (p. 21). It is a matter that varies with different writers from a pronounced backhand to a sharply inclined forehand slope, with most angles between well-represented in the population. Indisputably, and in accordance with this definition, a slant of about 60° forehand, prescribed by most writing systems, is by far the most common.

However, when the angle of inclination is related to the baseline, problems in semantics arise. A change in slant to something more pronounced is spoken of as an increase in slant, when, in fact, it is actually a decrease relative to the baseline. It is an increase only in its relationship to the vertical, which is the perpendicular to the baseline. Osborn (1929) speaks of backhand slopes of ≤15° that can only be thought of as relative to the vertical, which is indeed the slope of one of the systems of writing of his time. Harrison (1958b) speaks of enhanced slopes that one might interpret to mean greater slopes to the right. If slope is related to the baseline, however, these greater slopes are actually lesser.

As a solution to the confusion, it is proposed that slant or slope be related to the perpendicular or to the vertical. Lexical definitions of these terms suggest that vertical refers to a line upwards to some zenith point whereas perpendicular refers to a line that meets with another line at a right angle, such as the baseline of the writing. Accordingly, slope is defined as follows:

> **Definition:** Slope is the angle or inclination of the axes of letters relative to the perpendicular to the baseline of the writing.

This definition allows for the fact that some writings have ascending or descending baselines that can have an effect upon the slopes of letters. It can be readily understood, then, that as writing slopes lean further to the right or to the left, the angle increases and so the slope increases.

Using the slope of the stem of the capital "T" as the determinant, Wing and Nimmo-Smith (1987) observed, in a study of 61 subjects, that there was a statistically significant difference between the sexes, in that females wrote more upright (0.09 radians or ≈5.1525 degrees) than males (0.24 radians or ≈13.74 degrees). If the former is the more upright, then the angle of inclination must be considered relative to the perpendicular.

This study is somewhat in contrast to comments made in manuals of writing-system publishers that now place less emphasis upon slant. Stone (1962) states: "The slant (whether forward, vertical, or backhand) should be one which the pupil has success in keeping uniform" (p. 2). Purtell (1980) noted that newer commercial systems considered slant in writing as not of major importance.

Osborn (1929) treated the matter of slope extensively as a means of distinguishing between the principal writing systems of his time and as a usable feature for distinguishing in many cases between writers. There was, of course, on average, greater quality and consistency in writing at that time than can be found among today's writers, and the indicators of writing systems are now seldom reliable. In place of consistency in any respect, writing has become irregular for many persons and the value of measurement in the study of slopes in these cases is questionable.

On the other hand, a regular and consistent slope contributes substantially to the appearance and beauty of a writing. In mature writings, it remains fixed once it has been developed. Writers tend to display a variation in the slope of their executions over a range of 50° extending from ±40° forehand, to a backhand slope of ±10° left of the perpendicular.

At the same time, slope can affect legibility. Backhand slopes are more often foreign to normal experience and greater effort may be needed in reading the writing. On the other hand, the eye and the mind can more readily adapt to an enhancement of slope in the forward direction.

Harrison (1958b) claims that experiments have shown that small changes in slope are virtually impossible to achieve and maintain without impairing fluency, over a quantity of extended and reasonably skillful writing. Consequently, slope has been considered an important feature of writing identification.

Osborn (1929) maintained that a consistent difference of 15° or less in the slopes of two writings was indicative of different authorship. Harrison (1958b) qualified this rule by arguing that speed of execution must be considered. In his view, fast and undisguised writing will exhibit a small increase in forehand slope, from the vertical.

One should not confuse any discussion of slope by using the term *slope* to refer to ascending and descending alignments of words or lines of writing, as some authors (e.g., Harrison 1958b) have done. For the purpose of writing identification, the definition of alignment as being the relation of successive letters of a word, signature, or line of writing to an actual or imaginary baseline, is more accurate and appropriate, and less likely to be misunderstood.

While slope has lost its former significance as a system or individual characteristic, it continues to be a useful tool in the study of disguise. As indicated elsewhere, changes in slope are a favored process for affecting a disguise. Not surprisingly, it has been reported that a change from forehand to backhand is seven times more popular as a means of disguise than a change from backhand to forehand or from forehand to an enhanced forward slope from the vertical. This is understandable in that an increase in the forehand slope seems to have less effect upon the appearance of a writing than a change in the opposite direction, and an alteration in appearance is the change intended.

Although a change in slope affects the pictorial appearance of a writing it is accomplished at the expense of fluency and rhythm. Few writers are able to maintain, deliberately and extensively, a small change in slope. Furthermore, to defeat recognition, in many cases, a writer may think that a profound change in slope is all that is considered necessary to accomplish disguise.

While change in slope is difficult to maintain deliberately in the course of disguise and considerable variability may result, it must be noted that variable slope is not always evidence of disguise. Writings of poor quality usually exhibit variation in slopes. Other factors such as variation in size, spacing, and letter forms, that may accompany variability in slope, can be strongly indicative of a lack of skill or of incompetence rather than of disguise.

From the viewpoint of writing individuality, where this discussion began, slant or slope of writing can be a significant consideration (Figure 6.10). As with size and spacing, we find that slant must be approached in both its absolute and relative respects, absolute being

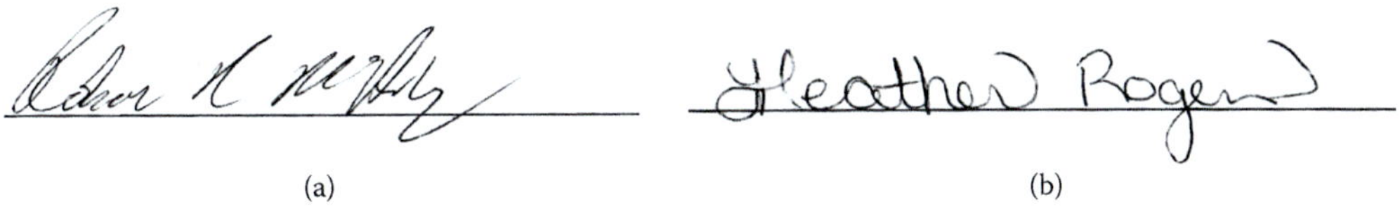

Figure 6.10 Examples of signatures with right slant (a) and left slant (b).

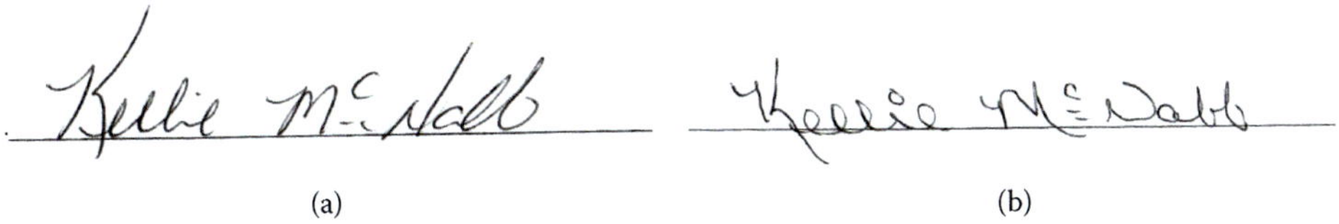

Figure 6.11 Comparison of natural and disguised signatures. (a) A genuine, natural signature with right slant. (b) A signature with left slant used as a feature to disguise the signature.

an estimation of the general slant of tall letters usually, and relative being the relationship between the slants of any two letters or parts of letters. However, not all people are consistent in writing slant. Some develop idiosyncrasies of slant insofar as particular pairs or groups of letters. As a result the relative respect of slant will be the more significant characteristic of the writing to be studied.

One of the problems in the study of writing slant or slope is the basis on which slant is to be judged, particularly bowl type letters ("a," "c," "g," "o," "q"), complex letter forms, ("r," "z"), and some numerals. Obviously, as others have suggested, one must reasonably, but arbitrarily judge the axes of bowls, loops, arches, and troughs in the vertical direction.

As in many aspects of handwriting, there are extreme diversions from the norm in slant that tend to be the more obvious cases. Of some import to the examiner is the fact that because slant is a more obvious feature of writing it can be the subject of more voluntary control. It may change in minor respects as a result of writing circumstances. As is noted elsewhere, a pronounced alteration in slant, for example, forehand to backhand, is a device commonly used for the purpose of disguise (Figure 6.11). Such a change is invariably blatant. On the other hand, unless writing circumstances may have a bearing on it, as Osborn (1929) maintained, a lesser but consistent difference in slant between two sets of writings is likely to be indicative of a difference in authors. Harrison (1958b) cautions, however, that an increase in the speed of execution of a writing correlates with an increase in its forward slope and the disparity in slopes must be carefully assessed.

6.2.1.7 Spacing

1. Interword and lateral expansion (between)
2. Intraword and lateral expansion (within)

There are several aspects of spacing within writing that become habitual with the individual and of value in the identification process. These include the wide, narrow, mixed, or uniform spacing between letters, words, and between lines on unruled sheets sometimes referred to as interlinear spacing. Habits of some significance also develop in the spacing between capital letters and lowercase or small letters in the same words (Figures 6.12 and 6.13).

Two other aspects of extended writing that might be included within this category are the dimensions and uniformity of margins, and the parallelism of lines on unruled paper. The present focus is on these aspects as elements of the arrangement of writing on the page.

Copybooks prescribe uniformity in spacing between letters in the execution of writing that is currently found only in better quality writing. At other levels of writing skill, habits of spacing evolve with pairs or groups of letters. Spacing and letter forms then combine to become units of habit and must be considered in that fashion rather than as separate forms or characters. Examples of this are frequently found in word endings such as "er," "ly," or "ing." Other letter combinations worthy of note are the "th" and the "wh." The result is an unevenness in the writing that

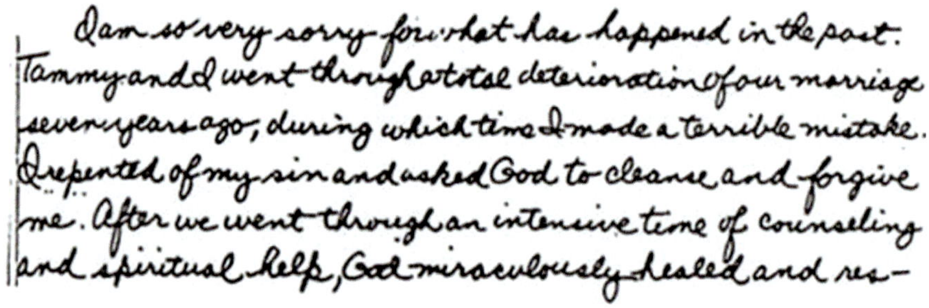

(a)

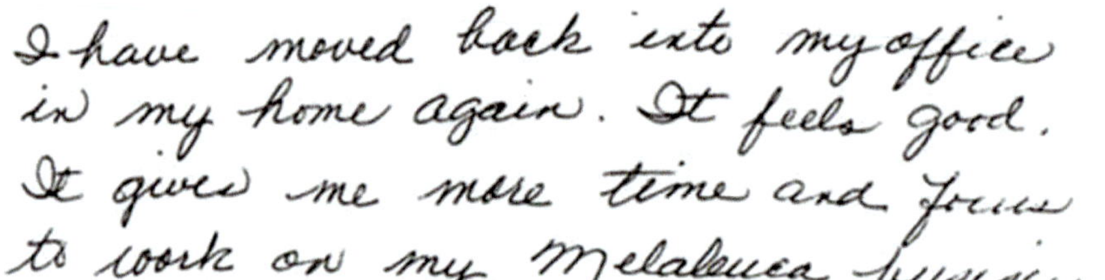

(b)

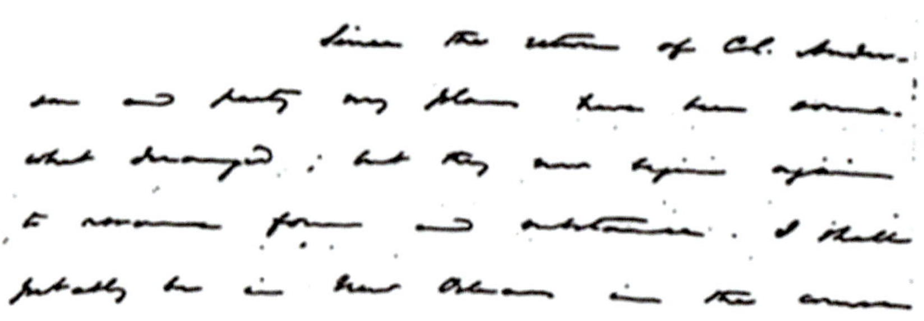

(c)

Figure 6.12 Illustration of interword and lateral expansion depicting (a) narrow, (b) uniform (balanced), and (c) wide interword expansions.

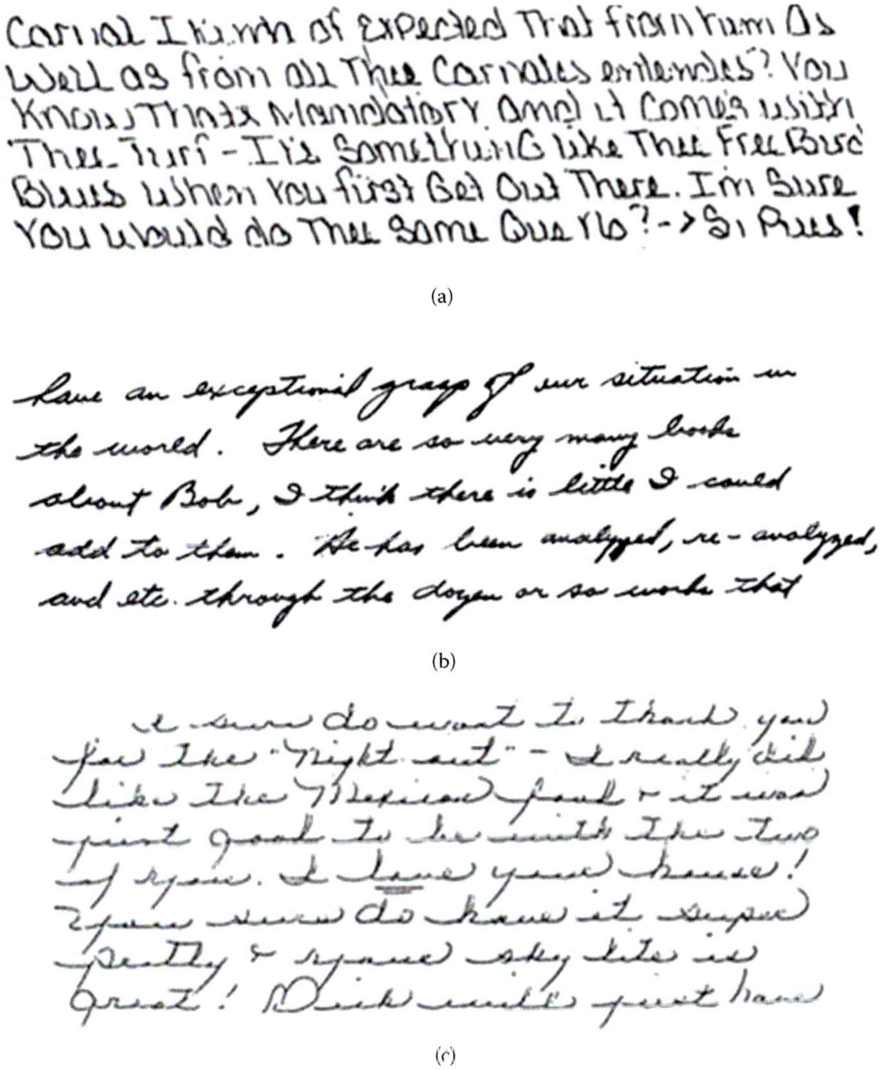

Figure 6.13 Illustration of intraword and lateral expansion depicting (a) narrow, (b) uniform (balanced), and (c) wide letter (intraword) expansions.

can be found to vary widely from writer to writer. The extremes in this variation are significant personal habits.

As mentioned above in the discussion of writing size, there are occasions when writing must be compressed in order to be accommodated in limited spaces. Such restrictions and accommodations tend to have greater effects upon interletter spacing than they have on letter forms or letter sizes, at least initially in the process of compression. The reason for this is simply that in order for the writing to be read, letter forms and sizes must be preserved to the extent possible. Of even greater import is the fact that, as Morton (1980) points out, this reduction is accomplished without fundamental alteration of the writing habits. She cautions, therefore, against attributing divergences in two writings to contractions due to space limitations.

Spacing is a matter that is not appreciably different in the writings of many people. There are writers, however, that deviate from the norm noticeably, and the value of this aspect of writing in writing studies increases accordingly.

One of the difficulties in the study of spacing lies in the method employed for judging its dimensions. A variation in the size of the writing will exhibit a corresponding variation in interletter spacing, making linear measures unreliable in writing comparisons. Harrison (1958b) suggests that linear dimensions of writing should be judged in terms of letter widths, a measurement that will reflect the proportionate contribution of spaces when the overall size of the writing is diminished. The exception to this will be writings that are insertions in restricted spaces that tend to sacrifice interletter space in the interests of legibility.

6.3 ELEMENTS OF EXECUTION

6.3.1 Abbreviations

1. Word contractions that eliminate letters
2. Letter combinations that sacrifice form in favor of speed

Within all of the books that have been written on writing identification, few authors have mentioned the topic of abbreviations. Osborn (1929) and Harrison (1958b) speak briefly of the abbreviations of the titles "Mister," "Mistress," and "Doctor" but there are numerous other titles and words that are contracted and subject to individual methods for so doing. Police and military ranks are almost invariably abbreviated. Political offices are frequently abbreviated and business positions are reduced to Mgr., for manager; Dir., for director, etc. There are a multitude of others many of which have been products of the current popularity of acronyms.

Of import to the examiner of handwriting is that the contemporary styling of abbreviations is, to a large extent, inconsistent and arbitrary. Among the masses of contractions, reductions, and abbreviations now employed, no set of rules can hope to cover all the possible variations encountered in the written and printed word. Variation in capitalization, spacing, and punctuation can be dependent on writer preference, selected style manual, or organizational policy.

How abbreviations are styled, then, can become a significant individualizing feature of writing (Figure 6.14). Among the many that examiners are likely to encounter will be abbreviations of the following:

Agency, association, and organization names
Company names (including Co. for company and Inc. for incorporated)
Compass points
Computer terms (e.g., CPU, RAM, ROM, OEM, DOS)
Contractions employing apostrophes (sec'y, ass'n, dep't)
Country names (USA, CAN, UK)
Days of the week (Sun., Mon., Tues. or Tue., Wed., Thurs. or Thu., Fri., Sat.)
Degrees (academic)
Geographical and topographical names (St., Mt., Pt., Ft., and postal addresses)
Latin words and phrases (etc., i.e., e.g., viz., et al., pro tem.)
Military and police ranks (Cpl., Sgt., S/Sgt., CSM.)

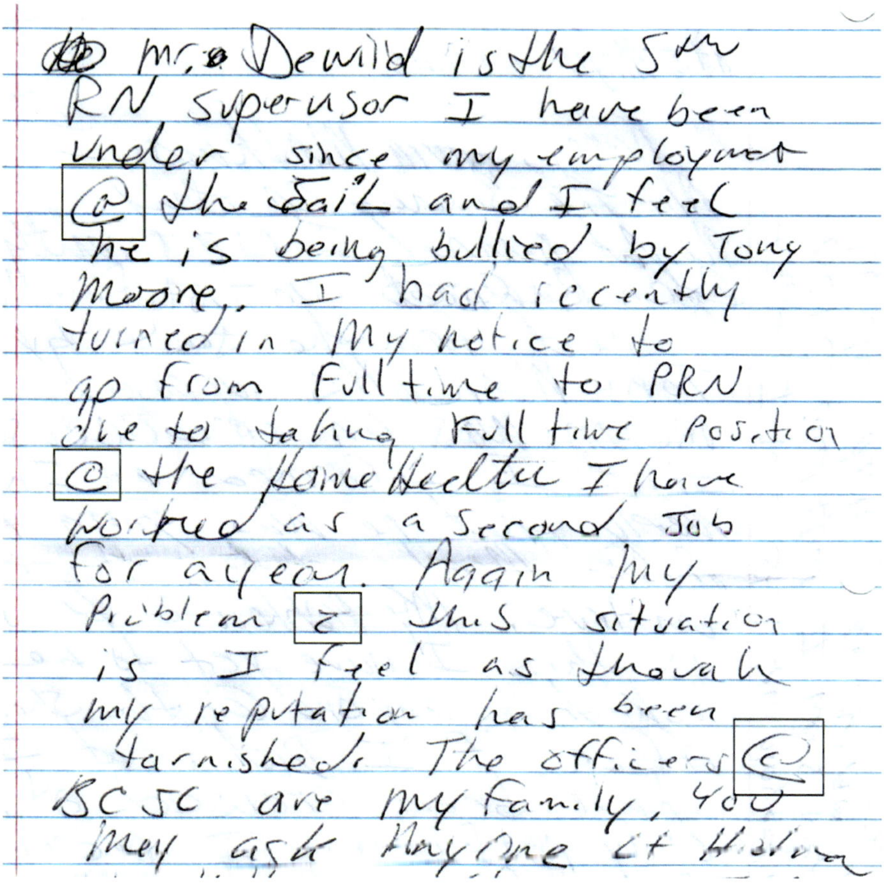

Figure 6.14 Illustration of handwritten note showing the use of the "at" symbol and the medical shorthand symbol bar c (meaning "with").

Months of the year (Jan., Feb., Mar., Apr., Jun., Jul., Aug., Sept., Oct., Nov., Dec.)
Personal names (Geo., Marg., Marj.)
Special characters (ampersand "&," dollar sign "$," octothorpe "#," pound "£")
Structural locations (Apt., Bldg. Ct.)
Thoroughfare designations (Ave., Blvd., Cres., Pkwy., Rd., St.)
Titles (including Hon., Rev., Sen., Mr., Mrs., Ms.)
Units of measure (cu. ft., sq. yd., km., kilo., sec., min., hr.)
Words and word groups (c/o, w/o, w/w, c.c., c.o.d.)

In what are said to be carry-overs from the secretary system of 400 years ago, there are some variations in the alignment or manner in which abbreviations are written that become habitual with current writers. It was the practice in that system to omit letters and elevate the last letter or letters of the word to indicate that a reduction had been made. The elevation of the "r" in M^{r}. or the "rs" in M^{rs}. are examples. Teachers in scientific fields are known to write "sol^{n}" for solution.

The special characters included in the list of abbreviations mentioned above are worth noting. They are not contractions of words as other abbreviations are. They are symbols that are used to represent words and, thereby, to economize on space or writing. In that sense, they have the same purpose in their use and for that reason we include them here. Some writers use them frequently, particularly the ampersand (Mr. & Mrs.) in addressing envelopes.

There is little or no instruction given in writing books governing the form, size, or structure of these special characters. Without guidance or restriction, individuals are left to develop these characters for themselves, and consequently they vary substantially from writer to writer. The result is that they become highly individual elements of writing.

Signatures are often illegible but are not normally abbreviated in the usual sense. What serves as an abbreviation of a signature is the inscription of sets of one or more of the initial letters of the name. When referred to collectively as a person's initials, they are ascribed some of the attributes of personal identity that the signature enjoys. These may, however, display little of the normal characteristics of the signature they are intended to represent. Because of their widespread use in authenticating, validating, and authorizing documents, a writer's initials can take on a character of their own that can be, in some cases, just as reliable and usable a means of identification as the signature itself. For many writers, initials tend to diverge more drastically from copybook prescription than extended writing. On the other hand, some initials are over simplified to little more than a single letter. The difficulty that initials present for writing examiners lies in the quantity and quality of evidence of similarity or dissimilarity, of genuineness or of spuriousness, that such limited writing may contain. Notwithstanding the fact that, for many writers, initials can be distinctive and unique, caution must be exercised in the comparison and evaluation processes, for the less writing involved, or the more inconsistent its execution, the easier the task of spuriously reproducing it.

There are numerous fashions in which letter forms and structures are abbreviated by the omission of elements, usually in the interests of fluency or speed. Initial upstrokes are frequently sacrificed (particularly in the "i," "t," and "h"), loops are reduced to single downstrokes (particularly in the "f," "h," "g," and "y"), retracings of staffs (as in "t," "B," "P," "R") are not performed. There are also writers that are aware of these omissions they are making and will occasionally return later to repair the deficiency by adding strokes. In these kinds of abbreviations, it will be noted that almost invariably it is the upstrokes that are sacrificed while the downstrokes, that are the more dominant strokes with right-handed writers, are retained.

6.3.2 Alignment

This concerns the relation of successive letters of a word, signature, or line of writing to an actual or imaginary baseline.

With or without the benefit of ruled lines, many writers exhibit an ascending (i.e., rising) baseline in their writing. Some maintain a horizontal baseline, while the baseline of others tends to descend (Figure 6.15). But whatever the tendency is it will likely be fixed. Some authors employ the term *line of writing* to describe a writing's conformity to this real or imaginary line. Alignment habits may be general and occur insofar as a signature, a word, or a group of words. They may also be specific to a letter and/or relative to a neighboring preceding or succeeding letter.

A study on alignment was reported by McClary (1997) respecting the writing of signatures and extended text by 200 subjects on both ruled and unruled paper. He found that the "baseline alignment is a repetitious writing habit and reliable factor in handwriting comparisons for the

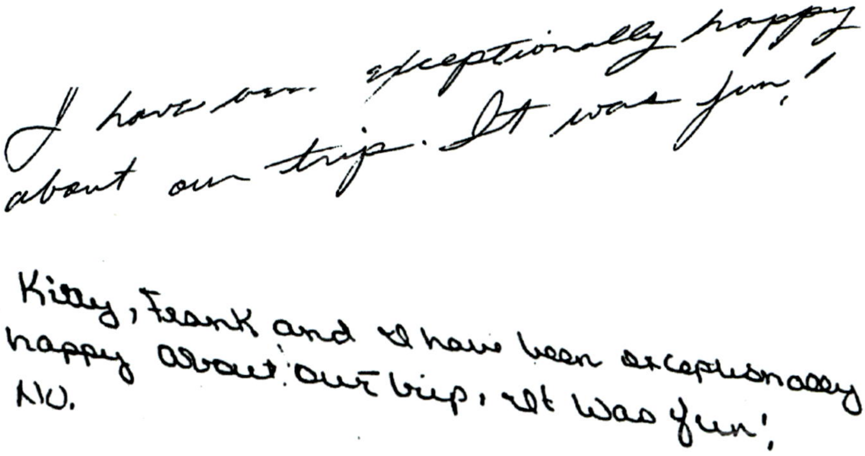

Figure 6.15 Forms of baseline habits on unlined paper.

purposes of identification or elimination. This is true more so with respect to signatures that are the more habitual of one's handwriting skills" (p. 35).

In addition to alignments, fixed habits will also be found, insofar as the location of signatures and other material written within a limited space (Figure 6.16). It is as though the width of the left margin, or the space to be left preceding the entry, was as fixed a practice as other habits might be.

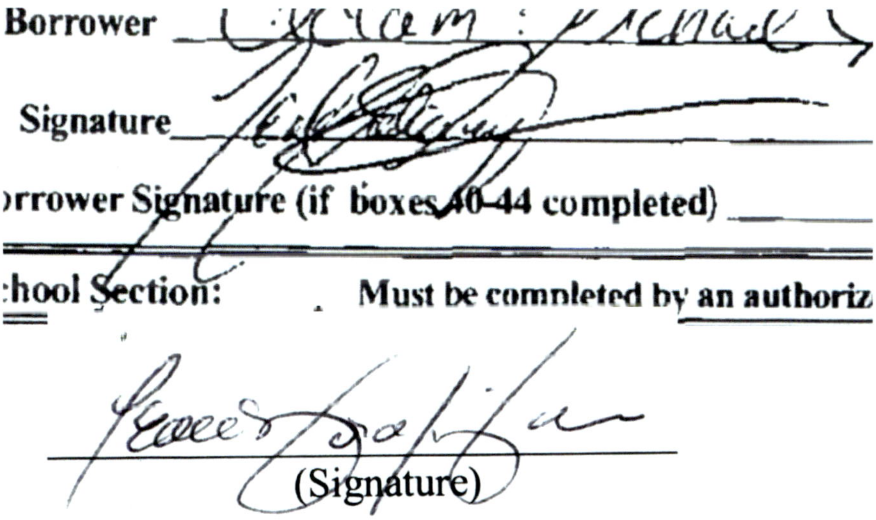

Figure 6.16 Signature differences in the interaction to the signature line with respect to the baseline of the writing. Top signature is written on the signature line. Bottom signature is written above the signature line.

6.3.3 Commencements and Terminations

1. Their length, direction, and path
2. Their taper (the abruptness with which the instrument approaches and leaves the paper)

Lowercase letters, particularly those following a capital letter, are frequently commenced with an initial stroke that is long and often intersects with the terminal stroke of the capital letter that precedes it. This is a common occurrence in the writing of the "r" in the abbreviations "Mr." and "Mrs." It is perhaps even more common in the writing of signatures. A long initial stroke, usually a secondary stroke, can occur, of course, with any lowercase letter in any initial position in extended text.

Furthermore, while copybook prescribes for termination in an upward direction for all lowercase letters, the strokes with which terminal letters in a name or a word are finished are found to vary substantially in the writing of different persons, if indeed, they are executed at all. Frequently, the terminal stroke will return to cross "t"s, apply accents, or simply to inscribe a characteristic underscore or rubric. This tendency seems to correlate with the fluency or speed of the execution of the signature.

Strokes with which lowercase letters are commenced and terminated, vary in both length, the direction of their paths, and their tendency to intersect with the strokes of other letters, according to the personal habits of the writer. Therefore, they can be significant individualizing elements of writing.

Another aspect of initial and terminal strokes that must be studied, although only indirectly as a point of identification, is the abruptness with which the strokes start or finish. In normal, natural, and reasonably fluent writing, these strokes exhibit a degree of taper, owing to the fact that they are created by a writing instrument that is in motion as it approaches or departs from the surface of the paper. Handwriting examiners have long referred to these tapered strokes as flying starts or flying finishes and have relied upon them as evidence of fluency and, therefore, evidence of genuineness. In spurious simulations of another's writing or signature, these strokes are found to commence and terminate abruptly, having noticeably blunt endings, as the application of the instrument to the paper is a more deliberate and conscious act.

In summary then, initial and terminal strokes to letters, words, or names must be considered insofar as their length, their direction, and/or their path, and their degree of taper, all of which will be present—if indeed, such strokes are present (Figure 6.17).

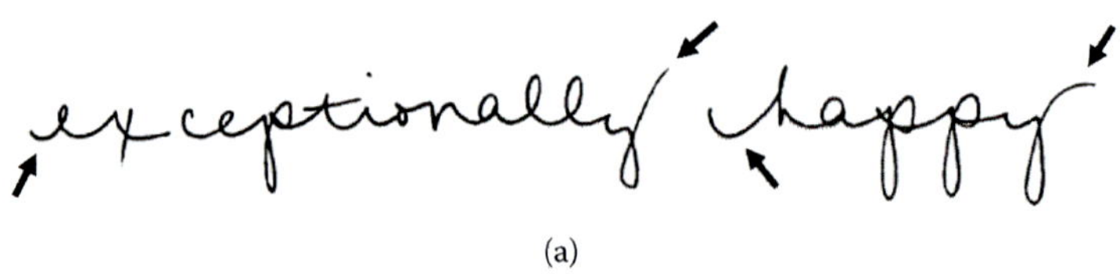

(a)

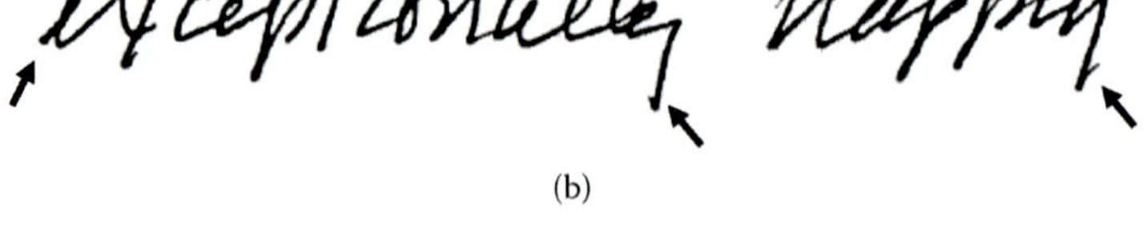

(b)

Figure 6.17 Two examples of different styles of stroke (a) commencements and terminations (b).

6.3.4 Diacritics and Punctuation

Punctuation marks are used in the English writing system to clarify the meaning of sentences by attempting to control the reading of a passage to correspond to certain elements of the spoken language. They also serve to clarify meaning by organizing certain grammatical elements in the structure of the sentence, regardless of how those elements might be spoken. Punctuation is intended to indicate pause, pitch, volume, and stress.

Two terms that are frequently used regarding the comma to describe patterns of punctuation are *open* and *close*. An open pattern is one in which the comma and other marks are used sparingly. A close pattern makes liberal use of punctuation marks, often putting one wherever grammatical structure will allow. In the examination of extended writing, an awareness of these two patterns of practice can be helpful.

Diacritics, or diacritical marks, are marks that are used with a letter or group of letters to indicate a sound value that is different from that of the letter(s) without it. Although the English language doesn't use diacritics, the French language and many others do. In the sparsely written material on the subject, some authors have referred to the "i" dot as a diacritic, but since the "i" has no alternative sound without the dot it fails to qualify for the term. It is an integral component of the letter much like the crossbar to the "t." It was introduced to distinguish the "i" from the numeral "1." In earlier writing (circa 1500), the "1" and the "y" had their vertical stems dotted, but the practice was switched in the seventeenth or eighteenth century.

Like some others, punctuation is an aspect of writing on which few of the recent authors have seen fit to comment. For Osborn (1929), it was one of 16 features considered under the general heading of arrangement, and in that respect, location of the punctuation relative to baselines was important. He cites a case in which the apostrophe was consistently but improperly used in many words where it didn't belong. This evidence supported the identification of the writer. He cites another case to illustrate the precision with which punctuation was reproduced in tracings that would not occur in natural writings.

Harrison (1958b) also comments on the location of "i" dots as being of some potential value in writing comparisons since few writers place them precisely over the staff. But there are other respects in which a study of the dot form or structure may be helpful. The "i" dot may be round, a stroke, a tick, or small "v," sitting upright or lying on the horizontal. In bubble writing, the dot is frequently executed as a small circle and located rather precisely over the staff. In the case of some writers, the dot may be omitted completely, or applied only occasionally.

Similar variations will be observed in the study of accents or diacritics in other languages. Few correspond closely to the copybook styles. It will be found, however, that since "i" dots and diacritics are somewhat carelessly and speedily applied during the writing process, and perhaps because of their size, they may vary substantially in both style and location.

Commas and periods are, of course, the punctuation marks most frequently encountered in examinations. Here too, little correspondence is found between their forms, sizes, and locations, and the copybook examples. For the most part, they are strokes that vary in length and direction, not dots, and are seldom curved. In the writing of many persons, little consistency in them will be found, but as with so many other writing elements, there are some individuals that are quite distinctive in the manners in which they punctuate and are reasonably consistent in their execution. Osborn (1929) suggested years ago, there can be consistency in the location of the comma relative to the word that it is inscribed to follow. Accordingly, this element of the study should not be overlooked.

While often a matter to be considered in signatures and extended writings, "i" dots and punctuation marks can be of particular assistance also in the study of envelope addresses. The writing of envelope addresses invariably provides ample opportunity for the writer to display his or her particular habits in this respect.

If the potential of diacritics and punctuation marks is to be realized in a writing examination and study, and request standards are likely to be available, it is important that those standards be prepared from dictation rather than from copy, in order that no assistance may be provided that might influence the use or location of dots, accents, commas, and periods.

6.3.5 Embellishments

Embellishments are flourishes, ornaments, paraphs, rubrics, and underscores.

Embellishment adds or extends strokes that are easily executed and are not essential to the recognition of the character or the word. It is the natural product of speed, fluency, or individual caprice. Although some terminal letters seem to lend themselves to embellishment, as the lower loops of the "y" and "g," the flourishes and ornamentation that a writer may develop follow no particular patterns and are as individualistic as a writing element might be.

A particular kind of embellishment of some years ago was a complex design or symbol located under or after the signature or name. It evolved into a more simplified pattern and eventually into a single flourish or understroke. This was called a paraph that was sometimes more in the nature of an initial, and that, according to the Oxford dictionary, originated about 400 years ago as a kind of security against forgery. Ellen (1989) claims that the same practice is followed even today by some writers for the same reasons. It may have been the forerunner to the current practice of initialing all pages of a document as protection against substitution or replacement. The underscore to a signature is often currently but improperly referred to as a rubric, for which Osborn (1929) may be given some of the credit as he gave both terms, *paraph* and *rubric*, the same meaning. Regardless of what term may be used to refer to them, underscores to signatures encountered today are not always limited to single lines, but may be double or even triple.

The rubric, in ancient documents, was an initial character or a heading, or underscore to such a character or heading, that was printed or inscribed in red or ocher ink to set it off as the beginning of the page or passage. More recently, it has been used to refer to marginal instructions or explanations in a manuscript that were invariably done in red ink. In the world of today, perhaps in the absence of employment as an embellishment to initial characters or headings, it is occasionally used to refer to the underscores that some writers apply to their signatures, or to some personal flourish that follows it.

In this discussion of the extraordinary strokes and patterns that are added to the writing of signatures, one cannot overlook the smaller but highly personal embellishments that are frequently executed in the first or final letters of words in extended writings that, for want of a better term, might be called ornamentations. The crossings of the "t" can also be somewhat ornate. These antics of the pen, as Osborn (1929) described them, are obviously intended to add a certain artistic quality to the writing. Of import to examiners of writing is that these ornamentations tend to be persistent habits of the writer (Figure 6.18). Writings with split nib or fountain pens that allow for some noticeable variation in stroke width, exhibit more of this kind of characteristic than writings with other instruments may. The shading of the stroke, that flexible nibs allow, is an inducement to writers to exploit the potential for this kind of ornamentation.

Figure 6.18 Embellished signature.

6.3.6 Legibility or Writing Quality

Legibility is not considered from the viewpoint of the density of the written line relative to the substrate that might be better described as visibility. Nor is legibility considered from the viewpoint of quality, as Osborn (1929) and Hilton (1982) have done, to refer to particular identifying factors or characteristics. Instead, there is a combined use of both of these terms, legibility and writing quality, as closely related measures of the excellence of a writing, each being a product of the other.

> **Definition:** Legibility and writing quality are the ease of recognition of letters, usually stemming from the adherence to copybook designs, and to a lesser extent, to copybook size, slant, and spacing.

When one thinks of legibility or writing quality as measures of the excellence of writing, it is realized that excellence must be considered from the standpoint of both the writer and the reader. From the viewpoint of the writer, excellence is the efficiency of production. Efficiency has to be judged on the basis of the quality of the stroke, the smoothness of the movement, and the economy of the action of the pen, that is often developed at the expense of letter formation (Figure 6.19).

As a measure of efficiency in writing, speed does not correlate well either directly or inversely. That which a reader may judge to be better quality takes slightly more time to produce, but in many cases this is because the pen travels a greater distance to complete the letters. At the same time, that which takes more time to produce is not necessarily of better quality, for the writing may lose some of its smoothness as the action becomes more deliberate and conscious.

Ease of recognition needs to be considered, and it is from this perspective that writing quality is more often judged. One cannot judge writing excellence, however, without addressing the question as to what makes writing good or bad.

One of the aspects of writing by which its excellence is judged is its uniformity. The lack of uniformity affects appearance even to the point of the writing's legibility. Uniformity or the lack of it is observed in alignments, letter slopes, and the consistency of shape in repeated letters or in different letters having common elements: for example, "a" and "d," "q" and "g," "y" and "j," "h" and "l, "m" and "n," "F" and "T," "P" and "R" (Figure 6.20).

In addition to uniformity, there are two other aspects of writing having a bearing on its excellence. These are the quality of the line or stroke producing the letters (see line quality) and the shapes of letter formations themselves. In the latter respect it cannot be denied that adherence to copybook design must contribute to excellence, if only because copybook styles have proven to be the least ambiguous designs for letters, which ensures their legibility. Nonetheless, there are handwritings that are quite legible that employ letter shapes that depart widely from copybook models. In these cases, it is found that the departure retains some of the basic elements of

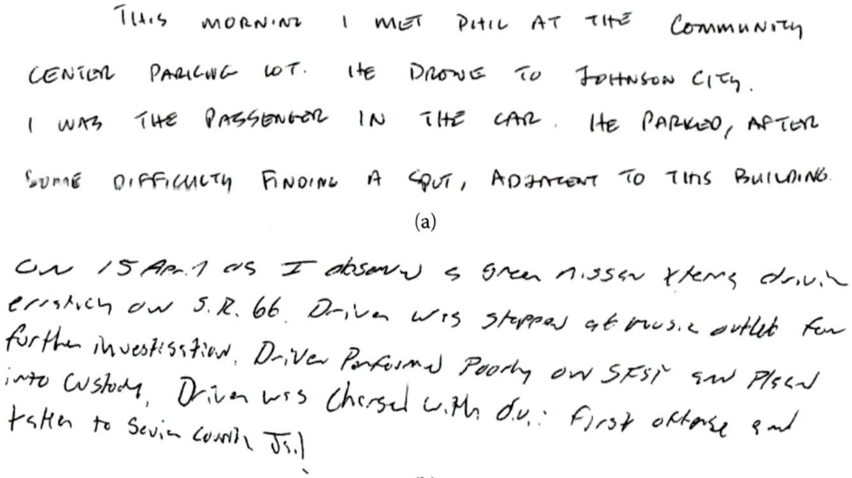

(a)

(b)

Figure 6.19 Examples of legible writing (a) written with simplified forms and illegible writing (b) also with simplified forms, but exhibiting poor writing quality.

letter design, or the modifications are sufficiently distinctive from one another that confusion and misinterpretation is avoided.

Writing movements, particularly the garlanded movement, when allowed to dominate the writing execution severely, renders many of the linear letters difficult to differentiate. The "m" and "n" resemble the "u," "v," and "w" very closely, and words such as *minimum* are extremely difficult to recognize or distinguish.

Poor legibility can also result from wide ranges in natural variation that permit some letters to be mistaken for others. Thus, as was stated earlier, uniformity or consistency in the various elements of writing, whether it be shape, size, slant, spacing, or other aspects contributes substantially to writing quality and consequently to legibility.

The importance of distinguishing between levels of excellence in writing is primary to the application of one of the fundamental principles of handwriting: a writer cannot exceed his maximum writing ability or skill without effort and/or training over a period of time. This principle is used to advantage in handwriting identification. Obviously, a writer who possesses limited skill in writing cannot be considered a potential author of a writing that was executed with indisputably greater skill, unless there are extenuating circumstances to account for the lesser skill at the time that standards were prepared.

Osborn (1929) made the point that illegibility and carelessness were frequent indications of genuineness, that grotesque and illegible signatures were thought to be better protected against forgery. That, of course, is now not true. Harrison (1958b) explains that legibility may be unrelated to the writing's artistic quality in that elegant and fluid writing may be difficult to read while irregular and arrhythmic writing may be read with ease.

Furthermore, consistency in letter designs and shapes fosters legibility. Wide ranges in variations confuse letter recognition and makes reading slow and laborious in deciphering words. Similarly extreme slopes, particularly backhand slants, introduce features that are foreign to a reader's normal experience to which the eye does not readily adapt and, thus, makes reading difficult.

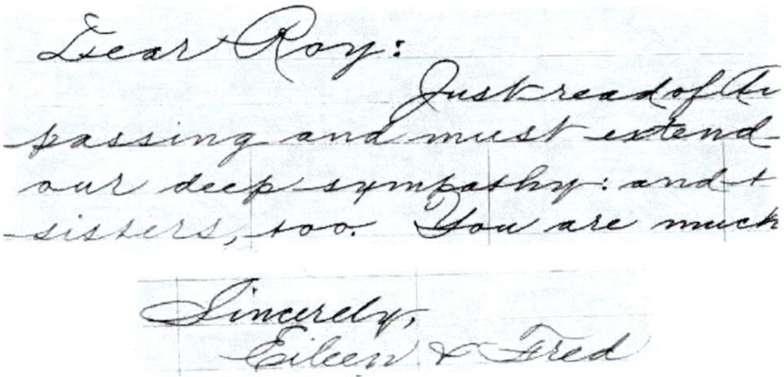
Dear Roy:
Just read of the
passing and must extend
our deep sympathy: and t
sisters, too. You are much
Sincerely,
Eileen & Fred

(a)

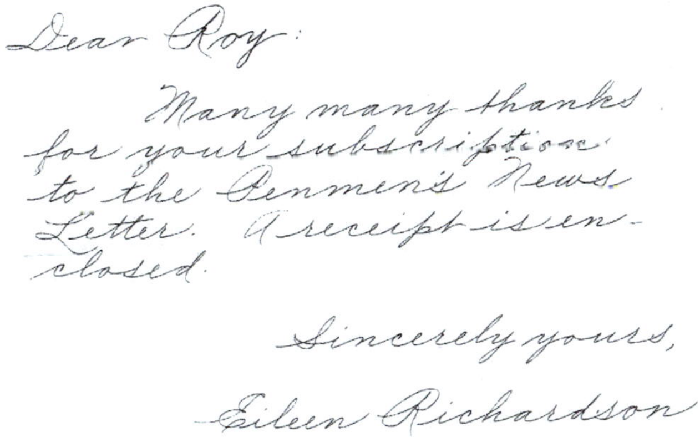
Dear Roy:
Many many thanks
for your subscription
to the Penmen's News
Letter. A receipt is en-
closed.
Sincerely yours,
Eileen Richardson

(b)

Figure 6.20 Writings of Fred (a) and his wife Eileen Richardson (b), both master penmen who followed the Mills (Rochester) system. Both were 84 years old at the time of writing. Note the striking similarity in many letter shapes, but also the subtle differences in the proportions of the "p," the angularity to the "y" and the style of "t" when a medial letter.

For these same reasons, writing that is excessively arched or garlanded, such as the rounded bubble writing of adolescents, can be quite illegible to many readers. More often, of course, the reason for illegibility is simply a lack of skill or carelessness on the part of the writer.

Regarding legibility in adolescent handwriting, Andersen (1964), in an investigation of the writings of 5,286 elementary and junior high school pupils, reported on five handwriting variables: legibility, size, slant, size uniformity, and slant uniformity. On average the quality of writing (i.e., legibility) of girls was better, and the writing was more vertical than that of boys. He also observed that legibility varied directly with uniformity in slant and with writing size. However, larger writings, while being more legible, were less uniform in size.

6.3.7 Line Continuity

This concerns the interruptions in or discontinuity of the writing line, occurring as a result of pen stops, pen lifts, or disconnections.

Nineteenth century writing systems and some foreign systems made a practice of executing some letters independently of the letters preceding them rather than in the uninterrupted continuous pen motion that modern systems prescribe. Consequently, disconnections occurred in specific places with specific letters. Today's systems, when they are followed meticulously, require that each word in lowercase be completed without the writing instrument leaving the paper. The crossing of the "t," the crossing of the "x," and the dotting of the "i" are acts that follow the completion of the word. Intraword disconnections, then, are elements of one's personal writing habits and vary profoundly from one to another.

Many foreign systems of writing are similar to lettering on this continent, in that letters are separately constructed. Oriental, Arabic, and East Indian scripts are of this kind, largely disconnected. North Americans do block lettering or pen printing with the same frequency of disconnections or pen lifts. When highly developed, disconnected writings of these kinds can display consistency and many features of individuality. When unskillfully produced, they can be spuriously reproduced more easily than connected writing.

Disconnections, or pen lifts as they are more frequently labeled, in the cursive writing of this continent, occur for several reasons. They may be due to a lack of skill in the movement control of the writing instrument. For some of this class, there is a need to interrupt the writing process to contemplate the next step. Erstwhile writers of script experience difficulties with letter connections in converting to cursive writing styles. Circular or bowl type letters, such as the "a," "c," "d," "g," "o," and "q," seem by virtue of their design to prompt a lifting of the pen before commencing the bowl. Indeed, writers of the old round hand system of the turn of the century were taught to lift the pen before beginning the body or bowl of such letters.

Disconnection occurring before and after some lowercase letters, such as the circular or bowl type letters, may be so pronounced that there is no vestige to be seen of the secondary or terminal strokes to these letters or to the letters that precede them. When the interruption in the movement of the instrument is of this magnitude, the disconnection is usually referred to by UK examiners as a hiatus.

Under the circumstances disconnections, when they occur in normal, natural, genuine writing of lowercase letters, usually occur between letters, or insofar as initial or terminal strokes are usually few in number for the whole word or name. On the other hand, capital letters are often written in separate segments and in that sense similar to the process in block lettering. Letters such as the "B," "D," "P," "R," "T," and "F," can be constructed of two or more separate strokes despite the requisite of the copybooks to produce the letter in one continuous action.

Harrison (1958b) cautioned that in his view writing habits respecting hiatuses were not fixed. He commented that it is not uncommon to find that slow writing by some individuals will be liberally garnished with gaps (i.e., pen lifts or hiatuses), yet another specimen by the same author will be almost devoid of pen lifts, far fewer hiatuses. Thus, the value of pen lifts and hiatuses will depend greatly upon the letters between which they occur. Before the "c," "d," "g," and "o," they will be common. After the "p" and "s," they may be common when these letters are written with closed bowls. Before the "e," "i," and "v," they will be uncommon, and after the "w," they will be uncommon as well.

Disconnections in genuine writing, whether they be pen lifts or hiatuses, are frequently obvious and seldom, if ever, corrected. With fluent writers, the motion of the pen may be continuous even if the line is not, thus producing tapers to the ends of the strokes. On the other hand, disconnections in spurious writing are much less obvious, and often patched, repaired, or retouched afterward (Figure 6.21). Patching and retouching requires a second, third, or more applications of the writing instrument that are usually obvious in examination by microscope.

Figure 6.21 Arrow shows example of discontinuity or pen lift.

In the examination and study of signatures, disconnections or pen lifts are classic symptoms of simulation by tracing methods. The reason claimed for this is that one who forges is the most severe critic of his or her own work and strives to perfect it.

The consequence of all of this is that dissimilarities in pen lifts can be of greater value in eliminating writers than similarities may be in writer identification, particularly in respect of circular or bowl type letters, unless the method of disconnection is very unusual. The retouching of genuine writing, if it occurs at all, is clearly apparent and made with strokes that are obviously intended to improve only the pictorial effect or to dispel potential problems for the reader in comprehension.

6.3.8 Line Quality

Osborn (1929) is credited with the introduction of the term *line quality*, but not all authors have understood it to mean the same thing. Others have described it as resulting from the level of freedom and the rate of velocity in the movement of the pen. For Harrison (1958b), it was better stated as quality of line. As indicated above, and as Hilton (1982) has used it, it has been suggested that line quality is the umbrella under which many elements of writing movement reside. To achieve much needed clarification, the terms should be divorced and separately defined.

> **Definition:** Line quality is the degree of regularity (i.e., smoothness and/or gradation) to the written stroke as may be judged from the consistency of its nature and of its path in a prescribed direction.

Osborn (1929) used the term *writing movement* as a matter of several writing elements forming a component of line quality. Line quality, or alternatively, the quality of the line is a matter that is depicted by characteristics independent of form or routes of pen action. As is delineated by this definition, the quality of the written line or line quality is the degree of regularity (i.e., smoothness or gradation) in the written stroke. It may be described as or judged from the consistency of its path in a prescribed direction. It varies from smooth to tremulous, from controlled to erratic. Its third dimensional characteristic, if it has one resulting from the application of pressure by the writing instrument, will vary from consistent, gradual, or rhythmic to irregular, sudden, or abrupt.

There is no doubt that many factors related to control (e.g., skill, state of health, age, velocity of the instrument, pen pressure, even quality of vision) are contributing factors to the quality of the line that may be produced. They are, however, contributors to line quality, and care must be exercised in the evaluation process to avoid improperly appending the evidence of line quality to the evidence of its contributing factors.

There are a number of other terms that presumably are used to reflect some level of line quality. Harrison (1958b) uses the term *fluency* as something that is absent in the execution of disguise. Furthermore, he employs the expression *fluency and rhythm* that implies that they are somewhat different qualities. Osborn (1929) did not use the term *fluency* precisely, but has defined a flowing hand to be a coordinated succession of movement impulses that glide into each other with a rhythm which is the final perfection of a fixed and cultivated habit. If fluency can be equated with a flowing hand, then Osborn's definition suggests that rhythm is an integral part of it. Osborn also speaks of skill and freedom and goes on to describe freedom in writing as that which is shown by the direction, uniformity, and clear-cut quality of the pen strokes.

One seldom speaks of fluency or freedom insofar as poor writings or simulations or disguises are concerned, for invariably they are not present. One should speak of line quality in these situations for, whether it is good or bad line quality, it will be present. Fluency, freedom, and other like terms simply refer to a generally higher grade of line quality, not always present, that is without any kind of tremor or erratic changes in direction or in pen pressure. Line quality then, being the more ever-present circumstance, is the preferred term (Figure 6.22).

6.3.9 Pen Control

This concerns the management of the writing instrument by the hand in generating a writing line. To organize information within the families to which they relate, point load (pen pressure), pen hold, and pen position are assembled as aspects of pen control.

1. Point load—the vertical component of the force applied to the nib, ball, or tip of the writing instrument, during line generation. Frequently called pen pressure, it may be (1) absolute: that is, constant through all the writing or (2) relative: that is, greater or lesser in some strokes. In either case, it will be evidenced by (1) shading and variations thereof, (2) the deposition of ink or graphite, and variations thereof, or by (3) the depression of the paper, and variations thereof.

   It is called rhythm, or fluency, or a flowing hand when it materializes as a harmonious and graduated recurrence.
2. Pen hold—the grasp of the writing instrument by the hand, mouth, foot, or prosthesis, determinable only (1) when the angle of the axis of a ballpoint pen and the plane of the writing surface is ≤45°, or (2) when shading is produced by a split nib pen.
3. Pen position—the orientation of the writing instrument relative to (1) the writing sheet or substrate, (2) the writing baseline, or (3) the writing stroke.

(a) (b)

Figure 6.22 Comparison of line quality: Writer (a) has irregular, hesitant line quality. Writer (b) has smooth, fluent line quality.

6.3.9.1 Point Load (Pen Pressure and Shading)

Pen pressure and shading, two facets of writing that at one time were considered to be separate entities but closely related, have generated a great deal of interest in published material on the subject.

Tytell (1995) has provided an excellent account of the role and the course of shading over the eras of the quill pen, the steel nib, and the fountain pen to the arrival of the ballpoint pen in the late 1940s. In the transition from one kind of instrument to the next, the diminution of shading was seen as the demise of important qualities and characteristics of skilled penmanship. Tytell comments:

> Today's common perception ... holds that the introduction of the ballpoint pen after World War II foisted upon the public a writing instrument unsuitable for proper shading. For the penman, the ballpoint was just another step in a steady descent of writing instruments. In the nineteenth century, the steel pen was compared unfavorably to the quill. In the twentieth, the fountain pen was criticized as inferior to the steel pen.

There has been some difficulty expressed in the early writings of this century in making a distinction, whether necessary or not, between shading and pen pressure. In consequence, terms like *unconscious emphasis* and *unconscious pressure emphasis* have been employed to clarify meanings, but not very well.

As Tytell reported, Osborn (1910) in his first edition of *Questioned Documents*, recognized a potential for confusion between pen pressure and shading.

> No very definite distinction can be drawn between pen pressure and shading in writing ... pen pressure refers ... to the involuntary placing of emphasis, smoothness of stroke, and quality of line in writing, as distinguished from that deliberate and voluntary emphasis that is ordinarily described as shading.

The confusion of terms was not fully resolved by Osborn (1929) in his second edition of the book when he wrote:

> Without careful definition this term *pen pressure* means nothing, and a term which perhaps would more clearly express what is here called pen pressure, as compared with shading, would be unconscious emphasis. What is termed *shading* is that more obvious increase in the weight of strokes which in many instances are in conformity with and grow out of the system of writing followed. Shading itself in a mature well-developed hand is, however, largely unconscious, so that the term *unconscious emphasis* may be somewhat misleading in that it would suggest that what is called shading is always consciously done. It is seldom that a handwriting made up of the finest and most delicate lines does not show throughout consistent variations in line widths due to variations in pressure, and this emphasis is what is here described as pen pressure, or unconscious emphasis, as distinguished from pronounced and perfectly evident shading. (p. 128)

Brewester (1932) reiterated Osborn's words in saying:

> Pen pressure may be defined as the weight or pressure, unconsciously applied to the pen during the act of writing, while shading is that conscious or voluntary pressure at first deliberately applied to certain parts, but afterwards becoming as much of an automatic act as any other unconsciously acquired writing habit. (p. 39)

As Tytell reports, Osborn was still not satisfied with his definition of pen pressure, and in another effort to curb the misuse of the term he wrote in 1946:

> one of the most significant qualities in handwriting, [is] often inadequately described as pen pressure, which without accurate definition means nothing … there is in writing, a delicate inconspicuous and almost wholly unconscious variation in line quality, weight of stroke, location of emphasis, smoothness of line, and manual skill that has high identifying value. This … is the result of the movement employed, the pen holding, body and arm position, and the habitual skill and speed that has been developed … the location and character of emphasis or unconscious shading, (and) the variation in this feature is one of the most important evidences of genuineness or forgery … The mere habitual location of extra pressure or emphasis in a character often is highly significant and the force, freedom, and speed of the writing is clearly shown by the quality of line or control of pen pressure, or whatever it may be called … The examination of line quality and unconscious pressure emphasis is especially important in alleged signature forgeries. (p. 292)

Osborn felt so strongly about shading and pen pressure that he had made for himself diagonal line measures, that is, glass grids with which he could measure and compare stroke widths from 1/30 to 1/200 in.

Hilton (1982) in his collection of definitions lists pen emphasis as "the act of intermittently forcing the pen against the paper surface with increased pressure. When the pen point has flexibility this emphasis produces shading," and goes on to define pen pressure as "the average force with which the pen contacts the paper" (p. 20).

Hagan (1894) made a similar distinction between average pressure and extremes of pressure in stating:

> In addition to the general measure of pen pressure found to occur throughout the writing of a signature, there must also be taken into account, in determining individual habit, the measure of comparative density occurring between the lighter and heavy lines of a signature, the points at which the shading emphasis commences and ends, and the facility with which it is accomplished. (p. 68)

Tytell cautioned that it would be wrong to suggest that persons as renowned as Hagan and Osborn, and as familiar with the calligraphy of their time, were off base or obsolete in their treatment of the subject of pen pressure and shading. Even Osborn, however, would allow that there might be something to gain from another perspective of the topic.

A review of these definitions and explanations raises some questions and prompts one to make some observations. Both Hagan and Hilton are saying that there is a general measure of pen pressure in any writing. It may range from light to heavy, but it is necessary to prompt the release of ink to the paper. Beyond that there may be localized variation in the application of this general measure of pressure that supplements the changes in stroke width at turning points that might emanate purely from the physical dimensions of the nib of the writing instrument and its orientation to the writing.

Osborn seems to have held the view, originally, that pen pressure was unconscious and involuntary, and that shading was deliberate and voluntary. He allowed that shading, initially induced by imitation, becomes, with practice, an unconscious and involuntary habit of the individual. The difference between pen pressure and shading, then, seems to be only in the magnitude of the effect attained.

Osborn (1929) defined pen pressure as unconscious emphasis. This term implies that shading, the alternative circumstance, is a relatively conscious act. Indeed, he says that shading is the more obvious and presumably deliberate and conscious increase in the weight of strokes.

Yet, shading, he says, in mature writing is largely unconscious. Thus, the term *unconscious emphasis* for pen pressure can, by itself, be misleading.

The crux of the problem which Osborn and others were endeavoring to resolve centered on magnitude—the magnitude of the variation in stroke width. The shading of writings of Osborn's era was extreme. It was decorative, and it was deliberate. To achieve it required a conscious effort. The literature says that it was much slower to perform. Mature writings, executed with speed and fluency, seldom displayed the same magnitude of variation in stroke width. Thus, when shading became less conscious, it also became less pronounced.

One might ask why a distinction between pen pressure and shading must be made at all. There is little ground for claiming them to be fundamentally different, other than in their visible properties. They are directly related in that they are cause and effect. Furthermore, it is virtually impossible to determine when shading would change from a deliberate act to one that is involuntary.

Shading, in its more extreme forms, is the product of pen pressure that is manifest in the widening or narrowing of the stroke, particularly with split nib pens, or in the production of impressions or troughs in the surface of the paper. Shading and indentations are the manifestations that can be observed, but the application of pressure on the pen, and consequently of the pen on the paper, is the action that becomes the habit of the writer (Figure 6.23). Therefore, shading is not the characteristic of the writer; pen pressure is. Shading is the manifestation, but pressure is the cause.

To be technically correct, pen pressure is not the term to be used, although it has been for a century. Point load, which is defined within the manufacturing industry of pens as the vertical component of the force applied to the writing tip during line generation is in fact what has been loosely referred to as pen pressure. Pen pressure has two components—a vertical component and a horizontal component, but only the vertical component is responsible for the shading of the line (Figure 6.24).

The application of pressure on the pen or the point load, then, which may result in shading, may be constant and heavy in the writing of some individuals, producing broad strokes throughout a writing, or constant and light. It may be rhythmic, occurring consistently with strokes moving in a particular direction, usually but not necessarily down strokes or strokes toward the wrist of the hand. It may be peculiar to particular elements of certain characters or it may be sporadic, having no apparent raison-d'être. It may be graduated or it may be impulsive.

What is being discussed here, and was by Hagan, Osborn, and Hilton, is merely the two qualities of pen pressure or point load: absolute pen pressure and relative pen pressure. These are two qualities that are similar to those previously spoken with respect to size in writing, and with respect to slant. Absolute pen pressure is that which is constant through all of one's writing. It may not always be obvious but it will be there. It is necessary for the writing instrument

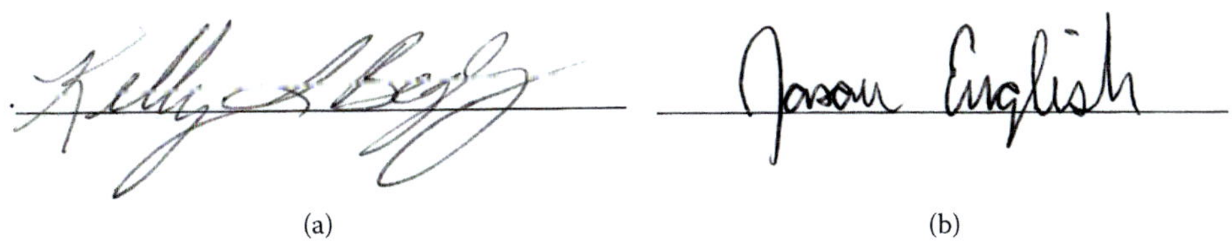

(a) (b)

Figure 6.23 Comparison of pen pressure: Writer (b) has heavier pen pressure and stiffer pen control than Writer (a).

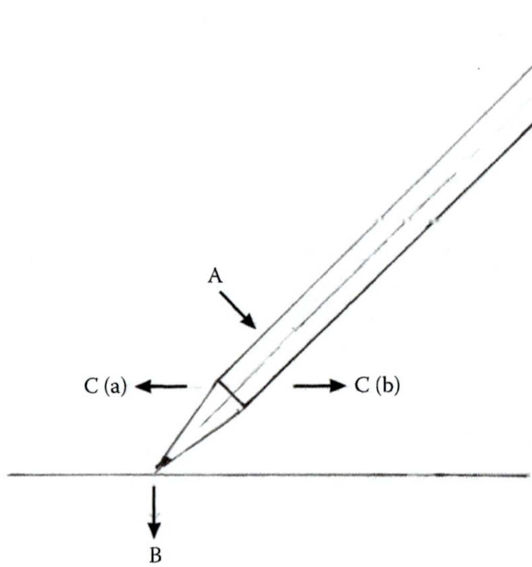

Figure 6.24 Directional components: A. "Pen pressure" by the writer (exerted perpendicular to the axis of the instrument); B. Point load [The vertical component, Responsible for indentations and shading (i.e., the separation of nib points)]; C. Travel action [The horizontal component, Responsible for line generation (a) Forward or sideward (as in upstrokes or crossings) (b) drag or backward (as in downstrokes)].

to generate a line. Relative pen pressure is that which is greater or lesser at certain locations in some strokes. It is responsible for that property of writing that is commonly referred to as shading.

On reviewing the effects of modern writing instruments on the classic attributes of writing, it must be acknowledged that the fundamentals of the movement of the instrument are essentially unchanged from the days of the nib pen. Only the visual track is different. Line quality is still a product of pen control, pressure variation, and fluency. The evidence depicting it may be diminished but it has not been demolished.

6.3.9.1.1 Kinds of Shading and Its Causes

Shading should be studied in terms of its nature, consistency or graduation, intensity, skill, and location. If it is faulty, it can be evidence of spuriousness. If it is correct, it can testify to genuineness.

Shading occurs, for the most part, because of the separation of the nib points due to the application of force against the writing surface. The separation ensues because of the curvature of the nib, which gives each half of the nib its own, but different arc. Each arc subtends an ordinate that runs at a small angle to the other. Pressure, or a point load upon the nibs causes each to bend along the lines of these ordinates, with the result that the tips move away from each other, thereby, widening the stroke they make.

The quill pen, the original split nib writing instrument, was frequently so resilient that evidence of nib tracks was difficult to find. The steel nib left no doubts. The gold pen or gold-tipped pen was a modification of the steel nib to overcome the corrosive action of the acids of ink on the steel. The softness of gold was overcome by the addition of iridium that greatly extended the life of the nib.

The reservoir pen was the forerunner to the fountain pen, in which an ink reservoir was attached to the back of the pen shaft to allow much more writing to be executed without requiring refilling or dipping the nib. Indeed, the length of the ink line without replenishing the supply in the pen is the principal means of differentiating the reservoir pen from the conventional steel pen.

The fountain pen extended the length of the written line between fillings to a much greater extent. It was initially more resilient and responded to pressure by broadening the stroke, but more recent products are not so reactive.

The greatly reduced use of split nib pens and the popularity of ball pens has correspondingly reduced the incidence of pronounced shading in writing of this era. Shading in older writings, or indeed in any writing, however, occurs for one or both of two reasons: the application of the vertical component of pen pressure that forces the separation of the nibs, and/or the use of broad tipped nibs that changes the width of the stroke according to the pen's orientation with reference to the generated line. When the principal ordinate subtending the full arc or curve of the broad tipped nib lies parallel to the direction of the stroke, the ink line will be broad, as broad as the width of the nib point, or greater with greater point load or pen pressure. When the direction of the ordinate crosses the stroke at right angles, the ink line will be narrow, as narrow as the thickness of the nib point, regardless of the pressure applied. In both cases, however, the point load (i.e., the pen pressure) could be the same. Between these extremes, the angle of the ordinate to the stroke of the writing and the pressure applied will determine the width of the written line. Thus, as a characteristic of writing or as a habit of identification value, it is preferable to speak in terms of pen pressure or point load rather than shading, and to avoid confusion with terms respecting the evidence of a particular pen hold or pen position, or the evidence of a choice of pen. Shading can be the product of one or more of these four factors.

There is reference to "the product of one or more of these four factors" because it is possible to shade a stroke without any appreciable application of pressure or point load. This is due simply to the physical dimensions of the nib point that is usually, but not necessarily, wider than it is thick. Consider the execution of a circle. From any fixed position there are two segments of the circle (usually but not necessarily top and bottom) at which the line width will conform to the thickness of the nib, thereby creating the pen's thinnest strokes. There are two other segments (the extremities of the circle, left and right) at which the line width will conform to the width of the nib, thereby, creating the pen's normally and naturally wider strokes. In the area of these latter segments of the circle, as the point load increases so does the stroke width.

No summarization of the topic of pen pressure could improve on the remarks of Tytell (1995) cited previously, for which reason they are quoted here in their entirety.

> A review of the patents granted for devices and methods, the scientific and technical literature, as well as the experimental data and findings all support the hypotheses that there are highly individual characteristics in [the] act of writing and that among the most individual and consistent of these is the pattern of pressure emphasis in writing a signature—the same conclusion found in the literature of document examination.

The basic principles of questioned document examination are explained fully in the various texts and articles studied by all students of the subject. It is not easy to reduce them to a few bare statements, like proofs in a geometry book, and any such attempt runs the risk of omitting a crucial detail. However, both the texts in document examination and the results of nondocument examiners working with dynamic handwriting analysis as a form of biometric identity verification support the following statements:

- Dynamic pressure patterns are an integral part of an individual's signature.
- Patterns of pressure emphasis show a high degree of interpersonal variation. They are highly individual to the extent that it would be exceptional to find two people with well-developed signatures of normal length and the same patterns.
- The pressure patterns of a well-developed signature of normal length are extremely difficult, if not impossible, to duplicate when imitating another's writing, especially when attempting to reproduce details of formation and method of production.
- As with all writing, there is some intrapersonal variation in these patterns from signature to signature.
- The amount of intrapersonal variation in pressure patterns is generally less than with other writing characteristics.
- In some individuals, these variations will be extreme, in others slight or virtually undetectable.
- For writing of individuals with a wide range of variation, more standards than usual may be required.
- As with all writing, there can be changes in these patterns over time.
- In some individuals these changes will be extreme, in others slight or virtually undetectable.
- Standards close to the date of the questioned material are generally preferable, especially where change over time is acute.
- The pressure distribution and pressure contrast of these pressure patterns can be considered along with other dynamic elements (the elements of line quality), such as speed of writing, for a fuller assessment of individuality.

Important to bear in mind in any study of shading is that the particular location of the shading of the stroke may be a function of the particular writer's pen hold, or the orientation of the instrument to the paper surface or to the writing line, that is called pen position. It might be also a function of the instrument employed. Together and in combination with pen pressure or point load they produced the result that was known as shading. Pen holds that were previously taught with penmanship, now vary substantially with the individual. Some writers are known to hold a pen in such a position that the horizontal strokes are widened (i.e., shaded) rather than the vertical.

6.3.9.2 Pen Hold (Grasp)

Insofar as any variation in width that might be observed in the writing line, the pen hold or grasp of the pen will make a difference. It is noted, incidentally, that grasp was a term used by early authors on handwriting to refer to the degree of rigidity or force with which the instrument was clutched, rather than simply the manner in which it is controlled within or by the hand. The various pen holds or grasps that are presently employed do not exhibit the same rigidity or force of former years. It has been observed, however, that individuals that hold the writing instrument in the more awkward fashion of a clenched fist tend to execute rounder forms of letters. Surprisingly, more recent studies show that, contrary to earlier teachings, unconventional pen holds do not necessarily slow the speed of writing execution (Sassoon et al. 1986).

Nevertheless, variation in the grasp of the pen or pencil occurs in a fashion that is more extreme in the writing of sinistrals, or even dextrals, utilizing IHP (the inverted hand position—see left-handed writing). In these cases, the slope of the instrument is in a direction away from the writer and the stroke on which greater emphasis might be placed will be in the direction of the wrist, and that is away from the writer. Consequently, if emphasis occurs it is likely to be found on what would otherwise be identified as upstrokes, rather than the downstrokes. This aspect of a writing is sought and studied if only to provide evidence of execution by a left-handed writer, or at least one using an inverted hand position.

6.3.9.3 Pen Position

The pen position may also make an observable difference. Generally, this is with reference to the orientation of the instrument to the writing line, or the orientation of the document to the writer. In this latter respect, people are quite consistent in the orientation they prefer with respect to the document, but can be quite different from one to another. Modern ballpoint pens, however, provide much less evidence of the orientation of the instrument to the paper or to the writing line than their predecessors. Consequently pen hold and pen position are not aspects of a writing that the examiner will have an opportunity to consider in most cases.

Pen position, defined earlier as the orientation of the instrument to the paper surface or to the document, is usually thought of as being in reference to the line of writing. Another relationship pertains to the angle at which the axis of the instrument meets the paper surface. Its importance lies in the fact that ballpoint pens, roller pens, and perhaps others have limitations to these angles at which the housing of the pen contacts the surface. This seems to be, as Nemecek (1974) reported, at about 45 degrees. At this angle, shadow and other lines created by the housing and writing substrate may appear. These conditions can be helpful in supplying evidence as to the writer's pen hold or grasp as well as the pen position that can be of some significance in certain cases.

In summary. It follows that if the writing is executed with a flexible instrument the shading observed can be a feature of some significance in the examination and study of handwriting for the purpose of its identification. The extent and location of shading depends upon the instrument, its grasp, and the manner of its manipulation. Pen pressure (and shading) tends to become more habitual and pronounced with signatures and other frequently executed segments of writing such as initials. Accordingly, its importance as a useful feature has been stressed (Moore 1983).

As the fountain pen, the principal split nib writing instrument currently available, is widely available in expensive pen formats and is the preferred choice of pen for signing or writing by many people who own or collect pens from manufacturers that distribute high-end fountain pens, shading of the ink stroke continues to be a factor to be considered in the identification of writing.

Pen Performance. This refers to the effects of instruments on the evidence related to pen control. Shading, or the variation in width of the line generated, is not the only consequence of variation in the point load. Depending upon the surface against which the writing is produced, and the type of writing instrument, some degree of indentation or embossing of the paper can occur.

Ballpoint pens frequently produce a groove in the paper that is observable and, to some extent, able to be judged under examination with a stereoscopic microscope. As a result of variations in the point load or pressure, the depth of the groove will be seen to vary, even if the width of the line remains apparently unchanged.

In initial studies of the ballpoint pen, Mathyer (1950) suggested that the stroke width of the instrument might vary from very narrow when against a hard surface, to that which represented the width of the ball when writing occurred against a soft or resilient surface, and the ink was deposited in a trough in the paper. There are, of course, some differences in ball sizes between fine and broad instruments, but given a particular instrument and a particular writing surface, there is not likely to be any measurable difference in stroke widths that will correspond to the shading of the split nib pen. Point load, or pen pressure, then, must be judged on the basis of the indentation observable by microscope in the paper surface, if indeed, there is any.

In a later study of ballpoint pens by Lyter et al. (1983), it was hypothesized that six factors affect the written line of ballpoint pens: the pen mechanism and ink, the writing speed, point load, writing angle, writing direction, and writing surface, only the first of which is not controlled by the writer. These factors manifest themselves in the written line in three ways: the line width, the line density, and certain anomalies called gooping, splitting, dotting, skipping, starving, and blobbing. The study was directed at the effect of the pen, the writing angle and point load on the width, line density, and the occurrence of the anomalies of splitting and blobbing.

The results indicated that, insofar as the 20 different kinds of ballpoint pens employed in the study, stroke width, density, and anomalies are attributable to both the writing instrument and the writer. This combination of factors appears to be inseparable, however, and therefore, their value in the identification of writers or instruments requires that for comparison purposes, instruments and writing conditions, that is, point load, writing angle, and paper type, must be duplicated.

Both line width measurements and line density measurements (i.e., the absorption of 580 nm light waves by inked line deposits) were ruled out as reliable factors for discriminating between either writers or writing instruments. As reported, fine point instruments could be differentiated from medium point instruments only at low angles of incidence to the paper surface.

Definitions of the technical terms used in the study include ballpoint pen, point load, writing angle, blobbing, dotting, skip, directional skipping, starving, splitting, and gooping. These terms are included in the glossary.

The porous point or fiber tip pen was the first to appear on the scene after the ballpoint pen. It delivers an aqueous ink through a feed system based on capillary action. Its relatively soft tip produces a flat ungrooved line. The ink deposits from this pen tend to be heavier than others and varies in dimension only insofar as the point type (fine, medium, broad) of the instrument selected. For this discussion, suffice it to say that pressure or point load makes no difference to the width of the written line.

In fact, there are two kinds of writing tips to these pens: one is made from a stiff perforated plastic and the other is a fiber or felt tip. The plastic is used in fine and most of the medium tips and the felt in broad tips. The porous tip tends produce a surplus of ink at stroke endings. Because of the aqueous nature of its ink, it may spread or bleed along the edges of the stroke, particularly on unsized paper. In these respects, then, it may create some apparent differences to writings executed with ballpoint pens, but not significantly greater than the differences that might occur in two writings with the same kind of pen (Hilton 1984).

Variation in point load does not result in apparent variation in stroke width, although the broader stroke, and the bleeding that occurs, tends to fill the counters of narrow loops, acute angles, and small gaps between strokes. Hence, open bowls of the "o" and "a" may be closed. Tapered stroke endings do occur, but are less frequently observed than in writings with other kinds of instruments.

The roller pen is another instrument manufactured in the early 1950s using aqueous ink in a ballpoint pen design, of two sizes, that is now seldom seen. The pen produces a ball track or groove much like the ballpoint pen, and a more dense ink deposit much like the porous point pen. Against a soft surface variations in groove depth may be observed as with other ballpoint pens. Against a hard surface and with a lighter point load, the groove may not be observable and the stroke resembles closely that of the porous point pen.

In the late 1970s, the porous point pen was supplanted by the plastic-tip pen having a tip of either plastic or fibers encased in a tube. The stiffness of this point is sufficient to create carbon copies that the porous point pen could not do. Furthermore, against a reasonably soft writing surface, the firmness of the point is sufficient to produce grooves or furrows in the writing line where the point load is greater. In any event, it is not likely to be as pronounced an indentation in the paper surface as the conventional ballpoint pen produces. Like the porous point pen, the dimension of the writing line, regardless of the point load, changes only insofar as the point size of the instrument selected (Hilton 1980).

Plastic-tip pens are capable of producing a fine writing line and thereby producing a slight groove or furrow even against a hard or less resilient surface. One instrument, the Pilot Razor Point was reported to produce a finer line than those of competitors and, consequently, were the most apt of its kind to emboss the paper. The Flair Hardhead produced a moderate width stroke, but, according to Hilton, no other plastic-tip pens were reported to produce the wide strokes of which some porous point pen were capable.

Hilton (1980) stated that fine pointed writing instruments are capable of reproducing the finer details of a person's writing. Broader points normally obscure these details with the result that certain significant aspects of fine line writing are lost in the broader, less distinct writing strokes.

The fountain pen remains the only split nib instrument that is capable of the shading and pressure characteristics of the pens of the past. It is also the only conventional writing instrument that provides a reasonable indication of pen hold and pen position.

6.3.10 Writing Movement

Writing movement is a term that is used in several different respects, and tends to adopt for itself a somewhat different meaning for each occasion. Traditionally, it is an attribute of writing that is observed in letter formations and intraword connections, that may be as follows:

1. Garlanded—counterclockwise movements predominate
2. Arched—clockwise movements predominate
3. Angular—straight lines take precedence over curves
4. Indeterminable—predominating movement uncertain

Thus, it is defined in this fashion:

Definition: Writing movements are (1) general variants in the predominating action of the writing instrument.

If differentiation can be made at all, these movements seem to fall into one of the three classes: garlanded, arched or arcaded, and angular (Figure 6.25). To be fully comprehensive, however, a fourth class must be added: indeterminable.

There are, as well, other more specific movements in the writing of a person that are particularly letter related. It may be the manner of combining the letters "of" to significantly modify the

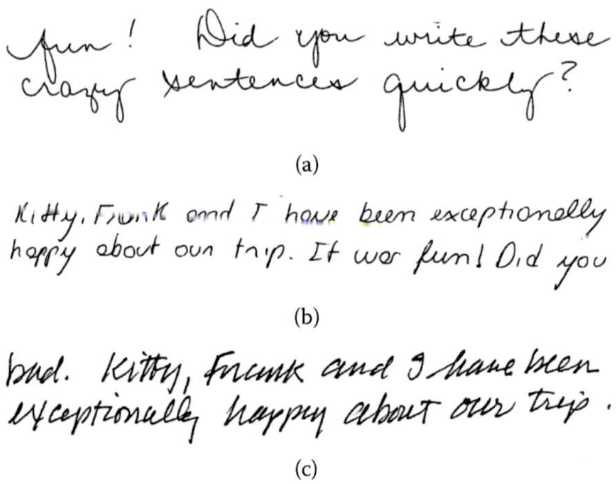

Figure 6.25 Examples of garland (a), arcade or arched (b), and angular writings (c).

construction of the upper loop of the "f," the arching of the connection in "on," or any one of a number of methods of executing initial or terminal letters or of executing letter combinations that are more frequently present in the written language. Such movements tend to sacrifice form in the interests of fluency and speed. It is not uncommon to find signatures that exhibit particular movements in the production of certain letters that may, in fact, render the letters quite indiscernible. Because of their greater frequency of use these movements become more fixed and less consciously executed habit patterns. To be complete, then, the definition must have a second clause that reads:

Definition: Writing movements are (2) specific variants in the union of two or more particular letters.

This definition describes a two-dimensional pattern of action of the writing instrument. In addition, variation in point load (i.e., the application of pen pressure) is also part of the action of the instrument, and may be present and observable in any particular pattern of movement in forming a letter or combination of letters. Thus, there is a three-dimensional pattern of the action of a writing instrument. All of this instrument action is what is included in the definition of writing movement.

Ames (1900) used the term *writing movement* to discriminate between the chief elements of the limb involved in the writing process: finger movement, finger and wrist movement, finger and forearm movement, or whole arm movement. These discriminations, however, are applicable to better qualities of penmanship that are seldom seen in the writing of current times. Osborn (1929) supports Ames' classes of movements and suggests five levels of quality that each kind of movement might attain. Harrison (1958b) used *writing movement* to refer to the various patterns of motion of the writing instrument, but not necessarily the dominant patterns. Hilton (1987) fails to define it precisely, but uses the term *line quality* almost synonymously with *writing movement* that is said to embrace several aspects of writing instrument performance, such as skill, speed, freedom, hesitation, and emphasis. Admittedly, these are factors that may contribute to the quality of the line, but there are other factors as well. It seems preferable to avoid a confusion of terms, to refrain from considering the terms to be interchangeable, but to allow them to enjoy distinctly different definitions.

6.4 ATTRIBUTES OF ALL WRITING HABITS

6.4.1 Consistency or Natural Variation

Definition: "Natural variation" is the imprecision with which the habits of the writer are executed on repeated occasions.

Natural variation is the current and popular alternative to the term *consistency* used in the old-fashioned penmanship classes. Consistency was an objective to be achieved. Natural variation was a condition to be avoided. Despite such teachings, mutability occurs and can be observed in any two or more examples of a person's writings, whether or not they are made on the same date, at the same time, in the same place. The reason for this mutability is simply that humans are not machines, and consequently, the executions of every writer vary to some extent from one occasion to the next. There is also variation occurring between writings made on different dates, on different documents, and with different instruments. The difference between these variations is usually just a matter of degree and may be greater or lesser depending upon circumstances.

With practice, the acquisition of skill, and the application of control, these variations diminish in their range, but writers are never totally without them. Skilled penmanship may exhibit the consistency that makes the imprecision difficult for the unaided eye to perceive, but a more precise method of judgment (e.g., a measuring microscope) will reveal it.

Natural variation is an attribute of every perceptual-motor task. There is natural variation to the basketball player's toss of the ball to the basket. There is natural variation to the shooting of a gun. Golf is a perceptual-motor skill to which there is natural variation that golfers are incessantly trying to explain or to control. The decrease of natural variation in perceptual-motor skills is the mission and intent of practice and training.

Natural variation in writing has been spoken of as if it was a general attribute that affects all of the aspects of writing in some common fashion. Hence, the use of the singular number. This, however, is not quite the case as there is variation in each of the discriminating elements of writing.

Some of the discriminating elements of writing may exhibit much wider variation than others. For example, the designs and shapes of the cursive letters "i" and "e" may be quite consistent. Indeed, there is little about them to vary. On the other hand the shapes and sizes of the loops to the cursive letters "g" and "y" and the formation of the capital letters "G" and "S," because of the number of curved strokes involved, may seldom be quite the same. Natural variation, then, must be thought of as an attribute of each element in the composition of a writing, having some cumulative effect upon the countenance of the total product. To be correct then, variations are plural in number and should be referred to as natural variations.

Osborn (1929) contended that the important and often unappreciated fact is that the variations in a handwriting are themselves habitual (Wing 1979). Whatever the difference may be between variations affected by differing circumstances, for the most part, variations tend to lie within ranges peculiar to the individual and to the elements of a writing. Accordingly, these fluctuations in a writing are said to constitute a writer's range of natural variations (Figure 6.26).

The range of variations in writings of different dates or documents or instruments, appropriately called asynchronous writings, tends to be somewhat greater than that of synchronous (i.e., same date, place, and time) executions. Furthermore, while variation will occur in the consistency of the same letter form (i.e., the graph), there may also be variation in the selection of the style (i.e., the allograph) employed. There are, for example, many writers that use two designs of the letter "r," one that has a cusp and a shoulder (the conventional form) and one that is a narrow "v" shape (the Palmer option), and each may have a use in particular letter combinations.

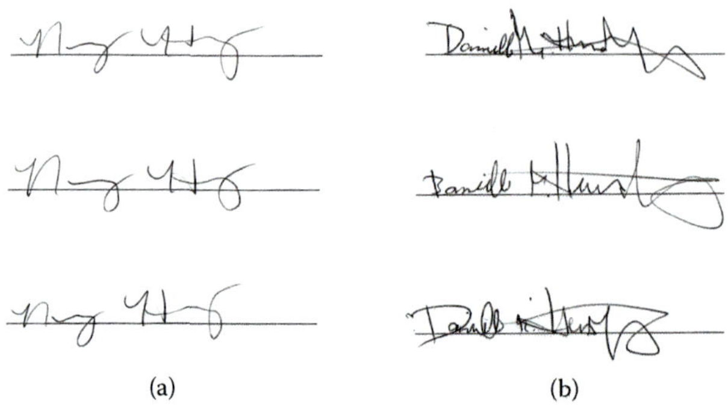

Figure 6.26 Natural variation in signatures. Writer (a) has minimal variation and writer (b) has a wider range of variation.

Others have two methods of crossing the "t" depending on whether it is in a medial or terminal position within the word. Some writers vary the allograph in a more fundamental fashion going from one style of writing to another, if only for certain graphemes and then only in certain locations in a word. Thus, block lettering or script may be mixed with cursive writing.

The more practiced the hand or the more skillful the writer, the more consistent is the product and the more limited is the range of these variations. But skill is not the only factor limiting or influencing variations, particularly insofar as the choice of design or allograph selected for many graphemes (i.e., letters). How much variation may occur will depend on the individual and the circumstances. Needless to say, standards for comparison may not always reflect the full range of variations of which the writer may be capable, or duplicate the circumstances responsible for some of the anomalies.

Speed and context can also be contributing factors to variation. Practiced writers that write quickly often tend to slur the execution of some letter combinations, especially word endings that can greatly affect the letter shapes, perhaps to the point of rendering them unreadable as individual letters. Recognition is achieved primarily by virtue of the context in which the words occur.

Wing et al. (1983) found that there is greater variation in an allograph (letter design) when it occurs in the initial position of a word than when it occurs in the medial or final positions of a word. Furthermore, an allograph is as consistent in the final position as in the medial position. The variation to which this study was directed is the more profound variation in allograph selection, not to be confused with the subtle changes occurring in the execution of the same allograph, to which natural variation normally refers. Thus, it was concluded, as Ellis (1979) had concluded before them, that the selection of the allograph (design) of a letter depends on the position of the letter in the word and the letters that precede it, or perhaps succeed it. Suffice it to say that variations, and the range of them, can be in some instances significant elements of the writing to be considered in both the identification or in the elimination of a writer.

Natural variation, then, in the execution of writing, is a term respecting the consistency of the attributes of its many discriminating elements that observation and study have revealed. It is sometimes used in a collective sense to refer to the level of imprecision exhibited by the writing as a whole on repeated occasions. As such, a statement about it constitutes an observation rather than a principle. It is a reflection of the degree of consistency between or within standards, or rather of the degree of consistency between samples of the discriminating elements of the standards. It is often an explanation for a disparity between standards and the unknown.

Collectively, it is a variable attribute of the substance (i.e., writing) or particularly of an element of the substance (i.e., any of the 21 discriminating elements of writing) under examination. It is a kind of attribute that fields of science such as chemistry and physics seldom have to consider, provided temperature, pressure, and purity are controlled.

In writing examinations, variation is an expected attribute of the standards, for which allowance must be made in the study of any apparent disparity between the standards and the unknown or questioned writing. The level of such disparity and the range of the writer's normal variation may be the principal factors on which the determination of authorship may turn.

There are some examiners that tend to confuse persistency with natural variation. A writer that is inclined to employ two or more designs (allographs) of a letter, perhaps a block letter and a cursive letter, perhaps an epsilon "e" and a conventional one, is said to display great variation in their letter forms. It is contended that while these different forms may be different styles in the construction of a letter, they are more correctly described as different allographs of the same grapheme. They are not the kind of subtle changes from one execution to the next to which natural variation is normally intended to refer. Natural variation is a property of a single allograph or design, a single method, a single writing movement that experiences a change due to imprecision when it is repeated.

6.4.2 Persistency

Persistency concerns the frequency with which a given habit occurs, when the occasion permits. The term persistency tends to be applicable particularly to the selection of the allograph to be used in any particular situation. As has been observed in studies, and reported elsewhere, the position of the letter within the word may determine the allograph chosen. It may be simply the purpose the writing is intended to serve that will prompt the change or selection. The inscription of addresses on envelopes is a case in point.

It might be argued that persistency and consistency (see point 18) are the same thing, and the use of both terms will be confusing. As aforementioned, *consistency* was the predecessor to the term *natural variation* in the language of penmanship, when excellence in it was being sought. Consistency was attained by the acquisition of skill that refined the execution of a character, a feature, or writing element, without altering or modifying its design. Persistency pertains to the more allographic or profound changes in an element of writing than natural variation does, and so the use of the two terms, *persistency* and *consistency* is justified.

6.5 COMBINATIONS OF WRITING HABITS

6.5.1 Lateral Expansion

Definition: Lateral expansion is the horizontal dimension of a group of successive letters and words.

Lateral expansion is the product of letter formation, letter sizes, and the spacing between letters and words and ranges from contracted to expanded (Figure 6.27).

Although letter forms and letter sizes contribute to lateral expansion, the principal contributor tends to be the interletter and interword spacing. This is an aspect of writing that is frequently distinctive and remarkably consistent with some individuals.

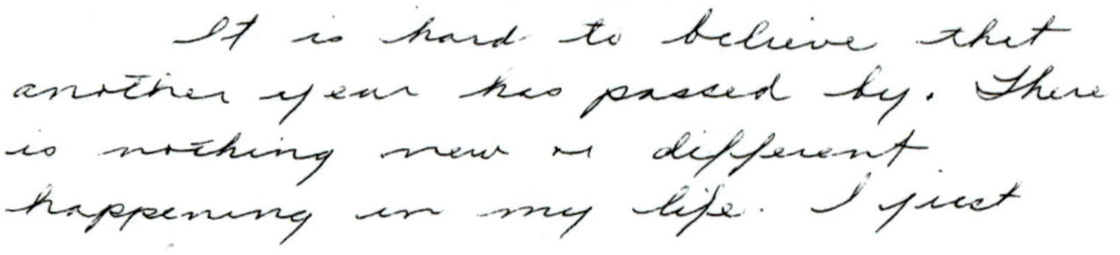

Figure 6.27 An example of considerable lateral expansion, the product or interword spacing, interletter spacing, and in some cases letter widths.

Consequently, lateral expansion is not a writing characteristic, per se, and may be difficult to judge for comparison purposes, except in special cases. Precise judgments can only be made on similar text material, and that is seldom available except in signature comparisons. Its particular advantage in the study of writings and especially signatures lies in it being cumulative. Minor disparities in the dimensions of letters and of spacing are accumulated across a signature, across several words or across a line of writing, that confirms the similarities in size and space aspects, if such are present, and renders differences more pronounced, if differences exist.

Some writers exhibit considerable lateral expansion. When this occurs, it is to be noted that an increase in interletter spacing correlates well with interword spacing. An increase in the vertical dimension or the size of the writing does not necessarily ensue. An increase in the vertical dimension of the writing, such as occurs with an increase in the size of letters, frequently results in a decrease in the space between letters or an apparent crowding of the writing.

6.5.2 Word Proportions

1. Vertical dimension versus horizontal dimension
2. The product of size and spacing

Osborn (1929) wrote:

> Genuine writing or genuine signatures show a certain definite and fixed proportion of height of letters to length of words. This is another of the distinctive ways in which the general appearance of a page of writing is changed by a different system of writing. This change may be very slight although in combination it changes the general appearance of writing in a striking manner. (p. 141)

Osborn said that the subtle or minute differences in writing, between systems or indeed, between persons, have a cumulative affect that is more obvious when greater quantities of writing (such as a page) can be considered.

6.6 SUMMARY

6.6.1 Artistic Quality

Artistic quality was not included in this catalog of writing features by which writing might be identified or differentiated. Admittedly, artistic quality is a term sometimes used in reference to writing in which many of its aspects, such as arrangement, size, proportions, line quality, and writing quality are of such kind and consistency as to be pleasing to the eye. It cannot be simply defined, however, any more than beauty can be defined, for it rests largely in the eyes of the beholder. Consequently, it is not an aspect of writing, or a writing habit of itself, that can be easily defined, described, or utilized in the identification process.

6.6.1.1 The 21 Elements in Review

In summary, the aspects of writing that become habitual with each and every writer, that are its discriminating elements, and that are the subject of examination and study in the process of handwriting identification or elimination are 21 in number. These include two combinations of habits and two common properties of habits, and are as follows:

1. **Elements of Style**
   a. ***Arrangement***
      i. Influenced by artistic ability, sense of proportion, and instruction received
      ii. The product of a group of habits
   b. ***Class of Allograph***
      The four styles of allographs
   c. ***Connections***
      i. Interword
      ii. Intraword
   d. ***Designs of Allographs and Their Construction***
      i. Correspondence to foreign/domestic or particular writing systems
      ii. Number, nature, position, sequence, and direction of strokes in letter composition
      iii. Use of two or more forms for the same letter
      iv. Capitalization—divergences from standard practices
   e. ***Dimensions***
      i. Proportions of elements of letters, that is, bowls to staffs, bodies to loops, arches to loops
      ii. Absolute sizes
      iii. Relative sizes of specific letters to specific letters or according to position in words
   f. ***Slant or Slope***
      i. Of the writing in general
      ii. Of letters or parts of letters in particular
   g. ***Spacing***
      i. Interword
      ii. Intraword
2. **Elements of Execution**
   a. ***Abbreviations***
      i. Word contractions that eliminate letters
      ii. Letter combinations that sacrifice form for speed
   b. ***Alignment***
      The relation of successive letters of a signature, a word, or line of writing to an actual or imaginary baseline
   c. ***Commencements and Terminations***
      i. Their length, direction, and path
      ii. Their taper (the abruptness with which the instrument approaches and leaves the paper)

d. ***Diacritics and Punctuation — Presence, Style, and Location.***
e. ***Embellishments***
Including flourishes, ornamentation, rubrics, and underscores
f. ***Legibility or Writing Quality***
Ease of recognition of letters or adherence to copybook form
g. ***Line Continuity***
The presence/absence of pen stops, pen lifts, or retracings
h. ***Line Quality***
The degree of regularity (i.e., smoothness and/or gradation) to the writing stroke as is judged from the consistency of its nature and of its path in a prescribed direction. It varies from smooth and controlled to tremulous and erratic.
i. ***Pen Control***
    i. Pen hold
    ii. Pen position
    iii. Point load (pen pressure)
        A. To be considered if and when determinable
        B. Evidenced by shading, greater deposition of ink or graphite or by the depression of the paper; called rhythm, or fluency, or a flowing hand when it materializes as a harmonious and graduated recurrence
        C. Absolute—occurring in all writing
        D. Relative—greater or lesser in some strokes
j. ***Writing Movement***
    i. Variants in the predominating action of the writing instrument; may be three-dimensional
    ii. Observed in letter formation and interword connections that may be:
        A. Garlanded — anticlockwise movements predominate
        B. Arched — clockwise movements predominate
        C. Angular — straight lines take precedence to curves
        D. Indeterminable

3. **Attributes of All Writing Habits**
a. ***Consistency or Natural Variation***
The precision with which the habits are executed on repeated occasions
b. ***Persistency***
The frequency with which a given habit occurs when the occasion permits

4. **Combinations of Writing Habits**
a. ***Lateral Expansion***
    i. Ranges from contracted to expanded
    ii. The product of spacing and letter formation
b. ***Word Proportions***
    i. Vertical dimension versus horizontal dimension
    ii. The product of size and spacing

Chapter 7

Special Problems in the Discrimination and Identification of Writing

7.1 IDENTIFICATION OF HANDWRITTEN INITIALS

Handwritten initials are an incidence of writing separate and apart from the execution of a signature. It is rather an execution in lieu of a signature, usually comprised of the first letters of some or all of the names involved.

Business practices make the use of initials a standard procedure in the authentication of documents, the approval of amendments, or the authorization of the action to which the document pertains. It has been suggested that initials are utilized in these instances simply as an abbreviated signature. This explanation for their wide use is not to suggest that initials will resemble any part of the signature of that individual in every case. In fact, the disparity may be surprising. In the majority of instances, however, a close study of one's initials will disclose at least some basic correspondence with the first or capital letters of the individual's signature.

Some writers adopt distinctive styles in their initials, and sufficiently so, that they provide ample evidence by which the writer can be identified. Authorizing or approving initials by persons in some authority are frequently accompanied by other abbreviations of the individual's rank or position, such as "A.B.C./R.N." or "D.E.F./Mgr.," "G.H./Sgt," "I.J./Sec'y," or "K.L./Dr," with or without punctuation or the slash shown here. The manner of punctuating and appending the rank or title can be quite individualistic and a significant element in the identification or elimination of a potential writer. In the majority of cases, however, the evidence within initials alone is qualitatively limited and quantitatively insufficient.

Initials are sometimes elaborately embellished, or hastily scrawled such that the letter forms they are expected to contain are unrecognizable. It is not uncommon to find that initials are underscored or encircled practices of which may not be a part of the individual's signature.

The initials of persons having less need to write them may display little consistency. Frequently, they are used simply to acknowledge receipt of an item, or an agreement to terms on a document (that may not be read or fully understood), and are commonly executed under a wide range of writing conditions and writing positions. For these reasons it is often stressed that when possible "request" writing standards for use in comparisons should be prepared under similar writing circumstances imitating awkward, uncomfortable, or inconvenient writing situations.

In some lines of employment, the initializing of documents as an authorizing or authenticating exercise is a frequent daily requirement and, consequently, becomes a well-practiced movement that reflects much greater consistency, greater perhaps than the signature. In a study of natural variation, Widla (1990) collected writing samples from 30 extramural students at law at the Silesian University (Poland) who, by virtue of their employment, were required to sign and to initial documents many times a day. It was reported that, over a period of six months, initials proved to be a more stable graphic product than signatures. This finding was based on the initials displaying, on average, a smaller standard deviation in physical dimensions than that of signatures from the same individuals. The results of this study are said to support the findings of Wallner (1975).

The potential for identification of the author will depend on the number of letters involved in the execution, the complexity of the movements, and the skill and consistency with which it is performed. The use of the microscope or of photographic enlargements, in the examination or illustration of evidence the initials may contain, is a recommended practice.

Although not numerous, cases are known to have occurred wherein initials, and in some instances signatures, have been deliberately written carelessly and illegibly to supply a plausible pretext for the eventual repudiation of the writing, that is, a later denial that the writing is genuine. As has been said elsewhere, disguise and distortion is a practice affecting the gross or more obvious elements of writing because they are the more consciously executed structures. Initials are, for the most part, a group of such gross features of an individual's writing. Consequently, disguise and distortion affects a more substantial portion of the limited amount of writing that initials provide. The examination and study of illegible initials and signatures must be conducted with such possibilities and limitations in mind.

Galbraith (1981, 1983) conducted two studies of initials and their relationship to the signatures of the same persons. She reported that size and relative heights may change, and that spacing usually changes by diminishing, displaying more crowding or less lateral expansion to the writing. It was found that punctuation, not present in the signature is often added to the initials. Even letter forms may be modified. The majority of her subjects in both studies (72% and 69%) disclosed some change in the initials as compared to the signatures, suggesting that they should be considered a special category of handwriting.

Cadola et al. (2013) carried out an experimental simulation study on simple signatures and initials and found that the forger subjects were not able to produce perfect or undetectable simulations of initials when they were submitted to document examiners for proficiency testing. It was reported that forgers had difficulty successfully emulating proportions, slant, and shape.

A wider range of variations is expected to be found in initials from people not required to use them on a daily or routine basis. This is probably due to the fact that there is no necessity to conform to any standards, thereby, allowing more freedom and individuality in developing the design of the final product.

Although initials may display much fluency they may also display a great deal of variation from one execution to the next. Because of their brevity, a deceptive simulation of the initials is much easier to achieve. Only a general outline of the genuine product is required to be reproduced to pass normal scrutiny, without regard to details. Consistency in the known standards of the initials, however, such as may emanate from the more practiced hands, is an indication of the range of variation within which a set of questioned initials may be expected to fall if they are genuine (Figure 7.1).

7.2 IDENTIFICATION OF NUMERALS AND SYMBOLS

Numerals and other non-alphabetic compositor's job case characters are those characters that normally occupy a space in the type case that was used for many years in the days when compositors set type by hand. This group of characters, plus the letters of the alphabet in both capital

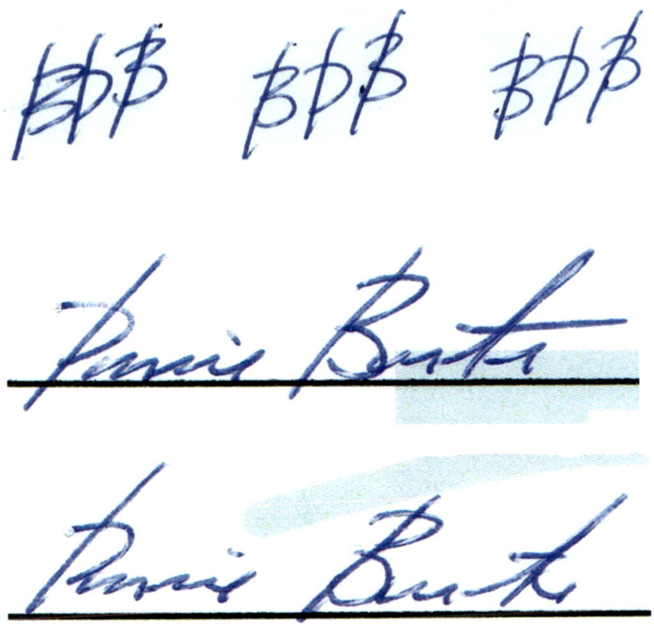

Figure 7.1 Initials of writer with signature specimens depicting similarities in letter construction for both.

and small letter size came to be known as the font of any style and size of type. The term *font* is unrelated to any particular typeface, a word we use interchangeably with type style. Modern usage tends to associate font improperly with the name of a typeface, as in a Bodoni font or a Times Roman font. A font can be defined as the complete collection of characters and letters (uppercase and lowercase) that one might receive if one was to purchase or procure a particular typeface, or type style.

There are, however, other characters that appear in conjunction with handwriting, such as check marks, cross marks, arrows, and other symbols of various shapes that are currently offered as type characters for the computer and are collectively called *dingbats* or iconic symbols.

7.2.1 Numerals and Textual Symbols

Hilton (1970) provided a general coverage of the subject of numerals, going so far as to suggest that a writer may be identified from the habits acquired in the writing of numerals alone. Horan and Horan (1984) reported on the correspondence they found between 675 (American) subjects and the review of numerals by Ansell and Strach (1975). In a later paper, Hilton (1986) describes some of the features that he noted in the Austrian writing of numerals.

Osborn (1929), Hilton (1982), and Conway (1959) have each made the point that numerals, and the signs and symbols associated with and frequently accompanying numerals, possess similar discriminating elements to those of the alphabetical cursive characters. Consequently, the examination and study of numerals does not differ fundamentally from that of any other aspect of writing. Numerals and other characters are found to vary with the writer insofar as structure, dimension, slope, spacing, system (in some cases), varieties of styles and shapes utilized, and even connections, although they are primarily independent executions.

Because of this independence, variations due to the influence of a preceding or succeeding character or numeral are limited. Distinctive relationships in dimensions of two or more numerals (i.e., relative heights or sizes) do occur, particularly respecting the cipher (zero), but the quantity of evidence of individuality is considerably reduced by the independence of the numerals.

For the most part, there is greater consistency in the writing systems followed in North America in the designs and structures of numerals and other characters than in the designs and structures of upper and lowercase letters of cursive writing. Furthermore, there are fewer, if any, optional forms for any numerals or characters suggested by any of the published systems, and less time is devoted to their development. Some pronounced differences are to be noted in the construction of other characters, such as the ($) dollar sign, the (¢) cent sign, the (%) percent sign, the (c/o) "in care of" sign, the (&) ampersand, the (@) "at" sign, and the writing of fractions, 1/2 or H. Numerals themselves, however, are much less distinguishable with any given system.

As a consequence of this greater consistency in writing systems, and the lesser influence of other numerals or letters or characters with which the numeral may be associated, it might be expected that there are fewer variations in the products by different writers. Indeed, one would expect that some numerals by design (e.g., the "0" and the "1") allow for little to be done as personal modifications. In a study of the numerals executed by approximately 110 writers, Giles (1996) found that the numerals "1" and "6" afforded the fewest number (three) of classifiable variations in design, and the "2" the greatest (eight). In fact, the "0" afforded as many variations in design (five) as the "8" and "9." The numerals "3," "4," "5," and "7" varied in (six) classifiable fashions. Among other things respecting the frequency of occurrence of some forms, Giles comments that the presence or absence of a crossbar to the numeral "7" divided her sample in half. Furthermore, she reported that this numeral and the numeral "1" were the most consistent in design among the writers of her sample.

While Giles' (1996) study records three to eight variations in design for each numeral, there are numerous subclassifications in most classified variations that are not reported. For example, the cross stroke to the "7" is a single category among six for this numeral, although it was apparently present in 50% of her sample. Cross strokes, however, may vary in length, position on the staff, and in angle of intersection.

For some writers, consistency in shape and design doesn't always prove to be the case. In normal written communications for these people, numerals are infrequent inclusions and for this reason are less practiced habits. Accordingly consistency in their execution can be poorer than that of textual material from the same individual. In her study, Giles (1996) found that significant numbers of persons (as many as 48%) employed two or more forms for any given numeral.

At the same time there are numerous occupations, including architects, engineers, and draftsmen, that are taught to write numerals in a prescribed fashion. Then too, there are lines of work that generate documents bearing numerals, symbols, or combinations of the two to express monetary amounts, dates, times, or prices, that become targets of dispute in civil and criminal litigation. These include accounting records, inventories, stock records, bank deposit slips, drawings, records of time, records of distance, logs, and even betting and gambling records. In many of these cases, by virtue of the nature of employment, the writer of the records may be sufficiently practiced to display much consistency in his or her writing of numerals.

Consequently, the role of natural variations in the study of numerals will vary with the writer's personal background and experience.

These circumstances prompted Ansell and Strach (1975) to study the classification of numerals as a first step in the future classification of block lettering (capitals) and ultimately cursive writings. In a report of their study of 1,080 (British) subjects, they have provided frequency of occurrence data (in percentages) of four to eight distinct variations in structure and/or design for each of the numerals "0" to "9." This differs only slightly from the aforementioned results obtained by Giles (1996).

In their study, Horan and Horan (1984) examined the numerals of 675 (American) subjects, using the Ansell and Strach (1975) system of classification and obtained corresponding results. As these authors point out, however, in the categories of variations in structure and design for each numeral, one category represented a clear majority of the subjects in each case. As a classification system, this circumstance tends to limit its usefulness in the discrimination process. It also furnishes a caution to the evaluation of similarities in numerals in the approach to their identification.

Other studies have shown (cited below) that the writing of monetary amounts on checks has been usefully classified to narrow populations of writers that may be potentially authors of questioned writings, usually on checks. Although these studies are few in number, and their use by examiners is not broad, they still constitute evidence in support of the argument that there is some empirical data available that can be applied to handwriting cases under certain circumstances.

Because of the wide diversity in the situations in which numerals and other characters may play a part, in addition to the 21 discriminating elements of writing, generally, the study of numerals and other characters, frequently, must consider many matters: the manners of ornamentation, the manners of simplification, the manners of utilizing the virgule or slash "/," the caret "^," the octothorpe "#," the plus sign "+," the minus sign "–," the equals sign "=," the percentage sign "%," the "in care of" sign "c/o," the methods of space filling (with straight lines or undulating lines), the alignment of digits in amounts or quantities, the writing of fractions, the underscoring of digits in some sets of numerals, the manners of writing monetary amounts with dollars "$," pounds "£," cents "¢,"the manner of writing ciphers "0" in pairs or triplets, and the manner in forming the "@" symbol.

Alford (1965) provided a classic example of a case in which the discrimination between the numerals of a small population of writers is possible while applying the Bayes Theorem and the likelihood ratio to handwriting examination. In this case, other circumstances narrowed the population of possible writers to four persons whose habits in executing the numerals "0" to "9" were sufficiently distinctive from each other to permit proper conclusions of authorship to be drawn.

As others have expressed, numerals, and this wide assortment of other characters, are matters that are given less consideration in the disguise or distortion of one's writing, or in the simulation of another's, when circumstances call for their inclusion in the questioned document. Their usefulness in writing studies and examinations, therefore, should not be overlooked or underestimated.

Although disguise in the execution of questioned numerals is less frequently encountered, Kelly (1998) drew attention to the fact that disguise in the execution of numerals may be attempted in the preparation of standards or request writings, for use in comparisons with questioned writings consisting largely of numbers. In Kelly's study of the methods of disguise employed by 200 subjects in the writing of numerals, she identified five techniques and reported their frequency:

1. Use of an alternate form for the numerals “2,” “4,” “7,” “8,” and “9” (45% to 62% depending on the numeral)
2. Increase in the size of the numerals (20%)
3. Adoption of a more formal version of the numeral (15%)
4. Change in slant, but not well maintained (10%)
5. Change in pen direction in the structure of the numeral (5%)

Srihari et al. (2003), using an extensive automated database sample of 3,000 images of numerals extracted from handwriting samples, found that some numerals are more distinctive or provide a higher degree of discrimination than others. This finding is not surprising in that some numerals are more complex. For example, the handwritten execution of the numeral “5” is more complex and requires the writing of more strokes versus the execution of the numeral “1.” Accordingly, the numeral “5” also offers more opportunity for variation from the copybook model and allows for the possibility of increased idiosyncratic design. Incidentally, Srihari et al. found that identification performance for the numeral “5” had the highest number while the numeral “1” had the lowest performance. However, the study found that analysis of single numerals did not perform well for verification or identification and recommended the analysis of multiple numerals.

In a similar study, Zhang et al. (2003) reported that alphabetic characters are more individualizing than numerals. The study was based on 1,000 handwriting samples from a US population. Using computational features (e.g., pixel density) as well as components from the 21 elements, Leedham and Chachra (2003) also reported that numerals had discriminatory value.

Numerals are the means of recording telephone numbers, illicit drug deals, bets or wagers, and the monetary amounts of debts, checks, and other transactions. In such cases, the quantity of questioned writing is often limited, the size of the document is often small, and the records on a given document may be the product of two or more persons. Thus, the examination of numerals and special characters warrants considerable care (Figure 7.2a and b).

7.2.2 Dingbats and Iconic Symbols

Within the general category of dingbats or iconic symbols there are *check marks* and *cross marks*. These are two of the other manually-executed characters that often enough become matters of dispute, and consequently, are subject to examination and study by handwriting examiners. Unlike numerals and other characters that are usually executed in conjunction with textual material of some sort, check marks and cross marks are seldom a minor part of a larger problem of writing identification. More often they are the principal issue in dispute and their identification, without the help of other material, is sought to establish the validity of a document or documents. They frequently occur with typewritten or printed text and may be the only handwritten element on the document.

Cross marks are the usual essence of disputes respecting ballots in election processes. They are usually one or two stroke structures situated with their components running roughly vertically and horizontally, or with two feet on the baseline and their components running diagonally. In both cases, the intention, if not the tendency, is for the strokes to intersect one another approximately in the center. The precision with which the intersections are made in the middle of the strokes can be a matter that varies between individuals, and serves to

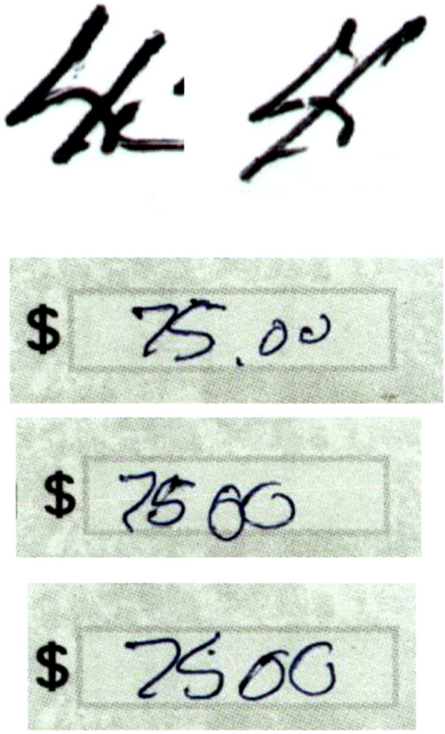

(a)

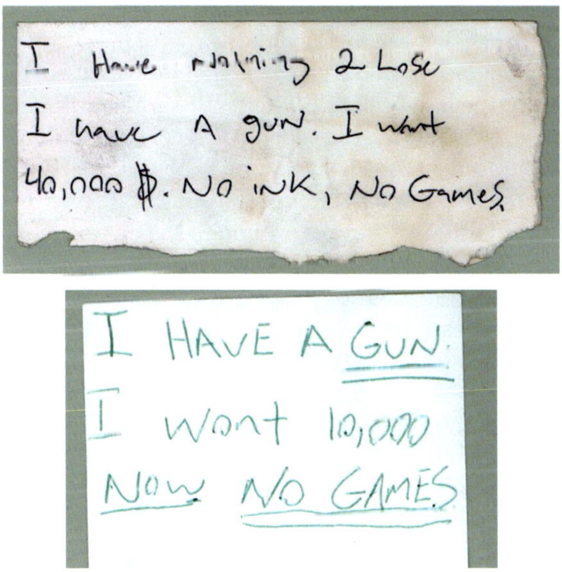

(b)

Figure 7.2 (a) Numerical formations of the number four by same writer and three variations of $75.00 by one writer and (b) two robbery notes depicting similarities in the number 0 formation.

distinguish the products of some writers from each other. The orientation of the strokes to the baseline, be it vertical or diagonal or some position in between, may also be peculiar to the individual and of discriminatory value.

The strokes of cross marks seldom meet at right angles to one another, and the angle itself may exhibit some consistency worth consideration. Furthermore, while the ideal structure is for the strokes to intersect in their middles, this is often not the case, and the pattern of balance, if there is one, may be of some significance. The quality of the lines, of course, can indicate the fluency with which the character was executed. Alternatively, a slow, drawn, deliberate production may say something about the act of writing or the writer.

It is generally presumed that cross marks are executed as two separate downstrokes, although on infrequent occasions when the character is small it has been noted that hastily executed cross marks may exhibit a pen drag from the bottom of the first stroke to the top of the second. Certainly, this is the structure prescribed by copybook, as a survey by Doud (1985) disclosed.

It is reasonable to assume that forgers of cross marks seldom or never work from masters. If and when known standards are available for comparison the questioned cross mark(s) can exhibit differences in skill or fluency, differences in movement or angles of intersection and differences in pen position.

Legitimate cross marks are, frequently, the extent of the writing ability of illiterates and bedridden individuals. The amount of evidence that they can provide will be limited in any case and the task of identification or elimination is especially difficult. As the identification process is based on the study and comparison of habits, illiterates and bedridden individuals are rarely sufficiently practiced in the execution of cross marks to have developed consistent habits in their production.

Check marks must be studied in a fashion similar to cross marks. The usual structure is comprised of two strokes meeting at an acute angle much like a printed "V," the first stroke of which is shorter than the second. The axis of the angle normally is vertical or slanting slightly to the right.

The conventional style of check mark varies with the writer in several respects: the size generally, the relative lengths or balance of the strokes, the slant of the axis of the angle, the placement of the mark with respect to the line or item of the text to which it refers, and the curvature or straightness of the strokes, particularly, the second. It has also been observed that some sinistrals (left-handed writers) reverse the orientation of the check mark such that the longer and final stroke extends off to the left. These aspects of the mark can serve to distinguish reasonably well between the products of different writers, although the degree to which a finding must be qualified depends on the case circumstances.

The inversion of the check mark "^," called the *caret*, is a symbol employed regularly as a direction along the baseline to indicate the location for the insertion of additional text. It should not be overlooked when the examination of the handwriting of the material to be inserted is being conducted. Much like the check mark, an insertion mark can possess its own style of individualization. While the conventional design of the check mark "u" is that which comes readily to mind when the subject is mentioned, there are numerous other methods of checking off articles in a list of items. The dash or hyphen ""– or -"" may be used. The period may be used. A short inclined line or diagonal may be employed, or even an arc or circle. Other symbols sometimes appear in questioned documents not always as check marks, but of some importance to the resolution of the matter in dispute. Arrows, brackets, and some styles of parentheses are but a few. These kinds of marks may afford fewer attributes to study and consider, but the approach in doing so remains the same. Indeed, one can move from these kinds of iconic marks to music symbols, mathematical symbols, and the like. A case study on the analysis of handwritten music symbols was reported by Jarvis (2010) who applied handwriting identification principles to determine authorship of music calligraphy on manuscripts.

What must be scrutinized carefully is the consistency between the standards and the questioned marks. If consistency does exist the weight of the evidence of common authorship may still be dubious. If consistency is blatantly absent a conclusion of nonidentity or elimination may be more demonstrable. In many cases, it will be found that the task of the examination is not unlike that of synchronous and asynchronous writings. The key lies in the consistency of the executions. The circumstances of the matter under investigation frequently limits the population of possible or potential writers to be considered, and this may have a bearing on the merit in any conclusion reached.

7.3 EXAMINING WRITING OF FOREIGN AND UNUSUAL SCRIPTS

In addressing the examination of handwriting in foreign scripts, it presupposes that the examiner is not skilled in any manner of writing other than one using the English (i.e., Roman or Latin) alphabet and Arabic (Brahmin) numerals. Other languages that use the Roman alphabet include French, Dutch, Belgian, Danish, Swedish, Norwegian, Spanish, Italian, German, Swiss, and others. This gives rise to another closely related question as to how important it is for the examiner to know the language in order to properly conduct an examination of handwriting in that language.

The task of conducting examinations of handwriting in other alphabets or methods of communication and the success achieved in doing so is well reported. There are many examples of studies and examinations that have been made in a wide variety of subjects including gang writing and graffiti (Davis 2008; Tong et al. 2011; Klivans 2013), shorthand (Brown 1967; Bradley 1988), handwritten musical calligraphy (Calvert 1980; Jarvis 2010), historical manuscripts (Huber 1960; Kroon-van der Kooij 1985; Srihari 2013), signatures on works of art (Mathyer 1974; Goetschel 1989; Hanna 1992; Harralson et al. 2012), and other unusual scripts (Huber 1955; Ellen 1999) (Figures 7.3a–c, through 7.5). Miller (1995) reported on the successful identification of the artist/originator of human figure drawings, following standard writing examination techniques (Figure 7.6). There are several published studies on the analysis and identification of foreign language handwritten scripts covered in Chapter 8.

The case records of most document examiners of reasonable experience will encompass matters whose study and investigation lay outside the scope of orthodox handwriting or document examination. Undoubtedly, if the study was reasonably successful, the matter is sometimes reported, if only to describe the uniqueness of the case and to credit the examiner with some merit in the approach to the examination.

Jacquin Keller (1985) and Hensel et al. (1973) used analytical approaches to the study of writings in foreign alphabets, principally Arabic, that were entirely independent of literacy or understanding of the language or the writing system. Hansel et al. reported that "forgery can be detected, handwriting identified, and typewriting compared by an intelligent illiterate who uses the criminalistics techniques commonly employed with toolmarks, firearms, and footmarks" (p. 143).

Hanna (1989), in describing her approach to the examination of Chinese characters, maintains that if the principles of identification and the appropriate preparatory steps are taken, an unfamiliar script may be intelligently studied. She draws a valid analogy to the examination of writings in the English language, produced during certain illnesses, under the

(a)

(b)

(c)

Figure 7.3 (a–c) Examples of graffiti.

Figure 7.4 Handwritten music calligraphy.

influence of certain medications, comprised of chemical or physical formulas, or mathematical equations etc. (e.g., scholastic examination papers) not within the normal purview of the document examiner.

Other studies of a more physical nature may also become a part of an examiner's repertoire, which are comparable to unusual writings in that the subject material is widely diversified and there are no prescribed methods of approach to the study. Is there a common approach to be taken in such cases that will ensure the legitimacy of the results? Epstein (1987) offers his approach to the examination of the Josef Mengele handwritings as a guide to any examination of foreign handwriting: "Some familiarity with the language … is necessary. It would be preferable to be able to read and write the language, thereby, being familiar with the basics of … alphabet, accentuation, diacritical marks, punctuation, word order, syllabication, capitalization, compounding, and orthography. This is, of course, the ideal, and we know that the ideal seldom occurs" (p. 109).Epstein recommends researching the foreign language through books, language instruction, and obtaining samples of the foreign handwriting under question.

As described in an earlier chapter, the examination of any kind of physical evidence should be approached as a process having three distinct stages: analysis, comparison, and evaluation. The analytical stage should address the elements of the material under examination that are subject to variation or change with each member of the population to which it belongs. These will be its discriminating elements. If this is not known at the outset, it will be necessary to collect sufficient samples of the same kind of material from different sources to clearly establish what it is that may vary from source to source, and to what extent. Ideally, this will consist of writing samples in the same language and alphabet as the questioned material and preferably containing the same letter or character combinations. The assistance of a translator may be necessary to ensure that writing characters are being properly identified, as some alphabets such as Cyrillic employ characters so similar to one another that only an understanding of the language can reliably distinguish between them (Muehlberger 1984). Furthermore, knowledge and understanding of the method of production of the subject material (e.g., the number of independent strokes

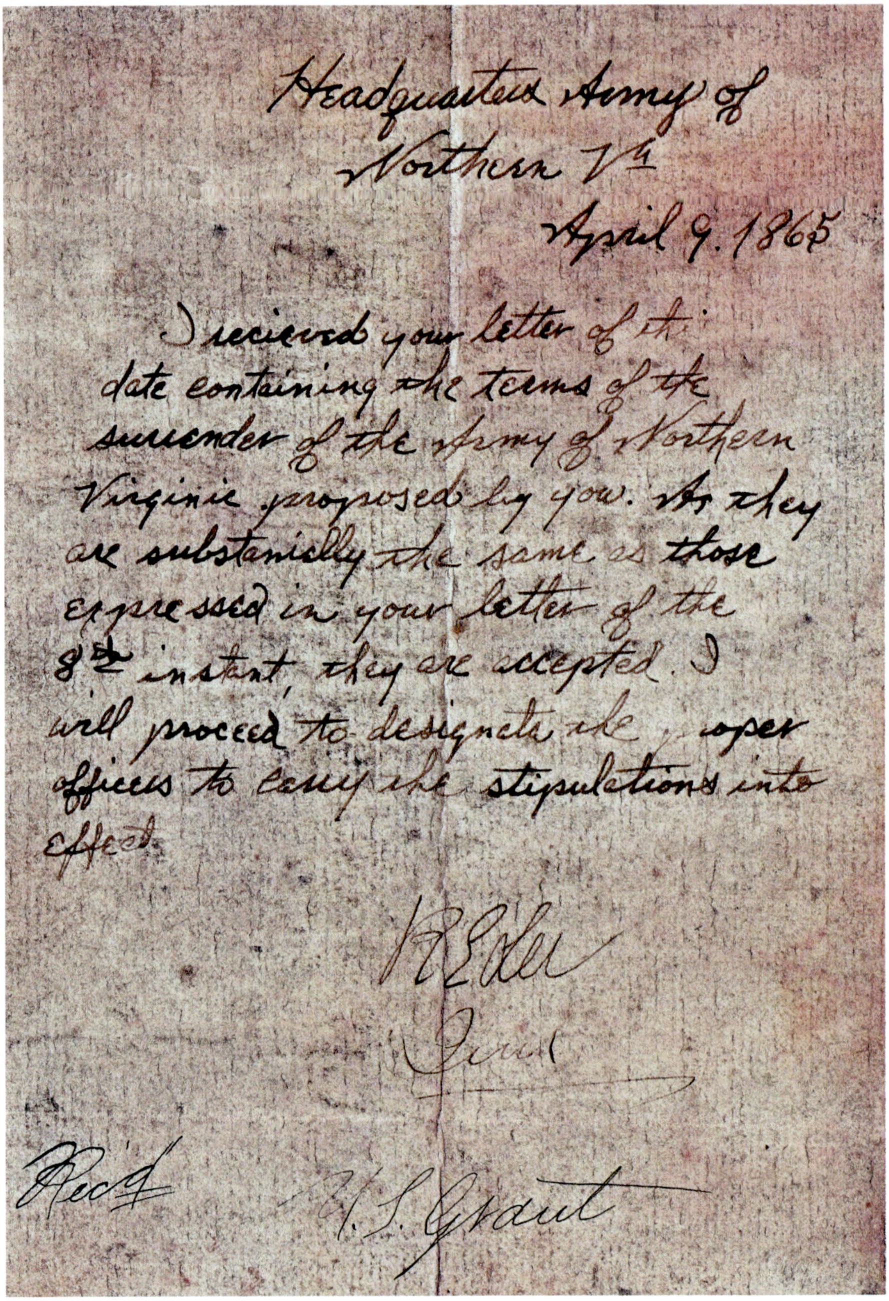

Headquarters Army of
Northern Va
April 9. 1865

I recieved your letter of this date containing the terms of the surrender of the Army of Northern Virginia proposed by you. As they are substanially the same as those expressed in your letter of the 8th instant, they are accepted. I will proceed to designate the proper officers to carry the stipulations into effect.

R E Lee
Genl

Rec'd
U. S. Grant

Figure 7.5 Example of a forged historical document. Despite the fact that the copybook style of writing is not accurate for the time period, the paper was artificially "aged" and has a watermark indicating it was manufactured in the 1980s.

Known
(a)

Questioned
(b)

Figure 7.6 Drawing (b) was found in a trash can in an elementary school classroom. Drawing (a) was identified as the same "artist" from having all the students in class draw a picture of their family.

and the order in which they are or should be executed) leads the examiner in the direction that makes the search for usable evidence more efficient. Hanna (1989) has illustrated the process commendably with respect to Chinese writing.

When the analyses of both the known and questioned materials is complete they have, thereby, each been reduced to an aggregate of elements that vary from source to source. The combination of these elements may serve to distinguish one member or group of members of the population from another, and the second stage of comparison may be initiated. If the analysis has revealed and isolated the variables of the matter, their comparison should not be overly complex. To ensure, however, that comparisons are being made between like elements it is wise to engage the services of someone competent to speak and write the language.

The third stage of the mechanism, evaluation of the significance of similarities or differences perceived through comparison, is the part of the process that is not normally a component of the examiner's experience. It is the most subjective aspect of the process that, in the majority of cases, is dependent upon the examiner's experience in other languages and alphabets, or in other types of examination. It is also the most important, for, what analysis has identified and comparison has disclosed only proper evaluation can render material. Exposure to large numbers of writings, or other samples of the kind that is the subject of the current study, may provide a crash course in evaluation, if it is used judiciously.

In a given case, it may be that the discriminating elements, that is, the varying elements, that the analysis has divulged are not fully independent of one another, but share with other variables some common heritage, as class or system characteristics would do. It may also be that comparison has disclosed similarity between these elements in the known and unknown materials under study. In such circumstances, because of their common heritage, the evaluation of such elements must be appropriately modified. The assistance of someone knowledgeable in the conditions or circumstances that might be common to groups of this foreign population or circumstances is frequently necessary.

The handwriting examiner is typically cognizant of the limitations of his or her experience and knowledge insofar as the particular material undergoing study. It is recommended that the report reveal that appropriate assistance was obtained before conclusions were drawn. Depending on the subject matter and the experience with which the examiner has with a specialty subject, the examiner should err on the side of conservatism.

The accumulation of information from various sources on various items responsible for or related to methods of communication, and its consolidation in a manner facilitating the examination of questioned documents is a process common to many scientific and quasi-scientific practices. The identification of inks, typewriters, printing devices, papers, and other products is dependent upon the assembly of knowledge from different manufacturers as to the characteristics and behavior of their products and the respects in which various products and their behavior are similar or different.

Similarly, the identification of writings in foreign languages using different alphabets is achieved by the assembly of information from various sources familiar with the alphabet and the language. The laws and principles discovered by research are utilized by other scientists in further studies of the same subject without having to repeat the original research, personally, to justify such use.

The function of the forensic scientist (in this case the forensic document examiner) lies in his or her use of the information obtained. That information must be evaluated in terms of its reliability and its significance for identification purposes, or its support of other conclusions that may be drawn from it. Once this process is understood, some progress may be made in identifying matters not within an examiner's normal purview. As reported earlier, problems respecting a foreign script or unusual writing system may be addressed with a measure of success. Typewritings may be identified with typewriters by persons never employed in typewriter factories. Printing methods may be distinguished from each other by persons never engaged as printers. Counterfeit currency may be recognized reliably as such by persons who never made a dollar.

7.4 ANONYMOUS WRITING

Anonymity in a writing is an author's device employed to prevent the association of the writer with the document, or the comments expressed on it. It may involve some method of disguise, some method of simulation, the inclusion of some method of deception or misdirection, or simply the omission of any conventional method of recognition of its source. Elsewhere, disguise is discussed in the section captioned Disclosers of Disguise and with simulation in the section captioned Flags of Forgery. Methods of deception or misdirection may go well beyond the realms of disguise and simulation. The omission of conventional methods of recognition of its source, usually limited to the omission of a signature or the adoption of a fraudulent or ambiguous identity, may involve a change in traditional or practiced methods of communication. A typical example would be a change from cursive writing to typewriting and delivery in some unorthodox fashion.

Invariably, these are attributes of anonymous letters, but they may also be aspects of the preparation or issue of fraudulent checks, hold-up or bank robbery notes, hotel registrations, and a multitude of other documents that may have the potential to identify and/or incriminate an individual in some manner. Anonymous letters as a group can usually be classified, according to their purpose. Casey-Owens (1984) and Harrison (1958a) both suggest seven categories, although their breakdowns into different categories are not quite the same. Casey lists them as threatening, obscene, extortion, nuisance, stool pigeon, racial, and guilty conscience. Harrison, on the other hand, lists them as threatening, indecent (obscene), blackmailing (extortion), practical jokes (nuisance), disparagement and/or recommendation (racial or stool pigeon), revenge, and spitefulness. Although the anonymous letter may be intended to serve one of seven or more different purposes, the general techniques for concealing the identity of the source remain the same: disguise, simulation, deception, or omission of identifiers.

In these cases, the examination and study of the handwriting, per se, does not necessarily change from that of other cases. What does change are the circumstances prevailing, and these may have a bearing on the examination.

1. Cursively-written anonymous letters, of a kind other than nuisance, guilty conscience, revenge, or spitefulness, tend to be reasonably lengthy productions. Hand-printed communications and paste-ups tend to be shorter, principally because their production is more labor intensive. For the same reason, typewritten letters may be shorter, unless typing is not strange to the typist. Frequently, limited hand printing is added to commercially printed greeting cards bearing some comment or verse that can be modified to suit the communication's objectives that are usually obscene or offensive.

   Longer handwritten letters, wherein disguise of one's writing or the simulation of another's has been attempted, may exhibit relapses to the author's normal or natural writing habits for short intervals, after which the disguise is resumed. Unfamiliar writing practices are difficult for most persons to maintain.

   Furthermore, in anonymous letters a page or more in length, it is frequently observed that as the writer approaches the end of his or her discourse, the disguise employed is not as assiduously pursued and more normal or natural writing ensues. Consequently, this is the segment of the document that should receive the examiner's particular attention.
2. Anonymous letters are usually intended to generate some kind of response on the part of the recipient that the sender often delights in observing. If the response is pleasurable to the sender, or if there is no indication of the letter having been received or of having elicited any response, the sender is frequently encouraged to issue another or a series of additional communications.

   The greater the number of anonymous letters issued, the greater the potential for collecting evidence indicating or identifying the source.

It is usually the case that the method of disguise employed in a first anonymous letter will not be consistently followed in subsequent letters. What was changed and how it was changed will escape the writer's recollection. This may benefit the writing examination in two respects. First, it is an indication of the elements of the writing that are not to be trusted as evidence of normal writing habits, and second, it provides an opportunity for normal writing habits to occur in subsequent letters that may have been concealed by disguise in earlier products.

3. Envelopes in which letters are sent may be as useful in writing examinations as the letters themselves.

   Writers develop habits in the manner in which they address an envelope, which evidence can seldom be found in the documents it contains. Occasionally, instances are encountered in which the letters and the envelopes are the products of different writers, particularly in those cases in which the assistance of a second party is obtained to write the letter, as a technique of deception.
4. Anonymous letters containing obscenities and profanities are as often the products of female writers as male writers.
5. Notwithstanding the lack of consistency within a single anonymous letter that one usually finds in disguised writing, there may be an abundance of consistency between letters executed on separate occasions.

   Although the particular effects of the method(s) selected for altering one's writing may be difficult for an individual to maintain consistently without practice, there is likely to be some consistency in the selection of the method(s) employed on repeated occasions. Parker (1989) reported on the similarities to questioned disguised writings found in court-ordered request writings, when the subject was required to disguise his or her executions. There are, obviously, limits to an individual's knowledge of and familiarity with the techniques that might affect an appropriate change.
6. Anonymous letters may contain indications of the nationality, age, education, gender, handedness, or occupation of the author.

   Assessment of these attributes is sometimes based on the study of sentence structure, grammar, idioms, spelling, division of words, and other such aspects of the text. Osborn (1929) suggested 53 of them in what he called "The Analysis of Language as a Means of Identification" (p. 397). There is no doubt that similarities and dissimilarities in these aspects of a text are difficult for an examiner to ignore, but the danger in infringing on the domain of the linguistic analyst without adequate qualification should not be disregarded. With respect to gender and handedness, a database analysis of a limited letter set was carried out by Taroni et al. (2014) to determine gender and handedness on the data set. The researchers applied a Bayesian approach for making inferences about gender and handedness that may be useful in anonymous letter cases, particularly in narrowing the population of possible writers.
7. A recipient of an anonymous letter (perhaps one of several) may be the author of the letter or instigator of the act.

   From the viewpoint of the writing examination, all recipients of anonymous letters should be included in the circle of potential authors.

As was intimated earlier, there are numerous anonymously written documents other than letters, or various types of personal communications. Hold-up or bank robbery notes are a classic example. Because of the limited written material that they contain, a first step in the course of investigation is usually an attempt to associate the writing with that of other similar documents appearing in other crimes or cases. The accumulation of written material improves the potential for the identification of the author.

The quest for anonymity in letter writing is invariably coupled with a sense of compulsion to repeat the act. The purpose of the anonymous communication will usually indicate to an investigator whether the recipient will be the same or different in a subsequent letter, and whether the number of communications is likely to be large or small.

Books on document examination frequently describe the techniques that might be employed in associating documents of this kind with others, or in relating them to particular sources. These techniques range from watermarks to paper cutters, to paper types, to inks, to commercially printed inscriptions, to paper stains, to indentations in the paper surface. Other documents that share similar properties may assist significantly in identifying the sources of them. Notwithstanding the wide range of aspects of a questioned document that may contribute to its identification or the determination of its origin, the process of study and examination of the writing or hand lettering thereon remains essentially the same.

7.5 THE CLASSIFICATION OF HANDWRITING

Historically, Ames (1900) and Osborn (1929) classified handwriting according to the involvement of the fingers, hand, and arm in the action of writing, usually one of four categories: finger movement, wrist movement, forearm movement, and whole arm movement. Neither of these authors provided a system for discriminating between the products according to the different movements. Indeed, the whole arm movement is an action that is almost exclusive to blackboard writing, or to some of today's graffiti writing, the circumstances of which will alone suffice to distinguish the movement. With the exception perhaps of graffiti or writing and painting on walls, the whole arm movement is seldom a matter to be considered in the process of writing identification.

Blackburn and Caddell (1909) claimed that all writing could be placed in 1 of 10 classes or categories. The system included the making of some measurements that may have been more practical insofar as the writing of their time than it is for current writings. Lee and Abbey (1922) devised a system of classification utilizing the criminal record forms of their days. It endeavored to tabulate eight factors of handwriting, each of which had as many as three subdivisions. As a system, it has been criticized as being too imprecise, providing merely a generalized categorical system for large numbers of writing samples.

Quirke (1930) developed what he referred to as his "Practical Scheme of Handwriting Analysis" in which he described 16 general qualities or features of writing followed by some 100 or more examples of each lowercase letter of the alphabet, then 13 points for attention in examining uppercase letters, 13 points for attention in examining numerals, 24 points for guidance respecting block letters, and 3 points respecting Roman numerals. There is some correlation between Quirke's 16 general features of handwriting and the 21 discriminating elements of writing (Chapter 6).

The law enforcement field has a distinctly different objective in mind with respect to handwriting classification systems. Their application has been, and still is, to facilitate the identification of the writers of fraudulent checks, hold-up or bank robbery notes, and anonymous and/or threatening letters, as an assistance to investigators. The observation had been made in the early 1940s that paper hangers, that is, check forgers, were frequently quite consistent and distinctive in their manners of writing bad checks.

The first published attempt in North America to classify elements of writing for this purpose was made by Livingston (1949) for the benefit of the Milwaukee Police Department beginning in 1944. The system grouped and filed the manners in which monetary amounts of the check were inscribed. Alignment and slant were also recorded. Other breakdowns were created in aspects such as writing skill, and material was classified simply as poor, medium, or good. The use of check writers and typewriters were given separate categories, as were names used.

By 1952, other law enforcement agencies had established "fraudulent check files" that endeavored to classify material according to the following:

- Manner of writing sums
- Method of production: written, lettered, or typewritten
- Names used
- Selected individual handwriting characteristics
- Idiosyncrasies, for example, the use of "only," "and," and "&," etc.
- Other peculiarities in production or passing of the checks

Smith (1954), a pupil of Robert Saudek in London, published a procedure for the classification of handwriting based on variations in six aspects of writing: pressure, form, speed, spacing, size, and slant that were broken into 59 subclassifications. The claim was made that the categories of the classification were measurable discriminations. For example: *spacing* is subdivided into *perfect*, *good*, and 12 divisions (4 each) of *fair*, *poor*, and *bad*. The objective of the classification process is not clear, but may be simply a method of organizing the information sought and accumulated in the course of a handwriting examination. It was, of course, one of the earliest attempts at classification since the writings of Quirke in 1930.

In a subsequent paper, Smith (1964) elaborates on the classification system by adding seven more aspects of writing to the previous six as further divisions. They are loops, "t" bars, capital "I," word units, mistakes, signature position, and special peculiarities, each of which is broken down into 8 to 20 subdivisions. From this it is clear, that what is offered is not a system of classification for the filing of writing samples, but rather, a delineation of the features of a writing that might be sought and studied in the course of a routine examination.

In 1955, Livingston put his classifications on McBee punch cards to facilitate searching and sorting, and in 1959, he published an illustrated article entitled *A Handwriting and Pen Printing Classification System for Identifying Law Violators*. By 1962, Livingston's system had expanded to include other breakdowns and the fraudulent check files of other agencies were exploring new ideas. Wrenshall and Rankin (1965) noted that classification had taken two forms:

1. Classification of inherent characteristics of handwriting, for example, skill, letter forms, etc.
2. Classification of variations in the arrangement of handwriting on a document, particularly the manner of completing a check form, sometimes referred to as *the completion method*.

The first of these two was the more desirable, but the second had proven more popular and practical, if only because it was less subjective and provided greater consistency between classifiers. Problems developed, however, when the completion method, which offered few subclassifications, produced unsearchable large collections of material in the more common categories. Further, criminals were found to change their method of completing a forged check from time to time, which frustrated the search for them from their products.

Interestingly enough, Wrenshall and Rankin in 1965 foresaw the use of the computer in handwriting classification and search at a time when information retrieval was, apparently, not a primary pursuit of computer programmers. Research into computer retrieval, however, had to be prefaced by research into the features of handwriting that might be classified for search purposes.

Schroeder (1971) described his procedure which tried to include some writing aspects into a system devoted largely to the completion method. It is not unlike the system R. Mally devised in Switzerland in the 1960s. Schroeder (1974), too, apparently saw the value of the computer in classification, but when his system was revised, it had reverted to the use of card wheels that had been discarded years before. Rather than employ the burgeoning electronics field to expand the system's potential, classification was considered to be merely an aid to the searcher's memory, which is the most efficient means of connecting new incoming checks with those already on file.

Despite the lack of optimism for handwriting classification expressed in the writings of Baxter (1973), there have been many changes in the approach to the subject. Initial studies suggested that all capital letters of the alphabet might be placed in 1 of 12 groups, which allowed for a degree of commonality between letters such as "F," "T," "M," "N," and others. Then the observation was made that some letters, for example, "Z" and "X," seldom appeared on checks while others were infrequent enough to question their value as classification categories within the system. The Metropolitan Police Lab in London in the late 1970s designed a simple system around the word *pounds* that invariably appeared on British checks. The number of subclassifications were too few, however, and the numbers of writers falling into some categories became unmanageable for manual searching.

A system unrelated to checks and their completion method but directed at the inherent writing characteristics was developed at the Zurich Kantonpolizei Laboratory, and described formally in a report by Angst and Erismann (1972). It employed a large number of writing features, selected from a prescribed one paragraph sample of writing, that were classified by a document examiner. The results of classification were entered into a computer to become the databank against which unknown writings could be checked in a search for correspondence. A simple "yes" or "not present" approach was taken in the system procedure to objectively classify and search for writings.

Nine aspects of writing were recorded in the databank, including:

1. Writing skill
2. Line quality
3. Slope
4. Size
5. Width (lateral expansion?)
6. Angularity
7. Type and degree of connection
8. Position of diacritics
9. Construction of cursive and block letters

Noticeably, these nine handwriting characteristics constitute almost half of the 21 single discriminating elements (two of which are combinations of two elements) of writing that are described in Chapter 6 and form the basis of the writing identification process.

Harvey and Mitchell (1973) describe a one-time classification sort and search system designed to scan samples from 1,046 writers to assist investigators in their quest for a particular murder suspect. The process involved three features related to the completion method of fraudulent check files and three additional features that would qualify as inherent writing characteristics that were present in a check involved in the commission of the crime. The combination was sufficient to permit a positive identification to be made. The authors of the paper spent time reviewing the use of the X^2 statistical test to assess the significance of two or more of these features occurring together. As it happened, and almost contradictory to their findings, the X^2 values obtained were too high to permit the acceptance of a null hypothesis: that two of the apparently unrelated features in the completion of the questioned check (the use of = between the numbers of pounds, shillings, and pence, and the indentation of the writing on the amount line), were in fact independent of one another. The suggestion is made that a larger databank may have been helpful.

Ansel and Strach (1975) attempted to classify the methods of 993 individuals in writing the numerals "0" to "9" in an exploratory study that would qualify as related to inherent writing characteristics. Their method provided four to eight subclasses for each numeral, but soon revealed that the "1" had little or no discriminatory value, the "2," "3," and "7" had only limited value, and the "0," "6," "8," and "9" provided the best division of samples. As it happened, using the X^2 test, as Harvey and Mitchell had done, the classification of "0" and "8" could not be established as independent of one another.

With a similar objective in mind, Allan et al. (1978), in a study of extended writing from 52 subjects, attempted to use measurements to obtain data that might be computerized to discriminate between the subjects and determine the consistency of the data in specimens taken a year later and in specimens that were disguised. Eight measurements were taken, including:

1. Number of lines taken to write a given passage
2. Margin widths
3. Paragraph indentions
4. Length of the last 10 spaces
5. Length of the last 11 words and spaces
6. Length of the first 10 spaces
7. Length of the first 11 words and spaces
8. Ratio of relative heights of letters with ascenders

The rationale for selecting these particular measurements, and the application of study results to actual case work, is not explained or suggested. While margin widths, paragraph indentions, and relative heights may be matters to be considered in case work, items 4 to 7 are much less likely to prove useful in the examination of other texts, and causes a reader to wonder about the point and purpose of their inclusion.

A second study by Allan and Pearson (1978) attempts to subjectively classify the uppercase "D" in the specimens obtained and to add this information to that provided by the previously taken eight measurements. The study results are difficult to comprehend and the task is not made easier by use of the terms *crime specimens* (to refer to what others would call questioned writings), *questioned specimens* (to refer to what others would call known writings of a particular writer, e.g., K1), and *file specimens* (to refer to what others would call known writings of 51 other writers, e.g., K2 to K52). These authors were likely influenced by Kind et al. (1979) who advocated the use of such terms in an attempt to consolidate the proliferation of terms employed in forensic science literature.

Ansell (1979) reviewed a number of the classification programs developed to that point, including unpublished work that he conducted with H. Prichard at the Metropolitan Police Forensic Science Laboratory in London. Eighteen parameters were used to classify samples of block lettering from 134 subjects that were successful in discriminating between all but three pairs of subjects. The 18 parameters are summarized as concerning:

- Design and shape of the "A"
- Commencement of the "A," "B," "D," and other letters
- Termination of the "G"
- Number of strokes in the construction of the "K"
- Centers of the "M" and "W" (long or short)
- Termination of the "U"

A radically different approach to handwriting identification was taken by the Bundeskriminalamt at Wiesbaden employing computerized image processing and pattern recognition. As described in Klement's (1983) report the more objective process of feature extraction by the computer supplants the more subjective study and classification of writing features by human examiners, with apparent success.

The research program, which acquired the title FISH (forensic information system of handwriting) captivated the interest of a group of scientists at the German BKA (Bundeskriminalamt) Laboratory for more than 10 years and after an investment of more than 12 million dollars, produced many publications including Hecker and Eisermann (1986) and Bross et al. (1987).

The German endeavor proved successful in creating a system for objective classification and measurement. Its setbacks included the cost of the equipment involved and the technical competence required to run the system. The duration of the necessary 6 months of training seems to be greater than that of the computer programs pursued in the United Kingdom and elsewhere. The Dutch government and the United States Secret Service have each acquired operational versions of the FISH system, the Secret Service having the only English version.

The Secret Service has established two databases in the 1990s: one in 1991 for protective intelligence, in relation to the president, vice president and public officials, and a second, authorized in 1995, to assist law enforcement agencies in cases respecting missing and exploited children. As Maguire and Moran (1996) have reported, the system is proving its worth in a manner that continues to grow. Apparently 33 "hits" were scored in the first 6 months of 1996.

Reporting from a police forensic science laboratory, Nicholson (1984) commented on a problem common to many manual systems:

1. The same character may be classified differently by different classifiers or by the same classifier on different occasions.
2. Tolerance must be provided in the system for natural variation from one occasion of writing to the next, the range of which varies with the individual writer.

Nicholson's system concerns itself with block lettering of all characters of the alphabet excluding the "C," "L," "O," and "S," and is based on (1) the number of pen strokes, and (2) the particular pen paths followed in the letters "E," "H," and "N." Variation is accommodated by permitting letters to be classified in each of two sub types, if necessary. Some provision is made for cursive forms and the tendency of some writers to interconnect certain printed letters. Nicholson's project had two stated objectives:

1. Permit linking crimes to one another and to known perpetrators
2. Accumulate quantitative information respecting frequency of occurrence of the features classified.

At the same time, Nicholson hoped to improve on previous systems by reducing the number of misclassifications due to ambiguities and felt that fewer categories for each letter would reduce the misclassification due to natural variation. In this system, letters were classified according to the number of pen strokes in letter construction and their order of execution. In a few cases, classification was made according to pen paths rather than pen lifts as the former was considered to be less variable. A pilot study of 140 subjects was conducted and while high frequency was encountered in some categories for some letters that seemed to reduce their discriminating value, it is reported that computer calculations confirmed that useful discriminating power had been achieved.

In a further study, Nicholson (1987) sought to determine whether pen path habits are less variable than construction habits involving pen lifts. This study was confined to samples of the block letters "B" and "E" taken from a standard passage of text prepared by 100 dextral subjects. The results confirmed the views previously held that pen path habits are less variable than pen lift habits. It was also observed, rather incidentally, that the letter "B" varied with its position within a word. Similar observations have since been made by other investigators respecting a number of other letters.

Hardcastle et al. (1986) pursued the matter of classification of block lettering on checks employing 32 features of each of 2,000 samples. These features included 18 of the letters of the alphabet, 10 numerals, and 4 general features (relative heights, style of date, sex and identity of writer if known). Only the manner of writing the date was carried over from earlier trial schemes as it was found that other completion practices varied or changed over periods of time. The classifications for each feature were coded and filed on a computer under a program that permits the operator to search the data by way of a single feature or any combination of features. The latter facility is reportedly used routinely with reasonable success.

Taylor and Chandler (1987) described a relatively simple classification program created for the Arkansas State Laboratory. It was based on the writing of eight lowercase cursive letters, to which was added categories for race and gender. Although it showed some promise it was limited to 500 files, which was the storage capacity of the home personal computer on which it was run. Of particular interest in the report is the statement that "classification is not the same thing as identification." The former is said to distinguish authors on the basis of handwriting patterns, whereas the latter is concerned with handwriting patterns plus individual characteristics "as well as a host of other features."

It is contended that the handwriting patterns described in this, or in fact employed in any system, and used to classify writings, are simply some of the discriminating elements, occurring in isolation or in combinations that constitute handwriting habits, that is, arrangements, designs and styles of allographs, unorthodox shapes, styles of diacritics, etc. Classification systems generally discriminate between writings on the basis of gross or lucid features, but identification requires the consideration of other more subtle or elusive and individualistic discriminating elements of the writing as well, not in place of, but in addition to the gross features. These more subtle and individualistic features simply do not lend themselves readily to classification.

Hardcastle and Kemmenoe (1990) sought features of cursive writing that would discriminate effectively between writers, and that occur frequently enough in the writing of checks to yield some investigative assistance. They selected 21 features including 6 lowercase letters ("d," "f," "i," "p," "t," and "u"), 2 uppercase letters ("C" and "F" as in "Cash" and "Fifty"), 15 numerals and general features taken from the scheme of classification for block lettering developed by Hardcastle et al. (1986). There were 1,000 samples in the test collection.

In summary, it may be said that classification began as a means of providing investigative leads regarding unknown authors of fraudulent checks by associating the handwriting with that of a known writer living or moving within a given area, or with other checks. The systems endeavored to record and to group in some prescribed fashion all of the fraudulent checks passed or presented within the area. If the system was well designed, the groups were small in size and writers within the group could be quickly and conveniently differentiated.

It worked well as long as the collections were relatively modest, as long as the perpetrators of this type of crime made few changes to their writing, and as long as their activity was confined to limited areas. But collections grew large and unworkable, perpetrators did change their manners of writing, and they became exceedingly transient. Other equipment such as typewriters, check writers, copiers, and printers became involved, and file classifications had to be expanded to accommodate such features appropriately. Other instruments of the criminal have begged to be included, such as anonymous, threatening, crank, obscene and insulting letters, false identification and travel documents, and hold-up notes as reported by Williams (1985) and by Noblett (1991). The last mentioned were used in a study of San Francisco's collection reported by Blake (1995), although the systems of classification for them are not described. In addition, any negotiable document having a monetary value (e.g., postal money orders, cash grain tickets, or poultry tickets) that has been repeatedly falsified has warranted some classification consideration and classification systems have been constantly challenged and taxed.

The advent of the computer and its potential for use in the analysis of handwriting was described at length by Teulings and Thomassen (1979). The particular application of the computer to handwriting recognition insofar as the developments in digital image processing (Kuckuck et al. 1979; Steinke 1981; Klement 1983), in pattern recognition (Klement et al. 1980; Impedovo and Abbattista 1982), in sonar analysis (De Bruyne and Messmer 1980), and in prototype deformation (Naske 1982), has received considerable attention by a number of scientists. Since 1987, the International Graphonomics Society (IGS) has published virtually hundreds of papers and publications related to the study of handwriting by way of computer applications. The objective underlying many of these studies has been the search for a validation process that serves to verify the identity of the individual executing a signature (Watson and Pobgee 1979), from which better methods of handwriting classification may ensue simply as a by-product. The research work carried out by IGS and similar research-based organizations (International Conference on Frontiers in Handwriting Recognition [ICFHR], International Community of Document Analysis and Recognition [ICDAR], and others) has afforded an almost limitless means for recording, classifying, and cataloging handwriting aspects such that subjectivity can be replaced by objectivity in analysis through computational analysis.

Certain limitations still prevail in the automatized analysis and verification of handwriting. Technology and its necessary components are costly and available only to certain laboratories. Ahmed et al. (2015) comment that current signature verification systems lack practical applicability and are not designed for real world casework involving handwriting other than signatures on documents. Further, the background information on documents may be difficult for systems to segment or extract. Much of the work on automatic signature verification has focused on signatures which, although important, represents only a part of the total casework carried out by experts who conduct examinations on a wide variety of handwriting-related areas.

Additionally, all of the work performed to date seems inclined to carry a rider, either stated or implied, that reads: "All identifications made by machines require confirmation by human experts" although research in this area has shown that computational analysis removes many of the factors concerning subjectivity and bias and performs better than layperson judgments.

Some studies have compared the accuracy of automatic handwriting verification systems to forensic handwriting experts. In one study, Liwicki et al. (2010) compared performance between automated systems and handwriting experts, but had difficulty comparing expertise because EERs (equal error rates) could not be calculated for human experts. In a difficult handwriting task, the handwriting examiners had 7.2% misleading opinions while 52.3% of the opinions were inconclusive. For the same task, automatic handwriting verification systems (seven in total) had a combined average EER of 66.1.

In a study on differentiating the handwriting of twins, Srihari et al.'s (2008) automatic handwriting verification system's performance was compared to that of document examination interns and laypersons. By comparison, the system had an error rate of 9.02%, document examination intern error rate was 4.69%, while layperson error rate was 16.51%. It was demonstrated that the automatic handwriting verification system's performance was better than laypersons, but less than document examiners.

More recently, Malik et al. (2014) evaluated forensic handwriting examination proficiency data compiled by LaTrobe University between the years 2001 and 2005 (four tests) and compared the accuracy of human examiners to automatic signature verification systems tested on the same material provided to the human experts. Not surprisingly, the results found that there was more variability in human performance than machine performance. On average, the machine outperformed human experts in three out of the four tests. Conversely, the best human examiner outperformed the best machine in three out of the four tests (by a considerable margin in some tests). The researchers commented that factors such as disguise continues to be a problem for both human experts and machines. Clearly, though, research with computational techniques has established the usefulness of automatic handwriting verification systems as a tool in the handwriting examination process.

7.6 ESTABLISHING THE SIGNIFICANCE OF WRITING HABITS

Handwriting identification has been criticized for the absence of statistical data to support its conclusions. The renowned French criminologist Bertillon (1898) said: "The investigation by the handwriting expert in the court will, in fact, only deserve to be referred to as a science from the day he creates tables of probability for the various letter shapes." Kirk (1953) and Rhodes (1963) were equally critical. Thornton and Rhodes (1986) described document examination (and must have meant handwriting identification) as a field "which has progressed more by judicial acceptance than by any attempts to elevate the practice to a more scientific discipline" (p. 12).

If empirical or statistical data is what Thornton and Rhodes were looking for they must have overlooked a number of publications in German, the writings of Popkiss and Moore (1945), Livingston (1963), the studies of Muehlberger et al. (1977), Ansell (1979), and Eldridge et al. (1984). This was all work that was designed "to permit the linking of crimes to each other, and to their perpetrators, and to provide the means to accumulate quantitative information which document examiners can draw on when reaching their conclusions" (Nicholson 1984, 415). Blake (1977) proposed the taking of objective measurements of stable handwriting forms in an attempt to validate methods.

Over a greater period of time forensic scientists in Europe have shown considerable interest in objectivity within the discipline. As Böhle (1993) reported, Mueller (1939) attempted to determine the frequency of occurrence of particular versions of seven letters, letter elements, and one numeral. Reitberger (1941) conducted similar studies that deviated greatly from Meuller's.

A feature catalog, developed in the former German Democratic Republic in the 1950s, failed to produce acceptable results. Bein (1967) criticized the practices of that time and called for objective rates of evaluation in handwriting expertise.

Mathematical methods are undoubtedly a method of making the analysis of handwriting more objective. Although they are not likely to replace fully the current working methods of the handwriting examiner, Böhle (1993) contends that "mathematical methods can back up some logical and theoretical methods used to recognize individualization in handwritings and extend the practical experience of the expert" (p. 41).

Since the beginning of the use of the computer in research, an increasing number of studies have been conducted in England and the Netherlands in attempts to produce empirical data and to apply measurement and statistical analysis to it that will expand an understanding of handwriting and supplant subjectivity with some degree of objectivity (Eldridge et al. 1984; Eldridge et al. 1985; Evett and Totty 1985; Wing and Nimmo-Smith 1987; Wann and Nimmo-Smith 1991). A measure of success has been achieved in the computerized classification of block lettering and cursive handwriting employed on personal checks (Hardcastle et al. 1986; Hardcastle and Kemmenoe 1990). The size of the files that have been created, however, is not large and accordingly their usefulness is limited. Other reports respecting the frequency of occurrence of particular handwriting features have been mentioned within the topic of handwriting and hand lettering classifications above.

Much of the early work done relative to the classification of writing suggests an attempt to provide frequency ratios that could assist in the evaluation of the significance of writing features. However, the study by Muehlberger et al. (1977) was the first to clearly state it and pursue it as an objective. The study involved an examination of request writings of 100 subjects and nonrequest writings of a similar number. The study was focused on the letter combination "th" as appearing in words such as "that," "this," and "the." The work classified and counted letter forms, relative sizes, proportions and positions of elements, and the alignment of the letters in the combination. A number of observations respecting forms and correlations were made, although, as the authors point out, the sample size was too small (200 persons) to generalize from the results.

As mentioned, Nicholson's (1984) police forensic science project had two stated objectives, one of which was to accumulate quantitative information respecting frequency of occurrence of the features classified. In this respect, a pilot study of 140 subjects was conducted and while high frequency was encountered in certain categories for some letters that reduced their discriminating value, computer calculations confirmed that useful discriminating power had been achieved.

Giles (1990) provides a further report on the program of the Metropolitan Police Forensic Science Laboratory in London mentioned earlier. The database that is searched along the lines of the program developed by Totty et al. (1982) respecting type styles, but dealing with the stroke structure of uppercase block letters, has been expanded to 1,100 files. It is reportedly not used to search for specific individuals but principally to provide some insight into the process of evaluation by offering actual data on feature frequencies. Thus, it functions in a support role in casework, if not in direct evidence.

Historically, the search for empirical data on the significance of writing features that might be found in frequency of occurrence studies was foreseen as a reasonable offshoot from and/or a target of classification. It began with Livingston's (1963) tabulation of characteristics in the lettering of 200 subjects, and was continued in the spirit of the reports and papers of Muehlberger et al. (1977), Huber (1990), Giles (1990), Horton (1992), and others.

Perhaps because there has been a continuing need to attempt to correlate the writings on fraudulent checks as an assistance to criminal investigators, the study of completion methods in the writing of fraudulent checks continued to attract the attention of government examiners. This is illustrated by the work previously cited by Hardcastle et al. (1986), Hardcastle and Kemmenoe (1990), and by the survey of Crane and Crane (1997). Tangential to these studies has been the search for information on the frequency of occurrence of the elements of writing dealt with by these studies.

Data has also been pursued at length in Europe. The aforementioned German endeavor to produce a feature catalog of significant features of Latin handwriting, under development for 20 years, was described by Böhle (1993). Based on a sample of 1,000 writings, 1,485 features of 20 minuscules, 532 features of 20 majuscules, and 207 features of the numerals "0" to "9," were combined to create a record of 2,224 features in total.

The usefulness of the catalog lies in determining within a questioned writing and a group of known standards whether they contain a corresponding combination of a number of the 2,224 features that have been cataloged. The respective values or levels of significance for each feature (i.e., frequency of occurrence) can then be used to calculate the significance of the feature combination.

The number of significant script features required to support an identification was initially thought to be 26, on average, that by employing a particular and somewhat complex formula, yields an identification value of 40.9. Studies suggest that this identification value might be set at a level as low as 20.4, by reducing the number of similarities required to support an identification. Böhle felt that the number of features cataloged (2,224) was too large for the system to be workable. The suggestion was also made that the sample size on which it is based (1,000) should be increased to 5,000 to provide greater reliability.

Among the problems encountered with the frequency of occurrence statistics that may be generated by these classification systems is that these statistics are not necessarily transferable over long distances, particularly between populations that are less transient or that have different origins. What may seem to be a discriminating feature between writers in one locale or in one kind of document may be less discriminating in another. To help counter language and cultural handwriting variables, the FBI (2007), through the coordinated efforts of scientists and computer engineers, developed the FLASH-ID (forensic language-independent automated system for handwriting identification). Essential biometric identifiers, known as the biometric kernel, are relied upon in making matches within the system. Using statistical algorithms across several handwriting features, statistical matches are made to writings already in the database. Using graph-based recognition technology, the accuracy rate for writer identification is 98% in a text with as few as 50 words. FLASH-ID uses a lossless data structure that ensures the integrity of the original graphic handwriting features. The system is also language independent, relying on graphical rather than linguistic features.

Another limitation involves the frequency of occurrence statistics that classification systems may produce that cannot be applied as a rudimentary calculation of probability regarding any particular combination of writing elements. When the respective significance of the discriminating elements varies from one to another, as they do in writing, each element must be appropriately weighted to determine the composition of the combination of elements necessary to support any conclusion of identity.

Welch (1996) provided the details of four cases in the United Kingdom in which large numbers of writing samples were manually scanned in search of as few as five or six particular elements of writing. Although these cases are offered as evidence of the heterogeneity of writing, they are limited evidence, but evidence nevertheless, that discriminating elements of handwriting can be employed to search and segregate masses of writers (as many as 600,000) into workable numbers for further, more detailed study. This is all that any system of classification is designed and intended to do.

Classification systems that may afford some evidence of frequency of occurrence deal primarily with major features. Needless to say, these are measurable features, and refinements of the classification process and the utilization of computers make the systems increasingly discriminating. The identification of writing, however, involves additionally and particularly the study of subtle features that may change with certain letter combinations, certain writing circumstances, or certain writer conditions. Two aspects of writing identification that are undoubtedly difficult to classify or measure, beyond general subcategories such as good, poor, and average, are writing movements and line quality.

However, computational studies have contributed to the assessment of line quality. Franke (2005) used a sophisticated robotic arm device to create ink traces with different pens on real substrates. The line quality or ink deposits of the traces were carefully examined with respect to pen tip force and relative ink density to create an ink deposition model that can be used not only in the objective study of line quality, but also for computational analysis.

7.7 DISTINGUISHING SYNCHRONOUS FROM ASYNCHRONOUS WRITING

Diversity notwithstanding, like many other questioned document problems, the question associated with synchronous writing is usually one of authentication, fabrication, or alteration. This requires a study in search of evidence that signatures, writings, or entries, purportedly made on different and separate occasions were, in fact, written at one and the same time. Or the study may be in search of evidence that signatures, writings, or entries, purportedly made on a single occasion were, in fact, the products of separate writing instances.

The particular circumstances will vary with the case, of course, and the resources available to establish the genuine or spurious nature of a document, or simply its history of production is seldom the same twice. Writings, typewritings, inks, papers, and writing instruments can all play a part in the study.

There is also some diversity in the manner in which authors refer to the two writing circumstances. Some use the terms *single entries* and *multientries*, others use *same time* and *different time*. Some call them *periodic entries*, others prefer to say *made separately* or *made sequentially*. Even the more ambiguous terms like *continuous* and *uninterrupted* and their antonyms are occasionally employed.

For the purpose of this discussion the term *synchronous* will be used and its antonym *asynchronous*. The Oxford Dictionary defines *synchronous* as: "happening at the same time, coincident in time, contemporary in occurrence, related to different events of the same time or period," but not simultaneous in the strictest sense as in a stroke-by-stroke reproduction. That would involve a mechanical or electronic device to create two or more writings from the same singular movement of the hand. Accordingly, the term must be broadened to mean *at the same time* to refer to writings normally occurring:

- On one occasion
- In the same writing position (sitting, standing, or leaning over)

- With the same media (pen and paper)
- On the same surface (table, counter, lap, or other)
- For the same purpose (two or more copies of the same document)
- By the same person
- In the same mental and physical state

These circumstances, insofar as the writings of signatures are concerned, are considered to be conditions exercising control of the internal and external influences on the writing. Moreover, writings executed after an interval or interruption of as little as an hour or less are not always thought of as happening at the same time. Interruptions in the writing process of even a quarter or half hour are likely to be accompanied by some adjustment in the writing position and/or in the orientation of the documents to the writer, that may have some effect upon the products written.

Although circumstances vary widely in matters in which this question arises, the issue of synchronous writings frequently centers on two or more signatures or sets of initials that are required to be executed in the completion of the same transaction. Or it may involve notes or records (e.g., medical records, inventory registers or research logs) written in the course of some continuing, but short-term action, examination, or study. Contracts consisting of a number of handwritten or typewritten provisions may also be subjects of dispute. On the other hand, the question of asynchronous writings more often is challenged insofar as the extended writings of the entries of records, diaries, logs, and the like, normally prepared over a period of days or weeks that are alleged to have been rewritten or amended to conceal an act of omission or to materially alter the record of events.

The matter of synchronous and asynchronous writings is closely related to the dating of documents or writings on which Osborn, Hilton, and Harrison have written at some length. The difference in the two approaches lies chiefly in the time frames that are usually involved. Dating studies are more often conducted on writings divided by substantial periods of time, often years, where paper and watermarks, aging or decrepitude of writing, changing of writing styles, and changing of machines (typewriters) or instruments (pens) can play a greater role in establishing periods of production of documents. On the other hand, synchronous or asynchronous issues tend to relate to time frames no longer than days, weeks, or months, for which the methods of Osborn (1929), Hilton (1982), and Harrison (1958b) seldom suffice.

The point to be remembered, however, is that the kind of evidence sought to differentiate documents in a broader time frame, for example, DOIs (dates of introduction) of pens, machines, or materials can sometimes be helpful in the study of documents within narrower time frames, when the circumstances happen to straddle pertinent DOIs.

In summary, it may be said that these studies invariably involve:

1. Records, such as tally sheets, compiled by inserting tally marks vertically (opposite particular names) or horizontally (to register a predetermined number)
2. Time books or time cards on which hours of work or days off and sickness are inscribed according to dates
3. Logbooks and records of an occupational specialty — ship's logs, medical logs, or records
4. Ledger sheets recording money transactions, formal or informal
5. True diaries of a personal or official nature
6. Pocket notebooks

The key to many of these handwriting studies is the matter of consistency. Synchronous writings are almost invariably consistent executions. Asynchronous writings are frequently not consistent. Synchronous writings are consistent in writing quality, line quality, size, slope, spacing, letter forms, pens, inks, and arrangement. If inconsistencies do occur there is often an apparent reason for them, for example, a change in writing instrument due to pen or ink failure. Unless they are particularly skilled executions, asynchronous writings should almost invariably display inconsistency. Such inconsistency can be expected to be of a magnitude comparable to the range of natural variation observed in collected writing standards of the author, for that, indeed, is what they are. Writings found to be synchronous or asynchronous, particularly in the creation of medical records, however, cannot be prejudged as to their pertinence or legitimacy without fully investigating the record-keeping practices of the institution or the individual.

In the study of these cases other factors may be available for consideration. Greater consistency may be evident in letter forms in synchronous writings or signatures of an individual that normally uses alternative or optional forms and structures for some letters. Intersections of the strokes of writings with one another may support or dispute the sequence in which questioned writings purport to have been produced. Document dates may not be consistent with the date of introduction of the printed form, or the particular kind of paper. Cards or sheets of paper allegedly taken from stocks serving various purposes over periods of time may be found, by aging characteristics or guillotine (paper cutter) characteristics too similar to one another to be consistent with their selection from stocks over long periods of time. Furthermore, surface indentations on one document may provide evidence of having been present and in a close relationship beneath another document when the latter was being prepared.

Keeler (1934) described the evidence she found in tally marks, tabulating election results, indicative of marks having been made in groups with greater speed, as opposed to the more deliberate writing of other tally marks, made separately and somewhat unpredictably, in disparate locations on a tally sheet. The former displayed *drag tracks* or connecting strokes between tally marks, whereas the latter marks were more irregular and unrelated to one another with typical blunt endings. The drag tracks of the former reflect a continuity of pen motion from one mark to another, and for such reasons, continuity is allied to consistency as keys to synchronousness. Marks may also be related by regularity in spacing, slant, and pen pressure. The irregularity of asynchronous writings is attributed to the necessity to change position of the arm or hand between the execution of each mark. Regularity and irregularity seem to have been the chief discriminating aspects of the writings to sort the synchronous from the asynchronous. Errors may also be helpful. In synchronous writings, they may be repeated in columns or rows, whereas in asynchronous writings they tend to be singular and/or isolated.

Harris and Mills (1963) summarized their findings as evidence of alteration ("the expanded record"), or fabrication ("the substituted or rewritten record"). Alteration is, of course, the objective of an asynchronous production, whereas fabrication is the usual objective of a synchronous preparation. The third line of forensic pursuit—that of authentication—might be investigated of course, from the perspective of either a synchronous or asynchronous parcel of writing. Under the category of alteration, they noted as evidence:

1. Crowding, squeezing in, or fitting of insertions around other material
2. Irregularities (i.e., inconsistencies) in slant, pressure, and quality
3. Presence of erasures, eradications, or obliterations
4. Irregularities (i.e., inconsistencies) in inks, writing instruments, typing ribbons, or machines

5. Lines intersecting with other lines, folds, perforations, tears, or holes in the paper
6. Presence or absence of indentations in subsequent pages
7. Inconsistencies in alignments

Under the category of fabrication, they noted:

1. Remarkable (i.e., unusual) consistency in writing quality, ink, margins, spacing, arrangement, and alignment
2. Bleeding of ink strokes, purportedly of different dates, into one another at intersections
3. Variation in preternatural paper characteristics between undisputed and disputed pages of the same record
4. Errors in the writing of dates in advance of their occurrence
5. Use and dating of forms in advance of their dates of introduction

Doud (1967) reviewed the frequency of occurrence of forms for the letter "e" ("e" vs. "*e*") and the numeral "4" (closed vs. open) in an allegedly asynchronous record. He compared these frequencies to those displayed by standards that were indisputably asynchronous. Again, the evidence was that the questioned material displayed consistency in forms that was not present in the normal, natural writing of the individual.

Beck (1974) summarized his review of diary entries as matters evaluated in terms of (1) consistency with statements made about them and (2) consistency of entries with each other. In the latter respect, he noted that synchronous writings tend to be more like each other in quality, size, shape, etc. than samples done at different times, which is simply the evidence of consistency that may also be found in the writing instrument employed, in arrangement and alignment, in size, proportions, slant, pattern of letter forms, and the use of options. As others have reported, Beck mentioned other evidence to be considered as including erasures and obliterations, ink offsets, and ink trails between entries, as well as aging or the soiling of pages.

Foley (1979) differentiates between the two basic situations as *single entries* (what is referred to here as asynchronous writings) executed independently of one another, and *multientries* (referred to here as synchronous writings) executed with little or no interruption or alteration of the writing position. He describes single entries as slower, more deliberate executions than multientries. The slower, more deliberate writings exhibit the classical symptoms: abrupt commencements and terminations of strokes, less slant, larger letters, shorter word length, heavier and wider strokes, and greater legibility. Multientries offer classical symptoms of greater speed: greater slant, poorer letter construction, tapering stroke endings, decreased pressure, greater word lengths, perhaps greater variation and decreased legibility.

Foley (1979) found that progressive increase or decrease in marginal alignments occurred in multientries or synchronous writings, whereas single entries seemed less influenced by the alignments of other entries. Single, asynchronous entries displayed greater randomness regarding the placement of handwritten notations on calendars synchronously and asynchronously. Foley's study also confirmed the work of Doud insofar as the frequency of occurrence of optional letter and numeral designs or design variations.

McCarthy (1981), in three case illustrations, reiterates what others had said, that asynchronous writings display:

1. Greater variation in:
   a. Writing styles
   b. Arrangement or location of written material

c. Use and manner of abbreviations
d. Methods of record production
e. Writing angles and in pen pressures
f. Writing inks, instruments and pen performance
2. Less evidence of progression in left hand margins
3. Less evidence of prior knowledge of text to be written
4. Less or no evidence of relatable indentations on pages behind or (in page substitutions) from pages above

Despite the finding of this kind of evidence in each of his cases, McCarthy (1981) declines to commit himself to positive statements respecting the production of the writings as being asynchronous or otherwise. Rather, he seeks to find a unique feature to contradict the nature of production purported by the text itself.

Foley (1985) repeats that synchronous writings display greater consistency than asynchronous executions and cites several cases that illustrate his point. In conclusion, and contrary to McCarthy (1981), he suggested that, on this and other relevant evidence, an examiner may reasonably conclude that writings or signatures were executed coincidentally.

Foley (1987) addressed the subject again with particular respect to signatures and states that signatures, whether synchronous or asynchronous, are normally expected to display a lesser degree of variation, although this is dependent upon the writer. Variation is greater, he maintained, where the external and internal influences change. Variation is less where external and internal influences are controlled or constant. External influences include:

1. Writing instrument
2. Writing position
3. Writing media (pen or pencil and paper)
4. Paper position relative to the writer
5. Writing space

Internal influences include:

1. Writer's state of mind
2. Writer's state of health
3. Formality or informality of the act
4. Level of trauma or pleasure to the act
5. Writer's state of intoxication or psychosis

Foley's study of approximately 400 signatures revealed, as expected, that signatures signed when documents were stacked and writing was synchronous and sequential, displayed the greatest consistency in alignment and size. Single or asynchronous signatures exhibited more variation, less speed, and greater legibility.

In summary, it is emphasized that adequate writing standards of a similar kind, for example, diaries or logs, are important to these examinations but difficult to find, if they exist at all. Many factors may contribute to a study including examination of the media (i.e., pens and papers), indentations of and on other pages of the record, statistics (frequencies of occurrence of writing idiosyncrasies), and offsets of ink or pencil on facing surfaces. Information respecting record-keeping practices is almost invariably helpful. Stains, soils, tears, staple holes, and other preternatural characteristics of the record must also be duly considered to ensure that the implied chronology of events in the history of the record is completely plausible. To begin with, however, as stated earlier, the key to synchronism versus asynchronism is found in the attribute of consistency, considered in conjunction with continuity (Figures 7.7 and 7.8).

Figure 7.7 Time altered on visitor log sheet which may indicate asynchronous writing. Ink differences may support this position.

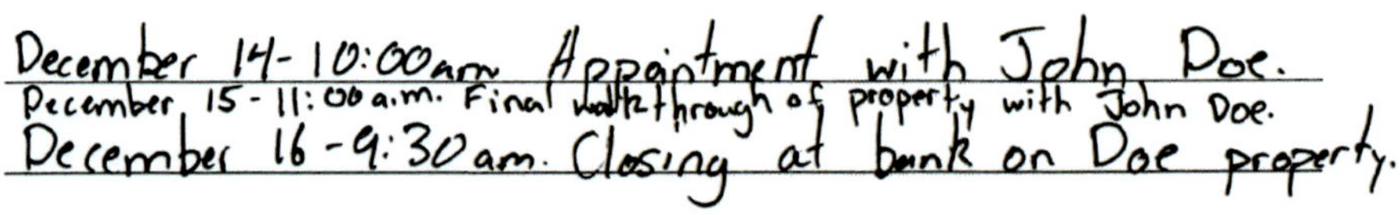

Figure 7.8 Insertion between lines with altered spacing may indicate the writing was not synchronous.

Chapter 8

Extrinsic Factors Influencing Handwriting

8.1 THE VARIABLES OF HANDWRITING

As an introduction to the factors discussed in Chapters 8 and 9, the following general comments are warranted. It is noted here, as well, that Huber and Headrick define certain variables or factors as *extrinsic* or *intrinsic* differently from some other authors.

There are numerous conditions and circumstances that contribute to the nature of normal writing and the quality of the writing performance. Some of these factors are variables that are extrinsic and, for the most part, not within the writer's voluntary control. They belong to the nature of the writer and include those factors that are physical in kind while others are mental. Age and infirmity are invariable extrinsic influences; sinistrality (left-handedness) is another frequently encountered; adherence to a particular writing system or skill in penmanship are two others.

Other variables are intrinsic and somewhat circumstantial. They are factors where the imitation of family and other practices, or the grasp of the writing instrument are two such influences. Included within these intrinsic factors are that set of temporary conditions, derived from hallucinogens, alcohol, hypnosis, stress, and fatigue that exercise their influence upon writing, regardless of the form it otherwise takes. All are influences to which one voluntarily submits, for other reasons.

8.2 EXTRINSIC FACTORS INFLUENCING HANDWRITING

8.2.1 Handwriting Systems

To some extent, the nature or appearance of one's writing is predetermined. Since it is an acquired perceptual-motor skill and it is generally not instinctive or hereditary, it is primarily environment, experience, and culture dependent. The writing systems one is taught, that follow patterns popular within one's country or particular population provide some basic characteristics of form, slant, proportions, movement, and size.

A number of earlier authors placed emphasis on the importance of writing systems in the study of handwriting. Osborn (1929) devoted an entire chapter to the subject (37 pages) and stated that in spite of the changes one's writing undergoes, the original system in which one is taught will still be visible in their writing in some way. Osborn advised that system and national characteristics should always be considered and evaluated in handwriting. He claimed further, and Hilton (1982) agreed, that evidence of the system learned may serve as an indicator of the writer's age since there have been definite periods during which particular writing systems were taught. Almost every writer on the subject has maintained that handwriting identification is based on the finding of a combination of similarities in class and individual characteristics, and class characteristics are invariably defined as those characteristics that result from such influences as the writing system taught, trade training, and education.

Prior to the time when the typewriter and now the computer began to dominate, communication methods and records were dependent upon calligraphy. Numerous occupations developed distinctive characteristics. There was a *small litorary hand* with wide word spacing, the *strong railroad style* having a fixed number of words per line, the compact writing of the *bookkeeper's hand.* There was the modified *round hand* with vertical slope, having wide spacing between letters that was known as the *civil service hand,* and there was also a large awkward, angular hand that was taught in certain exclusive schools for women (Osborn 1929).

Masson (1990) and Weiss (1982) reported on the lettering of draftsmen, architects, and architectural engineers that follow prescribed patterns of design or construction and can greatly limit individualization. The patterns of construction are sufficiently distinctive such that the occupational influence upon a writer may be recognized. For example, all strokes are executed in a downward direction. Circular letters such as "O," "Q," and "C" are formed using two or more strokes all of which are executed in a prescribed sequence. Generally, it seems engineers are allowed even less freedom to individualize letter styles than architects.

Herrick (1960a) published a comparative review of 19 commercial systems followed by schools of the United States in 1960. Beacom (1965) added 10 others to the review in 1965. Towson (1975) compiled a similar, but less detailed, review of the five systems taught in Canada during the period 1960–1970. Moon (1977) provided a slightly different list of 16 systems offered in 39 states of the United States. However, the 1980s marked the beginning of the demise of stipulated policy respecting handwriting in the schools, and now there is not a prescribed writing system in many areas, although there are many systems available. Vastrick's (1993) report is testimony to this. His survey, to which 28 states responded, revealed that 9 states had no specific system to offer pupils. The balance of 19 states identified 14 different systems that were being taught. An updated list of the copybook systems available is provided in Appendix A. With the introduction of the CCSS (Common Core State Standards) in 2009, which most US states adopted, the curriculum does not require cursive handwriting and only mentions handwriting training up to first grade. After first grade, states can choose how to continue handwriting training, or, eliminate handwriting training altogether (Saperstein Associates 2012).

As a result, the role of penmanship in the development of the individual has changed substantially over recent years, as many examiners have observed, and adherence to any writing system has not been aspired to or required. Harrison (1958b) recognized that a great deal of change from the system a person has been taught is to be expected as the person ages. He comments that "by the time adolescence is past and the handwriting has assumed the character it will certainly retain until senility or ill-health takes their toll, it may well be that comparatively few letters will conform at all closely to the original copybook design" (p. 296).

Miller (1972a) conducted a study of a selected sample of specimen writings from 128 former students of various ages of a specific school that had been in existence since 1909 (that had taught the Palmer writing system exclusively until 1936 and the Zaner Bloser system since that time). In his report, he declared that it is nearly impossible to correctly determine the handwriting system in which a mature writer was taught. Because the evidence of the writing system to which the individual was subjected in his or her formative years is unclear, its value may lie primarily in the study of writings prior to 1900.

In the survey of national handwriting systems that follows, the focus on certain systems is primarily based on available research about a particular handwriting system as it may pertain especially to handwriting examination questions. This survey is not meant to be comprehensive or representative of every handwriting system currently in use.

8.2.1.1 North American Handwriting Systems

Herrick (1960a), in his aforementioned study of the 19 writing systems in use in the United States in and about 1960, found that the greatest dissimilarities in the systems were the letter forms advocated, and the use of manuscript writing. In the cursive designs of the capital letters suggested by these systems, there were as many as 10 designs for one allograph (e.g., "F" and "R"). Most of the differences in these designs, however, were minor, and less than a dozen of the cursive capitals showed any really significant formation differences in even as few as two forms. The lowercase cursive letters showed even less variance.

The teaching of manuscript writing to the students, before their introduction to cursive writing, was the other major dissimilarity. While manuscript was employed in a large number of systems, it was not universal. Manuscript writing was introduced in US schools around 1920, and in the 1980s a majority of schools still taught it before they taught the cursive style, because the strokes involved are simpler and less varied (Figure 8.1).

Moon (1977) surveyed the systems being taught in schools in the United States with a view to relating them, if possible, to geographical locations. In 39 states, some 15 different systems were being followed. Some states employed two or more systems. The conclusion drawn was that it was not possible to determine the geographic origin of a person by the style of handwriting he or she was taught.

In a review of 35 of the commercial systems offered in various locations in North America, Regent (1989) took a different approach in search of the elements of upper and lowercase letters of the alphabet that all systems had in common, rather than those by which they might be

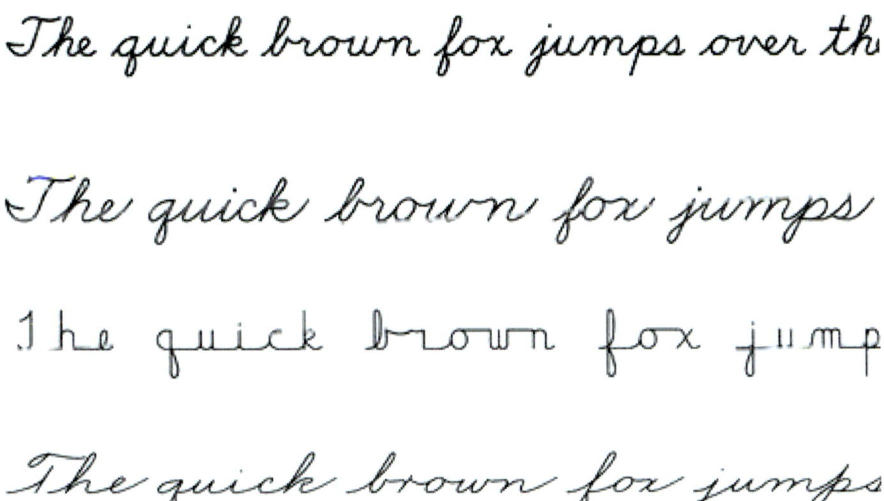

Figure 8.1 Commonly encountered copybook styles in the United States.

differentiated. His objective was to catalog the aspects of writing that should not be construed or considered to reflect class or system characteristics. Divergences in these aspects can then be rightfully categorized as individual characteristics. This study of cursive systems revealed a number of common elements including:

1. Uppercase letters "D," "L," and "Q" have an eyelet at the heel, of similar size, the axis of which runs parallel to but slightly above the baseline.
2. Descending loops of the uppercase letters "J," "Y," and "Z" are similar in shape and size, and the axis of each parallels the slope of the writing generally.
3. The center trough of the uppercase letter "G" forms a cusp with the final lower curve, which cusp is never as tall as the initial loop.
4. Loops of the uppercase "J" are executed in a clockwise direction.
5. Bowls of the lowercase letters "a," "d," "g," and "q" are similar elliptical or oval shapes that are closed at the upper right point of the ellipse.
6. Descending loops of the lowercase letters "g," "j," "y," and "z" are similar in shape and size, and the axis of each parallels the slope of the writing generally.
7. Loops of the lowercase "f" are executed in a counterclockwise direction.
8. Loops of the lowercase "f" do not intersect with one another or meet at a common point on the staff.
9. Loops of the lowercase "h" and "k" are similar in shape and length.
10. Arches of the lowercase "m" and "n" are rounded and of equal height and width.
11. The top of the lowercase "r" commences from a cusp on the upper left and proceeds as a descending compound curve to fashion a round shoulder on the right from which the stroke returns to the baseline.
12. The apex of the lowercase "s" is a cusp.
13. The stem of the lowercase "t" is a retrace.

Osborn (1929) states that the most significant handwriting characteristics are those that diverge from the copybook or system model. Osborn's assumption seems to have been that most writers follow copybook designs closely, which may have been the case in his time. Osborn implies that significance varies directly with divergence from copybook form or system style. Conversely, it might be held that the least significant characteristics are those that most closely resemble the prescribed copybook form. Huber (1963), in a study of the writings of 227 subjects, reported that neither of these tenets could now be supported. Copybook writing, that is penmanship of quality, is a rarity nowadays and accordingly, copybook forms are of greater value in the identification process—so much so, that quality in writing has become a writer's best defense against forgery.

It was also observed that some writers utilize some letter forms in, and perhaps only in, certain written text, such as the writing of "USA" on envelope addresses, that has developed as a habit. The form(s) may not appear frequently in any other text or when these letters are isolated from one another. As a law or fundamental principle, then, it is obviously more correct to say that the significance of a discriminating element of handwriting (a characteristic) varies inversely to its frequency of occurrence in similar text material in the writing of different persons.

It is generally presumed, as most writing systems tend to prescribe, that certain consistencies will prevail in the common elements shared by some letters. For example, the uppercase "P," "B," and "R" can be expected to display some similarity in the structure of the staff and the bowl. Consistency can also be expected in some elements of the uppercase "M" and "N," the uppercase

Figure 8.2 The "3-W" style commonly seen in Brazilian handwriting.

"F" and "T," the uppercase "I" and "J," the uppercase "V" and "W," and the lowercase "a," "d," "g," and "q." It might also be expected that some consistency would be found in the loops of the lowercase "l," "h," "b," and "k," or in the commencement of the uppercase letters "U," "Y," and "Z." These assumptions can be important in cases where limited standards do not contain samples of all of the allographs present in a questioned writing.

While similarities in the common elements of such allographs may prompt an examiner to presume that, in the general case, there would be similarity in another allograph sharing these elements if a sample were available, this assumption may not be invariably valid. Consequently, it may not necessarily follow that a difference in, say, the design of the "P" is indicative of a difference to be found in the design of the "R," if such an allograph were available to compare.

Kiser and Torres (1975) in a study of a sample of 588 incarcerated individuals of both genders and different ethnicity, also found that these assumptions are not fully supported. Inconsistencies occurred in these sets of letters in as many as 40% of their sample in some cases. However, there are limitations about generalizing from prison inmates to the general population.

Systems may develop within systems and can be far more localized than national, provincial, or state boundaries might suggest. Bellomy (1986) described the nature of Mexican-American communities, called *barrios* that developed in Arizona, Colorado, New Mexico, Texas, and particularly in southern California. For various reasons, these communities have produced street gangs, known as *vatos* that have been a part of the social structure of those areas for nearly a century. Part of a gang's guise or identity is the adoption and use of its own distinctive style of lettering referred to as *Barrio script* that is a particular modification of conventional hand printing, employed by the vato in gang writings on the walls of structures.

Additionally, influences can be exhibited with respect to particular letter forms, without altering the designs of any other letters of similar structure. Because of their prevalence among students in Florida, McCarthy and Williams (1987) referred to the unusual letter forms of the "J" and "W" in certain ethnic groups (Figure 8.2). But as Haywood (1991) has pointed out, this generalization may not be fully justified.

8.2.1.2 Latin American Handwriting Systems

Muehlberger (1988) has written on the class characteristics of Hispanic (i.e., Latin American) writers, large numbers of which have migrated to the southern United States, particularly from Cuba and Mexico. He has observed that there is a distinction between the older generations of

Hispanics, who were educated in private schools that provided instruction in penmanship, and the younger generations whose education was obtained in state-run schools that offered little in penmanship training. In consequence, older generation Hispanics frequently display a better quality of writing often based on the Palmer system, whereas younger-generation individuals exhibit a lesser quality of writing not readily associated with any particular writing system. It is reported that good penmanship acquired a status in years gone by that became a matter of personal pride. Then too, due to the level of technology, and the quality of record keeping in the Latin American countries, there is little doubt that penmanship was put to greater use by the educated portion of the population.

Many Hispanic writers share a tendency to ornateness in the formation of capital letters that produces embellishments and disproportionate increases in size that may reflect a European influence. The mixture of simplistic or lettered forms with cursive writing is not unusual. Whether it is due to the tendency to embellish or not, disconnections, hiatuses or pen lifts between letters are not uncommon. Mixtures of writing movements (e.g., garlanded with arcaded) have also been noted in the work of some writers, but this lack of consistency has not been explained. All of this may give Hispanic writings a character that is somewhat different from the normal writings of the United States and Canada. The geographical source of the influence, however, is not likely to be determinable.

Caywood's (1997) study of the impact of foreign education on handwriting illustrates a number of samples of writing purportedly receiving Spanish influence, from such countries as Mexico, Cuba, and other Hispanic countries. The copybook style for Spanish writings that he provided is, with a few minor exceptions, the Palmer method.

8.2.1.2.1 Jamaican Handwriting

In a study of the handwritings of 90 Jamaican women, Anderson (1982) reported a number of features that were common to many writers:

1. The lower case "a" and "d" and the upper case "A" commenced with a small internal curl within the bowl.
2. The lower case "c" and the upper case "C" commenced with a small curl.
3. The majority (62%) used lettering as opposed to cursive writing.
4. The majority (90%) printed the capital letter "E," and at least half of those executed the bottom arm with an undulating stroke.
5. The majority (80%) used an enlarged lower case style for the capital "G," and located the bowl above the baseline. As in the "a," "c," and "d," the letter was commenced with a small curl within the bowl in most cases.
6. A number of writers (38%) formed the loop of the capital "I" by adding a downstroke to the front of a staff. Similarly, the majority of writers (61%) added a downstroke to create the upper loop of the capital "J."
7. Some writers (40%) used the lower case "i" for the personal pronoun "I."
8. No cursive forms of the letters "K" or "k" were found.
9. The majority (90%) used the Palmer "r."
10. All writers formed the upper and lowercase "X" as two circle sectors, back to back, as is common in German writing.
11. Half of the writers commenced the numerals "2" and "9" with a small curl or hook within the upper curve, similar to many German writers.

12. Some writers execute a crossbar to the numeral "7" (36%), and a majority (66%) undulate the top bar.
13. It is also common for Jamaican women to use lower case letters to begin proper names of the days or months or for middle names or initials.

8.2.1.3 European Handwriting Systems

8.2.1.3.1 English (UK) Handwriting

There are a few particular observations respecting English writing systems worth considering in writing studies.

1. English writing tends to be more vertical.
2. The "M" and "N" is frequently of a Spencerian style, and similar to the styles of the English civil service hand, that was a modification of the old round hand (Figure 8.3).
3. English writers frequently add a period or a comma after the house number in a street address and after the abbreviations "Mr." and "Mrs."
4. English writers frequently introduce an eyelet to the union of the vertical and the horizontal strokes in the numeral "4."

8.2.1.3.2 French Handwriting

In a study of the signatures of 16 female youths from France, ages 11 to 24, 12 of whom were adolescents aged 15 to 17, Boisover (1993) reported that 15 of the 16 writers exhibited one or more of three particular characteristics: 13 writers added a rubric, 9 writers superimposed an initial with the capital letter of the surname, and 9 writers exhibited a distinctive ascending baseline. The study of two additional signatures from older persons having an origin in France revealed similar features, suggesting that the features noted are not necessarily peculiarities of the adolescent.

The explanation offered is that writing systems taught in schools in France tend to be fancier and that, consequently, signatures are fancier. An element of the writing that may contribute to the more ornate assessment of French writings is the inclusion of a small eyelet, often blind,

English civil service hand

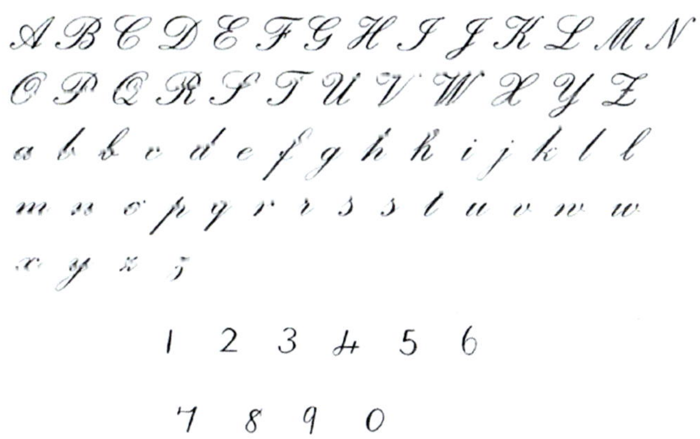

Figure 8.3 The English civil service hand.

to the commencement of the uppercase letters “H,” “I,” “J,” “K,” “V,” “W,” and “Z,” executed in a counterclockwise direction. It produces a short, trough-like, horizontal beginning to the letter. Large commencement curls are characteristic of other uppercase letters.

The addition of a cross stroke to the stem of the digit “7” is common in French cursive writings taught in France and in other French communities (e.g., in Canada). The use of guillemets, that is, horizontal chevrons «…» to enclose a quotation, rather than quotation marks, is another practice in French writing. The observation has been made that the writings of France tend to be smaller than those of their neighbors, Germany and Spain.

8.2.1.3.3 German Handwriting

Features of the German cursive writing systems (Figures 8.4 and 8.5) can be found often in the writing of neighboring countries such as Austria, Switzerland, and Poland. The Netherlands and the Scandinavian countries of Denmark, Norway, and Sweden also share many of these features that include:

1. In any quotation, the first set of quotation marks is located on or below the baseline. The last set is elevated.
2. Salutations are usually followed by an exclamation mark “!” rather than a colon “:”.
3. Apostrophes are not always used to indicate the possessive forms of nouns or pronouns, except when the name ends in an “s.”
4. A small u-shaped diacritic is placed over the letter “u” to distinguish it from the letter “n.”
5. German writing is frequently larger than that of other countries, just as French writing tends to be smaller.

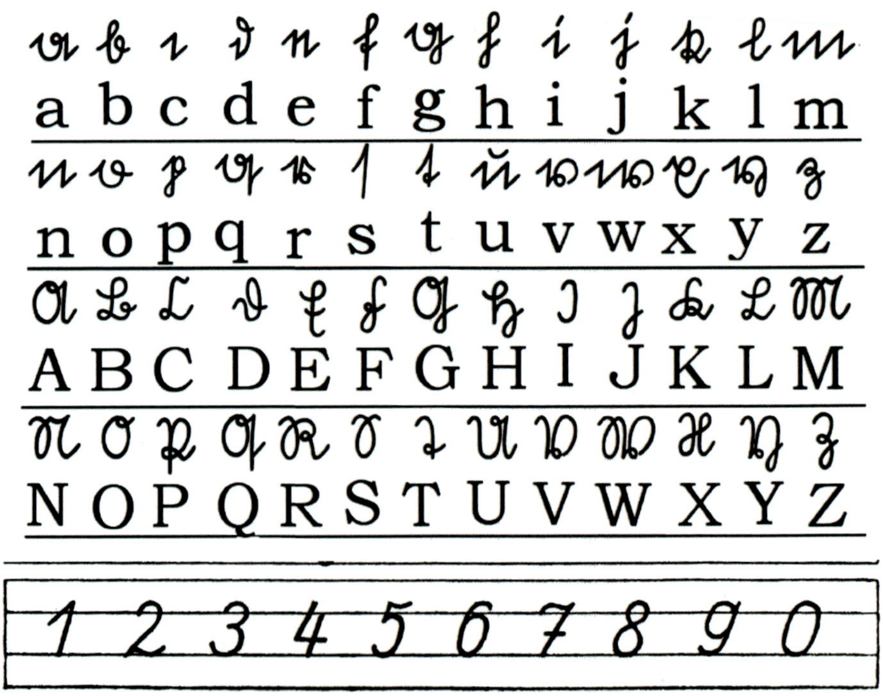

Figure 8.4 German copybook style.

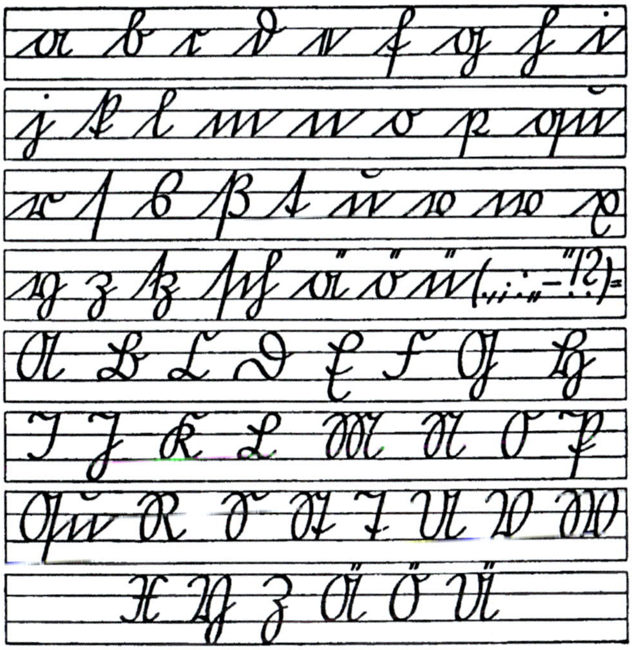

Figure 8.5 German–Suetterlin copybook style.

6. The bowls of cursive letters in German writing tend to be broader or more circular than those of English or North American writings, which are more oval shaped. As in other Cyrillic European writings the bowls may be overwritten by the same stroke.
7. Younger German writers tend to use the printed style of a letter as a capital. Older writers are more ornate in their executions.
8. Many German writers add an approach stroke to the figure "1," a cross bar to the figure "7," and commence the figures "2" and "9" with an inside curl or hook.
9. A medial or terminal lowercase "t" is frequently crossed in a continuous motion that begins at the base of a straight stem or staff, rises and loops in a counterclockwise direction to the left of the staff, and crosses it, usually at midpoint. Some copybooks omit the execution of the complete loop or buckle.
10. Large initial loops are omitted in the execution of the uppercase "I" and "J" in favor of a smaller single arch connected to the apex of the letter with two acute angles. Similar movements are employed to commence the "H," "K," "V," and "W"
11. The uppercase "G" is designed as an enlargement of the lowercase "g."
12. The contour of the arch of the uppercase "N" and the second arch of the uppercase "M" is interrupted by a shallow trough at the apex.
13. The shoulder of the lowercase "r" is troughed rather than rounded.

8.2.1.3.4 Polish Handwriting

In an examination of class characteristics present when Polish people write in English, 31 features were present in the Polish samples that could constitute class characteristics of Polish writing (Turnbull et al. 2010). Of those characteristics, 17 could be used to distinguish Polish writing from English writing.

8.2.1.3.5 Portuguese Handwriting

Behrendt (n.d.) reported that in a study of Portuguese writings, 6 of 14 subjects commenced the upstroke to the loops of the lowercase "l," "b," and "h" and to the staff of the "t" at a point well above the baseline, thereby, disconnecting the letter from any preceding letter. Breaks preceding other letters such as the "a," "c," "g," and "m" were also common occurrences. Behrendt attributes these breaks to a Portuguese writing system that teaches the commencement of these letters from an elevated point, and so considers it to be a class characteristic.

8.2.1.3.6 Spanish Handwriting

In Spanish writing systems, there is use of an inverted question mark "¿," to open an interrogative statement in extended texts.

8.2.1.4 Middle Eastern Handwriting Systems

With the increased focus on terrorist groups operating out of the Middle Eastern areas of the world, interest has emerged on the use of Persian and Arabic handwriting systems. Of the many varied handwriting systems employed in the Middle East countries, Arabic, Persian, and Farsi handwriting systems are most commonly encountered. While there are many similarities and few dissimilarities in the style of writings among these nations, the most prominent characteristic is the writing form of right to left. The Arabic alphabet is more commonly seen in Middle Eastern countries due to the proliferation of the Muslim holy book, the Qur'an, being predominately written in Arabic. Those trained in Persian, Arabic, and Farsi handwriting may display minimal individual characteristics due to the rigorous training received in the handwriting form (Abed et al. 2011; Ghods and Kabir 2013) (Figure 8.6).

There have been several published studies on the national characteristics of Arabic writing including a statistical study of 188 writers that examined features and variation (Al-Haddad et al. 2009). Writing samples from Morocco, Tunisia, Jordan, and Oman were collected to determine if a writer could be identified regionally (Al-Hadhrami et al. 2015). While some correspondence between writing and regions was found, classification was particularly marked when dividing the countries into North Africa and the Middle East. A study on the simulation of Arabic signatures included over 900 Arabic writers simulating four elements in two Arabic signatures. The relative difficulty to simulate the signatures in four characteristics (size, slant, baseline, and spacing) was evaluated and showed that slant and baseline were relatively easier to simulate than spacing and size (Al-Haddad et al. 2009). Other studies examined form, proportion, and line quality in Arabic signatures (Al-Musa Alkahtani and Platt 2009; 2011a) and also the ability of subjects to identify simulated Arabic writing (Al-Musa Alkahtani 2014). There are statistical studies related to variance in Arabic writing as well as the performance of handwriting examiners who are not fluent in Arabic performing handwriting identification in the language or the writing of Arabic (Al-Musa Alkahtani 2010; Al-Haddad et al. 2011). Statistically significant differences were not found between examiners who were or were not fluent in Arabic. These studies also support the ability of handwriting examiners to opine on identification in cases in which the writing examined is not the analyst's native language.

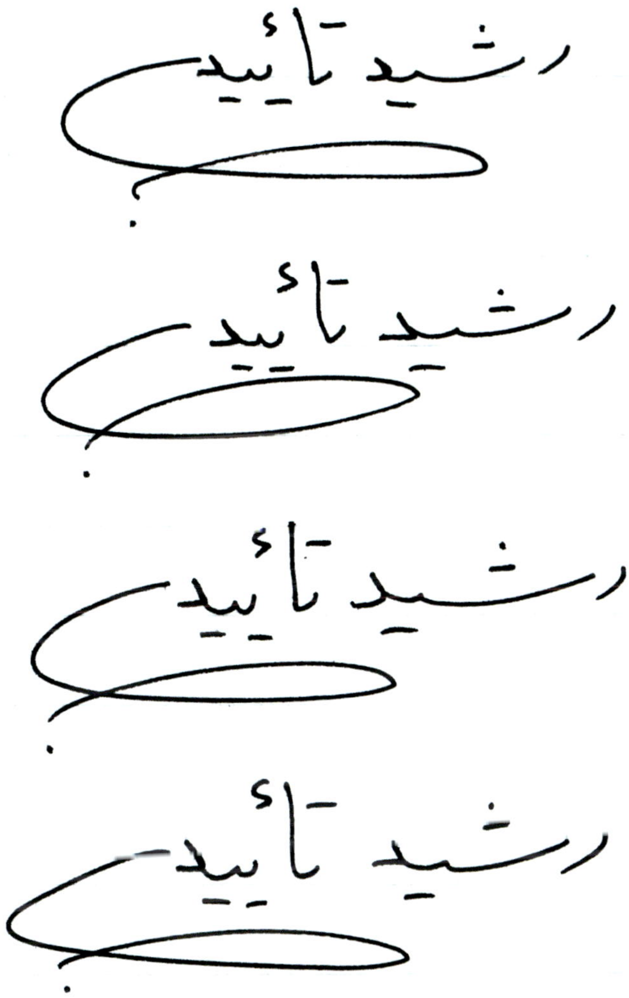

Figure 8.6 Four signatures written by the same person in Persian. Note the minimal natural variation shown between the signatures.

8.2.1.5 African Handwriting Systems

Ziegler (1988) provided a few samples of Nigerian handwriting that is mostly lettering and some signatures, with few comments as to the source of his material or the frequency of occurrence of the features that are illustrated. One feature noted is the profuse use of periods before initials and after signatures and numerical dates (e.g., 8/15/85.). He also noted that the cent symbol "¢," is frequently used with the dollar symbol (e.g., \$15:25¢), and that colons are used in amounts (\$15:25¢) and dates (e.g., 10:17:53). He provided samples of signatures with underlining. Little else is offered that might be particularly characteristic of the writing of the Nigerian population.

8.2.1.6 Asian Handwriting Systems

Caywood (1978) offers two examples of the English writing styles offered to Chinese, Japanese, and Korean students in the process of their learning to speak English. These copybook examples are not readily identifiable with known systems currently in use in North America, probably because both have been stripped of embellishments and flourishes, to facilitate the learning process. In this respect, they may correspond as closely to the D'Nealian system as to any other. Beyond that their usefulness is uncertain. Although there is no Chinese alphabet, there is an alphabet to transcribe the Chinese language (Figure 8.7).

Figure 8.7 Chinese alphabet example.

8.2.1.6.1 Hmong Handwriting

Tweedy (1995) reported that Hmong people (pronounced "Mong") originated in the northern portions of Laos, Thailand, and Vietnam, and in southern China. Many have moved, by way of refugee camps, to the United States after the war in Vietnam.

The Hmong people did not have a written language of their own until 1953, when one was developed for them by missionaries called the RPA (romanized popular alphabet). This alphabet was designed to use all of the letters of the Roman alphabet. On the heels of the RPA, another system of writing was developed that was called Pahawh Hmong, and used symbols created especially for the system rather than the Roman alphabet and letter forms. According to Tweedy, other systems or scripts have appeared on the scene since the late 1950s but none have become popular or survived (Figure 8.8).

Figure 8.8 Hmong handwriting example.

Tweedy's (1995) study of 107 samples of Hmong writings (68 males, 37 females, and 2 unknown), most of whom were taught to write before moving to the United States, failed to reveal any particular national characteristics that might serve to suggest a person of a Hmong background. There was a tendency (83%) to execute a lowercase lettered style for the allograph "b" (with a clockwise bowl and no loop). There was, however, a much greater tendency for Hmong writers to use lettered styles and fewer connections between letters. Frequently, not more than two letters would be joined. Beyond that the writings disclosed no particular class characteristics of value to a writing examination.

8.2.1.6.2 Vietnamese Handwriting

In a continuing study of the writings of Vietnamese that have immigrated to the United States since 1970, Torres (1987) provided a number of worthy observations in the nature of national characteristics. Vietnamese use the Latin alphabet in systems handed down under French rule. Correspondence with French writings can often be found. There are, however, other idiosyncrasies that may constitute national characteristics of their own. For example:

1. Signatures are highly stylized and written without breaks between the first, middle, and last names. It is typical of Vietnamese to place the signature in the middle of the signature line.
2. The "1" is frequently executed with an approach or secondary stroke.
3. The "2" is frequently executed with an initial curl within the upper curve.
4. The terminal stroke of the "3" is frequently without curvature.
5. The bowl of the "5" is often angular rather than all curved.
6. The staffs of "4," "7," and "9" often descend below the baseline.
7. The "6" commonly commences with a small hook.
8. Fewer than 50% of writers place a cross stroke on the "7."
9. The staff of the "9" frequently descends below the baseline; the bowl rests on the baseline with the resulted appearance of a letter "g."
10. Block letters frequently replace cursive capitals.
11. Lower case letter forms frequently replace capitals.
12. The lower loop of the "f" is executed clockwise.
13. Upstrokes to "b," "h," "l," and "k" frequently commence part way up the letter.
14. The bowl of the "p" is often open.
15. Terminal "t's" are often Palmer style. In other cases, the cross stroke is located to the right of the staff.
16. The "W" is sometimes formed by the overlapping of two separate "V"s.

8.2.1.7 Various National Handwriting Systems

Within the published and unpublished material written by document examiners it is frequently mentioned that writing systems are as nationalistic as languages, that the writing of a person taught to write in a foreign country retains a foreign accent. Hilton (1982) claims that "the presence of foreign writing characteristics is a strong indication of foreign background and particularly of foreign education" (p. 145). Among these authors, however, Hilton is the only writer who describes and illustrates a few of the foreign characteristics to be found in French, German, and Italian writings. Osborn (1929) provides a few samples of English writing without comment. Stangohr (1971) provides some 98 samples of writings or portions of samples of writings from around the world.

Caywood (1978) provided samples of writing from 15 transient individuals that had been educated in one country and were living in another, usually an English-speaking country. Their origins were mixed and included Ceylon, Greece, Iran, West Germany, Japan, India, Pakistan, Croatia, French Canada, and France. The samples are not accompanied by guidance as to what specific writing features may indicate the individual's country of origin or adoption.

McCarthy (1982), under the title *A Collection of Modern European Handwriting Systems*, describes a program for the assembly of samples of European writings to be pursued by the Forensic Document Laboratory of the Immigration and Naturalization Service, but offers only two samples of Cyrillic (Russian) writing without further comment. The United States Bureau of the Chief Postal Inspector (1954) produced a useful collection of standard alphabets most of which are in cursive writing styles from 28 nations around the world.

Work by Kroon-Van der Kooij (1987) provided five samples of four letters and two numerals (the uppercase "F" and "J," the lowercase "d" and "g," and the "7" and "8"), written by individuals from 10 different national backgrounds: the Netherlands, Surinam, Aruba/Curacao, Belgium, France, the United Kingdom, India, West Germany, Italy, and Spain. From these charts, certain national characteristics seem to emerge.

1. The Netherlands changed the system of writing taught in their schools in 1950 from a somewhat ornate style to one that is quite simplistic. Most capital letters are now quasi-printed forms without secondary strokes. The "F" is one such character in which the upper horizontal arm extends well to the left of the staff. This printed style is apparent in younger writers in the Netherlands. Surinam and Aruba/Curacao, both former colonies of the Netherlands, did not follow the 1950 change promptly as copybooks were evidently not available. France, the United Kingdom, and India also use a printed style, without the projection of the upper arm to the left of the staff. There is also a tendency to connect the strokes. West Germany is more cursive in style.
2. The "J" is a lettered style in the samples from France, the United Kingdom, and India.
3. The slope of the letter "g" tends to be vertical or backhand in the writings from France, the United Kingdom, and India.
4. The "7" is invariably crossed with, perhaps, the exception of India. The staff runs well through the baseline in the Netherlands, Surinam, and Aruba/Curacao, which is not surprising since the latter two are colonies of the Netherlands. The numeral sits on the baseline in all other country samples. The cross stroke in the Italian samples is quite consistently sloped downward to the baseline.
5. Construction of the numeral "8" seems to differ distinctly in the Netherlands and its colonies in that it commences with the counterclockwise formation of the lower bowl and ends with the clockwise formation of the upper bowl. The Surinam writings, however, include some samples in which the movement of the strokes appears to be in the opposite direction. The UK, West Germany, and Italy writings disclose a tendency to pirouette the structure of the figure so that its beginning and end meet at the center top.
6. The slope of the writing in the France, UK, and India samples tends to be vertical or even slightly backhand. The samples from West Germany, on the other hand, are clearly forehand leaning.
7. As far as the Belgium writings are concerned, it should be noted that the country is bilingual—French and Dutch. Belgian writings may follow the patterns afforded by either of these nationalities.

In 2003, Yalon consolidated a study of international handwriting into a single volume that included images of numerous handwriting samples from various languages including Chinese, Japanese, Thai, Hebrew, Arabic, Persian, Indian, Greek, Cyrillic, and the US print and cursive. There are comparative studies discussed and details about the language and graphic components of the handwriting. The book also included an extensive bibliography of over 240 references regarding non-Roman handwriting systems.

8.2.2 Physiological Constraints

8.2.2.1 Use of Foot or Mouth

Those that are not familiar with these types of cases find the ability of people to write with a foot or the mouth almost incredulous. Equally incredulous is that the written product may not be distinguishable in any particular fashion from the writings of any other person produced with a fully enabled hand. There are, of course, a number of factors involved. The individual that writes with the foot or the mouth does not have the facility of the hands to uncap the pen, hold the paper, turn over the page, manipulate an eraser, or the capacity to write on a horizontal surface at the elevation of a bank, business, or store counter. Nevertheless, persons incapacitated in this fashion from birth are capable of developing remarkable facility for adapting to the situation. The point is that when conditions are appropriate the writing itself resembles, in many respects, the general characteristics of the writing of any other individual.

This constitutes evidence that, in the mechanism of human writing, the mind is the principal component of this neuromuscular process. Raibert (1977), respecting footwriting and mouthwriting, has been commonly cited as supporting the concept of writing system independence in the motor process. Wellingham-Jones (1991c) reported a case of an individual who became a quadriplegic at the age of 26 as a result of spinal abscesses around the fourth and fifth cervical vertebrae of unknown etiology. Samples of postparalysis writing with an instrument held in the mouth are remarkably similar in letter forms, slant, loops, and proportions to samples of writing taken 2 years prior to the onset of the illness. The circumstances prompt the article's author to suggest that "handwriting is brainwriting."

Wann and Athenes (1987) describe a single case study of an individual with congenital absence of both arms who had 16 years of experience in footwriting and was employed in a clerical position. After a study of numerous aspects of the individual's writing, including form, pressure, speed, and velocity/curvature dependence the authors reported that there was little to distinguish the footwriting from the handwriting in size or form. However, interesting anomalies in letter formation were present. The directional preference for the formation for letters such as "e" and "o" was clockwise, contrary to all current writing practices of manual writers, the findings of Thomassen and Teulings (1979), and the samples of footwriting observed by Huber and Headrick. Writing speed was on average 60% slower than manual writers on similar tasks, but on the other hand, pressure and other aspects of writing performance were surprisingly similar.

This evidence tends to support the conclusion that the normal development in the use of an alternative motor system for writing will produce a script exhibiting the same control features observed in manual writing.

8.2.2.2 Use of Artificial Aids (Prostheses)

Artificial aids have been developed to satisfy the writing needs of particular individuals. More often than not, these are cases of persons that have lost the use of the dominant hand or arm due to accident or injury, or the inability to grasp the writing instrument owing to arthritis. These devices may be engineered to operate from the affected member (the arm or hand), from the head, or from a prosthesis designed to replace a lost hand or arm.

Studies have disclosed that after a period of practice with the artificial aid the ability to write reasonably well can be reacquired (Kelly 1975). This is not unlike the acquisition of skill in writing with the subdominant hand when circumstances make it necessary to do so. A common attribute of the writing produced with artificial aids may be observed in the lack of pen pressure that can be applied, so much so that ball point pens exhibit poor ink flow. Not surprisingly then, the preference of these writers seems to be the fiber-tipped pen. Furthermore, as in other situations in which new writing skills must be learned, the writing tends to be larger than normal, at least until the finer manipulations of the pen are accomplished.

8.2.2.3 Visual and Hearing Impairment

The writing of the deaf or hearing-impaired individual has not been the subject of frequent study. Indeed, it may be that it has been presumed that one's inability to hear would have little or no effect upon one's ability to communicate by pen and ink. This, of course, is not so. It may be also that these cases have been overlooked as to the numerous situations of a civil nature, for example, property transactions, wherein the validity of a signature of a hearing-impaired individual has been brought into question. Savage (1978) addressed the matter in some depth and provided a fairly comprehensive report on the various kinds of hearing loss and what might be expected of them in written products.

Hearing-impaired individuals are one of two classes: the hard of hearing, or hearing impaired, and the deaf. The hard of hearing are those who can identify through hearing (without visual receptive communication, for example, speech reading or lip reading), enough of its distinguishing features to permit at least partial recognition of the spoken language. With lip reading, the individual may comprehend more of the language that is furnished by vocabulary and syntax if it is a part of his or her linguistic code, that is, understanding of language.

A deaf person, on the other hand, is one who cannot identify enough of the prosodic and phonetic features of speech to permit recognition of word combinations. This individual relies mainly or entirely on speech reading or some other type of visual receptive communication. He or she may understand language in many instances, but his or her linguistic code will be much less developed, especially if hearing impaired or deaf from birth.

According to Savage (1978), traditionally there has always been a distinction made between the congenitally deaf (those who are born deaf), and the adventitiously deaf (those who are born with normal hearing that becomes nonfunctional through illness). Adventitious deafness is now less frequent since medical science has been able to treat and control illnesses such as rubella, meningitis, chronic respiratory infections, and otitis media, all of which caused deafness in the past.

To the number of adventitiously (illness-related) deaf persons must be added the large numbers of individuals that suffer hearing impairment with advancing age. These numbers are being constantly increased by the benefits of medical science in prolonging life, generally. The growth in the population wearing hearing aids is a reasonable indicator. However, statistics that reflect the constant change to the numbers of persons experiencing hearing impairment are not readily available, and consequently, there may be a higher frequency of hearing impairment in society than realized.

Years ago the term *deaf and dumb* was encountered in reference to the deaf, particularly among the younger age group. Use of the term, however, indicated a serious lack of understanding of the problem. Hart and Rosenstein (1964) demonstrated that deaf children are endowed, according to most psychometric test measurements, with normal intelligence and abilities. The deaf child, however, is maturing in a world that is stimulus-rich for others but is lacking in meaningful sound for him or her. Thus, he or she is compelled to master one of life's most vital tasks, language, without helpful aural experience. Under these circumstances, the deaf child was more often mute, a condition for which the term *dumb* was commonly substituted, along with its conventional, but, in this case, improper meaning.

The child, whether deaf or able to hear, is required to learn how to respond to and produce patterns of phonology, meaning, morphology, syntax, and function words. When language must be acquired by vision alone it is much more difficult to master without the benefit of linguistic stimuli. It is not surprising then that the hearing-disabled child is slower by some 3 years or more in his or her acquisition of language and educational attainment than his or her hearing-enabled counterpart. As a teenager, his or her reading vocabulary may be even further behind. Because of its importance as an educational tool, his or her underdeveloped vocabulary will greatly influence his or her academic progress, but this is not a valid reflection of his or her intellectual ability. Accordingly, the fallacy that the deaf are dumb should be completely dismissed, as Vernon's (2005) study clearly demonstrates.

Savage's (1978) study did not reveal any particular handwriting feature(s) or general property or properties common to the writing of the hearing impaired, by which their executions as a group might be distinguished. There is as much variation in writing habits, style, and system as is encountered in the writing of the hearing-capable population.

The principal characteristic by which the writing of the deaf deviates from that of the hearing-capable individual rests in the field of linguistics. Every language evolves a criteria governing sentence structure, word order, grammar, and punctuation under the general umbrella of syntax. Furthermore, in language there are lexical meanings to the separate words and structural meanings to word combinations. Both lexical meanings and structural meanings must be present and correct for an utterance to be intelligible. It has been held that deaf children acquire lexical meanings more readily than structural meanings, and it is this delayed mastery of morphology, syntax, and function words (verbs) that retards the development and utilization of proper sentence forms.

For the most part, the deaf child develops language through lip reading, but by this process he or she does not perceive every word of an utterance. The key words are caught or perhaps only the root words, for example, *man* instead of *men*, *work* instead of *worked*. Words not understood are ignored, as are function words that tie a communication together. To achieve meaning, the deaf child forms links between the words he or she has lip-read and fills in with nonverbal clues derived from the situation, the gestures and facial expressions of the speaker. Thus, there are two points to watch for in writings of the deaf: (1) emphasis on the use of key words, often leading to improper use of singular or plural forms, and (2) the omission of function words, such as definite and indefinite articles, for example, "the" or "a," and others like "for," "to," "by," "at," "in," etc. that serve to tie sentences together.

While word knowledge increases with time for the deaf, word usage progresses more slowly. At any age they display a persistency in the use of certain phrases, indicating an inability to apply normal variation and flexibility to written language. Furthermore, two types of errors are common to their written communications: one of substitution and one of addition. Substitution produces sentences like "A boy will running" rather than "is running," whereas, addition creates sentences like "A dog is be barking." Remarkably, the frequency of these errors persist, notwithstanding any growth in the person's vocabulary.

An error that does tend to diminish with age and vocabulary is that of word order, seen for example in verbs: "A girl playing is," and in noun/adjective relationships: "A dog brown." Studies of punctuation in the writings of the deaf from the perspectives of addition, omission, and substitution have revealed that the hearing impaired are equal to or superior to the hearing abled in this respect.

Some general observations regarding the writing of the deaf include:

1. There is a greater inclination at all ages to use nouns, rather than pronouns.
2. There is a greater inclination to omit verbs.
3. If articles such as "a," "an," and "the" are used, they are used in greater numbers than by the hearing population.
4. Greater difficulty is encountered in the use of prepositions, adverbs, adjectives, and conjunctions.
5. There is greater inclination to write short (but more) sentences of simple construction, employing limited vocabulary.
6. There is a greater tendency to commit errors in verb tenses, and lexical substitutions, for example, family for familiar or vice versa.

While these points are admittedly matters of linguistics, and some may argue that they are beyond the purview of the handwriting examiner, their inclusion here has been prompted by the intent to provide some insight for the examiner into the potentials of the subject for the identification or elimination of hearing-impaired individuals from their handwriting. Indeed, the points are not so complex that they cannot be appreciated by any reviewer without the aid of special knowledge of linguistics or the involvement of statistics.

Progress in the social acceptance and treatment of deaf persons in recent years has had its implications for handwriting examiners. The teaching of visual gestural language known as ASL (American sign language) has modified understanding of what to expect in the writing of the deaf.

The native language of the deaf person is not English, but ASL. ASL is a unique and distinct language that has its own principals of syntax, its own idioms, and its own problems in translating the English language, all of which can be helpful in determining whether a writing was executed by a person so restricted. ASL, however, is not so much a language as it is a code, one of several that have been created to teach English to deaf children. As a code or set of principles, ASL dictates rules for the sign language content of a communication that may also be evident in the extended writings of the deaf person. Kerr and Taylor (1992) have provided an outline of some of the characteristics of ASL, that such writings may exhibit and the reasons for them.

Points that they mention include:

1. In ASL, syntax is described as sign order rather than word order. Signs are arranged in the order in which the events they represent occur or occurred.
2. Signs are repeated to show plurality, for *few, many, some.*
3. Tenses are not incorporated in verb signs.
4. Verbs differ according to directionality.
5. In ASL, one sign is used for all forms of be. Signing frequently omits them.
6. There are no articles in ALS ("a," "an," or "the").
7. First and second person singular pronouns tend to be left to the end.

Kerr and Taylor (1992) summarized that the ability of the deaf person to use the English language in writing (or speaking) varies with the individual. Many documents written by them will exhibit linguistic evidence indicative of deafness. Determinations that the author is deaf, however, should not be based simply on the fact that the quality of English seems poor.

Studies of sinistrality in the handwriting of the deaf by Boyd (1967) have indicated that there is a lesser degree of dominance of one hand over the other, regardless of the hand preferred. This being the case, if evidence, such as that delineated above, is present in a questioned document that would indicate that it may be the execution of a hearing-impaired individual, the examination of samples from both hands of a hearing impaired suspect may be warranted.

Another matter of interest to those who examine handwriting is the observation that sinistrality is more common among the hearing-impaired population than among others. Studies of deafness due to external causes at or near the time of birth, of the prenatal and postnatal exogenous groups, disclosed that 16.7% were left-handed in writing, as opposed to 11% of the population, generally. Among the hereditary deaf group, the endogenous group, 30% were found to be sinistral (see Chapter 11).

In summary then, the manner in which a handwriting by a hearing-impaired person may be expected to differ from that of the normal hearing person must involve the field of linguistics. Under these circumstances, a single signature or a few words of text are not likely to provide adequate material for the purposes of indicating hearing impairment from an examination of the handwriting.

The writing of the blind or visually-impaired individual is quite a different matter. The characteristics it may exhibit will diverge to some extent depending on whether the vision loss occurred prior to the point in the individual's education when writing is normally taught, or after some experience in the writing process had been acquired. Then too, the written product will vary with the degree of the vision loss.

The terms *legally blind, functionally blind, industrially blind*, or *partially blind*, each of which is used relative to visual impairment, do not all mean the same thing to all persons. Legal blindness is defined as the condition of having not more than 20/200 corrected vision in the better eye. Partial blindness is the condition of having between 20/70 and 20/200 that also includes functional blindness and industrial blindness. Furthermore, there is a variety in kinds of visual impairment some of which have a bearing on one's writing ability. These encompass:

1. Congenital blindness—total blindness from birth.
2. Myopia—near sightedness. Good vision, but only at short range.
3. Hyperopia—far sightedness. Good vision, but only at long range.
4. Optic atrophy—damage to the optic nerve resulting in a small field of vision, restricting areas usable for reading and writing.
5. Retinitis pigmentosa—night blindness. Difficulty seeing under reduced illumination, particularly in artificial light.
6. Retinal detachment—separation of the retina from the choroid behind. A portion of the central field of vision is obstructed.
7. Cataracts—clouding of the lens resulting in a loss of detail.
8. Glaucoma—an elevation of pressure within the eye that may destroy side or peripheral vision.
9. Retinopathy—a swelling and leaking of retinal blood vessels. May cause blurring or obstruction of vision. Common among diabetics.
10. Macular degeneration—three types from different causes: the thinning or atrophy of the macula, the abnormal growth of blood vessels behind the retina, or the blistering of the retina. Principal effect is the distortion of the image in the field of vision.

Various writing aids have been offered to the visually impaired from time to time, none of which have been widely adopted. Templates have been designed as a column of long windows to accommodate lines of writing or lettering on a reasonably-sized sheet of paper, and others provide windows within which a signature might be executed. Templates provide problems for the execution of lower loops and descending staffs. Some templates employ elastic or wires to represent rulings or baselines. Still other techniques for the production of folds in a sheet of paper have been suggested. For example, the rolling of the sheet around a pencil, withdrawing the pencil and flattening the paper tube against the table surface to create parallel creases about one-half inch apart, is intended to provide tactile but not restrictive guides for the baseline of the writing. Related to this is the Marks system of writing that teaches the subject to locate the writing well above the guide lines to accommodate downward extending letters. Other instructional techniques encourage the production of letters in rectangular forms.

Understandably, as these types of writing aids imply, one of the principal disadvantages of a visually-impaired writer is the lack or loss of feedback information that the writer with normal vision experiences with each and every movement of the writing instrument. Without that information, the visually impaired must judge the form, length, and location of strokes without references. Partial vision can provide a few guides and the availability of these references or reference points may determine the quality of the writing or lettering that the subject is able to produce.

Understandably too, a well-practiced signature may represent the best quality of writing of which the subject is capable, and this quality may supply little evidence of the nature or extent of the impairment, particularly if the vision loss occurred long after writing habits had been established.

There are cursive writing systems offered that prescribe the construction of nearly all letters without the necessity to lift the pen from the paper. Cross strokes are formed as retracings ("t," "F"), or as a result of the retracing of other strokes ("H"). Where pen lifts must occur, as in "i" dots or "j" dots, the index finger of the other hand is employed to mark the position of the writing instrument at the point of leaving the paper, to which point the instrument is returned after the dot has been made.

Thus, the characteristics of the extended writing of the visually impaired or totally blind person that occur to a greater or lesser extent according to the degree of sight loss, the writing aids employed and the type of instruction received, if any, are likely to include:

1. Misalignment of letters with respect to one another, of words with respect to one another, and of writing with respect to a ruled or implied baseline
2. Inconsistency of spacing between letters and between words
3. Intersection of writing with other writing or printed material
4. Overlapping of letters or words, sometimes making reading or deciphering difficult
5. Flattening of letter bases, and the flattening and extending of connections in cursive writing, indicative of the use of a visual or writing aid
6. Execution of squared letter forms, particularly in hand printing, if certain kinds of writing instruction have been received
7. Infrequent pen lifts in cursive writing, and connections, frequently longer than necessary, employed to assist in positioning the succeeding letter
8. Absence of "t" crossings in cursive writing, or alternatively their construction as a continuous motion of the pen
9. Absence of "i" dots or "j" dots in cursive writing, or their consistent application and location over the stem of the letter, indicative of the employment of some means of assistance, such as another finger

10. Stunting of letter designs, particularly the upper and lower loops
11. Unrepaired or unretouched occurrences of pen failure creating voids in ink deposits in the strokes of ballpoint pen writing
12. Lack of fluency, or the appearance of tremor in strokes, owing to an uncertainty in the formation of letters or in the writing process
13. Infrequent introduction of hesitation marks or scratches at the beginning of letters or commencement strokes
14. Some increase in letter sizes from that of previous practices, if writing had been learned prior to the onset or occurrence of the impairment
15. Increase in vertical spacing between lines of writing

Other authors report features as characteristic of handwriting distortion caused by visual impairment. Features of handwriting written by those who are blind or visually-impaired reported by Beacom (1967) include: hand printing of the signature, poor alignment, preference for uppercase letters, square-shaped "r" forms, problems writing certain letters (e.g., "j," "b," "d," "k," "h," "f" as the retraced movement of these letters creates difficulty for blind writers), difficulties with the letters "t" and "i" due to the cross and dot formations in those letters, problems forming connectives between letters, lack of uniformity in size, illegibility, and incomplete signatures.

Lindblom (1983) reported that handwriting features associated with visual impairment include tremor, pen scratches, misalignment of words/letters, writing across or through other material, squared letters, overlapping of letters, ink errors, problems in writing certain letters, infrequent pen lifts, absence of "t" bars and "i" dots, inconsistent spacing, stunted letter designs, and flattened letter bases (due to use of visual aids).

In a forensic case study, Masson (1988) found that the handwriting was difficult to decipher because handwritten letters and words were written on top of another. Some of the primary effects of handwriting distortion included lack of baseline alignment, overwriting, entanglement, inconsistency in word and letter spacing, and erratic proportional relationships.

Komal et al. (1999) performed a statistical analysis of the writings of over 60 individuals who were blind or visually impaired. The results showed that the writers exhibited overlapping/intermingling letters, unusual/distorted letter forms, ink failures (because the subjects could not see that the pen was not working), problems with certain letters ("S," "A," "G," "P," "H," "K"), tremor, preference for capital letters, line quality problems, alignment, and inconsistent size.

The examination of the writing of the blind or visually impaired by handwriting examiners seems, for the most part, directed toward the identification of signatures as genuine executions of a given individual, or toward a reliable decipherment of executions that are difficult or impossible to read or to understand. In the latter cases, confusion occurs from the overlapping of words and letters and the extreme misalignments and irregular spacing of them relative to one another. The task then becomes one of identifying letters individually, and combining them appropriately to create words that can lead to sentences. While not an impossible task, it may be and usually is extremely time-consuming (Todd 1965; Beacom 1967; Bleuschke 1968; Lindblom 1983; Duane 1989).

Further to what has been said above, and particularly to item 5, individuals have been encountered whose sight is not significantly impaired but who practice straightedge writing, or what is referred to as *blind man's writing.* These individuals employ some device, such as a card or ruler that is positioned along the baseline of the writing to provide a buffer against which the writing instrument is deliberately run to inflict a horizontal but quite unnatural characteristic upon the execution. The intent of the writer is to give the writing an attribute that is both neat and unusual. A danger to the writing examiner lies in misinterpreting this characteristic as evidence of vision impairment.

The technique of producing simulated blind man's writing of this kind usually requires some ensuing action by the writer to add the lower loops and extenders to staffs that the straightedge device obstructs. The accuracy with which the elements are added is evidence of the ability of the individual to see reasonably well. The manner of executing and adding the descending elements can be of considerable value in writer identification. Some writers add one element at a time, some add the elements for a line of writing at a time, and others will complete the additions for a page of writing, at one and the same time. The regularity of straightedge writing in letter and word spacing, letter slopes, and letter forms is usually a reliable means of distinguishing between the products of individuals with and individuals without the ability to see. Morgan and Zilly (1991) have provided excellent examples of straightedge writing and some of the techniques employed to accomplish the effect.

8.2.3 Genetic Factors

8.2.3.1 Familial Relationships

The earliest published comment regarding the possibility of writing similarities due to familial relationships is by Chandler (1911). The article illustrates three cases in which some general similarity is noted between brothers, sisters, or father and son, but the similarity is not so great that current and competent examiners would be easily deceived.

Stevens (1964) noted the lack of published material on the resemblance in the writings of siblings as compared to that found in nonsiblings. The study conducted was a comparison of the writings from three control groups with the writings of eight members (seven female) of one family, all of whom were dextral writers, taught in the same school by the same teachers and with the Palmer writing system. The control groups were matched as closely as possible in age and gender, but were unrelated to each other. Nine elements were said to have been considered including stroke endings, continuity, slant, letter forms, proportions, size, speed, skill, and pictorial appearance.

The results indicated that there was greater similarity and less variation between the members of the family than there was in the control groups. The level of resemblance between some members of the family was remarkable, although discrimination could be made. One control group, eight inmates from a women's correctional institute, disclosed the greatest variation from writer to writer. Suffice it to say that family relationships, locale, and schooling can result in writings with considerable resemblance to one another that is greater than might otherwise be expected.

Münch (1987) reported on the similarity found in one case in the writings of a mother and daughter. The questioned material was limited to three sets of initials. While there were disparities between the questioned and known writings they were not so consistent or so fundamental that they could not have been attributed to natural variations, if the examination and study was not thorough.

A total of 212 family signatures collected from 53 families were examined in a study reported by Miller (1991). While nothing specific concerning genetic influence could be determined by the study, it was noted that over half of the families contained signatures that matched other family members especially among father/son and brother/brother. Miller advised that sufficient standards are necessary in cases involving the differentiation of family signatures.

A preliminary study was reported by Hladij (1999) who studied the handwriting of three generations. No significant similarities were noted between grandparents and grandchildren especially since the handwriting skill was better in the older generation than the younger generation. There was more similarity reported between children and parents, but it was not possible to determine if the similarity was caused by genetic influences.

In the writing of sinistrals, there is no evidence that left-handedness in writing can be related to familial sinistrality (i.e., left-handedness in brothers, sisters, and other relatives). Nevertheless, there is some support for a relationship between sinistral children and sinistral parents. Maternal left-handedness is associated with sinistrality in both male and female children, although paternal left-handedness can be associated with sinistrality in sons, but not in daughters.

8.2.3.2 Multiple Births

Writers who are the product of multiple births, that is, twins, triplets, quadruplets, or quintuplets, by virtue of their genetic background might develop or possess very similar writing habits that could make discrimination between them difficult. Thorndike (1915) and Kramer and Lauterbach (1928) wrote on the subject of similarity in the writing of twins, but not from the point of view of writing identification as the authors were not document examiners. Thorndike, however, does point out the dissimilarity in the writing of twins, and goes so far as to say that twins may be more easily distinguished by their handwriting than by their physical appearance.

Multiple births are classed as identical, that is, the products of the same egg, or fraternal, that is, the products of two or more eggs fertilized at the same time. Fraternal twins are stated to be no more alike than any other two siblings from the same parents. On the other hand, identical or same egg twins are likened to the left and right halves of one individual's body (Dahlberg 1951).

Beacom (1960), a former handwriting teacher, was the first of the document examination profession to tackle the subject. It was her recollection that the writing of twins differed sufficiently for discrimination purposes, but she was without empirical data to support her position. In a study of the writings of 50 pairs of twins, 19 pairs were identical and 31 fraternal. Twenty pairs were both male, 22 pairs were both female, and 8 pairs were mixed as to gender. The identical twins were always, of course, the same gender.

Four pairs of identical twins were mixed as to handedness, one dextral and one sinistral, a circumstance that prompts some to classify them as mirror twins. Three pairs of fraternal twins were similarly mixed as to handedness. Forty-three pairs were both dextral, and of some import is the fact that no pairs were both sinistral.

Writings were assessed with the assistance of the Ayers scale for writing quality on the basis of legibility, relative sizes, spacings, slant, and line qualities. Although some pairs received similar scores, this did not reflect similarity in their writings as different ratings were received by each member of the pair for different aspects of their writings, but sometimes resulted in a similar cumulative total.

Twins displayed comparable abilities to their siblings in cursive writing, lettering, and script writing. Notwithstanding their similarity in schools attended, teachers, and family environments, the writings of twins could be discriminated from one another without great difficulty given adequate specimens. Basic differences could always be found. Beacom (1960) also found some progression in the differences between siblings, probably resulting from differences in occupations as adults. There were no particular deviations in writing quality related to gender that were unlike other populations.

In an endeavor to determine whether twins displayed greater resemblance to one another in their writings than other siblings, Kramer and Lauterbach (1928) studied the products of 205 pairs of twins and 101 pairs of siblings. It was their finding that twins showed a greater degree of resemblance than other siblings, that same gender twins displayed a greater resemblance to one another than dissimilar gender twins, and, like Beacom (1960), resemblance does not increase with age. Where greater resemblance occurs, however, there may be factors other than genetics at work.

Gamble's (1980) study of 58 pairs of identical twins, 24 pairs of males and 34 pairs of females, claimed that no matter how closely two persons are alike and related to one another, their handwriting allowed them to be differentiated. He found 42 of his sets of twins were dextral writers, 15 sets were mixed and one set was sinistral. These statistics are slightly different to those of other studies, but the number of subjects is not large in any case and this may account for the difference from other studies.

Gamble's (1980) study was directed at seven elements of writing: (1) pictorial effect, (2) size, (3) slope, (4) speed, (5) writing quality, (6) proportions, and (7) letter forms. His finding was that identical twins can exhibit greater similarity in their writing than might otherwise be expected. Nevertheless, similarities in letter forms and general appearance are accompanied by a sufficient number of differences to allow an examiner to discriminate between individuals.

Beacom (1960) claims to have studied the writings of triplets, quadruplets, and quintuplets with similar results—that the issue of multiple births develop writing habits that are distinctive from one another and evidently independent of their genetic backgrounds.

Although the handwriting of twins can be differentiated, a handwriting examination study (Srihari et al. 2008) using computational analysis advised caution when approaching casework as error rates were higher in discriminating twin handwriting (12.91%) from nontwin handwriting (3.7%). The nonstatistical studies commented that some twin handwritings had remarkable similarity (Beacom 1960; Gamble 1980). In performing a detailed analysis, Gamble noted similarities in general appearance, size, slope, writing quality, and several letter characteristics. Differentiation of the twin handwritings was based on certain letter characteristics that did not match. A study on triplets reported that the sibling writings could be differentiated (Lines and Franck 2003).

Boot (1998) noted that certain mirror twins wrote with a high degree of graphic similarity. However, handedness of the twin could be established through stroke direction which led to identification in mirror twin writing pairs. Stroke direction between left- and right-handed writers showed that right to left horizontal crossings in the uppercase print letters "A," "E," "J," "T," "H," and especially the cursive *t*, were indicative of a left-handed writer (Franks et al. 1985). Handedness may play an important role in twin writing as a cognitive study reported a higher incidence of left-handedness among twins than single born (Annett 2006). In a case study, Harralson (2007) used stroke direction to differentiate the writing between identical mirror twins.

These findings support Boot's (1998) study that mirror twins can be differentiated through stroke direction. The findings also support previous studies and especially Srihari et al.'s (2008) study that twin writings can be differentiated, albeit through an analysis of microfeatures. Macro and style features, and sometimes critical writing elements, are not always useful in differentiating twin handwritings, especially when there is a high degree of graphic similarity.

8.2.3.3 Gender

The possibility of distinguishing the gender of the writer from his or her handwriting has been the subject of many investigations. Some studies have shown a trend a little above chance in judging gender from handwriting. There has also been the observation that, on average, female writers are more skillful at writing than male writers. For a more thorough discussion on this topic, see Chapter 11.

8.2.4 Physical (Normal)

8.2.4.1 Maturity, Practice, and Development

This section is directed at the normal and natural changes, if any, that occur to handwriting over the period of a lifetime. Harrison (1958b) comments that a developed handwriting has the potential for identification.

The development and progress of one's handwriting passes through four stages in the course of a lifetime: (1) the formative stage, (2) the impressionable or adolescent stage, (3) the mature stage, and (4) the stage of degeneration. Development is a matter of control. During the first two stages, the writing act is more deliberate and under greater voluntary control. During the latter two stages, the act is more involuntary and under progressively less control.

From these premises, the changes that occur during the first stage are seen in structure, fluency, and consistency. It is the learning stage for all persons, when letter designs are being developed and skills are being mastered. The changes occurring in the second stage may be quite pronounced in form or style, depending on the source of the influence responsible for the change. The desire to imitate another style may stem from many exogenous factors, both aesthetic and identification related (Bellomy 1875; Hecker 1981). Writing of the third stage is more consistent over longer periods of time, and likely to change only in fluency or design; the former usually being the result of writing frequency, and the latter usually being the product of a particular occupation. The fourth stage, associated with endogenous factors, is prompted largely by neurophysiological degeneration, the onset and the magnitude of which varies with the individual. It is the stage in which line tremors may become evident, shapes, slopes, and sizes become less consistent, and quality or skill in writing becomes progressively poorer.

A kinematic study (Rosenblum and Werner 2006) on the digitally-captured handwriting of healthy elderly persons (53 subjects ages 60–94) showed lower speed and pressure as well as longer pen down (on paper) and pen up (in air) time. Caligiuri and Mohammed (2012) provided a comprehensive discussion on research with respect to aging in handwriting and cited studies that also discuss age effects over a lifetime. Generally, elderly persons write more slowly and there may be increased variability. This topic is important to handwriting examiners who encounter cases where there may be significant differences in a person's age between the questioned material and the comparison samples.

8.2.4.2 Handedness

8.2.4.2.1 Dextrality or Right-Handedness

Approximately 90% of the population are right-handed insofar as handwriting is concerned. This is not to suggest that the same percentages will be found in the handedness of various activities including golfing, batting, holding utensils while eating, shooting or in any other activity in which a limb or an eye on a particular side of the body is chosen to direct or to execute the action. For many years, instruction in penmanship was tailored to the right-handed individual. The grasp of the writing instrument was prescribed and the orientation of the paper to the writer was directed. Notwithstanding these facts, right-handers appeared in small numbers that preferred the IHP (inverted hand posture) in which the axis of the pen or pencil was directed upward and away from the writer rather than toward the writer. A much greater number of sinistrals (left-handers) use the IHP. For more information respecting handedness, see Chapter 11.

8.2.4.2.2 Sinistrality or Left-Handedness

A comprehensive discussion of the indicators of sinistrality can be found in Chapter 11.

8.2.4.2.3 Ambidexterity

Some writers have been observed with the ability to write reasonably well with either hand. Among the recognized authorities in handwriting examination, Harrison (1958b) commented on ambidexterity. In his view, the individuals exhibiting this ability are probably persons who were sinistral in their early years, but who were persuaded to change to dextral in handwriting during the course of their schooling. Suffice it to say that, in most cases, the executions by the two hands will be similar in many respects, but divergences between them will be found in fluency or writing quality. The reason for this is may be due to the lack of practice that one hand will experience owing to the writer's inclination to use the other hand as a matter of personal preference.

8.2.4.2.4 Grasp

There are two primary postures of grasp: (1) normal posture (writing instrument directed away from writer's body) and (2) inverted posture (writing instrument directed toward the writer's body). For more information on this topic, see Chapter 11.

8.2.5 Physical (Abnormal State of Health)

8.2.5.1 Handwriting as a Diagnostic Tool

For the most part, the effects of an illness upon one's handwriting stem from and portray a loss of control or fluency (Wellingham-Jones 1991a). The result is a more erratic execution, exhibiting omissions, distortions (particularly in the formation of loops and compound curves), irregularities in the application of pressure, general illegibility, and increased inconsistency.

While writing skill and quality deteriorates progressively there are some recognizable aspects (i.e., habits) of the writing that persist. There is no logical reason for fundamental changes in writing habits to occur. Although the act of writing may involve a degree of effort, it is not deliberate and pressure controlled in the usual sense. It is never drawn.

The occurrence of micrographia in writing, that is a reduction in size, can occur as early as 2 years prior to the onset of Parkinson disease in some 10–15% of cases. Micrographia has also been observed in a few cases of cerebral syphilis and schizophrenia.

While the deterioration of handwriting is an accepted consequence of many kinds of illness, and simply of aging itself, there are few characteristics of this deterioration that may be identified with any particular illness, or family of illnesses. Age and illness eventually affects the neuromuscular coordination which alters the writer's ability to control the writing act. But the effect on the neuromuscular system is largely the same, regardless of the cause.

While a decline in writing ability and a loss of vigor is expected during illness, some signatures written during an illness do not reflect the expected writing weaknesses. This may be the case, particularly with illnesses of short duration and those that do not limit the individual's mobility or confine the person to bed. Being the most automatic element of a person's writing, signatures tend to be the most resistant to change. Consequently, some signatures written during an illness or recuperation are not altered sufficiently to hamper or to alter handwriting examinations (Hilton 1969a).

8.2.5.2 Illnesses Organically Related

8.2.5.2.1 Agraphia, Aphasia, Dyslexia, ADD, and ADHD

Agraphia, aphasia, and dyslexia are closely related conditions: *aphasia* is understood to be impairment of the power to use and understand words, although some definitions are broad enough to include impairment of all means of communication including speaking, reading, writing, and ciphering. To be precise, however, *agraphia* is the term that identifies the inability to write, or to write in an orderly fashion, as the result of brain lesions. *Dyslexia* is a more limited disturbance of the ability to read while *dysgraphia* is associated with impairment or disturbance in writing or written expression.

Aphasia usually stems from head injuries, strokes, brain infections, and tumors. It is frequently accompanied by paralysis (hemiplegia) from which the upper limbs recover more slowly than the lower limbs. More often, paralysis will affect the right side of the body rather than the left requiring dextrals to learn to write with the left hand in the recovery process, and reportedly as many as 90% of them succeed, over a period of 6 months. Furthermore, improvement in writing seems more difficult to achieve than improvement in speech. Ordinarily, as might be expected, the skills in writing do not fully return.

Most forms of aphasia affect one's ability to write and abnormal genuine writing is often disputed, particularly with respect to wills and financial transactions. Furthermore, senile aphasics are frequently the victims of fraud or miscreant influence. Accordingly, the correct interpretation of the symptoms of aphasia may be helpful in the study of aphasic's writing and the peculiar manners in which the writing process can be impaired, when such cases arise. With the current increase in life expectancy, the concomitant increase in strokes and the increase in motor accident injuries, there bodes a corresponding increase in the number of cases in which the writing of aphasics will be the center of argument.

Harris (1969) provided an excellent coverage of the disorder and its effects upon motor skills such as writing. Aphasics do not seem to be effected by a single symptom, but experience a combination of disorders involving reading, writing, and speech. Cases of pure motor agraphia (i.e., able to read and speak, but unable to write) are rare. The disorder attacks a person in a highly individual manner, and generalizations are seldom possible. Recovery is equally diversified. Persons afflicted under the age of 50 make more progress than others, but it is never possible to forecast the results of therapy. Suffice it to say, recovery is never complete.

Writing suffers in either execution or composition or both. *Motor agraphia* is an inability to write due to an inability to form letters, but ability to spell is retained. *Amnesic agraphia (or agnostic agraphia)* is an inability to spell, but ability to manipulate the writing instrument is retained. *Paragraphia* is an inability to write the correct words, but the ability to copy text is retained. When aphasia is accompanied by a degree of paralysis (hemiplegia), the individual must learn to write with the other hand. Recovery in penmanship ability varies but generally finds a plateau beyond which little improvement occurs.

Writing ability is not always effected by aphasia. Mental skills may suffer more than motor skills. Accordingly, the writing itself is not always a reliable indicator in recovered aphasics. The context, syntax, spelling, and repetition of names or words has to be considered. Peculiarities in arrangement and inconsistencies in spacing may also prove helpful.

Head (1963) classified aphasic disorders into four groups with symptomatic handwriting observations for each:

1. Verbal defects—the person knows what he or she wants to say but is unable to express correct words. May not be able to write, but writing of signature is last ability to disappear and first to return upon recovery.
2. Syntactical defects—the person speaks in a jumble of brief phrases, is confused and only isolated words are understandable. Composition is affected more than manual ability. Able to execute a letter, but unable to read it. Always executes a recognizable signature after experiencing the initial shock.
3. Nominal defects—able to describe an object, but unable to name it. May be able to write his or her name. Can copy text but unable to compose.
4. Semantic defects—may talk coherently in short phrases. Unable to compose or comprehend paragraphs. No significant effects on handwriting. May write in fast scrawl to avoid losing train of thought. Context may be confused, but writing is otherwise normal.

Although writing skill is often affected, one's inability to compose thoughts on paper is more frequently observed. The individual may be able to copy a text and produce a legible script, but writing from memory (e.g., the days of the week) may display great deterioration. It may result in the omission of small words such as articles, prepositions, and conjunctions, in accelerating the writing process sometimes to the point of skipping words, or in producing mirror writing. The execution of proper letter forms can be difficult. It seems that the capacity to manipulate the writing instrument can be retained, but there is a loss in the mental capacity to know what to write.

When writing is affected, and particularly in the case of the agraphic, the forms of letters may be irregular, and mistakes are made that may or may not be corrected. Alignments of letters and proportions are irregular, which Neudert (1963) attributes to disturbances of coordination. Some individuals have difficulty with numbers, but others that are unable to speak, read, or write may be able to solve mathematical problems. Some can count in proper sequence, but are unable to comprehend the meaning of the numerals.

As aforementioned, the extent of the disorder varies greatly with the individual. From the reader's viewpoint a written product can be confusing owing to the interchanging of words with similar sounds, usually rendering the sentence meaningless at first glance. Beacom (1970) offers several examples:

beat–heat	stamp–damp	hair–chair	locks–socks	gun–pun
pair–fair	sty–sly	tool–cool	wet–met	take–cake

Also provided are examples of misspellings of words containing double consonants, for example, *leter* for *letter*, *hamer* for *hammer*, *mater* for *matter*, *seling* for *selling*. Vowels may be changed and phonetically similar letters may be substituted: for example, *watur* or *watar* for *water*, *fathur* or *fathar* for *father*. Intermediate syllables may be omitted in long words, for example, *rember* for *remember*, or *infortion* for *information*. Occasionally, consonants are omitted, for example, *quater* for *quarter*, *coner* for *corner*, or *kitche* for *kitchen*.

Questions of mental competence are difficult to decide. There may be a tendency to erroneously classify all aphasics as the same or equal. It has been recommended that if an individual is capable of signing his or her name in a semilegible manner he or she should be allowed to do so, if the need for a signature arises. Harris (1969) noted that speech therapists consider writing to be an important kind of therapy for aphasics, and for that reason often retain dated exemplars in a patient's file, thus, providing a ready source of specimen material, if needed, for handwriting comparisons at some later date.

Dyslexia, on the other hand, is a learning disability that becomes apparent in children as a difficulty in learning to read and later as a problem with spelling. It is thought to be a maturational defect that lessens as the child grows older and is capable of improvement or correction, especially with the proper remedial assistance. It is usually a genetically-determined condition, appearing to affect more boys than girls, that is unrelated to intelligence, teaching methods, emotional factors, or sociocultural circumstances.

McCarthy (1984) has written on the subject principally because the matter was raised in cross-examination in a case in which a dyslexic was accused of an offense and the issue of dyslexia and disguise in the writing standards became significant. This raises an important consideration in the collection of standards from those who have conditions that have some features similar to disguise.

The condition becomes apparent when children experience difficulty in learning to read, because for a percentage of them some letters may be reversed (e.g., "b" for "d") or wrongly interpreted (e.g., "cut" for "cat"). Difficulties in learning are increased in developing writing skills. Because it is a problem, handwriting is, invariably, slowly and carefully executed to achieve legibility and accuracy. Consequently, the child suffers scholastically in traditional schools where time is limited or essay type of answers to questions are often required.

The slow, careful writing process results in large, well-formed letters with an almost vertical slant. Interletter spacing tends to be greater, reversals of letters sometimes occurs and "i" dots and "t" crossings are carefully formed and positioned; however, in some cases, these elements of the letters will be omitted completely. Misspellings and malformation of letters can make extended writings more difficult to comprehend. Dyslexics may err in transcribing words that sound the same but which have different meanings, such as *read* and *red*. Because of the difficulties experienced in writing, vocabularies in written text tend to be more limited, and the text itself tends to be brief.

Dyslexics sometimes make phonetic substitutions in their writings, producing *cum* for *come* or *rite* for *right*. Reversals are another common problem, in which *dog* is written as *bog*. Vertical reversals also occur in which letters such as "y" and "h" are exchanged, with the result that *yard* becomes *hard* and *hat* becomes *yat*. Reversals in sequence also occur, in which *rat* becomes *tar* and *form* becomes *from*. Mirror writing, in which the letters of an entire word are reversed, is also known to happen, but it is reported that it only occurs in sinistrals and only in cursive writing. Words with double letters are sometimes abbreviated by omitting one of the double letters. In other cases, all letters will be present but in improper order, or the spelling of the word may be completely irrational.

Dysgraphia is a severe writing problem related to dyslexia in which writing may be illegible, erratic, misshaped, and cramped (Figure 8.9). Cramping of writing is thought to be an endeavor to mask spelling errors. Copying is often a difficult task for the dyslexic or dysgraphic individual. He or she is prone to make the same types of errors in copying that are made in reading including reversals, omissions, and substitutions.

The acts of disguised and spurious writings require much more attention and concentration than is normal. The result is a decrease in writing speed, characterized by blunt initial and terminal strokes, heavy and even pen pressure, awkward movements, tremor, and irregular pen lifts. What should be of particular interest to examiners is that, as Hicks (1996) reported, many of these characteristics can be exhibited by the normal writing of dyslexics.

Figure 8.9 Example of a 14-year-old adolescent with signs of dysgraphia (e.g., mixing capitals with lower case letters, inconsistent size, misspelling).

In the taking of writing standards from the dyslexic, the difficulty they have in writing from dictation rather than from copy must be fully appreciated. The labor exhibited by the individual may be wrongly interpreted as an effort to disguise the writing act. With specialized training over a period of time, many of the problems can be overcome and the effects of the disorder upon the individual's writing will be significantly diminished. This suggests, that in the study of dyslexic's writing, the need for contemporary standards is particularly important, and the significance of evidence of a slow, drawn execution must be properly assessed.

The decrease in handwriting training in schools has resulted in a corresponding increase in handwriting variability. Logically, this variability increases with those with learning disabilities that influence handwriting. Akcin (2012) reported on the writing conventions of those with learning disabilities and found problems with illegibility, letters in reverse order, word mistakes, punctuation mistakes, and mistakes in use of capital letters. Langmaid et al. (2012) found that adolescents diagnosed with ADHD (attention deficit hyperactivity disorder) may have underlying motor impairment. In the study, ADHD subjects and healthy controls wrote handwriting-related tasks. The ADHD subjects showed inconsistency in handwriting size and the severity of the ADHD predicted poorer handwriting.

The topic of learning disabilities and poor handwriting skill is a relevant study to handwriting examiners. Cortiella and Horowitz prepared an updated report for the National Center for Learning Disabilities (2014). The report found that a disproportionate number of youth with learning disabilities (especially ADHD) and low literacy are in the juvenile justice or correctional system. This report suggests that those with learning disabilities may be more inclined toward criminal activities. Learning disabilities have been associated with adolescent depression and suicide (Bender 1999). McBride and Siegel (1997) opined that neurological dysfunction may be the root cause for learning disabilities that in turn lead to depression and suicide in adolescents. Learning disability is determined from the handwriting by evaluating spelling, grammar, syntax, and handwriting skill. It was found that there were significant deficiencies in these areas in the handwriting of adolescent suicides.

From a juvenile justice perspective, it is expected that suicide notes, anonymous or threatening notes to schools, and graffiti are more likely produced by those with low literacy, poor handwriting skill, and learning disabilities. Harralson (2007) reported on a case involving the analysis of an adolescent suicide note where learning disabilities contributed to the variance

Figure 8.10 Example of an adolescent writing in a graffiti style.

in the handwriting (Figure 8.9). It is not unusual for handwriting examiners to work on cases involving adolescent graffiti on school property. Weiderman (2012) reported on an alternate or illicit street literacy that develops with the practice of graffiti that can lead to proficiency or fluency in graffiti execution (Figure 8.10). Undoubtedly, those incarcerated who spend time practicing art, drawing, or calligraphy become fluent and proficient in these areas. Likewise, those who practice graffiti, using unusual writing instruments such as a spray paint can, would naturally become fluent in the writing of graffiti.

8.2.5.2.2 Alzheimer's Disease, Dementia, and Delirium

Alzheimer's disease is a degenerative, dementing disorder associated with memory loss and deterioration of other cognitive skills. Studies have indicated that there might be a slight hereditary disposition in some families, possibly combined with undetermined environmental factors. According to data collected by the Alzheimer's Association (2015), "an estimated 5.3 million Americans have AD [Alzheimer's disease]; 5.1 million Americans are age 65 years, and approximately 200,000 are age <65 years and have younger onset AD. By mid-century, the number of people living with AD in the United States is projected to grow by nearly 10 million, fueled in large part by the aging baby boom generation" (p. 332).

Behrendt (1982) claimed that Alzheimer's disease accounts for 50% of all senile dementia cases. It is further subcategorized as (1) SDAT (senile dementia Alzheimer's type), (2) Alzheimer's related dementia, and (3) Alzheimer's disease (Strub 1980). Alzheimer's disease is said to be senile dementia occurring before age 65, sometimes called presenile dementia. SDAT is said to refer to senile dementia occurring after the age of 65, a boundary that is an arbitrary one. Both conditions are pathologically similar. Alzheimer's related dementia refers to senile dementia arising from different causes, but sharing the same symptoms.

The symptoms are usually progressive, but the rate of memory loss varies from person to person. Infrequently, there is rapid deterioration. More often there are long periods in which little change is obvious (Trueman 1991).As one loses memory, one's ability to read and to write is also diminished. Words are forgotten, the thread of a conversation is lost, and there is a tendency for the person to repeat him or herself. As the disease progresses, the individual finds it difficult to concentrate on and finish a given task, even one as straightforward as writing his or her own name. For a while, the individual may succeed if given a model to follow, and then the process becomes too complex for him or her to decide how to start.

Behrendt (1984) reported that many persons experience the initial stages of mental degeneration, but retain physical strength and health such that their writing may display some symptoms of age, such as the omission or repetition of letters, the improper connection of words, but reveal no noticeable loss of writing skill or fluency. It seems that only when the mental ability to direct the motion of the pen is no longer available will the writing cease to be performed. Writings may be executed in any direction, but exhibit some evidence of strength and skill in the movement.

Diaz de Donoso (1993) provided two sets of samples of the writing of persons with Alzheimer's disease that illustrate the progressive loss of control over a period of time. As in many other situations, this loss of control affects the execution of curves initially, resulting in the production of angles or abrupt changes in direction in the writing line, and eventually in the demolition of recognizable forms.

As the condition progresses Alzheimer's patients experience emotional and personal changes in addition to cognitive impairment. They become confused, depressed, irritable, restless, anxious, and agitated. Medications are typically administered to offset these symptoms. The examiner of a handwriting from an Alzheimer's patient must, therefore, ensure that standards are obtained that reflect, if possible, the medical and mental state of the individual at the time a questioned handwriting is alleged to have been executed.

Studies relying on digital tablets in collecting data found significant impairment in those with Alzheimer's disease and mild cognitive impairment. Specifically, it was found that the Alzheimer's subjects and those with cognitive impairment "demonstrated slower, less smooth, less coordinated, and less consistent handwriting movements than their healthy counterparts" (Yan et al. 2008, 1203). Another study found that Alzheimer's patients exhibited increased variability in comparison to healthy subjects. This included variability in speed, velocity, and stroke length (Slavin et al. 1999; Schröter et al. 2003). The subjects also increased in perseveration (repetition of units or letter segments, so they repeated letter formations unnecessarily). These results were consistently shown whether the patients were taking medication or not. Another comparison of Alzheimer's patients with healthy controls showed that the patients exhibited an increase in temporal features while the pressure was lower (Werner et al. 2006). However, Caligiuri and Mohammed (2012) did report that these are sensitive or subtle handwriting impairments in Alzheimer's patients. They also reported that, as the condition deteriorates, the ability to produce a signature can fluctuate. Fluctuation in the condition of the patient is also evident in their writing as reported in a case study by Onofri et al. (2015). In their case study they presented writing samples showing the extreme fluctuation (discontinuity, fragmentation, spatial disorganization) in an Alzheimer's patient that occurred over three days.

8.2.5.2.3 Motor Neuron Disease and Amyotrophic Lateral Sclerosis or Lou Gehrig Disease

ALS (amyotrophic lateral sclerosis) is a form of MND (motor neuron disease) and is a degeneration of the muscles of the body resulting from a disorder of the nervous system. It is characterized by muscular weakness and atrophy, among other things, that are first evident in the hands and forearms in at least one-third of the cases. A progressive twitching is a common symptom, but one that does not necessarily affect the writing act as the twitching is spasmodic rather than constant, and not entirely beyond control by the individual.

ALS is progressive and continuous, and the increased weakness produces an increased inability to do simple things efficiently, such as writing. Progression of the disorder is relatively rapid, leading to paralysis and death in 2 to 5 years. Physical pain is not symptomatic. Mental ability, intelligence functions, and awareness are preserved even to the terminal stages. Frustration, stress, and depression are experienced due to the inability to direct the muscular system.

ALS strikes more men than women and usually at the age of 50 to 70 years. An exception to this was Lou Gehrig, of baseball fame, who contracted the disease in this thirties and died from it at the age of 38. In consequence, ALS is still commonly referred to as *Lou Gehrig disease*. Occasionally, ALS occurs in families in a manner that suggests that there could be a genetic transmission.

Conway (1985) reported on some of the handwriting indicators of ALS. Some variation in writing ability may be seen in subjects during the early stages of the disorder. With progression, the subject's ability to form and to connect letters is affected. Malformations and some illegibility occur. The writer's intellectual function, however, may not be impaired. When difficulties in pen movement are encountered and malformations ensue, little attempt is made to conceal or correct the mistake. As ALS affects the neuromuscular system, Caligiuri and Mohammed (2012) remarked that studies associated with fatigue and handwriting could also apply to those whose handwriting is affected by ALS.

8.2.5.2.4 Arthritis

Many physical factors may alter a person's writing, injuries and deformities to the hand and arm particularly. There are also diseases and injuries affecting the central nervous system; diseases and afflictions affecting muscles, ligaments, and joints of the writing hand that may temporarily or permanently alter one's writing. Perhaps the most common physical anomaly that tends to accompany age is arthritis and its related conditions.

Millions of people suffer from more than 100 different kinds of arthritis, and the number of cases increases annually with the extension of the normal life span. These ailments create degenerative changes in articular cartilages, particularly of the phalanges, resulting in pain and swelling of the joints. In advanced stages, they may lead to deformities in the hands and feet. Stiffness, discomfort, or pain may last from a matter of hours to one of days. A characteristic of the malady is that it afflicts more women than men.

Obviously, it is a condition that will have its effects upon writing, and one that may be encountered by the document examiner in the study of wills, deeds, bank documents, and perhaps in suicide notes. The question of import, in all cases in which alterations to the writing act may result from medical circumstances, is whether the effects may be misinterpreted as indications of a spurious execution of one kind or another.

Miller (1987) studied the writings of 420 subjects suffering from a diagnosed intermittent arthritic condition whose ages ranged from 56 to 78 years of whom 72% were female. Writing samples were taken from each subject while not suffering from an arthritic episode and able to write in a normal manner. A second writing sample was taken from each while enduring an arthritic episode during which they experienced difficulty. A third and a fourth sample was also obtained under similar sets of circumstances.

The study of these samples disclosed that changes occurred at least 48% of the time in each of 12 writing indicia that were claimed to be the aspects of writing that would be closely examined in cases of suspected forgery. These included (1) line quality, (2) pen lifts/separations, (3) retouching/patching, (4) angle/pitch, (5) pen pressure, (6) size/proportions, (7) alignment, (8) diacritic placement, (9) stroke formation, (10) loop formation, (11) beginning/ending strokes, and (12) circle formations.

It was reported that significant changes were noted in the afflicted writings of arthritics, particularly insofar as:

- Line quality (97% of samples)
- Size/proportions (93% of samples)
  - size was pictorially larger
  - spacings increased (greater concentration on letter forms rather than words, more deliberate or conscious writing)
- Retouching/patching (82% of samples)
- Loop forms wider, squared, shorter, with broken connections (78% of samples)
- Terminal strokes, heavier pressure, blobbed endings (48% of samples)

Noteworthy is the Miller's (1987) explanation of the frequency of retouching and patching as attempts in the arthritic writing of signatures to match the quality of normal signatures. It is expected that corrections of this sort would appear crude and obvious, and more likely to reflect the writer's concern for readability rather than writing quality. If an inability to control the writing instrument was responsible for the error that needed correction, then the retouching or patching would be conducted with the same lack of control and would likely achieve the same cumbersome results. On the other hand, retouching and patching done in the course of simulations (forgeries) tends to be less obvious, more subtle, often requiring examination by microscope to confirm its existence.

It has been observed that in some cases, the discomfort of writing for arthritics is sufficiently severe that the grasp of the writing instrument is changed. It is clutched rather than held, and its orientation to the paper surface and the line of writing may be profoundly changed.

More significant findings in Miller's (1987) study related to the examinations of signatures that were initially conducted without the extended writings or any knowledge of the malady suffered by the writers. In this case, 81% of the arthritic signatures were found to possess characteristics indicative of forgery. Of the signatures, 68% were classed as forgeries, and 32% were classed as inconclusive. However, when examiners were provided with all of the extended writings that accompanied the signatures, 92% of the findings were changed to authentic with the qualification *attempted to disguise*, presumably as an endeavor to account for the differences observed in the two sets of writings.

The results of the study prompted the author of the report to caution that, without the benefit of standards that are contemporaneous insofar as the state of the illness affecting them, differences in writings might be wrongly interpreted. Obviously, in cases involving arthritic writings, standards written a day before or a day after the date of execution of a questioned writing or signature, or of an arthritic episode, may not be completely satisfactory. He then used these results as an argument in support of his contention that the examiner should be provided with as much information as possible regarding the writer's physical and mental health prior to an examination or study.

The results of Miller's (1987) study raise a number of questions, one of which would relate to the competence of the examiners that conducted the examinations and misinterpreted the arthritic signatures as possessing characteristics indicative of forgery. As stated elsewhere, there are differences between spurious writings of signatures and altered executions by persons afflicted with such conditions as arthritis. The discomfort experienced by the act of writing, the effects of rigidity of the hand and fingers, the loss of fluency and speed of writing is evidenced in all elements of writing. The results are capricious and involuntary. The erratic movements produced are irregular, awkward, and unpredictable. On the other hand, spurious writings exhibit some intent to achieve a sufficiently fluent product to avoid attracting undue attention to its execution.

Huber and Headrick report that in most cases, the pain of arthritis is severe enough to discourage the individual from doing any writing whatsoever during an arthritic episode, unless absolutely necessary. They also noted that there are writing instruments that have a bearing on the discomfort the writer experiences, the smoother pens requiring the application of less pressure resulting in less discomfort. With respect to writing frequency, however, in a study of 36 arthritics (Dyer 2015), most of the subjects reported that they wrote daily even though the task was difficult for them. It was further noted in the study that the arthritics demonstrated slower speed and legibility in their handwriting.

8.2.5.2.5 Cerebral Palsy

Beacom (1968) provides a definition of CP (cerebral palsy) as "an abnormal alteration of movement or motor function arising from defect, injury, or disease of the nerve tissues in the cranial cavity" (p. 7).

With respect to prevalence, Oskoui et al. (2013) stated that CP occurs in 2.11 per 1,000 live births. Causes of CP include birth injuries, meningitis, encephalitis, or any other ailment that carries a very high fever. Many CP patients have learning disabilities, or hearing or sight disabilities, but the greatest incapacities experienced occur in the fingers and toes. There are several cerebral-palsied persons that are gainfully and professionally employed. While many are incapacitated, training and education for them is possible and available, and the signing of wills, credit card transactions and the writing of checks are among the functions that some can perform.

Beacom's (1968) examples disclosed lettering and cursive writings of varying qualities. Erratic movements and angularities are common. Consistency in form and in many other aspects of the writing is difficult for them to attain. Lettering or cursive writing tends to be large, in many cases. Better writing, however, can be achieved with practice and instruction.

8.2.5.2.6 Diabetes Mellitus

Diabetes mellitus and particularly low blood/sugar levels can affect writing performance. It is a condition believed to be experienced by at least 5% and perhaps as much as 8% of the population in North America, whether the persons afflicted are aware of their condition or not. Diabetes is an inability of the pancreas to supply sufficient insulin to maintain normal sugar concentrations in the blood stream to meet the body's needs for energy.

When sufficient insulin is not supplied by the pancreas, the concentration of sugar (glucose) in the blood increases progressively to the point where the individual becomes comatose. To prevent this, individuals may be injected with insulin subcutaneously to augment the supply from the pancreas and control the blood/sugar levels. While the body has a mechanism (a homeostatically regulated system) for ceasing the supply of insulin when not required, such a brake is not available to insulin that is injected and it continues to work regardless of the need for it. As a result, blood/sugar levels may move below the norms (hypoglycemia) and offsetting action must be taken by the individual in the form of the ingestion of food to moderate the sugar levels in the bloodstream.

Very low blood/sugar levels are known to affect human behavior in many respects, sometimes resulting in serious accidents or even death. There are blood/sugar levels below the normal, but above the level of complete loss of personal control at which people can function sufficiently well to execute signatures and some writing or initials. These levels are usually of relatively short duration, that is, 10 to 60 minutes, after which they progress to the point where control and consciousness are completely lost.

Towson (1971) studied the effects of low blood sugar levels on handwriting and the ability of handwriting examiners to identify correctly the writers under these circumstances. Writing samples were obtained from 28 subjects at normal blood sugar levels and at two levels of hypoglycemia induced by insulin injections.Towson found that there were highly significant correlations between low blood sugar levels and writing impairment. Furthermore, when impairment occurs competent writing examiners (13 lab personnel) were able to make a significant number of correct judgments as to writing impairment. Notwithstanding the impairment that occurred, examiners were able to correctly associate the writing samples with their proper authors more than 98% of the time. Impairment of the writing was exhibited by the following:

- Deterioration in line quality
- Uncertainty of letter forms, overwriting and wrong letter forms
- Deterioration of and abbreviation of letter forms
- Failure to maintain alignment or a consistent baseline
- Increase in pen lifts, pen stops and hesitations
- Increase in the overall size of the writing
- Inconsistency in writing slant

Of interest to Towson (1971) was that three of his subjects proved to be reactive hypoglycemic patients that tend to register abnormally high or low blood sugar levels three to five hours after the ingestion of food. Reactive hypoglycemia is a condition of fluctuating blood sugar levels that may occur in some cases in the early stages of the development of the disease. It can result in impairment of the handwriting, seemingly in a contradiction of the blood sugar levels the subject may experience.

Apart from reactive hypoglycemia, the impairment of writing will occur with diabetics almost exclusively in connection with low blood sugar levels, known medically as hypoglycemia. Elevations of blood sugar levels, known as hyperglycemia, are not known to have a noticeable effect upon writing other than that which might be expected as the individual progresses slowly into a comatose or sleep-like state.

8.2.5.2.7 Multiple Sclerosis

MS (multiple sclerosis) is a widespread neurological disorder, a chronic progressive disease with a variety of symptoms, some of which are noticeable in handwriting. Eighty-five percent of those with the disease are first diagnosed between 20 and 40 years of age. Sixty percent of those diagnosed with MS are women. Duration of the disease may be more than 25 years, and is increasing as technology increases life spans. MS follows a ritual of remissions and exacerbations in which the time between exacerbations decreases as the illness progresses. It is believed that the target of MS is myelin in the central nervous system, the fatty insulating sheath surrounding the axons (long single nerve-cell process) of many nerves in the body.

In a study of the writing of 23 MS patients, Wellingham-Jones (1991a) found that the disorder did, in fact, alter the writing of the subjects in a measurable fashion. Writings displayed irregularity, angularity, decreases in lateral expansion, and a decrease in speed of execution, tremor, and distortions. Word spacing and alignment were also affected. Fewer flourishes and narrower left margins were also noted. The study suggested that patients had difficulty in manipulating the pen and making flexible formations and connections. In general, it may be said that control and fluency are diminished.

Wellingham-Jones' (1991a) subjects were 7 men and 16 women, from the United States and Canada, between 29 and 75 years of age, that had been medically diagnosed as having MS. The writing samples were collected over a period of 5 years and consisted of extended writings of the subject's own generation. In descending order of frequency of occurrence, their physical symptoms included leg and arm weakness, coordination problems, tremor, fatigue, and visual problems. Obviously, the effects upon handwriting are consistent with the physical symptoms that the individuals experienced.

Hooten (1992) discussed a case study dating MS onset by handwriting. In a clinical study, Alusi et al. (2000) used handwriting samples and spiral drawings to develop a method to assess tremor in MS. In another clinical study, Schenk et al. (2000) provided handwriting tasks to 10 MS patients and 20 control subjects including a standard writing task, a closed loop task, and an open loop task. Both stroke duration and segmentation increased for the MS patients during the standard writing task in comparison to the controls supporting the researchers' hypothesis that MS patients employ a closed loop motor process in their handwriting.

8.2.5.2.8 Tremor

Ailments associated with tremulous writing include:

- Parkinson's disease
- Acquired agraphia
- Linguistic agraphia
- Nonlinguistic agraphia
- Spatial agraphia
- Progressive supranuclear palsy
- Huntington's disease
- Essential tremor

PD (Parkinson's disease) is considered to be a disease of the middle and older ages. The effect of the ailment upon handwriting is frequently profound, but equally profound is the effect of medications upon the uncontrollable tremor that is characteristic of the advanced stages of the disease.

Two other less-common conditions produce tremor, progressive supranuclear palsy and Huntington's disease. These, with Parkinson's disease and essential tremor, are classed as extrapyramidal disorders to identify them with the part of the neural system within the brain to which they are attributed. Progressive supranuclear palsy is much like akinetic Parkinson's disease, but has other characteristics observed in the face and eyes including the paralysis of eye movements. Huntington's disease is hereditary and is characterized by large jerks of the arm or hand occurring at random. It is called *choreic* because the legs are always moving as if dancing.

Essential tremor is a monosymptomatic illness that is common to all age groups and equally distributed between genders. It is considered to be a *postural tremor* (i.e., present but much less noticeable during the maintenance of steady posture) that is accentuated by voluntary movement creating disabilities during activities such as writing. The handwriting of essential tremor is typically large and tremulous in contrast to the effects of the tremor of Parkinson's disease (Figure 8.11). It is unlike the tremor of PD that is referred to as a *resting tremor*, present when the limb is at rest, but disappearing during action.

In a study by Boisseau et al. (1987) of the writings of 35 individuals suffering from these disorders, no particular characteristics were found in the handwriting that could be associated with any one of the four disorders. The administration of drugs was seen to affect a few letters or the

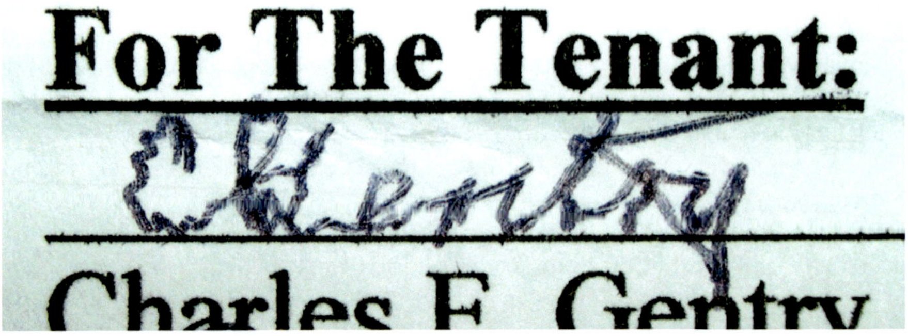

Figure 8.11 Example of a writer with Essential Tremor (ET).

general quality of the writing but the majority of the elements of writing were not significantly altered. In their view, tremors due to neurological conditions tend to produce greater and more erratic changes to or interruptions in the pen movement, that become more obvious with the progression of the responsible disorder.

Parkinson's disease is a degeneration of cells within the brain in an area called substantia nigra. As a result, there is a decrease in the amount of the neurotransmitter dopamine present in the cells that causes disturbances of a particular function and results in interference of motor control. The principle symptoms of the disorder are: (1) akinesia—the loss of muscular power, (2) bradykinesia—abnormal slowness of movement and fatigue, (3) rigidity—resistance to muscular action, and (4) tremor—oscillations of the hand at frequencies of three to five oscillations per second when the limbs are at rest. One of the classic features of this tremor is its presence during rest and its disappearance on purposeful movement. The tremor is usually aborted by the initiation of any willed act, but tends to reappear a few moments later, despite the continuation of the action. In most cases, the tremor is less pronounced during action than it is during rest.

Clinically speaking, Parkinson's disease is described as a disorder of the scaling of movements that are slow, but do not exhibit obvious problems in the selection and sequencing of muscle activity. Patients have normal patterns of muscle activation, but require more cycles of muscle activity to produce their movements (Phillips et al. 1991).

Males and females are equally affected by the disorder that tends to run in families 10–15% of the time. Its characteristic tremor is said to be asymmetrical, affecting one hand or both hands or both hands and the trunk. The disorder is progressive over periods of 10 to 20 years.

Handwriting difficulties have been suggested as one of the earliest symptoms of the disease. Patients have been observed to have problems with the size or speed of writing and report difficulties in the writing of signatures, as on checks. It appears that the effects are exhibited principally by the motor programs, since spelling and letter formation are not usually impaired.

According to Margolin and Wing (1983), linguistic agraphias are essentially disorders in spelling portrayed by letter omissions, substitutions, additions, and letter reversals, although letter morphology (i.e., forms) is preserved according to Marcie and Hecaen (1979). Nonlinguistic types of agraphia entail the production of faulty letter forms with intact spelling, and may entail a breakdown in morphology and in the sequencing of movements. Neither of these occur with PD.

As noted by Hécaen et al. (1956), some instances of agraphia are due to perceptual disturbances, caused by brain lesions, and may produce a particular combination of writing changes termed *spatial agraphia*. These changes include ascending or descending alignments, widening of the left margins and letter repetitions, but these also are not characteristic of PD.

Handwriting disturbance is frequently an early manifestation of PD and is widely accepted as a part of its clinical picture. The incidence, severity, and modifying features of the phenomenon are now becoming better understood. Certain characteristic size changes have led to the use of the term *micrographia* to identify and describe the condition in the writing of some Parkinsonian patients (Figure 8.12).

Micrographia, described as a reduction in the size of letters that is often progressive along a line of writing and/or down a page of writing (Figure 8.13), with no higher-order problems such as spelling or stroke errors, was first noted by Pick (1903). Several other investigators, most of whom published their results in German in the early 1920s, have studied the phenomenon from the viewpoint of its etiology, that is, its cause or origin, and its effects in the writing of Parkinson's disease patients.

Kinner (1925), in suggesting possible causes, reported the occurrence of micrographia in cases of cerebral syphilis and central arteriosclerosis. Gilmour and Bradford (1987) reported two cases in a study of 17 patients undergoing drug treatment for schizophrenia. The medications associated with treatment of schizophrenia are known to cause Parkinson's-type tremor among schizophrenic patients (Gervin and Barnes 2000).

McLennan et al. (1972), tried to describe the phenomenon more precisely and establish its incidence among patients with PD by studying the records of 800 Parkinsonian patients from which 95 cases exhibiting micrographia were selected. From this the incidence of micrographia was estimated at 10–15%.

Check signatures proved to be the standard source of writing samples executed prior to the diagnosis of PD. The study disclosed that patients with micrographia are unable to sustain normal sized writing for more than a few letters, if at all. There was a tendency to write progressively smaller as the end of the line approaches. Renewed effort produces temporarily larger writing, but this soon diminishes to even smaller writing than previous executions. Occasionally, patients can write larger with the assistance of guidelines, but without such guidelines the writing becomes small.

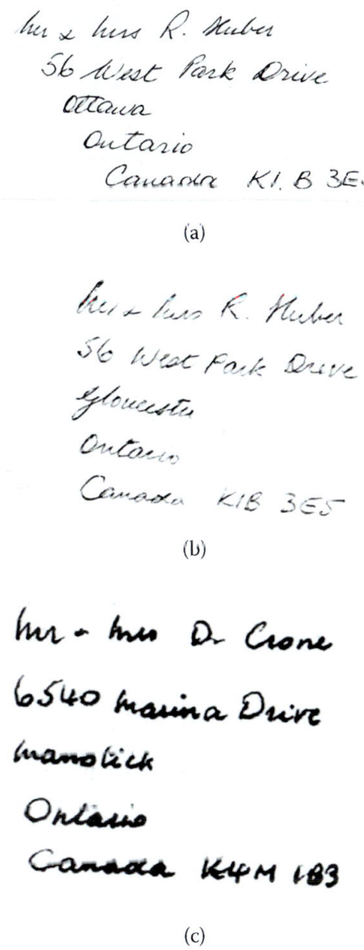

Figure 8.12 Micrographia in Parkinson's disease. In 10–15% of patients, their writing progressively diminishes in size and lateral expansion. The example shows the progression of diminished writing of a Parkinson's disease patient over a period of 10 years. 1984 (a) 1992 (b) and 1996 (c).

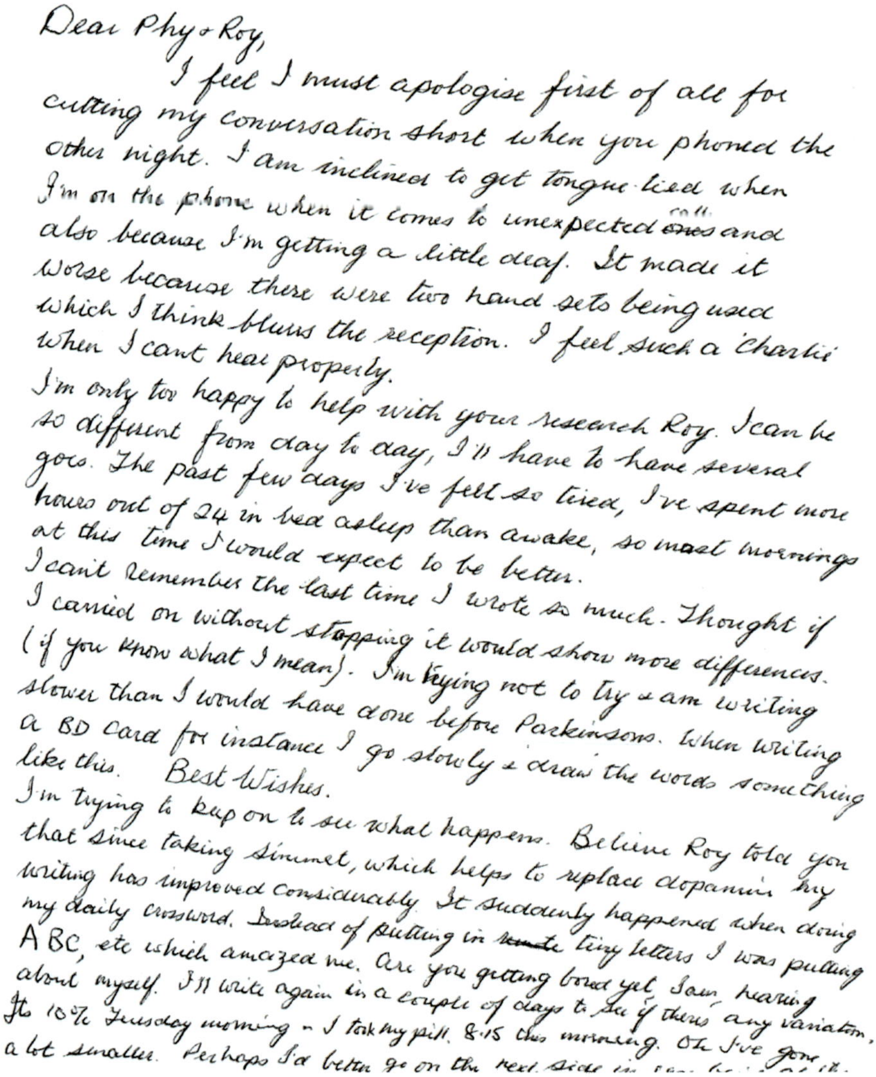

Figure 8.13 Another example of micrographia, illustrating the tendency for writing to diminish across the page and down the page.

McLennan et al. (1972) charted the course of the changes in the writing of 17 patients, for 6 years before and after the onset of PD. This study revealed that changes were observed at least one and sometimes 2 and 3 years in advance of the onset and diagnosis of the disorder, and that micrographia developed in some cases 4 to 5 years following. Micrographia appears to be a very definable symptom in at least 5% of all PD patients, and in as much as 30% of those patients who will later develop more advanced micrographia.

No correlation has been found between micrographia and the side of the body affected by PD. Neither is it related to the handedness of the writer. Furthermore, tremor and rigidity that are two of the four principal attributes of PD show no correlation with micrographia. Former writing characteristics are reasonably well preserved. McLennan et al. (1972) reported that many samples of micrographic signatures would, if enlarged, superimpose well on other earlier written signatures. Suffice it to say that the phenomenon of micrographia remains unexplained. It can only be said that it originates within the central nervous system.

Tarver (1988, 1989), on the strength of a study of 16 PD subjects, claimed that he found no support for the existence of micrographia in the writing of his subjects. At an occurrence rate of 10–15% that McLennan et al. (1972) reported, out of an examination of the writings of 800 Parkinson's disease patients, it is not surprising that small samples might contain no evidence of its existence. Furthermore, there are sources (Margolin 1984) other than McLennan that have confirmed its actuality.

There are few instances wherein handwriting may be used as a diagnostic tool by medical practitioners in advance of other symptoms. Parkinson's disease is one of the exceptions. Although the percentage of patients displaying micrographia is small, it may serve as a specific prodrome of what is developing or will develop in a period of up to 4 years.

The administration of the medication L-dopa makes a greater amount of dopamine available to the brain, a therapy that can have spectacular results permitting those otherwise disabled limbs to function near-normally for 10 to 20 years, although in some cases the efficacy of the drug can decline in 5 to 7 years. In a study of 91 patients by Stellar et al. (1970), 75% showed marked or partial improvement. They reported that mild tremor was lessened in a small number of cases, and that rigidity, bradykinesia, facial masking, voice, gait, and handwriting disturbances were often greatly diminished, although toxic side effects occurred in a high percentage of patients.

Patients with Parkinson's disease, however, may experience dyskinesia (excess, unintentional or involuntary movement) as a side effect of drug therapy. These unwanted movements can occur in the process of handwriting and interfere with letter formation. Problems of letter formation and spelling are also observed in other disorders and must be carefully judged if to be used as indicators of PD.

Much research has been and continues to be conducted in an endeavor to better understand the difficulties experienced by Parkinson's patients in the execution of writing. Teulings and Stelmach (1991) attempted to quantify writing deficits in Parkinson's patients through the use of signal-to-noise analyses. Phillips et al. (1991) endeavored to study the extent to which several measures of handwriting quality might discriminate between the handwritings of two control groups (young adults and elderly) and Parkinson's patients, particularly as a result of the tremor that Parkinson's patients usually experience. Studies of this type need to be monitored for the knowledge they provide respecting the neuromuscular process that underlies the writing act.

Both Harralson (2005, 2008) and Caligiuri and Mohammed (2012) have contributed to reviews on the extensive literature on how PD affects handwriting. More importantly, these authors have also examined PD and other motor disorders to determine if the handwriting distortion caused by these disorders inhibits identification of the writer and can be effectively differentiated from simulation. Harralson et al.'s (2008) experiment comparing the kinematic differences between movement disorder patients and forgers demonstrated that the groups performed differently with the forgers writing more slowly and less fluently than the movement disorder patients (which included both PD and essential tremor (ET) writers). Harralson et al.'s study was cautionary though in stating that movement is easier to assess with online data than it is through assessment of the static, paper-based handwriting trace. Caligiuri and Mohammed also carried out an experimental study which showed some similar results. In their study, three patients (resting tremor PD writer, micrographic PD writer, ET writer) provided online signatures which were then compared to a writer forging the signatures online. Examining the kinematic results, in some trials, the handwriting exhibited greater dysfluency in the simulations. The authors commented that forgers may have difficulty scaling their handwriting down to effectively imitate micrographia, a finding at variance with the Harralson et al. study (which found that some writers of the forger group were especially skilled at imitating the rigid and small movements of the micrographic PD writings). Caligiuri and Mohammed stated that forgers may tend to scale their writing down in order to imitate tremor and sometimes simulated tremor may increase inefficiency and dysfluency.

8.2.6 Medications

Medications have been suggested as the cause of changes in writing by many authors. Gilmour and Bradford (1987), cited in the discussion of Parkinson's disease, found that neuroleptic drug treatments for schizophrenia did produce changes in individual writings, but the nature and extent of these changes were quite variable between subjects. Furthermore, the nature of the change insofar as line quality varied from an improvement to a deterioration. It was their conclusion that "the effect of drugs (i.e., medications) on handwriting is dependent on the type of drug administered, the individual's sensitivity to it, and the points at which the handwriting is sampled during drug treatment" (p. 138).

Neuroleptics are drugs used in psychiatric treatment of some disorders that can cause a reversible Parkinson-like state, exhibiting the characteristics of rigidity, akinesia and tremor at rest. The principal medications used to treat Parkinson's disease are (1) L-dopa, to control the motor abnormalities, and (2) anticholinergics, to control the resting tremor. The first can cause choreic movements called dopa-induced dyskinesia. The second may result in impairment of recent memory.

The principal medications used for ET are propranolol and primidone that decrease the amplitude of the oscillations during movement. In Huntington's disease, neuroleptics are said to slightly relieve the frequency and amplitude of choreic movements, but at the expense of some Parkinson-like symptoms.

Haase (1961) studied the relationship between the therapeutic response to a neuroleptic agent and the handwriting changes that are produced. For some time prior to his study, antipsychotic drugs were and still are frequently administered to patients with mental illness (e.g., schizophrenia) to render them more amenable to psychotherapy. Sometimes there is a slowing of the motor activity typically found in patients with Parkinson's disease.

It was Haase's (1961) theory that small doses of neuroleptic drugs produce fine motor changes often not apparent to the clinician. These changes manifest themselves in the handwriting of the patient. Haase suggested five primary handwriting changes indicative of fine motor neuroleptic effects: stiffening, cramping, size reduction, a lessening of slant, and shakiness. His terms, however, warrant some thought. Stiffening and cramping are certainly conditions of the hands, but say little of the effects manifest in the writer's script. Shakiness presumably produces a degree of tremor in the written line that may be the meaning the author intended.

Haase (1961) demonstrated that the efficacy of chlorpromazine, reserpine, and analogous drugs is associated with their effects on fine extrapyramidal movements as seen in handwriting. Studies of other drugs with similar actions have confirmed his findings (Simpson 1970).

The neuroleptic effectiveness of a drug depends on the affinity the drug has for the extrapyramidal system and on the dose given.

The term *extrapyramidal system* was first used by Wilson (1912) to refer to those parts of the CNS (central nervous system) that were concerned with motor disorders. The term is used clinically and anatomically to refer to one of the three principle motor systems in humans: the pyramidal system, the cerebellar system, and the extrapyramidal system. Each is thought of as a separate entity and considered to be an independent structure. Lesions (abnormal structural changes due to injury or disease) within each of these systems result in distinctive disturbances in motor activity.

The fibers of the pyramidal system pass through the medullary pyramid. Injury to this tract produces paralysis of voluntary movement. The cerebellar system comprises the cerebellum and the pathways to and from it. It is believed to be concerned with the coordination of movements as opposed to the initiation of voluntary movement. Lesions of this system result in tremor with movement, incoordination, dyssynergia, and ataxia. The extrapyramidal system is made up of a number of paired nuclei and associated pathways. The term *basal ganglia* is often used as an alternative term. Lesions of the extrapyramidal system often result in abnormal movements (e.g., tremors) that usually are present at rest. There are also abnormalities of station and postural reflexes. This system is thought to be concerned particularly with the maintenance of posture as opposed to initiation or coordination of voluntary movement.

The term extrapyramidal disease ties together a number of clinically defined disease states that share a number of related symptoms. The clinical signs and symptoms that help to tie these disease states together fall into four groups: (1) hyperkinesia (abnormal involuntary movements), (2) akinesia (slowness or poverty of spontaneous movement), (3) rigidity, and (4) loss of normal postural reactions. The principle disorder within this group was described by Parkinson (2002), after whom it was named, as: "Involuntary tremulous motions with lessened muscular power in parts, not in action and even when supported with a propensity to bend the trunk forward and to pass from a walking to a running pace, senses and intellect being uninjured" (p. 223).

The Haase (1961) study compared the action of four stronger neuroleptic drugs to chlorpromazine insofar as their effects upon handwriting. These included prochlorperazine, trifluoperazine, fluphenazine, and thioperazine. The results were essentially the same for all drugs and were observed to be the extrapyramidal handwriting manifestations of (1) stiffening, (2) diminution (reduction in vertical dimension), and (3) narrowing (reduction in horizontal dimension). Weeks after treatment with the drugs, the writings of the patients returned to normal fluency and dimensions.

Hart (1985) outlined some of the adverse effects of three groups of drugs: antipsychotic drugs, tranquilizers of the phenothiazine type, and potent synthetic analgesics. Of the first group, lithium is mentioned as one having adverse effects upon muscular coordination that may be accompanied by tremor. Tranquilizers may have adverse effects depending upon the dosage of the drug and the duration of administration. A CNS disorder called *tardive dyskinesia* may occur that is characterized by involuntary movements of the extremities, among other things. These involuntary movements may result in a jerky writing that is abnormal in appearance. This may be accompanied by blurred vision that would also have its effects upon writing. The effect of drugs within the third group, classed as potent analgesics, is not as great upon the CNS as the first two, but blurred vision or double vision can occur that will have a detrimental effect upon handwriting to varying degrees.

The point of Hart's (1985) paper is that the effects of these drugs may resemble the characteristics of disguised writing, and need to be carefully studied. They are drugs that can be easily obtained and may be taken for maladies other than those for which they are usually prescribed. She lists the drugs within the three groups as taken from the *Physicians' Desk Reference.*

The importance of discriminating accurately between disguise and the effects of these drugs stems from the position taken by the courts in the United States that the presence of disguise in court-ordered writing samples is tantamount to contempt. This places an onus upon the examiner to responsibly determine whether a disguise has been deliberately attempted. Concern over the risk of misinterpreting the effects of drugs and some medical conditions on handwriting is often expressed. The risk is admittedly present when the material under examination and/or the competence of the examiner is limited. Hopefully, the indicators of disguise provides some of the guidelines by which reliable discriminations can be made.

A study by Glogowaski (1963) at the Orthopedic Department of the University Hospital in Munich, of the effect of treatment with valium on the handwriting of 27 patients, aged 8 to 16 years, resulted in a demonstrable improvement in coordination of the handwriting mechanism. While the changes are described as "an objective qualitative improvement in handwriting" (p. 2448), there is little information as to the nature of the illnesses for which the subjects were being treated or precisely what changes were responsible for the improvement.

Antipsychotic medications typically prescribed for schizophrenia can cause a variety of movement disorders including tardive dyskinesia, akathisia, dystonia, Parkinsonism, tremor, bradykinesia, postural abnormalities, muscle rigidity, tremor, reduction in size of handwriting, and rhythmic disturbances in handwriting (Gervin and Barnes 2000). Kinematic research into how medications affect schizophrenics showed that handwriting can be used as a clinical monitor for medication side effects and is a more reliable measure than observer-based ratings (Caligiuri et al. 2010). Comparing the psychiatric patients to healthy controls, it was found that the patients exhibited slower and less fluent writing than controls. Handwriting differences were also observed in response to varying doses of psychotic medications on different days when evaluating patient handwriting.

Caligiuri and Mohammed (2012) presented a tabulation of several psychotropic medications and each of their potential side effects on the motor system including tremor, dystonia, bradykinesia, dyskinesia, akathisia, Parkinsonism, muscle weakness, muscle twitching, and muscle relaxation.

8.2.7 Infirmity

8.2.7.1 Stages of Development, Age, and Senility

It is generally accepted that an individual's handwriting changes throughout a lifetime. As stated earlier, handwriting progresses through four stages in the course of a writer's life. It begins with (1) the formative or learning stage that is followed by (2) the impressionable or adolescent stage, sometimes called *the puberty stage*. The third stage is (3) the maturity stage that is the longest and in which the writing is most consistent. The fourth stage is (4) that of degeneration, sometimes referred to as *the senility stage*, during which writing quality, pen control, and fluency suffer progressively. Changes may occur during any of these stages depending on circumstances, but particularly so and understandably during the early stage when it is developing, and the late stage when it is deteriorating. The progressive deterioration of writing skills in the elderly, that is, the fourth stage, is the topic that has been covered in response to handwriting signs of senility and age. There are also temporal or short-term changes occurring in handwriting resulting from illness, disease, or injury, the effects of which diminish or disappear completely with recovery from the condition.

In modern writing, a style has been noted, particularly among adolescents that has been given the name *bubble writing* largely because of its predominant roundness. In addition to being round, it is usually large, vertical, and compacted in that little space is provided between letters for connections. Relative heights of letters or of elements of letters are also distinctive in that supralinear and infralinear letters (those having ascenders and descenders such as "d," "f," "g," "h," "j," "k," "l," "p," "y," and "z") do not have vertical dimensions that are not much greater than linear letters (i.e., "a," "c," "e," "i," "m," "n," "o," "r," "s," "u," "v," "w," and "x"). The staffs of the letters "d" and "t," that tend to be looped by many other writers, are retraced as copybook prescribes. The letter "b" frequently exhibits a clockwise structure in the bowl, giving it a printed appearance. Other tendencies that seem to be associated with bubble writing include the construction of the "8" as two separate circles, the dotting of the "i" with a small circle, and the production of punctuation marks as circles. It is a writing style popular with over 40% of the female subjects, all of whom were adolescents, in studies reported by Masson (1988) and Cusack and Hargett (1988).

Some bubble writers are consistent and characteristic, and are readily identified with the class. There are also numerous other writings that are described as a modified round style or modified bubble writing, that are not as clear and distinct a group of variations from conventional writing practices, and exhibit greater individuality than the classic bubble writing.

It is suspected that bubble writing may be a passing phase in the maturing of the writing of adolescents and particularly females. It occurs at a stage in writing development when experimentation is common. Individuals that use it are known to be able to revert to a more conventional writing style at will. Its origin is vague, but its transmission among adolescents may be a matter of intentional imitation. Bubble writings by different individuals may have a great deal of resemblance and their differentiation can be difficult.

A Canadian study of the writing of adolescents within the native populations of Saskatchewan by MacInnis (1994) failed to find any significant evidence by which native and nonnative adolescents might be distinguished from one another. Some distinction was observed, however, between male and female subjects of his study that may be related to the prevalence of a roundness in the writings of females of both natives and nonnatives, not unlike the modified bubble writing mentioned.

8.2.7.2 Guided Hands

8.2.7.2.1 Deathbed Signatures

With the decline in writing ability, illness affects the writing consistency. Because of a decline in coordination, signatures will vary between themselves in somewhat erratic ways. There may be the occurrence of extraneous, false strokes. As quality diminishes, letter designs, relative heights, slant, and alignments lose their former stability. The product may appear deceptively false.

The effect of a terminal illness upon writing may not be consistent. Relapses occur even at times close to death when, for unknown reasons, or due to medication, spells of writing control may return, perhaps to be lost again hours or days later. As illnesses progress, however, and death approaches, one's ability to control a writing instrument diminishes to the point where little that is legible can be executed. Normally, there are few signatures written when in this condition, but almost too frequently, it is at this stage when wills are made or revised and the choice of beneficiaries and bequests become subject to dispute.

Terminal illnesses, in their last stages of progress, produce signatures that are often accompanied by false starts. The writing is erratic and letters are poorly formed. Terminal strokes and final elements of these signatures may display more fluency than any other part as though there was some relief from a strenuous ordeal. The study of these signatures for the purpose of identifying the handwriting is made more difficult by the lack of contemporaneous standards, which is usually the case.

8.2.7.2.2 Guided-Hand or Assisted Signatures

Often enough it is alleged that a second party endeavored to assist the testator in executing a signature by holding the hand and guiding it through the movement. For a broad treatment of this topic, see Chapter 11 regarding the attributes of assisted-hand and guided-hand signatures.

There are corrective effects upon a subject's handwriting ensuing from drugs and other medications administered to the patient. There are, for example, drugs that will suppress the tremors characteristic of Parkinson's disease for periods of time but not permanently.

8.2.8 Mental State of Writer

8.2.8.1 Emotional Stress

Stress or extreme emotional states related to or causing stress can influence handwriting movement. McNally (1974) depicted it as a condition that interferes with fluency in that it makes the process a more conscious endeavor with increasing care and attention to details. The product is more drawn than written. In short, it possesses many of the characteristics that are observed in spurious writings or signatures, and for that reason, caution in its study is advised.

The element of emotional stress is not only a condition peculiar to the questioned writing, but can enter into the execution of the so-called request writings of a subject. Its effects can be noted in some exaggeration of the range of natural variation that a writer may exhibit. It has been suggested that stress in some degree has a part in most of the cases that an examiner studies. Girouard (1986) noted that research has demonstrated that stress affects both physiological functioning and psychological health. Girouard further stated that it is difficult to isolate the effects of stress as it influences the whole organism. Frederick (1968) sought evidence of stress in the writings on suicide notes and noted that the examiners in the study were significantly better than laypersons at distinguishing genuine suicide notes from the fabricated notes (45 sets of notes were used in the study).

Longstaff and Heath (2003) noted that writers with tremor or motor system degradation had a harder time adapting to writing conditions where mild stress was introduced through the presence of a "loud, annoying sound" (p. 92). However, healthy controls were able to adapt and maintain control by increasing pen pressure, while the tremor group decreased pen pressure. Loud noises seemed to be the trigger for tremor associated with PTSD (post-traumatic stress disorder) in a case study (Walters and Hening 1992). When the patient was startled, his or her handwriting became bigger, showed inconsistencies, and exhibited tremor similar to psychogenic tremor. The patient's normal handwriting was moderate in size, exhibiting only a fine kinetic tremor.

8.2.8.2 Nervousness

Nervousness has been suggested as a cause of fine tremors or some lack of fluency in writing. Research in this area is understandably difficult as the induction of a nervous state in a subject in a test situation may not be easily accomplished.

According to Carney (1993), Elble and Koller (1990) discussed task-specific tremors such as orthostatic tremor and primary writing tremor. Primary writing tremor is defined as a tremor that is induced primarily, but not only, by the act of writing and other similar motor activities, such as handling a knife or screwdriver. Alcohol, Inderal, and Mysoline all reduce primary writing tremor, but they are ineffective against other tremors such as those of Parkinson's disease. Whether primary writing tremor is, in fact, a consequence of a state of nervousness in some individuals is not known, but might warrant further investigation.

8.2.8.3 Instability (Mental Illness)

In studies to test the hypothesis that patients' signatures may have a useful potential in the making of psychiatric diagnoses, some evidence has been found that the signature size in the manic group and in the organic mental disorder group of patients at one hospital was significantly larger than that of control groups (Baig et al. 1984).

There have been some studies on the writing of individuals experiencing DID (dissociative identity disorder—formerly known as multiple personality disorder). This is a psychopathological and psychophysiological phenomenon that is offered with increasing frequency as an explanation for certain kinds of conduct or actions. It is described by Schwid and Marks (1994) as a dissociative disorder in patients that have experienced childhood abuse or neglect and that are dissociation-prone. It is reported by Cohen and Giller (1991) that people with dissociative disorders tend to be intelligent, creative, resourceful, and articulate. Authorities agree that DID patients suffer a great deal and are generally relieved when their disorder is diagnosed.

DID is defined as two or more distinct personalities that exist in one person, each of which is dominant at a particular time. Switching from one personality to another occurs when the subject has difficulty dealing with specific conflicts, and feels threatened by a particular situation. Of importance to document examiners are the reports that the handwriting of the subject changes notably when the individual switches from one personality to another.

In view of this change, problems arise for document examiners in ensuring that questioned and specimen writings are executed under the same prevailing personality. Huber and Headrick reported on a case in which an examination and study of handwritings was required to determine which of the personalities indicated by the writings was likely to be the executions of the normal or nonafflicted personality. The psychiatrist's interest in this determination rested in the desire to administer medication for the condition only during the normal nonafflicted state of the patient.

Schwid (1995) provides examples of the writing of four of the nine personalities of one subject, in which there are size changes, proportion changes, quality changes, and changes in lateral expansion. Despite such changes, given adequate standards, document examiners have been able to associate the writings of the various personalities of a subject as the products of one and the same physical being. Schwid and Teulings (2013) reported on a longitudinal study of a DID patient using dynamic measurements and found that that there were both static and kinematic differences between the writing samples of the personalities.

8.2.9 Injury

Injuries that impair the movement of the writing arm or hand will afflict the control of the writing instrument. The result, usually, is erratic movements or sudden changes in direction, or an obvious inability to execute some finer or more complex maneuvers of the pen or pencil.

From a handwriting examination perspective, it is important to bear in mind that injuries are usually temporary. Unless some permanent damage to the arm or hand has occurred, writing ability will be regained over a period of time, although depending on the injury recovery may not be 100%. The dates on which the injury occurred and on which the questioned or standard writings were executed may become important and should be noted. The quality of the questioned writing should be consistent with the ability of the writer on the particular date of its purported execution.

Yancosek and Mullineaux (2011) studied the nondominant handwriting samples of those who were injured and had lost the use of their dominant hand. Two evaluators were able to match the dominant to nondominant handwriting samples with 89–100% accuracy. Ellison (1978) reported on the action tremor present in the writing samples of patients with severe head injuries.

Chapter 9

Intrinsic Factors Influencing Handwriting

9.1 INTRINSIC FACTORS INFLUENCING HANDWRITING

The reader is referred to the comments regarding *The Variables of Handwriting* that is found as an introduction to Chapter 8.

9.1.1 Imitation

Beyond the various writing systems to which writers are exposed, individuals are influenced by what they see and like in the writing of others. In many cases, individual tastes turn in certain directions, or the artistic sense expresses its preferences. Imitation is probably one reason why the handwritings of classmates, close relatives, and those who have lived together for a long period of time, often have so much in common (Harrison 1958b). Certainly, as noted elsewhere, sinistrality and the adoption of the inverted-hand posture, have some factors to them that may be hereditary or be simply the imitation of parents or siblings. Hecker (1981) described the changes that occurred in one 16-year-old German female's writing that occurred coincidentally with the adoption of a different culture.

It is typical of the acquired handwriting styles occurring in particular teacher–pupil relationships, in professional and social groups, and in the fashionable or popular writings of a social strata at a particular time. The permanence of the changes will likely depend on the duration of the interest in the group or individual adopted as the model.

9.1.2 Circumstantial

There are factors influencing writing that vary with circumstances under which the writing is executed. Osborn (1929), Harrison (1958b), Hilton (1982), and Ellen (1989) have each commented on the effect that circumstances may have upon writing, usually under the broad caption of "writing conditions." For the most part, these comments have dealt with extreme circumstances and the claims that have been made in defense of unskillful simulations.

For example, the writing is claimed to have been executed against walls, on the roofs of cars, in moving vehicles, upon one's knee, or on a clipboard held in the hand. It is well known that writing up against walls, on the roofs of cars, in moving vehicles, writing on one's knee, or while standing without stable support for the document, or in a confined space at the bottom of a document are conditions that often occur with genuine executions of *recipient* or attesting signatures. Consequently, the use of these conditions as excuses for apparently poor writing is understandable. It is also well known that writings under these circumstances may be distorted, erratic, and imprecise. Retraces are difficult to execute and bowls of letters are not carefully closed. There are other circumstances, or variations in normal circumstances, such as changes in the nature of the writing instrument or changes in the nature of the document being signed are less extreme and, accordingly, their effects upon the writing may not be as pronounced. There are six circumstantial factors that an examiner should consider:

1. Writing media employed
2. Writing posture, including stance and orientation to paper
3. Writing purpose
4. Writing space available and location
5. Writing surface and support
6. Writing environment

9.1.2.1 Writing Media

Osborn (1929) devoted a full chapter to the effect of the writing instrument upon writing as well as the identification of the writing instrument. He discussed the products of various types of split nib pens and pencils of the time. Insofar as their effects upon the writing of an individual, he had only to say that the flexibility of the split nib permitted one to consider pen pressure and pen position relative to the written stroke as significant matters of habit for the writer and, accordingly, important elements in the study of writing for the purpose of identification.

His comments respecting pencil writing dealt particularly with the fact that it tended to conceal many aspects of writing that were important to consider in the process of identification, including line quality (tremor and fluency), line continuity, pen lifts, pen position, retouching, overwriting, and even pen pressure. Furthermore, pencil writing, particularly with hard leads, usually requires more pressure, that is a greater point load, than split nib pen writing to produce a pronounced line, and allowance must be made for this in the handwriting study and comparisons.

The split nib, but less flexible, fountain pen has replaced the steel nib pens, and technology has provided a plethora of other kinds of writing instruments for today's use that range from ballpoint pens (using viscous ink), porous point pens having felt, fiber, or plastic tips to roller ball pens (using less viscous or fluid inks).

Studies by Mathyer (1950, 1969) and Hilton (1984) of the writing produced by these common writing instruments have enabled examiners to discriminate reasonably well between their products. The task of handwriting identification is not assisted, however, as the softer but more stable instrument points tend to conceal matters of line quality (tremor and fluency), line continuity, pen position, pen pressure, pen lifts, and even overwriting. Thus, in many respects, the problems provided by the pencil have been revived. And the absence of a pen track, as occurs with felt tips, is reminiscent of the old quill pens.

In two short studies (34 subjects and 19 subjects) of the work of felt-tip pens of different widths, Masson (1985, 1992) reported that the effect of this instrument upon the writing is merely superficial. In a few cases, however, a very broad-tipped pen induced the writer to increase the size of his or her writing, although the increase was not extreme. More substantial problems arose from the difficulty in following the continuity of the line made by the felt-tip pen, and establishing unequivocally the occurrence of pen lifts or disconnections.

As Mathyer (1969) pointed out, the influence of the writing instrument upon the writing of an individual is rarely very significant. If there is an observable difference between the writings of a given person made with different instruments, it may be due as much to that person's personal preference for, or comfort in using, a particular instrument as it is to the effects of the instrument itself.

The writing instruments that Mathyer (1969) was referencing (e.g., ballpoint pen, pencil, fiber pen, rollerball) are still widely used and of relevance in the study of the effects of writing instruments on handwriting. With the advancement of technology, other types of "pens" or writing instruments are now used in addition to the inking pen. In electronic signature capture technology, the signing instrument may be a blunt stylus on a digital tablet, a mouse signing electronically on the monitor, or a finger signing on an iPad or iPhone. The effects of these types of instruments were studied by Harralson et al. (2011) who examined and compared subjects signing with an inking pen, a digital pen, and a mouse. Not surprisingly, it was found that when subjects signed with a mouse there was considerable deterioration in the signature form.

9.1.2.2 Writing Posture

The effects of extreme conditions are highly variable and little can be proffered as to what may be expected in any given situation. Nevertheless, Grant (1974) reported on a distorted writing alleged to have been written under unusual circumstances. It was claimed that it was written while standing at a cluttered counter when the writer was holding a weight of unwieldy tools in the other hand. Standards were obtained when circumstances were duplicated and a remarkable correspondence in the writings was revealed.

Supporting the position that conditions are highly variable from writer to writer, Equey et al. (2007) carried out a study with subjects writing in four different positions. On average, variance was low, but they did report extreme variation with some subjects. Sciacca et al. (2011) reported on the results of subjects writing while standing, lying, or kneeling on vertical or horizontal supports. An increase in variability was found when subjects were lying and kneeling while writing vertically. In the other conditions, Sciacca et al. reported that the handwriting remained stable. Thiéry et al. (2013) carried out an online analysis of signatures produced by subjects in four positions, but also collected samples on different days to account for natural variation. They did not find a general trend regarding the different writing positions as it varied with the subjects. An important finding was that the day-to-day variation seemed to influence the writing more than the position. In a study by Dziedzic (2016), text and signature samples were collected from 50 healthy subjects who wrote in varying postural positions (sitting, lying with pen and paper on lap, lying with pen and paper on desk to side of bed). Dziedzic was simulating the postures that occur in cases where patients are signing documents from a bed. There was reported variation in pen pressure, left margins, baselines, and middle zone letter height. A blind test, however, indicated that the variation caused by posture did not influence the ability to accurately identify the author of the writing.

9.1.2.3 Writing Purpose

The writing of signatures is a more conscious act when being inscribed on formal or legal documents of some significance. More care is exercised in the site of the signature, if only because the act is at least witnessed if not directed by other parties. For some people, care is simply warranted, and given to the execution of the signature, that results in a better quality of writing, pictorially, than it might otherwise exhibit. Consequently, the care that the writing of the signature receives usually improves letter forms and regularity at the expense of fluency.

Case experience seems to be the source of evidence in support of these statements. Osborn (1929), Harrison (1958b), and Hilton (1982) barely mention the fact that the purpose of the document may have an effect upon the writing. Nevertheless, it is only reasonable to assume that, for persons not frequently required to sign formal documents, the act of doing so will be a matter of greater importance and, consequently, a more conscious endeavor.

9.1.2.4 Spatial Limitations

There is an assumption that writing within a confined space will have an effect upon the writing. It is a question that arises more frequently, and for obvious reasons, with respect to signatures that are required to be applied to printed forms of various kinds that seem to exhibit little respect for people with longer names. There are other occasions when extended writings are voluntarily confined by their nature when they are executed as interlinear insertions in a handwritten or typewritten document.

Morton's (1980) study of signatures provides some empirical data that indicates that a limitation of space may affect a signature in one of two fashions: (1) a reduction in lateral expansion only, that is, a compaction of the writing length with little change in vertical dimension or (2) a miniaturization of the writing in both vertical and horizontal directions, particularly if a vertical limitation was imposed upon the signature. Although interletter spacing is shortened when lateral expansion is reduced and long commencement and terminal strokes may be altered, there is little change to other aspects of the writing such as form or relative heights and no evidence of a significant change in writing fluency. On the other hand, as might be expected, miniaturization has little effect upon any of the writing aspects other than absolute size. Horizontal limitations did not result in miniaturization in all cases, however, vertical limitations invariably did.

A recent study of the signatures of 62 subjects by Bey and Ryan (1998) may be in conflict with Morton's (1980) findings. The report of these authors indicates that a reduction in the vertical space available does have an effect upon the relative heights of some letters, which they say was to be expected. They also report that they found a strong relationship between the space available and the occurrences of variation in a person's signature. This is not variation in the sense in which the term is normally used, but rather an observable change in five writing characteristics: letter spacing, legibility, relative heights of uppercase to lowercase letters, relative heights of uppercase to uppercase letters, and change in baseline tendencies.

Like Morton (1980), Bey and Ryan (1998) were endeavoring to identify some of the changes that might occur in signatures written in a confined space, for which allowance must be made in the study and comparison of handwriting. When due allowance is made, neither of these studies suggest that the task of identification is made overly difficult or impossible.

More recently, Simsons et al. (2011) looked at the effect of constraints on signatures and reported that the size of the signature was affected along with other variations including reduced complexity, reduced fluency, hesitation, and extra artifacts. Burkey (2012) examined spatial constrictions for signatures and handwritten entries that included additions to prewritten material, and letter and numeral alterations. Changes observed when examining the handwriting samples of over 150 participants included height, width, and letter spacing (Figures 9.1 through 9.3). Burkey also noted that writers had a tendency to not write over existing handwritten lines and termed the phenomenon "reflex of avoidance."

9.1.2.5 Writing Surface and Support

Many claims have been made in defense of poor simulations that the questioned writings, usually signatures, were executed under extreme conditions, but little research has been conducted to dispute these claims, except as might be demanded by particular cases. For the most part, the circumstances of these cases are extreme, as in writings on the flesh of dead bodies.

There are, however, numerous other sets of circumstances, closer to the norm for writing that may alter the written product. Hecker (1983) examined the effects of four writing instruments—ballpoint pen, pencil, fiber-tip pen, and felt-tip pen—against 10 different surfaces and using two

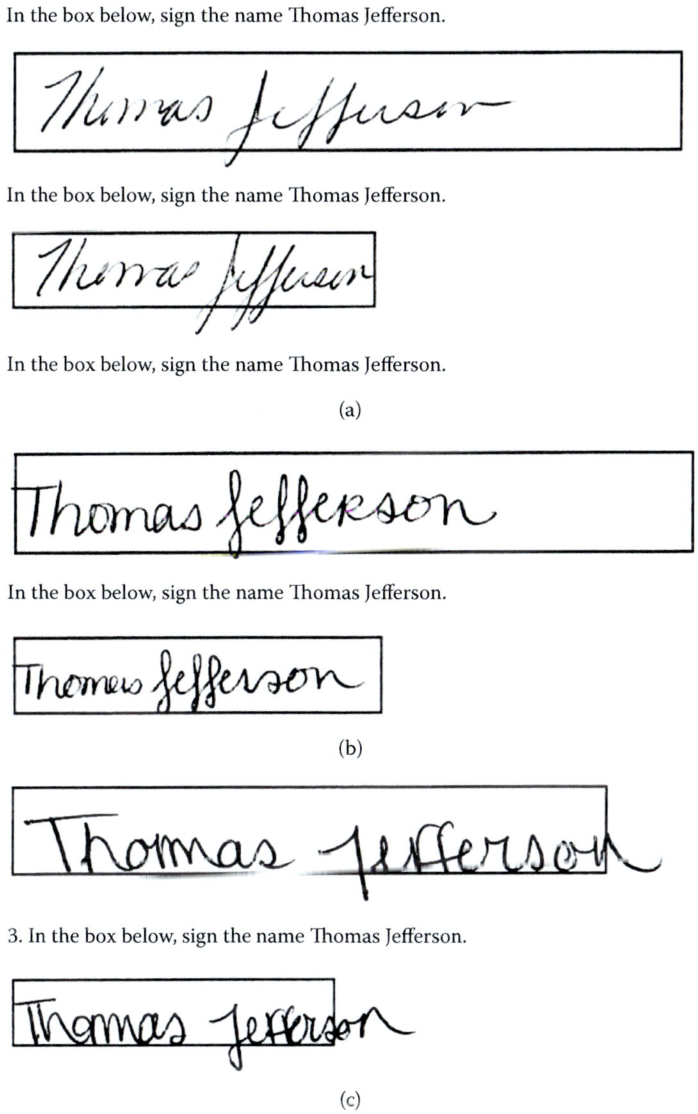

Figure 9.1 Three individuals asked to sign the name Thomas Jefferson within boxes. Note that person A started using the same size but horizontally compressed the last name to stay within the box (a). Person B horizontally compressed the entire signature to stay within the box (b). Person C disregarded the box for the most part (c).

different weights of paper: copy paper (25–39 g/gm) and typing paper (60–90 g/gm). As might have been expected, his results showed that effects depended upon:

- The thickness of the paper
- The type of writing instrument employed
- The hardness of the supporting surface

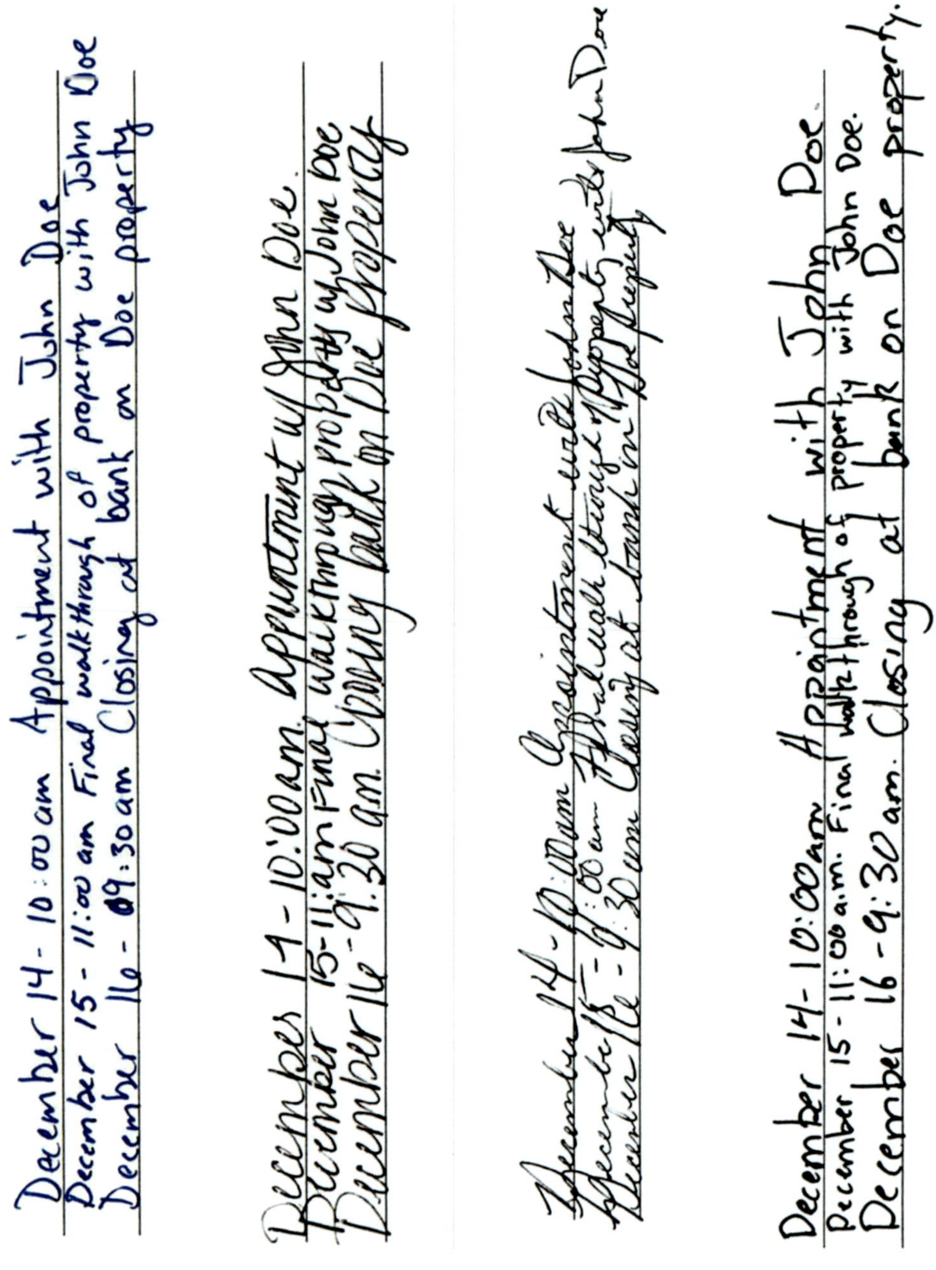

Figure 9.2 Four writers asked to insert a sentence between December 14 and December 16. Note the vertical compression used to attempt to avoid writing across existing lines of writing.

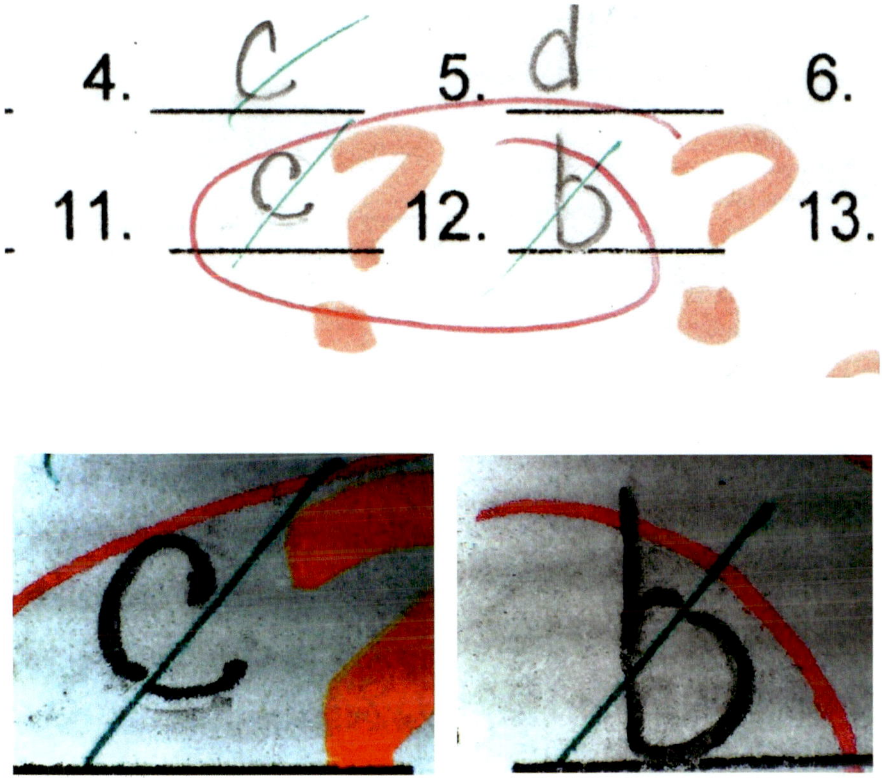

Figure 9.3 Pencil erasures and changes to answers on an exam after grading. Note the avoidance to write across the inked lines by the writer—referred to as "reflex of avoidance."

Hecker (1983) observed that, with thinner papers, the structure of the supporting surface was more apparent in the writing, but depended to some extent on the nature of the writing instrument. He also noted that sharply-pointed instruments (pencils) pierced papers more frequently on soft support surfaces than others.

The fine structure of a support surface became particularly obvious when a soft pencil was used. On the contrary, fiber-tip pens provided the least evidence of the nature of the support surface. When the "amount of relief" to the surface is near negligible there is little deflection of the instrument and the surface structure is not well reproduced, but hard pencils may enhance it. Regularly patterned surfaces tend to produce regularly patterned marks in the paper as the instrument runs across it.

Fiber-tip pens were found to provide fewer clues to supporting surface characteristics and felt-tip pens provided the fewest, as one might have expected. Coarse-structured surfaces interfered with the movement of the writing instrument to the extent that, on occasion, garland movements were converted to arcadic. Extremely coarse-structured support surfaces such as corrugated cardboard provided different effects depending on the orientation of the writing to the direction in which the ribs of corrugation ran.

Hecker (1983) cautioned against misinterpreting deflections in pen movement that may be simply accidental characteristics as indications of irregularity in support surfaces. He also noted that embossing on the reverse (back) of the document viewed with oblique lighting may yield evidence as to the surface structure on which the document was written.

Major irregularities in surface structure, such as cracks in a table top, can cause the writing instrument to change direction and follow the irregularity some distance. Such is a localized or isolated circumstance that may not be repeated if the writer takes evasive action. Hecker's (1983) studies were made of general conditions of surfaces which might affect any or all lines of writing across them.

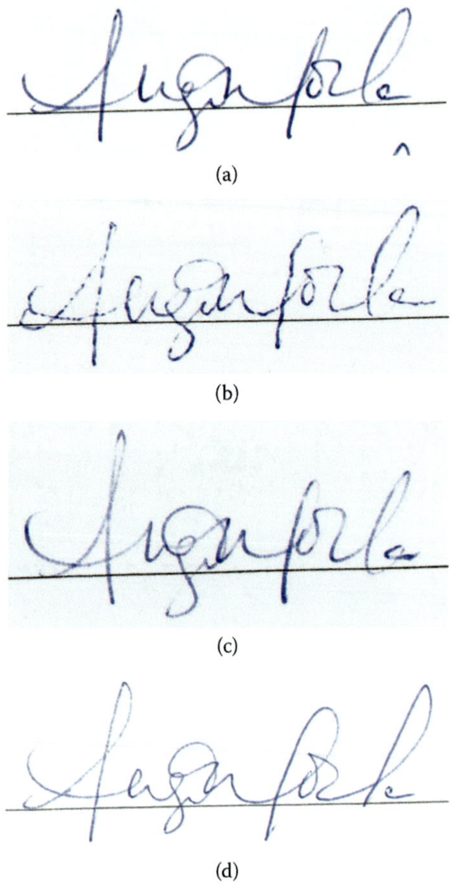

Figure 9.4 Four signatures written on different surfaces (a) normal, (b) concrete, (c) fabric, and (d) plaster. Note the changes in line quality.

DeAngelis (1997) examined writing surfaces and reported that uneven surfaces can influence the regularity of line quality through breaks, skips, and corrugations. Herkt et al. (1999) also reported on the line quality irregularity that is a by-product of writing on an uneven backing surface. Miller and Harralson (2005) carried out a systematic study involving 113 subjects writing on seven different uneven surfaces (concrete, brick, wood, plaster, leather, fabric, and Pebble Tec®). They found that surfaces such as concrete, brick, and Pebble Tec produced corrugated line quality with heavy pressure. Softer surfaces, such as fabric and leather, produced wider ink line width and false starts (Figure 9.4). Wood and plaster exhibited both smooth parts in the line quality interspersed with occasional breaks or tremor depending on how the pen interacted with occasional unevenness of the surface. The researchers commented on the importance of examining original documents in cases when the writing surface is in question as inspecting the back of the page or signature (where there is heavy embossing when writing on an uneven surface) helps to discriminate between writing on an awkward surface in comparison to simulation.

Other reports by Totty (1981) and Leung (1986) described the examination of lettering (and Chinese writing) on the soft skin surfaces of corpses. Taylor and Hnilica (1991) discussed the examination of lettering present on a corpse that they found to be self-inscribed prior to death. Brown (1985) describes the examination of writing on the hard metal surfaces of fairly large copper tubing (2 inch diameter). In all cases, some evidence was found by which the lettering could be associated with the authors, although not definitively. Many factors had a bearing on these examinations, including the effects of the movement of the flesh with the writing instrument, and the curvature of the pipe. A principal obstacle in all cases was in obtaining appropriate standards for comparison (Figures 9.5 and 9.6).

9.1.2.6 Writing Environment

Numerous environmental circumstances are suggested or claimed as conditions responsible for changes in writing, particularly of signatures. Frequently, the condition alleged must be considered, not in isolation, but in combination with some other condition. Subdued lighting may have little effect on the writer, unless he or she suffers from impaired vision. Low temperatures may have little effect, unless writing is executed while wearing apparel on the hands that is heavy or restrictive, or unless body temperature is diminished and shivering is induced.

Cheng (2007) carried out a study involving subjects wearing three types of gloves (disposable, thin cotton, and thick cotton gloves) while producing various handwriting samples. While Cheng commented that the observable differences in the subjects' handwritings would not preclude an examiner from identifying the handwriting, he mentioned that writing pressure, size, and spacing showed differences along with the presence of some pen slips and awkward strokes.

When finger movement is restricted, the control of fine writing movements is restricted, and some change in their fluency or quality of execution will occur. Writing becomes more of a whole hand or forearm movement that is often unfamiliar to the writer and may, therefore, have its effects upon the fine movements that are required, until some adjustment to the circumstances is made by the writer in the course of longer texts or successive signatures.

Figure 9.5 Writing substrates may be walls, refrigerators, or car doors as illustrated. And, the "ink" may be blood, lipstick, or spray paint (as in the case of graffiti).

9.1.3 Temporal States

In a review of 30 papers on the subject of drug-induced changes to handwriting, Gross (1975) described, and criticized when necessary, the work of different investigators. His introduction sets out the reasons for the interest in the subject as being the tangible and measurable effects of many pharmacological agents in altering the user's muscular coordination:

> Complex motor skills, including handwriting, have frequently been utilized to assess these temporal malfunctions. There are several advantages in utilizing handwriting.... First, the analytic sample is easily obtained and provides a permanent record. Second, since handwriting is one of the most complex, coordinated human activities, intrusions upon the nervous system should

Figure 9.6 Murder scene where a woman was found drowned in the bathtub with a handwritten threat on the shower panel, written in red permanent marker.

> logically produce alterations in one's usual writing pattern. Finally, since it is such a well-habituated act, handwriting should provide a conservative measure of the actions of pharmacological agents (p. 375).

The potential of handwriting in research involving therapeutic administrations of antipsychotic and anti-Parkinsonian drugs has become evident. The use and abuse of many different pharmacological agents in contravention of the law and the consequences of such abuse within a forensic arena has stimulated the interest of handwriting examiners called upon to identify the writings of the users that become the perpetrators of other crimes. It comes as no surprise, then, that the drug most often studied in relation to handwriting changes has been alcohol.

Gross's (1975) criticisms of the studies conducted are directed largely at the methods employed. They deal with design components that work of this kind should address. First: many of the studies were conducted without the administration of placebos, necessary to verify that effects are legitimate, not psychosomatic or resulting from other variables. Second: few studies employed the double-blind technique in which neither the subject nor the investigator is aware of whether treatment or placebo is being administered, to control expectation effects. Third: the statistical analyses of data were often descriptive rather than inferential. Thus, the differences in the effects on handwriting could not be accurately or objectively assessed.

These criticisms notwithstanding, there is a degree of consistency in the results reported respecting the effects upon handwriting that serve as a guide to examiners. This guide encompasses where and what changes occur, whether or not such changes are measurable at low, or indeed, any level of drug influence. Furthermore, Gross (1975) advanced that psychological stability tends to influence the degree and direction in which one's handwriting is apt to change following drug ingestion. Despite the variation in the location and extent of change, however, the discriminating elements involved remain the same.

9.1.3.1 Alcohol

Questions frequently arise in matters under litigation respecting the effects of drugs, particularly alcohol and hallucinogens, upon the writing of the individual, which has prompted numerous studies to be conducted. Questions concerning the authorship of signatures on consent forms usually acquired during a DUI arrest are likely documents to come under dispute involving the influence of alcohol.

There may be no other aspect of handwriting identification that has received as much attention and undergone as much research as the effects of alcohol on handwriting. It may be because it is so frequently proffered as a prevailing condition at the time of signing a document, when the writing itself becomes the center of dispute. The argument contending that the writer was intoxicated at the time is proposed to contest the writer's knowledge and responsibility for his or her actions.

It could be that in research on alcohol and writing, it is not difficult to muster a body of willing subjects not wanting financial remuneration for their time. Furthermore, in recent years instruments for the testing of breath alcohol levels in vehicle operators has been introduced. Understandably, the need has emerged to train users of the equipment in real-life situations to develop their skills in order to obtain valid and reliable results from test processes. This has made available a body of subjects whose capabilities in numerous other tasks, such as writing, can be conveniently and coincidentally tested or measured.

Technically, alcohol is a toxic substance and a poison to the human body. When ingested in any amount (e.g., the first social drink) it results in a state of intoxication (i.e., poisoning), almost immediately. This is not to say that, at this point, intoxication affects behavior. Nor is it to say that the level of intoxication is detectible to an observer or is a fact of which the subject is conscious. Furthermore, drunkenness is a state of impairment of the faculties, not too precisely defined, and usually applied in a nontechnical sense to high levels of intoxication.

Ethanol, the kind of alcohol that is consumed as a beverage, is a reasonably moderate poison and one that the body can tolerate or contend with in limited quantities. While in the body, it is a depressant drug affecting the central nervous system much like anesthetics such as ether or chloroform. The alcohol, ethanol, is often referred to in the vernacular as *grain* alcohol. The more lethal kind of alcohol found in many household items, and sometimes consumed by addicts with devastating if not deadly results, is methanol, referred to in the vernacular as *wood* alcohol.

Alcohol, almost the entire dose of alcohol in a beverage, is absorbed through the walls of the gastrointestinal tract within 30–75 minutes of consumption. It is distributed throughout the body by the blood system. It resides in the tissues of the body in proportion to their water content. It is eliminated from the body by metabolism (95%) and as a relatively unchanged component of urine, sweat, and expired breath (5%). It leaves at a rate of about one ounce of liquor per hour for a 160-pound male. Digestion is not required. Food in the stomach, particularly starches and fats, may serve to slow the rate of absorption somewhat.

The blood alcohol concentration (BAC) is the amount of alcohol in blood, expressed in various ways, at any point in time. The same amount of liquor will produce a lower concentration of alcohol to blood (BAC) in a large person than it will in a small person, simply because the larger person has more water in the body in which the alcohol is distributed. In order to attain higher BAC levels, one must consume a number of ounces of liquor within a relatively short span of time, to offset the body's natural rate of elimination of one ounce per hour, and to build the concentration.

Alcohol is metabolized in the body by an oxidation process involving enzymes. The enzymatic systems reduce the level of BAC in chronic drinkers at a faster rate than nondrinkers. An alcohol tolerance can develop, in some cases. These enzymatic systems may be responsible for the greater ability of some chronic drinkers to carry out complicated tasks while under the influence. This retention of capabilities is the reason chronic drinkers can exhibit fluent, normal writing at BAC levels higher than nondrinkers.

Tolerance is a word with many meanings in technical alcohol discussions. *Blood alcohol tolerance* usually refers to the concentration of alcohol (BAC) needed to produce measurable changes in particular behavior or performance (e.g., vehicle operation or handwriting). This is a tolerance that varies with different individuals or with the same individual on different occasions. It is the tolerance that induced lawmakers to limit BACs to certain levels for motor vehicle operation, as deterioration in performance was measurable at those levels. The performance of neuromuscular tasks by many persons, particularly those requiring high levels of muscular coordination (such as handwriting) may be measurably altered at BAC levels as low as ≥0.05% (Baird 1969).

Then there is *body tolerance*, that is the amount of alcohol required to affect different people (or the same person on different occasions) to the same degree or to the same change in performance (e.g., the ability to stand without wavering, to walk a straight line or to bring the ends of two fingers together with arms outstretched). This is a tolerance that varies with the individual owing to differences or variations in the rates of absorption, metabolism, and elimination. It is the sense in which the layman uses the term *tolerance for alcohol*.

The literature on alcohol and writing tends to classify people in one of four categories: nondrinkers, social drinkers, chronic drinkers, and alcoholics. The lines of demarcation between the last three groups are not always clear, at least in the minds of the drinkers. Then too, the first three groups are often referred to as normal drinkers, distinct from alcoholics.

Alcoholism has been classified as a disease, the nature and origin of which has long been debated. The prevailing view for years was that it was an emotional disorder that when treated and resolved allowed the individual to return to normal drinking practices. The newer and more enlightened view is that alcoholism is a disease entity in itself that is physiological in origin. This school holds that the behavior pattern of the alcoholic is the result rather than the cause of the disease that can be arrested only by total and continued abstinence from alcohol.

Beck (1982) has provided an excellent description of the alcoholic and his or her attendant problems giving us some explanation for the tremors occurring in the patient's writing, and some insight into the improvement in writing performance that accompanies the alcoholic's first drinks after a spell of sobriety. Beck explains that while the nonalcohol drinker has two handwriting states (sober and intoxicated), the alcoholic has three handwriting states (sober, intoxicated, and in withdrawal).

The studies conducted are attempts to answer a few fundamental questions:

1. Does handwriting contain evidence of a writer's consumption of alcohol within a certain time period prior to execution? If so, what evidence?
2. Does this evidence, if any, correlate reliably with the writer's BAC?
3. Could the evidence of intoxication in handwriting be mistaken for another condition/ circumstance, or vice versa?

Bogan (1958) systematically outlined the several changes that occur in writing, speech, and behavior in the course of progressive intoxication. He stated:

> The choice of words and subjects in writing shows the same loss of inhibitions which may be noted in speech and actions. Handwriting at an early stage is apt to be larger and heavier and more ornate than usual. There may be a tendency for the writing to rise or fall, and to vary in the size of letters. Later, the changes become more marked and the letters less legible, with more misspellings, crossing outs or erasures, overwriting, and with excess duplications, insertions, omissions, or transpositions of strokes, letters, or words similar to the corresponding changes in the enunciation of spoken language. The writing becomes more scrawling and illegible and eventually merely a sprawling line before the person becomes entirely unable to scribble (pp. 48–49).

Historically, several investigators have researched the effects of alcohol on handwriting including Nousianen (1951); Rabin and Blair (1953); Tripp et al. (1959); Resden (1959); Packard (1960); Duke and Coldwell (1965); Doulder (1965); Hilton (1969b); Anderson (1974); Doud (1975); Beck (1982); Galbraith (1984); Goyne and Kittel (1985); Conway (1991); Watkins and Gorajczyk (1996). Their combined research shows:

1. The ingestion of alcohol results in handwriting impairment, although the BAC at which it becomes apparent, and the elements of writing affected varies with the individual, his or her drinking practices or history, and the circumstances under which the writing is done.
2. The quality of writing deteriorates progressively with the elevation of BAC, and more profoundly in extended writing than in signatures.
3. The legibility of writing deteriorates progressively with the elevation of BAC, partially due to the distortion of letter forms.
4. The dimensions of writing increase with the elevation of BAC. A given word or text will occupy more space.
5. The lateral expansion of writing increases with the elevation of BAC.
6. The alignment of writing deteriorates progressively with the elevation of BAC.
7. The irregularity of letter slopes increases progressively with the elevation of BAC.
8. The point load of the writing instrument (pen pressure) increases or may become irregular with the elevation of BAC.
9. The speed of writing decreases markedly with the elevation of BAC.
10. Errors, letter omissions, and overwritings increase in frequency with the elevation of BAC.
11. Erratic movements or sudden changes in the writing line or tremors may occur with the elevation of BAC.
12. Abnormalities in allograph selection may occur with the elevation of BAC.
13. There is no particular residual evidence of impairment in the writing of a normal drinker during the period following the return to sobriety (the hangover period).
14. The influence of alcohol on writing can vary somewhat with the individual's temperament, state of health, emotional state, or with fatigue.
15. The quality of writing of an alcoholic may not be fully recovered during the withdrawal (sober or hangover) stage of his or her drinking behavior.
16. The quality of writing of a sober alcoholic may be improved initially by the ingestion of alcohol.
17. Tremor is a likely characteristic of the writing or line drawing of chronic drinkers and alcoholics, drunk or sober that may be reduced or eliminated at low levels of BAC.

In determining the ways in which alcohol alters handwriting, the results of the studies are consistent, although the methods of judgment are somewhat imprecise and lack specificity. As Gross (1975) has done, others have challenged the reliability of some studies. Reports on some aspects of writing such as point load (pen pressure) and speed are less consistent with one another, perhaps because procedures and blood/alcohol concentrations are not entirely comparable.

The listing of these 17 changes that may be found in the writing performance of persons consuming alcohol is not to suggest that all will be present and to the same degree in any particular drinker's writing sample at any given BAC. The reason for changes at all is evidently due to alcohol's depressant action upon the central nervous system. Beyond that the similarity between individuals or between the effects on the same individual on different occasions diminishes.

Studies that have attempted to use changes in handwriting as a measure of the level of intoxication or BAC of a subject have not yet proven successful. Duke and Coldwell (1965), did find a degree of correlation between them that has not been pursued, a task that would be complicated by differences in body tolerance.

The tendency for most persons to write larger, poorer, and with less regularity under the influence of alcohol suggests that alcohol inhibits the finer movements of muscular coordination or motor control (Figure 9.7). However, as Galbraith (1984) reported, a few individuals have been observed to write smaller, which seems to contradict the theory. The likelihood is that there are factors involved in these special cases that are not fully understood.

A study by Stinson (1997) endeavored to validate selected prior studies of the effects of alcohol consumption upon handwriting. On the strength of a study of 26 subjects, agreement was found in changes observed as compared with the reported observations of earlier studies. Difficulty was encountered, however, in attempting to compare quantified results, owing to the vagueness of the language used in the previous works. Terms such as *few* or *increased, appeared more* and *did not appear to have an effect* were too imprecise to facilitate comparisons.

Purtell (1965) is one of the few writers to mention the effect of alcohol when taken in conjunction with or in addition to some other forms of medication or drug abuse such as meprobamate (a tranquilizer). While other drugs and/or medications by themselves may not significantly alter a person's writing, when combined with the ingestion of alcohol they tend to potentiate the effects of the alcohol. On the other hand, it has been claimed that alcohol increases the sedative

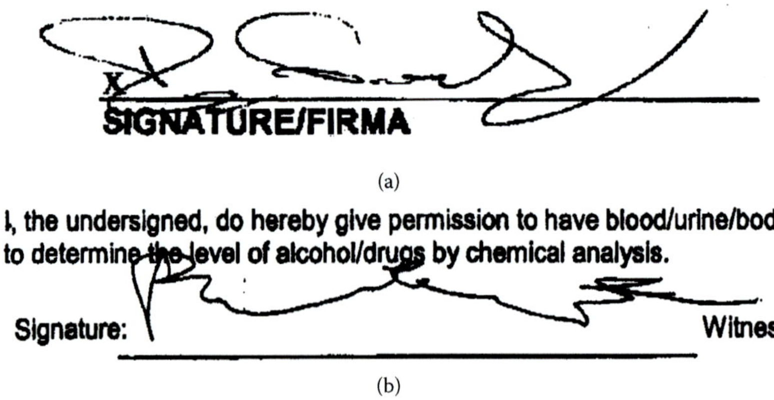

Figure 9.7 Example of the influence of alcohol on writing. The normal signature of a writer (a). The same writer under the influence of alcohol (b).

effect that any other drug may have on the central nervous system. There is limited information as to the consequences of the combination other than to note that the alterations to the writing are more pronounced at lower levels of BAC.

Brun and Reisby (1971) conducted a study of handwriting changes resulting from the effects of alcohol, meprobamate, and their interaction. In two experiments involving 38 subjects (28 males), and 40 subjects (29 males), it was found that the interaction of alcohol and meprobamate produced more errors than either drug alone, while each drug produced more errors than a placebo. The greatest measurable changes in handwriting occurred from the interaction of alcohol and meprobamate, however, there were few measurable changes resulting from meprobamate alone. While no single handwriting change was found to be drug specific, writing consistency and stability appeared to be most reflective of drug ingestion. Other reliable indices of drug effects were found to be fluctuations in letter size and pen pressure, as well as undulating baselines. In the second experiment, the subjects were grouped by psychiatric interview into four categories using the Taylor manifest anxiety scale. Interestingly, the handwriting of the subjects in the group displaying the fewest personality disturbances was the least affected under any of the drug conditions.

Tripp et al. (1959) demonstrated that normal persons possess superior writing ability to alcoholics in tests of pressure variability, ataxia, and speed, and further that the tougher the task the greater the difference. Under the influence of ethanol, however, the performance of normal subjects was impaired while that of alcoholics showed marked improvement. To this extent, then, what happens to one's writing under the influence of alcohol depends upon the drinking history of the writer.

With respect to the influence of alcohol consumption and alcohol dependence, Phillips et al. (2008) reported on the results of a kinematic study that factors such as word height and width may be affected when drinking alcohol. However, they also mentioned that the handwriting of those who are alcohol dependent showed less influence. Aşıcıoğlu and Turan (2003) carried out a comprehensive statistical study involving 73 subjects whose writing samples were evaluated before and after alcohol consumption. In the alcohol condition, results showed handwriting increases in word length, height of upper and lower case letters, height of ascending letters, height of descending letter, spacing between words, angularity, tremor, and tapered endings.

Hilton (1969b) commented on the fact that the changes to writing that result from alcohol are, in the initial stages or at low levels of BAC, not unlike some symptoms of other conditions (i.e., fatigue, carelessness, and simulation). For this reason, hasty conclusions should not be drawn that alcohol is the only cause for perceived handwriting distortion.

9.1.3.2 Hallucinogens and Recreational Drugs

Much like alcoholics, persons addicted to drugs such as heroin, cocaine, and the many varieties of them, initially experience a certain state of well-being with the ingestion of the drug during which performance in any neuromotor task is improved over that in a state of withdrawal or abstinence. Important to note, as well, is the fact that effects similar to those of alcohol are obtained in writing under the influence of other drugs such as lysergic acid diethylamide (LSD-25) and 2-brom lysergic acid diethylamide (BOL-148).

Cases arise involving the writing of wills or other communications in conjunction with or prior to the taking of drug overdoses resulting in death. Checks and receipts are sometimes signed while in a drugged state, after which, and on return to a normal state, the writer may have no recollection of the writing act. As with alcohol, it can be a defense offered by an accused person who has been linked to a document on the strength of writing, or other evidence.

Hallucinogenic and addictive drugs of most kinds, like alcohol, have an effect upon the neuromuscular system, and while the effects are somewhat varied there is some consistency in the conditions reported. In a well-conducted study of the effects of seven different drugs on the handwriting of five subjects, Hirsch et al. (1956) compared the results obtained from the oral consumption of:

Lysergic acid diethylamide (LSD-25)
Lysergic acid ethylamide (LAE-32)
Dd-1-brom lysergic acid diethylamide (BOL-148)
Ethyl alcohol
Ergonovine (ergometrine)
Pervitin or methedrine (methamphetamine hydrochloride)
Scopolamine (hyoscine)
No. 1 tap water placebo
No. 2 tap water placebo

Several precautions were taken. Each substance was given on a separate day. No two subjects received the same drug on the same day. About four hours after receiving each substance, the subject was required to copy a poem one paragraph in length. Each drug was diluted in 200 cc of water and only the alcohol had a taste and an odor. The principal results are summarized as:

1. The effects of the different substances varied with the individual.
2. Under the influence of LSD-25, alcohol, and BOL-148, three subjects wrote much larger, that is, occupied more space, than after the placebos, and two wrote smaller. Under ergonovine, subjects generally wrote smaller.
3. The greatest number of errors and the greatest number of erasures, deletions, corrections etc., tended to occur under scopolamine. This drug produced feelings of extreme drowsiness that may have been responsible. No erasures, etc., were made after ergonovine, and only one erasure was made after BOL-148.
4. The greatest irregularity and carelessness in writing occurred after alcohol, scopolamine, and LSD-25. The most noticeable effects followed LSD-25 ingestion. Irregularity in letter size, word spacing, slant, and lack of control characterized the writing of four subjects under the influence of LSD-25. One subject wrote smaller. The other drugs had no widespread marked effects.

Fisher et al. (1966) conducted studies regarding the effect of the hallucinogen psilocybin on psychomotor performance, and particularly on handwriting. It was their finding that at peak levels of the drug on two male subjects, there were substantial increases in the size of writing, the rate of writing, and the pen pressure (point load) exerted. Other investigations of the effects of lysergic acid diethylamide (LSD) on an index of handwriting referred to as the handwriting pressure curve (HPC) by Thuring (1960) proved less conclusive.

Legień (1984) employed a handwriting test with some success in the diagnosis of narcotic addiction. Legge et al. (1964) examined six measures of handwriting size as indices of the effects of different concentrations of nitrous oxide (NOH), the anesthetic gas that is a central depressant drug. Nitrous oxide produced a systematic increase in the size of handwriting that varied with the concentration of the NOH. The six aspects of size that were measured consisted of (1) the number of words in two lines of writing, (2) the average baseline lengths (horizontal dimension) of 10 key words, (3) the average vertical dimension of minuscules in the key words, (4) the average vertical dimension of infralinear letters (e.g., "y" and "g") in five key words, (5) the average vertical dimension of supralinear letters (e.g., "l" and "h") in five key words, (6) the vertical dimension of the tallest supralinear letter.

The baseline length (horizontal dimension) of words was found to be the most sensitive and reliable index; it is relatively quick and simple to measure and might have some practical application. Why nitrous oxide produces a systematic increase in writing size that correlates with the concentration of the dose administered is not explained, but the suggestion is made that it acts on neuromuscular control in such a way that only relatively coarse movements can be made. The effect is not unlike that of alcohol.

In a later study of the same drug on handwriting, Legge (1965) observed that the drug appeared to have acted on processes subserving judgment, and increased the subjects' tolerance for errors in alignment. Under the drug's influence, misalignments were accepted that were not tolerated when performing without the drug.

Dhawan et al. (1969) examined the effects of two stimulants (caffeine and methamphetamine), two depressants (chlorpromazine and phenobarbitone), and a placebo on handwriting in a double-blind test situation using the elements of writing employed by Legge et al. (1964). Briefly, they found that the time taken to copy a passage decreased under the influence of methamphetamine but increased under phenobarbitone. They found that the average length of words and the vertical dimension of key words increased under the stimulants caffeine and methamphetamine, but was unaffected by the depressants chlorpromazine and phenobarbitone. The authors felt that the tests were not sufficiently sensitive to differentiate reliably between the different types of centrally acting drugs.

Peters et al. (1976) studied the influence of 9-tetrahydrocannabinol (THC) (hashish), the active ingredient of cannabis sativa (marijuana), in a number of sensory, motor, cognitive, and perceptual tasks, but not specifically handwriting. The effect was minimal but consistent. Performance was less efficient and more variable. Even at high dose levels, THC failed to produce gross alterations, but there were consistent, subtle decrements on a variety of performance measures. Klonoff et al. (1973) is reported as obtaining more pronounced results in other similar tests, which suggests that factors other than THC may be involved.

Many studies have been conducted of the effects of alcohol on performance when taken in conjunction with other drugs. Zirkle et al. (1960) found that there was a greater (synergistic) effect on human performance and judgment from a combined dosage of meprobamate and alcohol than from either of these drugs taken singly. Indeed, the effects were greater than those found in an earlier study (Zirkle et al. 1959) of alcohol and chlorpromazine that is generally considered to be a stronger drug.

Several studies have been conducted of the effects of marijuana (THC) and alcohol in simulated driving tests. THC has been found to have a stronger effect on one's ability to estimate time and distance, but that both drugs slowed one's reaction time. Few studies have been reported regarding the combined effects of THC and alcohol on handwriting. Foley and Miller (1978) studied the handwriting of 12 individuals under the influence of marijuana, alcohol, and a combination of the two relative to control samples taken in advance. Of the 12 subjects, 8 were judged to be habitual users, smoking marijuana at least twice a week. The others were less frequent users. The authors found that:

1. After smoking one marijuana cigarette, there was little or no change in the subject's handwriting.
2. After smoking three marijuana cigarettes, some changes were observed in the writing of subjects with little prior experience with THC. There was some increase in size and some alteration to letter forms.

3. After smoking five marijuana (THC) cigarettes, there was a general increase in letter sizes, some deviation in alignment and greater carelessness in execution.
4. After consuming three 12 oz. cans of beer, subjects increased writing speed, letter sizes, and lateral expansion. Some changes in relative heights of letters and letter slopes were also observed.
5. After consuming three 12 oz. cans of beer and smoking three marijuana (THC) cigarettes, subjects revealed changes to their writing similar to those observed after the ingestion of alcohol alone. The authors suggest that the gross changes observed when consumption of the drugs was combined was probably due, principally, to the effect of the alcohol.
6. Marijuana (THC) smoking in moderate amounts had less effect upon handwriting than did alcohol. The combined effects of alcohol and THC are evidently not synergistic.

Foley and Miller (1978) explained that the neuromuscular activity necessary to produce normal writing is directed by the CNS (central nervous system). The marked effect of alcohol on writing is due to its depression of the CNS. Although THC also affects the CNS, it does not greatly depress the activity that directs manipulative functions, such as handwriting. Thus, THC produces emotional or mood changes, a *high* for example, without impairing the individual's ability to write.

In the body of literature that is available, there is some variation in the effects obtained by drugs on handwriting. As Gross (1975) pointed out, psychological stability influences the degree and direction in which one's handwriting is apt to change following drug ingestion. According to Gross, "there is reason to believe that these drug-induced graphomotor reactions are proportional to one's psychological reactions" (p. 390). Anderson, a neurologist, was cited by Wellingham-Jones (1991b) and pointed out that certain drugs interfere with neurotransmitter function which cause disturbances in handwriting. The handwriting changes or disturbances are nonspecific but are not diagnostic of any particular drug. With respect to drug rehabilitation, Davidson (2010) reported a case study involving a patient in rehabilitation for heroin use who showed considerable improvement in the legibility of his handwriting during and after rehabilitation.

Although it is not expected that other recreational substances such as caffeine and nicotine would have a dramatic influence on handwriting, studies have shown that they can indeed affect writing. In studies about the effects of nicotine and caffeine on motor tasks, Tucha et al. (2004, 2006) found that both nicotine and caffeine improved handwriting performance specifically in kinematical or movement measures such as increased speed, velocity, and fluency.

9.1.3.3 Hypnosis

Hypnosis is a trance-like condition or an induced state that resembles sleep in which the subject is highly responsive to suggestion. Although there is no record of an actual case in which writing under hypnotic influence is alleged to have occurred, it is a possible circumstance that some document examiners have been curious to explore. Does handwriting change under hypnosis, and/or can it be made to resemble another individual's writing or signature? If it was so, the potential for this as an argument in civil and criminal matters is significant. Bowers (1976) stated that the behavior and perception of those hypnotized become sensitized to the hypnotist's communication, but there are varying degrees of hypnosis. Some are able to go into a deep hypnotic state while others may not be able to achieve the state at all.

In a study of 17 subjects and their ability to simulate or forge signatures when hypnotized, Nemecek and Currie (1972) found that neither hypnosis nor posthypnotic suggestion improved the subject's ability to simulate or forge another's signature. In fact, most subjects reported that under hypnosis, the writer was more relaxed to the point at which writing was an effort.

Blueschke (1985) claimed that judges in British Columbia have posed the questions about whether hypnosis has an effect on handwriting, whether it can be used to write the perfect forgery, and whether it can be used to disguise one's handwriting successfully. His study of 26 subjects disclosed that in some cases handwriting under hypnosis deteriorated, but the degree of deterioration varied with the individual. Furthermore, the subject's ability to simulate another writing or signature did not improve. The question of disguise was not addressed.

In a study on hypnotic states and automatic handwriting, Walsh et al. (2014) had participants evaluate their own handwriting after hypnosis and reported that some participants did not recognize their own handwriting when it was written under hypnosis. Writing form was affected with a change in visual appearance when comparing prehypnotic writing to writing under hypnosis. The extent to which this change affected handwriting was not measured.

9.1.3.4 Fatigue or Physical Stress

There are two forms of stress that a person may experience: emotional stress and physical stress. Fatigue is the physical form of stress. One can find mention of the effects of fatigue upon writing in papers dealing with alcohol, but little that describes in any detail what the effects are. Hagan (1894), Osborn (1929), and Harrison (1958b) have commented briefly on fatigue, but the source of their knowledge is not indicated. Nousianen (1951) reported on the changes occurring in writing after the subject had run up four flights of stairs. In these, he observed that the lateral expansion of the writing had increased significantly.

Of the earlier recognized authorities, Hagan (1894) and Harrison (1958b) mentioned fatigue, but simply as one of several factors that may influence handwriting, without further elucidation as to how fatigue may influence handwriting.

Nousianen (1951) reported on the changes in the writing of one subject in executing a sentence of 18 words after having run up four flights of stairs. He noted changes that resembled those produced by intoxication, particularly an increase in lateral expansion but without an apparent increase in height.

Roulston (1959) reported on a study of 30 writers under extreme and moderate states of fatigue, and fatigue localized to the writer's forearm. His subjects were healthy males of similar age (early 20s) that were required to write a modified version of the *London Letter* under four different test conditions. He observed an increase in vertical height (109 out of 120 cases) in both lowercase and uppercase letters, without a significant change in proportions or relative heights and an increase in letter width or lateral expansion (23 subjects out of 30). Insofar as the spacing between words, Roulston found both expansion and contraction (15 subjects out of 30), but noted that whichever tendency was exhibited it remained consistent. Slope was not significantly influenced, nor was speed, rhythm, or fluency habits. Only minor deterioration was noted in writing quality that tended to produce a scrawl and exhibit less care. In only one case was greater pen pressure displayed. No evidence of tremor was found. Remarkably, fewer patchings and overwritings occurred in writing under fatigue. Minute movements tended to be enlarged, but there was no fundamental change to most writing habits. There was some propensity to abbreviate, to commit spelling errors, and to omit punctuation and diacritics ("i" dots). There was no apparent difference between the effects of forearm fatigue and general body fatigue. In either case, however, there was some difference in the effects that varied with the severity of the fatigue.

Remillard (1970), in a study of 21 high school students, endeavored to determine whether there was a degree of impairment to a person's writing that would correlate with the pulse rate of the heart under different levels of exertion. He studied further what the nature of the impairment would be and whether stress-impaired writing could still be correctly associated with its author. Remillard's results disclosed that physical stress, producing abnormally high pulse rates, did in fact impair the individual's writing performance, but the reading of pulse rates can only be considered an indicator of the level of stress being experienced by the subject. It cannot be construed from this study that pulse rates are totally responsible for the degree of impairment, although they may be a contributing factor. Impairment of the writing in this case was judged on the strength of the following:

1. Deterioration in letter formation, coupled with overwriting and corrections
2. An increase in lateral expansion, particularly of the spacing between letters, and a frequent misjudgment of the length of words at the ends of lines
3. A tendency to write larger
4. A reduction in the speed of writing, accompanied by an inconsistency in point load (pen pressure)
5. Failure to maintain good alignment or a proper baseline
6. General failure in writing quality and greater carelessness

Notwithstanding the impairment of the writings in these fashions, a group of 15 competent writing examiners were able to associate the writing samples of each subject correctly (100% accuracy) at various levels of stress. These results are obviously consistent with the findings of Roulston (1959) that were reported earlier. An interesting closing comment by Remillard (1970) was that the impairment of writing resulting from physical stress, produced by running various distances was generally similar to, but not as pronounced as, the impairment resulting from the ingestion of alcohol.

Among healthy writers, Provins and Magliaro (1989) reported that fatigue causes deteriorative effects in handwriting. Poulin (1999) stated that research on healthy writers has shown that fatigue affects those with poor writing skill more severely and found that fatigue can result in an increase in size, length, lateral spacing, errors, baseline variance, speed, and slope. Chang et al. (2015) found that the manner in which some adult writers extend their wrists is associated with writing fatigue and pain. In the study, the test subjects who experienced pain wrote in a wrist position that was less extended than the control group who did not experience pain while writing for prolonged periods of time. Fatigue-inducing handwriting tasks of 157 third-grade students with both good and poor handwriting were evaluated (Parush et al. 1998). The results showed that the handwriting of both groups was affected adversely by fatigue but those with poor handwriting skill were more influenced by fatigue.

It is generally believed that those with movement disorders become fatigued more easily when performing handwriting tasks than healthy writers (Figure 9.8). A study conducted by Harralson et al. (2009) with 10 motor-disorder patients (PD and ET) and seven age-matched healthy controls requested that subjects complete 24 handwriting and drawing tasks. The first trials were compared to the final trials to detect any deterioration of the writing. In comparing the two groups, the trend observed was that the controls were faster than the patients in both conditions. However, in comparing the conditions among the individual subjects, some motor-impaired and/or fatigued writers used unorthodox strategies to handle tasks involving repetitive writing that can cause deterioration of their handwriting (i.e., switching from cursive to printing).

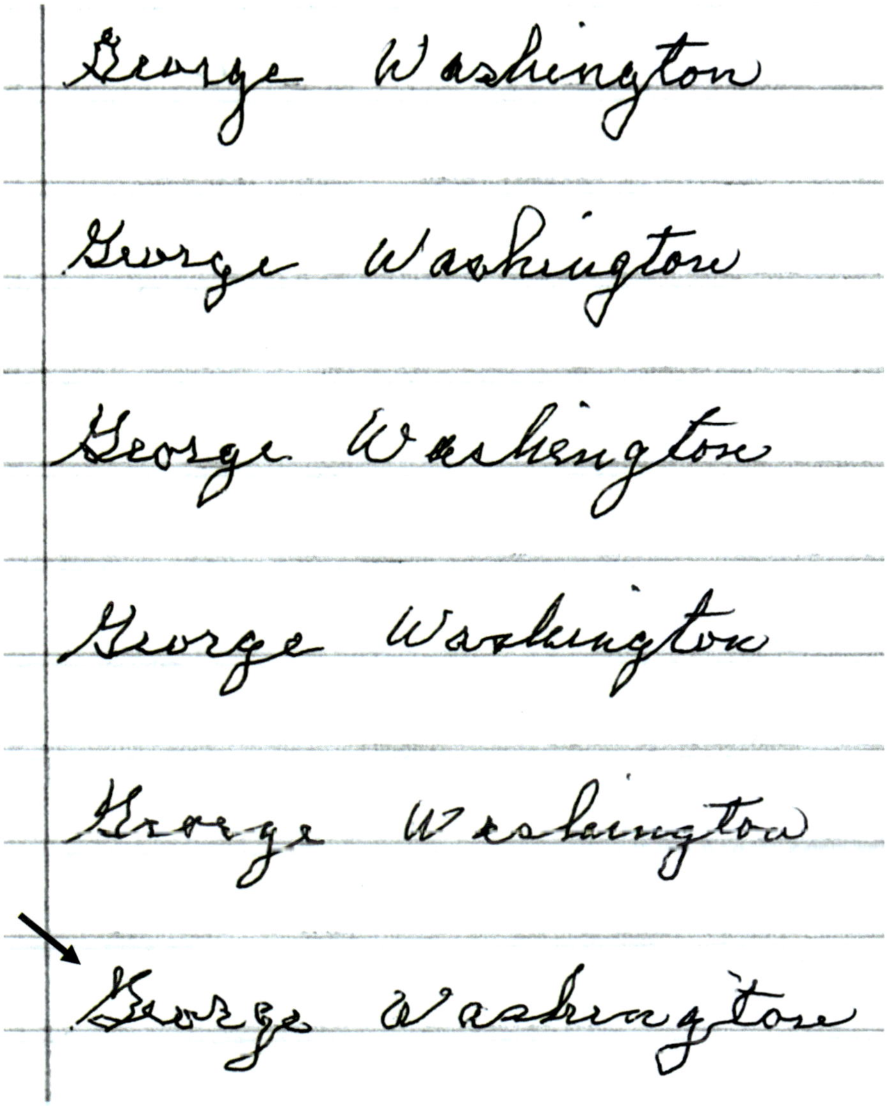

Figure 9.8 Bottom sample shows increased tremor in an essential tremor patient in a sequential writing task.

Overall, the movement disorder patients showed more variability than healthy controls when performing repetitive writing tasks that can cause fatigue.

In summary, fatigue has some influence on the control of the writing instrument that tends to increase the expansion of the writing horizontally. This expansion may be noted in the enlargement of the more minute movements of the writing process and suggests a trend in the writing toward a scrawl. Generally, fatigue occurs in commonplace business transactions that require the signing of multiple documents such as in real estate transactions. Handwriting fatigue may also be intentionally induced during request standard sessions which require persons to produce a large number of handwriting samples.

9.1.4 Literacy and Education

The part of this topic related to illiteracy is discussed further in Chapter 11. In this section, education is discussed as an influence on handwriting. Broom and Basinger (1932) attempted to judge intelligence from samples of penmanship from 30 subjects. Among the authorities on handwriting identification, Harrison (1958b) commented that skill in paragraphing reflects the educational status of the writer. He suggests further that punctuation and spelling, presumably when correctly executed, may also be indicative of a reasonable level of education. It is logical to expect an educated person to be more competent in the written language, and more capable of sorting and organizing thoughts, from which proper paragraphing and punctuation ensues. However, Harrison further noted that correlation is not to be expected between artistic quality (i.e., writing skill) and education or intelligence that has been the evidence proffered by written prescriptions executed by medical professionals.

With respect to literacy, education, and handwriting skill, Tucha et al. (2008) opined that there is too much focus on the visual aspects of handwriting skill (i.e., neatness, legibility) and not enough attention on the automaticity of handwriting which is the real hallmark of a person who is experienced in handwriting performance. Automaticity in handwriting is revealed through speed and fluency while a lack of automaticity is indicated by slow writing with effort and attention placed on the handwriting act. Research carried out by McCarney et al. (2013) support automaticity as a sign of literacy stating that as automaticity develops in school children, working memory is devoted to compositional writing tasks instead of focused on handwriting mechanics. Their study on 284 school children showed correlations between lower literacy and poor handwriting skill while recommending that school children increase automaticity in handwriting in order to increase literacy levels.

Chapter 10

Requirements and Results

10.1 STANDARDS REQUIRED FOR HANDWRITING COMPARISON

Writing standards, or exemplars as they are sometimes called, are of two kinds: collected standards or request standards. Collected standards are those samples of writing or lettering that have been executed in the normal course of business or social activity, and are usually unrelated to any matter in dispute. Request standards are those writings that are executed at the request of a document examiner, investigator, counsel, or some other person involved in the process under litigation.

From the viewpoint of the examiner of handwriting, collected standards are the preferred material to work with in most cases, for it is the more normal and natural product. Collected standards, however, consisting of similar texts to that of the questioned writing, such that they will contain similar letters, letter combinations and letter locations may not exist, or may be difficult to find.

Request writings, on the other hand, are frequently influenced by the circumstances and the knowledge that they are to be the subject of some examination. If the writer of the request writings is, in fact, the author of some writing in dispute, it is not unusual to find that the specimens are altered from the person's normal writing in some manner. If the writer of the request writings is not the author of the disputed material, the circumstances themselves may induce a degree of nervousness that may have some effect upon the fluency of the writing.

Handwriting comparisons require samples of writing from those individuals who are considered to be potential authors and meet the following conditions:

1. They are sufficient in number to exhibit normal writing habits in executing the questioned text or parts thereof, and to portray the consistency with which particular habits are executed.

   Since humans are not inanimate machines operating mechanically within narrow tolerances, natural writing has in its elements a degree of variation from one writing occasion to the next, the range of which is peculiar to the person. Writing standards should be sufficient to portray the range of those variations. For skilled or practiced hands, a half dozen signatures or one or two pages of extended writing might prove adequate. For others, the requirement might be greater. Suffice it to say, one can never have too much.
2. They include some samples in original ink.

   Original ink samples have a three-dimensional character to them, with which aspects of instrument control, particularly pen pressure (point load), and pen position, may be observed or calculated. These properties of the writing may be important in examinations or studies.

3. They consist of both collected and request samples.
   Collected standards, in addition to being more representative of normal writing habits, are also indicators of the degree of reliance that can be placed on request writings that may or may not be deliberately altered. Also, they can be more contemporaneous with older questioned documents. On the other hand, request writings can provide duplication of the letter combinations of the questioned material.
4. They duplicate the conditions or nature of the questioned writing.
   Many things may influence a person's writing, from the writing instrument and writing circumstances to the writer's age or temperament. The extent to which they can be duplicated in writing standards is the extent to which these variables can be controlled. Thus, the comparison should be made of like material, of similar age, similar letters or letter combinations, similar words, names or phrases, written under similar conditions, and with the same media (instrument and paper). Much that has been written on standards of comparison is directed at the control of these variables (Hilton 1941, 1965, 1967; Hodgins 1967). A comparison of general writing features, such as size, slant, and proportions, may not provide sufficient evidence from which definitive conclusions can be drawn.

Control of the variables, however, means having at least:

1. *Similarity of texts.* The comparison of writing habits necessitates having the same habits of form and other writing elements executed under the influences ensuing from the same level of habit hierarchy (i.e., letter, word, or phrase). To reproduce the influence of one letter or letter combination upon another one is compelled to duplicate the text.
2. *Similarity in writing circumstances.* It is common knowledge that variations in instruments, writing position, and writer's condition can have considerable effect upon the written product which may complicate the identification process. This last factor underlies the importance for contemporaneous writing standards, if possible.
3. *Similarity in writing purposes.* The nature of the document, the intent of that which is written, and the audience to whom it is directed may make significant differences to the manner in which writing is executed. Personal notes and handwritten business communications may contain little that corresponds in these respects.

10.2 QUANTITIES OF HANDWRITING STANDARDS REQUIRED

Osborn (1929) was not specific about the quantity of handwriting standards required for a comparison, but he made some comments that are open to challenge. Respecting the examination of signatures he states: "Five signatures constitute a more satisfactory basis for an opinion than one, and that 10 are better than five" (p. 27). Following this he cautions: "It is dangerous to base a positive and final conclusion that a suspected signature is genuine on a comparison of it with only one genuine signature, unless it is a highly individualized and skillful signature" (p. 27). He states further that "a suspected signature … may contain so many inherent qualities indicating that it is not genuine that one good standard signature may be sufficient on which to base a positive opinion that it is not genuine" (p. 28). Clearly from this, one can reason that under certain circumstances he was prepared to reach positive conclusions of either identification or elimination on the strength of an examination of a single standard. Almost in contrast, he adds that it is not always helpful to examine more than 25 to 75 signatures except in unusual cases. Insofar as extended writing is concerned he says: "For comparison with a disputed letter, one good complete standard letter may be sufficient ... but even ... more writing should always be obtained if possible" (p. 27).

In an endeavor to provide some guidance to investigators, Hilton (1982) went so far as to suggest that five or six pages of continuous writing should be adequate for comparison with questioned extended writings, and 20 or more separate signatures should be adequate for comparison with questioned signatures. Others have suggested fewer, perhaps only half those numbers. Certainly, in many cases, half of Hilton's recommended quantities are all an examiner is likely to receive.

One should not try to answer the question of quantities until one has addressed the issue of the need for numbers in standards, whatever those numbers might be. This need stems from two factors of writing: habituation and natural variation. The fact that habits of the writer are involved says something about the standards needed to conduct a study. Single or limited examples of any element of human conduct are insufficient to substantiate reliably that the conduct is habitual. Admittedly, in fluent and skillful writing it is assumed that another sample from this individual will look very much the same. It is a presumption, however, based solely on experience with other writers, not this one, and science avoids presumptions as a general rule. This highlights the core of the problem that standards frequently present.

The habits studied comprise the discriminating elements of writing that are present in the questioned material. Many of these discriminating elements will involve specific letters or combinations of two or more letters in particular relationships to one another. As a result it is important, if not imperative, that the writing standards with which comparisons are made consist of similar letters and combinations of letters as will occur in similar words, names, texts, or signatures written under comparable circumstances. Except in request writings, it is seldom that a few standards will meet these requirements, and, as was said before, request writings are not always reliable.

Furthermore, there is the matter of natural variations to contend with that may be broad or narrow, depending on the individual and the circumstances. Should they be broad, as occurs in less skillful writings, only greater quantities of standards, and particularly collected standards, will properly portray its nature and range. The variables affecting writing have a greater influence on less skillful writing than on skillful writing. Larger quantities of collected standards afford a better opportunity to study writings in which the variables have been duplicated and are, thereby, controlled.

Notwithstanding such suggestions, sight unseen, there is no simple answer to the question as to how many writing samples will be required, as the requirement will vary with the writer and the circumstances. In the interests of practicality, Hilton's (1982) recommendations as to numbers may be a reasonable target even if somewhat ideal. In most cases, there are too few standards and seldom are there too many standards.

10.3 FINDING SUITABLE STANDARDS

There are a multitude of sources that may bear signatures, letterings, or extended writings suitable as standards for comparison. Frequently, some of these sources do not occur to most when searching for standards, but are readily recognized as sources with good potential when they are suggested. For that reason, the following list of possible areas of exploration are offered in the hope that if, in themselves, they don't prove to be productive they may suggest other areas that will offer potential sources of standards.

Accounts, charge	Bank deposit slips	Certificates of birth
Accounts, time payment	Bank money orders	Certificates of death
Address change forms	Bank safety box records	Certificates of marriage
Affidavits	Bank signature cards	Charge accounts
Agreements, business	Bank withdrawal slips	Charity pledge cards
Agreements, car rental	Bar tabs	Chattel mortgages
Agreements, financial	Bibles, family	Checks, bank, business
Agreements, rental	Bills of sale or lading	Checks, bank, personal
Agreements, separation	Birth certificates	Chits, bar
Applications, bond	Birthday cards	
Applications, credit	Bonds, surety	Church records
Applications, employment	Book flyleaves	Club records
Applications, insurance, various	Business correspondence	Community service records
Applications, license	Car rental agreements	Contest entries
Applications, loan	Cards, bank signature	Contracts
Applications, membership	Cards, birthday	Cooking recipes
Applications, passports	Cards, Christmas	Corporate records
Applications, permit	Cards, credit	Correspondence, business
Applications, utility service	Cards, florist	Correspondence, personal
Assignments	Cards, get well	Courier receipts
Attendance records		Court records
Authorization letters	Cards, identification	Credit cards
Autograph books	Cards, membership	Credit card purchases
Automobile insurance applications	Cards, pledge	Currency exchange records
Automobile licenses & applications	Cards, report	Death certificates
Bank deposit authorizations	Cards, union	Declarations
Deeds	Military records	Records, attendance
Delivery receipts	Minutes, meeting	Records, bank
Depositions	Money orders, bank	Records, church
Diplomas	Mortgage releases	Records, convention
Discharge papers	Mortgages	Records, employment
Divorce documents	Naturalization papers	Records, library
Drafts, correspondence	Options	Records, political party

Continued

Driver's licenses	Orders, automobile service	Records, school
Employment records	Orders, bank money	Records, tax
Estimates	Orders, merchandize	Records, union
Examination papers	Orders, purchase	Records, voting
	Orders, repair	Registers, funeral
Fingerprint records, civil	Passes	Registers, guest
Fingerprint records, criminal	Passports	Registers, hotel and motel
Foreign currency drafts	Pawnshop records	Registers, narcotic purchase
Greeting cards	Paychecks	Registers, poison purchase
Grocery lists	Payroll deduction authorizations	Registers, visitor
Guardianship papers		Rental agreements, automobile
Guest registers	Personnel records	Rental agreements, residential
Health cards	Petitions	Reports, accident
Hospital records	Pledge cards	Reports, committee
Hotel and motel registers	Post cards	Reports, credit
Identification cards	Power of attorney	Reports, executor
Insurance applications, various	Premise access records	Reports, trustee
Insurance claims	Probate records	Requisitions, stores
Insurance releases	Proxies	Requisitions, supply
Investment accounts	Purchase orders	Requisitions, tool
Invitations	Real estate listings	Social security cards
Labels	Receipts, cash payment	Stock transfers
Leases	Receipts, courier	Tax returns
Letters	Receipts, delivery	Time sheets
License applications	Receipts, express	Traveler's checks
Licenses, automobile	Receipts, freight	
Licenses, business	Receipts, personal property	Visitor registers
Licenses, drivers	Receipts, refund	Waivers
Licenses, fishing	Receipts, registered mail	Warrants
Licenses, hunting	Receipts, rent	Welfare records
Licenses, marriage	Receipts, storage	Wills
Marriage certificates	Receipts, telegram	Withdrawal slips
Membership cards	Receipts, witness fee	Work orders
Memoranda		Working papers

10.4 PREPARING REQUEST STANDARDS

Bearing in mind that, ideally, writing standards should reflect the normal, natural, unconscious writing habits of the individual, there are three key words that provide the necessary guidance in obtaining request writings: dictate, duplicate, and isolate.

10.4.1 Dictation

It is a cardinal rule that request writings should be prepared from dictation, leaving the subject free to make his or her own decisions as to how material is arranged or spelled. Only the writing style, that is, block letters, script or cursive writing should be stipulated. If the manner of signing or preparing particular kinds of documents, for example, personal checks, is of special interest, then blank documents of the same type should be supplied for completion. The speed of dictation should prompt the subject to write as rapidly as he or she may do comfortably. In so doing, the writer is compelled to direct attention more so at what is being written rather than how it is being written.

10.4.2 Duplication

As the general rules for writing standards indicated, the duplication of the writing conditions and circumstances is a means of controlling the variables that may influence a writing. This control can be exercised conveniently in the production of request writings, whereas, duplication of writing conditions in collected samples is much more difficult to achieve. On the other hand, the variable produced by time cannot be controlled in request writings. If a questioned writing is alleged to have been executed at some time in the past, only collected standards of the same vintage will portray the writer's capabilities and practices of that period.

10.4.3 Isolation

To avoid biasing the standards in any fashion it is a basic rule that the questioned writing should never be exposed to the subject from whom writing samples are being taken. Depending on the individual and the instructions given, exposure of the questioned document may have one of two consequences.

1. It may induce the subject to imitate, unintentionally, the features of the questioned writing, which diminishes the significance of similarities found in a subsequent handwriting study. The danger is that evidence might be generated that could wrongly incriminate an innocent person.
2. It may induce the subject to modify or to omit features that he or she considers to be similar to the questioned writing, to avoid association with it, which diminishes the significance of differences found in a subsequent handwriting study. The danger is that evidence might be generated that could wrongly exonerate a guilty person.

If isolation of the questioned material is not maintained, the handwriting examiner, unaware of the circumstances under which the standards were obtained, would be at a distinct disadvantage in evaluating the evidence that has to be considered, and is likely to overestimate or wrongly estimate its worth in the identification process.

Not only should the questioned writing be isolated from the subject, but each sample of writing should be removed from view immediately upon completion, and thus, writing samples are isolated from one another. Deliberate alterations to writing, if they are attempted in the writing of the standards, are difficult to maintain consistently from one sample to the next, because they are unnatural and not habitual practices. Thus, their nature may become self-evident, and particularly so, if the alteration has to be repeated from memory and not from a model, that another sample might provide.

10.5 STANDARD TEXTS FOR REQUEST WRITINGS

A number of attempts have been made to compose a standard or universal text for request writings that contain two or more examples of each letter of the alphabet in upper and lowercase, all of the numerals and some of the various punctuation marks. Osborn (1929) provided what has come to be known as the *London Letter* in his first edition of *Questioned Documents*. It has been the standard and most widely used text in past years but is less popular now. It reads:

> Our London business is good, but Vienna and Berlin are quiet. Mr. D. Lloyd has gone to Switzerland and I hope for good news. He will be there for a week at 1496 Zermatt St. and then goes to Turin and Rome and will join Col. Parry and arrive at Athens, Greece, Nov. 27th or Dec. 2nd. Letters there should be addressed: King James Blvd. 3580. We expect Charles E. Fuller Tuesday. Dr. L. McQuaid and Robt. Unger, Esq., left on the 'Y. X.' Express tonight. (p. 34)

Osborn (1922) later composed the *Dear Sam* and *Dear Zach* letters, modifications of the *London Letter* that also contained all of the upper and lowercase letters and the numerals of the English alphabet. The latter has also been referred to as the *Idaho Letter*. They read:

> Dear Sam:
> From Egypt we went to Italy, and then took a trip through Germany, Holland and England. We enjoyed it all but Rome and London most. In Berlin we met Mr John O. Young, of Messrs. Tackico & Co., on his way to Vienna. His address here is 1497 Upper Zeiss Str. care of Dr. Quincy W. Long. Friday, the 18th, we join C. N. Dazet, and leave at 6:30 A.M. for Paris on the "Q.X" Express and early on the morning of the 25th of June start for home on S. S. King.
>
> Very sincerely yours.

> Dear Zach:
> Well, the old class of "16" is through at last. You ask where the boys are to be. Val Brown goes on the 24th to Harvard for law. Don't forget to address him as "Esq." Ted Updike takes a position with the N.Y. N.H. & H.R.R., 892 Ladd Ave., Fall River, Mass. and Jack McQuade with the D.L. & W. at Jersey City, N.J., 400 E. 6th St. Wm. Fellows just left for a department position in Washington; his address is 735 South G St. At last accounts Dr. Max King was to go to John Hopkins for a Ph.D. degree. Think of that! Elliott goes to Xenia, Ohio, to be a Y.M.C.A. secretary. I stay here for the present. What do you do next? How about Idaho?
>
> Yours truly, and Good bye. (p. 50–51)

Purtell (1963) criticized these letters as not being too useful with subjects of limited education or lower intelligence. He found the names and passages too unusual for the average individual involved in criminal cases in the mixed populations of metropolitan areas: in a sense too foreign to foreigners. It was reported by Hall and Hardcastle (1987) that in a study of European writing, a text of 200 words executed once in block letters and once in cursive style was the most that could be obtained from subjects without them becoming uncooperative. Two samples of such a letter in either style is probably all the request writing of this kind that one could expect a cooperative subject to provide.

Other attempts at a universal or multipurpose text that might serve for different kinds of criminal cases have since been made. The most noteworthy of these is the study by Hall and Hardcastle (1987) who provided a draft of a new letter with certain reservations. It is a text of approximately 200 words that reads as follows:

> Dear All,
> I'm sorry that I haven't written to you for quite a long time but I have been very busy since April. I enjoy this new job more than the old one and it's only about an extra hundred yards or so for me to walk up the road from the station. What I don't like though is that my employers are paying my wages by cheque into my bank that is way across town. Cash every week would be so much easier because you know how lazy I am without a car. On Friday it took us no less than fifty minutes getting to the bank and back. There were six people in front of me in the queue — two with jumbo size zip up bags of money for paying in. The first of them was fairly quick but the next one hadn't sorted his out properly so it took absolutely ages for the cashier to serve him. I don't know why she couldn't refuse and make him go away and do it all again.
>
> Anyway, how is Mr Pounds getting on? He was very lucky he did not receive a major injury when that big box of equipment fell and knocked him out at work. And they all said he just got up after as if nothing had happened!
>
> Well, must stop now. See you soon.

The text was composed after a study of 42 passages of varying length from 21 authors totaling 69,340 words to determine average word lengths, letter frequencies, letter pairs, and common words. It was Hall and Hardcastle's (1987) view that texts such as this might be used in cases involving anonymous letters, that a design might be deliberately biased to serve cases of check fraud, or cases concerned with signatures. An appropriate text sample, however, could not be designed to reconcile these three different types of questioned writings. Hence, they concluded that the universal specimen is not a viable proposition.

Given the wide variety that exists in the nature and kinds of questioned documents, this conclusion is not surprising. No single letter model can contain all of the possible letter combinations or other features of writing, such as those related to arrangement or the methods of writing checks that may be present in the disputed material. The methods of writing signatures are, for many people, distinctively different from textual writing.

Universal or standard letter formats, however, should not be expected to reflect all writing possibilities. Their purpose is to provide an adaptable vehicle, a document whose elements such as names, places, words, or phrases, even the expression of monetary amounts, should be replaced by those occurring in the disputed material, and a more normal and natural execution of the writing can be obtained. Request writings in the form of word lists, alphabets, and isolated names tend to produce a more deliberate and artificial product, in which writing habits may be less fluently performed.

Nevertheless, many law enforcement agencies and forensic document laboratories have designed forms for the taking of request writings. Purtell (1963), while working in the Chicago Police Scientific Crime Detection Laboratory, was one of the first to publish usable formats. They sometimes consist of individual upper and lowercase letters of the alphabet, include a list of names that might correspond to questioned signatures, and occasionally a passage of extended text (Figure 10.1a and b).

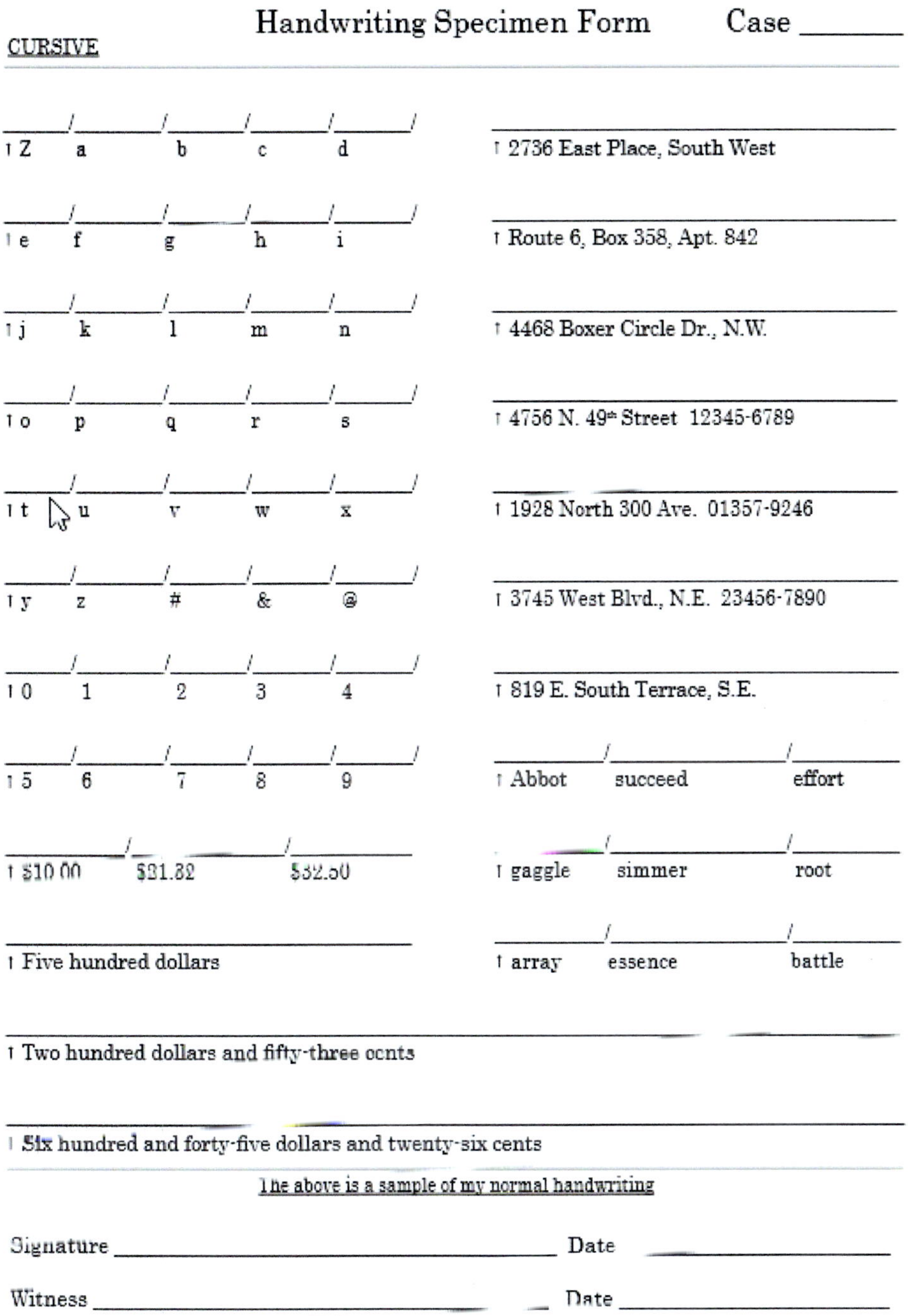

Handwriting Specimen Form Case ______

CURSIVE

↑ Z a b c d

↑ 2736 East Place, South West

↑ e f g h i

↑ Route 6, Box 358, Apt. 842

↑ j k l m n

↑ 4468 Boxer Circle Dr., N.W.

↑ o p q r s

↑ 4756 N. 49th Street 12345-6789

↑ t u v w x

↑ 1928 North 300 Ave. 01357-9246

↑ y z # & @

↑ 3745 West Blvd., N.E. 23456-7890

↑ 0 1 2 3 4

↑ 819 E. South Terrace, S.E.

↑ 5 6 7 8 9

↑ Abbot succeed effort

↑ $10.00 $21.82 $32.50

↑ gaggle simmer root

↑ Five hundred dollars

↑ array essence battle

↑ Two hundred dollars and fifty-three cents

↑ Six hundred and forty-five dollars and twenty-six cents

The above is a sample of my normal handwriting

Signature ______________________ Date ____________

Witness ______________________ Date ____________

(a)

Figure 10.1 (a and b) Examples of handwriting specimen forms to request exemplars from subjects.

(Continued)

HANDWRITING EXEMPLAR FORM

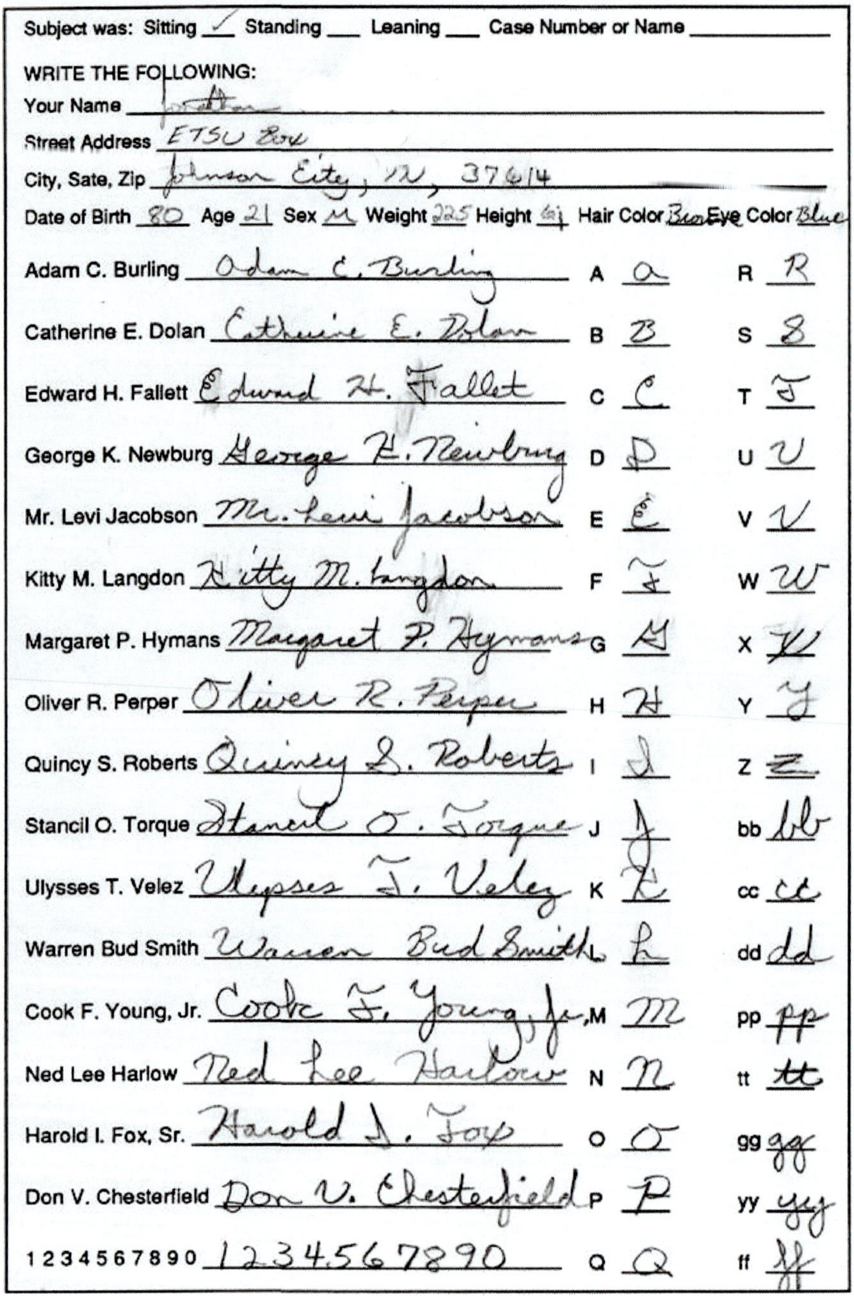

Subject was: Sitting ✓ Standing ___ Leaning ___ Case Number or Name ________

WRITE THE FOLLOWING:

Your Name ________

Street Address ETSU Box

City, Sate, Zip Johnson City, TN, 37614

Date of Birth 80 Age 21 Sex M Weight 225 Height 6'1 Hair Color Brn Eye Color Blue

Adam C. Burling	Adam C. Burling	A	R
Catherine E. Dolan	Catherine E. Dolan	B	S
Edward H. Fallett	Edward H. Fallett	C	T
George K. Newburg	George K. Newburg	D	U
Mr. Levi Jacobson	Mr. Levi Jacobson	E	V
Kitty M. Langdon	Kitty M. Langdon	F	W
Margaret P. Hymans	Margaret P. Hymans	G	X
Oliver R. Perper	Oliver R. Perper	H	Y
Quincy S. Roberts	Quincy S. Roberts	I	Z
Stancil O. Torque	Stancil O. Torque	J	bb
Ulysses T. Velez	Ulysses T. Velez	K	cc
Warren Bud Smith	Warren Bud Smith	L	dd
Cook F. Young, Jr.	Cook F. Young, Jr.	M	pp
Ned Lee Harlow	Ned Lee Harlow	N	tt
Harold I. Fox, Sr.	Harold I. Fox	O	gg
Don V. Chesterfield	Don V. Chesterfield	P	yy
1234567890	1234567890	Q	ff

(b)

Figure 10.1 (Continued) (a and b) Examples of handwriting specimen forms to request exemplars from subjects.

10.6 LEGAL REQUIREMENTS FOR WRITING STANDARDS

Per rules of evidence in North America regarding admissibility, one of four conditions usually serves to qualify a writing standard for acceptance.

1. The standard is acknowledged by the writer, to the court or to another party who is prepared to testify to such acknowledgment.
2. The writing of the standard was witnessed by a party who is prepared to testify to the action.
3. The standard is identified as the product of the writer by a party who is familiar with his or her writing through some business, social, or family relationship.
4. The circumstances surrounding the standard make a conclusion that a particular person executed the writing to be the only reasonable conclusion that the court may reach.

Obviously, the latter two methods of proof are open to challenge more so than the former two. Furthermore, greater latitude is allowed in civil cases than in criminal matters. The requirements of the law, however, must be borne in mind, for a denial by the court to admit any of the standards may significantly alter the findings of the handwriting examiner based on the remainder of the writings.

If the proof of a particular standard is likely to be challenged or is doubtful for other reasons, and these circumstances can be anticipated, the examiner should be advised so the writing examination can be conducted in stages that will determine first, the results that can be supported by the more limited material, and subsequently, the results that are supported by the standards as a whole.

10.7 RESULTS EXPECTED FROM HANDWRITING EXAMINATIONS

Insofar as handwriting examinations are concerned, the results of an examination are dependent upon the amount and significance of the evidence that the study discloses. This may be hampered by restriction to photocopies or inadequate standards. It may also be that the questioned writing is too brief to contain a sufficient combination of writing habits to support a conclusion, as is frequently the case with initials or numerals. Given the appropriate material in both nature and amount, definite conclusions are normally achievable. Unfortunately, such circumstances are not always encountered.

10.7.1 Photocopies, etc.

When dealing with reproductions of questioned or disputed handwriting, such as photocopies or facsimile transmissions, care must be exercised in the manner of reporting results. When a handwriting examiner identifies a writing appearing in a photocopy, he or she is, in fact, identifying a writing that is not on the paper of the photocopy, but on another document that the examiner has not seen. Whether writing appearing in the reproduction is an actual inscription on the document on which it purports to reside, only an examination of the original document will determine. Learned examiners are aware of the ease with which photocopies can be falsified. Findings must be so worded, then, that they clearly indicate:

1. The identification is of a writing on a document of which the material at hand purports to be a trustworthy reproduction.
2. The findings are subject to confirmation of their existence as original writings, upon examination of the original document.

10.7.2 Conclusions versus Opinions

Some controversy has been noted in the views of examiners as to whether the results of their examinations should be expressed as conclusions or as matters of opinion. It may be that the legal need for a definition and classification of the kind of testimony that an expert gives might otherwise be considered inadmissible, has contributed to some confusion in nonlegal minds. *The Shorter Oxford English Dictionary* defines *opinion* in the traditional legal sense as: "The formal statement by an expert or professional person of what he (she) thinks, judges or advises upon a matter submitted to him (her)."

This is the name given to the kind of testimony that a professional might provide. It says nothing about the substance of that testimony or the basis on which that statement has been established. It suggests that it is deemed to be advice. Some examiners, in response to the challenge that their testimony is merely an opinion, have argued that they offer a considered opinion. In the nonlegal sense Oxford defines *opinion* as the following:

- An estimate of a person or thing
- A belief, a view, a notion
- Something seeming to one's own mind to be true
- A belief of something as probable
- A judgment resting on grounds insufficient for complete demonstration

This suggests clearly the basis for the opinion, from which its reliability may be judged. The attributes of this definition tend to be completely incongruous with the concept that competent/experienced expert witnesses hold of the task they have performed, the findings it may yield, and the testimony they may offer in the legal context. It is not a belief, or something seeming to be true, or a judgment resting on insufficient grounds for demonstration. There is much more physical evidence in support of the findings than these expressions convey. On the other hand, *Oxford* defines *conclusion* as the following:

- An outcome
- A final determination
- A judgment arrived at by reasoning
- An inference, induction, or deduction

These terms are far more appropriate to describe the results of a handwriting study or document examination. Handwriting examiners, as do persons engaged in other forensic science pursuits, make judgments or determinations by reasoning and inductive inference. Accordingly, they reach conclusions, that, when reported as testimony in courts of law and other public forums, qualify for admission under the terms prescribed for a class of testimony inappropriately captioned, perhaps for want of a better title, *opinion evidence*.

Some examiners believe that their findings must be expressed as opinions to comply with their understanding of the law respecting expert witness testimony. The rules of law do not govern how expert evidence is determined or expressed, however, but only how it will be received. The issue over opinion evidence arose many years ago, and provision was made to allow it in the courts in hypothetical situations in which there was no factual or physical evidence before the court. In such cases there would be an estimate, a belief, a view or a something seeming to be true, based on no actual grounds or grounds insufficient for demonstration. There is no analogy to the current situations in which physical and factual evidence is an essential element of the expert witness' testimony.

In its review of forensic science, the National Research Council (2009) (the committee who prepared the NAS report) included the scientific interpretation and reporting of results in handwriting identification. The NAS report mentioned the use of five-point scales and cited a nine-point scale published by ASTM. The NAS report mentioned that these scales are subjective and also mentioned that "the scientific basis for handwriting comparisons needs to be strengthened" (pp. 5–30).

Much of the published research testing the proficiency of handwriting examiners from LaTrobe University's Forensic Expertise Profiling Laboratory (FEPL) has utilized a five-point scale for the expression of opinions (Found and Rogers 2008). The difference between the LaTrobe scale and the ASTM or SWGDOC scales was the exclusion by LaTrobe of gradations of *probable* and *probably not*. Kam et al. (2001) reported using the ASTM scale in a study on signature authentication.

10.7.3 Qualified Opinions

When definite conclusions cannot be reached, qualified opinions are sometimes expressed. In the light of what has just been said it is clearly more correct to refer to them as *qualified conclusions*. They are in the form of statements of probability such as, "There is a very strong probability that writer A wrote Q."

Statements of this kind are supposedly statistical inferences, but are semantically untenable. The statement that anyone "probably wrote" anything has no sensible meaning. Only two semantically tenable statements can be made about writing: (1) that writer A wrote Q, or (2) that writer A did not write Q.

The objective of a probability statement respecting the identification of a writing can be only to signify that, if accepting the proposition that A wrote Q and act accordingly, the risk of error is low, although the statement may not indicate precisely how low. Probabilities are measures of the likelihood of either one of the two statements, (1) or (2), being correct. The probability cannot be attached to the action, that is, the act of writing, of the statement itself.

According to Huber (1980), a semantically tenable qualified opinion would be written in the form: *The probability that a person selected at random would possess the correspondence in writing habits found in this questioned and known material is remote, very remote or extremely remote.*

Because it is not the common language of the layman, this wording lacks the ostensible strength of the semantically incorrect or untenable probability statements that have been and are being employed. On the other hand, Huber and Headrick thought that there is no reason why a finding cannot be expressed in terms that both justify and explain the reason for a modification to the wording, such as: *To be semantically tenable, only one of two statements can be made respecting the relationship of writer A to the questioned writing Q: (1) that writer A wrote Q, or (2) that writer A did not write Q. On the strength of the evidence in the documents at hand, there is a strong probability that the statement (1) is that which is correct.* When the correspondence between the questioned and known material is of such magnitude or significance that the probability of another person's writing exhibiting such correspondence is too remote to warrant practical consideration, a definitive conclusion of identification is justified.

Probabilities derived from statistical data, as these statements imply, are expressed mathematically as a ratio of likely occurrences of any event divided by the number of possible occurrences of the same event. So, given that there are a number of similarities and no disparities between questioned and known writings, how many other persons might exist in a population of, say, 1,000, that would have the same quantity and quality of similarities as the known writings exhibit? If the expectation is fewer than 10 persons, then, if it is resolved that the given writer executed the questioned document and acted accordingly, the risk of error is less than 1%, or the likelihood of being correct exceeds 99%.

$$P = \frac{\text{Number of likely occurrences}}{\text{Number of possible outcomes}} \times 100 = \frac{10}{1000} \times 100 = 1$$

P = 0.01% or 1% chance of error, conversely 99% confidence.

As the likely occurrences of other persons with similar writing habits approaches zero, the ratio of likely occurrences to possible occurrences also approaches zero so that P≈0 (that which never happens). Conversely, as the likely occurrences approach the number of possible occurrences (that which happens every time), that is, the finding of these similarities to a questioned writing in that of any person selected at random, the ratio nears the value of 1. Thus, probability values range from 0 (that which is impossible) to 1 (that which is a certainty).

Probabilities are measures of the risk of error in positive statements, or the likelihood of an alternative explanation for a given set of circumstances. Since the only two semantically tenable statements one can make about a writing are (1) that the writer of A wrote Q, or (2) that the writer of A did not write Q, then the task of the examination is a matter of determining which of these statements is likely to be correct, on the strength of the physical evidence that has been found.

To each of these statements there is always a risk of error or a likelihood of an alternative explanation. In the first case (the identification statement), insufficient evidence may enhance the risk of error. In the second case (the elimination statement), unusual writing circumstances may be misinterpreted or overlooked and result in an error: document Q may have been written when A was ill, or when A was intoxicated, or when A was writing against a wall, etc. Whenever these measures, that is, the risk of error or likelihood of a plausible alternative explanation, are small but not inconceivable, qualified conclusions are reached and expressed as qualified opinions, as legal minds would refer to it. When these measures are very small and too remote to be practical considerations, positive conclusions are reached.

It has been argued that examiners making statements of probability should be prepared to translate them into mathematical values. There is no other way to explain or to describe in precise terms what is meant by *a strong probability* or *a very strong probability* to an intelligent audience. Only mathematical numbers will indicate the relative certainties intended by the two expressions. Despite the reluctance of some handwriting examiners to involve statistics in their work, Hilton (1958) pointed out that "when the examiner states that in his opinion two writings were written by the same person, he has actually applied the theory of probability (without mathematics)" (p. 127).

Statistical proof underlies all scientific investigation, and the tool is the same for all disciplines. As Dixon and Massey (1951) stated: "There does not exist a theory of statistics applicable only to economics or only to education. There is a general theory of statistics which is applicable to any field of study in which observations are made" (p. 2).

The allegation has been made, frequently, that sufficient data has not been assembled to establish the frequency of occurrence of any particular discriminating element of handwriting, from which its significance for identification purposes might be calculated. There is a line of argument, however, that supports the view that some arbitrary values can be ascribed to probability statements to reflect the magnitude of the risk of error the statement is intended to represent.

The risk of error that might be implied by *a strong probability* may be judged, arbitrarily, to be less than 1%. How much less need not be expressed. The examiner is saying the chance of encountering another individual with as much similarity in their writing in a random selection from the same population is less than 1 in 100 persons. The estimate of that probability is based solely on his or her experience, which is comprised of what has been observed or read or heard.

Similarly the risk of error implied by the expression *a very strong probability* might be judged, arbitrarily, to be less than 0.1%. The intended meaning is that the chance of encountering another writer with the same degree of similarity in a random selection from the same population is fewer than 1 in 1,000 persons.

Admittedly, such statements are founded entirely on an experience-based judgment, and while their accuracy cannot yet be statistically demonstrated, at least they reflect the level of confidence that the examiner has in his or her finding. One should also be confident that the error in the statements will be an underestimation of the level of probability that the evidence supports. The examiner, however, is left to him- or herself to set the figures that reflect what he or she has in mind when qualified opinions are expressed.

Obviously when the risk of error exceeds 5% and the chance of encountering another writer with the same degree of similarity is thought to be equal to or greater than 1 in 20 persons, the conclusion pointing to an identification is not very strong. In this respect, the numbers speak for themselves.

10.8 LEVELS OF CERTAINTY IN HANDWRITING IDENTIFICATION

The principle of identification that has been followed for many years was stated earlier by Huber (1959): "When any two items possess a combination of independent discriminating elements (characteristics), that are similar and/or correspond in their relationship to one another, of such number and significance as to preclude the possibility of their occurrence by pure coincidence, and there are no inexplicable disparities, one may conclude that they are the same in kind or have a common source" (p. 276).

While this principle provides a general criterion for drawing a definitive conclusion, it does not stipulate how many characteristics or what level of significance is required. At this point in time it is virtually impossible in some fields of forensic science to state arbitrarily how much evidence and what kind is necessary to reach a certain conclusion. How many striations on a bullet or in a tool mark does one need? How many similarities in the discriminating elements of a handwriting does one need? These are subjective judgments that have been conscientiously made by examiners who are usually fully cognizant of the dangers involved.

In the absence of an appropriate formula and in the interests of reliability, it is the rule of competent writing examiners to limit one's conclusions to those that may be drawn by any other equally competent examiner after a study of the same material. Although this rule is not overly explicit, it introduces an element of conservatism, or a caution that may serve to avoid serious error.

There is little difficulty in finding examiners that will agree on definitive or positive conclusions. Nonetheless, no one will state precisely what their respective level is that a positive conclusion would represent on a probability scale, other than to hold that the quantity and quality of the evidence of similarity precludes the possibility that it would occur in the writing of another randomly selected person by pure coincidence. In fact, there are differences in the levels at which certainty is reached by each examiner. As long as personal experience prescribes, simply, that conclusions exceed the level of certainty at which the risk of error would give any examiner cause for concern, no attempt is made to define the levels precisely. The argument is closed in the form of a question. What would be gained? Perhaps only the satisfaction of consciously moving in the direction of orthodox scientific method, but this should be reason enough.

Obviously, there is little to be gained when the evidence is overwhelming. It is only when evidence nears the lower limits for positive conclusions that examiners have arbitrarily set for themselves, that divergence occurring in the findings of examiners is seen. As the strength of the evidence diminishes, conclusions such as "a very strong probability...," "A strong probability...," "It is highly probable...," "It is probable...," "There is evidence to indicate...," and a multitude of others make their appearance in reports and testimony.

There are few topics respecting writing identification on which more has been written by a greater congregation of persons than on the subject of probable conclusions or qualified opinions. Whether or not qualified opinions should be expressed at all is an issue that has long been debated. Those that oppose their use may do so from a lack of understanding of statistical inference and may wish to avoid discussions of it from a witness box. There are, however, good reasons for the use of statements of probability.

Principal among them is the fact that, as Trueblood (1963) stated, all conclusions, whether positive or not, are expressions of probability and it is important for this to be recognized. Moreover, examiners are no better equipped to articulate the level of probability chosen for a positive conclusion than they are for a qualified one. Further, the legal profession should be made aware that their process of reaching conclusions is, in principle, the same as that of the scientist. The court's own criterion for establishing the guilt of a person—"beyond a reasonable doubt"—discreetly avoids stipulating "with certainty" or "beyond any doubt." Whittaker (1973) challenged, yet cautioned, criminalists: "It is the responsibility of the criminalist to command the written and verbal skills necessary to make crystal clear to his listener of what exactly the probative strength level of the identification consists" (p. 184).

McElrath and Berman (1956) stated: "The scientist, too, never proves everything 'with certainty' or 'beyond a doubt;' the best he can ever hope to say is that he has established a fact 'beyond a *reasonable* doubt.' The difference between the experimental and the legal situations is that the scientist has learned how to calculate the probability of the doubt. This has been the contribution of statistics" (p. 589). The search for truth seems reason enough for handwriting examiners to engage statistics to assist them in the definition and clarification of the levels of certainty, confidence, or probability, in order that conclusions being drawn are more precise reflections of the truth.

Hilton (1958) wrote an excellent dissertation on the relationship of mathematical probability to handwriting identification, but confined his remarks to cases in which unqualified opinions were expressed. His comments were directed particularly at the criticisms of Kirk (1953) respecting the absence of probability data in published material that had prompted Kirk to say: "Handwriting analysis, despite statements to the contrary, cannot be truly 'scientific' until such serious omissions as these are repaired" (p. 475). Hilton pointed out some of the difficulties in collecting and classifying the writing data that Kirk insisted someone should assemble. Not the least of these is the allowance to be made for natural variation in the measurement of discriminating elements, the uncertainty of the degree of independence between elements and the unsuitability of some elements to any process of measurement. In this regard Hilton mentions such aspects as skill, speed, shading (i.e., pen pressure), and writing quality.

McAlexander et al. (1991), in a review of some 60 different manners of enunciating conclusions, has suggested nine expressions (*identification, strong probability, probability, evidence to indicate, no conclusion, indications did not, probably did not, strong probability did not, elimination*) to reflect levels of certainty without locating them precisely on the continuum of probability from 0 to 1. Ellen (1979) has proposed a scale of five expressions (*identification, high probability, could or consistent with, inconclusive, no evidence and likely to be by different persons*) and argues that fewer divisions on the scale permits them to be more easily defined. The problem with these expressions is that they mean different things to different people. Both authors attempt at some length to explain exactly their intended interpretations. Terms suggested for forensic odontologists are even less precise (Dailey 1987). Scott (1988) cited several cases in which testimony of handwriting examiners was expressed in a wide variety of manners, some very poorly, and each was accepted by the courts.

Leung and Cheung (1988) thoroughly reviewed the practices and views of 40 examiners worldwide. Their survey provides 16 divisions and the probability levels (in percentages) for many of them. Noteworthy in their report is the variation in the zero points on the scale, and the directions in which the scales run. This survey disclosed that there is much diversity in the use of percentages as measures of certainty. Confusion stems on occasion from the placement of the zero and the 100% points of the scale. Some run levels of certainty in descending order from 100% for definite-positive, to 0% for definite-negative. Others used percentages as indicators of the degree of certainty in opposing scales of identification and elimination, starting from 0% for the level of an inconclusive finding.

The latter practice introduces another uncertainty into the process, for the point of inconclusiveness is not precisely determined, regardless of the direction that the scale is running (i.e., toward an identification or an elimination). Huber and Headrick preferred to think in terms of a single scale for identification respecting any particular writer, wherein levels approaching 0% are indications that it is almost an impossibility for this writer to have executed the questioned material. In statistical language, the level of inclusiveness is 0.5 or 50%, and a level of 50% means that the toss of a coin would be as reliable an indicator of the writer's involvement as the handwriting.

It has been maintained in other writings (Huber and Headrick 1990), that the only means available to examiners to convert observations and evaluations (or judgments such as conclusions) that are qualitative, subjective, and private, to forms that are quantitative, objective, and public, is by means of numerical values that are communicable. Not surprisingly, criticisms are now being voiced in different locales. For example, McKenna (*US v. Starzecpyzel* 1995) and Found and Rogers (1995) have commented regarding the vagueness of the expressions used and advocated, and their interpretations.

Brown and Cropp (1987) ventured to propose conversions for the findings in all fields of forensic science in suggesting four levels of approximate probability commencing at 0.5, the statistical level of chance. These consisted of Possibly (0.5–0.9 or 50–90%), Probably (0.9–0.99 or 90–99%), Very Probably (0.99–0.999 or 99–99.9%) and Almost Certainly (>0.999 or >99.9%). Any attempt to use probabilities (statistics) to reflect the likelihood of things happening in the real world requires that examiners understand certain statistical terms, and three of them in particular: *randomness*, *independence*, and *clustering*.

10.8.1 Randomness

When it is said that there is a strong probability that writer A wrote Q, it implies that the chances of *selecting at random* another person in the same population with similar writing characteristics (i.e., discriminating elements) is very low.

Randomness is the property of the process of selection that gives each person in the population possessing a particular combination of a number of items (e.g., writers with 10 particular discriminating elements) the same chance of being the sample selected. In the toss of a coin, randomness ensures that heads and tails have equal opportunities to occur, but it does not guarantee that a head (or if you wish a tail) will occur every second time.

Randomness allows one to calculate the approximate predictability of occurrences by relative frequencies, the degree of approximation depending, by the law of large numbers, on the number of observations (i.e., features) being considered.

10.8.2 Independence

Events are said to be independent if the probability that one of them will have a certain outcome is the same no matter what the outcome of all the other events may be. For example: the occurrence of an epsilon "e" in a person's writing should be independent of the occurrence of a Palmer "r" or a Palmer "t."

In writing examinations, the matter of independence means that a number of class, national, or system characteristics cannot be considered to be as many separate pieces of evidence, but can only be considered collectively as one.

10.8.3 Clustering

Many events in the real world seem to happen in clusters: accidents, deaths, successful rolls of the dice (e.g., "I'm on a roll"). It seems that clustering affords a basis for forecasting the observations in an otherwise random sequence. The more often that "black" pays the more likely "red" will appear in the next event. Nonetheless, as long as the events are independent of one another and the selection is random, the likelihood of a particular result, like the ones on which wagers are made, are not improved.

One of the impediments to progress in the understanding of the application of statistical inference to writing examinations is in the conflict between the meaning of *probability*, as a statistician might use it, and the more vernacular sense of the layman. As has been pointed out (Huber 1980), to be semantically tenable one cannot say, "There is a strong probability that writer A executed Q." One can only say, "Writer A did or did not write Q."

In fact, what is said when using probability expressions is that if acting on the assumption that "writer A wrote Q" the likelihood is that the examiner will be correct. Indeed, Webster defines *probability* as "a likelihood, something that, judged by present evidence, is likely to be true." But how likely? To paraphrase Oxford's definition of *probable*, if it is said, "Writer A probably wrote Q" the examiners is making a statement that is worthy of belief. But how worthy? And how much more worthy (or likely) is a strong probability than a probability?

There is no alternative to numbers that is available to examiners to define precisely what is meant by *probability*, *strong probability*, *very strong probability*, or any similar expression, to indicate the respective levels of certainty that each represents.

If thinking of percentage probabilities in the lexical sense that Webster has suggested, rather than the statistical sense, that of representing "the likelihood of being true," it may help to understand the proposals of Brown and Cropp (1987), cited earlier. These authors have suggested that expressions of *probability* should be considered as lying between the 90 and 99 percentages, which is to say that the risk of error in identifying the wrong person is no greater than 1 in 10 and may be as small as 1 in 100. They suggest that an expression of *very probably* should be considered as lying between the 99 and 99.9 percentages, which is to say that the risk of error in identifying the wrong person is no greater than 1 in a 100 and may be as small as 1 in 1,000. A finding of *almost certainly* is anything greater than 99.9%, that is a level at which the risk of error in identifying the wrong person is less than 1 in 1,000. These are ratios that should be within the comprehension abilities of most examiners and may be worthy of adoption, at least until more reliable data is available.

Huber and Headrick suggested that percentages such as these might be thought of as risks of error or duplicity. A statement of a 90% probability means that the chance of finding in another sample of writing as much correspondence in writing features as these known writings exhibit would be 1 in 10, if a writer was selected at random from the same population. Similarly a 99% probability lowers the odds to 1 in 100, and a 99.9% probability represents a chance of 1 in 1,000 of encountering another writer in the same population with a similar combination of writing characteristics.

At the same time, because of the clustering phenomenon mentioned above, one must use caution in applying this kind of probability thinking to particular cases. A chance of 1 in 1,000 does not mean that there cannot be two or three writers exhibiting the same degree of correspondence in a particular sample of 1,000 persons.

However, if more than 10% of a population would display as much similarity in writing characteristics (i.e., a less than 90% probability respecting the known writer) the risk of error or duplicity is high, the likelihood of a conclusion of identification being true is low, and the evidence of identity cannot be very strong. If more than 1% of the population would display this degree of similarity (i.e., a less than 99% probability), the risk may be lower because the evidence is stronger but not overwhelming. Suffice it to say, any qualified opinion that is thought of or translated into a probability of identification of a magnitude of less than 0.9 or 90% says little for the strength of the evidence, the risk of error, or the likelihood of being true. The writings of Brown and Cropp (1987) implied as much.

Attempts have been made by knowledgeable people to apply the various probability theories to handwriting examination with little success (Karlsson 1987). Two of the reasons for this is the lack of empirical data respecting the frequency of occurrence of writing elements, and the absence of apparent concurrence as to what aspects of a writing constitute significant elements of identification value.

Leung and Cheung (1988) have suggested an 11-point scale running from a midpoint 0, for inconclusive, to ±5 for positive identifications or eliminations that might be used somewhat arbitrarily to clarify the level of certainty in the mind of the examiner. Such a scale implies that the differences between the levels of the scale are more or less uniform. It also implies that the difference between an inconclusive finding and the lowest level of a significant probability is not particularly strong. As the Brown and Cropp (1987) scale intimates, the term *probable* should be applied to levels ≥0.9 or ≥90%, and allowed to move rather exponentially up the scale from there.

Herein lies the difference in the approaches to probability scales, as conceived by the layman and the statistician. Probability applied to writing identification should not be thought of, necessarily, as a linear regression in which changes between levels are uniform or regular. It may run exponentially, on a scale in which the levels of probability (or risks of error) constantly change. The change in probability at any point is proportional to the level of probability already attained. This is *curvilinear regression* in which probabilities follow a curve rather than a straight line, similar to compound interest.

In writing studies this means that at higher levels of probability on the scale, a small quantity of additional evidence would contribute greater toward an identification than the same quantity would contribute at lower levels.

Even if qualified opinions are defined in these very broad terms some progress will have been made in the direction of greater consistency between examiners, the comprehension of findings, and the examiners' intended meanings. When examiners begin thinking and speaking alike, it is presumed that they are using the same scientific methods.

Thornton (1997) admonished forensic experts when he wrote: "We have tended to reject statistics and probability because we generally don't understand them, and to concede their validity forces us to admit to our ignorance as to how they would be implemented.... To master statistical models to explain much of our evidence may be a slow, reluctant march through enemy territory, but we must begin to plan for that campaign" (p. 758).

Similar concerns were raised by the National Research Council (2009) in the NAS report. In that report, it was mentioned that when presenting results, forensic practitioners use various subjective terms that are not interpreted similarly across the disciplines (or even by handwriting examiners) and can have various interpretations in the courtroom. Recommendations for further research and standardization as to the interpretation and use of opinion terminology was urged in the NAS report.

10.9 CAUSE OF ERRORS IN HANDWRITING EXAMINATION

Osborn (1929), Harrison (1958b), and Hilton (1982) have commented on the circumstances that lead to erroneous conclusions in handwriting identification. Beck (1995) has dealt particularly with three of them. In summary these circumstances include:

1. Inadequate, fallacious or self-serving standards for comparison
2. Quantitative insufficiency of questioned writing
3. Lack of comprehension respecting the discriminating elements of writing
4. Lack of appreciation for the writing movement underlying the form
5. Improper assessment of divergences
6. Overevaluation of class or system characteristics
7. Overlooking or ignoring disparities
8. Omission of intercomparison of standards to confirm common authorship
9. Influence of external information respecting the matter
10. Incompetence on the part of the examiner

Other factors have also been suggested, including a suspicious attitude or predisposition toward the matter and the documents. Owing to the fact that in North America, cases are submitted to examiners from sources that represent one side of an issue or the other, it is difficult for the examiner to avoid the prejudice that accompanies the submission of material. Objectivity is then put at risk and every component observed in the questioned document may be approached as suspicious.

Some of the circumstances responsible for errors are classed as human factors such as competition, dishonesty, recognition, or ego. The misinterpretation of facts and the misapplication of scientific principles have also been cited. These can occur in any field of forensic science, and on this, Howard (1986) has written, suggesting the establishment of an independent testimony review board.

Gencavage (1987) drew attention to the need to examine extended writing closely for the subtle evidence that may exist in a word, a line, or a paragraph having been inserted in a document by a second writer. While evidence of another author can be quite pronounced, every examination should be thorough enough to avoid the errors that haste and assumption can create.

It has been said that handwriting and hand lettering identification lends itself readily to unintended bias on the part of the examiner, and bias can lead to error. It is, admittedly, one of the few disciplines of forensic science that depends primarily on a subjective analysis and evaluation of evidence. Most document examiners are aware of this and attempt to be as objective as possible, using sophisticated measurements when they can. Complete objectivity is difficult to achieve, however, because of (1) the circumstances under which the examiner is summoned, and (2) the fact that the identification process is precariously subjective.

Nisbett and Wilson (1977), and Miller (1984) reported that there were unconscious factors at work on human behavior that could account for bias, prejudice, fear, and stereotypes. Applying social-psychological schools of thought to bias among document examiners, it can be seen that a subjective conclusion by the examiner may have been influenced by social interaction, situation, and/or past experience. In a criminal situation, the police may be convinced of the guilt of the accused. Their preoccupation is with procuring sufficient evidence to obtain a conviction. Knowingly or otherwise, the police may communicate their belief to the document examiner in a social interaction. The examiner may assume the existence of other evidence to indicate the guilt of the individual and such unconscious beliefs have the potential to create bias. In a civil action, an attorney may provide the same bias influence on the examiner in expressing his or her own conviction of his or her client's innocence. This bias may receive support if the questioned and known writings/letterings exhibit some pictorial similarity. The expectation of payment for an opinion may also have a subtle influence.

Miller (1984) attempted to test the hypothesis that document examiners are influenced by the social interaction between themselves and the police or attorney requesting their services, and by the situation in which they were requested to do the examination. Twelve college students, trained in the forensic examination of questioned documents, were divided into two groups and provided with fictitious evidence of a case of forgery of checks. The first group was provided with (1) a synopsis of facts concerning the investigation, (2) the suspect's name and his or her handwriting examples on a request exemplar form, and (3) three checks allegedly written by the suspect. Group one was advised that the police had two witnesses that would testify that they saw the suspect write and pass the checks. Group two was supplied with the same three questioned checks and writing exemplars from two additional suspects. They were not advised of expected witness testimony and were simply asked if any of the three suspects wrote any of the questioned checks. In fact none of the suspects had written any of the checks.

The conclusions reached by the examiners supported the bias hypothesis. Four of the examiners in the first group wrongly identified the suspect as the writer of the checks. One examiner was inconclusive and one examiner was correct. All six of the examiners in group two correctly eliminated all three suspects. Miller (1984) admits that his experiment was superficial. His examiners were university students and the questions are left unanswered respecting their course of training, their trainers, or their experience. His point is simply that bias is difficult to control and offers three suggestions to limit its effects. First, information should not be provided regarding a writer's possible involvement with a written document. Second, writings from more than one suspect should be submitted, and thirdly, when possible, collected specimens from writers should be submitted.

Dror and Charlton (2006) carried out a study on fingerprint examiners and found that two-thirds of the examiners who were provided with additional biased, contextual information changed their opinion. Dror and Cole (2010) looked at expert perception in forensic pattern recognition and commented that the same expert may arrive at a different conclusion when examining the same evidence under different contextual conditions. Stoel et al. (2014b) revisited the study carried out by Miller in 1984 and commented that little concerning the management of bias had changed in forensic casework.

There has been considerable attention on the topic of bias in forensic science, especially since the release of the National Research Council's (2009) NAS report. The report's committee recommended research studies on the effects of contextual bias in forensic science. It also recommended that standard operating procedures be implemented in forensic laboratories to minimize the effects of bias. With respect to irrelevant contextual information, Found and Ganas (2013) reported on the measures that the Victoria Police Forensic Services Department in Australia have taken to counter the effects of bias. Specifically, it has modified its procedures to reduce biased information from the handwriting examination process. Sulner (2014) discussed how cognitive and motivational biases adversely influence decisions, opinions, and testimony of handwriting examiners. Stoel et al. (2014a) maintain that in forensic cases involving handwriting evidence, the examiner should only focus on the handwriting trace and not be influenced by other factors such as the paper, ink, language, etc. surrounding the handwriting trace.

With respect to confirmation bias, Kukucka and Kassin (2014) carried out a study in which participants were provided with information concerning the purported confession of a defendant involving handwriting evidence. This knowledge tainted the perception of the participants leading to erroneous opinions about the guilt of the writer.

There are those that will argue that some contextual information pertaining to the case is useful especially with respect to unusual conditions surrounding the execution or signing of the document (e.g., health, medications, awkward signing conditions, etc.). Another argument centers on laboratory resources. The examination of the writings of a second or third subject in a lineup process would be a cumbersome addition in laboratories that are already backlogged with casework and short on personnel and resources. Even in civil matters, examination of additional subject handwriting samples increases time and cost to the client. Champod (2014) opined that there are some latent dangers in shielding the examiner from contextual information that may be relevant to proper procedures in collecting and examining evidence.

It seems fitting to end this discussion of the reasons for and means of avoiding error with the comments of Cole (1964) who stated that the standard or base of experience to which the document examiner refers every new examination does not remain static. It is subject to small changes day by day, especially in the early years of experience. A period of success will tend to make the standard more liberal. A single error or near miss will raise the standard as a protection against repetition. Over a long period of time, the standard becomes more efficient and permits the greatest number of useful judgments with the best protection against error.

Chapter 11

The Diagnosis of Handwriting Identification

11.1 THE PERFECT FORGERY

There is no practical way of knowing whether or not perfect forgeries have been created (in this discussion, the word "forgery" is used to represent "simulation" in handwriting). Being perfect, they necessarily escape detection. Forgeries that have been detected must be something less than perfect. Under certain circumstances, forgeries can and have been produced that have been exceedingly difficult for the most competent examiners to detect. Under most other circumstances, forgeries are frequently produced which, while not readily detected by lay persons, are within the capacity of the competent examiner to recognize as spurious executions.

11.2 AUTOFORGERY

Normally, *autoforgery* would be defined as a forgery of one's signature created by oneself. This, however, is a contradiction of terms for a forgery must be, by definition, an execution performed by another person. The observation must be made, then, that there is no such thing as autoforgery. Thus, the question becomes: whether or not a person can so subtly alter his or her signature that its alteration will pass casual scrutiny and, under normal circumstances, will be accepted as genuine. At the same time, the signature will, by virtue of some omission, modification, or addition of a less conspicuous handwriting attribute, deceive handwriting examiners into concluding and believing that the signature is spurious.

In a study of 20 subjects, Cole (1973) found it to be beyond the capacity of the persons in his study to accomplish the task posed by autoforgery. He did, however, find that a few subjects revealed what he considered to be a potential for an appropriate handwriting change that a period of practice might develop. On the other hand, his subjects were given a week to practice and were asked to submit only their most successful efforts. One wonders, then, whether additional practice would significantly alter the results, and whether the subjects themselves would be able to appreciate the improvement. Furthermore, it is assumed that the subject is aware of the nature of the change to his or her handwriting that would be appropriate.

The circumstances under which an individual might pursue this kind of action are probably remote, but Cole (1973) described two scenarios involving large sums of money in which the denial of signatures containing minor defects converts the question posed above from the hypothetical to the more realistic form. Notwithstanding the few instances in which a person might be disposed to fabricate an irregular signature of this kind, there are numerous other instances in which a faulty memory coupled with a minor irregularity in the writing may induce an individual to honestly or dishonestly deny its execution. The handwriting examination on these occasions must address the issues of natural variation, accidental occurrence, deliberate modification, and true difference.

11.3 PROFESSIONAL FORGERS

McCarthy (1970, 1984) and Buglio and Gidion (1977) have reported on the skill of a few known individuals at producing freehand simulations of various person's signatures. The five individuals on whom these studies focused were relatively skilled, and with one exception, were non-criminal freehand forgers, who had only an avocational interest in simulating signatures that had prompted them to practice. None of the products of these persons was judged to be beyond the capacity of competent examiners to detect as spurious, given adequate standards. Osborn (1929) wrote, years ago, that it is a rare occurrence that one will be inclined or have the skill to execute such a simulation.

Totty (1995) investigated the ability of one individual who, by virtue of training and profession, might be expected to succeed in creating accurate reproductions of signatures. The subject was a graphic artist, with professional training at college and university in the field, and 10 years practical experience in the preparation of copy for advertisements, sales literature, and packaging. He was a skilled artist and accustomed to making accurate freehand drawings from sketches or outlines. He had no interest in the simulation of signatures and had never previously attempted to do so. He was asked to copy the signatures of four individuals, working at his own speed, under his own conditions, using materials of his own choosing, without restriction as to time or extent of practice. The object of the exercise was to study the ability of a skilled person in copying signatures under optimum conditions.

The results were that overall pictorial accuracy and a high level of skill and fluency was achieved. The classic symptoms of forgery, that is, tremor, poor line quality, hesitation, and pen lifts, were almost entirely absent although some pen lifts and blunt stroke endings did occur. The subject paid less attention to details of letter designs and it is to these more subtle features that the examiner's attention is directed when the work of a professional must be taken into account.

Ordinarily, however, the existence of professional, competent forgers exists for illicit purposes and their services may be engaged for a price. Although the skills of a professional forger or penman are not expected in most ordinary cases, the possible occurrence of a perfect forgery needs to be acknowledged. Expertise exists among calligraphers and both calligraphy and art are hobbies practiced among criminals in prison. Incarceration provides the requisite practice time necessary to hone skills in calligraphy. Cases involving autographed sports memorabilia, celebrity autographs, historical documents, and signatures on art works are more likely to attract professional forgers (Figure 11.1). The expertise of professional forger Mark Hofmann, who created forged historical documents and sold them to the Mormon Church, is a well-documented case (Launius et al. 1988).

What is meant by a *perfect* forgery is really a subjective judgment of the forger's ability to deceive, and that will vary with the circumstances under which the forgery is scrutinized and the perceptivity of the scrutineer. It can also vary with the kind of signature involved. Shorter signatures, those in which letter forms have diminished to simply undulating lines, and those, wherein proper structure and design has been sacrificed in favor of embellishments that almost invariably suffer from great variation from one execution to the next, make a good reproduction

Figure 11.1 Subject was told to sign her name normally (a) and then disguise her signature as in auto-forgery (b and c).

more difficult to discriminate from the genuine. However, just as there are degrees of proficiency in the act of writing, there are degrees of proficiency in the act of executing forgeries, and it may well be that the fruits of some of the best have escaped detection, in the course of their examination or inspection.

Buglio and Gidion (1977) reported on the ability of one individual who displayed remarkable talent and speed in simulating the signatures of others. As a demonstration of his talent, he produced a simulation of the signature of each of 32 individuals that was combined randomly on a single sheet with 11 genuine signatures. These examples were employed in a study of the level of this simulator's competence in duplicating signatures. The authors claim that the simulations are reasonably good reproductions. They can be distinguished upon careful and thorough examination by competent examiners, with the benefit of the 11 standards for comparison on the same sheet, notwithstanding the fact that the spurious signatures were randomly distributed among the genuine executions. This is a somewhat ideal situation in which a comparison might be made. What the results might be if one was to encounter a signature in isolation, or had less suitable standards for comparison, are questions to be considered. A further question is raised as to whether any of the spurious signatures could be positively eliminated.

As Buglio and Gidion (1977) pointed out, their single subject cannot constitute a threat to the profession of handwriting examination. Nevertheless, they do acknowledge that the finding of this one person with the prerequisite ability to simulate the writings of others reasonably well compels one to allow that there may exist others within the population possessing equal or greater skill. The likelihood of such a person being involved in a given and particular case is a proposition that depends on many ancillary factors including accessibility, awareness, availability, and amenability to a fraudulent act. When all factors are considered, the likelihood of there being an involvement of a willing person, having the necessary qualifications, at the right time and place, seems remote.

A point that may be of some interest to readers is that the simulator in the study was left-handed and professed to experience greater difficulty in duplicating the writings of the two left-handed persons among the group of 32. No reasons are offered for this. The adept penman in this case was an individual with some drawing, if not artistic, ability. He was well educated, holding a PhD in criminology and membership of the American Academy of Forensic Sciences. Should an examiner be concerned about the prospects of a given questioned signature being the work of someone that is particularly adept at duplicating another person's writing? A few observations can be made that may be helpful:

1. Simulated forgeries of high quality will probably display little or no evidence of the slowness or lack of fluency that is normally one of the hallmarks of spuriousness.
2. Standard signatures of poor quality call for equally poor quality in their duplication, however, the simulation may in fact display a superiority in writing style or writing quality.
3. Writers are known to have deliberately altered their writing styles in their signatures with limited practice and in a limited period of time.
4. On questioned checks, witnessed endorsements may be poorer than unwitnessed maker's signatures, even if both are in the same name.
5. In skillful simulations, the differences between the questioned signature and the known standards will be more subtle. Their study must be more carefully conducted, standards must be more contemporary in time and, if possible, should be prepared or produced under more comparable circumstances.

McCarthy's (1984) study of the work of two adept penmen provides a number of valuable observations respecting his two subjects that are worth bearing in mind should the possibility of this rare quality of simulation occur:

1. Deceptive simulations of unskilled writing can be accomplished with little or no practice.
2. Skilled simulations done from memory can be as deceptive as those made with a model at hand.
3. With proper standards the author of some simulations can be identified.
4. Simulations of signatures in a foreign alphabet may be difficult for a simulator to produce, but equally difficult for an examiner to detect.
5. Retouching of skilled simulations is an infrequent occurrence.
6. Flying starts and finishes can occur in better quality or skilled simulations.
7. Reduction in the size of a simulation from that of a model is achievable, but requires some practice.
8. Simulations will equal the size of the model if there are no space constraints.
9. Two simulations of the same model by the same skilled simulator may be near superimposable.

10. Deceptive simulations may not provide sufficient evidence that they are spurious, but conversely, when doubt exists, it should not be assumed that they are genuine.
11. Deceptive simulations can appear among the standards for comparison.
12. Practice on several documents from which one is selected to be proffered will result in a better quality of what then becomes the questioned signature.
13. The methods employed by skilled simulators will vary.
14. The simulations of two different skilled simulators are distinguishable under optimum conditions.
15. Simulators of great skill have an unusual capacity to remember complex images and forms, but may not believe that they have special eidetic (power of recall) capabilities.

A noteworthy study by Dewhurst et al. (2008) involved a proficiency study of 42 handwriting examiners. Over 3,000 opinions were expressed by the test subjects examining 100 questioned signatures that were written by a population that included laypersons and calligraphers. The results showed that the examiners were four times more likely to provide an erroneous opinion on a simulated signature penned by the calligraphers in the study.

11.4 ATTRIBUTES OF ASSISTED OR GUIDED-HAND SIGNATURES

Invariably, the writing involved, when assistance is needed, is a signature, although there have been exceptions to this rule. Terms used to refer to the action include (1) *inert-hand*, (2) *guided-hand*, (3) *assisted-hand*, and (4) *forced-hand*, and are intended to reflect the different levels or degrees of voluntary action on the part of the signatory, or the requirement for help. The term *aided-hand* has been employed in lieu of *guided-hand* or *assisted-hand* but without further definition. The term *death-bed signature* has also been used, but it is even less specific as to the method of production and only indicative as to place and time. For clarification the terms are defined as follows:

The *inert-hand* is completely involuntary, incapable of motor activity and the signatory may be conscious or even unconscious. It has been suggested that completely illiterate persons might appear in this group when their ignorance of the document is being exploited. Foley and Kelly (1977) describe the state as *total incapacitation*.

The *guided-hand* and *assisted-hand* actions are attempts to define slightly different situations that may disclose slightly different characteristics. The *guided-hand* situation is one in which the person providing the guidance usually dominates the writing process and provides the greater portion of control. The *assisted-hand* situation is one in which the person assisting provides help to a lesser degree, perhaps only to the point of steadying a tremulous arm or hand, without actually directing the movement of the writing instrument. These latter two terms refer to what Foley and Kelly (1977) called *partial incapacitation* and relate to a continuum of signatory abilities ranging from little or none to near normal.

Signatures of *inert-hands, guided-hands*, or *assisted-hands* are often the products of a line of thinking that a writing instrument must be in the hand of the signatory, even if mentally or physically incapable, in order for a signature to be accepted as legally valid. Occasionally, they appear as the products of young children in some expression of greeting or gratitude directed at family and relatives, where parents are, obviously, the guiders or assistants.

The *forced-hand* is a term that Locard (1951) and Mathyer (1963) employed to refer to somewhat, although not entirely, theoretical situations of a criminal nature in which the signatory is forced to write against his or her will, by threats, constraints, or extortion. It is alleged to have occurred with people and prisoners in World War II (1939–1945) and more recently in the incarceration of hostages on the international scene.

To avoid misunderstanding as to which of the individuals involved in the writing act reference is being made, authors resort to such terms as *guider* and *guided*, or *assister* and *assisted*. But *guider* and *assister* are not normally found within English lexicons. The term *signatory* is used to refer to the person whose name is being inscribed upon the document and who is the individual requiring the assistance or guidance. The term *coadjutant* refers to the individual providing the enabling aid.

The *inert-hand*, by its very name and nature, provides no evidence to associate it with the signatory. On the contrary, the signature of an inert-hand may be identifiable with the person controlling the movement of the writing instrument. The impediment provided by the signatory's hand results in less regularity in the writing, greater angularity, pen stops (halts), and disconnections. It also effects the forms and locations of diacritics and "t" crossings. Locard (1951) cited a case of a quadriplegic who wrote well prior to incapacitation. As a product of entirely passive collaboration, the signature to a will was unlike the signatory's former writing or that of the guider, except for the fact that it reflected a writing style, Anglaise de Sacre Coeur, corresponding to that of the individual, that is, the coadjutant, controlling the signatory's hand.

Almost invariably, the questioned writing or signature and the relevant action within this category are referred to as *guided-hand* or *assisted-hand* signatures. The guidance or assistance required ranges from minimal—the steadying of a tremor, to complete—the maneuvering of the hand through the course of the writing act.

The assistance provided and its effect upon the written product varies with the level of dominance of the coadjutant's hand that is assisting or guiding the signatory's hand. As may be expected, if the signatory is passive the coadjutant will dominate and the signature tends to acquire characteristics of the latter. If the signatory is not completely passive and the coadjutant endeavors to dominate, conflicts occur in the execution of writing elements. If the assistance rendered is minor, the effect on the written product may be little, or indeed, unobservable.

Assistance at this level will amount to either a steadying of the arm, or a steadying of the hand, and the degree of interference with the writing process will differ somewhat from case to case. The steadying of the hand requires greater pressure and control, and consequently, the results will be more distorted. Needless to say, both steadying methods involve some conflict, but a steadying of the arm is less restrictive for the signatory and, accordingly, the product will be closer to the individual's writing prior to the onset of tremor or disability.

In the extreme, the participation of the signatory may be no more than a resting of the hand on the arm or hand of the individual doing the actual writing. Or it may be limited to a grasping of the end of the writing instrument. This is a practice having some historical significance in that it was followed a century ago in the application of signatures of Indian band leaders to treaties with governments. Hence, came the expression: "The laying on of hands."

Many cases, however, appear to be within the group where conflict is evident. Irregularities in the writing occurs due to a lack of harmony and coordination of movement impulses between the two hands involved (Hilton 1969a). As Osborn (1929) pointed out, guided-hand signatures exhibit uneven alignment and inconsistent spacing between letters, and these are two of the less conscious elements of handwriting. They also display abrupt changes in direction, disconnections, superfluous strokes, as in false starts, and a general decrepitude of the writing. These then, are the symptoms of genuineness. Conversely, smoothness, continuity, shading, pen control, careful retouching, and the meticulous joining of stroke endings can be construed as evidence of spuriousness.

Such conflict tends to produce a more angular product and a reduction in writing size. Alignments that an unassisted writer has difficulty maintaining can be substantially improved. Furthermore, in situations of conflict, the coadjutant tends to anticipate the pen movement. Consequently, the level of conflict is greater and the influence of the coadjutant is more pronounced in the execution of more unusual or peculiar letter formations or writing movements.

It is to be expected that the speed of the writing act will be slowed because of the conflict. Letter dimensions are irregular, spacing is broader, pen pressure becomes greater than normal for either party and letter forms are generally larger. Ascending and descending strokes and loops tend to be longer than customary and executed with greater pressure. Foley and Kelly (1977), however, found in their study that assistance for their subjects tended to reduce writing size.

Contributions to the conflict of hands may result from differences in the normal and natural practices of the two parties, particularly where differences are pronounced in writing slants and in the progression and locations in which diacritics are applied. Some writers are in the habit of dotting the letter "i" and crossing the letter "t" immediately after completing the letter, whereas other writers apply them after completing a group of letters or the entire word.

Few of the authors of books on handwriting identification of a century ago, other than Osborn (1929), have mentioned the subject of guided-hand signatures in their dissertations. Frazer (1901) devoted several pages to the measurement of questioned signatures of this kind for the purpose of discriminating between the elements of the writing emanating from the guided and those emanating from the guider. This apparently proved to have limited results, quite out of proportion to the amount of work involved.

As Sellers (1962) maintained, where conflict between the hands is great, it may render the product almost unidentifiable with either individual. The signature produced will be erratic in size, in spacing, in slant, in alignment, in commencement and terminating strokes, in speed or fluency, and in skill. The opposition between the hands yields false starts, grotesque characters, deviating movements, and pen jabs into the paper that can be destructive. This latter feature, however, when present, can of itself be evidence that the signature was guided.

Different views have been expressed as to whether guided-hand signatures are valid or not. Sellers (1962) raises the issue as to whether unconscious individuals, incapacitated individuals unable to resist, illiterate individuals ignorant of the purpose of or need for the signature, and/or any individual lacking the mental, physical, or oral facility to register or indicate disagreement with the process should be protected from the assumption that the writing of their name attests to anything. Along this line of thinking, Mathyer (1963) made the point that the more evidence one can find in the questioned signature of the signatory's normal writing characteristics, the more evidence there is that the signatory participated voluntarily.

Skelly (1987) argues that without any evidence of awareness or consent the matter must be left to the courts to decide. McNally (1976) maintains, similarly, that guided-hand signatures are products of the person doing the guiding, the coadjutant, coupled with aberrations and distortions resulting from the particular writing conditions. Along the same lines Mathyer

(1963) states that, in European countries, a signature created by or with an inert-hand, a guided-hand, or an assisted-hand would not constitute a signature, in that it is not the product of a series of more or less rapid reflex movements. Rather, it should be referred to more correctly and simply as a written name.

There is, however, an even more fundamental controversy. Notwithstanding the many pages that have been written on the subject, there are those that question whether an actual guided-hand or assisted-hand signature exists. Harrison (1958b) states that every guided or assisted-hand signature examined by him has been declared a forgery. It may be this experience that prompts him to stress the importance of obtaining, at the outset, precise details of the manner in which the questioned signature is alleged to have been inscribed in order that the evidence within the signature can be considered as to its plausibility under the claimed writing circumstances. His view of the dubious nature of guided-hand signatures was shared by Ruenes (1975) who wrote that the guided-hand is an inadequate story invented to explain the poor quality of a forgery.

It seldom occurs that more than a single signature of these kinds is disputed in a matter under civil or criminal litigation. Jones (1986), however, describes a case in which a claim was made that certain signatures written over a period of time were genuine but assisted, as the writer had suffered from an injury to the hand. The point of this paper is the contention that in cases where several signatures are involved, the effect of assistance should vary in location within the signature from one execution to the next. Control, under such circumstances, is never consistent or constant, but vacillates from guider to guided and signature to signature. Apparent defects in the signatures, then, are not likely to occur in the same manner and location over a purported period of time. When it does, the evidence it provides of spuriousness is impressive.

There is an aspect of these cases that must not be overlooked. It is the reconstruction of the circumstances under which the signature is purported to have been executed. Gähwiler (1984), Mathyer (1963), and Sellers (1962) all recommended that the examiner duplicate the circumstances that allegedly occurred during the production of sample signatures. As reported earlier, Grant (1974) described a classic example of a signature, the authenticity of which was disputed, written while standing at a counter holding a weight of unwieldy tools in the other hand, which circumstances significantly altered the execution of the signature. Circumstances must always be considered a variable influencing the written product.

In the majority of instances, the signatory will be in bed and partly or fully reclined. Seldom will he or she be sitting upright. Support for the writing is frequently improvised. Under these circumstances, it can be quite inconvenient for a second person, the coadjutant, using the same hand as the signatory, to control or conduct the movement of the hand and arm while writing (Figure 11.2). Frazer (1901), in his comments referred to earlier, claims that assistance is usually given by "passing the arm around the body of the invalid or otherwise incapacitated writer, and supporting the writing hand" (p. 152).

In one of the few research studies conducted and reported involving larger samples from actually incapacitated persons (53 subjects), Foley and Kelly (1977) noted the difficulties encountered in orienting the two parties to one another and reported that: "It was necessary to make several attempts on different days to obtain … samples" (p. 227). Obviously, circumstances will have a significant contribution upon the written product.

A point that most writers on the subject have made is that appropriate standards for comparison are seldom or never available. A person incapacitated in this fashion is unlikely to execute any other document without considerable difficulty and will avoid doing so. Examiners of

(a)

(b)

Figure 11.2 (a) Signature of Adolph Hitler identified as a forgery. (b) Photo is purported to be genuine.

handwriting must therefore extrapolate from standards of an earlier or later date, and such a process is sometimes difficult to do and frequently subject to challenge.

11.5 CHARACTERISTICS OF DISGUISE

Writings are disguised, be they extended writings, letterings or signatures, with the sole objective of concealing the writer's identity. Disguised writings serve various purposes:

1. They may avoid recognition of the writer by the reader, as in the writing of both short and long anonymous communications, threatening or extortion letters, "hate" mail, "nut" mail, and obscene letters (Figure 11.3).
2. They may be subsequently denied by the author, more often involving the writing of one's own signature, as in autoforgery.
3. They may avoid association of the writer with the writing of an incriminating document as frequently happens in the production of court-ordered writing samples. They may be intended to avoid association with the writing of hold-up notes, or with the writing of fictitious checks and endorsements on stolen checks. They may be an attempt to conceal a relationship with the application of fictitious names or signatures to electoral documents, or other official records. Within this group are the writing standards obtained from charged or incarcerated individuals including fingerprint forms, bond forms, as well as exemplar forms and personal effects forms.

Each of these situations is sufficiently different that they produce evidence of somewhat different natures. Generally speaking, that which is obvious and superficial is disguised while

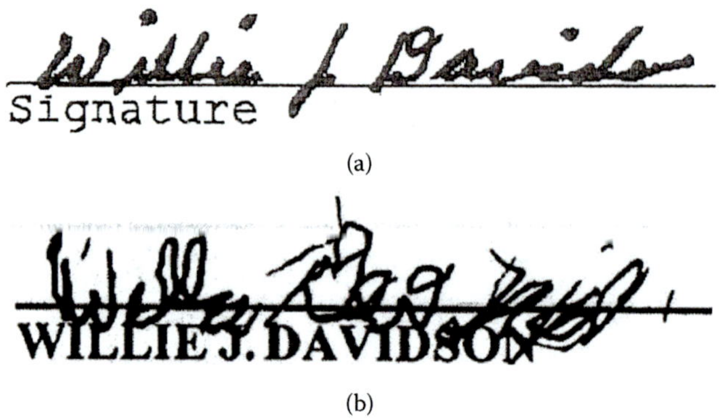

Figure 11.3 Normal signature (a) compared to a guided-hand signature taken at the hospital (b).

that which is done less consciously and is less conspicuous (and, therefore, may be more individualistic) is usually overlooked. Consequently, the more significant writing elements frequently escape disguise. The intent of the writer seems to be to alter the pictorial effect of the writing. When delicate inconspicuous parts of a writing are executed consistently on repeated occasions, and especially if they are written freely, it is safe to conclude that they are elements that are not disguised.

Disguise in writing is a topic on which much has been written and from a number of different perspectives. A number of these publications use the term *intentional disguise* which is a redundancy of words since an intent is implied by the word *disguise*. Osborn (1929) contended that there are four changes to the writing that are popular in anonymous letters or extended writings, as methods of disguise: (1) a change in slant, (2) a change in size and/or proportions, (3) a change in style, usually from cursive to block lettering, and (4) the invention of unusual letter forms (Figure 11.4). Saudek (1929) reported a list of 17 points relating to disguise in English writing. Mansfield (1943) followed with a list of 52 points. Each of these authors somewhat arbitrarily ascribed levels of difficulty in accomplishing certain changes to one's writing to effectively disguise it. None, however, provided reliable information as to the kinds of changes that are more popular, more effective in achieving disguise, or more deceiving to the public or to the practicing document examiner.

Harris (1953) reported that in an investigation of 100 disguised writings, 12 particular aspects of writing were altered, to which Harrison (1958b) added two more. Alford (1970) in a study of 135 subjects, Herkt (1986) working with 72 writers, and Konstantinidis (1987) with 98, reported on similar studies that can be consolidated into a list of 30 changes that may occur, singularly or in combinations, intentionally or as by-products of other changes, in writings wherein disguise has been attempted. These consist of the following:

Frequency of occurrence		Nature of change
1.	common	in slant
2.	common	in capital letter designs
3.	common	in lower case letter designs
4.	common	in commencement (approach) or terminating strokes
5.	common	in dimensions (size) of writing

Continued

6.	common	in style, that is, cursive to lettering or script or vice versa
7.	common	in hand used
8.	common	in spacing
9.	common	in upper and lower extenders (stems, staffs, or loops)
10.	common	in speed or fluency of writing
11.	common	in movement to greater angularity
12.	common	to grotesque letter forms
13.	common	to flourishes or embellishments
14.	common	in pen stops
15.	common	in pen lifts
16.	common	in connections
17.	infrequent	in care or writing quality
18.	infrequent	to copybook style
19.	infrequent	in letter proportions
20.	infrequent	in an increase in pen pressure
21.	infrequent	in patching, retouching, or overwriting
22.	infrequent	in alignment
23.	infrequent	in arrangement
24.	infrequent	in diacritics and punctuation, being altered or omitted
25.	infrequent	in special characters, signs, or symbols
26.	infrequent	in numerals
27.	rare	to a previously learned system
28.	rare	to simulate age or illiteracy
29.	rare	in spellings and misspellings
30.	rare	in writing direction (to backward or mirrored writing)

Many of these changes occur in either of two directions: slant may change from forehand to backhand or vice versa, or simply to or from the vertical, size may increase or decrease, spacing may be enlarged or reduced, speed may be increased or decreased, pen stops and lifts may be more frequent or fewer. Writing quality, that usually tends to deteriorate, may on occasion improve with the care and/or consciousness that the act of disguise invokes. Individuals are known to merely change their writing instrument, presumably expecting it to have the desired effect.

In his summary, Alford (1970) stated that the elements most often changed drastically affected the pictorial appearance of the writing. Other changes that may occur are in writing elements such as the lower loops of "g" and "y" that simply lend themselves to modification or substitution. Somewhat remarkably, Alford, contrary to his expectations and the principle of escape for the inconspicuous, found that nearly 15% of his subjects altered their use of diacritics and punctuation. Konstantinidis (1987) found similarly in 19% of his Swedish subjects. Notwithstanding these findings, Alford and Bertocchi (1974) make the point that disguise seldom results in an alteration to punctuation marks, diacritics, and symbols, and that in studies they conducted these features contributed substantially to the identification of disguised

Figure 11.4 Example of disguise used in threatening and anonymous letters.

extended writings. This was consistent with the accepted principle that the less conspicuous features of writing, for which there are few readily conceived alternatives, are less subject to change and, thus, are of greater identification value.

Keckler (1988) sought to deal with the possible criticism of other studies that results may be unreliable due to differences in the motivation underlying the action of real criminals and that of the socially well-adjusted subjects of academic research. In his study of the writings of 400 felons he found 16 modes of disguise, which corresponded closely to the 12 methods of disguise reported by Alford (1970).

Herkt's (1986) study of disguise in the writing of signatures disclosed that 20 of the changes listed were observed. In summary, he, like Alford (1970), reports that the most favored methods of disguise were those that endeavored to alter the more obvious features of the signature, such as slope, care, pictorial appearance, capitals, supralinear and infralinear letters, and commencement and terminal strokes. Some of the conditions he observed, particularly hesitation and retouching, as well as changes to alignments, pen pressure, and pen lifts may have been unintentional by-products of the process rather than elements of the selected method or methods of disguise. Two other observations were made that are worth noting. The length of the signature and the space available to execute it had no significant effect upon the method of disguise employed.

Konstantinidis (1987) conducted a similar study of 98 subjects from a Swedish viewpoint, principally because national Swedish handwriting systems underwent changes in 1943, 1968, and again in the mid-1980s, each of which tended to simplify letter designs to facilitate the process of learning to write. While the popularity of some techniques varied from that found in other studies, the results were much the same. Herkt (1986) and Konstantinidis both commented, rather incidentally, on the fact that some changes occurring in disguised writing may be the unintentional by-products of other deliberate action.

Regent (1977) and Jamieson (1983) attempted to isolate the effects of a deliberate change in slant upon other aspects of the writing, without there being any particular intent to disguise. Regent found that in changing slant, 50% of writers used less space, 10% used more space, and 40% were unaltered. Also, 82% displayed an increase in pen pressure, 7% a decrease, and 11% were unchanged. In writers changing letter forms there was a greater tendency to alter the capital "S" and the capital "Z." The tendency to loop the "t" staff was greater when the slant went from forehand to backhand, whereas retraced "t" staffs dominated any changes from backhand to forehand writing. The tendency to loop the staff of the "d" was greater when slant was changed in either direction.

Jamieson (1983) found, as expected, that letter forms did not change with the change in slant. Of his writers, 80% reversed the direction of their normal slant, and 20% increased the slant in its normal direction. There was no clear tendency in altering spacing between words or letters: 25% of the writings displayed a noticeable loss in line quality; 35%, an increase in the frequency of retouching; 65% increased the size of loops (7% were smaller). On unruled paper, baselines ascended 67% of the time and descended 14% of the time. Finally, as others have contended, the adopted slope was not consistently maintained in 62% of the cases.

Related to these studies is another of more recent publication by Halder-Sinn and Wegener (1992). They observed that a change in slant can be more pronounced and maintained more consistently if it is the only modification that the individual is attempting to pursue. If modifications to one or more additional features are attempted, the change in slant is modified and the writing becomes more vertical. This is attributed to the "overtaxing of the control function in a multiple disguising task" (p. 905).

Kropinak's (1965) study primarily examined the effectiveness of four particular methods of disguise: (1) change of pen hold, (2) change of slant, (3) change to lettering, and (4) change of writing hand, which also revealed a relationship between some aspects of the results. Cramped pen holds affected writing quality but little else. Change of slant affected arrangements, and in some cases letter size, but little else. The change to lettering yielded a script rather than normal printing or block lettering. Printing tendencies in cursive writing, if and when they existed, went unchanged. Improper letter forms were common. Change in writing hand produced poorer writing quality, increased pen pressure and greater inconsistency. Connection practices were unchanged. There was an evident tendency to use copybook letter forms. Embellishments and diacritics did not change. Worth noting is that Kropinak observed that there is less deterioration in writing quality when a normally left-handed writer changes to the right hand than conversely. It may be that many left-handers have received some instruction, at some time in writing, with the right hand without being permanently converted, and there are some residual effects.

Parker (1989) made a further observation respecting signature disguise that is also worth bearing in mind. His experience suggested that the kind of disguise that an individual might employ tended to be consistent from one occasion to the next, as a request for disguised signatures evidently revealed.

The methods that one might employ in disguising one's writing are numerous and the manners in which the writing may be altered are equally numerous. The method selected is unpredictable and, as Galbraith (1979), Crane (1973), and Keckler (1988) have observed, there is no apparent correlation between education, gender, or motivation and the method chosen or the skill and success of the endeavor. Hull (1993) has provided some evidence that the number of changes occurring in a disguised handwriting increases with the level of formal education of the writer. Persons with less education tended to change to lettering and changed arrangements, while more educated individuals changed a greater variety of writing aspects such as lowercase letters, speed, spacing, size, approach strokes, numerals, and special characters.

The effectiveness of any one method or combination of methods will depend to a large extent on the amount and nature of the writing being disguised and the talents of the particular writer. In these studies, it has been found that some individuals are much less capable than others, for no apparent reason.

Similarly, the prospects of identifying the author of disguised material also varies. While studies have revealed the competent examiner's ability to penetrate disguises in the majority of cases, it has to be admitted that in some cases it can't be done. In the previously cited report of Whiting (1997), one individual had succeeded in adopting two identities and two distinctly different writing and signing styles. Behnen (1993) reported two cases, one in which an individual exhibited two styles for the writing of his signature, and another in which the writer exhibited five styles of writing of signatures, although some of these may be simply the effects of some consistency in a chosen disguise upon relatively short productions. Although these cases are rare, the fact remains that the interpretation of differences in some circumstances is precarious.

Insofar as the anonymous letter writer is concerned, it has been repeatedly observed that writing is so automatic that the author, particularly when the document is of some length and his or her attention is absorbed by the thoughts being expressed, almost inevitably lapses into his or her natural hand. This may occur intermittently throughout the document and frequently toward the end.

Osborn (1929) maintained further that illiterate anonymous writing frequently consists of a combination of script forms and Roman capitals, or pen or pencil printing, and that often this writing contains original or freak forms of letters, abbreviations, or punctuation marks that are individual creations and are of the utmost significance as evidence of individuality. At the same time, he cautioned that assumed illiteracy was often the disguise adopted by anonymous letter writers and that such cases warranted a thorough study.

It should not be overlooked that anonymous letters can sometimes be associated with individuals by the materials used, such as pens, inks, papers, writing pads, envelopes, as well as the writing. Even postmarks, traces of obliterated or erased writings and typing, or their impressions, left on the anonymous letter itself or on an underlying sheet, have proven to be helpful in tracking a document to source.

While under special circumstances handwriting may be successfully disguised, the disguises ordinarily adopted are ineffective. The author of an anonymous letter of any considerable length, and particularly a series of letters, can in most cases be identified, given adequate standards. In many serial cases, perhaps 20% of them, the writer is one of a number of supposedly innocent recipients of the letters, and perhaps more often than not the writer is female.

It also happens that in instances where a series of anonymous letters have been issued at intervals, the disguise employed is apt to be partially disregarded or almost entirely forgotten after the first few issues. There are also cases on record in which the only person to have received the anonymous letters is the writer him- or herself. Assumed illiteracy is sometimes encountered as a disguise in an anonymous letter.

While document examiners have dealt with disguised writings for years and regarded the fact of disguise as simply an obstacle in the course of handwriting identification, recent decisions in case law regarding court-ordered exemplars have changed the role of the document examiner to a great extent. In *People v. Igaz*, 326 N.W. 2d, 420 (Mich. App. 1952), the US Appellate Court ruled that the defendant, in attempting to disguise his handwriting, did not comply with the order requiring him to provide exemplars.

Thus, as Hart (1985) has pointed out, a defendant who disguises court-ordered exemplars of writing provides grounds for contempt proceedings, the proof of which rests solely on the shoulders of the handwriting examiner. It has now become just as important to prove disguise as it is to prove the subsequent writing identification. Accordingly, there must be criteria developed to establish disguise and to eliminate other less incriminating explanations for changes in writings such as abnormal variations, writing circumstances, or the influence of drugs and medical ailments.

Coupled with the changes in aspects of writing listed above, the principal and most persistent distinguishing feature of disguised executions is likely to be inconsistency: in size and forms of letters, in spacing, and in writing quality, when compared to the normal natural writing of the individual. Obviously, inconsistencies will be more evident in longer writing samples.

Writers of articles on various topics, including arthritis and drugs taken as medications, have mentioned the risks of wrongly interpreting the effects of these conditions or circumstances as evidence of disguised writing or forgery. In some cases, however, the concern for misinterpretation may be unwarranted. There are principles and practices characteristic of disguise that make it recognizable from the normal, natural writings of other persons and from the normal, natural writing of its author, as the foregoing has endeavored to delineate.

Furthermore, if drug or ailment-altered writing can be improperly identified as disguise, and an author of court-ordered writing samples, thereby, wrongly incriminated as knowingly refusing to comply with the order of the court, then it must be allowed that disguised writing can be improperly identified as drug-affected writing and its author wrongly exonerated. Hence, the discipline must assume some responsibility for clearly discriminating between the written products of these two situations.

It is not known if the loss of control, fluency, and consistency resulting from drug ingestion or medical ailment is evidenced in all elements of a writing. It is capricious and involuntary. A reduction in the speed of writing may be partially responsible. The changes to writing provoked by disguise are evident in major features and escape the subtle features. They are deliberate and voluntary. The speed of writing and fluency is not necessarily affected. They frequently include extreme distortions of the writing movement. The erratic movements of drug and ailment-altered writing are irregular and unpredictable, whereas the supposedly erratic movements that disguise may include have a more regular nature and location to them. Misinterpretation of the evidence can occur, but should not occur when the amount of writing and, consequently, the amount of evidence is adequate.

Nonetheless, recent studies on disguise have shown that this factor is a problematic area in handwriting identification for examiners. It has been recognized in published research on handwriting examiner proficiency testing that disguised writing increases a handwriting examiner's number of misleading and inconclusive opinions. Bird et al. (2010a) found that in comparison to laypersons, handwriting examiners had lower misleading rates but higher inconclusive rates, indicating the handwriting examiners' conservative approach when expressing opinions on problematic areas such as disguise. In another study carried out by Bird et al. (2010b), they reported that handwriting examiners are correct in detecting that there is a problem with disguised signatures, but that the misleading opinion is a result of attributing incorrect authorship.

Mohammed et al. (2011) examined differences between genuine, disguised, and autosimulated signatures using electronic signature technology so that dynamic handwriting features of each signature could be captured for evaluation and comparison. The disguise study collected 1,800 signature samples of different types of signatures that were printed, cursive, or mixed in style. The subjects were asked to provide examples of genuine, disguised, and autosimulated samples that were then measured using handwriting movement capturing software. The handwriting factors examined included duration, size, velocity, jerk, and pen pressure. It was found that changes in handwriting factors were dependent on the style used, and that changes in handwriting velocity and size were caused by the writer's change in handwriting style during a disguise strategy.

11.6 CHARACTERISTICS OF WRITING DEVICES

There are manually-operated devices for inscribing a signature, such as rubber stamps, and mechanically-operated devices for inscribing a signature or any other writing, such as photocopiers, facsimile machines, or even printing presses. Each kind of device has its own particular characteristics, or "set of fingerprints," by which it may be discriminated from the normal and natural writing executed by persons with pens or pencils.

For the most part, manual, mechanical, and electronic devices produce images of a signature that are two-dimensional. If there is a third dimension, the impression into the paper, the point load observed in the writing line is constant. There is no evidence of the variation in pen pressure that normal, natural writing usually exhibits.

Most manual, mechanical, and electronic devices produce what is referred to as a *static* impression, created without (horizontal) movement in the direction of the plane of the paper. Actual writing is a *dynamic* impression, created only as a result of some horizontal movement of the writing instrument over the plain of the paper. Static and dynamic impressions differ particularly in the manner in which the writing media (ink or graphite) is deposited on the paper surface. While static impressions are without any directional evidence, dynamic impressions frequently, if not invariably, contain directional evidence. The reason for this lies in the fact that the fibers of the papers surface are being employed as a friction agent to drag ink or graphite from the instrument. As a consequence, ink or graphite tends to accumulate along the edge of the paper fibers facing the approach of the pen or pencil, to a greater extent than along the opposite sides.

Admittedly this kind of directional evidence, visible clearly with the aid of a stereomicroscope, is more pronounced with pencils and with some types of inks than with others, but it is a condition that should be studied. If there is an accumulation of ink or graphite deposits on either side of the fibers, it may be evidence of a dynamic rather than a static impression.

Dynamic impressions by manual, mechanical, or electronic devices are found in the production of multiple signatures by machines such as the Signo-Graph for the signing and authenticating of as many as 20 stock certificates, bonds, and similar monetary or negotiable instruments at the same time. This is accomplished by coupling a number of writing instruments to a master pen that is manipulated by the signing official. Single enlarged or reduced reproductions of signatures may be created with the aid of a pantograph machine, but neither of these machines have the capability of duplicating the third (vertical) dimension of the writing, to replicate properly the pen pressure or point load throughout the signature.

A machine called the Autopen was invented in 1958 by R. M. de Shazo for the reproduction of signatures, one at a time, in a device in which a prepared matrix is housed that controls and maneuvers the pen. Signatures can be repeated by setting the speed of the machine as fast as an operator can insert and replace the documents under the pen. Dynamic characteristics are induced in the writing by the movement of the turntable beneath the pen, rather than a left to right motion of the pen across the paper.

The dynamic nature of the Autopen signature gives each product additional symptoms of an authentic execution. It has been a relatively popular machine, used by many government officials, insurance companies, airlines, and fund-raising organizations. Because the movement of the pen is controlled by the matrix, each new signature executed will be a very close duplication of the last. Changes will only occur with the wear of the matrix that is plastic or metal.

The more observable defects in the signature are the result of operator settings of the machine. These were described and illustrated by McCarthy and Winchester (1973) that also dealt with such questions as whether the product of a robot writer is a legal execution, and whether a given execution can be associated with the matrix employed to produce it. Certainly, the signatures produced warrant close study and examination for many reasons.

Somewhat in the nature of a manual device, Radley (1983) reported that he had encountered 10 presumably spurious signatures (8 executed with a ballpoint pen and 2 with a felt-tip pen) that were evidently prepared with the assistance of a stencil. The stencil enabled the perpetrator to control the movement of the writing instrument and allow it to be manouvered through curves and loops at greater speed, to produce a more deceptive fluency. Radley found that usable stencils could be cut from reasonably thick material following the outline of a genuine signature. His observations of the results of this rather unusual production method were that (1) the signatures were quite superimposable executions, (2) there was a consistently heavy point load (pen pressure) within the strokes, and (3) there were irregularities in the lines at the point of stroke intersections that he called *kinks*.

The Autopen has been updated with computer technology to include flash memory drives, smart cards, security features, and LCD display screens. Automated Signature Technology (2011) produces a machine that works with a card (similar to a credit card) containing an image of the signature. The card is inserted into the device, and then a pen connected to metal arms reproduces the signature image onto the page.

Kulvicius et al. (2012) reported on the developments in neuro-engineering that are producing technology that mimics not only the static features of the handwriting, but its fluency and movement. A robotic arm was engineered using a combination of neurotechnology and computational neuroscience which helped develop fluid and smooth movements in the robot arm that can simulate handwriting movement. The engineers found that producing smooth movement was challenging due to the complex movement patterns in handwriting that involve joining handwriting trajectories. The technology can produce accurate movements in both position and velocity with fluency, or in simpler terms, the robotic arm can mimic the form features of the handwriting as well as the speed features of the movement.

11.7 CHARACTERISTICS OF FORGERY

Generally speaking, criminal codes of Western civilizations define *forgery* as the making of a false document with the intent that it should be used or acted upon as genuine, and, for the purpose of the law, "making a false document" includes altering a genuine document in any material part.

Forgery is probably not the oldest of crimes known to civilization but there is no doubt that it has occurred ever since man first recorded his thoughts on papyrus. Whether or not forgery has always had something of the present definition, certainly in principle, it is the same. The public attitude toward it, however, has profoundly changed. Until the 1500s, and because of the illiteracy rates of the lower classes, forgery was more common among royalty and the upper classes. This era saw forgery flourish among the clergy since they constituted a significant portion of the people who could read and write. Consequently, the occurrence was tolerated and did not become a statutory offense in England until 1562.

To the forger of modern times, given the necessary skill, time, and resources any document may be reproduced at a deceptive level. Absolute security is almost impossible to provide within the document itself. In forgeries, the workmanship, the modus operandi, or method of operation may vary from the clumsy and obvious endeavors of the inept to the almost undetectable productions of the adept, and the materials involved may be equally variable.

One of the more disturbing consequences of the forging of checks is that many of the generally accepted security practices are now no longer trustworthy. Sophisticated and expensive printing formats, company stamps, check writers, check protectors, and bank certification stamps are all devices available to the forger and are capable of deceptive duplication. They may be used to give his or her work a more authentic appearance. As a means of protection, their reliability is, consequently, diminished.

Certainly, the signature is the principal target of the forger, and insofar as this element of writing is concerned forgeries tend to fall into one of four types; (1) the simply spurious execution, (2) the freehand simulation, (3) the traced simulation, and (4) the transferred signature. Although it is a less frequent occurrence, the forgery of other extended writings, including letters, holographic wills, personal notes, diaries, and other handwritten records is also attempted and often receives greater publicity, perhaps because of the monetary aspects involved. The Howard Hughes will (1986), the Howard Hughes autobiography fiasco (1975), the Benito Mussolini diaries (1968) and the Adolph Hitler diaries (1983) are four prominent cases. The task of forging extended writings is different in many respects from that of forging signatures and for that reason the evidence to be considered changes distinctly.

The Hughes' will, his autobiography, the Mussolini diaries and the Hitler diaries are instances that demonstrate the ingenuity and/or talent of the individual and the extent of the labor that the forger is prepared to devote to the production of extensive false instruments when the calculated financial return appears adequate. In each case, the documents were sufficiently deceptive to delude authorities and some reputable document examiners, but each had failings that a careful and appropriate examination of the handwriting and the paper on which it resided would disclose (Grant 1969; Cabanne 1975; Grant 1985; Michel and Baier 1985; Harris 1986). The eventual identification of the Hitler diaries as spurious documents proved to be a classic example of the difficulties one may encounter in the examination of writings in a foreign language, the need for a thorough investigation and confirmation of the reliability of the standards supplied, and the assurance of their adequacy in nature and contemporaneousness.

Forgery, however, is a legal term that, while it describes the act, also implies some illicit motivation. This text confines itself to the matter of distinguishing spurious writing from the genuine, and *spurious* will be intended to refer to that which is not executed by its purported author. Accordingly, where understanding will not be impaired the term *spurious* will be used.

Spurious writings of all kinds usually exhibit at least one common symptom of their fraudulent nature: it is not so much their divergence in form from the genuine writing, but a drawn and hesitating quality of line, particularly at points that should be freely written. Furthermore, a simulation of another person's writing, be it extended writing or a signature, must in some measure resemble that which it is intended to duplicate. Osborn (1929) believed that most errors in identifying writing are due to the improper assumption that this general correspondence of writing characteristics is proof of genuineness. On the other hand, it must be acknowledged that a simulation of another's writing may sometimes be produced that, while suspicious, cannot positively be declared to be spurious. Nevertheless, one of the writing features most characteristic of spuriousness and most often occurring is the lack of fluency (Harrison 1958b). Accordingly, it has long been held that it is easier to produce a forgery with a pencil than with pen and ink, for the pencil is less inclined to show the evidence of a halting, tremulous movement that lacks continuity. It may fail to disclose pen lifts, pen position, retouching, or overwriting as clearly as a pen.

Simply spurious signatures are encountered in cases in which the perpetrator has no access to a sample of a genuine signature to use as a model or does not care to mimic the genuine signature. This happens when checks are stolen. In such cases, there is usually little correspondence between the spurious signature and the genuine. There may be odd flourishes or embellishments to the writing, presumably added as a kind of disguise, or to give it an ambience of authenticity.

In other situations, perhaps after some previous study or practice in copying from a model, the simulation of the signature is attempted from memory, as in the case of an endorsement to a check written in front of a teller at a bank or on an electronic signature capture device. Understandably, the product may be a mixture of some features of a writing that recollection can provide, together with such contributions as the writer's own habits or inventions may suggest to complete the writing task. As may be expected, the components of a signature that are remembered sufficiently to be included are likely to be the major or more obvious ones.

Depending upon their length, the letters involved, the quality of the writing and the writing circumstances, however, the simply spurious writing may, by coincidence, resemble the genuine products to a deceiving degree. Discrimination is even more difficult when the writing is limited to a matter of initials. For the most part, however, differences will be obvious and discriminations can be made. The argument often offered in support of the spurious is that it was executed under unusual circumstances (on a moving train, on the roof of an automobile, on one's knee) which accounts for its disparity from the normal genuine product.

The study of the differences must, therefore, be made as to whether they are differences in the fundamental aspects of the writing or simply in matters such as size and design that could conceivably fall within the wider range of variation that unusual writing circumstances might produce.

Perhaps the most telling characteristic of simulated signatures is poor line quality that reflects the level of consciousness in the writing act. Simply spurious signatures, however, are more often freely and fluently written and line quality can be misconstrued as indicative of genuineness. Then too, because most people's writing changes slightly but steadily with time, and signatures are known to be changed in style rather distinctly in many cases by choice of the writer, it is particularly important that handwriting comparisons be conducted with contemporary standards.

Although it is not often that a writer of a forged signature will include enough of his or her own writing characteristics in it to allow him or her to be identified with it, the potential for doing so is, understandably, greater in the execution of that which is simply spurious.

Freehand simulated signatures are the most common kind of signature imitations. While it is reasonable to expect that imitations will resemble in some ways the writing being imitated, they tend to deviate from the genuine in three principle respects: form, line quality, and stroke continuity (Figures 11.5 and 11.6).

The reproduction of letter forms suffers particularly in complex letter designs in which compound curves are involved. Because the simulation process requires reasonable attention to detail and form, and a consciousness of the writing act in attempting to follow an unfamiliar design, there is, frequently, a loss in the smoothness or fluency of the writing line commonly referred to as the *tremor of fraud*. This lack of fluency may be discerned in abrupt changes in stroke direction.

In a study by Masson (1996), the loss in line quality occurred in the overwhelming majority of freehand simulations and resulted in a line quality that was inferior to both that of the model being simulated or that which was normal for the simulator. Worth noting is the fact that in some 50% of the cases the resultant line quality was no different whether the simulation was made freehand or by tracing. In the other 50% of the cases, the tracings were the poorer. Also worth noting is the fact that the line quality in some simulations and tracings produced in this study was only marginally diminished.

This loss in line quality and the reasons for it prompts some examiners to suggest that the more conscious and deliberate act of simulating tends to result in drawings rather than writings. With the reduction in writing speed or fluency and the resultant loss in line quality, there is, as might be expected, a tendency for initial and terminal strokes to exhibit blunt endings.

The poorer quality of line usually present in freehand simulated signatures, often described as tremor of fraud, may be accompanied by varying and abrupt changes in pen pressure, and an absence of any regular contrast in point load between upstrokes and downstrokes. There is likely to be unequal distributions of ink and interruptions in the movement of the writing instrument

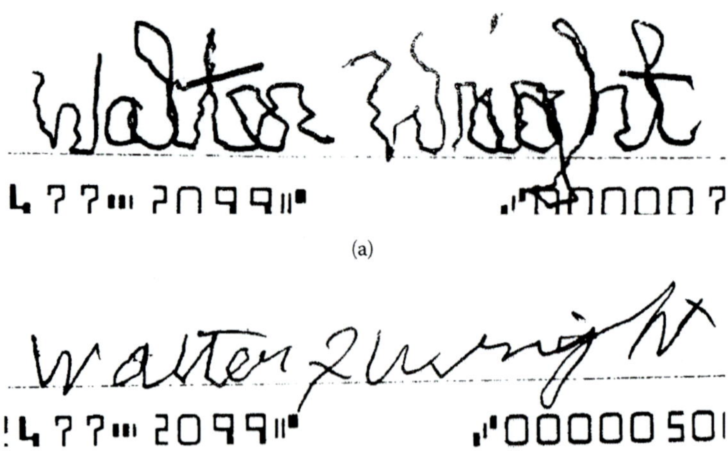

(a)

(b)

Figure 11.5 Example of an attempt to simulate tremor associated with a forged signature. (a) Forged signature. (b) Genuine signature. Note the adherence to baseline on the forged signature.

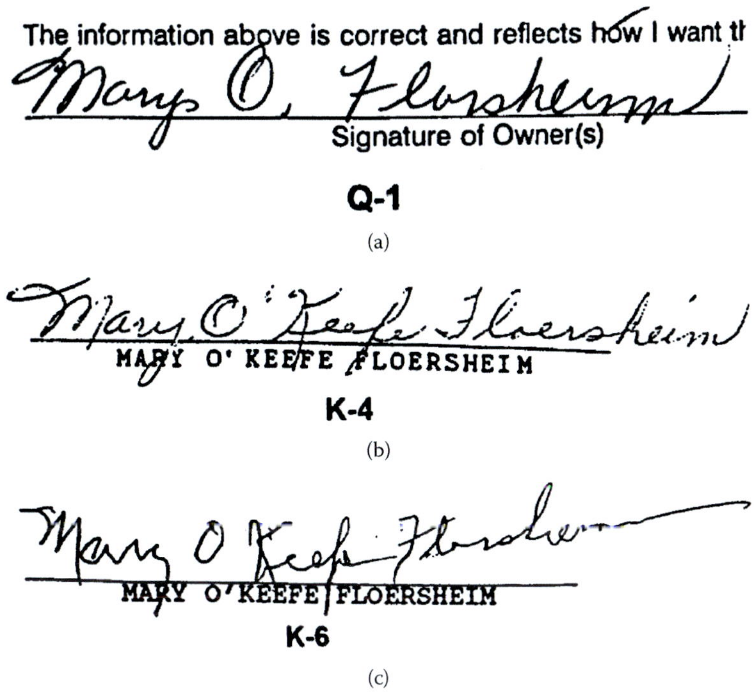

Figure 11.6 Example of a simulated (forged) signature using a model signature. The (Q) signature (a) was purportedly signed a few days after the known signature (K-6) (c). The forger used an earlier signature as the model (similar to (b) K-4).

in the middle of curves or even straight lines. It must be distinguished from the tremor of age, the tremor of illiteracy, and the loss of control that may occur with certain illnesses.

Conway (1982) has commented on the not uncommon finding in simulations that they deteriorate and differ more from authentic signatures toward the end of the signatures. In effect, the task of sustaining a good simulation is more difficult the longer the signature.

A hallmark of spurious simulations can be found in line continuity (Figures 11.7 and 11.8). Simulations frequently contain too many pen lifts or pen lifts in the wrong locations. Masson's (1996) study of simulations of signatures by 22 writers revealed that more than 60% of the freehand simulations contained at least one pen lift or area of patching. Pen lifts, however, are more readily seen in the strokes of fluid inks, whereas in pencil and ballpoint pen writings it may prove difficult to determine the location of pen lifts with certainty. Letter alignments is another less conscious element of the signature that frequently escapes the attention it deserves in the simulation process. Furthermore, spurious simulations may contain patching or retouching in some areas, to improve their correspondence to the master being copied, or to conceal errors in the imitation.

The patching and retouching of a letter or part of a letter is not always evidence of spuriousness. Some persons are known to have contracted the habit of going over elements of what they have written to improve on imperfections, and the practice is repeated whether the retouching is needed or not. The examination of several samples of writing will likely indicate the consistency and nature of such practices. Then too, these patchings and retouching are seldom as subtle or inconspicuous as are found in spurious writings.

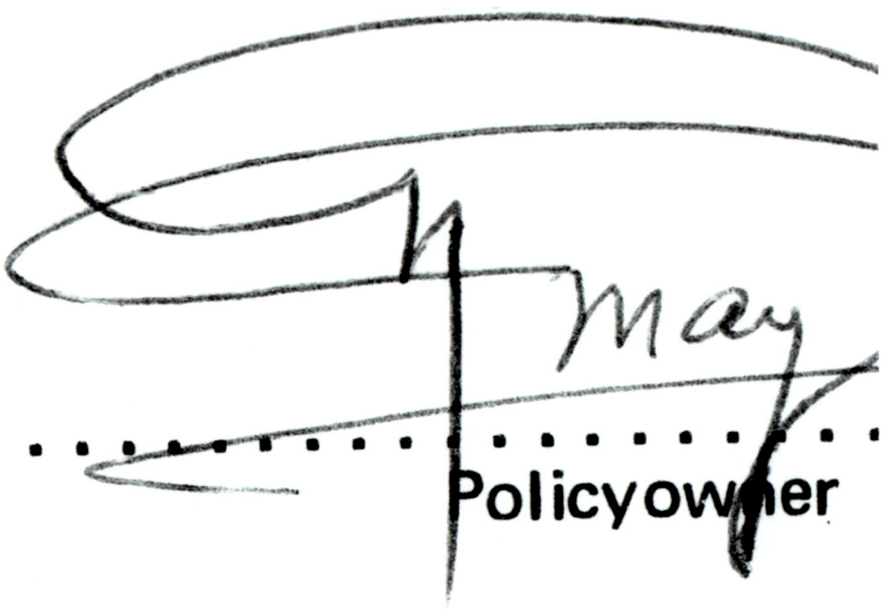

Figure 11.7 A freehand simulation of a signature in which there is a lack of fluency in the flourishes above, a discontinuity (pen lift) between the flourish and the commencement of the "M" and a retouching in the loop of the "y," all of which are indications of simulation.

Figure 11.8 A genuine signature (left) and a freehand simulation of it, exhibiting blunt endings, retouching, and a lack of fluency.

Complex or unusual letter structures and designs can be misinterpreted by one who is simulating (or tracing) a signature such that the particular movements of the writing instrument in the model or genuine signature are not duplicated. These conditions when occurring can be particularly significant.

Simulated forgeries involve a double process: the discard of one's own writing habits, most of which are unconscious acts, and the assumption of the unfamiliar characteristics of another writer, many of which are not fully perceived. This results in a mental and physical conflict for the individual, the magnitude of which will determine the success to be achieved. Furthermore, it has been commonly observed that, in simulations of signatures and writings, attention is directed at the obvious features of the writing rather than at the less consciously executed aspects (Figure 11.9). Experiments by Leung et al. (1993) and Herkt (1986) have now provided

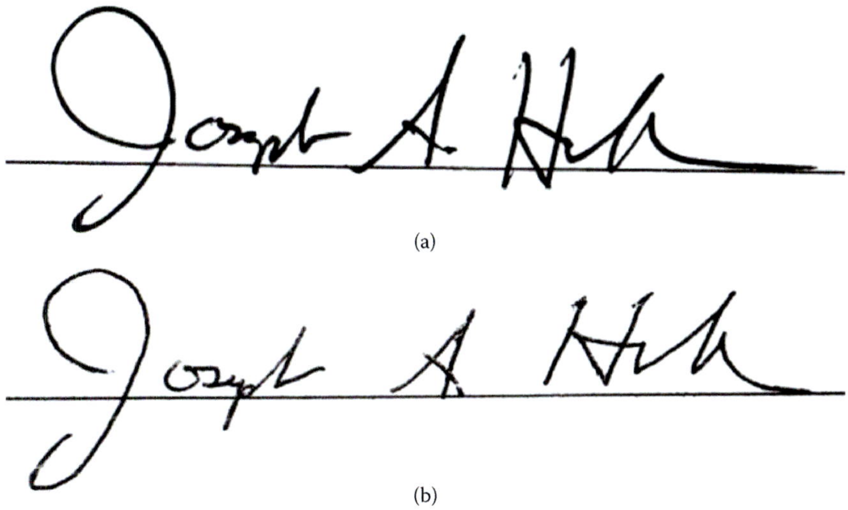

Figure 11.9 A genuine signature (a) and a freehand simulation of it (b). Note the patching of the "ticks" in the capital H and the lack of fluency giving the simulated signature a "drawn" appearance.

empirical data confirming the generally accepted viewpoints of the past. The examination and study of simulated signatures can continue to be conducted from these premises.

The writings of Osborn (1929) and Hilton (1982) on this subject and the findings of Herkt and Leung et al., (above) are elucidations and evidence of the principles of exclusion and inclusion, in handwriting identification. One cannot exclude from one's writing those habits or discriminating elements that one is unaware of possessing. Furthermore, one cannot include in one's writing those habits or discriminating elements of another's writing of which one is unaware as being present or significant.

Another fundamental related to freehand simulations that must be borne in mind is the principle of interference. This well-established psychological principle holds that it is more difficult, rather than easier, for an individual to duplicate (writing) habits that are similar to, but discriminable from one's own, because of the difficulty of maintaining a subtle or minor change to one's normal or natural tendencies. Subtle changes would be those related to proportions, relative heights, alignments and economies of movement. Less subtle changes that would be more easily accomplished and maintained would include those occurring in capital letter formations, slope, size, embellishments, and extremes of contraction and expansion.

Horan (1985) reported that forgers tend to write smaller in order to avoid detection, apparently on the premise that a smaller writing will conceal evidence of spuriousness. This might be a valid contention if the reduction in size was being made photographically, but such testimony as pen lifts, retouching, loss of fluency, or tremors are just as evident in the writing regardless of the dimensions it happens to possess. Horan's study of 482 samples of simulated signatures (i.e., forgeries), disclosed that fewer than 18% of them exhibited any significant reduction in size. In fact, a larger percentage (25.1%) exhibited a notable increase in dimensions.

In summary then, hesitation, unnatural pen lifts, patching, tremor, uncertainty of movement as exhibited by abrupt changes in the direction of the line, and a stilted, drawn line quality devoid of free normal writing movements combine to reveal the true nature of the spurious simulation of a signature (Hilton 1982). In multiple forgeries, there may be less variation from one spurious signature to the next than there is in the collected signature specimens from the individual whose signature has been violated.

A study by Dewhurst et al. (2015) challenged the reliance on pen lifts as a strong indication of simulation. In the study of over 2,000 simulated signatures, it was found that 12% of the simulated signatures actually showed fewer pen lifts than the genuine signatures. Although more pen lifts were reported in 22% of the simulated signatures, the study does show that reliance on pen lifts alone may not support an opinion of authorship without taking into account other handwriting factors.

For the most part, the task of determining that a simulation is spurious is not insurmountable, but quite routine. The question frequently posed, however, is whether the author of simulated writings, particularly signatures, can be identified with his or her product. Obviously, the prospects will vary with the nature and amount of writing involved (i.e., extended writing vs. signatures), the respect for letter form in the writing being simulated, the level of penmanship that it reflects, and the quality of the simulation. Certainly, the closer the simulation comes to duplicating the writing being copied the less evidence it is likely to contain of the hand that engenders it. Conversely, poor simulations may be expected to contain features that reflect some of the natural writing habits of the author. Whether or not the evidence will be sufficient from which to draw definitive conclusions will depend on the circumstances and the evidence in each particular case.

The model from which the simulation was made is rarely available for examination with the simulation. When it is, it can be of some assistance in extracting those features in which attempts have been made to duplicate the model, and focusing on the balance that is more likely to exhibit some correspondence to the writing of the author, as Muehlberger (1990) has pointed out.

Traced simulations of signatures are almost invariably produced by techniques that yield drawings rather than writings. Only an exceptional individual can trace a signature accurately with a fast, fluent pen movement. A study by Osborn (1984), however, disclosed that the quality of line of the tracings varied somewhat with the nature of the writing instrument (ballpoint pen, fiber-tip or felt-tip, and roller ball pen) that was employed. The tremor that is characteristic of tracings was more difficult to observe in products of the fiber-tip pens. The wider line of this kind of pen, its handling characteristics and the manner in which the ink took to the paper were all considered factors contributing to the quality of the tracing.

In addition to its revealing line quality, the primary evidence of spuriousness in a tracing is its correspondence to the model from which it was created, or the correspondence of a number of tracings to one another. Absolute correspondence is not found in genuine signatures, even if they are the executions of a well-practiced writer.

Traced signatures usually depart from genuine signatures (1) in fluency that is the result of greater speed of execution in normal, natural writing, (2) in line quality that a tracing lacks, (3) the presence of pen lifts and/or retouching that is indicative of the uncertainty of the writing instrument movement, and (4) the attendance of guidelines in the form of graphite or carbon lines or indentations. Notwithstanding these respects in which the spurious tracing will differ from the genuine product, it has long been held that tracings, by their very nature, are not likely to contain sufficient evidence of the discriminating elements of the perpetrator's writing habits to allow the author to be identified (Harrison 1964). Muehlberger and Vastrick (1992), however, provided an example of an instance in which the circumstances of the case limited the number of potential authors to a small population. Within these limitations it was possible to select the writer possessing the few discriminating elements within his or her writing that appeared in the questioned material, to support a conclusion of identity.

A typical tracing contains a rather uniformly heavy stroke without the variations in pen pressure characteristic of natural writing. Also symptomatic of tracings are frequent interruptions in the movement of the writing instrument that may be found as full pen stops or as pen lifts in abnormal locations that display some care and accuracy in the subsequent application of the instrument to the paper. These hesitations or interruptions provide the individual with a momentary opportunity to review and to plan the ensuing course to be taken by the pen. Imperfections in the product are often corrected or concealed by patchings or retouchings. Depending on the method of production, microscopic examination may disclose that tracings exhibit carbon traces, pencil traces, or simply indentations in the paper that do not precisely coincide with the ink strokes of the signature.

Generally speaking, tracings exhibit a reasonably close adherence to the letter forms and dimensions of the signature being duplicated. Complex or unusual letter structures may not be correctly interpreted, however, and a lack of correspondence in this respect may be significant in a study of genuineness.

There are a number of techniques that are employed in the tracing of signatures, none of which are particularly successful in producing deceptive products. Basically, they are variations of (1) a transmitted light technique, sometimes called direct tracing, (2) a carbon creation or pencil line technique, (3) an excessive pressure technique also called projection tracing, and (4) a tracing paper method.

- In the first procedure, the document is appropriately positioned over the genuine signature being traced, and against a glass surface behind which a strong light source (such as a window, a headlight, a projector, a photographic printer, or a lamp) is situated. The outline of the genuine signature that can be seen through the spurious document is followed carefully with the writing instrument. A pen may be used to produce a final product directly or a pencil may be employed to create a light outline that is overwritten later and the outline erased (Figure 11.10). The quality of the product will depend upon having reasonably translucent documents, having documents without interfering printing or writings on their backs, and keeping the spurious document tight against

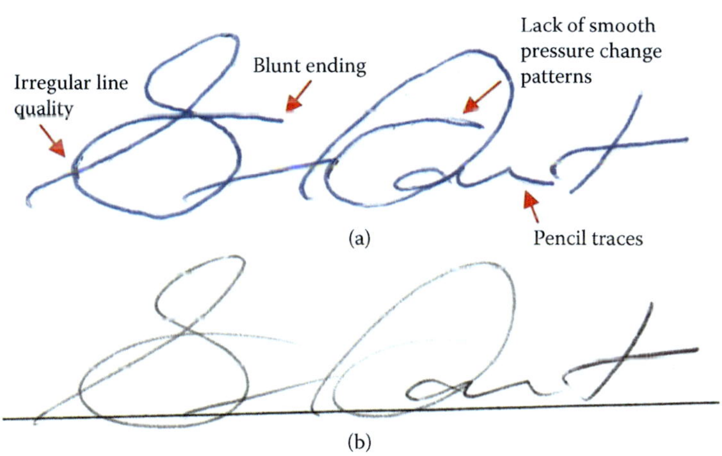

Figure 11.10 An example of a genuine signature (b) and a traced signature (a) using pencil to create the signature and then a ballpoint pen to create the "inked" signature.

the genuine signature so that its image is clear and precise. The technique can leave indentations in and around the genuine signature used by which it can be associated with the tracing.

- In the second method, the genuine signature to be traced is positioned over the spurious document, a piece of carbon paper is inserted between them and the outline of the genuine signature is followed by overwriting with a pen or an inkless instrument. The carbon impression on the spurious document is then overwritten with a pen after which the carbon deposits can be removed with an art gum or soft eraser. If the removal of the carbon is not complete, its presence can be seen under a microscope or detected with infrared photography and the process of production can be established.
- In the excessive pressure technique, the genuine signature is positioned over the spurious document on a somewhat soft surface, for example, several sheets of paper or a writing pad, and the strokes of the signature are overwritten with a pen or similar instrument with sufficient pressure to create an observable impression in the document beneath. The impression is then inked in by following the course of the furrow with a pen. The impression in the paper of the spurious document remains obvious under oblique lighting and examination under a microscope usually discloses a failure of the ink and the impression to coincide at all points (Figure 11.11). The study of impressions in documents is sometimes facilitated by scrutiny of the reverse side with parallel or oblique lighting techniques. As in other tracing processes, the application of pressure and/or ink to the genuine signature provides evidence by which it might be associated with the tracing created.

Figure 11.11 Oblique or grazing light to show indentations where a signature was traced using a stylus to create a pressure groove and then ink to fill in the grooves. Note the difficulty in staying within the grooves when applying the ink.

In these three techniques, impressions or outlines may be produced that need to be removed, for, as Harrison (1958b) claimed, the most devastating evidence of a tracing is the presence of a guideline or traces of it. The search for traces of guidelines should be concentrated around the ends of strokes, as graphite or other evidence in these areas cannot be as readily attributed to the instrument employed for overwriting. Penciled guidelines, however, may be erased completely, in which case the close correspondence in design between the spurious and its master, together with the classic lack of fluency in the copy, may be the only evidence on which one has to rely.

Harrison (1958b) also cautioned that the presence of suspicious impressions alone is not reliable evidence that the signature is spurious. It may be simply that the signature bearing the suspicious impression is the genuine signature that was used as the model from which another signature, that is spurious, was traced. To be significant as evidence of spuriousness, the impressions should extend beyond the ends of the ink lines.

On rare occasions, genuine signatures have been overwritten on documents as a result of legitimate handwritten changes that were made later. The overwriting is simply an endeavor to achieve some consistency in the color or kind of writing ink for all elements of the document. Overwritings have also been made to genuine signatures that have experienced ink failure or fading on the part of an exhausted writing instrument. In such cases, evidence of the progressive failure must be sought under the microscope in the traces of the original writing not completely concealed by the overwritings, perhaps with the help of the discriminating techniques of infrared radiation.

One should not overlook the situation in which several copies of a document or several documents require signatures on the same occasion, and genuine signatures are executed while the several papers are superimposed on one another. In such cases impressions of one signature may be left in the document beneath it. Depending on the consistency of the writer and the consistency of the signature locations on the sheets, innocuous impressions may be mistaken as grounds for suspicion.

- The tracing paper technique reported by Harrison (1958b) and Herkt (1986) is an alternative to the carbon paper method for applying a carbon outline of the genuine signature on the false document. Tracing paper is laid over the signature to be traced and an outline is created on it by running a soft pencil or pen over the lines of the signature that can be seen through the tracing paper. Following this, the back of the tracing paper is given a graphite rubbing with the side of a sharp pencil and the tracing is laid over the spurious document. Overwriting the outline of the signature on the obverse with a suitable instrument will then transfer graphite on the reverse to the document beneath in the outline of the signature that is then overwritten in ink to create the final product. While the method is more tedious than the others, it leaves no evidence behind on the genuine signature by which it can be associated with the tracing other than the correspondence in outline that there may be between the two.

A discourse on traced signatures should not overlook the fact that, when writing with ballpoint pens, there are some circumstances that provide genuine signatures with the characteristics of traced executions. De la Pena (1991) described a case in which ink failure in a genuine signature prompted an overwriting by the author using a second instrument. This yielded close correspondence between the impression of the first execution and the ink of the second, suspiciously similar to the symptoms of a tracing. Walters and Flynn (1974) reported that the metallic plating on the housings of some ballpoint pens tended to be rubbed off and left along the ink lines of writing done on zinc oxide photocopy paper, when the angle of the pen to the paper surface was low enough to permit contact. These deposits produced a guideline, shadow, ghost image parallel to the writing line that lasted for a few letters until the plating in that location was worn off. The shadow line could be misconstrued as evidence of a tracing process, if not studied closely. Vastrick (1982) found other instances of what he called *sister lines* that might be observed under other circumstances, in which genuine writing might be mistakenly identified as spurious.

Notwithstanding what has been said of these four tracing techniques there is no reliable line of distinction between skillful freehand simulations and tracings in all cases. Some of the defects may be the same, and tracings may diverge from the model as much as dexterous simulations.

The transferred or transposed signature is the unwanted progeny of modern technology. Since the advent of Scotch tape, the development of dry transfer lettering, and the invention of the photocopier, document examiners have speculated on and studied the potentials for machines and materials to facilitate the transfer of genuine signatures from one document to another.

The fundamental characteristic of transposed signatures is that they lack any evidence of pressure of the writing instrument into the paper. Furthermore, when dry transfer or photocopier techniques are employed, the ink of the strokes can be seen microscopically to be deposited, perhaps in some quantity, on the surface of the document rather than impressed into the substrate. In this respect, it has been likened to intaglio or "relief" printing, although the vertical dimension the ink deposit can acquire is considerably less. The materials used are recognizable and sometimes provide evidence by which the product can be identified with a source.

Transposition by transparent tape can be accomplished with pencil writings, but encounters problems with some ball pen inks. The release of the graphite or ink in the new location is usually encouraged by burnishing the back of the tape with a burnishing tool or ballpoint pen, similar to the procedure for depositing dry transfer characters. Even when release of the graphite or ink can be achieved, the adhesive of the transparent tape is often reluctant to leave the paper surface and fiber disturbance or adhesive can remain as telltale evidence of the encounter. To prevent this, the document may be deliberately torn and the tape left on the paper to imply that it is there to repair the tear. In other cases the document is photocopied to conceal the presence of the tape and the original is then conveniently lost or destroyed. Solvents may also be used to separate the tape from the paper, but not without the risk of reaction with the ink.

Greater use of dry transfer lettering has been found in criminal cases in which attempts have been made to duplicate the printing of corporate or private negotiable instruments, such as payroll checks. In most cases, however, the authenticating signatures to these documents are reproduced by other processes or are simply spurious executions.

Much has been written to describe other techniques in detail (Gamble 1970; Hodgins 1973; Kraemer 1979; Carney 1980, 1983; Tappolet and Ottinger 1982; Welch 1986; Ellen 1989). One technique that has been mentioned in papers is that of gelatin transfers. These differ slightly from other transfers in that the original signature is not totally removed from its document, but a quantity of its ink is lifted by a gelatin medium and deposited on the second document. The line is not as crisp or as deep in color and the ink is different in its manner of bonding to the fibers of the paper (Gencavage 1984). Still another technique for producing a number of replicas of the same signature was reported by Radley (1983) in which stencils, cut from plastic photocopying sheets or pantographs, were used as guides for the movement of the writing instrument.

A review of many of these older transfer techniques is useful especially when working with older documents which is a relevant part of any document examiner's caseload. In modern times, the transfer method is more frequently carried out using computer technology. Using simple desktop computer technology, which is widely available, one can scan a signature, cut the image from the source document, and transfer the image to a new document (Figure 11.12). Manipulations can be made to the signature so that it can intersect with a signature line or other text in a natural way. The signature can be colored to blue ink to make it look like an original ink signature when it is printed using a color printer. Other manipulations can be made to the signature so that it is not an exact match of the source signature. Color copiers are advanced to the extent that to the unaided eye, the document and its signature may appear to be an original signed with ink. Handwriting examiners should use caution when examining purported originals and look for signs of handwriting indentation and especially examine the ink under a microscope to ensure the purported original is indeed signed in ink (Figure 11.13). Transferred signatures presented as copies rather than originals present limitations for the examiner. Examiners should report the limitation concerning copies when

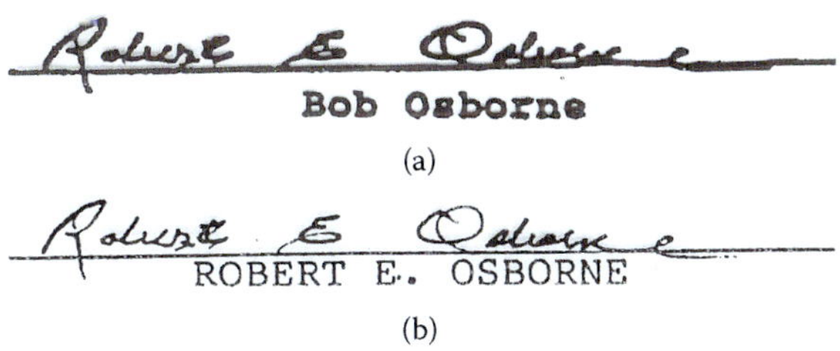

Figure 11.12 Example of a "cut and paste" signature using computer software to digitally scan and then paste the image of a genuine signature onto a fraudulent document. (a) This signature was "pasted" onto a contract dated 2003 and then copied on a copy machine (no original exists). (b) This signature was the model signature found on a deed signed in 1991. This illustrates the importance of examining originals rather than copies if authentication of the document is necessary.

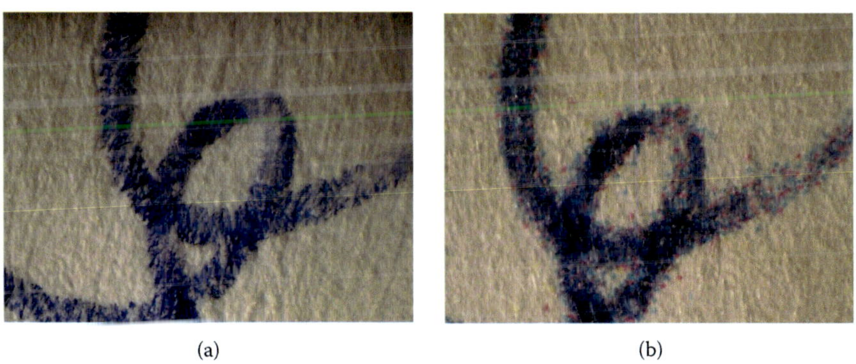

Figure 11.13 Signature (a) magnified is a "wet-ink" signature created with a blue ink ball point pen. Signature (b) magnified is a digital image created on an inkjet printer. Note the color in (b) was created by small dots of red, blue, and yellow inks.

presenting opinions about handwriting authorship. Transferred signatures using computer technology may be undetectable to handwriting examiners unless they are provided with the original source signature for comparison.

11.8 THE INDICATIONS OF GENUINE WRITING

Over many years the International Association of Master Penmen and Teachers of Handwriting have fought a losing battle for excellence in handwriting. Writing examiners shared their concerns, if only because excellence in whatever one does is its own best defense against duplication. It applies to any skill or personal performance. It pertains to the printed document or to the handwritten document. Thus, quality in writing is its own best protection against forgery, and quality in handwriting is reflected in fluency, forms or shapes, and consistency. Along the same line, Osborn (1929) maintained that the most effective protection of a signature is skill in that no one can successfully imitate a writing more skillful than his or her own.

It follows then that where one finds fluency in the quality of the line, adherence to copybook form and consistency or uniformity in other aspects of the writing such as slope, size, proportions, and spacing, the conclusion is reasonable that the writing is genuine. One can expect these conditions to be accompanied by the application of graduating pressure on the nib, ball, or point of the instrument (point load), and some difference in it between upstrokes and downstrokes. Evidence of fluency is frequently found in the tapering of endings of commencement and terminal strokes, sometimes referred to as *flying starts* and *flying finishes*. Other evidence will probably include speed, carelessness, and inattention to detail, as well as delicate, inconspicuous movements, consistently repeated, especially if written freely.

There are also occasions on which carelessness, speed, reasonable variation, and even illegibility are earmarks of genuineness. Obvious but inexplicable omissions may be further symptoms. The determining factor is the level of consciousness of the writing process that may be evident. Except in the executions of the aged or infirm, genuine writings more often reflect a concern for what is being written rather than how it is being written.

Errors made will be more obvious and corrections attempted less carefully performed, particularly so in the writing of the aged or infirm. Under these circumstances, elements of the writing may be clumsily overwritten. Indeed, physical infirmity may produce signatures that are broken, unfinished, and completely divergent from those written in a state of good health, but in these circumstances their very nature will be indicative of genuineness.

Questioned documents bearing writings of some length can introduce other factors that are indicative of genuineness, particularly natural variation. It must be present, and will be found to have a distinctive range peculiar to the writer, even in the short frequently occurring words such as "and," "of," "but," "the," "my," and other articles and possessive pronouns. These words warrant special study. In spurious handwritten documents words like these have been noted to take on a rubber-stamp effect due to their unnatural consistency. The same concern for natural variation must be directed at cases involving two or more signatures in the same name (Muehlberger 1982).

Initials, individual letters, and even some signatures provide such limited material to study that the evidence available may not be so profound. Initials and signatures are sometimes allowed to degenerate into little more than a nondescript mark, the letters of which often cannot be positively deciphered. They may be executed, however, in a distinctive way with great fluency and speed that can distinguish them from the slowly drawn imitation. In the extreme case of the illiterate, unable to inscribe more than an "X," it has long been held that a cross mark by itself is insufficient to show evidence of genuineness or a lack of genuineness.

Tangential to the study of the writing elements themselves, there are other aspects of the document worthy of the examiner's consideration. An obvious ink failure, particularly if clumsily rectified, or a failure wherein no attempt is made to complete the signature or writing, is often the kind of carelessness characteristic of genuineness. In extended writings, the study of composition, facts stated, idioms, grammar, division of words, titles, abbreviations, folds, aging, soiling, cut or torn edges, paper size or type, all may contribute something to the determination of the authenticity of the document, of the writing on it, or of the history of its production.

Since fluency is so important in the determination of genuineness it must be noted that the signature is the single element of one's writing that is done more automatically, hence more fluently, and with less awareness of the writing process. Even the poorest of writers of other material can have reasonable fluency in their signatures.

11.9 INDICATORS OF ILLITERACY

Illiteracy in writing seems at the outset to be a contradiction in terms. It is usually one's inability to write at all which warrants him or her being labeled illiterate. The inability, however, may apply only to writing in other languages or in using non-Roman alphabets. For example, literate English-speaking people are usually illiterate in Arabic or the languages employing the Slovak alphabets. As a result of the movement of masses of immigrants, refugees, and international trade and communication, it is not unusual to encounter individuals of reasonable intelligence that are illiterate insofar as the Roman alphabet is concerned. This is not basic illiteracy, however, and the effects upon handwriting may not be the same.

The hallmarks of basic illiteracy are hesitation and a kind of tremor characterized by a general irregularity of the line that is due to a lack of skill and a mental uncertainty as to design and form, and to a general muscular clumsiness from unfamiliarity with the writing process. In tremor of illiteracy, the changes in direction are not apt to be as numerous or as abrupt as in tremor of age or weakness. In the latter kinds, omissions of strokes or parts of letters are not common. Nevertheless, there have been cases in which the tremors of illiteracy, age, and illness have been difficult to distinguish from each other.

Basic illiterate writing, even on ruled paper, frequently shows a pronounced irregularity in alignment. On unruled paper, illiterate writing tends to go uphill across the sheet or page. Both conditions probably stem from the lack of practice and control of the movements of the writing instrument. In other cases, basically illiterate writers will press the pen or pencil too hard, cutting the paper or breaking the point. The pen strokes are strong but uneven, and few elements will be symmetrically designed.

Disconnections or pen lifts tend to be more frequent with illiteracy. These disconnections are more closely related to letter designs rather than writing movements. Fluent writers do not stop the motion of the pen each time it is raised. Its continuous motion will be noted in the tapered ends of strokes as it leaves or approaches the page, whereas the unpracticed hand will begin or terminate strokes bluntly.

Frazer (1901) observed that signatures attempted by illiterate persons are comprised of separate strokes or letters. There is an apparent absence of any model as a whole in the writer's mind. Illiterate writers have been known to develop peculiar characteristics that are purely individual inventions, probably due to their lack of skill or their lack of familiarity with a proper letter form. Overwritings may occur in locations that make no particular sense. Osborn (1929) claimed that illiterate writers are not respecters of margins and write on both sides of a sheet, but this implies the production of more writing than the basically illiterate person would be capable of performing. He may have been referring to persons of limited literacy, of course, who could conceivably have occasion to execute a longer document.

Common indications of limited literacy are faulty arrangement of words, lines, paragraphs, and pages indicating general unfamiliarity with the writing process, and errors in punctuation. Variation in letter form is often much less in the writing of the less literate than in that of the practiced writer, who may alter the form or allograph with the location of the letter in the written word. Osborn (1929) claimed that looped letters in basic illiterate writing often tended to slant too much because the upstroke is made nearly straight.

Less literate individuals may misspell the same word differently on different occasions. Misspellings sometimes follow pronunciation, especially in proper names. Uncommon names may be misheard, then mispronounced, then misspelled. It is claimed that anonymous letters have been traced to source through mispronunciations, evidenced through misspellings that have later been recognized.

As previously intimated, writers initially taught to write in Arabic, Hebrew, or Yiddish, which languages are written right to left, may have difficulty developing fluency in writing English or other languages from left to right. If used only occasionally, their Roman alphabet executions may continue through a lifetime to be hesitating, conscious acts characteristic of the unpracticed hand or of forgery. Where a supposedly "Western world" style of signature, at least, is necessary to conduct business, a series of strokes may be developed that bear little resemblance to characters of the Roman alphabet, but which are sufficient collectively to be acceptable to the banking or legal fraternities.

A classic example of illiteracy is writing with an "X." Writing with an "X" may appear not only among illiterate writings but can also appear in the writings of those who have lost the ability to write due to a disability. Due to the limited written material associated with the single letter "X," examiners need to proceed with caution in providing conclusions of identity of nonidentity in such cases. There is little about writing an "X" that may be considered individualizing in its shape or production. Due to the limited complexity in writing an "X," little may be construed in terms of identity in such cases.

Illiteracy has been successfully simulated in some of these aspects and has sometimes been employed as a method of disguise in anonymous letters. Inconsistencies of these sorts do not support a pretense of illiteracy. When used it is evidenced by attempts to convey the impression of limited educational qualifications through:

- Improper grammar (perhaps combined with the subjunctive forms of verbs)
- Incorrect punctuation (perhaps combined with proper hyphenation)
- Spelling errors in simple words (with proper spelling of difficult words)
- Use of "I is" or "you was," (with otherwise proper sentence structure)
- Use of "i" for "I"

11.10 HANDWRITING SIGNS OF SENILITY OR AGE

The writing of all persons changes progressively and steadily with the passage of time. The extent of the change will depend on a number of factors: the amount of writing done, the state of health of the writer, and the particular stage in life of the individual. Kapoor et al. (1985) found in a study of 50 subjects over a 10-year period that changes occurred in 40% of the writers, but that the changes were less marked and there were fewer of them in persons over the age of 45. The extent of change in signatures may differ from that in extended writings of the same individual. For these reasons, writing standards obtained for comparison purposes must be as comparable and contemporaneous as possible. From a slightly different perspective, Lester et al. (1983) in a study of the writing of a sample of 2,168 subjects (20 to 69 years), in a search for indicators of age, observed that few measurable differences were found that might be reliably related to any age group in 40 aspects of writing.

The writing of older persons, the ill or the infirm, is characterized by its evident lack of control of the writing instrument. Strokes of the writing tend to be rough and made with considerable pressure. They are likely to exhibit more breaks in line continuity. Letter forms may be awkward and in many locations it seems that the direction of motion of the pen is unpredictable. Lack of control is frequently evident at the point of application of the pen to paper.

Loss of control is usually progressive though not necessarily linear, and its onset may be heralded by tremor, that is simply a deviation from the normally smooth and uniform writing stroke. Natural tremor, being involuntary, is apt to be comparatively uniform along similar elements of the writing. It may be minor or severe. When minor, it may be prompted by the writing process much like a state of nervousness. When severe, the writing may exhibit considerable departures from normal letter designs.

Tremor, however, can be of different types having different characteristics. That which document examiners refer to as tremor of age or infirmity has been defined by Hilton (1982) as: "A writing weakness portrayed by irregular, shaky strokes" (p. 21). Harrison (1958b) defines tremor as: "Frequent deviations and discontinuities in the smoothness of the line" and the tremor, if it is genuine, will be consistent and continuous throughout a writing (p. 339). Hilton maintains, on the other hand, that a tremulous signature or writing may exhibit sporadic moments of freedom and fluency (Figure 11.14).

There are other causes and kinds of tremor besides the tremor of age or infirmity. Boisseau et al. (1987) introduced the term *essential tremor* that they claimed to be a common

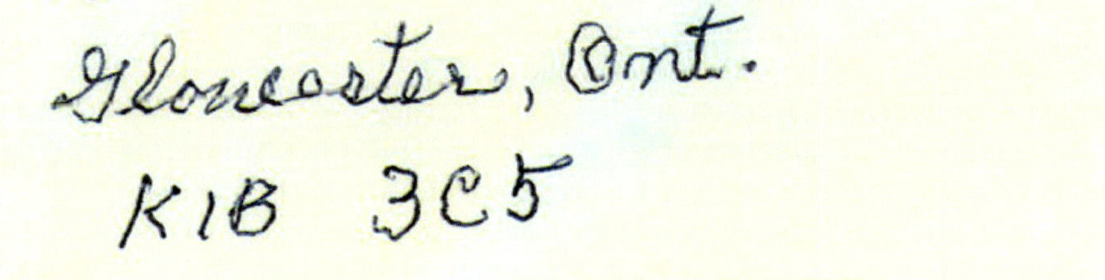

Figure 11.14 An example of the tremor of age. At the time of writing, this individual was 90 years of age. Note the erratic movements, particularly in what should be smooth curves.

neurological condition causing tremor of the arms often leading to difficulties with handwriting. Carney (1993) reported that Elbe and Koller (1990) defined tremor generally as an involuntary, rhythmic, and sinusoidal movement. The authors go on to define essential tremor (ET) as a "monosymptomatic illness" with a prevalence (4 to 60 per 1,000 persons) that increases with age, but is common to all age groups and equal in the sexes. It is a postural tremor (i.e., present, but much less noticeable during the maintenance of steady posture) that is accentuated by voluntary movement creating disabilities during activities such as writing. The handwriting is typically large and tremulous in contrast to the effects of the tremor of Parkinson's disease.

ET can begin at any age, even childhood. It is a much more benign and common disorder than Parkinson's disease. Its course is extremely variable. It begins insidiously and progresses slowly. Although ET usually disappears during rest (sometimes said to be an active tremor) and appears with action of the limb, it may not always do so in advanced cases. On the other hand Parkinson's disease is said to be a resting tremor that is apparent when the limb is not in use, but disappears when put into action.

As noted elsewhere, there are two other conditions, much less common, producing tremor: Progressive supranuclear palsy and Huntington's disease that, along with Parkinson's disease and ET, are classed as extrapyramidal disorders that identifies them with the part of the neural system within the brain to which they are attributed. Progressive supranuclear palsy is much like Parkinson's disease but has other symptoms observed in the face and eyes. Huntington's disease is depicted by large jerks of the arm or hand occurring at random.

According to Boisseau (1987) et al., in their study of the writings of 35 individuals suffering from these disorders, no particular characteristics were found that could be related to any of the four disorders. The administration of drugs was seen to affect a few letters, but the majority of the elements of writing were not significantly altered. Tremors, due to neurological conditions, tend to be more gross and erratic changes to or interruptions in the pen movement, that become more obvious with the progression of the responsible disorder.

According to Carney (1993), the authors Elbe and Koller (1990) also discuss task-specific tremors such as orthostatic tremor and primary writing tremor. *Primary writing tremor* is defined as a tremor that is induced primarily, but not only, by the act of writing and similar motor activities, such as handling a knife or screwdriver. Carney also notes that alcohol, Inderal, and mysoline all reduce primary writing tremor, but they are ineffective upon the tremor of Parkinson's disease.

It is also to be noted that tremors can be induced by the ingestion of numerous common drugs including nicotine, alcohol, lithium, caffeine, thyroid hormone, and cardiac antiarrhythmics. On the other hand, as Behrendt (1982) reported, the effect of tremor on handwriting can be diminished by the administration of mild sedatives.

Tremor of age in signatures is often accompanied by uneven alignment or a signature may apparently disregard the writing baseline. Furthermore, tremors of age, weakness, and illiteracy are not always distinguishable from each other. Tremor of age and tremor of weakness, however, beyond their many similar characteristics that make them indistinguishable, have about them a certain carelessness or abandon that marks them as genuine.

Feebleness is characterized by a general lightness of the stroke, and much tremor. It is accompanied by a decline in the design of a signature, not to be confused with the kind of change that occurs with haste or negligence. Terminations of strokes are often accompanied by the application of pressure. Despite the loss of control, the correct ideas of letter forms underlie the writing (Figure 11.15).

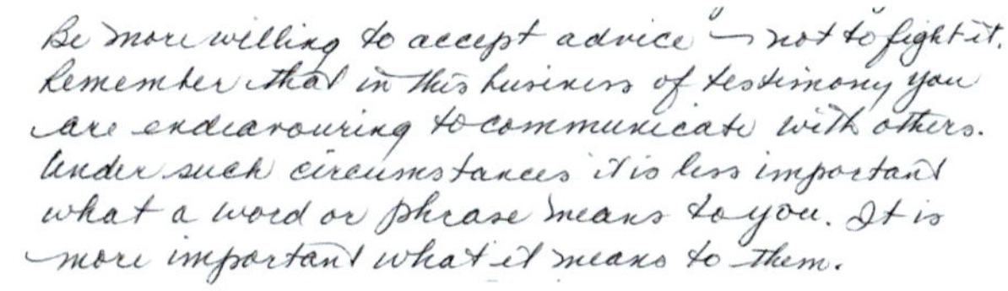

(a)

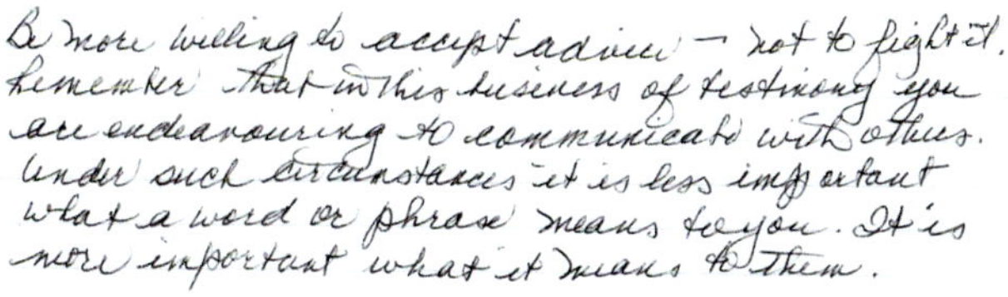

(b)

Figure 11.15 Changes in writing with age and/or time. Writing (b) was executed at age 77, 24 years after writing (a). Note the subtle changes that have occurred. (b) is less consistent in alignments, less consistent in letter sizes, and exhibits more angularity to troughs and arches. The slope of the writing of (b), relative to the vertical, is slightly less than that of the writing (a). Although fluency has been retained, these changes have resulted in some loss in skill or writing quality.

In summary then, age and infirmity may be seen in the deterioration of one's writing quality over time owing to the gradual and progressive loss of control of the writing instrument. This becomes evident in the following:

1. Loss in fluency (i.e., skill) or in the smoothness of curves and lines
2. The appearance of fine tremor
3. Deterioration in the quality and structure of letter forms
4. Irregularity of letter and word alignments
5. Irregularity of interletter and interword spacing
6. Irregularity of the widths of loops
7. Inconsistency in the locations of commencement strokes
8. Inconsistency in the direction and length of terminating strokes
9. The occurrence of erratic movements, and irregular, shaky strokes
10. The occurrence of "false starts" and inexplicable movements at the beginning of a signature or of a writing
11. General reduction in pen pressure, but an application of pressure in terminal strokes

In a sense, the progressive loss of control of the pen or pencil results in an expansion of natural variation in many of the aspects of writing that are mentioned here. The decline in form and skill or quality affects legibility. Erratic movements affect letter forms in manners that are beyond the ability of the writer to carefully and neatly correct (Hilton 1975). In more serious cases, letters or parts of letters may be repeated without any apparent attempt to correct such occurrences.

The changes in writing ability or quality are seldom extreme over short periods of time. Furthermore, writing ability can vary from one occasion to another such that relapses to better writing quality may sometimes be observed. Vision can also be a victim of age and some of the conditions that appear in writing may be due, in part at least, to the impairment of sight.

The deterioration of one's writing due to a particular illness, particularly if the individual is aged or infirm, is not likely to produce symptoms that can be associated with any particular illness. Loss of control in writing is simply that, and one can only speculate in most cases as to the cause. Nevertheless, it may have a trait to it that can distinguish it from the effect of attempts at spurious simulation.

When an individual suffers infirmity to the extreme, he or she is oftentimes confined to bed due to his or her inability to stand without support. Consequently, any writing one may wish or have to do must be executed under conditions that are bound to impair the quality of anyone's written product, and this too may have a bearing on the conditions noted above that may be observed.

When infirmity develops to the point where the ability to control the writing instrument is insufficient to produce an intelligible or decipherable inscription on paper, it is frequently necessary for another person to provide assistance in the control of the hand, and since these occasions usually involve the application of a signature to a document, they are referred to as *guided-hand-signatures*.

11.11 INDICATORS OF SINISTRALITY (LEFT-HANDEDNESS)

There has always been a small proportion of the population that displayed a preference to perform certain manual tasks in a manner that seems to oppose that of the majority. When members of the left side of one's body tend to dominate the action it is called *sinistrality*, or left-handedness, and when, as with most people, the right foot, right leg, right hand, right arm, or right eye tends to receive some preferential consideration it is called *dextrality* or right-handedness.

The human phenomenon of handedness has been of interest to psychologists and pedagogues for many years. Its definition in the broadest sense as the preferential and consistent use of the same hand during the performance of skilled uni-manual tasks (Porac et al. 1983) is complicated by the fact that with some individuals it is not necessarily consistent in the performance of an assortment of tasks. Richardson (1978) and Annett (1970) found that of seven tasks employing the hands, that is, writing, throwing, cutting with scissors, playing with a racquet or bat, brushing one's teeth, striking a match, hammering a nail (males) or threading a needle (females), handwriting proved to be the most reliable index of handedness. For the purpose of this discussion, sinistrality refers only to the use of the left hand in the act of writing or lettering.

For reasons that many writers of numerous papers, articles, and books have tried to explain, society has for centuries condemned rather than condoned the individual born with the inclination to left-handedness. In English and other languages, use of the left hand has been associated with awkwardness, stuttering, weakness, uncleanliness, and numerous other equally disparaging characteristics. Some writers have noted that 90% of chimpanzees are left-handed (Beacom 1961). Thorton (1985) and Barsley (1966) list many famous individuals who were left-handed.

The Phoenicians, a Semitic tribe who inhabited the Mediterranean coast, are credited with the origin of writing. Studies have proven that the direction of their writing was from right to left, as is still the practice with Hebrew and Arabic. This was followed by boustrophedon writing in which the direction of writing alternated with every line. Finally, as students of history contend, the Greeks settled on writing from the left to right that became the convention of Roman writing and styles that developed in societies to the north and west of Rome. Under these circumstances, it has been argued that Arabs and Hebrews were primarily left-handed writers, but there seems to be little substance to the argument. Nevertheless, there is not an acceptable explanation for the alphabet being written from left to right, although it is obvious that when it is executed by the right hand the product can be more conveniently observed.

In elementary schools, left-handed pupils seldom receive standardized instructions delineating a proper writing posture. Consequently, there is remarkable between-subject variability. There are, however, two principal positions adopted by sinistral writers that are generally referred to as the inverted-hand posture or position (IHP) and the noninverted hand posture or normal handwriting position (NHP). The common criteria defines the first as one in which the hand is placed above the line of writing and the writing instrument grasped so that it points generally toward the bottom of the page. This position seems to be correlated, though not invariably, to the tendency to slant the page to the left of vertical, as is done by dextrals. The second is described as one in which the hand is placed below the line of writing and the instrument is grasped to point generally toward the top of the page. This position seems to be correlated to the tendency to slant the page to the right of vertical. Guiard and Millerat (1984) have suggested a more reliable criteria for identifying the IHP: the slant of the page relative to the vertical (inverters to the left and noninverters to the right), the slant of the writing forearm relative to the vertical edge of the sheet (inverters perpendicular and noninverters parallel), and the position of the nonwriting hand on the page (inverters below and to the left of the writing point and noninverters to the right and often above the writing point). The latter tendency is comparable to the position of the left hand with a noninverted right-handed writer.

McKeever and VanDeventer (1980) chose to subdivide the IHP into two classes: normally inverted (in which the point of the pen or writing instrument is directed toward the writer and the bottom of the page), and markedly inverted (in which the point of the pen is directed to the left of the writer). In their study, however, only 3 of 65 left-handed writers fell into this category.

A third, but much less frequently employed, position of the hand has been observed in young sinistral writers that is described as parallel, in which the hand is neither clearly above nor below the line of writing (Bryson and MacDonald 1984). These findings report that most young sinistrals with this propensity eventually change to a fully IHP. Furthermore, studies of young female sinistrals show an early preference for the noninverted writing position, in contradistinction to their opposite sex. It should also be noted that Allen and Wellman (1980) reported finding, quite remarkably, a number of dextral writers employing the parallel position, but the tendency apparently declines with age and maturity in writing.

This discussion would not be comprehensive if mention was not made of the fact that the IHP is not peculiar to left-handed writers exclusively. It was observed by astute investigators, such as Gould (1908) in larger studies more than a century ago that there were a number of dextrals using the inverted-hand posture for writing. More recent studies, by Porac et al. (1983) of 450 triads of father/mother/offspring revealed that 4.7% of the parents and 9.1% of the offspring that wrote with the right hand employed an IHP. One may speculate that the rise in the frequency of IHP in the younger generation is a consequence of the lack of attention that penmanship now receives in the school systems, but the authors suggest that a complex, multicausal mechanism may be involved.

The incidence of inversion in right-handers varies between 1 and 10%, whereas the estimates of inversion within left-handers ranges from 30 to 75%. The point to note is that inversion does occur with both dextral and sinistral writers that studies and discussion should not overlook.

Nor should one overlook the rare, but nonetheless, real occurrence of sinistral writers that invert the paper position (IPP), but not the pen. This interesting orientation of paper, pen, and person results in the reversal of stroke directions, as in IHP writing, but also alters the relationship of the writing to a ruled or imaginary line. It does not sit on a baseline, but hangs from a clothesline so to speak, and, insofar as the writer is concerned, is executed upside down from right to left rather than left to right. Despite this highly unorthodox approach to the writing act, reasonable writing skill is still achievable.

Despite numerous efforts made by researchers to find relationships between the writing posture of left-handers and neurological causes, none has yet to be confirmed. The most parsimonious working hypothesis seems to be that the phenomenon of IHP, at one time thought to be an abnormal phenomenon, is definitely normal and represents an adaptation by sinistrals born of necessity: the need to see what has been written. Other studies have shown that the IHP produces more consistency in letter slants than the noninverted hand position (NHP), which supports the theory that the IHP is more a matter of adaptation to technical demands than anything else. Even this approach has been challenged on the grounds that right-handers executing Hebrew or Arabic from right to left do not generally develop an IHP while a proportion of Hebrew and Arabic left-handers do. Perhaps of even greater import is the fact that the incidence of IHP in left-handers, regardless of the gender of the writer, is lower among Israelis than Americans (Shanon 1978).

The incidence of IHP, a writing position that has never been taught anywhere, but is a recognizable pattern of writing conduct across many countries and several generations, has increased in recent years in parallel with social permissiveness respecting this writing behavior (Figure 11.16). It develops with maturation and writing practice and this observation is clearly consistent with the hypothesis that the IHP is an adaptive kind of behavior (Guiard and Millerat 1984).

Clark (1934) asserted that in Western civilization the writing systems have been oriented toward right-hand writing. Left-handers are forced to adapt to a system that is not suited for left-handers. In recent years, society has been more tolerant and accommodating toward left-handedness. This more permissive attitude toward left-handers in the early school grades, or the decline of interest in and need for quality penmanship may, in part, account for the increase in

Figure 11.16 A sinistral writer employing IHP (inverted-hand position).

sinistral tendencies in handwriting. The earlier constraints upon unorthodox writing practices may explain the report by Beukelaar and Kroonenberg (1986) that in a sample of 331 left-handed Dutch persons none born prior to 1940 used the left hand for writing.

Much has been studied and recorded in endeavors to explain left-handedness and to identify its causes. The subject is of interest to writing examination, however, primarily because of its effects upon the writing of the individual and the potential for distinguishing sinistrality from dextrality in the written product. In the course of these studies, a number of long-standing notions have been challenged and dispelled. For example, Trankell (1956) and others have provided substantial evidence that writing with the left hand is not necessarily poorer or slower than writing with the right. In the days of steel-nibbed pens and slower drying inks, however, there was a greater chance of young writers smudging their work (Barsley 1966), and undoubtedly this condition influenced a reader's judgment. Peters and McGrory (1987) have settled any dispute with their findings that "the writing performance of right-handers and left-handers, when writing with the preferred posture, was well matched" and that the performance of inverted writers was by no means inferior to that of noninverted writers (p. 20).

To put sinistrality into perspective for the purpose of handwriting identification, the frequency of occurrence of left-handedness in the populations, and the frequencies of the different hand positions that are employed should be considered. The reason for this is simply that handwriting characteristics may change depending on whether the writing instrument is being pushed or pulled across the paper surface.

Beacom (1961) reported that the incidence of sinistrality may be as much as 30% at infancy, and 11% in adulthood. The latter is double the percentages for adults reported in 1945. Furthermore, the numbers are larger for males than for females. Clark (1957) reported that a survey of 72,238 Scottish children in 1953 disclosed that 6.7% of males and 4.4% of females (i.e., 5.5% overall) were left-handed writers. Then, in a second survey of 5,790 Scottish children in 1956, she reported 8% of boys and 6% of girls (i.e., 7% overall) to be sinistral. A 1964 to 1965 survey of English children indicated 11.3% of males and 8.8% of females to be left-handed. Peters and Peterson (1978), in a sample of 5,910 Canadian school children, found 11% to be sinistral, provided by 11.9% of the males and 10 % of the females. Spiegler and Yeni-Komshian (1983) in a study of 1,816 American university students, their siblings, and their parents, found a 13.8% incidence of left-handedness provided by 15.2% of the males and 12.6% of the females. Furthermore, the incidence of familial sinistrality, that is brothers, sisters, and other relatives (not parents) being left-handed, had no significant effect upon the subjects of the study. However, the incidence of left-handedness was effected by parental handedness in that maternal left-handedness could be significantly associated with increased sinistrality in both sons and daughters, whereas paternal left-handedness could be significantly associated with increased sinistrality in sons, but not in daughters. While parental sinistrality produced left-handedness in the offspring to levels as high as 22% this study did not support the findings in other reports that ran as high as 87.5%. McKeever and VanEys (1989) are now suggesting that grandparents may have a significantly greater effect than parents do upon the occurrence of IHP left-handedness in children. A further study by Peters (1986) of 2,194 German school children revealed that 9.5% of the males and 6.9% of the females wrote with the left hand. The difference between the German and Canadian figures was ascribed to the significantly lower incidence of left-handedness among females, but the lower levels of left-handedness among German children suggest that pressures against the use of the left hand may be more operative within the German sample.

These studies suggest some growth in numbers over half a century and a persistent difference in the incidence of sinistrality between genders. Other studies that have attempted to correlate the condition with such matters as academic discipline and immune disorders have met with little success (Temple 1990). Levy's (1974) graph of percentages of left-handed writers that displayed a sharp increase from 1932 (2.2%) through 1947 (8.2%) plateaued at around 11% from 1960 to 1972. In a study of 580 subjects of various ages, Horton (1992) reported that 64 (11%) were sinistral. Berthold (1995) found that in a small sample of 25 subjects, mainly those in their 20s, three (12%) wrote with the left hand.

Having established an acceptable national average (11%) for sinistrality recent studies of the subject have directed their attention at other aspects of the phenomenon. For example, no correlation was found between left-handedness and irrational thinking, but some correlation has been noted between left-handedness and the season of births (Rogerson 1994).

Iwasaki et al. (1995) suggested that the percentage of sinistrals in many populations tends to drop continuously with the age of individuals over 30 years. The persistent conversion of left-handed writers to right-handedness in earlier generations is suggested as one of several causes. Eglinton and Annett (1994) presented evidence that found the proportion of nonright-handers is higher in children with specific reading problems (e.g., dyslexic).

It was mentioned earlier that sinistrality is more common among the hearing-impaired population than among others. Studies of deafness due to external causes at or near the time of birth, the prenatal and postnatal exogenous groups, disclosed that 16.7% were left-handed in writing as opposed to 11% of the population generally. Among the hereditary deaf group, that is the endogenous group, 30% were sinistral.

The incidence of IHP among left-handed writers is another matter that has been given much attention. While Peters and Pedersen (1978) had found in Canadian children approximately 40% of sinistral males used the IHP and 29.75% of sinistral females (many writers were not classified by their procedure), McKeever (1979) reported on the results of two studies that found the incidence of inversion in American university students to be 75.8% in males and 44.2% in females. In a later study, Peters (1986) reported that in his sample of German school children, 65.25% of sinistral males used the IHP and 58.75% of sinistral females did the same, but the difference between the genders may not be significant for the sample size involved. Levander and Schalling's (1988) study of Swedish college students found 60.4% of males and 38.9% of females utilized IHP.

As these studies point out there is clearly a preference in males for the IHP that is not found among females. This may be at least partly due to a higher sensitivity in females to social pressures against the use of the IHP. Also worthy of note is that Peters and Pedersen (1978) as well as Bryson and MacDonald (1984) observed a significant increase in the incidence of IHP over grades 1 to 5 or 6 in schoolchildren of both genders which may be related to an increase in proficiency in rapid cursive writing, or due in part to the growing permissive attitude toward left-handers in recent years. Also worthy of note is that Levander and Schalling observed that self-assessment of the IHP produced a notably lower frequency of inversion, perhaps due to a reluctance of left-handers to identify themselves with the awkward hand posture. Also of significance to handwriting examiners is the findings of this latter study that 76% of noninverters and 48% of inverters chose hand printing or lettering as their normal style of writing. This and other studies suggest that for left-handers, the inverted-hand posture is more often the posture of choice for cursive writing.

The evidence of sinistrality in handwriting has received little attention until recently. Lester et al. (1982) in a study of 2,168 people, sought evidence in some 40 aspects of writing by which left-handed writers could be differentiated from right-handers, and failed. Totty et al. (1983) endeavored to find a dependence of slope in handwriting upon the gender and handedness of the writer, and while results suggested that right-handers and males tended to write with a greater forward slope than left-handers and females, the figures did not achieve statistical significance.

Wing (1980) in a study of the neurological controls affecting the amplitude (height) of handwriting found that there was no difference between the handedness or the gender of writers in the height of the writing produced. In this respect, he supported the findings of Reed and Smith (1962) that there was no difference in the writing performance of left and right-handed people. In general, prior to this decade, little was known of the differences between right- and left-handed writings and there was no completely reliable technique for determining the hand used.

Harrison (1958b), Conway (1959), and Beacom (1961) have offered the following indications of left-handed writing:

1. Smudging or messiness (due to IHP?)
2. Terminal strokes upwards and to the left (due to IHP?)
3. Inconsistent slopes to letters
4. Heavier pressure on upstrokes than downstrokes (due to IHP?)
5. Right to left horizontal strokes, tapering and curving upwards at left end (due to IHP?)
6. A tendency to vertical slope or backhand
7. Right to left "t" crossings (due to IHP?)
8. Right to left "i" dots and punctuation marks (due to IHP?)

As suggested by the question in parenthesis (above), it may be that this evidence was reported without considering the hand position as a likely cause. The tendency to write more vertically, contended earlier, is supported by studies by Goodnow and Levine (1973), Goodnow (1977), and Nihei (1980).

Somewhat contrary to others, Zitzelsberger (1958) cautioned that the elements of skill and speed, slant, size, proportions, and alignment were not always reliable indicators of sinistrality. This has now been supported by more recent studies previously discussed. Stroke direction was, in the past, more readily determined by the graphite deposits in pencil writings, or the tracks of split nibs in ink writings. More recent research argues that, although the evidence is sometimes subtle, whether it be determined by: (1) the location of graphite deposits from pencils on the edges of paper fibers as seen under the microscope, (2) the spread of the tracks of split nib pens that are now less frequently encountered, or (3) the burr striations of ballpoint pens; the study of stroke direction in particular letters seems to offer the greatest promise for distinguishing the sinistral writer from the dextral at the present time.

The potentials of stroke direction in sinistrality determination was suggested by a number of individuals. Fryd (1975) dealt with the cross stroke to the block letter "T." Shanon (1979) studied cross strokes in the lowercase cursive "t" and the upper case "H," the crossbar to the "7" and the Hebrew letter Daleth, in the writing of dextral and sinistral Americans and Israelis, as well as in the drawing of a horizontal straight line. All right-handers with only one or two exceptions, whether English or Hebrew, executed these strokes from left to right. Among left-handers, higher percentages of Hebrew writers than English writers executed the strokes from right to left, the direction Hebrew writing normally takes. Brandt (1976) observed that right to left horizontal (RLH) strokes never or very rarely occurred in the writing of right handers. Although these strokes did not occur in all writing of left-handers, he concluded—and many will now concur—that when they did occur they were a reliable indication of the product of a sinistral. Nicholson and Hartley (in a National Child Development Study [1966]) are reported by Franks et al. (1985) to have noted the tendency of some left-handers to execute the figure "0" in a clockwise manner. Although statistics are not provided, Thomassen and Teulings (1979, 1983) commented on the fact that they found a larger proportion of left-handers than of right-handers tended to write the digit "0" in a clockwise fashion. Coincidentally, Connolly and Elliott (1972), in a study of the painting strokes of children, found that left-handers frequently drew horizontal strokes from right to left and tended to make clockwise curves.

The burr striations found in ballpoint pen writing are described as the linear voids that occur with most ballpoint pens when curves in the stroke tend to change the rotation of the ball and expose a part of its surface lacking in ink (Mally 1956; Hilton 1957; Snape 1980; Franks 1982). These voids invariably move from the inner to the outer radius of the curve in the direction of the stroke. Franks et al. (1983, 1985) attempted to determine more precisely the potential that stroke direction may have for discriminating left-handed writing from right-handed writing. These were broader studies of curved and almost straight horizontal strokes in lettering, numerals and the bowls of cursive letters, such as "g" and "d," that suggested some significant differences in writing performance. For many left-handers circular forms were executed clockwise (39%), whereas right-handers almost invariably (99%) moved the pen in a counterclockwise direction. Furthermore, horizontal strokes were executed from right to left (RLH) by 69% of the left-handers but never by the right-handers. In their sample of 347 left-handed writers, stroke direction in one or more of the target letters "O," "A," "E," "J," "T," "H," "G," "Q," "F," "t," "o," "g," "q," and the numerals "5," "9," and "0," indicated sinistrality in some 276 (80%) of the writers. A problem encountered in these studies was that stroke direction was determinable by burr striations in only a percentage of the writing samples that varied (22% to 97%) with the target letter or numeral. Clearly the tendency to produce striations varies with the ink and/or writing instrument.

Unfortunately, there is no information from these studies as to whether RLH and clockwise-executed zeros are characteristics peculiar to inverted-hand writers only or are shared to some extent by all kinds of left-handed writers. It seems obvious to some that these unusual grips (e.g., IHP) will result in some difference in letter forms, even within the sinistral sector of the population. Further studies are necessary, however, to establish what these differences may be and how they correlate with the IHP.

Using computerized database methods, Liwicki et al. (2007) were able to correctly classify right-handers from left-handers in a database of over 200 writers with an 85% accuracy rate. It was commented in the study that the reason why the rate was so high may be due to the way the letter "o" is written differently by some left-handers.

11.12 INDICATORS OF GENDER

M. Alfred Binet (1906), a French psychologist, claimed that, in French writing of that era, gender could be determined accurately in 75% of the cases. In the ensuing decades, a number of investigators attempted to duplicate Binet's work with American writers, but the accuracy achieved was notably lower. Two of these investigators were Downey (1910) and Newhall (1926). Young (1931) summarizes the results by saying simply: "There appears to be good evidence for the view that the sex of the writer can be determined from handwriting in a manner superior to chance" (p. 486). His results led him to state that untrained judges are able to determine the gender of the writer from handwriting with an average performance 11% better than chance. The words *untrained judges* are emphasized as none of these studies were conducted with the assistance of trained handwriting examiners.

Since there was a success rate slightly better than chance in identifying the gender of the writer some investigators sought to determine what aspects of the writings constituted the gender signs that judges were using to indicate gender. Young (1931) reported several adjectives and phrases offered by his 50 (25 male) judges in making their assessments.

Middleton's (1938) study involving 200 judges (100 male) provided 10 reasons influencing judgments:

1. A woman's writing is neater.
2. Women write more slowly and achieve greater finish.
3. A woman's writing is prettier.
4. Men tend to dot the "i" with a dash instead of a dot.
5. When a man does write well, his writing is likely to be almost perfect.
6. Men write larger than women.
7. Any backward writing or printing is likely to be the writing of a woman.
8. The use of an epsilon "e" is likely to indicate a woman's writing.
9. A woman's writing is likely to be more readable than a man's.
10. Men press harder on their pens than women.

Reasons 1, 2, 3, and 9 seem to relate to or stem from quality of writing or penmanship. This is consistent with the findings of Starch (1913) that females are superior to males in handwriting quality and slightly superior in speed, but the differences found were small. Broom et al. (1929), in a study of 40 randomly selected sample writings (18 male), had similar findings that regularity, curves, conventional form, and uniformity of slant were characteristic of samples most frequently judged to be feminine handwriting. Conversely, irregularity, unconventional form, angles, and nonuniformity of slant were characteristic of samples most frequently judged to be masculine handwriting. Tenwolde (1934) simply stated that "the advantage discovered in average penmanship quality favored the girls" (p. 705).

Newhall (1926) declined to report the criteria that his judges reported as he felt unable to determine which criteria were actually used and which were rationalizations. He does go so far as to say that: "The handwriting most frequently judged to have been written by men appears characteristically different from that most frequently judged to have been written by women" (p. 151).

Of particular interest is the fact that, notwithstanding the consistency in these gender guides, the success rates in distinguishing the gender of the writer seldom exceeded 66% of the judgments made on average. Evidently, substantial numbers of males and females do not fit their respective patterns.

In the United Kingdom and Canada, at the beginning of the twentieth century, the angular system of writing was taught exclusively to women in ladies' schools, and served to be indicative of gender. The angular system was not taught in the United States, but, because it became a fashionable style, it appealed to women anywhere, and so was imitated.

Osborn (1929) wrote that "the distinctive, angular, woman's hand is usually coarse and heavy and often of a sprawling awkward character with abnormally wide spacing between words and between lines and with horizontal concluding strokes to words" (p. 140). Handwriting has changed significantly in more recent years and the gender indicators of a century ago are no longer available. What indicators today's writings provide are not numerous and, just as gender guide indicators were 100 years ago, they may be misleading.

Gender is often indicated by the choice of words, cumbersome use of expressions or idioms characteristic of males or females. Threats of violence tend to be masculine, however threats using words such as *horrid* and *awful* are invariably feminine. Remarkably enough, in anonymous letters, the excessive and awkward use of profanity or lewdness is also a feminine characteristic.

Osborn (1929) maintained that the writing of women is, as a rule, more delicate containing more superfluous peculiarities and mannerisms. It is generally more finished. Shading, if present in older writings, is likely to be in bunches, particularly at ends of words. Heavy shading of every stroke, and jabs of the pen, is more often masculine. Studies of more recent times have generally confirmed Osborn's statements. Hodgins (1971) determined that good quality, small size, neatness, and fluency with carefulness were the bases for judging a writing to be that of a female.

Evidently, there is no historical basis for quality, neatness, and fluency being more characteristic of female than male writing. This seems the more remarkable when it is recalled that education, including penmanship, was, generally, the prerogative of males until the latter part of the nineteenth century. Bookkeeping, accounting, record keeping, and correspondence were male domains, almost until the advent of the typewriter in the late 1880s, when "typewriter" was a title accorded the female who mastered the mechanical keyboard.

Notwithstanding the apparent correlation between quality, neatness and fluency, and the gender of the writer, Hodgins (1971) found, as did Goodenough (1945) before him that accurate determinations as to gender could only be made in about 66% of the writings examined. Furthermore, Hodgins' panel of 25 judges consisting of 11 document examiners, 11 lay persons, and 3 master penmen, were not successful in making a correct gender determination of any one of 40 writing specimens 100% of the time. Totty et al. (1983) sought to correlate gender and handedness with writing slope, but found that the overlapping nature of the distributions would not permit it. Although their results suggest that males and right-handers tend to write with a greater forward slope than females and left-handers, but the results did not achieve statistical significance.

Fluckiger et al. (1961), in their review of the literature published between 1933 and 1959, stated that pressure seems to be the most important clue to gender, among all the clues considered. Along these lines Cambridge (1972) propounded that an evenness of and somewhat greater "pressure emphasis" in vertical strokes was indicative of masculinity, whereas an evenness of and somewhat greater "pressure emphasis" in horizontal strokes was indicative of femininity. Nevertheless, as Hodgins (1971) suggested, despite the fact that determinations of gender may be made with accuracy better than chance, the proportion of errors is high. The level of accuracy was not sufficient to warrant the use of handwriting to infer the gender of the writer.

Several studies have been conducted in search of psychosexual symbolism. It has been argued that handwriting need not be congruent with physical sex, but may simply reveal psychological masculinity and/or femininity of the writer. Lester et al. (1982) claimed that 11 of 40 aspects of writing significantly differentiated males and females in all age groups from 20 to 49. Anderson and Wolowitz (1984), attempting to test the claims of Freud (1900), found evidence in the proportions of the capital letter "I," when used as the personal pronoun, that seemed to confirm the male's preference for elongating constructions in contrast to women's better balance of proportions in the letter's construction.

Hecker (1996) reviewed and listed the success rates of 30 studies, conducted between 1906 and 1991, that endeavored to determine the gender differences in writing with reasonable accuracy. The results ranged from 57% accuracy to 94% with a mean of 71.7%. With these results, arguments have arisen as to how gender is defined: whether biologically or physiologically, whether psychologically in terms of femininity/masculinity, or in terms of dominance. Furthermore, there seems to be at least two methods of judging writing for gender indicators. One group takes a holistic approach and seeks evidence in the general character of the writing, or the appearance of the writing as a whole. Other researchers have sought to measure specific features (e.g., slant or size) in search of a correlation with gender. Another criticism of the methodology has been directed at the variability of the populations from which the samples were drawn. Goodenough (1945) and Hodgins (1971) suggested that the rater's gender had a bearing on the results, females being superior to males in judging the gender of writers, whereas earlier investigators did not seem to agree.

Hecker (1996) ran two studies of the digitized writing images in the FISH data pool. One employed pattern recognition and image processing techniques for feature extraction and classification. The second was a more traditional view of the digitized handwriting image in the FISH system in terms of conventional features such as slant, shape of loops, etc. Hecker's sample consisted of 96 males and 96 females between the ages of 16 and 40 years selected from writings in the FISH data base.

For comparison, the same samples were examined by 21 handwriting experts (4 females) of one of the German State Crime Labs, and 50 lay persons (22 females). The lab examiners and lay persons correctly judged the gender of the writer in 63% of the cases, the experts performing only slightly better than the nonexperts (64.7% vs. 62.3%). The writings of males were judged correctly by the experts in 76.5% of the cases and of females in 61.8% of the cases. There was considerable variation in the results of the raters.

Insofar as the computer data was concerned, discriminant analysis found higher coefficients for measured features such as the length of ascenders, the shape of upper loops and the size of lower loops. Factor analysis suggested three factors having some bearing on this type of study: the size of writing, the slant of writing and the shape of writing. The best rate of correct matches with gender was 72.4%, and the mean success rate resulting from computer-assisted feature processing was 71.5%, that can only be said to be superior to the 63% success rate of examiners and the 62.3% of nonexperts, but hardly acceptable.

It is Hecker's (1996) view that there are no group-specific handwriting features that can be attributed to the gender of writers. Females and males do exhibit different mean values for their various writing features, but there is invariably a large area of overlap. The only general statements that Hecker ventures to make are that females tend to write larger (contrary to the findings of others), more rounded, and more upright than males.

More recently, in a study carried out by Beech and Mackintosh (2005), laypersons were provided with 120 samples and asked to judge gender from handwriting. The study reported that the laypersons were able to judge the gender accurately in approximately 70% of the samples. The researchers evaluated the laypersons descriptions for the writing samples to determine why each sample was judged as male or female. The most common descriptions used for female samples included rounded, neater, circular, bubbly, and curvier. The judges described male writing as messier, smaller, more slanted, more scribbling out, spiky, and angular.

Using a computerized automatic handwriting recognition system, Liwicki et al. (2007) achieved a 67% accuracy rate in judging gender from online writing samples which surpassed the human raters used in the same study (57% accuracy). In another study by Liwicki et al. (2011), combined online and offline features were evaluated using an automatic handwriting system achieving a 68% accuracy rate. In an offline study using a dataset of over 1,000 writing samples in English and Arabic, Al Maadeed and Hassaine (2014) reported a 74% accuracy rate in predicting gender from handwriting. In a statistical study, Al Musa Alkahtani and Platt (2011b) found some indication that women may be better at signature simulation then men.

11.13 INDICATORS OF WRITING WITH THE NONDOMINANT HAND

In the discussions of dextrality and sinistrality in handwriting many terms have come into use to refer to the writing produced by the *other* hand. Some call it the *nonpreferred* hand, others the *unpracticed* or *unaccustomed* hand or the nondominant hand. Still others refer to it as the *awkward* or *unskilled* or *weak* hand and there are those who elect to call it simply the *off-hand* or *opposite* hand writing. Some of these designations are not as correct or descriptive as one would like to use. For dextral-sinistral writers (who were originally left-handed writers, but were trained to use the right), the left hand is hardly the nonpreferred hand. Moreover, the writing of these individuals with their left hands is often quite skilled, though it may or may not be as skillful as that produced by the hand enjoying greater or more frequent use. To say it is unskilled, however, would be an underestimation. It is equally incorrect to call it the weak hand, for it may well be the stronger of the two.

Except for the rare individual who is fully ambidextrous insofar as writing is concerned, the many studies of writing with the other hand are consistent in their findings. Regardless of the nature of the material under study, be it lettering, signatures, or extended cursive writing, when one changes to the "other" hand to hold the writing instrument, there is some loss, however great or small, in writing quality, fluency, or skill.

To induce some consistency in the language of writing examination, it appears much more appropriate to refer to the products of the other hand as writing or lettering of the nondominant hand. The terms selected must be equally applicable to both dextral and sinistral writers, yet indicative of the preference held by the individual.

From the viewpoint of forensic handwriting examination, any discussion of sinistrality or left-handedness must address the matter of nondominant hand writing regardless of the term chosen to indicate writing hand preference, be it *nonpreferred, awkward, unskilled, opposite, unaccustomed, subdominant,* or *weak* hand. For the most part, such writings appear in matters in which the writer has a reason to conceal his or her identity, such as in anonymous or threatening letters, or in hold-up notes presented with a demand for money. In these cases, writing with the nondominant hand is a chosen method of disguise, though the effectiveness of it is a matter that the writer seldom considers. There are also other instances, of course, in which the writing hand must be changed due to disease, injury or amputation.

Studies of the effectiveness of a change of hands to accomplish disguise have shown that, insofar as a sinistral using the right hand, in as many as 80% of the cases competent examiners have been able to accurately associate nondominant hand writing with that of the normal hand, and 87% of the time insofar as a dextral using the left hand (Comeau 1973). Comeau offered these results as support for Harrison's (1958b) contention that it is very difficult for most people to disguise their writing merely by using their unaccustomed hand. Comeau's samples consisting of 34 dextral and 6 sinistral were small, however, and thus, reliability of the study is somewhat in doubt.

In an earlier study, Stevens (1970) found 200 files of prison inmates in Wisconsin correction institutions containing sample signatures apparently executed with both hands. While some success appears to have been achieved in distinguishing nondominant handwritten signatures from normal regnant executions, the task was exacerbated by the fact that standards were limited to single samples from each hand.

A point that Stevens (1970) makes is that nondominant hand or awkward handwritten signatures, because of the loss of skill that they almost invariably exhibit, may be mistaken for traced signatures, writings of the aged or infirm, or simply ordinarily unskilled handwriting. Consequently, more specific characteristics are needed to discriminate between nondominant handwritten signatures and others that are executed under unusual circumstances.

While the use of the nondominant hand is addressed in most of the more recently published books on document examination, principally as a method of disguise, the formal studies that have been conducted and reported in the literature are relatively few. Harrison (1958b),

Conway (1959), Stangohr (1968), Anthony (1996), Sperry (1990), Zimmerman (1991), and Dawson (1985, 1993) have each claimed success in the identification of nondominant handwritings. These have been referred to variously as awkward hand, weak hand, or unaccustomed handwritings or letterings. The authors have described observations that these cases have proffered. Empirical data based on large samples, however, is limited. Nevertheless, what is available supports a number of general statements respecting writings of the nondominant hand.

Mature and practiced handwriting is substantially the product of the mind, implemented through a level of manual dexterity or muscular coordination peculiar to the individual. The mental picture of writing and of its characteristics does not change for the writer with a change of the hand chosen to operate the writing instrument.

Some have maintained that the difference between the writings of the dominant and the nondominant hands is due to a difference in manual dexterity and also to a difference in the neurophysiological processes that are involved (1985). While this may be so, there is little information as to precisely which changes are due to a difference in writing skill and which are attributable to a different mental process at work.

Whatever the reason for it, the writings, letterings, and signatures executed with the nondominant hand, as compared to those of the dominant hand, invariably display a loss of skill and fluency that is manifest in a number of fashions:

1. A reduction in writing speed that may result in a poorer line quality displaying tremor, abrupt changes in pen pressure and/or disconnections between letters of cursive writing (Figure 11.17).
2. A noticeable loss of pen or muscular control that is evident in the execution of curves, loops, eyelets, the retracing of staffs or stems between arches, and the quality of straight lines, such as "t" crossings, possible abrupt directional changes in lieu of smooth turns.
3. An inability to maintain consistency and quality in letter forms, letter sizes, letter alignments, terminations, and the finer movements with which some letters are constructed and others are connected.
4. An inability to maintain consistency in the slope of the writing or in particular letters, and perhaps a tendency to write more vertically.
5. A more deliberate inscription of diacritics and punctuation marks, although the pattern of use by the individual is not likely to change.

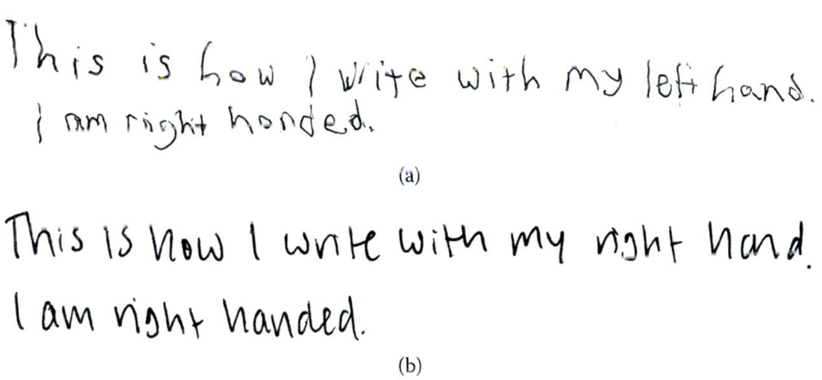

Figure 11.17 Example of nondominant handwriting (a). The writer is right-hand dominant (b).

6. The omission or abbreviation of initial and terminal strokes, however, terminal strokes are known to be somewhat variable in length and direction.
7. Some simplification of complex letter forms.
8. Hesitation and/or pen stops that may indicate some uncertainty as to succeeding movements.

Consistency between the written issues of the two hands can be expected in the following:

1. The relative sizes of internal letters in words, according to Hotimsky (1972). Relative sizes, however, may be subject to considerable modification. The control of the pen by the subdominant hand is, understandably, more difficult, and attention has to be concentrated on the creation of recognizable letter forms, regardless of normal writing habits. Relative sizes of letters tend to approach copybook. Indeed, as a general rule, any handwriting written under difficulty tends to lose its individuality and approach the copybook standard.
2. The basic designs of less complex letter forms, according to Newman (1975).
3. General lateral expansion. It has been suggested that writings of the subdominant hand will exhibit some increase in size, but studies of larger samples of writings, such as Newman's 120 subjects, did not prove this to be the case. One can expect an enlargement of the finer elements of writing, however, if only because the subdominant hand is not likely to function with the same dexterity as the other.

Greater consistency is to be found between the nondominant and dominant handwritings of sinistral rather than dextral writers. Generally speaking, left-handers produce a better quality of writing using their right hand than right-handers do with their left. It may be that most sinistrals have had some experience earlier on in an endeavor to convert or be converted to right-handers.

A study on the transfer of the handwriting hand after an injury showed that raters were able to match writing samples correctly between left- and right-handed samples with 89–100% accuracy (Yancosek and Mullineaux 2011). However, the caution expressed by Stevens (1970) and others bears repeating. Without adequate standards in number and kind, the writings of the nondominant hand can be easily confused with that of the aged or infirm, or mistaken for a spurious execution of one kind or another.

Chapter 12

Handwriting, Document Analysis, and Electronic Media

12.1 DOCUMENT EXAMINATION SCOPE OF WORK

Per Huber and Headrick, there are nine areas that frequently fall within the scope of study of the document examiner:

1. *Handwriting examinations*—including hand lettering and signatures
2. *Imprint examinations*—including those produced by manual devices (rubber stamps, dater stamps, and some postal cancellation stamps), mechanical devices (typewriters and check writers), electronic printing devices (typewriters, computer printers, time clocks, and cash registers), and including the manufacture of counterfeits (currency, negotiable instruments, travel documents, licenses and various personal credentials and identification documents)
3. *Reprographic examinations*—including photocopies, facsimile reproductions, machine generated writings and photographs
4. *Writing media examination*—including instruments, inks, and papers
5. *Dating examinations*—including absolute determinations (i.e., dates of introduction (DOI) of products) and relative determinations (i.e., the sequence of ink strokes with other ink strokes, printings, typewritings, perforations, and folds)
6. *Examination of falsifications and alterations*—including removals (i.e., erasures), changes, insertions, and substitutions
7. *Examination of invisible, faded, obscured writings and impressions of writings*—including those on charred documents
8. *Examination of preternatural paper characteristic*—including tears, fasteners (i.e., paper clips and staples), cuts, and perforations
9. *Miscellaneous examinations*—including envelope tampering, adhesives, laminations, typist's characteristics, and linguistics

In addition to identifying or eliminating particular persons with a questioned writing, some of these various examinations might be further described as endeavors to determine:

1. Whether and what alterations have occurred to the document
2. Whether writing media (i.e., instrument, ink or paper) is related or similar to that of known sources
3. Whether writing abnormalities occurred, for example, age, infirmity, alcohol, or drugs
4. What can be said about the typewriting or electronic printing, if present, and its relationship to particular machines?

5. What was the sequence in which two or more inscriptions were executed?
6. What was the sequence in which inscriptions, folds, or perforations occurred?
7. What were the absolute dates of origin of inscriptions?
8. What can be said about the nature or source of the materials involved?
9. What can be said about a document's preternatural characteristics?
10. What can be said about the indentations a document may bear?
11. What can be said about the original text of a faded, erased, obliterated, or charred document?
12. What can be said about the process and/or the equipment involved in producing the document?
13. What can be said about the integrity of the printed document (i.e., genuine or counterfeit or perhaps valid or forged)?
14. What is the generation of the reproduction (e.g., a [2] copy produced from a [1] copy produced from an [0] original)?

The Scientific Working Group for Forensic Document Examination (SWGDOC) published its *Standard for Scope of Work of Forensic Document Examiners* in 2013 and defines the document examiner's job description: "The forensic document examiner makes scientific examinations, comparisons, and analyses of documents in order to: (1) establish genuineness or nongenuineness, or to expose forgery, or to reveal alterations, additions, or deletions, (2) identify or eliminate persons as the source of handwriting, (3) identify or eliminate the source of typewriting or other impression, marks, or relative evidence, and (4) write reports or give testimony, when needed, to aid the users of the examiner's services in understanding the examiner's findings" (p. 1).

12.2 DOCUMENT ANALYSIS AND NONHANDWRITING EXAMINATIONS

Examinations of documents for purposes other than handwriting identification frequently require examination of original documents. Other requirements on the part of the examiner include:

1. Knowledge of products and product manufacture
2. Experience with materials and their performance
3. Understanding of appropriate technologies
4. Knowledge of scientific method and its application in testing

Generally, nonhandwriting examinations are conducted in the following ways:

1. Study of the consistencies and inconsistencies of various aspects or elements of the questioned document
2. Comparison of the particular characteristics, features or properties of a document or of the inscription thereon, that may be either physical or chemical, with the known or recorded characteristics emanating from formulations or particular processes of production
3. Use of special instrumentation:
   a. Stereomicroscope
   b. Low power magnification, using episcopic (reflected) and diascopic (transmitted) light facilities

c. Photographic facilities
d. Electrostatic facilities
e. Sources of ultraviolet and infrared radiation and a means of observing the fluorescence they promote
f. Appropriate physical or chemical analytical facilities
g. Collections of standard products, including type styles, writing instruments, writing inks, writing papers, and watermarks

Some examinations in the practice of document examination deal with factual matters (e.g., a feature or condition is present or absent), and are, therefore, more objective in nature. In such cases, definitive statements can frequently be made. In other instances involving documents with printed inscriptions, investigative leads and other information respecting the source of the document can be obtained through a study of the typestyle of the lettering. Typestyles employed on typewriters, printers, and facsimile machines may be searched against collections of typestyles that are constantly being produced and upgraded. These collections will permit a style to be identified by name or design, and in some cases can provide information as to the equipment on which it might have been installed.

The association of a questioned document with a particular piece of equipment is a more complex task depending usually upon a fault in the equipment that makes itself evident in the printed product in some atypical fashion. The level of certainty in a conclusion of identity respecting a given machine will vary with the uniqueness of the fault or circumstance of the machine. Suffice it to say, with today's constantly changing technology, an examiner is constantly challenged as to the adequacy of his or her knowledge.

The identification of inks, differentiation of inks, and relative age of ink inscriptions are questions that frequently arise in document examination. Proving whether the ink is the same or different between two samples may require the knowledge of an ink chemist. Most document examiners do not specialize in chemical ink identification or in questions involving ink age, but many document examiners have training in ink differentiation and general ink identification through visual characteristics. Differences between, for example, ballpoint ink and fluid ink can frequently be differentiated using visual techniques. The document examiner may be able to illustrate the effects of differences in the physical/chemical properties of inks, if such differences are present. If the inks appear visually similar, chemical techniques or special instruments (e.g., ink chromatography) may need to be employed in order to prove chemical similarity. While many studies have been published on ink analysis, Brunelle and Reed (1984) and Brunelle and Crawford (2003) have written foundational texts on the forensic examination of ink and paper.

A forensic document examiner may not be a specialist in all areas of document examination. For example, there are those who specialize in the examination of inks or typewriting. However, the document examiner needs to have at least a fundamental knowledge in all areas of document examination and its associated testing so that the examiner may more fully know his or her own limitations and provide guidance about appropriate tests or analyses. Even when a document examiner is consulted about a handwriting identification problem, there may be multiple questions associated with the document that requires knowledge about paper, print processes, and ink line sequence, especially in cases involving signature image manipulation or transfer to other documents (Figure 12.1). In such cases, the examiner needs to know the appropriate tests and protocol in conducting a complete examination of the document.

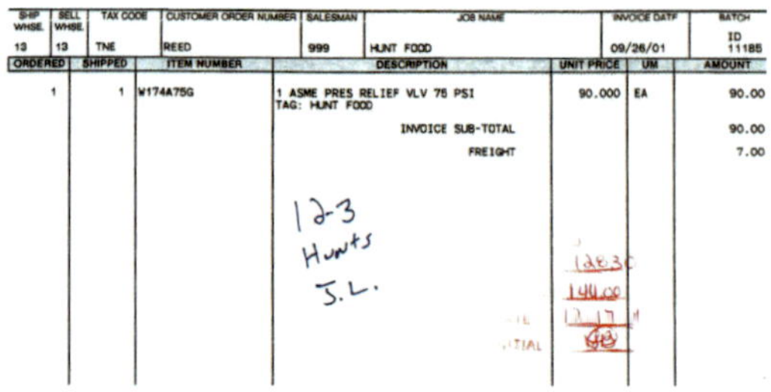

(a)

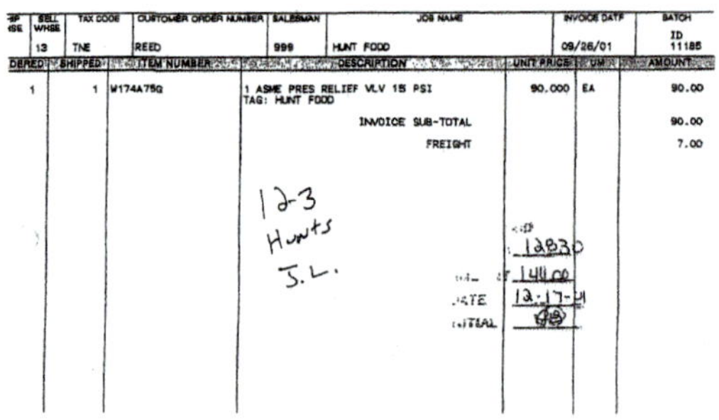

(b)

Figure 12.1 Example of an altered document. A boiler blew up and killed two workers in a plant. A safety inspection showed that the pressure relief valve exceeded the recommended pressure. A 15 psi valve was recommended but a 75 psi valve was installed. A review of the invoice (a) on file with the victim company showed a 75 psi valve was purchased. However, the installing company produced a xerographic copy of an invoice (b) showing a 15 psi valve was installed. The installer attempted to alter the invoice by deleting the number 7 and pasting a number 1 in its place using a common photographic software program. The item number identifying the part is actually for a 75 psi valve.

12.3 DIGITIZED HANDWRITING AND NONORIGINAL DOCUMENTS

In order to analyze a signature digitally, and examine nonoriginal documents, there is a greater need to understand the technology behind digitization. In the modern, computerized world, digital technology has revolutionized images in television, film, music, and photography. While advances in digitization of signatures has allowed the digitization of handwriting when writing a signature on a digital tablet, digitization of signatures has been occurring for several years through scanning, facsimile, and photography of documents.

The process of digitization involves the conversion of information (such as documents) into bits or bytes. These bits are points or samples of information. The higher the number of bits, the higher the resolution and closer approximation the digital process has to the analog signal. Resolution is typically measured in pixels. There are two primary ways of acquiring digital information. With handwriting, the digital signature can be scanned from a source document, or the signature can be captured using a digital device such as a tablet and stylus. Special software can be involved in capturing the signature digitally, or the tablet and stylus serve as a replacement for a mouse and the signature can be drawn and captured onto the computer screen.

Digitization of signatures is quite a different process from what is popularly referred to as a "digital signature." The nomenclature in the area of digital signatures is confusing and frequently a term can mean two or more types of signatures from a technical viewpoint. A digital signature in computer security terms refers to an algorithm-based, computer-encoded "signature." This type of "signature" is comprised of encrypted computer code and has no resemblance in process or product to a manuscript signature written on a digital tablet (which can be referred to as an electronic, biometric, or dynamic signature). A digital signature is a secure mathematical formula that is encrypted so that the receiver of the document knows the document has been sent by the intended sender. The National Institute of Standards and Technology (2009) defines a digital signature as "an electronic analogue of a written signature" (p. 9).

An electronically-captured signature is one in which the signer employs conventional methods in physically signing a signature, except instead of using traditional ink and paper, the signer writes on a tablet or screen with a stylus or fingertip. This type of signature is also referred to as a biometric or dynamic signature, which is recorded using online handwriting capturing methods that record not only the spatial properties of a signature, but also temporal characteristics such as the velocity and duration measurements (Figure 12.2). Capturing a signature "online" refers to recording the handwriting movement in real time, usually on a digital tablet.

A digitized signature could also refer to a pen and ink signature that has been scanned or faxed and thereby "digitized" for purposes of storage, capture, or even handwriting verification. Scanned handwriting is also used in handwriting recognition software. These types of signatures are also referred to as offline signatures, because the static image of the signature is digitized with no biodynamic information available (Figure 12.3). Digital and electronic signatures are sometimes used together to secure an electronically-captured handwriting signature onto a document. Some systems use both the digital and electronic signature together, while other systems employ only one type of signature.

The digitization of handwriting has made modern inventions such as handwriting recognition technology and automated forensic handwriting analysis technology possible. Handwriting recognition is the technology used to convert handwritten characters into text-based characters using optical character recognition. Initially, such technology was used by scanning documents and converting the handwritten characters into text read on a computer screen. However, now handwriting recognition is also used to convert online handwriting into text-based characters. In the first process, the handwriting is considered "offline" meaning that the handwriting is scanned and recognized from static handwriting on a document. "Online" handwriting recognition refers to the conversion of handwriting into text while the person is writing in real time on a tablet.

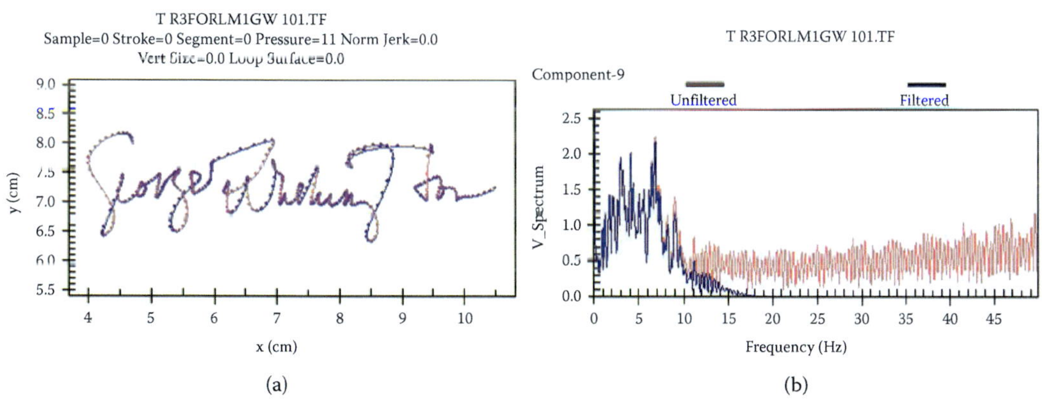

Figure 12.2 Example of a handwriting sample (a) and its frequency spectrum data captured on a digital tablet using NeuroScript MovAlyzeR software (b).

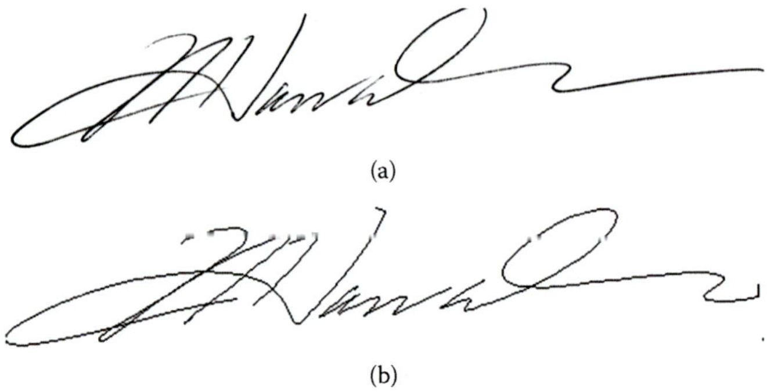

Figure 12.3 A normal pen and paper signature (a) and a signature captured using a digital tablet (b). Note the ragged or blocky appearance of the digital signature.

In handwriting recognition, handwriting feature extraction and classification are used in the process of optical character recognition (or OCR). Handwriting recognition technology is also used in handwriting identification research. An example of such research involves the application of a system originally intended as a handwriting recognition system, used by the United States Postal Service for reading postal addresses. This system was used in an experiment that proved the individuality of handwriting (Srihari et al. 2002). Aside from signature and document authentication and verification, handwriting recognition is also used for check processing in banks, address recognition, and research of historical documents.

Digitization of handwriting or signatures involves scanning and facsimile. The quality of the handwriting is dependent upon the resolution quality of the scan, measurable in dots per inch (dpi). Low resolution will cause the signature to produce a pixelized or digitized effect that can make the line quality of the signature appear ragged. Higher resolution will reduce the pixelized look, but under high enough magnification, pixels are observed instead of the characteristics of the ink line quality.

Digitization is also seen in digital photography of signatures in addition to electronically-captured signatures. In order to smooth the line quality of enlarged images, a digital processing feature such as interpolation is used. When there is a known set of captured data points, as frequently found in electronically-captured signatures, further processing can be achieved through interpolation. Rather than gathering 200 sample points per second, 100 sample points can be gathered and interpolation is used to fill in the gaps. In mathematics, regression analysis or curve fitting is used to construct new data points between the range of known data points. Interpolation is also used in digital photography, especially in optical zoom features which fill in the gaps between points of digital data when enlarging the image. Some scanner software also uses interpolation.

Analysis of digitized handwriting presents some challenges in handwriting examination. First, a computerized signature image is much easier to manipulate on documents than the hard copy version of a signature on paper that required a duplicate copy and mechanical cut and paste techniques, sometimes involving tape and scissors. Digitized handwriting provides a simpler, cleaner process that leaves less evidence of transfer on the final manipulated version.

The discussion of digitized handwriting brings up the topic of copy quality and its impact on the analysis of handwriting. Copy quality is a variable that can influence the accuracy of a conclusion by an examiner and the quality of the copy is a factor that examiners need to take into consideration when rendering conclusions. Standards of practice recommend qualifying or limiting conclusions when analyzing copies and this is one of the limitations that should be discussed in an examiner's report. The SWGDOC Standard for Examination of Handwritten Items (2013c) states that examination of nonoriginal documents is a potential interference or limitation. The standard specifies that examining from original writing is preferable and that if original writing is not submitted, the examiner is to request the original. The standard specifies that "if the original is not submitted, evaluate the quality of the best available reproduction to determine whether the significant details of the writing have been reproduced with sufficient clarity for comparison purposes and proceed to the extent possible. If the writing has not been reproduced with sufficient clarity for comparison purposes, discontinue these procedures and report accordingly" (p. 2). Slyter (1995) discusses copy quality when examining signatures and factors that into his recommended standard of practice as a potential limitation.

Historically, poor quality handwriting images were a by-product of multiple generation copies from photocopy machines that caused the photographed handwriting image to deteriorate and distort. Other effects that contributed to poor quality images included poorly operating or poorly maintained copy machines, low toner settings, or a machine low in toner producing an image that is too light or distorted to produce noticeably fine detail.

While many of these issues are still inherent problems when working with copies or reproductions, digitization has other effects. While the scanner in a copy machine or printer can be set to a high resolution (depending on the machine), the storage and processing demands are high. Many documents are scanned at low resolutions (e.g., bank checks) to keep storage requirements to a minimum and to allow faster processing of files. For example, a signature scanned at 70 dpi will have far less information or detail available for examination than a signature scanned at 600 dpi. If scanned in a black and white setting, without grayscale, other details pertaining to the signature's dynamic movement are also not recognizable (Figure 12.4). Pixel gradients, black-white transitions, and average gray value of pixels is digital language that expresses line quality and ink trace features that are relied upon in automatic handwriting verification research. These types of features are typically evaluated by a handwriting examiner with a microscope and are considered line quality characteristics.

In spite of the limitations associated with copies, document examiners are able to render accurate conclusions when working with copies. Found et al. (2001a) did not find differences in opinions expressed by examiners when provided with originals or copies. Found and Rogers (2005) carried out a proficiency study using both originals and copies and determined that examiners are able to offer accurate conclusions from copies. For several years, Found and Rogers offered proficiency tests on signatures and handwriting through LaTrobe University's Forensic Expertise Profiling Laboratory. They submitted digitized images to document examiners for

(a) (b) (c)

Figure 12.4 A handwritten letter K appearing in a photograph (a) as a xerographic copy (b), and scanned on a flatbed scanner (c). Note the pixelated scanned image due to low-resolution scanning.

testing purposes. The test materials were typically full color, high-resolution images provided both in printed and digital formats. Found and Rogers were able to characterize examiner proficiency in several published studies using nonoriginal materials. Dawson and Lindblom (1998) tested document examiners assessing line quality from photocopies and found that the examiners could identify ink line characteristics from average quality photocopies and were able to make accurate judgments regarding line quality. In the study, they noted that in a few instances "striation patterns and ink gooping were misinterpreted as pen lifts, hesitation and patching on the photocopies" (p. 189).

The copies submitted to examiners were characterized as "average" in the Dawson and Lindblom (1998) study. In the Found and Rogers (2005) study, the signatures submitted for examination were written with a ballpoint pen and serially photocopied twice in order to provide examiners with examples of second-generation copies. While document examiners are able to provide accurate conclusions when working with copies, the copy quality needs to be assessed as there are a number of cases in which the copy quality is so poor that a conclusion cannot or should not be rendered. While there is some subjectivity in the evaluation of copy quality, but when poor quality copies are examined, the examiner needs to provide qualifying conclusions.

Found and Bird (2016) devoted an entire module in their standard of practice to the topic of nonoriginal handwriting and addressed several issues concerning examination of copies. A primary reason why examiners are cautious with copies concerns manipulation and manufacture of signatures and handwriting using mechanical or electronic methods. A genuine signature can be manually or digitally copied from one document and pasted, placed, or inserted onto another document. The document is recopied or printed essentially forming a new document. Historically, the characteristics associated with manual or mechanical cut and paste techniques include, for example, shading around the edges of the cut and pasted signature, isolated signatures that do not overlap or are misplaced with respect to the document, misalignment, and other characteristics. These types of characteristics frequently do not occur in digitally manipulated documents. If the source document is available for analysis, the original and copy of the signatures can be compared to determine that they are the same. However, the source signature may not be available. Further, signatures can be digitally manipulated so that they do not resemble the source signature thereby creating alternate versions of the source signature. When working with digital copies, there may not be evidence on the questioned document or comparative evidence from another document to make determinations as to its authenticity. Due to these factors, it is common practice for document examiners to provide qualifying statements in reporting conclusions concerning the limitations associated in working with copies.

The copies or nonoriginal documents provided to document examiners are likely to come in many different formats. Examiners work with digital photographs of varying quality. Resolution on most digital cameras can also be changed. Photographs of documents are also taken with cell phone cameras and submitted to document examiners. Digital photographs submitted may be high-resolution, close-up images of handwriting that allow for analysis of line quality detail and can be enlarged for demonstrative purposes. Enlargement of average resolution images results in a highly pixelated image not useful for analysis or demonstration. It is obvious that digital photographs that are blurry or out of focus are not useful, but examiners may receive photographs taken of writing or graffiti on walls, bathroom stalls, cars, or in similar unusual places or surfaces where lighting conditions were poor or it was difficult to obtain close-up images of the writing. These may be the only photographs available if the writing was subsequently removed. In such cases, the examiner may need to rely upon poor quality photographs that do not provide the sort of detail available from high-resolution images.

It is not uncommon for examiners to receive electronic files of low resolution, black and white images of bank checks that are also distorted or compressed in size. Examiners may also be provided with hard copies of mortgage or banking documents bearing a poor quality, digitized image of a signature without realizing that the signature may have never been written in ink on paper. Instead, it may be a copy of a digitally-captured signature written on a digital tablet with a blunt stylus. Electronically captured signatures are sometimes stored and the images of the signatures provided for analysis without any context as to the instrument used or on what surface the signature was written.

Purported original documents need to be evaluated carefully and verified that the documents are indeed original. The sophistication of color copy printers is such that they are used to counterfeit currency. To the unaided eye, a high-resolution color copy of a document with a signature signed in blue ink may appear original, especially if the preparer of the document wrote over the signature creating pressure indentation to simulate a real ink signature. Typically, a microscopic analysis of the ink line is necessary to differentiate between printing effects and ink effects. For these reasons, document examiners need to be prudent in assessing nonoriginal documents and appropriately qualifying their conclusions.

12.4 DIGITAL AND ELECTRONIC HANDWRITING

With the advent of digital or electronic signature technology, the handwriting examiner is called upon to examine handwriting produced on digital tablets and converted to a digital ink image. Harralson (2013) provided an introduction to the topic and developed a method for the analysis of electronic signatures for document examiners. That discussion is summarized here along with other more recent studies.

In 2000, a bill was passed in the United States making digital signatures as legally binding for contracts as manuscript signatures written with an ink pen on paper. The European Union passed a similar law in 1999. Digital signatures are in widespread use internationally, although not in all countries. The Electronic Signatures in Global and National Commerce Act of 2000 specifies a general rule of validity with respect to electronic signatures: "a signature, contract, or other record relating to such transaction may not be denied legal effect, validity, or enforceability because it is in electronic form" (Federal Trade Commission 2001).

There has been an attempt to define a digital or electronic signature and to understand comprehensively what an electronic signature may represent from a legal perspective. The act provides several definitions for terms used throughout the document. Specifically, "electronic signature" is defined as "an electronic sound, symbol, or process, attached to or logically associated with a contract or other record and executed or adopted by a person with the intent to sign the record." This definition clearly shows the broad use of the term "electronic signature" which could be an algorithm based digital signature or an electronically-captured handwritten signature, and does not distinguish between these two types of electronic signatures.

Mason (2010), in a review of electronic signatures globally, found that "there is no specific provision for the concept of an advanced electronic signature in the Act" (p. 331). Mason sets forth that a signature is an intentional act that encompasses not only ink on paper but also includes wax seals as a type of signature. As such, Mason specifies several intents that can be construed as electronic signatures: typing a name onto a document, an e-mail address, clicking "I accept" icon, a PIN, a biodynamic signature, a scanned signature, and a digital signature. According to

Mason, “a biodynamic signature of a manuscript signature uses a special pen and pad measure and records the action of the person as they sign. This creates a digital version of the manuscript signature” (p. 333).

12.4.1 Electronic Handwriting Hardware

The digital tablet is an important component in the capture of digitized signatures. There are an ever-growing number of devices involved with signature and handwriting capture including tablet PCs, PDAs, mobile phones, and other devices. The different tablet devices available on the market can influence the quality of the handwriting signal (Figure 12.5). Commercially-available tablets manufactured by Wacom and used extensively in handwriting research, rely on electromagnetic induction to transmit and receive information to and from the stylus. The stylus also contains electronics for receiving and transmitting information. These signals help establish the position of the stylus on the tablet. Other tablets that exclusively receive information from the stylus can result in less white noise in the signal. Alonso-Fernandez et al. (2005), in a handwriting verification experiment, found that certain tablets perform better due to the sampling frequency oscillation.

Tablets are able to receive signal information from the stylus without the stylus touching the tablet. This helps in determining the location of the stylus above the tablet (known as pen position), pen tilt, and x and y positions on the tablet. One of the characteristics analyzed from the information above the tablet surface involves air strokes (the strokes produced in the air when a person is breaking between letters or words and creates a pen lift). Some of the unique handwriting features captured by the digitization of signatures allows for novel methods in forensic handwriting examination.

Touchpads or touch screens are also used for producing signatures. Some devices allow for writing with both the stylus and the touchpad interchangeably. The touchpad is pressure-sensitive to the fingertip. Research has shown that there are user performance differences in point-selected tasks between the touchpad and the mouse (Akamatsu and MacKenzie 2002). The touchpad, along with one’s fingertip, is all that is needed for signing one’s signature. No additional devices, such as stylus or mouse, are necessary. This technology increases convenience and allows for signing signatures on laptop computers, tablet computers, and on cell phones. Point-of-sale signatures using a touchpad-based cell phone connected to a credit card capturing device are widely used Figure 12.6).

Convenience is a primary factor for the popularity and widespread use of touchpad-based signatures, but the physical limitations of these signatures do not allow for handwriting

Figure 12.5 Four signatures of the same person as signed on a police officer’s handheld PDA device.

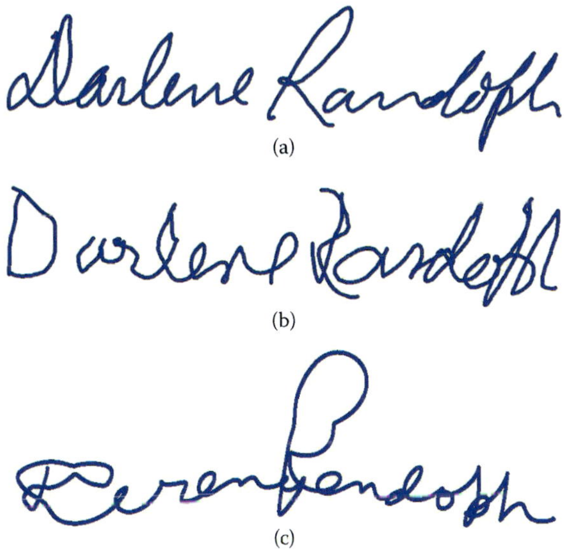

Figure 12.6 A writer signing signature with a stylus (a), finger (b), and with a mouse (c).

precision. Research into touchpads has shown that error rates are a problem when the device is held in the hand, but the errors are also due to the small size of the strokes in comparison to the width of the fingertip (Isokoski and Kaki 2002). Handwriting was developed using fine-tipped writing instruments like quills, fountain pens, ballpoint pens, and the stylus. The breadth of the fingertip in writing small, narrow movements diminishes the precision in the fine detail of the signature.

A digital pen or stylus is used in conjunction with digital tablets, tablet PCs, and mobile devices. Electronic ink is the digitized handwriting seen on a digital display and is sometimes converted to print characters using handwriting recognition technology. Not all graphic signatures are captured using a stylus as some systems allow users to use a mouse to sign the signature. There are manufacturers that state that such signatures are forensically reliable, even though using a mouse is highly awkward for the signer. In fact, research has shown that signing with a mouse may render a signature unreliable, especially when it is compared to nonrepresentative samples (Harralson et al. 2011). Signatures can also be signed with the tip of a finger, using a pressure-sensitive touchpad. While this type of signature may allow the writer more control over the fine motor movements than a mouse, touchpad finger signatures are still more awkward in comparison to signing with a pen on paper or even with a digital pen or stylus.

Computer technology has created new writing instruments, although some make the handwriting task uncomfortable and awkward. Many of the stylus pens used with graphics tablets are constructed similar in shape to a real pen. When the signer holds the stylus, it feels like a pen and allows for natural handwriting movement. Some styluses are outfitted with plastic pen nibs that glide across the surface of the tablet in a slippery way. A sensor within some of the more sophisticated digital pens can detect pressure and using pressure on the stylus on the tablet replaces clicking on a mouse.

While the stylus allows for writing a signature with greater detail and precision than writing with a fingertip, not all styluses have the same level of technological sophistication.

Especially when signers encounter point-of-sale devices, the stylus can be notoriously bulky and awkward—ill-fitted to the task of producing a detailed and accurate signature. Some are as simple as a plastic stick with a pointed tip, with no associated electronics inside the pen. Some devices that produce "digital ink" on the display (the trace left behind on the surface of some digital tablet displays) have a plastic stylus attached to the pad. Others are the equivalent of writing with what feels like an unsharpened crayon or a stick with a wide tip. There are soft stylus nibs with broad rubber tips that prevent scratching the surface of the display. Some large stylus nibs are not conducive to writing inside small signature-sized tablet boxes. In some instances, the broad stylus is comparatively too large for the small size of the tablet or display associated with the stylus. Harralson et al. (2011) carried out a study comparing the handwriting samples between three different "pens" (inking digital pen, digital stylus, and mouse). In the experiment, it was found that there was decreased complexity, fine detail, and coordination in some of the signatures written with noninking pens.

Some pressure-sensitive pads allow for both a stylus and a fingertip, and signing with one's finger is popular on iPhones and other similar pads of different dimensions. The same dimension problems also apply between a small tablet or display and a fingertip signing a signature. A fingertip is usually too broad and blunt for the size of the display and does not allow for the production of fine detail frequently associated with pen nibs. However, Robertson and Guest (2015) were able to find some features (e.g., jerk, size, duration, pen travel distance) that allowed for potential biometric uses when examining signatures produced on touch-screen tablets.

Many tablets can also be used with a mouse. While signing one's signature with a computer mouse is not particularly intuitive or natural, it is encouraged by some companies that advertise electronic signature technology. This type of signing creates multiple levels of challenge for producing accurate and consistent signatures. The mouse is awkward and does not allow for the traditional "tripod" grip on the pen which allows for maximum manual control in handwriting. Further, watching the writing on a computer screen instead of on a tablet or paper can also seem awkward and unnatural, especially if the writer has problems directing the mouse to sign within a certain field or box on the computer screen. The mouse, just like the stylus, also has differing degrees of accuracy depending on the device.

12.4.2 Examination of Electronic Signatures

What constitutes or defines a "digital signature" is broad in scope, and the terminology for this technology-based signature is inconsistent. Because there is variance in terminology relating to digital, electronic, and biometric signatures, these terms are also defined in the glossary. Harralson (2013) developed a methodology and categorized the three types of electronic or digital signatures in which a document examiner may be consulted: (1) digital cryptographic signature; (2) biometric or dynamic handwritten signature; (3) and static handwritten signature.

While analysis of a digital cryptographic signature is beyond the scope of most handwriting examiners, as it does not involve a physical "handwriting" process, it is still mentioned as part of the methodology because it represents a limitation in the scope of work of handwriting examiners. Document examiners receive analysis requests about cryptographic-based "signatures" so it is important to include these digital algorithms as part of the methodology and their subsequent limitations for handwriting examiners. Document examiners can educate themselves about the security requirements for digital signatures and their analysis so as to give clients and investigators more informed advice about their analysis and refer to a digital evidence specialist when appropriate. It is sometimes important for document examiners to know how a digital signature may be a part of the digital signing process as digital signatures and electronic handwritten signatures are sometimes used together in signing a document. In these instances, digital evidence specialists and forensic handwriting examiners may need to work together in the document analysis. It is recommended that document examiners develop a broad understanding of digital signatures so that they can guide clients about the correct type of analysis. Laypersons may not know the difference between digital signatures and handwritten electronic signatures.

A handwritten biometric signature involves the capture of computerized data, usually a combination of online and offline characteristics. If no biometric characteristics have been captured, but there is a graphic representation of a handwritten signature presented for analysis, then the examiner needs to treat the signature as an electronic static signature. Additionally, even if it is known that biometric data was captured but is not presented to the examiner or is for some reason unavailable, the examiner still needs to limit the opinion according to the guidelines for static signatures. When biometric data is available, the examiner should also make inquiries about how the data was stored and transmitted in order to ensure that the data is reliable. An inquiry about the signing conditions (tablet and stylus used) in addition to the quality of the data (hertz rate) is all a part of the analysis and should be reflected by the level of opinion provided.

The next step in the analysis of biometric or dynamic signatures involves handwriting feature analysis. At this stage, the examiner evaluates the individualizing character of the captured handwriting features as well as their reliability both in terms of standards already established in forensic handwriting examination, and available research about online dynamic features. There are numerous features that can be used in analysis, but research has shown that certain characteristics are more consistent and reliable than others. Some of the well-known features that can be analyzed via online methods include duration, stroke sequence, velocity, acceleration, pressure, and other factors.

The features that showed consistency and reliability included the speed of the x and y coordinates, the x and y coordinate sequence, and the angle with the x axis (Lei and Govindaraju 2005). The most significant features included pressure measures, vertical and horizontal position, pen azimuth, pen elevation, velocity measures, acceleration measures, and radius of curvature (Richiardi et al. 2005). Features with stronger results included total time, various velocity and acceleration measurements, average pressure, length, and pen-down time (Tariq et al. 2011). In selecting robust online features, Liwicki (2012) listed several measurements that included horizontal and vertical positions, pressure, acceleration measures, pen azimuth, and pen elevation, comparing features between genuine and simulated signatures across three classifications (size, complexity, and legibility). Nicolaides (2012) studied measures associated with acceleration and reported on their usefulness in signature examination. Ahmad et al. (2013) reported that pen pressure was a distinctive feature. Linden et al. (2016) found that signature size, trajectory length, and signature time were features useful in distinguishing between genuine and simulated signatures.

Insufficient or unreliable handwriting characteristics would result in an inconclusive opinion, especially if there were no comparable specimens available for comparison. It has been noted by researchers and developers of handwriting verification systems that one characteristic alone is not sufficient to establish handwriting identification; it is the combination of characteristics that establishes identification (Srihari et al. 2002; Franke et al. 2004).

Even if the questioned signature was captured with sophisticated biometric or dynamic data, the comparison signatures also need to be comparable with the questioned signature. Just as in any forensic signature case, the number of comparison samples need to be adequate, contemporaneous, and written under similar conditions. So, if the electronic signature was written with finger on a touchpad, ideally the comparison signatures would also be written in a similar manner. Some systems have a database of signatures used for enrollment, but many of these systems only capture a few signatures which may not be adequate depending on handwriting factors such as complexity and range of variation. When there are a sufficient number of biometric signatures available and captured under similar conditions, the dynamic and static features available in biometric or dynamic signatures can allow for conclusive opinions. When only static signatures are available for comparative analysis (these may be digitized or pen and paper signatures), qualified opinions may be possible especially if a stylus was used in creating the biometric signature.

Harralson et al. (2013) evaluated the effects of static and dynamic handwriting data on examiner proficiency. Student document examiners initially examined both genuine and simulated static electronic signatures. The students were later provided additional dynamic information associated with the signatures. The results showed a decrease in erroneous conclusions when the students were provided both static and dynamic information.

The third signature type, static handwritten signatures, can also be referred to as digitized signatures and were discussed in the previous section. These signatures are captured on an electronic device, but no biometric data or computer files are associated with the digitized image. The examiner may receive the signature either as a digitized electronic page (such as a PDF file with an image of the signature on the document) or as a hard copy print-out. Because of the digital manipulation that can occur with these signatures, it may not be possible to conclusively associate the signature with the document and the examiner may be limited to making opinions about the handwriting characteristics of the signature only. Evaluating the resolution quality of the signature is important. Any digitized signature should be evaluated for electronic signature production. Sometimes examiners receive hard copies of questioned signatures not realizing that the questioned signature had been written with an electronic device. If the signature was signed on a device and then transferred and embedded onto the document, the digitized signature may have an awkward or unnatural size with respect to the signature space on the document. The signature may also not interact with the baseline or surrounding signature area. Signatures that are embedded onto documents may also be reduced in size. A digitized signature with poor resolution (highly pixelated) and limited handwriting characteristics should be evaluated with caution, and inconclusive opinions are recommended. High-resolution quality in combination with comparison signatures captured in a similar electronic environment can lead to qualified opinions that take into account the limitations associated with digitized signatures.

Chapter 13

Evaluating Document Examiner Competency

13.1 SOURCES FOR COMPETENT DOCUMENT EXAMINERS

While there is no single source for information respecting the qualifications and competence of practicing document examiners, there are a few established organizations that offer certification programs and publish a list of their certified members. The American Board of Forensic Document Examiners (ABFDE) and the Board of Forensic Document Examiners (BFDE) publish, annually, a list of practitioners whom they have tested and certified and who are, thereby, entitled to the designation *diplomate*. The National Association of Document Examiners (NADE) also publishes a list of certified practitioners on its website.

The American Society of Questioned Document Examiners (ASQDE) was established by Albert S. Osborn in 1942. Later, other professional organizations offering levels of membership and/or certification were established. These include the NADE, an organization founded in 1980, and the Association of Forensic Document Examiners (AFDE), formed in 1986. The certification programs offered by these organizations include requirements to demonstrate continuing proficiency in their respective continuing education programs. Certification renewal in these programs is required every 5 years.

In 2000, the Forensic Specialties Accreditation Board (FSAB), with support and assistance from the American Academy of Forensic Sciences, the National Forensic Science Technology Center, and the National Institute of Justice, established a board to accredit forensic specialty certification boards. FSAB requires comprehensive testing, adherence to a professional code of ethics, and continuing education. While FSAB accreditation is not mandatory, it provided a step toward the consolidation and unification of certification in the forensic sciences. Currently, the National Institute of Standards and Technology (NIST) oversees the Organization of Scientific Area Committees for Forensic Science (OSAC) which is facilitating the development of standards and guidelines for a broad array of forensic disciplines. The goal is to help unify and consolidate the minimum standards required for training, certification, and examination procedures in the forensic fields. NIST recommends that certifying bodies should be accredited to ISO/IEC 17024 (International Organization for Standardization, 2012).

13.2 EVALUATING PROFICIENCY AND COMPETENCE

13.2.1 Academic Qualification

Within the profession it is generally agreed that a baccalaureate degree from a recognized university is a first requirement, preferably in a field of science, but psychology, mathematics, and other fields might also be considered appropriate. Universities in the United States offer degrees in forensic science that devote some coursework to the subject of document examination.

It is generally held that university education reflects a basic level of intelligence and understanding that document examination requires. The ASQDE, AAFS, ABFDE, and BFDE all currently require a 4-year university degree as a minimum level of academic achievement.

13.2.2 Training

University training in document examination was reviewed in more detail in Chapter 3. Forensic document examination graduate-level degrees are offered at East Tennessee State University and at Oklahoma State University. Both programs are offered in online formats making them more widely accessible to students in the United States and internationally. Both programs state that a degree in forensic document examination does not qualify one to become certified in a professional organization or to practice professionally. After completing university courses (which are usually components of broader forensic or criminal justice programs), the student needs to obtain practical, supervised experience in order to complete the recommended 2-year training.

In the United States, many private practitioners were formerly trained in municipal, state, and federal forensic laboratories in major cities. It must be emphasized, however, that while government labs are the institutions in which training is received by a large number of examiners, there is little standardization in the training programs provided largely due to the fact that they are based on the apprenticeship system. Some government document examination laboratories consist of one or two individuals who endeavor to train their own replacements. Similarly, many private practitioners employ understudies that assist in the preparation of exhibits for court purposes, the maintenance of collections of samples, and assistance with casework. From this, the understudy's interests are expanded to develop into an apprentice. It is difficult to judge the quality of the training or the competence attained by the trainee by the laboratory in which the training was obtained. Appropriate standards are lacking, and it is for this reason that certification boards have been created.

The Scientific Working Group for Forensic Document Examination (SWGDOC) (2013a) outlines specific areas that a student needs to learn in order to meet minimum recommended training requirements. It should be noted that courses in other forensic disciplines such as fraud investigation or graphology do not qualify one as a document examiner. Further, a student requires more training than one correspondence course can provide. A single correspondence course does not meet the minimum 2-year training requirement promulgated by SWGDOC.

Among recognized practitioners, it is generally agreed that training requires 2 years to complete and must be acquired under the direct supervision of a qualified instructor who has sufficient training, experience, and credentials. The reason for this is that proficiency depends upon the proper selection of appropriate evidence, the assessment of its significance, and some familiarity with scientific method. The first two of these are matters that vary with the material under examination, and therefore, cannot be found in books. Assistance can only be obtained from teachers and by experience, and tutorage couples the experience of the tutor with that acquired by the student, which is particularly important for novices in the field. Similarly it might be argued that examiners who work alone are without the benefit of the variations in the experience of others and the consequent modifications to evaluations. Obviously self-taught individuals are at a distinct disadvantage and run the risk of repeating undetected errors.

13.2.3 Professional Affiliations

A reasonable indication of proficiency in document examination, that is, the level of skill acquired, may be obtained from a review of the professional associations in which membership is held. These organizations are interested in attracting the most qualified practitioners in their field and are, therefore, sufficiently concerned about the qualifications of their present members to weed out or avoid those who would reflect adversely on the reputation of the group. Unfortunately, however, the standards for some groups or associations are not equal to those of others, and the affiliation with such groups will not speak to the same level of qualification.

Another indication of proficiency may be obtained from the elected offices and appointments held in professional organizations. This kind of acceptance by one's peers is a measure of the respect enjoyed by the individual among those who should be in the best position to judge competence.

13.2.4 Quality and Quantity of Publications

Many fields of science consider published material to be a measure of an individual's qualification for two reasons. First, it is material that is publicly available for review and assessment. Second, it is frequently subject to peer review prior to publication. Standards of peer review, however, vary widely and one needs to know something of the review board and journal policy to properly judge the quality of the publication's material.

13.2.5 Summary

Qualification is judged on the basis of the following:

1. Level of achievement in a recognized academic institution
2. Type and duration of training received
3. Qualification of the instructor(s)
4. Professional memberships held and the affiliations enjoyed
5. Offices held in professional associations
6. Number of contributions to the literature on the subject and the nature of the journals in which they have been published
7. Program of continuing education followed
8. Scope of the services offered
9. Dimensions of the experience acquired
10. Ability to supply information and provide answers concerning competency

Competence can also be evaluated on the examiner's curriculum vitae (CV), and in the capacity of his or her facilities to handle the task, as indicated by (1) equipment utilized and (2) resources available. The examiner's facilities and resources need to be sufficient in order to properly conduct an examination. There seems little justification in offering services as a document examiner or purporting to conduct an examination unless that examination and study is going to be complete.

Document examination (of which handwriting identification is a principal component) is a study to determine the history of the events that have occurred to a document. Although this text primarily addresses the topic of handwriting identification, it cannot be divorced from the media with which and on which the writing has been executed. It is not uncommon for signatures to be identified as genuine, but other evidence to reveal that the signature was not inscribed to the document when in its present form. An examination of the writing of the signature without any consideration of the other evidence is hardly complete and is a disservice to the client. The examiner must therefore possess facilities for:

1. Examination of writing strokes microscopically and stereoscopically, under a variety of lighting conditions
2. Study of writings while superimposed upon one another, with transmitted light
3. Precise measurement of the physical dimensions of the document and of the writing, lettering, or printing thereon
4. Study and recording of the reaction of inks, papers, and other materials to radiations beyond the visible range of the electromagnetic spectrum, that is, in the ultraviolet and infrared regions
5. Examination and study of indentations in the document produced by writings on other documents executed while superimposed upon the document under examination
6. Recording photographically or otherwise what other facilities have revealed

The examiner without the facilities to examine completely all aspects of the document on which a questioned writing resides may never know what segments of significant evidence has escaped his or her study nor can the examiner provide relevant guidance as to the types of tests that may be required beyond his or her scope of services.

13.3 MAINTAINING PROFICIENCY IN DOCUMENT EXAMINATION

The most efficacious means document examiners have for maintaining skills, gaining and testing new knowledge, and improving performance is through professional affiliations and participation in professional organizations and their meetings. Some of these conduct workshops in particular areas of the work.

In North America, certification by ABFDE, BFDE, and NADE requires the diplomate or certified member to demonstrate every 5 years, by courses taken, meetings attended, and papers presented and/or published, that one is current in knowledge of the subject. This may be one of the greater virtues in these certification programs for there are a number of document examiners who, for one reason or another, have left the field for a number of years and who, upon retirement or termination of their present employment, reenter the field and offer their services to the public as though inactivity over a period of time has no effect whatsoever upon the state of their knowledge or their skills. There are also a number of document examiners who may have been certified by a professional organization at one time, but did not maintain current membership and their certification has expired through lack of continuing education participation.

In the absence of a professional licensing system or some appropriate form of control by courts or the profession itself, the risks of the lack of continuing education to clients, to courts, and to the examiners themselves are not likely to be avoided. Although there are several self-designated document examiners and schools and organizations professing certification, a certification program that requires periodic continuing education has greater professional standing and credibility.

13.4 EXPERT WITNESS QUALIFICATION

It seems generally agreed that, by definition, an expert witness is a person who possesses special skills or knowledge, acquired by way of training or experience, not normally possessed by the layman, and is, thereby, permitted to draw conclusions or to express opinions that are otherwise inadmissible in testimony.

One school of thought has held the view that a level of competence is implied by the definition, notwithstanding the fact that it may be difficult to stipulate a level to satisfy all disciplines. Furthermore, the level of competence so implied is greater than that which can be achieved by simple exposure to the document examination laboratory. Were that not so, every secretary of every document examiner (or indeed of any other forensic specialist) would be qualified to testify as an expert witness. In fact, some secretaries have professed, after a period of time, to be competent examiners, but their level of competence has not been widely recognized within the discipline. It hardly warranted stating that legal authorities did not have this broad a coverage in mind when the qualifications of the expert witness were being considered and defined.

Historically, at least, the bottom line for qualification as an expert witness is legally defined as "that which can provide appreciable help to the court" and no more. There is no other formula for ascertaining whether a witness is indeed an expert or should be considered to be an expert in a particular field. Practical experience is important, but is rarely a sole criterion. The same may also be said of academic achievement. The law prefers to deal with levels of competence primarily as a guide to the weight to be given to the testimony. This situation prompted Imwinkelried (1982) to comment: "At least in federal practice, it is almost inconceivable that an expert will be kept off the witness stand altogether for lack of competency" (p. 37).

With what is referred to in the United States as the *Daubert* standard, the court acts as gatekeeper in the admission of expert witness testimony in federal courts and in many state courts throughout the United States. Three US Supreme Court cases (the *Daubert* trilogy) contributed to the revision of Rule 702 in the US Federal Rules of Evidence (the *Daubert* standard). In *Daubert v. Merrell Dow Pharmaceuticals* (1993), evidence offered through expert testimony was evaluated for its scientific reliability rather than evaluated via the *Frye* general acceptance test. In *General Electric Co. v. Joiner* (1997), a judge has the discretion to exclude expert testimony. In *Kumho Tire Co. v. Carmichael* (1999), the judge may act as gatekeeper in all expert testimony including nonscientific testimony. In 2000, Rule 702 was adopted which provided guidelines for the acceptance of expert testimony. The guidelines specify that a witness who is qualified as an expert by knowledge, skill, experience, training, or education may testify in the form of an opinion or otherwise if:

1. The expert's scientific, technical, or other specialized knowledge will help the trier of fact to understand the evidence or to determine a fact in issue.
2. The testimony is based on sufficient facts or data.
3. The testimony is the product of reliable principles and methods.
4. The expert has reliably applied the principles and methods to the facts of the case.

Merlino et al. (2007) evaluated US federal court cases in which document examination expert testimony was excluded and found that the exclusion was based on both expert qualifications and practice of document examination as a science. Regarding expert qualifications, judges specifically mentioned lack of nonacademic training, lack of skill with respect to subject matter, experience, publication record, and reputation as factors that precluded expert testimony.

The influence that an expert's qualifications may have on jurors should not be underestimated. In a study on the influence of forensic expert testimony on juror judgments, it was found that the qualifications and experience of the expert had more influence on jurors' judgments than forensic technology and scientific testing (Koehler et al. 2016).

13.5 RELEVANCE OF TRAINING IN OTHER FORENSIC DISCIPLINES

Notwithstanding the fact that the identification process of analysis, comparison, and evaluation underlies several other disciplines of forensic science, the steps of analysis and evaluation are different for each discipline and must be learned separately and independently. The greater the disparity in the materials to be examined in different disciplines, or in the natural laws governing their creation, their composition or their behavior, the less relevant training in other areas of forensic science has to the questions of handwriting examination.

In Chapter 5, there was a discussion about how handwriting examination differs from the examination of other materials in forensic science. As previously mentioned, writing is the conscious and deliberate issue of an animate body, whereas the material other disciplines examine is an involuntary issue of an animate body or a property of an inanimate one. Consequently, this difference in the voluntary control of the issue makes substantial changes in the approach to evidence. Other fields of forensic science examine and study properties, reactions, and attributes of material substances that are the consequences of constitution or composition. In these respects, there is consistency between different samples of the same material.

Handwriting identification is an examination and study of a particular facet of human behavior or performance that is depicted by personal habits of behavior. There is less, perhaps much less, consistency between samples which is referred to as natural variation. The consistent material substances involved in handwriting examinations are simply the substrates on which the behavior is recorded. Accordingly, the education, training, and perspectives of a person practicing in other disciplines differs significantly from that of a person practicing in the field of handwriting examination.

It has been assumed by some courts that there is a fundamental knowledge common to all forensic science disciplines, just as the many rules of evidence and procedure prevail throughout the various divisions of law. Or, it has been assumed that there is a basic education in forensic science after which specialization or field selection occurs, as in law or medicine. Other than an understanding of scientific method and a fundamental sense of evidence, however, the many fields of forensic science have little in common. There is some connection between the pattern-based forensic sciences which include latent print examination and handwriting examination. However, these pattern-based forensic disciplines have little in common with DNA or toxicology.

13.6 PROFESSIONALISM AND ETHICS

Professional and ethical codes of conduct are cornerstones in forensic science professions and organizations need to promulgate and enforce codes of conduct among its professional members. If the profession has outlined and reached standards of practice and professional and ethical conduct, this is a measure in which the justice system and clients can use to ensure the competency of the examiner.

Godown (1970) expressed the view that a professional organization was based on agreement with regard to the following: (1) Certification procedures, (2) educational and training standards, (3) promotion of research, and (4) standards of practice (ethical and practical). Flores (1988) explains that professionalism is commonly described as a complex set of role characteristics involving:

1. Specialized knowledge and training
2. Autonomous decision-making authority in matters of importance to society
3. Dedication to public service
4. That aspect of professionalism, usually implied, that marks the standard of responsible behavior

Ravetz (1971) offered four criteria that distinguish a true learned profession from a craft, a trade, or an occupation that provides a particular service.

1. The client needs a service, is unable to satisfy the need for his or herself, and, thereby, is dependent upon and vulnerable to the professional's services.
2. The client is not competent to assess the adequacy or quality of the service.
3. Recognized competence in the set of tasks is legally restricted to those certified to have completed a training of a scientific character.
4. In exchange for the monopoly of practice, the group accepts responsibility for the achievement of the aims of clients.

In these criteria, there is an essential fiduciary element, a vesting of trust, at least to a reasonable degree, and professionals are expected to honor this trust. Abuse of professional authority, incompetence, or malfeasance is a betrayal of the client's trust. Whatever legally rendered monopoly (e.g., licensing or certification) that the profession enjoys may be put at risk. Thus, the profession must maintain standards of work to protect the interests of clients, and a code of behavior is necessary to prevent the relaxing of standards and the neglect of client's interests.

Every major profession has established a professional code of ethics for its members, defining the duties and moral responsibilities that members are expected to follow. It is based on the primacy of the purpose of the task: serving the client's interests. As a guiding principle, the professional ethic is necessary if the fiduciary relationship is to be justified and preserved, indeed, reinforced, and the client's fear of being exploited or poorly served is to be rationally assuaged.

Additionally, given the claim of autonomy that most professions make, and assuming a posture of self-regulation, the professions have historically established these rules of conduct to assure the quality of services and to promote a sense of responsibility for the moral consequences that ensue. Moreover, self-regulation and adherence to professional codes enhances the profession's public image and, thereby, aids in sustaining its integrity in the mind of the public.

In recent years, increasing public criticism of the routine activities of professionals has precipitated a new interest in the normative aspects of professionalism. Consequently, major professions have undertaken the task of revising their codes of ethics as an expression of their commitment to ethical behavior. Furthermore, the education of professionals has increasingly focused on ethical issues. Academic curriculums are including courses on ethics and professionalism. There has been increased discussion of and a growth in the literature on professional ethics illustrating the serious thought being given to the moral dimensions of professionalism.

Flores (1988) claimed this interest focuses almost exclusively on examining the issues and responsibilities of professionals as defined by the rules promulgated in codes of ethics. The rules and principles that these codes incorporate provide a framework for evaluating professional activities and advocating condemnation when they are breached. Unfortunately, this exclusive emphasis on rules can create the mistaken impression that being professionally proper means no more than observing a variety of rules governing the conduct of one's routine activities. Professionalism so conceived is reduced to rule-governed behavior involving simply the application of formal codes. While this approach has its value in giving professionals general guidance as to how they ought to act, it can distort understanding of some fundamental aspects of professionalism.

Rules provide little perspective as to the virtues and ideals essential to professionalism, or to the kind of person one should be in addition to how one should act, in order to be considered a true professional. What is missing in the picture of professionalism as rule-governed conduct is reference to the virtues and ideals that make the duties and responsibilities incorporated in codes intelligible as moral rules. Without this foundation, codes may be seen as an ideology involving rules of behavior that simply promote the self-interests of the profession. On the other hand, reference to virtues such as honesty and integrity and to ideals such as truth and justice deepens understanding of what it means to be a professional, and of how professionalism must imply something more than mere rule-governed behavior.

The standard concept of professionalism focuses attention on how one should act, and particularly whether each act conforms to the rules. Flores (1988) maintained, however, that professionalism conceived as a virtue regards action to be of secondary importance to the question of what kind of person the professional is—the moral quality of one's character. Professionalism, thus conceived, is a way of living that is bound to certain habits of character and mind, such as honesty, impartiality, integrity, and public service. Because of such traits, one is disposed to act in ways consistent with the rules, not as an obligation defined by the rules, but rather as a consequence of the kind of person one is.

This difference in focus rests on adopting a set of ideals involving a commitment to excellence and a dedication to serve the common good that defines the kind of person one should be or become. In pursuing these ideals, one develops certain habits, attitudes, and dispositions that fashion the quality of one's mind and character. Hence, how one acts will depend not on one's will to follow rules, but rather on the moral goodness underlying one's character. Hilton (1974) spoke along these lines when he said that ethics is far deeper than a set of rules. It has to be an inborn or developed basic honesty which precludes the worker from undertaking anything which is not completely and fully honorable. It is not a matter that can be legislated.

Thus, the concept of professionalism is a commitment to the ideal of excellence in the exercise of professional skills. Indeed, because professional practice generates goods of value to both society and the profession, the professional who is committed to ideals of excellence will normally uphold standards of conduct that go beyond those an ordinary individual accepts. In addition, dedication to the ideals of integrity, justice, wisdom, and truth will convey honor to the profession and command respect from others. Thus, the definition of a professional should, morally speaking, include recognition of a variety of ideals that underpin the virtues central to professionalism.

For Newton (1981), a profession is an aggregate whose members:

1. Possess a specialized art, skill, or capacity, requiring long and difficult education, and extended practice
2. Individually and/or collectively render a service to individual clients and to society in that practice
3. Are employed full-time and for pay in the practice of the art or skill

This definition differs from that of Flores (1988) in its distinction of a profession on the basis of remuneration versus dedication. Indeed, the remunerative aspect that Newton (1981) includes has provided the particular criteria that commonly distinguishes the professional from the amateur. The dedication to public service that Flores embraces keeps the present discussion within the realm applicable to science. Furthermore, somewhat as a by-product, the professional, by possession of specialized skill, is one who retains his or her professional identity regardless of employment status. For professional status to be correctly conferred, there must be an extensive educational basis, full-time practice, and a special relationship between practitioner and client centered upon service. Elements will be differently emphasized in different professions, but invariably all will be present.

Like Flores (1988), Newton (1981) also distinguishes between the internal and the external aspect of any group of rules or guidelines for a field of practice. The internal is the larger, more serious aspect with which the professional begins—one's ideals and virtues. The external is the more visible, logically coherent, enforceable aspect—the code of ethics, to which the professional subscribes. The internal aspect, one's ideals and virtues, has its roots in each individual; the external is always linked to a professional organization, as a code of ethics, and is the product of its political process.

Neither aspect alone is satisfactory as an ethic. The internal ethic is apt to be ill-formed, and more a personal expression of feelings or a conscience, rather than a set of examinable rules. As for the external aspect, as a set of rules to be applied more or less mechanically, it can hardly be adequate to the infinite variety of situations that present as ethical dilemmas. Then too, practices that the ethic is supposed to guide may change to meet varying conditions putting a strain to adapt on practitioners and organizations alike, and the maintenance of a rational ethic may be an all but impossible task.

Forensic scientists have been especially targeted, perhaps because every finding becomes public, subject to challenge, and the population of available forensic scientists has grown substantially. Only the limit of resources to pursue the challenge limits the number of disputes. Nevertheless, findings and qualifications of alleged forensic scientists have been found to be false, and these few individuals have discredited disciplines.

The special nature of scientific enquiry demands the adoption of an ethical code if work is to be done fittingly. Social mechanisms, individual actions, and commitments must then be engaged if this code is to be enforced and maintained. The health and vitality of scientific inquiry are not guaranteed, either by the objects of inquiry or by the social aspects of the work. Unless there is an effective scientific ethic, even more refined than a professional ethic, the delicate and sensitive work of science will not continue to be well governed or well performed. The importance of a professional ethic should be obvious, then, to any aspiring scientific pursuit and its practitioners, including the examination of handwritings (Hilton 1988).

When given appropriate thought, the following eight provisions warrant a place in the personal or collective codes of ethics endorsed by handwriting examiners:

1. Apply appropriate principles of science and of logic, in accordance with scientific method, to the examination and study of written or lettered inscriptions on any material substrate.
2. Ensure that the scope of the examination and study is objective and appropriate to the task(s) presented by the document(s).
3. Ensure that the conclusions drawn and/or findings discovered are in accordance with, and not misrepresentative of the physical evidence present, and its proper interpretation; report them clearly, concisely and impartially.

4. Acknowledge one's personal limitations and those of the discipline in the resolution of questions posed.
5. Respect the confidentiality due a matter under examination as long as it is under investigation, and as long as that confidentiality is sustained by the client and his or her counsel.
6. Maintain technical competence and professional skills through continuing education.
7. Exhibit and maintain a commitment to excellence in the exercise of professional skills, and to the ideals of integrity, wisdom, and truth.
8. Endorse and adopt for personal use, such standards of practice as may be or become preferred practices for the conduct of handwriting examination.

In approaching the topic of quality control, Knight (1989) stated: "We possess—or perhaps suffer—the most stringent form of quality control in the form of cross-examination in the courts, where any malpractice, omissions, or fudging is very likely to be revealed both by opposing Counsel and through him by the expert on the 'other side'" (p. 59). Obviously, Knight had no doubts that forensic scientists counsel lawyers regarding the work and testimony of other forensic scientists. Such involvement provides a kind of quality control, and quality control is healthy for the profession. Other examiners have commented on the controversy as to whether opposing experts should critique the work of other examiners or report their conduct (Sellers 1968; Alford 1975; McNally 1988; Lindblom 1991). The controversy stems from the motivation of the opposing expert. In reviewing the work of another, is the opposing expert assisting counsel in confusing the issue and obstructing justice on behalf of the client's interests, or, is the motivation based on a genuine critique of the examiner's work to ensure that standards of practice are properly adhered to and applied?

There are difficult situations that document examiners encounter involving the testimony of other expert witnesses, and in some the findings of the other witness are right, but for the wrong reasons. There are other situations in which testimony respecting the identification of a signature is only part of the examination the circumstances demand. Further work would show the document to have been signed in blank, or that material has been added to the document above the signature that alters the intent of the document that it had when the signature was applied. Thus, an expert should counsel a lawyer in cross-examining another expert witness when (1) the pursuits of justice may be jeopardized, and/or (2) the reputation of the discipline is put at risk.

Other dilemmas arise out of a difference in the evaluation of the evidence within the writing—one examiner considers it sufficient to identify a writer while another considers it only adequate to support a qualified conclusion, for example, a strong probability. If the second examiner testifies does he or she defeat justice? Assuming that the second examiner is correct in his or her evaluation or honestly feels so, if handwriting evidence is being overevaluated, or underevaluated, the testimony of the first examiner may influence the court to place too much, or too little, reliance upon the handwriting in reaching a decision. This, in fact, may be action that defeats justice. Putting a proper evaluation on physical evidence cannot be defeating justice, but only promoting it. The issue must not be confused by a consideration of whether the testimony tends to incriminate or to exonerate an individual, whether it supports or weakens a particular side of a case. Physical evidence should be allowed to speak, but only as loudly as it deserves.

It is the responsibility of the competent examiner to do what is necessary to reflect a level of skill, professionalism, and scientific sagacity that will preserve or enhance the reputation of the discipline when it may be at risk, and to ensure that evidence is properly interpreted. The provisions of a code of ethics would allow for involvement in such a matter by a concerned and competent examiner subscribing to such codes. The issue, however, cannot always be so simply resolved. What are the proper techniques, proper assertions, and proper practices? Are these not matters of opinion on which many practitioners will find that they differ? And if this is so, are judicial forums the proper arena for the resolution of these differences? Handwriting experts are not alone in contending with such disputes. Many cases can be cited in which medical experts have testified in opposition to one another as to proper standards of practice (Harris and Mills 1963).

Chapter 14

Science and Handwriting Identification

14.1 DEFINING SCIENCE

Certainly, any dissertation on document examination needs to address the question as to whether handwriting identification, as it is presently conducted, qualifies as a science. This chapter provides definitions of science and scientific method against which the discipline may be judged.

Little is more often encountered, but less often understood than science, scientists, and scientific method. Numerous attempts have been made to provide precise definitions and while each has merit none has, as yet, been universally accepted, or has adapted readily to ever-advancing knowledge and technology. To some extent, the reason is that the proliferation of new fields of scientific study and the sophistication of study methods in all fields are constantly subjecting established definitions to modification. Science in itself is an evolving process.

Science began as a branch of pure learning that aimed at intellectual satisfaction. Science is not the only branch of pure learning, however, and must be distinguished from other academic-pursuit branches such as economics, history, mathematics, or philosophy. At one time, science was considered to have but a handful of divisions, for example, chemistry, physics, or astronomy. Today, science has branched into hundreds if not thousands of specialties.

However, Campbell (1952) concluded that science is a single whole. He asserts that the divisions between its branches are largely products of thinking without ulterior significance. His definition of science is as profound as one is likely to encounter: "The study of those judgments concerning which universal agreement can be obtained" (p. 27). Campbell's definition serves as a nucleus for the description of science. Understanding of it is assisted if one thinks of judgments as being observations or experiences that may be acquired from empirical studies or experimentation.

In applying this definition expressly to handwriting identification, Huber and Headrick made the observation that there are 21 discriminating elements of writing that may serve to differentiate the products of any one person from another. It was their intention that the proposed handwriting elements should acquire universal agreement as it would constitute a step in the continued growth of handwriting examination as a science. Other observations that examiners have made, for example, the heterogeneity of writing, also need to be continuously investigated and tested. As such, and finding universal agreement, the field continues to climb essential steps as a scientific endeavor. As the number of observations grows on which agreement is reached, the disputed observations or judgments are discarded. Laws are made, that, in turn, obtain universal agreement.

In a similar vein Sullivan (1949) wrote: "The essential distinction between science and art consists in the fact that science makes appeal to universal assent, whereas art does not. A scientific statement is open to verification by anybody, whereas a work of art appeals only to people with certain sensibilities ... music means nothing to a man who is tone deaf. Science deals with a public world, whereas art is concerned with a private world" (p. 169).

What is important in Campbell's and Sullivan's definitions is the requirement for *universal agreement* that distinguishes science from other branches of pure learning. It follows that scientific method is simply the framework within which universal agreement in the theories, laws, and principles of a field of science may be sought and realized.

Universal agreement, however, is only one of the two distinguishing characteristics of science. Another hallmark of science is that it endeavors to define data as precisely as possible through measurement (Margenau and Bergamini 1964). The kinds of measures employed vary a great deal, but by this means, a numerical value can be assigned to a fact, that before had only subjective sensory or esthetic value. The process of measurement is vital to science for a number of reasons:

1. Measurement is the most convenient means of establishing a meaningful rank/order for information. Order is needed to file/retrieve information and to establish relationships between their parts.
2. Measurement enables distinguishing between minutely different yet similar properties.
3. Measurement enables confirming constancy in a property, without which it is no longer a property.
4. Measurement is necessary for the purpose of communication and verification. Science is science only where there can be universal agreement, and verification is essential to achieve such agreement.
5. Measurement is essential to the discovery of laws in which properties are involved. When unable to measure a property, one is unable to articulate a law governing it.

Indeed, measurement is the only process available in which to convert observations, properties, and evaluations that are qualitative, subjective, and private to forms that are quantitative, objective, and public, and that are, therefore, communicable (Huber and Headrick 1990). This statement is of great significance to handwriting identification and of equally great significance to science for it is the second characteristic of science that distinguishes it from the arts and other branches of pure learning. What sets science apart from art is *universal agreement* and *measurement*.

To communicate information to all persons regardless of their understanding of the language involved, science has learned that numbers are the least ambiguous, most specific means available. So, measurement became the integral requirement of science, by way of which universal agreement can be obtained. Huber and Headrick expressed the conviction that if there is any hope of achieving accuracy and precision in examination results, and any aspiration to acquire the mantle of science for the discipline, examiners must embark on the pursuit of measurement in handwriting identification. As such, Found et al. (1994) stated: "If the field of forensic handwriting examination is to be considered a scientific endeavor, then the move toward the inclusion of objective measurement as part of the overall comparison methodology must be made" (p. 195).

In the minds of some persons, there is an aura placed about science and scientists that suggests that what is done in their laboratories is complex and beyond the layperson's comprehension. On occasion, it has been employed as a defense mechanism by some handwriting experts to avoid having to answer direct questions about their expertise. But, as Quine (1957) expounded, science should be comprehensible to the layperson, for science is not a substitute for common sense but an extension of it. It is noted that science's fundamental distinction from common sense rests in a single word: system. Quine (1957) further said: "The scientist introduces system into his quest and scrutiny of evidence. System, moreover, dictates the scientist's hypotheses themselves" (p. 5).

Osborn is reported by Swett (1959) to have written years ago about an attempt to marry document examination to science. He is reported to have said that the scientific spirit need not develop an attitude of timidity, but rather develop an attitude of caution. Extended knowledge and experience will develop the ability to draw correct inferences from what may seem slight evidence, but the inference will still be drawn from actual evidence.

Sellers (1942) argued, in a similar vein, that the scientific approach to a questioned document problem is the unbiased systematic application of all of one's knowledge acquired through experience, research and study, and the search for facts. It is adequate observation to which is applied correct reasoning. Sellers went on to say that the scientific approach might, in fact, lessen the complexity of any questioned document problem.

Cole (1946) was one of the first to tackle the question of whether handwriting identification is science and provided the response that many others have adopted when required: "In the sense that it is classified, formulated, and verifiable knowledge gathered by observation, research, and experiment, it is *scientific knowledge*" (p. 4).

Casey (1968), without employing a strict definition of the term, argued that handwriting identification is a science because it employs the concepts of the method of science in its general research and a scientific approach to its practical problems. Generally, valid science follows proven procedures in seeking answers.

14.2 HANDWRITING EXAMINATION AND SCIENTIFIC METHOD

Scientific method is the offspring of a branch of philosophy called epistemology (from the Greek episteme, *knowledge*, and logos, *theory*). Margenau and Bergamini (1964) reported that scientific method was initiated in the seventeenth century when Francis Bacon offered the scientist a fourfold rule of thumb for their work: (1) observe; (2) measure; (3) explain; and (4) verify.

Webster's (1995) defines scientific method as: "Principles and procedures for the systematic pursuit of knowledge involving the recognition and formulation of a problem, the collection of data through observation and experiment, and the formulation and testing of hypotheses" (p. 912).

In somewhat more specific language, students of the subject have modified Bacon's rule to read: (1) pose a question, (2) collect evidence, (3) hypothesize, (4) deduce its implications, (5) test experimentally, (6) accept, reject, or modify the hypothesis. Experimental testing (step 5) is an aspect of the process that the forensic nature of most handwriting examinations will not permit. If it did, the task of identification would be made simpler, for the standards obtained would be reasonable duplications of the several circumstances of the questioned writing, and the variables which oftentimes influence the writing act would be astutely controlled. Instead of the more ideal experimental situation, one is compelled for the most part to work with only that which is available, and draw conclusions from observations, as astronomers have done for centuries.

It may be said that scientific method has four corners to its character:

1. Recognition and formulation of the problem
2. Systematic pursuit of knowledge
3. Collection of data through observation and/or experimentation
4. Formulation and testing of a hypothesis

There have been characterizations of the scientific method from a slightly different viewpoint. It is said that the philosophy of the scientific method is to strive constantly for objectivity. It orders knowledge so that it may be considered in proper and logical sequence. It classifies knowledge as the only systematic means to its organization and retrieval. It advances verification as the most reliable form of proof. It utilizes observation and/or experimentation designed expressly to control variables. It is constantly critical of itself. It entertains no dogmas, maintains no absolutes or infallibility, and is both cautious and skeptical. These two approaches to scientific method are not in conflict, but tend to supplement one another. The first is simply a procedural outline for the task, whereas the second is a policy of conduct for carrying out the procedure.

Scientific knowledge is distinguished from other knowledge by (1) the method by which it is created or collected, (2) a systematic extension of common sense, and (3) sound skepticism. When these three factors are combined, they are referred to as *scientific method*. Judge McKenna, in his decision in *US v. Starzecpyzel* (1995), quoting Green (1991), states: "Scientific methodology today is based on generating hypotheses and testing them to see if they can be falsified; indeed, this methodology is what distinguishes science from other fields of human inquiry."

The consequence of the scientific method is the acceptance, rejection, or revision of the hypothesis. It has a condition that it employs the principles of logic and reason to draw conclusions from the information the study produces. If science is a systematized body of knowledge, scientific method is the framework for or method of acquiring and using it, regardless of the nature of the matter under study.

14.3 HANDWRITING AND MEASUREMENT

The assignment of numbers to represent facts is a necessary ingredient of most, if not all, disciplines of science. It must be pursued in handwriting identification if it is hoped to achieve universal agreement. The studies of handwriting for identification purposes have always considered measurable elements, such as size, relative heights, spacing, and other factors from the static trace.

Computerized methods have been designed to assist in the measurement of numerous handwriting factors (e.g., line lengths, distances between points, areas within loops, and angles of intersecting strokes). Using computational methods, Found et al. (1994) reported development of a computer program to compare measurable properties in handwriting. Srihari and Leedham (2003) carried out a survey of computer methods in handwriting examination and reported on the development of systems such as the forensic information system for handwriting (FISH), WANDA, and CedarFox.

There are computerized methods for measuring dynamic factors in handwriting as well (e.g., duration, velocity, acceleration). Methods of extracting dynamic handwriting measures are surprisingly not new. Freeman (1918) and Saudek (1929) performed experiments in child and adult handwriting using motion-picture photos and cinematographic exposures taken at speeds of 1/25 of a second (also known as the Freeman unit) to obtain information about the speed of writing. Tripp et al. (1957) endeavored to measure handwriting variables such as pressure and speed. For this, a specially designed writing instrument was used to record pressure in terms of the *perpendicular vector* (i.e., force applied perpendicular to the axis of the pen), the *parallel vector* (i.e., force applied parallel to the axis of the pen), and the *table vector*, that is now referred to as *point load*. Point load is in fact the product of the vertical components of the other two vectors. Extracting dynamic information from the static trace, through location of interaction points on the writing trace produced by movements of muscle-joint systems, was proposed by Hardy (1992). Dynamic information on factors such as speed, velocity, and other characteristics can be observed from the static trace and correlated with the characteristics of forgery reported in the document examination literature (Hilton 1993; Leung et al. 1993). Sophisticated software programs that record handwriting from digital tablets for experimental research have included OASIS and NeuroScript MovAlyzeR.

The International Graphonomics Society (IGS) and other groups with related interests have published virtually hundreds of studies to better understand the writing process, determine what might be measurable, and offer formulas for diagnosing the results. In these studies, the computer and the digital tablet have played a major role. The computerized, automated analysis of writing features has been reported by several authors and a number of scientific publications have been produced concerning the measurement of handwriting. Early studies using computational measurements included Van der Plaats and Van Galen (1990), and Brault and Plamondon (1993).

To a large extent, the focus in this area of research has been on the development of automated signature verification, the merits of which are now widely recognized. The handwritten signature is considered to be one of the best means of personal identification. It is a kind of identification that must be produced or created anywhere and at any time, unlike passwords or ID (identity) cards that must only be possessed. The security of passwords has its weaknesses and ID cards have the inherent risk of loss or theft. The computer must be engineered to recognize a touchstone that will discriminate between the genuine product and the spurious or the "coincidentally similar" writing of another person.

Much research has been directed at dynamic techniques in which computer input is acquired during the writing process, as in signature verification for access control purposes. But progress has also been made in static techniques where input is acquired from the completed writing as it appears on a document or a sheet of paper.

A review of the literature and a state of the art survey, with a list of approximately 180 published references, was provided by Plamondon and Lorette (1989). This survey focused principally on the two applications: identification and verification. Identification is the system for selecting a writer, if present, from a reference database, on the basis of some specific attributes of extended writing. A verification system, on the other hand, endeavors to accept or reject a particular writing, usually a signature, by a one-to-one comparison of the elements of the writing with one or more reference standards in an electronic storage. The identification system is the electronic development of the manually conducted classification systems introduced by Livingston (1963). The verification system is an attempt to computerize the standard bench work of the document examiner, but in a small fraction of the time required.

Historically, one of the instruments developed and marketed in the 1990s was by Rediffusion Computers the SIGNCHECK signature verification system designed to verify static signatures on checks. A study by Totty and Hardcastle (1986) found the system unsuitable at that time for forensic applications and of questionable value to banks and like institutions. Another study by Brocklehurst (1985) employed a computer to digitize signatures and data reduction techniques to obtain coded descriptions of signatures. In tests of "simply spurious" signatures, rejection rates of 97% were obtained at thresholds that accepted 90% of genuine signatures.

The computerized and automated identification and verification of handwriting is based upon many of the computerized methods that originated in handwriting recognition technology. Srihari et al. (2002) explained the fundamental difference between handwriting recognition and handwriting identification technology: handwriting recognition filters out individuality in order to capture the common elements of handwriting, in order to convert it to text, or in searching for a particular word that may be common between samples or writers. Handwriting identification is focused on exactly the opposite, as its intent is to capture the individuality and uniqueness of handwriting and how that individuality differentiates it from other samples that employ the same handwritten letters or text. Handwriting verification systems also employ mathematical and statistical formulas for comparison and matching of handwriting in a database to establish identification.

FISH was designed to help automatize the document examination process and increase efficiency through the computerized ability to scan, digitize, measure, store, and compare questioned and known handwriting samples. FISH measurements include letter characteristics such as height and distance of letters. WANDA, designed to interface with FISH, has advanced features, including additional handwriting measurements and modules that represent systematic handwriting examination procedures (Franke et al. 2004). The first procedure includes data acquisition which is the capture of handwriting through offline methods (such as scanning) or online methods (digital tablet input). The measurement module is based on pattern-recognition techniques that aid in the development of adding a measurement for allograph matching. Measurements include height, slant, and width of characters and baseline measurements. Automatic feature extraction is based on the premise that it is the combination of unique characteristics that establishes handwriting identification; one feature alone is not sufficient to establish identification.

A significant study that established the individuality of handwriting in forensic identification employed an automated system that was originally invented for postal address handwriting recognition (Srihari et al. 2002). This study reported on the underlying process generally used by automated handwriting systems. In the study, the three phases of the automated analysis included handwriting data collection, feature extraction, and validation to establish a statistical model for handwriting identification. For data collection, samples of representative types of handwritings were used to build a 1,500 sample handwriting database. In the feature extraction phase, the handwriting samples were scanned and converted into binary (black and white) samples.

In the feature extraction phase, Features were identified as quantitative measurements from different levels of the handwriting extraction phase. The features were measured from the samples and feature vectors developed. Several features were extracted for study including conventional features that are observable by human document examiners and computational features which are extracted and normalized using computer algorithms. The conventional features were extracted from the 21 discriminating elements compiled by Huber and Headrick.

For statistical analysis, an artificial neural network (ANN) was employed in the study. Artificial neural networks are mathematical or computational models that are used to model relationships and find patterns in data. ANN is based on machine learning and artificial intelligence, useful for data mining and pattern-based analysis. ANN also works well with Bayesian procedures, a statistical method useful for determining probability in forensic analysis. In the study, an ANN was trained to examine within-writer and between-writer variances at the document, paragraph, word, and character levels. The data was analyzed for identification of a writer against other writers (identification), as well as for comparing the writing of a document to another writing to verify that it is written by the same person (verification). Results showed that the system had a 98% accuracy rate for identification and a 96% accuracy rate for verification. The high performance of the system's method was based on just a few macro and micro features, but the authors pointed out that such identification or verification could not be determined by a single feature, indicating that handwriting identification and verification is dependent upon a set of features. Additionally, the results were based upon features that are used by document examiners, as well as on features that are computationally based, suggesting that computers can provide statistical analysis and inference that is not possible with the more traditional methods of handwriting examination.

Driven by the development of biometric systems, advancement in automated forensic handwriting analysis includes online feature analysis and sophisticated algorithms. There are intelligent systems that extract both offline and online features as well as what is referred to as global and local features. Global features are associated with signature "properties as a whole," while local features refer to "properties specific to a sampling point" (Tariq et al. 2011, 11).

Algorithms such as dynamic time warping (DTW) are used in online handwriting and signature systems which match handwriting samples using temporal and spatial characteristics captured in real time. Niels and Vuurpijl (2005) describe DTW in handwriting examination as a "technique that compares online trajectories of coordinates (i.e., trajectories in which both spatial and temporal information is available)" (p. 218). DTW can be described as following two similar writing patterns, and moving the "time" forward at variable rates so that the writing patterns will be at the same time at corresponding turning and reversal points. DTW is useful in comparing the similarity in the sequence between two handwriting units or samples even if they are produced in different time lengths. This technique would be particularly useful in online handwriting systems.

The hidden Markov model (HMM) is another algorithm that is used in both online and offline systems for sequence modeling in handwriting. This algorithm helps to process handwriting data not as single allographs or units, but as sequences of letters. The algorithm predicts stroke sequence: the stroke that follows next depends on the preceding stroke. For example, after an upstroke is produced, the chance of a downstroke is very high. HMM is especially useful for temporal pattern recognition where the output of the handwriting pattern is recognizable, but the process of the handwriting is not known. The HMM provides information about sequence when modeling handwriting and is used in automatic signature verification (Kashi et al. 1997).

A Gaussian mixture model (GMM) "is a parametric probability density function represented as a weighted sum of Gaussian component densities. GMMs are commonly used as a parametric model of the probability distribution of continuous measurements or features in a biometric system" (Reynolds 2008). GMMs are also used in handwriting verification systems sometimes in conjunction with HMMs.

Gannon Technologies Group has developed what is referred to and trademarked as Graph-based Recognition Technology, a technique similar to isomorphic graph matching. While Gannon is partially relying on traditional handwriting recognition techniques, it has further developed a method for handwriting identification that is biometric in nature. Handwriting-derived biometric identification is enabled through the use of recognizing and associating each graph element in a body of writing to an alphabet letter (Gantz et al. 2005; Miller et al. 2017). Because each graph may involve the calculating of hundreds of measurements, Gannon has developed a technique called the biometric kernel that reduces the measurements to the ones that are biometrically unique or identifiable to the writer. The biometric kernel of that writer is then used to compare to the other writing samples in the database to locate other possible matches in the database. The technology extends to cursive elements, or pictographs, in connected handwriting as well as the ability to recognize connected parts of text graphically instead of isolating parts exclusively to a single alphabetical unit (Walch and Gant 2004).

Clearly, the methods developed in handwriting identification demonstrate that handwriting is measurable and allows for statistical analysis. The methods being employed in these efforts to harness the efficacy of the computer do evidence clearly that the basis has been accepted—that handwriting identification meets the measurement criteria for science.

14.4 STANDARDS OF PRACTICE

In order for handwriting examination to be considered a science, the document examiner must employ the laws of science as the foundation from which work will proceed. The examiner must systematically pursue knowledge, recognize and formulate the problem, collect data through observation or experimentation, and formulate and test one or more hypotheses. In brief, the examiner must follow the accepted course of scientific method. Finally, the conclusions reached must be only those that reason and/or logic can support. Without standards of practice, handwriting identification cannot be practiced as a science.

The work of the handwriting examiner is two-phased: (1) examination, and (2) study. The term *examination*, as used in the expression *document examination*, has been employed, almost since the inception of the discipline, as an all-inclusive term covering the various aspects of the work, from writer identification, writing machine discriminations, to sobriety determinations.

Document examination should be conducted on the basis of the three fundamental elements that are characteristic of any scientific pursuit: (1) building on the universally accepted principles of a science, (2) following the process ordained as *scientific method*, and (3) employing the science of reason, that is, the principles of logic, to draw conclusions from the information any study provides.

The NAS Report (2009) discussed the importance of standards and guidelines for quality control and their importance associated with bias, consistency, validity, and reliability. "Standards reduce variability resulting from the idiosyncratic tendencies of the individual examiner—for example, setting conditions under which one can declare a 'match' in forensic identifications" (p. 7–7).

There are conflicts within forensic science as to professionalism and the application of science by practitioners. These conflicts arise in handwriting identification because the field does not adequately control the admission of persons having questionable qualifications and competence. Some examiners that have had limited instruction or are essentially self-taught have made themselves available to the legal profession and to private individuals, neither of whom are in a position to judge their competence. In the absence of a legally established licensing system, mandatory standards of competence, or broadly accepted appropriate academic qualification, some examiners use improper techniques, practices, and assertions that place the reputation of the discipline at risk and the pursuit of justice in jeopardy. The NAS Report (2009) commented that in spite of the number of standards in the forensic sciences, "their voluntary nature and inconsistent application make it difficult to assess their impact" (p. 7–10).

In a plea for greater professionalism, Godown (1970) asserted that a professional organization is based, in part, on unification with regard to standards of practice, ethical and practical. Cole (1980) appealed for a set of standards of practice falling within the document examiner's code of ethics dealing more specifically with the description of documents and the writing of reports. Purdy (1985) advocated a quality control system based on the development of a methods manual prescribing axioms governing the handling of documents, the examination of documents, and the writing of reports.

Osborn (1929) prescribed standards of practice under different headings including the care of questioned documents, the examination process, a 76-point checklist covering all aspects of a document where significant facts may be found, and the issuance of reports. The standards of practice that Cole and Godown were seeking were a consolidation of the best of the respective standards for the time. Slyter (1995) developed a detailed and systematic standard for the examination of signatures that adheres to scientific method including a thorough and hierarchical list of handwriting elements and quality controls pertaining to the evaluation of the quality and quantity of samples. Huber and Headrick offered the following model as a recommended standard of practice.

14.4.1 Standards of Practice for the Examination of Handwriting

14.4.1.1 Recording of Material

1. A document* on which a writing or lettering is or may be present, that is the subject of an examination and described in a report, shall be identified as an *item* and given an alphabetic or numeric designation. It shall be designated an *exhibit* only if it has been so designated by a judicial forum to which it has been submitted.
2. An item that is the subject of an examination, to which reference is made in a report, shall be described in sufficient detail to discriminate it from any other item of a like nature that may be involved in the same matter.

14.4.1.2 Protection of Material

3. Items that are the subject of an examination shall be kept, whenever possible, in clear plastic or cellophane covers and direct contact with them by the hands, writing instruments, and other devices shall be minimized or avoided completely.
4. While documents are in an examiner's custody nothing shall be done to them that will alter their physical state or condition, without the consent of the party for whom they are being examined or his or her counsel.

14.4.1.3 Approach to Examination and Study

5. Whenever possible, an examination of handwriting shall proceed from a study of the known to the unknown. In the process, notation shall be made of the following:
   a. The discriminating elements and their range of variation exhibited by the known
   b. The degree of correspondence that is found in the discriminating elements of the unknown
6. The examination of textual writing in a language in which the examiner is not fluent shall not be conducted without a printout of the text that identifies each allograph, or the assistance of a person competent to do so.

14.4.1.4 Basis and Reporting of Results

7. A definitive conclusion respecting the identification of a questioned writing or signature with provable standards shall be based on (1) the presence of a number of similarities in writing habits, in combination, sufficient in significance to preclude their occurrence by coincidence, and on (2) the absence of inexplicable disparities.

* For the purpose of these standards, "a document" is considered to include any portion of paper, or of like material or any other substrate on which writing or lettering is or may be present.

8. In the writing of reports, statements reflecting the consequence of a finding, for example, that a signature is genuine or spurious, or is a forgery are not to be expressed.
9. Reports respecting a writing/signature appearing in a photograph or photocopy must be phrased to ensure that the findings are understood to relate to a writing or signature on another document, as yet unseen, of which the photograph and/or photocopy examined purports only to be an honest, reliable reproduction.
10. The findings of a handwriting examination are reasoned conclusions drawn from observed and evaluated physical evidence. They should be expressed as *conclusions* in the lexical sense, despite the fact that when stated orally in a civil or criminal litigation they may sometimes constitute opinion testimony in a legal sense.

14.4.1.5 Certainty of Conclusions

11. A definitive statement respecting the identification of a signature and/or of a writing is a moral certitude based on a matter of probability at a level that implies that the probability of any other occurrence, while not impossible, is too remote to be considered practical. Accordingly, a conclusion drawn from a writing study is not and cannot be expressed as an absolute certainty.
12. When a questioned signature or writing is examined in isolation from known standards of particular writers, and if appropriate evidence is present, it may be described as "exhibiting classic symptoms of genuineness or spuriousness," but such symptoms are insufficient to support a definitive statement.

In 1997, the Technical Working Group for Questioned Documents (TWGDOC) began developing standards of practice for document examiners. This group was renamed the Scientific Working Group for Forensic Document Examination (SWGDOC) in 1999. From 2000 to 2012, standards of practice were developed by the American Society of Testing and Materials, International (ASTM) and practicing document examiners using a formal protocol that included strict adherence to ASTM practices in the development of standards. ASTM published over 20 standards pertaining to document examination tests and practices, and these standards were routinely relied upon by most document examiners practicing in the United States. The standards included methods for the examination of handwriting, altered documents, paper, ink, typewritten items, indentations, printer technology, and other technical examinations related to document examination. The standards also included terminology for expressing conclusions, scope of work, and training requirements.

In 2012, SWGDOC resumed publication of the standards all of which are available on its web site (www.swgdoc.org). Under different organizations, these standards have evolved with advancements in science and technology. Fundamentally, they adhere to the recommendations made by Huber and Headrick, but the SWGDOC standards are broader in scope providing detailed practice and methods for a wide variety of tests in document examination.

The European Network of Forensic Science Institutes (ENFSI) developed the *Best Practice Manual for the Forensic Examination of Handwriting* (2015). The ENFSI standard is a comprehensive 40-page manual including appendices on training requirements, detailed procedures for examination and comparison that includes illustrations of handwriting features, and a flow diagram.

The Documentation of Forensic Handwriting Method: A Modular Approach by Found and Bird (2016) offers a comprehensive method flow diagram. The standard describes in detail each phase of the method including illustrations of handwriting factors fully supporting each phase with numerous citations from published studies.

Standards of practice are not laws or regulations. Nevertheless, while compliance is not compulsory, noncompliance places an onus upon the examiner to defend the decision not to follow prescribed standards of practice. What should be of even greater importance to document examiners, however, is the message of reassurance that standards convey to the public and to the courts that the discipline is sincere in its endeavors to unify procedures to ensure competence, consistency, and reliability in results. Standards of practice are essential to science. Although seldom recognized as such, scientific method is the foremost standard of practice for scientific study.

14.5 REPORTING RESULTS

The National Research Council (NAS report), in its 2009 review of forensic sciences, made several critical comments and recommendations for improvement with respect to reporting results. NAS recommended that forensic reports should follow scientific method in their format and reports, and include sections on method and materials, procedures, results, conclusions, and identified areas of uncertainty. NAS stated that reports should be complete and thorough to the extent that they allow for an unbiased scrutiny of the conclusion. There was criticism directed at the brevity of many forensic reports that merely include the items examined and a conclusion without any scientific methodology explained. The NAS Report recognized the existence of standards to explain opinions or terms (e.g., the SWGDOC standards), however, the NAS committee also found that many forensic professions or examiners do not use the standards or terms consistently, or, that some of the terms are vague or imprecise.

Found and Edmond (2012) lent support to the recommendations made by the NAS committee regarding reporting results. In a paper on reporting on the comparison and interpretation of pattern evidence (including handwriting examination), they advocate a transparent approach to forensic report writing that allows for the evaluation of the opinion by both practitioners and those in the legal community.

Found and Bird (2016) provided more detail about reporting in their modular method of handwriting examination. They state explicitly: "All reporting, whether verbal or written, must be transparent, clear and complete. As a minimum, reporting must include the following elements: [1] A statement of propositions utilized in the evaluation of the evidence [2] A statement of the relevant background information provided to the examiner [3] A statement of any assumptions made by the examiner, including those assumptions tested as part of the examination process [4] A statement of limitations affecting the assessment or evaluation of the evidence [5] An explanation of the potential effect if there is any to change to propositions, assumptions or limitations in terms of the outcome of the examination" (p. 67).

Found and Bird (2016) also discuss the use of probability scales and advocate that they may be misleading. While they commented that handwriting identification is still in the process of embracing empirical approaches, they recommend forming conclusions within the framework or language of likelihood ratios (e.g., "evidence provides very strong support for proposition X over proposition Y" [p. 68]).

Most authorities on the subject of technical report writing place emphasis on audience analysis, a term intended to direct attention to the questions: who might read the report, and, what might they expect to learn from the report? The forensic scientist has, in point of fact, two audiences: one comprised largely of lawyers, law enforcement people and lay persons (few of whom may be technically oriented), and the other consisting of scientists or technically competent personnel interested in reviewing the procedure followed and the evidence found. The first audience is primarily concerned with the final results, that is, the conclusions drawn. The second audience is primarily interested in the conclusions and whether the premises for them have been properly established.

Some forensic science laboratories and their personnel have opted to address only the non-technical audience and, in so doing, to omit the material that only the technically competent reader might fully comprehend. Certainly, this simplifies the task of report writing, for it reduces it to a matter of expressing conclusions or listing findings without having to provide justification or accountability. The end is offered without revealing the means. There is a danger, however, that shortcuts of this kind in the exposition may induce an abbreviation of the examination since details of it do not have to be described. Furthermore, the practice tends to violate the rules for proper technical reports that numerous authorities have been advocating for many years. Certainly, it eliminates all elements of persuasion that Houp and Pearsall (1984) consider essential.

In the United States, Rule 26 of the Federal Rules of Civil Procedure prescribes the manner in which forensic science reports must be prepared to be acceptable as evidence. These requirements include:

1. A complete statement of all opinions and the basis for each opinion offered
2. All data relied upon to support the opinion
3. A curriculum vitae that includes a listing of all papers written and published in the last 10 years
4. Copies of all documents to be used at trial
5. A list of all depositions and court testimonies rendered in the last 4 years
6. A statement of the compensation expected to be received by the examiner

While Rule 26 provides some gatekeeping measures on the part of the court in requiring the expert to provide a more complete report with respect to the basis for opinions and data relied upon to support the opinion, there is, however, too much variety in the approach to handwriting problems and perhaps even more in the manner in which reports are written. There has been an appeal for the development of a battery of performance standards that might describe, in part at least, the manner of conducting examinations within the framework of a given code of ethics.

Huber and Headrick advocated a number of self-evident standards regarding the writing of reports that should be universally acceptable to all examiners. In some respects, but not all, the proposals they made are similar to the outline of Purdy (1982). Some examiners argue that they are required to comply with the administrative policy of an employer at the expense of such standards, but such convention verges on the questionable practice of subjecting scientific reports to the critique and control of nonscientific personnel.

Scientific reports should have the structure of critical argument suggested by Huth (1982), which consists of (1) a question or hypothesis that is posed, (2) presentation of the evidence pro and con bearing on the question, (3) assessment of the evidence, and (4) the conclusion that is reached. Reports of scientific research or investigation generally follow this structure, but include one or two additional elements: (5) the means by which the investigator gathered the evidence bearing on the question or hypothesis, must be described in detail sufficient to enable another investigator to replicate the research or study, and (6) the evidence gathered by the investigator must be separated from that available in the scientific literature.

The format widely used in many scientific fields divides and sequences the content of the report to fall under the general captions of introduction, methods, results, discussion, and if necessary, references, whether or not these five captions are used. These captions are readily applicable to reports respecting traditional research projects, but their appropriateness to the daily bench work of the document examiner is less obvious. Indeed, the components of Huth's (1982) critical arguments (1 to 4) with their additional two elements (5 and 6) appear to be more pertinent to the daily tasks of the forensic scientist, rather than the research scientist.

Huber and Headrick maintain that a proper report should have in its composition five elements:

1. A section to describe the material studied and to satisfy the legal requirements respecting *continuity*
2. A section to set down the objective or purpose of the study
3. A section to report the data found that the study has taken into consideration
4. A section to report the findings or conclusions drawn from the evidence found
5. A section to accommodate miscellaneous matters that are not essential ingredients of the work that was performed or the results achieved

The first may be captioned *description* and takes into account the possession of all items examined. It should be common practice to insert the purpose of the study as the second section under the caption *examination(s) requested.* All technical or scientific work must have a purpose even if it is simply the study of an unknown, without any particular goal in mind. Forensic science examinations have a purpose and they should be stated at the beginning of a report. They are, in fact, the hypotheses that are being pursued (e.g., that subject K.1 wrote item Q or that item Q was not written by subject K.1).

The third section may be captioned *data* or *observations* and serves to describe the nature of the material, its adequacy or otherwise, and the observations that have been made that will serve as the basis for any conclusions that might be drawn from the facts found. This is the factual evidence provided by the physical objects that have been studied. Without it in the technical report, there are no grounds for drawing inferences.

The fourth section may be captioned *conclusions* or *findings* and is confined to statements that can be made and supported on the strength of the evidence that the study revealed. Conclusions are the inferences that may be drawn from the factual evidence within the report, but it must be borne in mind that not all findings are conclusions. Some are observations made with the assistance of particular technical devices. The fifth may be captioned *remarks* and provides a section for comments or advice that are not necessarily an integral part of the study conducted.

The organization of a technical report in a manner such as this ensures that it has a proper beginning, an informative body, and a logical and understandable ending. It starts with premises that lead to conclusions so the syllogism is complete. Handwriting identification or document examination is only worthy of the label *science* when its endeavors and principles achieve a measure of universal agreement.

A second examination by another competent investigator should produce the same results. To demonstrate the scientific nature of the discipline, the first examiner should welcome reexamination by a peer. It is responsible scientific practice on the part of the examiner to produce a document that clearly charts the course of his or her examination in a manner that others may follow. Work must be reported in a fashion that allows for it to be replicated by a second or a third investigator. Agreement between investigators is the goal to achieving universality, one of the two criteria of science.

14.6 IMPROVING THE SCIENCE OF HANDWRITING IDENTIFICATION

In the ruling of Judge McKenna (*US v. Starzecpyzel* 1995), it was stated that forensic document examiners are not scientists, but are more in the nature of skilled craftsmen; that their opinions may be less precise, and do not have the demonstrable certainty that some sciences have. This ruling prompted many document examiners to rethink the state and nature of their profession.

The points made in the decision of Judge McKenna correspond in many respects to the criticisms expressed by Risinger et al. (1989) in their widely-cited paper published in the *University of Pennsylvania Law Review*. Indeed, Saks was a witness in the *Starzecpyzel* case. The law review article stimulated a critical response from a number of authors (Buglio and Wiersema 1989; Crown 1989; Scott 1989; Wenderoth 1989; Galbraith et al. 1995, and others). Much of the criticism toward Risinger et al. may have stemmed from their obvious agenda to indict the discipline of handwriting identification. Similarly, the McKenna decision generated arguments for many years. With perhaps two exceptions, all of the responses that initially sprang from the Risinger et al. article and the McKenna decision were reactionary in nature; attempts to rationalize, justify, and criticize the criticisms. Initially, Found and Rogers (1995) and Huber (1995) were proactionary; prepared to concede that a problem existed and offered some direction to rectify the situation.

Huber and Headrick provided criteria for the admission of a discipline respecting the study of handwriting into the scientific community. These criteria constitute an appropriate basis from which the science of handwriting examination can be practiced. Briefly, in order for a document examiner to claim the practice of scientific methods in handwriting identification, the examiner must demonstrate both in conduct and explanation concerning the operations of the discipline the following at an acceptable level:

1. Reliability of the behavior that will be the subject of study: that is, handwriting
2. Reliability of interpretation:
    a. conspectus reliability: the agreement between examiners as to what constitutes evidence in a given sample, and how significant it is (interrater reliability)
    b. inference reliability: the consistency of judgments across different samples from the same writer (test–retest reliability)
3. Discriminative reliability of the process: the consistency of judgments across samples from different writers, including simulations
4. Validity of premises: habituation and heterogeneity of the population (i.e., the uniqueness of handwriting to the individual)
5. Validity of process: the level of accuracy of assessments or analyses, across samples from different writers, or from the same writer
6. Skill in analysis: the level of education and special training required versus intuition

14.6.1 Reliability of the Behavior

It is believed that handwriting is stable, at least over short periods of time. The ability of most people to recognize familiar writing is testimony to that belief. If writing was not stable, recognition would not occur. Yet, although each person may have experienced handwriting recognition, most are not in a position to explain why.

Stability and consistency in writing features, however, has been established in and demonstrated by several objective published studies. Harvey (1934) obtained samples from 50 subjects two months apart and measured 16 handwriting variables. He found a correlation between samples of each subject of 0.77. Birge (1954) had two raters measure five writing variables in 50 samples from the same subject, and obtained an average correlation of 0.97. Lockowandt (1976) quoted studies (by Timm, Fischer, Prystav, and others) that have yielded high correlation coefficients for measured handwriting characteristics (most beyond 0.90) indicative of great consistency between samples from the same writer. Squire (1968) focused particularly on the stability of handwriting and obtained specimens of writing from 26 subjects at a two-week interval. The nine characteristics studied and measured (looping of the letter "l," closing of the letters "a" and "o," degree of slope, etc.) revealed consistency for all the characteristics studied, with the exception of slope. This may be an indication that slope is subject to a wider range of natural variation.

From a practical perspective, the vast majority of cases involving questioned writings of various kinds and of various ages have been correctly and properly associated with standards of writing from an equal number of persons, in the course of civil and criminal litigation. Valid identifications and valid eliminations could not and would not have been possible if the discriminating elements of handwriting on which the examinations depended were not stable over periods of time of various lengths. In summary, research evidence and practical experience affirms the stability of the behavior of writing and its reliability as a subject of study.

14.6.2 Reliability of Interpretation

14.6.2.1 Conspectus Reliability

Conspectus reliability in handwriting identification is universal agreement as to what is evidence in a set of standards and its significance. Obviously, there must be universal agreement within the discipline as to the evidence that will be considered. This is not to suggest that all examiners evaluate that evidence the same way—although this should be the ideal—but only to clarify and to achieve agreement as to what it is that will constitute evidence and the language employed to refer to it.

The NAS report (2009) commented that there needs to be a consensus among the forensic sciences concerning terminology and standards of practice. This is in line with the *Daubert* Rule 702 (2000) guidelines that mention that the court consider whether the technique relied upon by the expert has been generally accepted within the relevant scientific community.

14.6.2.2 Inference Reliability

Inference reliability, as it pertains to handwriting identification, is the consistency of judgments made on the basis of different standards from the same writer (technically termed *test-retest reliability*) and introduces a number of conditions upon which proof of reliability will depend.

The several sets of standards from the subject will have to provide the same or very similar textual material to ensure that, qualitatively and quantitatively, the same evidence will be present. It is then a matter of simply proving the stability of writing generally, the criterion referred to as *the reliability of the behavior*, that was previously concluded as adequately demonstrated by the research conducted and the practical experience gained.

If, however, it is proposed that the examiner work from standards of different textual material, then it must be recognized that each set of standards may contain different sets of evidence, having different levels of identification value. Within different sets of standards, evidence may differ in both kind and quantity. As long as the standards are adequate in number and the examiner offers consistent judgment to include differing levels of certainty within the same upper or lower quadrants of the scale of probability, then the examiner can offer conclusions. By this approach, allowance is made for some difference in evidential values.

If the judgments of different sets of standards are to be made by the same examiner, and consistency in results is the principle object of the study, it may be difficult to obtain. Exposure to one set of standards may influence the outcome of a second examination of a second set of standards by the same examiner.

On the other hand, judgments of different standards by different examiners is a common occurrence in contested cases. Consistency in results between examiners working with different standards would appear to provide substantial support for the reliability of inferences that may be drawn from writing, if, and only if, it can be assumed that both examiners are considering the same universal standard for kinds of evidence. In other words, after conspectus (interrater) reliability has been achieved.

It is not an uncommon practice, in a number of cases, for examiners to have been employed by an opposing party and asked to conduct a second examination frequently with a different set of standards than those relied upon by the first examiner. In the vast majority of these cases, the standards submitted to the two examiners are quite different in kind and number. Ideally, it should be rare that two examiners fundamentally disagree if provided with the same materials for examination. When disagreement does occur, qualifications, competence, and/or experience of the examiners are usually equally dissimilar. Thus, for the purpose of the present discussion such exceptional cases of disagreement can be disregarded. Insofar as the vast majority of cases are concerned, there is a general lack of record as to those cases in which agreement occurs in order that a compilation can be made that allows this information to serve as evidence of inference reliability.

14.6.3 Discriminative Reliability of the Process

Discriminative reliability pertains to the accuracy of judgments made across samples of writing from different persons, including those that are simulations of another person's writing, despite the process of imitation employed. In fact, it is an exceedingly important corollary to one of the two premises underlying writing identification: the heterogeneity of writing. If the process employed is not capable of discriminating between the writings of any two individuals, examiners are without the means of proving that writing is, without exception, heterogeneous. Furthermore, examiners are without a facility for knowing when and if, in their examination and study of the heterogeneity of writings, they are being deceived.

Huber and Headrick suggested a compilation of 21 discriminating elements of writing that serve to discriminate between any two writers of a given population, and to differentiate between the genuine and spurious executions respecting any single writer. The ability of the process to discriminate hinges largely on a proper and thorough study of the heterogeneity of writing, which is the next constituent of the criteria to be established. If the process does not discriminate in all cases, some revision of Huber and Headrick's 21 discriminating elements, or of an examiner's capabilities and facilities, may be required. The study of the heterogeneity of writing will likely provide an answer to the question of the discriminatory reliability of the process, as a corollary to the fundamental question respecting the uniqueness of writing. If the heterogeneity of writing can be proven by the process being used, then the process has been vindicated and must be reliable.

If a study of heterogeneity is to be conducted in accordance with scientific method, the examiner must be prepared to acknowledge that a null hypothesis could be the result; that is, that the process is not capable of discriminating between the writings of all persons. It may be learned, however, what the margin of error of the process may be, and what must be done to reduce that margin.

Harris (1958) remarked on the similarity he found in signatures of the same names, particularly those consisting of six letters or less. His study also disclosed that some letters provide less variation in form or design from one writer to the next, and that other somewhat peculiar letter forms can become popular and appear more frequently than might be expected. Accordingly, the discriminative ability of the writing examination process must be considered with regard to the kind and quantity of writing to be involved in the study, if valid results are to be obtained.

Document examiners now have empirical support for the hypotheses that (1) handwriting is sufficiently unique to the individual to permit discrimination between writers, and (2) competent examiners are sufficiently capable of discriminating between writers with acceptable low levels of error. These studies are discussed at the end of this chapter.

14.6.4 Validity of the Premises

Handwriting identification is based on two underlying premises that may, when both have been proven, constitute the scientific principles on which the work is based.

14.6.4.1 Habituation

People are primarily creatures of habit and writing is a collection of habit hierarchies of at least three levels: (1) letter habit, (2) word habit, and (3) phrase habit. These habits are employed according to the degree to which the action process is subjugated to the thought process. Writing habits are neither instinctive nor hereditary, but are complex processes that are developed gradually. Handwriting, or indeed footwriting, mouth-writing or typewriting, is a neuromuscular behavior that develops as an acquired perceptual-motor skill. It involves successively higher stages of integration as learning proceeds.

In handwriting comparisons, letters, combinations of letters, words, or phrases must be considered according to the degree to which they constitute a collective habit. It is a classic example of synergism in which the whole constitutes more than the sum of its parts. Accordingly, the influence of adjoining letters upon one another will vary according to the role these letters play in words or phrases that have become writing habits as units, rather than as individual letters. Variation in shape and movement can be expected to occur in relation to this factor.

14.6.4.2 The Heterogeneity of Writing

The uniqueness of writing to the individual is a subject that has been discussed in Chapter 3. In the context of addressing the present topic, some previous statements bear repeating. Handwriting identification is predicated on the heterogeneity of the writing of the population; that is, on the principle that handwriting is unique to the individual. The argument in support of this contention, however, stems largely but simply from the truism that "nature never offers her handiwork to us in facsimile." Thus, people are likened to leaves or to stones, no two of which have been found to be precisely the same.

Any two items of nature may be distinguished from each other if the scale of judgment that is used is appropriate and sufficiently precise. Whether or not the method employed in handwriting examination is fitting and sufficiently precise to discriminate between the writings of any two individuals is the initial challenge that has to be addressed

Questions worthy of investigation are whether a sample of the population can provide sufficient information respecting the differences between writers to indicate (1) what the probability of deceptive duplicity might be, and (2) to what extent deception may be an inverse function of the size or quantity of the writing specimen.

14.6.5 Validity of the Processes

This is related to, but not an alternative for "the discriminative reliability of the process" previously discussed. The issue is the process's ability to discriminate between (i.e., to differentiate) the writings of different persons. Further, there is inquiry as to the process's ability to recognize (i.e., to identify), with reasonable certainty, two writings as being products of the same person.

Admittedly, the two problems utilize the same discriminating elements in their determinations. The task of discrimination, however, relies on the evaluation of differences, whereas the task of identification procures its support from the evaluation of similarities. The level of accuracy of the assessments made by examiners from casework is not likely to prove to be a credible source for the data needed. On the other hand, this should not be a difficult situation to simulate in test material.

14.6.6 Skill in Analysis

The roles of skill, training, intuition, and education in the performance of an examiner is a matter that many have spoken about, but not in a fashion that delineates their relative merits. A Studies by Kam et al. (1994) and Wetstein et al. (1994) showed that trained document examiners were significantly more successful at identifying handwriting than lay persons.

Some organizations have insisted upon academic qualifications, at an undergraduate degree level at least, for admission or certification, without any particular stipulation as to the program of institutional learning. The result has been that the academic backgrounds of document examiners are widely diversified. However, there are specific advantages to a university training with respect to the professionalism of the examiner:

1. University education, even that which is not directly related, ensures the possession of the minimum level of intelligence necessary.
2. University education can provide some direction in abstract and analytical thinking, vital aspects of the occupation of any document examiner.
3. Handwriting is a human behavior, an understanding of which is practicably obtained through the psychology courses offered by universities.
4. The basics of ink chemistry and an understanding of the electromagnetic spectrum is knowledge needed and practicably obtained through university courses.
5. An understanding of statistical analysis is essential to the application of measurements to the examination of writing, if it is to rate as a branch of science. This is practicably and perhaps only obtained through university courses.
6. To justify being accepted by other disciplines within forensic science, practitioners must offer reasonably corresponding backgrounds.
7. Professional competence in forensic science, like justice itself, must not only be done, but must seem to be done. It is essential to secure the client's and the court's confidence. A university education is germane to this acquisition.
8. Growth and development in the discipline of handwriting identification or document examination will occur only in conjunction with growth in intellectual stature and the gain of broader and more profound understanding of various branches of science. University education is the practical route to this end.
9. Self-instruction alone cannot meet these needs.

It is recognized that there is a need for an education in the sciences as the basis for the development of skills in this unique discipline. If this cannot be articulated and demonstrated professionally, the ability to frame handwriting identification in scientific method may be beyond the reach of some examiners. Current standards for document examination training recommend that, at a minimum, the examiner should have an undergraduate degree prior to their training as a document examiner. The adoption of academic study by professional organizations as a preferred standard might change the capabilities and qualifications of the next generation of examiners. The advantages of education to the conduct of the work might then be articulated and indisputably demonstrated. Furthermore, it might so consolidate the thinking of competent examiners that fewer disparities would be found in the testimony and reports of practitioners.

In summary, the transformation of handwriting identification into a science must begin with the establishment of conspectus reliability and the heterogeneity of writing. The ability of the process employed to discriminate between writers, and the nature and quantity of writing necessary to do so reliably, follow as two further aspects of the work that will have to be addressed. Finally, at some point in time, a general agreement should be reached as to the program of higher learning to be followed by students in preparation for work in the discipline, if only to more appropriately equip future examiners.

It brings the discussion back to the *Starzecpyzel* (1995) ruling that identified handwriting identification as "purely practical in nature," stating that handwriting examiners are "nonscientific expert witnesses," and that handwriting examination is "closer to a practical skill, such as piloting a vessel, than to a scientific skill." The court was even critical of the use of terms such as *scientific* and *laboratory* by document examiners, alleging that it is an attempt to gird themselves in the trappings of science to garner some of the respect science traditionally enjoys.

This criticism may be unfair if not invalid. There are a number of kinds of investigations conducted as part of a document's study that are clearly within the parameters of science. The chromatographic analysis of the composition of inks, the chemical analysis of paper additives, the botanical analysis of paper fibers, the optical examinations of the responses of writing media in the ultraviolet and near infrared regions of the electromagnetic spectrum are but a few.

In these areas, however, document examination is not performing as a science in its own right. Rather it is employing the precepts and principles of various branches of science to pursue its studies. It relies on the principles of chemistry in its study of inks. It uses the precepts of botany in its study of papers. It employs the laws of physics in its studies of UV (ultraviolet) and IR (infrared) radiations. Even Risinger et al. (1989), in their criticism of document examination cited earlier, allowed that many kinds of document examination employ techniques based on principles of applied science. As such, document examination is a combination of many kinds of applied science.

14.6.7 Summary

In summary, the pursuit of the aforementioned six criteria is necessary to achieve the station of a science. Several are interdependent, however. There must be some agreement on the evidence to be considered (conspectus reliability) before the discriminative reliability of the process can be tested. Furthermore, establishing the heterogeneity of handwriting will depend on the reliability of the process being employed to make discriminations. If the process is too fallible, it may require revision. It appears, however, that conspectus reliability is deserving of priority treatment.

In many respects, the criteria established by Huber and Headrick is also referred to in the US Federal Rules of Evidence. Per Rule 702, the court will allow the testimony of expert witnesses if they meet the following criteria: (a) the expert's scientific, technical, or other specialized knowledge will help the trier of fact to understand the evidence or to determine a fact in issue, (b) the testimony is based on sufficient facts or data, (c) the testimony is the product of reliable principles and methods, and (d) the expert has reliably applied the principles and methods to the facts of the case.

14.7 CONCLUSION

Found and Rogers (1995) stated succinctly: "The future of our profession is based on learning from the types of criticisms that have been raised and recognizing that some of the traditional beliefs in the field must be abandoned" (p. 26). The traditional beliefs that Found and Rogers referred to concerned the infallibility of the practitioner and the method. Prior to *Starzecpyzel* (1995), practitioners and the methods they employed had not been empirically tested.

Historically, many reports and studies have been presented or published over the years, but too large a percentage of these have been anecdotal in nature, that is, case histories or descriptions, lacking empirical data. In past research, conclusions were often based on samples too small to be reliable. The lack of solid research and nonadherence to a scientific process resulted in the previously discussed criticisms from Risinger et al. (1989) as well as Risinger and Saks (1996), Saks and VanderHaar (2005), Risinger (2007), adverse rulings to handwriting identification in the court, and the criticisms reported in the NAS report in 2009.

As a response to these criticisms, considerable strides have been made in advancing handwriting examination as a scientific practice. Prior to and subsequent to the publication of the NAS report, there have been hundreds of studies on components of handwriting examination that firmly establishes the scientific viability of the field (Harralson et al. 2015). Based on the numerous scientific studies that have appeared since *Starzecpyzel*, many of the criticisms raised in reviews such as those written by Risinger, Saks, and the NAS report (2009) have been addressed, demonstrating a response by the field and researchers to the criticisms.

In a review of handwriting examination in the NAS report (2009), specific issues with respect to handwriting variability (interpersonal variability compared to intrapersonal variability) were noted. Essentially, the NAS committee stated that there was a need for more scientific research in handwriting examination:

> The scientific basis for handwriting comparisons needs to be strengthened. Recent studies have increased our understanding of the individuality and consistency of handwriting and computer studies and suggest that there may be a scientific basis for handwriting comparison, at least in the absence of intentional obfuscation or forgery. Although there has been only limited research to quantify the reliability and replicability of the practices used by trained document examiners, the committee agrees that there may be some value in handwriting analysis. (p. 5-30)

The NAS report cited three studies recognizing the scientific basis for handwriting comparison (Kam et al. 1997; Sita et al. 2002; Srihari et al. 2002). However, the committee commented that the scientific basis for handwriting comparison needs to be strengthened. The committee also pointed out that according to two of the cited studies regarding proficiency, document examiners had erroneous rates of 6.5% (Kam et al. 1997) and 3.4% (Sita et al. 2002), respectively. The NAS committee recognized the work by Srihari et al. which addressed the individuality of handwriting.

While the NAS report cited a few studies of importance (Kam et al. 1997; Sita et al. 2002; Srihari et al. 2002), there were other proficiency studies that could have been cited (Kam et al. 1994; Found et al. 1999; Found et al. 2001; Kam et al. 2001; Found and Rogers 2003; Kam and Lin 2003; Found and Rogers 2008; Dewhurst et al. 2008). These and other more recent studies demonstrate examiner proficiency across a variety of handwriting tasks (see Chapter 4).

The application of statistics and computational methods to inter- and intrawriter variation has been addressed in several studies using a variety of mathematical algorithms. Schomaker (2007), Bulacu (2007), Tan et al. (2009), Kalera et al. (2004), and Parziale et al. (2016) represent a small sample of the published research on the computational analysis of handwriting identification and verification. Other studies have addressed the use of likelihood ratios in handwriting (Davis et al. 2012; Marquis et al. 2011; Hepler et al. 2012; Taroni et al. 2012, 2014; Tang and Srihari 2014).

Srihari and Singer (2014) commented that there should be a combined role between practitioners and computerized analysis stating that "human examiners provide handwriting characteristics while computational methods provide the necessary statistical analysis" (p. 1083). Marcelli et al. (2015) recommend a combined approach of forensic handwriting examination best practices with pattern recognition methods. Collaboration between the handwriting examiner and the computer seems to be a viable approach in the continued advancement of the scientific practice of forensic handwriting examination.

Chapter 15

Terminology

15.1 UNDERSTANDING TERMS

Every discipline, whether scientific or not, has a language of its own. There are terms that the practitioners of the discipline have found or coined to more precisely describe their work or the materials with which they deal. Indeed, it has been suggested that a discipline without a language of its own has made little progress as consistency in terminology and methods is necessary for scientific practice.

Hilton (1982) compiled a fairly comprehensive collection of terms that was organized into six categories: general terms, handwriting, typewriting, altered documents, other identification problems, photographs and other reproductions. He mentioned that "there is a need for both standardization and simplification of terms ... [u]nlike most scientists, the document examiner is not primarily concerned with discussing his findings with highly trained associates but with presenting his conclusions clearly to the layman" (p. 14). A glossary focusing on technical terms associated with electronic handwriting was compiled by Harralson (2013).

Published standards of practice typically have a glossary or list of terms defined. The Scientific Working Group for Forensic Document Examination (SWGDOC) (2013a) publishes a standard on terminology related to documentation examination. SWGDOC also defines specific terms in other standards such as the *Standard for the Examination of Handwritten Items*. The European Network of Forensic Science Institutes (ENFSI) *Best Practice Manual for the Forensic Examination of Handwriting* (2015) has a basic listing of common terms used by handwriting examiners in presenting results. Found and Bird's *Forensic Handwriting Method* (2016) has a more extensive glossary that focuses on the technical aspects of handwriting examination.

The field of graphonomics has had some influence on terminology as the level of research being conducted is demanding greater precision in the nomenclature used and their meanings. As such, some of the terms used in studies involving computerized, online handwriting measurement have been incorporated. The following are terms that are being and have been utilized, respecting the examination of writing with the meanings that they should convey. A few terms have been added that respect other examinations within the purview of the document examiner that may serve to broaden the reader's understanding of the scope of the work.

15.2 GLOSSARY

Abbreviation: A shortened form of a word or title.

Acceleration: Handwriting features which show change or increase in velocity or speed; the rate in which handwriting changes velocity.

Accent: A mark indicating an emphasis on a syllable or word or quality of a vowel sound, sometimes called diacritics or diacritical accents. It may be positioned above, below, or through the alphabetic character.

Accent	Name	Example	Accent	Name	Example
´	acute	á	¯	Maoron	Ā
`	grave	à	˘	Breve	ă
^	circumflex	ê	¨	diaeresis	ä
~	tilde	Ã	¸	cedilla	ç

Acronyms: Abbreviations of private and governmental agencies or organizations in which the initial letters of the words in the name are written and spoken as a single word, for example, NATO.

Affix: A morpheme attached to a word root, a prefix, or a suffix.

Alignment: The spatial organization of the writing pattern, its linear arrangement of words and intervening spaces, and their accommodation on the page.

Allograph: A writing or signature made by one person for another; or a style (block capital, print script, or cursive form) of one of the 26 graphemes of the English alphabet or of the ligatures and other symbols that accompany it (Ellis 1979).

Allolog: Different forms of a word created by adding an affix, for example, hope to hoped.

Alphabet: A system of writing in which a set of allographs represent the graphemes of a language.

Ambidexterity: Equal skill and facility with both hands.

Ampersand (ampassy): The sign, "&," used as a symbol for "and" in several hundred languages.

Ample letter: That which encompasses more than the standard inner space in a given letter. Characterized by fulsomeness and expanded ovals and loops.

Apex: Up-pointing or down-pointing free-ending juncture of two stems, for example, "A," "M," "V," or "W."

Aphasia: The loss of a previous ability to speak, or impairment of the power to use and understand words.

Apostrophe: The superscript sign, " ' ," used to indicate the omission of a letter from a word, the possessive case, and certain plurals.

Appendage or paraph: A final pen-flourish of a free sweeping line made over or under a name written as a signature; sometimes a simple terminal stroke or dot.

Arc: Part of a circle; a bow-like curved line.

Arcade: The rounded style used to form the arches of the cursive letters "n," "m," and "h."

Arch: The rounded hump or top curve of such letters as "n," "m," and "h."

Arm: A horizontal or upward-sloping short stroke starting from the stem of a character, ending free, for example, "K," "E," or "F."

Arrangement: The order or organization of a written inscription on a sheet.

Ascender: Part of the lowercase letters extending above the body or x-height, for example, "b," "d," "h," or "k," usually a loop, but including the stem of the "t."

Assisted writing: The result of a guided hand, produced by the cooperation of the two minds and two hands of two persons.

Asterisk: A star-shaped symbol or figure, "*," used to indicate a reference to a footnote or an omission.

Autograph: A person's signature, his or her handwriting; a manuscript in an author's own handwriting.

Axial direction: In the direction of the axis.

Balloon: Printing that resembles speed ball-pen lettering.

Ballpoint pen: A writing instrument having as its distinguishing feature or characteristic a writing tip containing a rotatable ball that contacts the writing surface for the purpose of depositing the writing fluid.

Ball terminal: Small round globe, found at the end of some printing strokes, for example, "r" and "g."

Bar: Horizontal or oblique short final stroke of some cursive letters, not to be confused with terminal strokes.

Bar, connecting: Intermediate stroke, connecting strokes of a letter to other strokes, usually a dual-staffed letter.

Bar, cross: A stroke intersecting the stem or main portion of the letter; a cross stroke.

Baroque: Certain stylistic tendencies of the seventeenth and eighteenth century arts, characterized by exuberance and extravagance—grotesque, whimsical—used in reference to older designs of currency.

Base line: The horizontal real or assumed line upon which letters reside.

Beard: A slight hook preceding the body of a letter, not to be confused with that frequently forming a part of the initial stroke.

Beginning strokes: See strokes, initial.

Bitmap: A mosaic of dots or pixels defining an image, including dot matrix imprints. The smoothness of the image contour depends upon the fineness of resolution and the number of dots or pixels per inch.

Blind eyelet: An eyelet formation of such small size or narrow width that it has been filled in.

Blind loop: A loop formation that has been completely filled in with ink.

Blobbing: The accumulation of ink on the exterior of the point assembly of a ballpoint pen, that drops intermittently to the surface being written upon.

Block formation: Letters set so closely together within a word as to make the word stand out as a compact unit or block.

Blotter image: A natural, involuntary record on a blotter or similar substrate of script, figures, etc.

Blunt ending: The effect produced on commencement and terminal strokes of letters, both upper and lowercase, by the application of the writing instrument to the paper prior to the beginning of any horizontal movement; an action that usually omits any beard, hitch, knob, or tick.

Boat: A dish-shaped figure consisting of a concave stroke and a straight line, sometimes forming the base of letters.

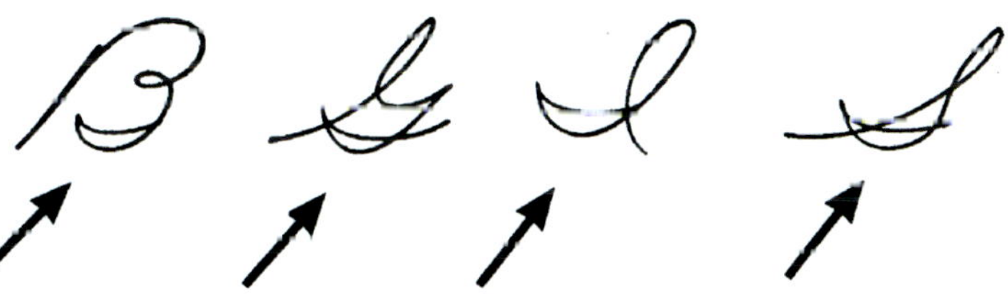

Body: That portion of a letter, the central part, that remains when the upper and lower projections, the terminal and initial strokes, and the diacritics are omitted.

Body-height: See x-height.

Bold face: A heavier version of a regular typeface; used for emphasis or visual effect.

Boustrophedon: Writing in which alternate lines are written in opposite directions and even have the posture as well as the direction of reversed letters.

Bow: A vertical curved stroke, as in capitals "D" and "C."

Bowl: The line fully enclosing a counter; a complete bowl, formed by a curved stroke only; a modified bowl, in which the stem forms a side of the bowl.

Braces: Two symbols ( ), used to connect or segregate written material.

Bracket or fillet: A wedge-shaped structure joining a serif to a stem.

Braille: A system of representing letters, numerals, etc., by raised dots that a visually-impaired person can read by touch.

Brush: Balloon-style printing extended to a script.

Buckle knot: The loop followed by a horizontal stroke that is sometimes used to complete letters such as the "A," "f," and "t."

Buckles: The means by which an element of a letter ties itself to the staff, as in the letters "K" and "R."

Burring: A division of a written line into two or more, more or less equal portions, by a noninked area generally running parallel to the direction of line generation, but moving away from the radius of a curving stroke, sometimes referred to as "splitting."

Cane: See "strokes, walking cane."

Capital letter or capital: Uppercase or majuscule (see also "uncial").

Caret: A mark, "^" used to show where something is to be inserted in written or printed matter.

Character: Any typed or handwritten mark, sign or insignia, abbreviation, punctuation mark, letter, or numeral, whether legible, blurred, or indistinct.

Check mark: A mark usually consisting of a short downward stroke, made with considerable pressure, followed by a lighter upward stroke at an angle toward the right (or to the left, as constructed by most, if not many, left-handed writers).

Chevrons: Horizontal (see "guillemets").

Cicero: A typographic unit of measurement used predominantly in Europe. It consists of 12 Didot points, each measuring .01483 inch. Thus, a cicero is .1776 inch or 4.511 mm.

Cipher: The arithmetic symbol "0," representing naught or zero.

Clockwise: The direction in which the hands of the clock move.

Coadjutant: One who works together with another; the individual providing enabling aid to a signer or signatory of a document, when required.

Codicil: A supplement to a will, the purpose of which is to alter or augment the provisions of the already executed will.

Collected standards: A sample of writing made during the normal course of business or social activity, not necessarily related to the matter in dispute.

Colophon: A short note at the end of a book, usually handwritten, giving details of its author and the making of the book. Also, the emblem or device of a publishing house, carried on the spine, title page, or back of a book.

Concave: A curved stroke that projects to the left or downward.

Condensed face: A typeface that has narrow letter widths.

Conjoined letters: Two letters that have been written in the common manner, such that the terminal stroke of the first is the initial stroke of the second.

Connectedness, degree of: The extent to which letters within a word are joined without lifting the writing instrument from the paper.

Connecting stroke: An expression commonly used to refer to the fusion of the terminal stroke of one lowercase cursive letter and the initial stroke of another, having no identifiable or describable entity of its own (see "conjoined letters").

Connection subtypes:

Unsupported—the body of the letter does not follow or retrace the stem.

Supported—the body of the letter rests against or retraces the stem.

Looped—the initial stroke forms a loop with the stem of the letter.

Contraction: A form of word abbreviation wherein one or more letters are omitted.

Convex: A curved stroke that projects to the right or upward.

Copybook: A manual of writing instruction that places models before the learner, to be copied.

Counter: A printer's term for the fully or partially-enclosed interior white space within a character, as in the "a," "b," "c," "d," "e," "g," "j," "o," "p," "q," "s," and many capitals.

Counterclockwise: The direction opposite to the movement of a clock's hands.

Counterstroke: A stroke that originates from a movement that stresses a direction opposite to the expected one.

Crossbar: The connecting horizontal stroke between two stems of a letter, as in "A" or "H," or the projecting horizontal stroke necessary for the formation of a letter, as in the cursive "t," or the printed "f."

Cross mark: A crude "X" used historically by those who could not write. Still used by illiterates and, if properly witnessed, can be legally accepted as a signature.

Crotch: Space where an arm or an arc meets a stem at an acute or obtuse angle.

Crown (cap): The horizontal (sometimes undulating) stroke forming the top of some letters; found only in majuscules, "T," "F."

Cursive: A form of continuous writing in which letters are connected to one another, and designed according to some commercial system; the most common allograph of a grapheme.

Curtailment: An abbreviation wherein the last letter(s) of a word are omitted.

Curvilinear: Consisting of or contained by a curved line or lines; opposite of rectilinear.

Cusp: The point at which two curved lines meet.

Dash: Short, usually horizontal, hastily written stroke.

Delta: Fourth letter of the Greek alphabet, "δ," the Greek d.

Dent: Slight hollow formation.

Descender: A part of a letter extending below the base line, as in "g," "j," "p," "q," "y."

Dextrality: Right-hand preference, as opposed to sinistrality or left-hand preference.

Diacritical mark or point: A sign added to a letter or symbol to give it a particular phonetic value. An accent. Sometimes used to refer to the dots over the "i" and "j."

Diagonal stroke: See "virgule."

Didot system: A typographic measuring system, used in Europe and based on the Didot point, similar to the US-English pica system (see cicero).

Digital ink: Some digital pad devices have active displays which show the handwriting trace on the electronic display at the pen and time location at or near real time. The trace on the display is referred to as digital ink.

Digital signature: A mathematical algorithm comprised of a private key and public key that is used for authenticating an electronic document. Digital signatures are mathematical data, not handwritten signatures.

Digital tablet. A computer input device that enables the user to draw, write, or sign a signature in a way similar to writing on a pen or pencil with paper. The tablet serves as the "paper" surface. Writing on the tablet allows for the digitization of the drawing, writing, or signature (also computer tablet, digitizer, digitizing tablet, drawing tablet, graphics tablet).

Digraph: A group of two successive letters representing a single sound or a complex sound that is not a combination of the sounds ordinarily represented by each in other occurrences, for example, "ph" in digraph, "ch" in chin.

Diphthong: The combination of two vowels in succession, the sound of which begins with one and ends with the other, for example, "oil," "boy," or "out."

Directional skipping: A skip that may occur after an abrupt (≥90 degree) change in the direction of line generation.

Disguise: The consequence of any deliberate attempt to alter the elements of one's own writing.

Disguised writing: The writing of a person who is deliberately attempting to alter his or her usual writing habits in the hope of concealing his or her identity.

Dismembered letter: A letter that lacks a structural part, is separated into parts, or has a part cut off.

Displacement: A stroke or letter written in one zone when it normally belongs in another.

Document: Any material that carries a communication, explicit or implied.

Dominating stroke: An extended horizontal stroke above a word; it may be an extended t-bar.

Dot: A minute, roundish, solid mark. Also called a point or period. It signifies interruption, stop, or silence.

Dotting: The deposit of small amounts of extraneous ink on the paper, occurring with predictable regularity under given conditions.

Double-length letters: Small or lowercase letters that have components that extend both above and below the x-height of the letter, for example, "f."

Downstroke: That part of a letter made when the writing instrument is moving from the top to the bottom of the letter, or a stroke directed toward the bottom of the paper.

Drag line: A very thin or light stroke of a writing instrument in areas where its movement is not normally recorded.

Duct: A stroke drawn or traced.

Ductus, link or junction-connected: The continuous line that joins two letters.

Ductus-broken or junction-broken: The disconnected or noncontinuous stroke between two letters.

Dynamic: In electronically-captured handwriting, refers to temporal features such as velocity, pressure, and duration. The dynamics of the signature refer to the movement patterns of the handwriting.

Dys-: Destroying the good sense of a word, for example, "dysfunction."

Dysgraphics: Inability to write or draw with any skill (Beacom).

Dyslexia: A disturbance of the ability to read.

Ear: the small stroke projecting from the top of the lowercase "g" in the printed letter. Sometimes given to a similar element of the printed letter "r."

Electronic signature: Handwritten signature that is captured on an electronic device using a stylus and digital tablet, or a digital pen. The law does not distinguish between a digital algorithm signature and a biometric signature. They are both considered electronic signatures even though they are different "signing" processes (also E-signature).

Elision: An abbreviation usually made for metrical and linguistic reasons that frequently affects the pronunciation of the word.

Ellipsis: A mark "...", used to indicate the omission of a part of quoted material or of words needed to complete a sentence.

Em space: A typographic unit of horizontal space, equal to the point size of any font.

En space: A typographic unit of horizontal space, equal to one half of the point size of any font.

Ending stroke: Finishing stroke of a letter.

Endstroke: The terminal stroke of a written form, word, or letter.

Endstroke obliteration: An endstroke that thrusts abruptly to the left, bisecting a word or signature crosswise.

Epistle: A letter or communication, especially a formal one.

Epsilon: The fifth letter of the Greek alphabet, "ε," representing the letter "e."

Escapement: The spacing of the letters or characters along the line of typewriting; the pitch.

Essential tremor: A common neurological condition causing tremor of the arms, and/or hands.

Exclamation mark: A punctuation mark "!," used after an exclamation.

Exemplar: An example of a person's writing, a standard for use in comparisons, a "collected" or a "request" specimen.

Expanded typeface: A typeface that has wide letter widths.

Expansion: The spread of writing, usually horizontally, upon the writing space.

Extended writing: Writing, usually cursive, of a textual nature, of any amount, but other than a signature.

Extensions: Ascending and descending stems and loops of bizonal and trizonal letters.

Eyelet: A small, round or oval formation beginning or closing a curve or spiral, or completing the inside shape of a round letter, for example, "e," "D," or "w."

Eyelet, blind: An eyelet formation of such size or width that it is "filled in."

Facsimile: An image of printed matter that has been transmitted electronically.

Feathering: The condition in which the writing/printing fluid spreads laterally in a pattern that usually follows the direction of the surface fibers away from the written or printed line. Characteristic of intaglio printing involving extreme pressures of the plate on the paper; thus, also called *gushing.*

Fixed spacing: Uniform horizontal spacing of the characters of a type font, as opposed to proportional spacing that varies with the design of the character.

Flourish: A decorative pen stroke that serves only as an ornament.

Flow-back: An increase in the density of an ink line caused by the run of excess ink along the finish of a stroke, occurring when the pen is lifted from the paper.

Fluctuation: Alternating changes of direction, position or conditions, that is, alternating acceleration and deceleration of writing speed, or alternating expansion and contraction of the writing pattern.

Fluency: Freedom, and other like terms, referring to a generally higher grade of line quality that is smooth, consistent, and without any evidence of tremor or erratic changes in direction or pen pressure.

Fluorescence: The phenomena in which some substances absorb light and reemit part of it as light of a longer wave length. Fluorescence ceases when incident or exciting illumination ceases.

Flying finish: The diminishing taper of a terminal stroke when the motion of the instrument does not stop at the completion of a word, or the minute barb sometimes growing out of it.

Flying start: The growing taper of an initial stroke, or the delicate initial hook, that appears where the motion of the instrument precedes actual writing.

Folio: Originally, four pages of text on a single sheet of paper.

Font (= fount): A complete set or collection of letters, figures, symbols, punctuation marks, and special characters that are of the same design and size, for a particular typeface.

Foot: That portion of the downstroke of a letter, written or printed, touching the base line.

Forced hand: A person's signature or writing executed while the hand was under the physical compulsion or control of another person.

Forward oval: An oval made by a clockwise circular motion.

Fount: See "font."

Fraudulent handwriting: The forgery of a signature, a word, a figure, a number of lines of writing, or of an entire document.

Freehand simulation: A fraudulent signature that is produced by copying or imitating the style and size of a genuine signature, without the use of physical aids or involving a tracing process.

Garlanded: A writing style in which rounded trough-like strokes and movements dominate.

Global feature: Handwriting feature extracted for the entire signature unit.

Gooping: The accumulation of excessive amounts of ink on the exterior of the point assembly of a ballpoint pen as a result of the rotation of the ball that is usually transferred to the paper surface immediately after the direction of rotation is substantially changed.

Graph: The pattern of ink on the paper representing, for that writer, a particular allograph.

Grapheme: The smallest identifiable unit of writing; not divisible; the abstract concept of a letter of the alphabet.

Graphics: Of, or pertaining to writing or drawing.

Graphoanalysis: A registered trade name that identifies the system of handwriting analysis taught by the International Graphoanalysis Society.

Graphometry: A method of characterizing a handwriting by measurement of the proportionate values of the angles and ratios of the heights and widths of letters.

Graphonomics: The study of the science and technology of handwriting and other graphic skills (coined in 1982), or the scientific study concerned with the systematic relationships involved in the generation and analysis of writing and drawing movements, and the resulting traces of writing and drawing instruments, either on conventional media, such as paper and blackboard, or on electronic equipment.

Graphonym: Two different words or letter combinations that, when written cursively, appear nearly identical. Rare in English, but includes "win/urn," "bi/lr," "d/cl," etc.

Greek "e": See epsilon.

Guided-hand signature: A signature that is executed while the writer's hand or arm is steadied or assisted by another person.

Guillemets: Horizontal chevrons, « ... », used in French to mark quotations.

Guilloche: Free swinging, asymmetrical curves; a succession of smooth convoluting lines that intersect themselves, characteristic of intaglio security printing.

Gutter: The space between printed columns of text.

Habit: Any persistently repeated element or detail of writing that occurs when the opportunity allows.

Hairline: A very thin stroke.

Hand lettering: A disconnected style of writing in which letter design usually follows that of the uppercase printed character. Hand printing.

Haplography: The unintentional omission in writing or copying of one or more adjacent and similar letters, syllables, words, or lines.

Harpoon: The snapped-back ending of a written stroke; shaped like a harpoon.

Hertz (Hz): A unit of frequency. For example, the number of cycles or periods per second of the harmonious waves in handwriting or the number of samples per second when recording handwriting.

Hiatus: A gap in a writing stroke of a letter formed when the instrument leaves the paper; an opening; an interruption in the continuity of a line.

Hind link: The stroke by means of which a letter links with a preceding letter.

Hitch: The introductory backward stroke added to the beginning of many capital letters and some lowercase letters.

Holograph: A document written entirely in the handwriting of the person whose signature it bears.

Homographs: The writing of "homonyms."

Homonyms: Words that are both pronounced and spelled the same, but have different meanings, for example, lead (verb) and lead (noun).

Homophones: Words that sound alike, but have different spelling and meaning, for example, stair and stare. In ancient writings they were different symbols with the same phonetic value or sound.

Hook: A small curved stroke.

Horizontal chevrons: See "guillemets."

Horizontal dash: A punctuation mark "—" used to indicate a break or omission.

Horizontal line: The base line of writing or printing, or a line parallel to it.

Horizontal malalignment: A typewriter alignment defect in which the character prints to the right or left of its proper position.

Hyphen: A punctuation mark "-" used to connect the parts of a compound word or the syllables of a divided word.

Iconographs: The first attempts by neolithic man to depict objects and ideas.

Ideographs: Picture symbols and stick figures employed by neolithic man to graphically represent objects and ideas in drawings on cave walls.

Imprimatur: A license to print.

Inert hand: An execution of writing in which the person holding the writing instrument exercises no motor activity whatever, conscious or unconscious. The guide leads the writing instrument through the medium of the hand of the first person. The writer may be feeble or a complete illiterate.

Infralinear letters: Small or lowercase letters that have components that extend below the baseline of writing, for example, "g," "j," "p," "q," "y," and "z."

Initial stroke: The first stroke of a letter or a word.

Initial spur: The long initial rising stroke of a letter.

Interline: The insertion of additional words between the lines of a written document.

Interlinear spacing: The distance between the baselines of two successively occurring lines of writing.

Interstice: An intervening space between things, for example, between fibers in paper or between lines of writing.

Inverted posture: That in which the point of the writing instrument is directed toward the body of the writer.

Italic: Type that slants forward.

Joint or juncture: The point or position at which two or more strokes meet within a letter.

Justified. Vertically-aligned side margins; line lengths of equal measure.

Kerning: The spacing of two letters closer together than customary when their designs leave too much intercharacter white space.

Kinematic: The physics of motion in handwriting.

Knob: A round lump or bulge, as in the copybook design of the lowercase cursive "k."

Lacunae: See "hiatus."

Lateral expansion: The horizontal dimension of writing produced by the width of letters, the space between letters and words, and the width of margins.

Lateral writing: characterized by wide letters and spacing.

Left-handed curve: A stroke that is made in a counterclockwise direction.

Leg: An appendage; usually a lower extension from the body, as in "R" and "K."

Legibility: The ease with which a reader recognizes individual letter and character shapes.

Letter: Any drawn, written, printed, or typed character, lowercase or uppercase, that can be recognized as an allograph of the alphabet of any language.

Lexical: Pertaining or related to the words of a language (hence *dyslexia* meaning a disturbance of the ability to read).

Ligature: A group of connected characters treated typographically as a single character; sometimes a stroke or bar connecting two letters.

Limb: See "leg."

Line measure: The length of a line of printing expressed in picas, points, or ciceros.

Line quality: A term characterizing the visible record of the stroke of writing. It is the product of a combination of factors including speed, rhythm, shading, pen pressure, and pen position. The degree of regularity (i.e., smoothness or gradation) in the written stroke as may be judged from the consistency of its path in a prescribed direction. It varies from smooth and controlled to tremulous and erratic.

Linear letters: Small or lowercase letters having no components that extend above or below the x-height, for example, "a," "c," "e," "i," "m," "n," "o," "r," "s," "u," "v," "w," and "x."

Link: The stroke connecting the top and bottom segments of a lower case printed "g."

Lithographic printing: See "lithography."

Lithography: Printing from a smooth surface plate that has been treated so that the printing areas are ink attracting and the nonprinting areas are ink repelling.

Local feature: Handwriting feature based on a single data point.

Look-through: The appearance of paper when viewed by transmitted light, thus disclosing the texture or formation of the sheet.

Loop: The circular figure formed when a line crosses itself, as in the cursive letters "e" and "l."

Lower loop: A loop extending below the baseline; a descender.

Lowercase letters: Small letters of the alphabet as opposed to capital letters; minuscules.

Luminescence: The visible glow of certain substances (e.g., components of some inks) when subjected to stimulation by electromagnetic radiation, electric fields, or heat. Luminescence embraces fluorescence and phosphorescence.

Main script: The most important stroke of a letter (see "stem").

Majuscule: The capital or upper case forms of letters. Uncials.

Manuscript writing: A disconnected form of writing using many printed letter forms, frequently taught to children in elementary schools as the first step in learning to write.

Margins: The space at the top, bottom, and sides of the page that frames the body of written, typed, or printed matter.

Microphotography: The term used in Europe for the making of large photographs of small objects, usually through a microscope. In the United Kingdom and the United States this is called photomicrography, and microphotography is used to refer to the technique of making microscopically small photographs by the process of optical reduction.

Mid-arm: The cross stroke in letters such as "H" and "A."

Midline: The line halfway between the baseline and headline of writing or printing, either real or imaginary.

Minim: A short, vertical stroke on the baseline, for example, the legs on an "m."

Minuscule: The small or lower case forms of letters, as opposed to capitals.

Mirror writing: That runs in the opposite direction to the normal pattern; starts on the right side of the pages and proceeds from right to left, with reversed order in spelling and turning of the letter images.

Model signature: A genuine signature used to prepare a simulated or traced forgery.

Moiré: A pattern that is the mathematical solution to the interface of two periodic functions. Most moiré patterns are generated by figures that consist of lines, but lines are not strictly necessary. They may be interacting figures having some sort of solid and open regions of any geometric form. In its simplest form, a moiré pattern arises from the imperfect superimposition of two sets of equidistant parallel lines.

Money bag: A vernacular term sometimes used to describe an inflated, oversized lower loop.

Monogram: A character composed of two or more letters interwoven together, the letters being usually the initials of a formal name.

Morpheme: The meaningful constituent of a word; the "root."

Natural variation: The imprecision with which the habits of the writer are executed on repeated occasions (Huber), or the divergence of one execution from another in an element of an individual's writing that occurs invariably in the graph but may also occur in the choice of the allograph (Huber), or normal or usual deviations found between repeated specimens of any individual's handwriting or in the product of any typewriter or other record making machine (Hilton).

Neck: See "link."

Nodule: A small, rounded mass or lump of ink caused by an excessive deposit; the result of gooping in some ballpoint pens.

Nonce word: A word coined to fit a special situation.

Normal posture: That in which the writing instrument is pointed away from the body of the writer.

Numeral: Any drawn, written, printed, or typed character representing a quantity, of which numbers are formed; a digit.
Oblique: See "virgule."
Obliteration: The blotting out or smearing over of writing, lettering, or printing to make the original invisible or undecipherable.
Obverse: The side that bears the principal design; the front or principal surface of anything.
Octothorpe: The symbol, "#," used to represent the word *number*, when it precedes one or more digits, or the word *pound* when it succeeds one or more digits.
Off-its-feet: The condition of a typeface that prints heavier on one side or corner than the remainder of the character.
Offline: Handwriting or signature written with pen on paper. Also refers to the analysis of a static signature. Some electronically-captured signatures may be analyzed through their graphic, static forms without the aid of temporal data (also "static").
Offset printing: See "lithography."
Online: Handwriting or signature written using handwriting capture technology. In capturing an "online" signature, temporal, dynamic characteristics are recorded such as duration and velocity (also "dynamic").
Optical Character Recognition (OCR): In handwriting, conversion of handwritten characters or images into computer text.
Orthography: The principles by which the alphabet is set into correspondence with the speech sounds; the art of spelling.
Oval forms: Bowls of letters that have an oval shape, for example, "a," "d," "g," "o," "q."
Paradigm: A pattern, an exemplar, an example, or model.
Paraph: A flourish or sweeping line, stroke or dot, above, through or below a signature; an appendage; a rubric; the figure formed by the flourish of a pen at the conclusion of a signature.
Parenthesis: Either or both of the upright curved lines used to mark off explanatory or qualifying remarks, for example, "( )".
Patching: Retouching or going back over a defective portion of the writing stroke; retracing.
Pen emphasis: The act of intermittently forcing the pen against the paper surface with increased pressure.
Pen hold: The manner in which the writing instrument is held in the hand; includes the pen position relative to the paper surface, the direction of the instrument relative to the writing line and to the writer.
Pen lift: An interruption in a stroke due to the removal of the writing instrument from the paper.
Pen position: The angle relationship between the axis of the pen and the paper.
Perfins: Pinhole designs, initials, or numerals, made through stamps (after 1860 in Great Britain, and 1908 in the United States), coined from "perforated insignia."
Period: A punctuation mark " . " indicating a full stop and placed especially at the end of sentences.
Phoneme: A symbol representing a phone (i.e., a distinctive sound), abstracted from spoken words.
Phosphorescence: A kind of fluorescence that continues for a time after the stimulating light source ceases.
Photomicrography: The making of large photographs of small objects often via a microscope (on this continent and in the United Kingdom). See also "microphotography."

Pica: A unit of measure of printer's type, approximately $\frac{1}{6}$ inch or 12 points typically used for vertical measurement. Also a term used to denote conventional monotone typewriter typeface that has a fixed character width of 10 to the inch.
Pilcrow: A proofreader's mark to indicate a paragraph's beginning, "¶."
Pitch: See "escapement."
Point: The basic typographic unit of measurement of fonts, line spacing, rules and borders; there are 12 points to a pica and 72 points to the inch; typically used for vertical dimensions.
Point load: The vertical component of the force applied to the tip of a writing instrument during line generation.
Polyphones: Symbols having more than one phonetic value.
Pressure: The amount of force exerted on the point of the writing instrument, technically termed *point load*. Pressure may manifest itself in line quality, that is, thickness and shading of the stroke; also noted in the amount of indentation in the paper surface.
Proportional spacing: That varies with the design of the character of the font.
Proportions: The comparative relations between letters and parts of letters.
Pseudo expansion: The result of wide interspaces between narrow letters.
Pump handle: A term some give to the projecting element of the printed "r."
Question or query mark: A punctuation symbol, "?," written at the end of an interrogatory sentence.
Rebound: A typewriter defect in which a character prints a double impression with the lighter one slightly offset to the right or left.
Recto: In printing, the right-hand page of an open book, hence, the front of the leaf, as opposed to the back or verso.
Reference collections: Collections of typewriting, check writer specimens, inks, pens, pencils, papers, etc. compiled and organized by the document examiner as standards of the products.
Request standards: Writing samples written at the request of another person.
Retouching: Touching up to correct or perfect a graphic execution.
Retracing: That portion of a letter in which a downstroke is superimposed upon an upstroke, or vice versa.
Reverse: That side of a page or document that does not bear the main device or inscription.
Reverse curve: A section of curve where its radius changes to an opposite direction; an undulation.

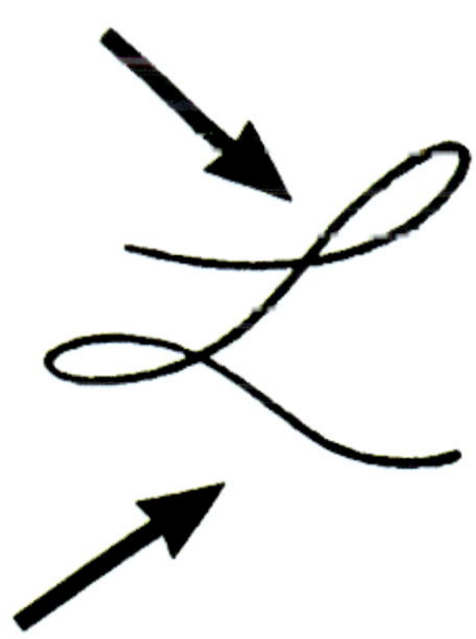

Rhythm: A harmonious recurrence of stress, impulse, or motion; sometimes used to classify writing quality, for example, smooth, intermittent, or jerky.

Ribbon impression: A sample of typewriter text made directly through a fabric or carbon film ribbon.

Right-handed curve: One that is made in a clockwise direction.

River: Gaps in the writing or printing pattern that form a straggling white stream down the page.

Rubric: A flourish after or under a name written as a signature, an underscore or underline. In ancient times it was a red ornamental letter at the beginning of a chapter or a division of a manuscript.

Sans serif: A class of typefaces without serifs.

Sawtooth: See "serrations."

Script: Handwriting as distinguished from printing or lettering; cursive writing.

Semicolon: A mark of punctuation, ";", indicating a degree of separation, intermediate between the comma and the period.

Serif: A broadening of the ends of the main strokes of a character; may be of many designs and sizes.

Serrations: Roughness along the edges of an ink line seen under a microscope.

Set: The width of an individual typewritten letter.

Set-off: The unwanted transfer of ink from one sheet of paper to the back of the sheet above.

Shading: Stressed contrast between thin upstrokes and thick downstrokes. A widening of the ink stroke due to the added pressure on the writing instrument.

Shaft: See "stem."

Shoulder: A joint, bridge, or hump on top of the small cursive letter "r" between the up and downstrokes; the curved arches of the "h," "m," and "n."

Signatory: A signer, with another or others; a person whose name is being inscribed on a document who requires assistance in doing so.

Signature: The name of a person, or mark representing it, as written by himself or herself.

Sinistrality: Left-hand preference, as opposed to dextrality or right-hand preference, particularly in writing.

Skeletal stem: Letter extensions made without the required loop formation.

Skip: The self-recoverable, temporary interruption (without deposition of ink) in an otherwise continuous writing line.

Slant: The angle or inclination of the axis of letters relative to the baseline of writing.

Slash: "/ ", see "virgule."

Soldered break: A corrective retracing by which the writer attempts to fit together the two ends of a broken stroke so that no hiatus remains.

Solidus: The diagonal line used to separate; amounts in English currency, for example, 12/6 for 12 shillings, 6 pence, or the numerator and denominator in fractions, for example, 1/2 (see virgule).

Spacing: The distance between letters or words (see also "interlinear spacing").

Speed "r": The round hand, Palmer, or Mills "r"; the "v" type "r."

Spine: The main slightly curved stroke of a lower case or capital "S."

Spiral: That portion of a letter executing a spiral formation, popular designs of commencement and termination in older styles of writing.

Splicing: A term used to denote the slight overlapping of two strokes after an interruption in the writing action.

Splitting: The division of an ink line into two or more, more or less equal portions, by a noninked area running generally parallel to the direction of the stroke, sometimes called *burring.*

Springboard: An initial stroke commencing far below the baseline and to the left of the stem.

Spur: A small projection off the main stroke seen on some printed uppercase "G"s; or the short lateral finishing stroke found in the lowercase "b," "v," and "w."

Spurious signature: A fraudulent signature in which there was no apparent attempt at simulation or imitation.

Staff: That portion of the letter forming the backbone.

Starving: A condition in which there is an inadequate flow of writing fluid to the writing surface.

Static: Handwriting produced using pen-and-paper methods, with no online data captured. Static signatures can also be digitized versions of electronic signatures (also offline).

Stem: The main or heavy stroke of a letter to which the other parts are attached.

Stress: See "pressure."

Strike-through: The condition in which the writing fluid has traversed vertically through the paper so as to appear on the underside of the sheet opposite the written line.

Stroke: A single written line, either ascending, descending, or lateral in the formation of a letter or any of its parts.

Subscript: A character or symbol written next to and slightly below a letter or number.

Superscript: A character or symbol written next to and slightly above a letter or number.

Supralinear letters: Small or lowercase letters that have components that extend above the x-height, for example, "b," "d," "h," "k," "l," "t."

Swash: A fancy flourish replacing a terminal stroke or serif.

Symbol: In writing, a character that is used to represent something that might be expressed in one or more words, for example, "$," "@," "#," "%," "£," "¢," and is considered part of a typing or printing font.

System: See "writing system."

Tail: A terminal or ending stroke; sometimes used to refer to the leg of an "R" or "K," or to the final element of the "Q."

Tenting: A term used to describe a letter that contains a tent shaped form.

Terminal stroke: The last stroke of a word; endstroke.

Textual writing: That pertaining to a text, extended writing, usually cursive, but not inclusive of a signature.

Tick: Any superfluous small stroke preceding or succeeding the body of a letter.

Tilde: A small stroke or mark used in writing or printing placed above certain letters in some languages to denote a change in sound; a diacritical mark.

Trace: The mark, track, rail, or imprint of a stroke.

Traced forgery: Any fraudulent signature executed by a manual, mechanical or electronic endeavor to follow the outline of a genuine signature.

Tremor: A lack of smoothness, due to lack of skill, consciousness of the writing act or to the deliberate control of the instrument in copying or tracing, or an involuntary, roughly rhythmic, and sinusoidal movement.

Tremulous: An unsteady, wavering stroke produced by an involuntary vibratory motion of the writing hand.

Trough: The bend, crook or inner side of a curve opening upwards, or, the valleys of letters such as "u," "v," "w," and "y."

Typeface: The name of a particular design of printed characters and symbols.

Typeface family: A range of typeface designs that are variations of one basic style of alphabet.

Uncial: A script writing style of the fourth to ninth centuries that introduced what became minuscule or lowercase forms to the alphabet.

Undercurve: A forward oval movement in an upstroke.
Undercut: A connection that falls below the base of the succeeding letter.
Uppercase letters: A printing term for capital letters; majuscules.
Upper loop: A loop extending above the baseline or the height of linear letters; an ascender.
Upstroke: A stroke directed toward the top of the paper.
Velocity: The vector describing both speed and direction of the handwriting stroke. It can be described by a horizontal or x coordinate and a vertical or y coordinate.
Versal letters: Those that mark important parts of the text, used for headings and words written at the beginning of books or chapters; often distinguished by size, color, and ornamentation which tends toward curves and flourishes.
Verso: The left-hand page of a book or the reverse side of a leaf; opposite of recto.
Vertex: The apex, top, or crown; the highest point of a letter.
Vertical expansion: Product of the height of letters and distance between lines.
Vertical misalignment: A typewriter alignment defect in which the character prints above or below its proper position.
Vertical stroke: An upright stroke perpendicular to the baseline of the writing.
Vertical writing: Perpendicular to the baseline, upright writing.
Virgule: A short oblique stroke "/ ", between two words indicating that whichever is appropriate may be chosen to complete the sense of the text in which they occur; a dividing line as in dates, fractions, etc. Also called a diagonal, solidus (in English currency and in fractions), oblique, slant, and slash mark. Used to mean "or" (as in and/or), or "per" (as in miles/hour). Separates figures of a date (e.g., 2/10/97).
Visible light: Rays that can be seen by the human eye, but are only a part of the complete spectrum of so-called electromagnetic radiation. Rays of other parts of the spectrum cannot be seen but can be detected.
Walking cane: A term sometimes given to the initial loop and stem of some capital letters when the curvature and design suggest the resemblance.

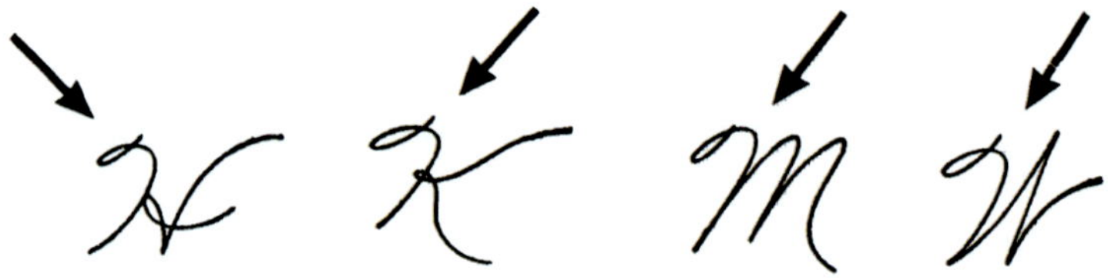

Whirl: The curving upstroke, usually on letters that have long loops, but also on some styles of the capital "W."
Whorl: A form composed of spiraling strokes, produced by a loose, circling writing movement.
Writing: The act of generating a line.
Writing angle: The included angle measured from the plane of the writing surface to the longitudinal axis of the pen when in the writing position.
Writing movement: A three-dimensional pattern of the action of a writing instrument; variants in the predominating action of the writing instrument.
Writing offset: The transfer of fresh ink upon contact with another document producing a mirror image of part of the writing.
Writing speed: The rate of line generation, sometimes wrongly regarded to be the rate of word generation, that varies with the size of the writing.

Writing system: The combination of basic letter design and writing movement prescribed by a publication or taught in a school.

Wrong-handed writing: Any writing executed with the opposite hand from that normally used; writing of the nondominant or nonpreferred hand.

X axis: Horizontal axis in the plane of the paper upon which the pen tip position is projected in recorded handwriting yielding a value for the x coordinate.

X-height: The height of the linear letters (no ascenders or descenders).

Y axis: Vertical axis in the plane of the paper upon which the pen tip position is projected in recorded handwriting yielding a value for the y coordinate.

Z axis: perpendicular to the plane of the paper. The height of the pen above the paper can be expressed by the projection of the pen tip position on the z axis. In practice there are no pen movement recording devices that measure the pen height. Instead, most pen recording devices measure the axial pen pressure. This is the pressure exerted upon the pen tip along the direction of the pen barrel. Pen pressure is often treated as the z coordinate.

Appendix A: Systems of Writing in North America

The systems of writing in North America are as follows:

4 Kids Publications
A Beka Book
American Book Company
J. J. Bailey (Sir Isaac Pitman & Sons (Canada) Ltd.)
Beckley-Cardy Company
The Bélanger System (Province of Quebec)
W. S. Benson & Company
Beta Books (publication used by Colorado private schools)
The Bobbs-Merrill Company
Bowman Noble (formerly Noble and Noble)
Cavanaugh and Myers
City of New York, Board of Education
Colonial, (American Southern Publishing Company)
Courtis-Shaw
Creamer
D'Nealian (1978) (Scott Foresman & Company)
C. E. Doner's Everyday Writing (Zaner-Bloser Co.)
Ecoles Chretiennes (Province of Quebec)
The Economy Company
For Little Folks/Catholic Heritage Curricula
The Forest-Ouimet System (Province of Quebec)
Frank Schaeffer Company
Freeman
Freres Maristes System (Province of Quebec)
Goodfellow
Graves
Graves Prewitt
Haan-Wierson (Allyn & Bacon Publishing Co, Boston)
I. Z. Hackman Company
Hall & McCreary Company
Hall-Savage
Handwriting Without Tears
Harcourt Brace Jovanovich (HBJ) Publishers

Harlow Publishing Corporation
Harr Wagner Publishing Company
Hausam
Hayes Publishing Ltd. (Burlington, Ontario and Niagara Falls, N.Y.)
Jenn (Jenn Publishing Co., Louisville, KY)
Kelly-Morris
Kirk & Freeman
Kittle
Landmark Freedom Baptist Curriculum
Laurel Book Company
Lister
Locker
Lyons and Carnahan (Lyons & Carnahan, Meredith Corp. Chicago)
McGraw-Hill (Webster McGraw-Hill Book Co.)
H. B. MacLean Method
McDougal, Littell & Company
Memoria Press (New American Cursive)
E. C. Mills System (Rochester)
New Laurel
Noble & Noble Publishers, Inc. (Later Bowman Noble)
Nystrom
A. N. Palmer Company
Peed
Pedia Learning, Inc.
Peterson Directed Handwriting System (MacMillan Publishing Co.)
Pitman Publishing Company (also produced Bailey System)
Public School Publishing Company
Putnam-Mills
Reason to Write (A publication used by Colorado private schools)
Reid-Crane
Rice
Rinehart
R. E. Rowe
Chas. Scribner's Sons
E. G. Seale and Company
Self Development (Educational Self Development Inc., Greensburg, PA)
Les Soeurs de la Congregation system (Province of Quebec)
Silver Burdett (Silver Burdett Co., Morristown, NJ)
Spirit Masters
A. F. Sprott's Metronomic System (Sir Isaac Pitman & Sons (Can.) Ltd.)
SRA (Science Research Associates, Inc., Chicago)
Steckbaugh (A publication used by Colorado private schools)
Steck Company

Steck-Vaughn (formerly the Steck Company)
Stone, Smalley & Cooke, (The Bobbs-Merrill Company)
C. E. Strothers & J. W. Trusler
Tamblyn
Teach Me Joy
Therapro, Inc.
Waldorf (their own system, in Colorado)
Zaner-Bloser, Inc.

References

Abed, H. E., Kherallah, M., Margner, V., & Alimi, A.M. (2011). Online Arabic handwriting recognition competition, Arabic database and participating systems. *International Journal on Document Analysis and Recognition, 14*(1), 15–23.

Adams, J. A. (1976). Issues for a closed-loop theory of motor learning. In G. E. Stelmach (Ed.), *Motor Control: Issues and trends*. New York: Academic Press, 87–107.

AHAF-American Handwriting Analysis Foundation. (2016). *The truth about cursive handwriting: Why it matters in a digital age?* American Handwriting Analysis Foundation. Retrieved from: http://www.campaignforcursive.com/ (accessed November 11, 2016).

Ahmad, S. M. S., Ling, L. Y., Anwar, R. M., Faudzi, M. A., & Shakil, A. (2013). Analysis of the effects and relationship of perceived handwritten signature's size, graphical complexity, and legibility with dynamic parameters for forged and genuine samples. *Journal of Forensic Sciences, 58*(3), 724–731.

Ahmed, S., Malik, M. I., Denge, A., & Liwicki, M. (2015). Extraction of signatures from document images for real world applications. *Journal of the American Society of Questioned Document Examiners, 18*(2), 67–78.

Aitken, C. G. G. (1987). The use of statistics in forensic science. *Journal of the Forensic Science Society, 27*(2), 113–115.

Akamatsu, M., & MacKenzie, I. S. (2002). Changes in applied force to a touchpad during pointing tasks. *International Journal of Industrial Ergonomics, 29*(3), 171–182.

Akcin, N. (2012). The perspectives of primary school teachers on the evaluation and remediation of the compositions of students with learning disabilities. *American International Journal of Contemporary Research, 2*(3), 68–75.

Alewijnse, L. C., van den Heuvel, E. C., & Stoel, R. D. (2011). Analysis of signature complexity. *Journal of Forensic Document Examination, 21*, 37–49.

Alford, E. A. (1965). Identification through comparison of numbers. *Identification News*, July, pp. 13–14.

Alford, E. F., Jr., & Bertocchi, M. P. (1974). *Punctuation as an aid in examining disguised writing*. Paper presented at the meeting of the American Academy of Forensic Sciences, Dallas, TX.

Alford, E. F., Jr. (1970). Disguised handwriting. A statistical survey of how handwriting is most frequently disguised. *Journal of Forensic Sciences, 15*(4), 476–488. doi: 10.2307/1139667.

Alford, E. F., Jr. (1975). Responsibilities and the document examiner. Paper presented at the meeting of the American Society of Questioned Document Examiners, Colorado Springs, CO.

Al-Haddad, A., White, P. C., Cole, M. D. (2009). Examination of a collection of Arabic signatures. *Journal of the American Society of Questioned Document Examiners, 12*(1), 35–53.

Al-Haddad, A., White, P. C., & Cowell, A. M. (2011). The use of principal component analysis to provide objective methods for the examination of Arabic signatures. *Journal of the American Society of Questioned Document Examiners, 14*(1), 3–18.

Al-Hadhrami, A. N., Allen, M., Moffatt, C., & Jones, A. E. (2015). National characteristics and variation in Arabic handwriting. *Forensic Science International, 247*, 89–96.

Allan, A. R. & Pearson, E. F. (1978). *A comparison of handwriting characteristics, part II*. Unpublished manuscript.

Allan, A. R., Pearson, E. F., & Brown, C. (1978). *A comparison of handwriting characteristics, part I*. Paper presented at the 8th meeting of the International Association of Forensic Sciences, Wichita, KS.

Allen, M., & Wellman, M. M. (1980). Hand position during writing, cerebral laterality and reading: Age and sex differences. *Neuropsychologia, 18*(1), 33–40. doi: 10.1016/0028-3932(80)90081-0.

Allport, G. W., Vernon, P. E., & Powers, E. (1933). *Studies in expressive movement*. New York: The Macmillan.

Al Maadeed, S., & Hassaine, A. (2014). Automatic prediction of age, gender, and nationality in offline handwriting. *EURASIP Journal on Image and Video Processing, 2014*(1), 1–10.

Al-Musa Alkahtani, A. (2010). The ability of forensic handwriting examiners to judge the quality of signature simulations in an unfamiliar writing system. *Journal of the American Society of Questioned Document Examiners, 13*(2), 65–69.

Al-Musa Alkahtani, A., (2014). Arabic-illiterate forensic handwriting analysis: A pilot study to further investigate the ability of Arabic-illiterate examiners to judge the accuracy of simulations of Arabic signatures, compared with Arabic-literate examiners. *Journal of the American Society of Questioned Document Examiners, 17*(1), 3–9.

Al-Musa Alkahtani, A., & Platt, A. W. (2009). Relative difficulty of freehand simulation of four proportional elements in Arabic signatures. *Journal of the American Society of Questioned Document Examiners, 12*(2), 69–76.

Al-Musa Alkahtani, A., & Platt, A. W. (2011a). A statistical study of the relative difficulty of freehand simulation of form, proportion, and line quality in Arabic signatures. *Journal of Forensic Sciences, 56*(4), 950–953.

Al-Musa Alkahtani, A., & Platt, A. W. (2011b). The influence of gender on ability to simulate handwritten signatures: A study of Arabic writers. *Journal of Forensic Sciences, 56*(4), 950–953.

Alonso-Fernandez, F., Fierrez-Aguilar, J., & Ortega-Garcia, J. (2005). Sensor interoperability and fusion in signature verification: A case study using Tablet PC. *Advances in Biometric Person Authentication, Lecture Notes in Computer Science, 3781*, 180–187.

Alusi, S. H., Worthington, J., Glickman, S., Findley, L. J., & Bain, P. G. (2000). Evaluation of three different ways of assessing tremor in multiple sclerosis. *Journal of Neurology, Neurosurgery & Psychiatry, 68*(6), 756–760.

Alzheimer's Association. (2015). 2015 Alzheimer's disease facts and figures. *Alzheimer's & Dementia: The Journal of the Alzheimer's Association, 11*(3), 332–384.

American Standards for Testing and Materials International. (2005). *Standard guide for minimum training requirements for forensic document examiners.* ASTM E2388-05, West Conshohocken, PA: ASTM International.

American Standards for Testing and Materials International. (2007). *Standard guide for examination of handwritten items.* ASTM E2290 – 07a.

Ames, D. T. (1900). *Ames on forgery: Its detection and illustration, with numerous cause célèbres.* New York: Ames-Rollinson.

Andersen, D. W. (1964). *Correlates of handwriting legibility.* Paper presented at the meeting of the American Academy of Forensic Sciences, Chicago, IL.

Anderson, D. J. (1982). *Foreign influence and identifying characteristics of writing systems.* Paper resented at the meeting of the Canadian Society of Forensic Science, Halifax, NS, Canada.

Anderson, G. J. (1974). *Varying effects of alcohol on handwriting.* Paper presented at the meeting of the American Academy of Forensic Sciences, Dallas, TX.

Anderson, T., & Wolowitz, H. (1984). Psychosexual symbolism in the handwriting of men and women. *Perceptual and Motor Skills, 59*(1), 233–234. doi: 10.2466/pms.1984.59.1.233.

Angst, E., & Erismann, K. (1972). Auswertung von anonymen und pseudonymen Handschriften mit electronischer Datenverabeitung. *Kriminalistic, 26*, 60–66.

Annett, M. (1970). A classification of hand preference by association analysis. *British Journal of Psychology, 61*(3), 303–321. doi: 10.1111/j.2044-8295.1970.tb01248.x.

Annett, M. (2006). The right shift theory of handedness and brain asymmetry in evolution, development and psychopathology. *Cognition, Brain, Behavior, 10*(2), 235–250.

Ansell, M. (1979). Handwriting classification in forensic science. *Visible Language, 13*(3), 239–251.

Ansell, M. & Strach, S. J. (1975). *The classification of handwritten numerals.* Paper presented at the 7th meeting of the International Association of Forensic Sciences, Zurich, Switzerland.

Anthony, A. T. (1984). *D'Nealian: A new handwriting system.* Paper presented at the meeting of the American Society of Questioned Document Examiners, Nashville, TN.

Anthony, A. T. (1996). *Examination of unaccustomed-hand signatures.* Paper presented at the meeting of the American Academy of Forensic Sciences, Philadelphia, PA.

Aşıcıoğlu, F., & Turan, N. (2003). Handwriting changes under the effect of alcohol. *Forensic science international, 132*(3), 201–210.

Askov, E., Otto, W., & Askov, W. (1970). A decade of research in handwriting: Progress and prospect. *Journal of Educational Research, 64*(3), 100–111.

Automated Signature Technology. (2011). Ghostwriter: Easy to use, tough enough for any task. Retrieved from http://www.signaturemachine.com/ (accessed June 23, 2012).

Baier, P. E., Hussong, J., Hoffman, E., & Klein, M. (1987). *The Mannheim bibliography of document examination 1987.* Mannheim, West Germany: University of Mannheim.

Baig, M. S. A., Shen, W. W., Caminal, E., & Huang, T.-D. (1984). Signature size in the psychiatric diagnosis: A significant clinical sign? *Psychopathology, 17*(3), 128–131. doi: 10.1159/000284029.

Baird, J. B. (1969, April). *The pharmacological effects of alcohol.* Presented in a Breathalyser training course, Crime Detection Laboratory of the Royal Canadian Mounted Police, Regina, SK, Canada.

Barsley, M. (1966). *The left-handed book.* Toronto: Ryerson Press.

Baxendale, D., & Renshaw, I. D. (1979). The large scale searching of handwriting samples. *Journal of the Forensic Science Society, 19*(4), 245–251. doi: 10.1016/S0015-7368(79)71294-1.

Baxter, P. G. (1970). The training of questioned document examiners. *Medicine, Science and the Law, 10*(2), 76–84.

Baxter, P. G. (1973). Classification and measurement in forensic handwriting comparisons. *Medicine, Science, and the Law, 13*(3), 166–84.

Beacom, M. (1960). A study of handwritings by twins and other persons of multiple births. *Journal of Forensic Sciences, 5*(1), 121–131.

Beacom, M. (1961). Was this document written with the left hand? *Journal of Forensic Sciences, 6*(3), 321–330.

Beacom, M. (1965). *A survey of handwriting systems by states and territories in the U.S.A.* Paper presented at the joint meeting of the American Society of Questioned Document Examiners and RCMP Crime Detection Laboratories, Ottawa, ON, Canada.

Beacom, M. (1967). Handwriting by the blind. *Journal of Forensic Sciences, 12*(1), 37–59.

Beacom, M. (1968). Handwriting of the cerebral-palsied. *I. D. News, 18*(11). 7–15.

Beacom, M. (1970). *Handwriting by aphasics.* Unpublished paper. Presented at the meeting of the American Society of Questioned Document Examiners, Houston, TX.

Beardsley, M. C. (1954). *Thinking straight: A guide for readers & writers.* New York: Prentice-Hall.

Beck, F. A. G. (1964) *Greek education, 450-350 B.C.* London: Methuen.

Beck, J. (1974). *Evaluation of handwritten diary entries.* Paper presented at the meeting of the American Society of Questioned Document Examiners, Milwaukee, WI.

Beck, J. (1982). *Handwriting of the alcoholic.* Paper presented at the meeting of the American Society of Questioned Document Examiners, Boston, MA.

Beck, J. (1995). Sources of error in forensic handwriting evaluation. *Journal of Forensic Sciences, 40*(1), 78–82. doi: 10.1520/jfs13764j.

Beech, J. R., & Mackintosh, I. C. (2005) Do differences in sex hormones affect handwriting style? Evidence from digit ratio and sex role identity as determinants of the sex of handwriting. *Personality and Individual Differences, 39*(2), 459–468.

Behnen, A. P. (1993). *Disguise and alternate writing styles.* Paper presented at the meeting of the American Society of Questioned Document Examiners, Ottawa, ON, Canada.

Behrendt, J. E. (1982). *Problems associated with the writing of senile dementia patients.* Paper presented at the meeting of the American Society of Questioned Document Examiners, Boston, MA.

Behrendt, J. E. (1984). Alzheimer's disease and its effect on handwriting. *Journal of Forensic Sciences, 29*(1), 87–91. doi: 10.1520/JFS11638J.

Behrendt, J. E. (1989). The status of training for questioned document examiners in the United States. *Journal of Forensic Sciences, 34*(2), 366–370. doi: 10.1520/JFS12645J.

Behrendt, J. E. (n.d.). *An examination of exemplars taken from non-English speaking writers.* Paper presented at the Meeting of the American Society of Questioned Document Examiners.

Bein, W. (1967). *Statistische Häufigkeitsuntersuchungen.* Kriminalistik und forensische Wissenschaften, Berlin, 8996.

Bellomy, D. A. (1975). *Barrio script.* Paper presented at the meeting of the American Society of Questioned Document Examiners, Colorado Springs, CO.

Bellomy, D. A. (1986). *Barrio script Mexican-American gang writing.* Paper presented at the meeting of the American Society of Questioned Document Examiners, Savannah, GA.

Bender, W. N., Rosenkrans, C. B., & Crane, M. K. (1999). Stress, depression, and suicide among students with learning disabilities: Assessing the risk. *Learning Disability Quarterly, 22*(2), 143–156.

Bergamini, D. (1963). *Mathematics.* New York: Time.

Berthold, N. (1995). *Principle number one, uno, eins.* Paper presented at the meeting of the American Society of Questioned Document Examiners, Chicago, IL.

Berthold, N. N., & Wooton, E. X. (1993). *Class characteristics of Latin American hand printing.* Paper presented at the meeting of the American Society of Questioned Document Examiners, Ottawa, ON, Canada.

Bertillon, A. (1898). *La comparaison des écritures et l'identification graphique.* Paris: Revue Scientifique. Retrieved from https://books.google.com/books?hl=en&lr=&id=f9v2lR2BM90C&oi=fnd&pg=PT6-&dq=Bertillon+%22La+comparaison+des+ecritures%22&ots=ztOgGK-kSj&sig=DQxpCnCj5Xp8chRfup3kYCt_PjY.

Beukelaar, L. J., & Kroonenberg, P. M. (1986). Changes over time in the relationship between hand preference and writing hand among left-handers. *Neuropsychologia, 24*(2), 301–303. https://doi.org/10.1016/0028-3932(86)90066-7

Bey, R. F., & Ryan, D. J. (1998). *Limited writing area and its effect on a signature—A preliminary study.* Paper presented at the meeting of the American Academy of Forensic Sciences, San Francisco, CA.

Binet, A. (1906). *Les révélations de l'écriture d'après un controle scientifique.* F. Alcan, Paris.

Bird, C., Found, B., Ballantyne, K., & Rogers, D. (2010b). Forensic handwriting examiners' opinions on the process of production of disguised and simulated signatures. *Forensic Science International, 195*(1), 103–107.

Bird, C., Found, B., & Rogers, D. (2010a). Forensic document examiners' skill in distinguishing between natural and disguised handwriting behaviors. *Journal of Forensic Sciences, 55*(5), 1291–1295.

Bird, C., Found, B., & Rogers, D. (2012). Forensic handwriting examiners' skill in detecting disguise behavior from handwritten text samples. *Journal of Forensic Document Examination, 22*, 15–23.

Bird, C., Stoel, R. D., Found, B., & Rogers, D. (2011). Skill characteristics of forensic handwriting examiners associated with simulated handwritten text. *Journal of the American Society of Questioned Document Examiners, 14*(2), 29–34.

Birge, W. R. (1954). An experimental inquiry into the measurable handwriting correlates of five personality traits. *Journal of Personality, 23*(2), 215–223. doi: 10.1111/j.1467-6494.1954.tb01150.x.

Blackburn, D., & Caddell, W. W. (1909). *The detection of forgery.* London: C. & E. Layton.

Blake, M. (1977). *Handwriting individuality, can we prove it?* Paper presented at the meeting of the American Society of Questioned Document Examiners, San Francisco, CA.

Blake, M. (1995). Are we seeing the same thing? Results of a survey presented to forensic document examiners. *International Journal of Forensic Document Examiners,* 1(1), 32–39.

Bleuschke, A. (1968). *Handwriting of the blind.* Unpublished manuscript, Royal Canadian Mounted Police Crime Detection Labs.

Blueschke, A. (1985). *Regression and/or attempted simulation of handwriting by hypnosis.* Paper presented at the meeting of the American Society of Questioned Document Examiners and the RCMP Crime Detection Laboratories, Montreal, QC, Canada.

Bogan, E. (1958). Handwriting, speech and behavior changes. *Journal of the American Medical Association, 168*(1), 48–49. doi: 10.1001/jama.1958.63000010014013.

Böhle, K. (1993). Cataloguing significant features of handwriting as an aid to objectivising evidence in the investigation of handwritten script. *Journal of Forensic Document Examination, 5*, 41–58.

Bohn, C. E. (1974). *Fundamentals pertaining to signature exemplars.* Paper presented at the meeting of the American Academy of Forensic Sciences, Dallas, TX.

Boisover, G. (1993). *Signatures of teenage French girls.* Paper presented at the meeting of the American Society of Questioned Document Examiners, Ottawa, ON, Canada.

Boisseau, M., Chamberland, G., & Gauthier, S. (1987). Handwriting analysis of several extrapyramidal disorders. *Canadian Society of Forensic Science Journal, 20*(4), 139–146. doi:10.1080/00085030.1987.10756952.

Boot, D. (1998). An investigation into the degree of similarity in the handwriting of identical and fraternal twins in New Zealand. *Journal of American Society of Questioned Document Examiners, 1*(2), 70–81.
Bowen, J. (1972). *A history of western education. Vol. 1: The ancient world: Orient and Mediterranean 2000 B.C.-A.D. 1054*. London: Methuen.
Bowers, K. S. (1976). *Hypnosis of the seriously curious.* Montgomery, CA: Brooks/Cole.
Boyd, J. (1967). Comparison of motor behavior in deaf and hearing boys. *American Annals of the Deaf, 112*(4), 598–605.
Bradley, J. H. (1988). *Shorthand identification.* Paper presented at the meeting of the American Society of Questioned Document Examiners, Aurora, CO.
Brandt, V. (1976). Changes in graphic characteristics in writing executed with the abnormal writing hand. *Zeitschrift fur Menschenkunde, 40*, 344–410.
Brault, J.-J., & Plamondon, R. (1993). A complexity measure of handwriting curves: Modelling of dynamic signature forgery. *IEEE Transactions on Systems, Man, and Cybernetics, 23*(2), 400–413. doi: 10.1109/21.229453.
Brewester, F. (1932). *Contested documents and forgeries.* Calcutta: The Book Company.
Brocklehurst, E. R. (1985). Computer methods of signature verification. *Journal of the Forensic Science Society, 25*(6), 445–457. doi: 10.1016/S0015-7368(85)72433-4.
Broom, M. E., Thompson, B., & Bouton, M. T. (1929). Sex differences in handwriting. *Journal of Applied Psychology, 13*(2), 159.
Broom, R. H. & Basinger, M. (1932). On the determination of the intelligence of adults from samples of their penmanship. *Journal of Applied Psychology, 16*(5), 515–519.
Bross, F., Eisermann, H. W., & Klement, V. (1987). *Experiments on the writer recognition with interactively measured features.* Unpublished manuscript.
Brown, C. D. W. P. (1985). *The identification of handwriting on a convex surface.* Paper presented at the meeting of the American Academy of Forensic Sciences, Las Vegas, NV.
Brown, D. N. (1967). *Shorthand individuality.* Paper presented at the meeting of the American Academy of Forensic Sciences, Honolulu, HI.
Brown, G. A., & Cropp, P. L. (1987). Standardised nomenclature in forensic science. *Journal of the Forensic Science Society, 27*(6), 393–399. https://doi.org/10.1016/s0015-7368(87)72787-x.
Brun, B. & Reisby, N. (1971). Handwriting changes following meprobamate and alcohol: A graphometric-graphological investigation. *Quarterly Journal of Studies on Alcohol, 32*(4), 1070–1082.
Brunelle, R. L., & Crawford, K. R. (2003). *Advances in the forensic analysis and dating of writing ink.* Springfield, IL: Charles C. Thomas.
Brunelle, R. L., & Reed, R. W. (1984). *Forensic examination of ink and paper.* Springfield, IL: Charles C. Thomas.
Bryson, S. E., & MacDonald, V. (1984). The development of writing posture in left-handed children and its relation to sex and reading skills. *Neuropsychologia, 22*(1), 91–94. doi: 10.1016/0028-3932(84)90012-5.
Buglio, J., & Gidion, H. M. (1977). *Another adept penman.* Paper presented at the meeting of the American Society of Questioned Document Examiners, San Francisco, CA.
Buglio, J., & Wiersema, S. J. (1989). *An examination of assertions concerning the validity or reliability of handwriting identification expertise.* Paper presented at the meeting of the American Society of Questioned Document Examiners, Arlington, VA.
Bulacu, M. L. (2007). Statistical pattern recognition for automatic writer identification and verification. Dissertation. University of Groningen.
Bunker, M. N. (1959). *Handwriting analysis: The art and science of reading character by grapho analysis.* Nelson-Hall, Chicago, IL.
Buquet, A. (1981). Handwriting examination background and current trends. *International Criminal Police Review, 36*(352), 242–246.
Burkey, L. C. R. (2012). Reflex of avoidance in spatial restrictions for signatures and handwritten entries. Electronic theses and dissertations, p. 1421. Retrieved from http://dc.etsu.edu/etd/1421 (accessed January 2, 2017)
Cabanne, R. A. (1965). *Recruiting and training document examiners for United States Postal Inspection Service identification laboratories.* Paper presented at the meeting of the American Society of Questioned Document Examiners and RCMP Crime Detection Laboratories, Ottawa, ON, Canada.

Cabanne, R. A. (1975). The Clifford Irving Hoax of the Howard Hughes Autobiography. *Journal of Forensic Science, 20*(1), 5–17. doi: 10.1520/jfs10236j.

Cadola, L., Margot, P.A., & Marquis, R. (2013). Are simple signatures so easy to simulate? *Journal of the American Society of Questioned Document Examiners, 16*(2), 3–11.

Caligiuri, M. P., & Mohammed, L. A. (2012). *The neuroscience of handwriting: Applications for forensic document examination*. Boca Raton, FL: CRC Press.

Caligiuri, M.P., Mohammed, L.A., Found, B., & Rogers, D. (2012). Nonadherence to the isochrony principle in forged signatures. *Forensic Science International, 223*, 228–232.

Caligiuri, M. P., Teulings, H.-L., Dean, C. E., Niculescu, A. B., & Lohr, J. B. (2010). Handwriting movement kinematics for quantifying extrapyramidal side effects in patients treated with atypical antipsychotics. *Psychiatry Research, 177*(1), 77–83.

Calvert, J. R. (1980). The identification of hand-printed musical scores. *Journal of Forensic Science, 25*(3), 619–623. doi: 10.1520/JFS11264J.

Cambridge, J. (1972). *Factors relating to the identification of masculinity and femininity in questioned handwriting*. Paper presented at the meeting of the International Association of Forensic Sciences, Edinburgh, Scotland, UK.

Campbell, N. R. (1952). *What is science?* New York: Dover.

Canada Evidence Act 1868 (Sc) (Can.).

Caponi, A. I., & Berardi, L. A. (1966). *Training and education of questioned documents examiner in Argentina*. Paper presented at the Second International Meeting in Questioned Documents, Copenhagen, Denmark.

Carney, B. B. (1980). Transfer of pencil writing by cellophane tape. *Journal of Forensic Science, 25*(2), 423–427. doi: 10.1520/jfs12149j.

Carney, B. B. (1983). *Transfer of pencil writing by cellophane tape—An update*. Paper presented at the meeting of the American Academy of Forensic Sciences, Cincinnati, OH.

Carney, B. B. (1993). *A new tremor in handwriting*. Paper presented at the meeting of the American Society of Questioned Document Examiners, Ottawa, ON, Canada.

Carroll v. State, 634 S.W.2d 99, 276 Ark. 160, 276 A.R. 160 (1982).

Casey, M. A. (1968). *Is handwriting identification a science?* Paper presented at the meeting of the American Society of Questioned Document Examiners, Lexington, KY.

Casey-Owens, M. (1984). The anonymous letter writer—A psychological profile? *Journal of Forensic Sciences, 29*(3), 816–819. doi: 10.1520/JFS11740J.

Caywood, D. A. (1978). *Handwriting styles based upon cultural education*. Paper presented at the meeting of the International Association of Forensic Sciences, Wichita, KS.

Caywood, D. A. (1997). *The impact of foreign education on the handwriting of individuals learning English as a second language*. Ottawa: Shunderson Communications.

Cha, S. H., Yoon, S., & Tappert, C. C. (2006). Handwriting copybook style identification for questioned document examination. *Journal of Forensic Document Examination, 17*(4), 1–14.

Champion, J. (1750). *The Parallel ; or, Comparative penmanship exemplified, etc.* London: John Bowles.

Champod, C. (2014). Research focused mainly on bias will paralyse forensic science. *Science and Justice, 54*(2), 107–109.

Chandler, R. H. (1911). Abstracts from current periodicals. *Scientific American.*

Chang, S. H., Chen, C. L., & Yu, N. Y. (2015). Biomechanical analyses of prolonged handwriting in subjects with and without perceived discomfort. *Human Movement Science, 43*, 1–8.

Cheng, Y.-S. P. (2007). A study on the influence of wearing a glove on handwriting by Chinese in Hong Kong. *Journal of the American Society of Questioned Document Examiners, 10*(1), 29–41.

Clark, M. (1934). *Psychology of the elementary school subjects*. New York: Farrer & Rinehart.

Clark, M. (1957). *Left-handedness: Laterality characteristics and their educational implications*. London: University of London Press.

Cohen, B. M., Giller, E., & Lynn, W. (Eds.). (1991). *Multiple personality from the inside out*. Baltimore, MD: The Sidran Press.

Cole, A. (1946). Cross examination. *Royal Canadian Mounted Police Gazette, 4*.

Cole, A. (1962). Qualified vs. no conclusion reports. *Identification News, 12*(4), 6–7.

Cole, A. (1964). *Qualifications in reports and in testimony.* Paper presented at the meeting of the American Society of Questioned Document Examiners, Denver, CO.
Cole, A. (1973). *Autoforgery.* Paper presented at the meeting of the American Society of Questioned Document Examiners, Silver Spring, MD.
Cole, A. (1980). The search for certainty and the uses of probability. *Journal of Forensic Sciences, 25*(4), 826–833.
Cole, L. (1950). *A history of education: Socrates to Montessori.* New York: Rinehart.
Comeau, G. W. (1973). *Left-hand writing vs. right-hand writing of the same person.* Unpublished manuscript, RCMP Crime Detection Laboratories, Sackville, NB, Canada.
Common Law Procedure Act, 17 & 18 Vict. Cap. 125 (1854).
Connolly, K., & Elliott, J. (1972). The evolution and ontogeny of hand function. In N. Blurton Jones (Ed.), *Ethological studies of child behaviour* (pp. 329–383). Cambridge: Cambridge University Press.
Conway, J. V. P. (1959). *Evidential documents.* Springfield, IL: Charles C. Thomas.
Conway, J. V. P. (1982). *Authenticity v. simulation.* Paper presented at the meeting of the American Society of Questioned Document Examiners, Boston, MA.
Conway, J. V. P. (1985). *Effects of aging and physical/mental disorders on handwriting, Part 1—Amyotropic lateral sclerosis.* Paper presented at the meeting of the American Society of Questioned Document Examiners, Montreal, QC, Canada.
Conway, J. V. P. (1991). *Effects of alcohol on the writing process.* Paper presented at the meeting of the American Society of Questioned Document Examiners, Orlando, FL.
Cormeau-Velghe, M., Destrait, V., Toussaint, J., & Bidaine, E. (1970). Normes de vitesse d'écriture: étude statistique de 1844 écoliers belges de 6 à 13 ans. *Psychologica Belgica, 10*(2), 247–263.
Cortiella, C., & Horowitz, S. H. (2014). *The state of learning disabilities: Facts, trends and emerging issues* (3rd ed.). New York: National Center for Learning Disabilities.
Coulmas, F. (1989). *The writing systems of the world.* Cambridge, MA: Basil Blackwell.
Crane, A. (1973). *An examination of the influences of sex and education on disguised writing.* Reported by John H. Hodgins at the meeting of the American Society of Questioned Document Examiners, Washington, DC.
Crane, A. J., & Crane, S. L. (1997). A frequency study of cheque-writing styles. *Canadian Society of Forensic Science Journal, 30*(3), 113–136.
Crépieux-Jamin, J. (1889). *L'écriture et le caractère.* F. Alcan, Paris.
Crépieux-Jamin, J. (1892). *Handwriting and expression.* K. Paul, Trench, Trübner & Company, London.
Crépieux-Jamin, J. (1933). *ABC de la graphologie.* Paris: F. Alcan.
Crown, D. A. (1989, Fall). Statistical articles. *American Society of Questioned Document Examiners Newsletter.*
Crumbaugh, J. C. (1986). Graphoanalytic cues. In *Scientific aspects of graphology* (pp. 47–58).Ed., Nevo, B., Charles C. Thomas, Springfield, IL.
Cusack, C. T., & Hargett, J. W. (1988). *A comparison study of the handwriting of adolescents.* Paper presented at the meeting of the American Academy of Forensic Sciences, Philadelphia, PA.
Dahlberg, G. (1951). An explanation of twins. *Scientific American, 184*(1), 48–51.
Dailey, J. C. (1987). Identification strength scale [Letter to the editor]. *Journal of Forensic Sciences, 32*(2), 317–318.
Daniels, J. (1990). *Unusual formation of cursive lowercase letter "p."* Paper presented at the meeting of the American Society of Questioned Document Examiners, San Jose, CA.
Daniels, P. T., & Bright, W. (Eds.). (1996). *The world's writing systems.* NY: Oxford University Press.
Daubert v. Merrell Dow Pharmaceuticals, Inc., 509 U.S. 579, 113 S. Ct. 2786, 125 L. Ed. 2d 469 (1993).
Davidson, R. A. (2010). Ataxia after 'Chasing the Dragon': A case of heroin induced toxic leukoencephalopathy. *UBC Medical Journal, 1*(2), 43–45.
Davis, K. A. (2008). Graffiti formats: Are they gangs or graffiti crews? *Journal of Gang Research, 15*(2), 1.
Davis, L. J., Saunders, C. P., Hepler, A., & Buscaglia, J. (2012). Using subsampling to estimate the strength of handwriting evidence via score-based likelihood ratios. *Forensic Science International, 216* (1–3), 146–157.
Dawson, G. A. (1985). Brain function and writing with the unaccustomed left hand. *Journal of Forensic Science, 30*(1), 167–171. doi: 10.1520/jfs10977j.

Dawson, G. A. (1993). An identification of handprinting produced with the unaccustomed left hand. *Canadian Society of Forensic Science Journal, 26*(2), 61–67. doi: 10.1080/00085030.1993.10757459.

Dawson, G. A. & Lindblom, B. S. (1998). An evaluation of line quality in photocopied signatures. *Science & Justice, 38*(3), 189–194.

Dawson, G. E., & Kennedy-Skipton, L. (1966). Elizabethan handwriting 1500–1650: A guide to the reading of documents and manuscripts. New York: Norton.

DeAngelis, C. M. (1997). Effects of writing surface and author's position on handwriting. *Journal of Questioned Document Examination, 6*(2), 10–17.

De Bruyne, P. & Messmer, P. (1980). Authentication of handwritten signatures with sonar. In R. W. De Vore, J. S. Jackson, & K. Fellbaum (Eds.), *Proceedings, third international conference: Security through science and engineering, September 22–26, 1980, Berlin, Germany* (pp. 169–172). Lexington, KY: Office of Engineering, College of Engineering, University of Kentucky.

De la Pena, J. E. (1991). *Can an apparently false signature turn out to be genuine?* Paper presented at the meeting of the American Society of Questioned Document Examiners, Orlando, FL.

Dewhurst, T. N., Ballantyne, K. N., & Found, B. (2015). Exploring the significance of pen lifts as predictors of signature simulation behaviour. *Journal of the American Society of Questioned Document Examiners, 18*(2), 3–16.

Dewhurst, T. N., Found, B., Ballantyne, K. N., & Rogers, D. (2014). The effects of extrinsic motivation on signature authorship opinions in forensic signature blind trials. *Forensic Science International, 236*, 127–132.

Dewhurst, T., Found, B., & Rogers, D. (2008). Are expert penmen better than lay people at producing simulations of a model signature? *Forensic Science International, 180*(1), 50–53.

Dhawan, B. N., Bapat, S. K., & Saxena, V. C. (1969). Effect of four centrally acting drugs on handwriting. *Japanese Journal of Pharmacology, 19*(1), 63–67. doi: 10.1254/jjp.19.63.

Diaz de Donoso, G. R. (1993). *Alterations in handwriting caused by Alzheimer's disease and abuse of drugs.* Paper presented at the meeting of the American Society of Questioned Document Examiners, Ottawa, ON, Canada.

Dibowski, J. R. (1975). Proving negative conclusions. *Identification News, 25*, 11–13.

Dick, R. M. (1964). *Qualified opinions in handwriting examinations.* Paper presented at the meeting of the American Society of Questioned Document Examiners, Denver, CO.

Dick, R. M. (1966). *Handwriting identification vs. elimination.* Paper presented at the meeting of the American Society of Questioned Document Examiners, New York, NY.

Diringer, D. (1968). *The alphabet: A key to the history of mankind* (3rd ed., Vol. 1). London: Hutchinson.

Diringer, D., & Freeman, H. (1953). *The alphabet throughout the ages and in all lands.* London: Staples Press.

Dixon, W. J. & Massey, F. J. (1951). *Introduction to statistical analysis.* New York: McGraw-Hill.

Doud, D. (1975). *Some pitfalls in testimony relating to alcohol consumption and handwriting.* Paper presented at the meeting of the American Society of Questioned Document Examiners, Colorado Springs, CO.

Doud, D. (1985). *X marks the spot.* Paper presented at the meeting of the American Academy of Forensic Sciences, Las Vegas, NV.

Doud, D. B. (1967). *Letter form variations as related to suspect calendar and diary entries.* Paper presented at the meeting of the American Society of Questioned Document Examiners, San Francisco, CA.

Dougherty, M. L. (1917). History of the teaching of handwriting in America. *The Elementary School Journal, 18*(4), 280–286.

Doulder, H. C. (1965). Examination of a document case. *Journal of Forensic Sciences, 10*, 433–440.

Downey, J. E. (1910). Judgments on the sex of handwriting. *Psychological Review, 17*(3), 205. doi: 10.1037/h0072159.

Dror, I. E., & Charlton, D. (2006). Why experts make errors. *Journal of Forensic Identification, 56*(4), 600.

Dror, I. E., & Cole, S. A. (2010). The vision in "blind" justice: Expert perception, judgment, and visual cognition in forensic pattern recognition. *Psychonomic Bulletin & Review, 17*(2), 161–167.

Duane, W. D. (1989). *Macular Degeneration (a low vision impairment) and its effect on handwriting.* Paper presented at the meeting of the American Society of Questioned Document Examiners, Arlington, VA.

Duke, D. M. (1980). *Handwriting and probable evidence*. Paper presented at the meeting of the International Association for Identification, Ottawa, ON, Canada.
Duke, D. M., & Coldwell, B. B. (1965, August). *Blood alcohol levels and handwriting*. Paper presented at the joint meeting of the American Society of Questioned Document Examiners and the RCMP Crime Detection Laboratories, Ottawa, ON, Canada.
Durina, M. E. & Caligiuri, M. P. (2009). The determination of authorship from a homogenous group of writers. *Journal of the American Society of Questioned Document Examiners, 12*(2), 29–38.
Dyer, J. (2015). *The impact of hand osteoarthritis on the handwriting of elderly people: A clinical trial of assistive technology*. Doctoral dissertation, Unitec Institute of Technology.
Dziedzic, T. (2016). The influence of lying body position on handwriting. *Journal of Forensic Sciences, 61* , S177–S183.
Eglinton, E., & Annett, M. (1994). Handedness and dyslexia: A meta-analysis. *Perceptual and motor skills, 79*(3), 1611–1616. doi: 10.2466/pms.1994.79.3f.1611.
Elbe, R. J., & Koller, W. C. (1990). *Tremor*. Baltimore: John Hopkins University Press.
Eldridge, M. A., Nimmo-Smith, I., Wing, A. M., & Totty, R. N. (1984). The variability of selected features in cursive handwriting: Categorical measures. *Journal of the Forensic Science Society, 24*(3), 179–219. doi: 10.1016/S0015-7368(84)72315-2.
Eldridge, M. A., Nimmo-Smith, I., Wing, A. M., & Totty, R. N. (1985). The dependence between selected categorical measures of cursive handwriting. *Journal of the Forensic Science Society, 25*(3), 217–231. doi: 10.1016/S0015-7368(85)72394-8.
Ellen, D. (1989). *The scientific examination of documents: Methods and techniques*. Chichester, UK: Ellis Horwood.
Ellen, D. M. (1979). The expression of conclusions in handwriting examination. *Canadian Society of Forensic Science Journal, 12*(3), 117–120. doi: 10.1080/00085030.1979.10757324.
Ellen, D. M. (1999). Handwriting examination of unfamiliar scripts. *International Journal of Forensic Document Examiners, 5*, 424–429.
Ellis, A. W. (1979). Slips of the pen. *Visible Language, 13*(3), 265–282.
Ellison, P. H. (1978). Propranolol for severe post-head injury action tremor. *Neurology, 28*(2), 197–197.
ENFSI (European Network of Forensic Science Institutes). (2015). *Best practice manual for the forensic examination of handwriting* Wiesbaden, Germany: ENFSI.
Epstein, G. (1987). Examination of the Josef Mengele handwriting. *Journal of Forensic Science, 32*(1), 100–109. doi: 10.1520/JFS12331J.
Epstein, G., Larner, J. F., & Hines, M. (1992). *The status of training for questioned document examiners in the United States*. Paper presented at the meeting of the American Academy of Forensic Sciences, New Orleans, LA.
Equey, C., Marquis, R., & Mazzella, W.D. (2007). Influence of writing position on the dimensions of signatures. *Journal of ASQDE, 10*, 53–59.
Evett, I. W (1983). What is the probability that this blood came from that person? A meaningful question? *Journal of the Forensic Science Society, 23*(1), 35–39.
Evett, I. W. & Totty, R. N. (1985). A study of the variation in the dimensions of genuine signatures. *Journal of the Forensic Science Society, 25*(3), 207–215.
Fairbank, A. (1970). *The story of handwriting: Origins and development*. London: Faber and Faber.
Fairbank, A. J. (1955). *A book of scripts* (3rd ed.). Harmondsworth, UK: Penguin Books.
FBI (Federal Bureau of Investigation). (2007). *The FBI laboratory report 2007*. Retrieved from http://www.fbi.gov/about-us/lab/lab-annual-report-2007 (accessed September 23, 2012).
Federal Rules of Civil Procedure. Rule 26.
Federal Rules of Evidence. Rule 702.
Federal Trade Commission. (2001). *Electronic signatures in global and national commerce act*. (E-SIGN), 15 U.S.C. §§ 7001-7003.
Fisher v. The Queen, 130 C.C.C. 1 (1961).
Fisher, M. P. (1992). Proposed curriculum for an apprenticeship as a forensic document examiner in private practice. *Journal of Questioned Document Examination, 1*, 2.
Fisher, R., England, S. M., Archer, R. C., & Dean, R. K. (1966). Psylocibin reactivity and time contraction as measured by psychomotor performance. *Arzneimittel-Forschung, 16*(2), 180–185.

Flores, A. (1988). What kind of person should a professional be? In *Professional ideals* (pp. 1–11). Ed., A. Flores, Belmont, CA: Wadsworth.

Fluckiger, F. A., Tripp, C. A., & Weinberg, G. H. (1961). A review of experimental research in graphology: 1933–1960. *Perceptual and Motor Skills, 12*(1), 67–90. doi: 10.2466/pms.12.1.67-90.

Foley, B. G. (1979). Handwritten entry research. *Journal of Forensic Sciences, 24*(2), 503–510.

Foley, B. G., & Kelly, J. H. (1977). Guided hand signature research. *Journal of Police Science and Administration, 5*(2), 227–231.

Foley, B. G., & Miller, A. L. (1978). *The effects of marijuana and alcohol usage on handwriting*. Paper presented at the meeting of the International Association of Forensic Sciences, Wichita, KS.

Foley, R. G. (1985). *Nearly identical signatures: A supplemental exposition*. Paper presented at the meeting of the American Society of Questioned Document Examiners, Montreal, QC, Canada.

Foley, R. G. (1987). Characteristics of synchronous sequential signatures. *Journal of Forensic Sciences, 32*(1), 121–129.

Folkes v. Chadd, 3 Doug. 157 (K. B. 1782).

FSAB (Forensic Specialties Accreditation Board). (2016). Retrieved from http://www.thefsab.org/ (accessed September 20, 2012).

Found, B. & Bird, C. (2016). *Documentation of forensic handwriting method: A modular approach*. Victoria Police Forensic Services Department & Forensic Science South Australia, Macleod, Victoria, Australia.

Found, B., & Edmond, G. (2012). Reporting on the comparison and interpretation of pattern evidence: Recommendations for forensic specialists. *Australian Journal of Forensic Sciences, 44*(2), 193–196.

Found, B., & Ganas, J. (2013). The management of domain irrelevant context information in forensic handwriting examination casework. *Science & Justice, 53*(2), 154–158.

Found, B., & Rogers, D. (1995). Contemporary issues in forensic handwriting examination: A discussion of key issues in the wake of the *Starzecpyzel* decision. *Journal of Forensic Document Examination, 8*, 1–31.

Found, B., & Rogers, D. (1996). The forensic investigation of signature complexity. In M. L. Simner, C. G. Leedham, & A. J. W. M. Thomassen (Eds.), *Handwriting and drawing research: Basic and applied issues* (pp. 483–492). Amsterdam: IOS Press.

Found, B., & Rogers, D. (1998). A consideration of the theoretical basis of forensic handwriting examination. *International Journal of Forensic Document Examination, 4*, 109–118.

Found, B., & Rogers, D. (2003). The initial profiling trial of a program to characterize forensic handwriting examiners' skill. *Journal of the American Society of Questioned Document Examiners, 6*, 72–81.

Found, B., & Rogers, D. (2008). The probative character of forensic handwriting examiners' identification and elimination opinions on questioned signatures. *Forensic Science International, 178*(1), 54–60.

Found, B., & Rogers, D. (Eds.). (1999). Documentation of forensic handwriting comparison and identification method: A modular approach. *Journal of Forensic Document Examination, 12*, 1–68.

Found, B., & Rogers, D. K. (2005). Investigating forensic document examiners' skill relating to opinions on photocopied signatures. *Science & Justice, 45*(4), 199–206.

Found, B., Rogers, D., & Herkt, A. (2001a). Comparison of document examiners' opinions on original and photocopied signatures. *Journal of Forensic Document Examination, 14*, 1–13.

Found, B., Rogers, D., & Herkt, A. (2001b). The skill of a group of document examiners in expressing handwriting and signature authorship and production process opinions. *Journal of Forensic Document Examination, 14*, 15–30.

Found, B., Rogers, D., & Schmittat, R. (1994). A computer program designed to compare the spatial elements of handwriting. *Forensic Science International, 68*(3), 195–203. doi: 10.1016/0379-0738(94)90358-1.

Found, B., Sita, J., & Rogers, D. (1999). The development of a program for characterizing forensic handwriting examiners' expertise: Signature examination pilot study. *Journal of Forensic Document Examination, 12*, 69–80.

Franck, F. E. (1996). *Objective standards: Fingerprint identifications vs. handwriting identifications*. Paper presented at the meeting of the American Society of Questioned Document Examiners, Washington, DC.

Franke, K. (2005). *The influence of physical and biomechanical processes on the ink trace: Methodological foundations for the forensic analysis of signatures*. Doctoral dissertation, Artificial Intelligence Institute, University of Groningen, The Netherlands.

Franke, K., Schomaker, L. R. B., Veenhuis, C., Vuurpijl, L. G., van Erp, M, & Guyon, I. (2004). WANDA: A common ground for forensic handwriting examination and writer identification. *ENFHEX News, 2004*(1), 23–47.
Franks, J. E. (1982). The direction of ballpoint penstrokes in left-and right-handed writers as indicated by the orientation of burr striations. *Journal of the Forensic Science Society, 22*(3), 271–274. doi: 10.1016/s0015-7368(82)71489-6
Franks, J. E., Davis, T. R., & Totty, R. N. (1983). *The Discrimination of left and right-handed writing.* Paper presented at the meeting of the American Society of Questioned Document Examiners, Lake Tahoe, NV.
Franks, J. E., Davis, T. R., Totty, R. N., Hardcastle, R. A., & Grove, D. M. (1985). Variability of stroke direction between left-and right-handed writers. *Journal of the Forensic Science Society, 25*(5), 353–370.
Frazer, P. (1901). *Bibliotics or the study of documents* (3rd ed.). Philadelphia, PA: J. B. Lippincott.
Frederick, C. J. (1968). An investigation of handwriting of suicide persons through suicide notes. *Journal of Abnormal Psychology, 73*(3, Pt.1), 263–267. doi: 10.1037/h0025871.
Freeman, F. N. (1918). *The handwriting movement: A study of the motor factors of excellence in penmanship.* Chicago: University of Chicago Press.
Freud, S. (1900). *Interpretation of dreams.* London: Hogarth.
Frye v. United States, 315 F.2d 491 (9th Cir. 1963).
Fryd, C. F. M. (1975). The direction of pen motion and its effects on the written line. *Medicine, Science and the Law, 15*(3), 167–171.
Gahwiler, H. (1984, January). Unauthorized assistance by a third person at the signing of a will. *Journal of the Forensic Science Society, 24*(6), 607.
Galbraith, N. G. (1979). *Another look at disguised writing.* Paper presented at the meeting of the American Society of Questioned Document Examiners, Rochester, NY.
Galbraith, N. G. (1981). Initials: A question of identity. *Forensic Science International, 18*(1), 13–16. doi: 10.1016/0379-0738(81)90134-1.
Galbraith, N. G. (1983). *Initials: A special category of handwriting.* Paper presented at the 35th meeting of the American Academy of Forensic Sciences, Cincinnati, OH.
Galbraith, N. G. (1984). *Alcohol: Its effect on handwriting.* Paper presented at the meeting of the American Society of Questioned Document Examiners, Nashville, TN.
Galbraith, O., Galbraith, C., & Galbraith, N. G. (1995). The principle of the 'drunkard's search' as a proxy for scientific analysis: The misuse of handwriting test data in a law journal article. *International Journal of Forensic Document Examination, 1*(1), 7–17.
Gamble, D. J. (1970). *Dry transfer printing.* Unpublished manuscript.
Gamble, D. J. (1980). The handwriting of identical twins. *Journal of the Canadian Society of Forensic Science, 13*(1), 11–30. doi: 10.1080/00085030.1980.10757337.
Gard, C. (1937). *Writing past and present: The story of writing and writing tools.* NY: The A.N. Palmer Company.
Gaudette, B. D. (1986). Evaluation of associative physical evidence. *Journal of the Forensic Science Society, 26*(3), 163–167.
Gencavage, J. S. (1984, May). *Facsimile signatures produced by gelatin transfer duplicators: Recognition and identification.* Paper presented at the meeting of the American Society of Questioned Document Examiners, Nashville, TN.
Gencavage, J. S. (1987). Recognition and identification of multiple authorship. *Journal of Forensic Sciences, 32*(1), 130–136. doi: 10.1520/jfs12335j.
General Electric Co. v. Joiner, 522 U.S. 136, 118 S. Ct. 512, 139 L. Ed. 2d 508 (1997).
Gervin, M., & Barnes, T. R. E. (2000). Assessment of drug related movement disorders in schizophrenia. *Advances in Psychiatric Treatment, 6*, 332–343.
Ghods, V. & Kabir, E. (2013). A study on Farsi handwriting styles for online recognition. *Malaysian Journal of Computer Science, 26*(1), 44–57.
Giles, A. (1990). *Increasing the level of objectivity in handwriting examinations.* Paper presented at the meeting of the American Society of Questioned Document Examiners, San Jose, CA.
Giles, A. (1996). *Figuring it out.* Paper presented at the meeting of the American Society of Questioned Document Examiners, Washington, DC.

Gillett, M. (1966). *A history of education, thought and practice.* Toronto: McGraw-Hill.

Gilmour, C., & Bradford, J. (1987). The effect of medication on handwriting. *Canadian Society of Forensic Science Journal, 20*(4), 119–138. doi: 10.1080/00085030.1987.10756951.

Girouard, P. (1986). *The influence of stress on writing.* Paper presented at the meeting of the International Association of Questioned Document Examiners, Toronto, ON, Canada.

Glogowski, G. (1963). Aktuelle Probleme der Spastischen Extremitätenlähmung. *Münchner Medizinische Wochenschrift*, pp. 2448.

Godown, L. (1970). *Marks of the professional.* Paper presented at the meeting of the American Society of Questioned Document Examiners, Houston, TX.

Goetschel, C. (1989). *Problems of identifying disputed signatures on works of art.* Paper presented at the meeting of the American Society of Questioned Document Examiners, Arlington, VA.

Good, I. J. (1985). Weight of evidence: A brief survey. In J. M. Bernardo, M. H. DeGroot, D. V. Lindley, & A. F. M. Smith (Eds.), *Bayesian statistics 2: Proceedings of the second Valencia international meeting, September 6–10, 1983* (pp. 249–270). Amsterdam: Elsevier.

Goodenough, F. L. (1945). Sex differences in judging the sex of handwriting. *The Journal of Social Psychology, 22*(1), 61–68. doi: 10.1080/00224545.1945.9714182.

Goodnow, J. (1977). *Children drawing.* Cambridge, MA: Harvard University Press.

Goodnow, J. J., & Levine, R. A. (1973). "The grammar of action": Sequence and syntax in children's copying. *Cognitive Psychology, 4*(1), 82–98. doi: 10.1016/0010-0285(73)90005-4.

Goodtitle d. Revett v. Braham, 4 Term. Rep. 497 (1792).

Gould, G. M. (1908). *Right handedness and left handedness with chapters treating of the writing posture. The rules of the road, etc.* Philadelphia, PA: J. P. Lippincott.

Goyne, T. E. W., & Kittel, H. R. (1985). *Do "hangovers" impair writing ability?* Paper presented at the meeting of the American Society of Questioned Document Examiners, Montreal, QC, Canada.

Grant, J. (1969). Mussolini diaries forgeries. *Journal of the Forensic Science Society, 9*, 43–44. doi: 10.1016/s0015-7368(69)70486-8.

Grant, J. (1974). *The effect of posture on a signature.* Paper presented at the meeting of the International Association of Forensic Sciences, London, UK.

Grant, J. (1985). The diaries of Adolf Hitler. *Journal of the Forensic Science Society, 25*(3), 189. doi: 10.1016/s0015-7368(85)72391-2.

Gantz, D. T., Miller, J. J., & Walch, M. A. (2005). Multi-language handwriting derived biometric identification. In D. Doermann (Ed.). *In Proceedings of the 2005 Symposium on Document Image Understanding Technology*, College Park, Maryland. (pp. 197–209). University of Maryland

Green, M. D. (1991). Expert witnesses and sufficiency of evidence in toxic substances litigation: The legacy of Agent Orange and Bendectin litigation. *Nw. UL Rev.*, 86, 643.

Greenwood, B. R. (1983). *Proficiency standards for document personnel (abilities, duties, knowledge and skills).* Paper presented at the meeting of the American Society of Questioned Document Examiners, Lake Tahoe, NV.

Gross, L. J. (1975). Drug-induced handwriting changes: An empirical review. *Texas Reports on Biology and Medicine,* 33(3), 370–390.

Guiard, Y., & Millerat, F. (1984). Writing postures in left-handers: Inverters are hand-crossers. *Neuropsychologia, 22*(4), 535–538. doi: 10.1016/0028-3932(84)90051-4.

Haase, H. J. (1961). Extrapyramidal modifications of fine movements: A "conditio sine qua non" of the fundamental therapeutic action of neuroleptic drugs. *Revue Canadienne de Biologie, 20*(2), 425–449.

Hagan, W. E. (1894). *A treatise on disputed handwriting and the determination of genuine from forged signatures: The character and composition of inks, and their determination by chemical tests: The effect of age as manifested in the appearance of written instruments and documents.* Albany, NY: Banks & Brothers.

Halder-Sinn, P., & Wegener, K. (1992). Controllability of the slant in simple and multiple strategies for disguising handwriting. *Perceptual and Motor Skills, 74*(3), 905–906. doi: 10.2466/pms.74.3.905–906.

Hall, M. G. & Hardcastle, R. A. (1987, August). *Is a universal handwriting specimen feasible?* Paper presented at the 11th meeting of the International Association of Forensic Sciences, Vancouver, BC, Canada.

Handwriting Without Tears. (2016). Retrieved from: https://www.hwtears.com/hwt (accessed December 15, 2016).

Hanna, G. A. (1989). A preliminary classification of the writing elements of Chinese characters. *Journal of Forensic Science, 34*(2), 439–448. doi: 10.1520/JFS12654J.

Hanna, G. A. (1992). Art forgery: The role of the document examiner. *Journal of Forensic Science, 37*(4), 1096–1114.

Hardcastle, R. A., & Kemmenoe, D. A. (1990). A computer-based system for the classification of handwriting on cheques. Part 2: Cursive handwriting. *Journal of the Forensic Science Society, 30*(2), 97–103.

Hardcastle, R. A., Thornton, D., & Totty, R. N. (1986). A computer-based system for the classification of handwriting on cheques. *Journal of the Forensic Science Society, 26*(6), 383–392.

Hardy, H., & Fagel, W. (1995). Methodological aspects of handwriting identification. *Journal of Forensic Document Examination, 8*, 33–69.

Hardy, H. J. J. (1992). Dynamics of the writing movement: Physical modelling and practical application. *Journal of Forensic Document Examination, 5*, 1–34.

Harralson, H. H. (2005). Handwriting characterization and differential analysis of Parkinson's disease and essential tremor. *Journal of the National Association of Document Examiners, 28*, 19–37.

Harralson, H. H. (2007–2008). Differentiating the handwriting of twins. *Journal of the National Association of Document Examiners, 29*(1), 24–32.

Harralson, H. H. (2008). *Forensic handwriting examination of motor disorders & forgery: Research and applications.* Saarbrücken, Germany: VDM Verlag Dr. Müller.

Harralson, H. H. (2013). *Developments in handwriting and signature identification in the digital age.* Waltham, MA: Anderson.

Harralson, H.H., Jarvis, M.W.B., Barabe, J., & Miller, L.S. (2012). Forensic analysis of painted signatures on artwork. *Proceedings of the Australia & New Zealand Forensic Science Society*, Tasmania, Australia.

Harralson, H. H., Teulings, H.-L., & Farley, B. (2008). Comparison of handwriting kinematics in movement disorders and forgery. *Journal of Forensic Document Examination, 19*, 41–52.

Harralson, H. H., Teulings, H. -L., & Farley, B. G. (2009). Handwriting variability in movement disorder patients and effects of fatigue. In A. Vinter & J.-L. Velay (Eds.). *Proceedings of the 14th Biennial Conference of the International Graphonomics Society*, 13–16 September 2009, Dijon, France. (pp. 103–107). Université de Bourgogne, Dijon, France.

Harralson, H. H., Teulings, H.-L., & Miller, L. S. (2011). Temporal and spatial differences between online and offline signatures. In E. Grassi & J. L. Contreras-Vidal (Eds.), *Proceedings of the 15th International Graphonomics Society Conference, June 12–15, 2011, International Graphonomics Society, Cancun, Mexico* (pp. 34–37).

Harralson, H. H., Teulings, H.-L., & Miller, L. S. (2013). Proficiency of forensic document examination students examining static and dynamic electronic signature data. In M. Nakagawa, M. Liwicki & B. Zhu (Eds.), *Proceedings of the 16th Biennial Conference of the International Graphonomics Society, June 13–16, 2013, International Graphonomics Society Nara, Japan* (pp. 22–25).

Harralson, H. H., Waites, E., & Will, E. J. (2015). A survey of forensic handwriting examination research in response to the NAS Report. In C. Rémi, L. Prévost, & E. Anquetil (Eds.), *Drawing, Handwriting Processing Analysis: New Advances and Challenges. Proceedings of the 17th Biennial Conference of the International Graphonomics Society.*

Harris, J. (1969). *A questioned document examiner looks at aphasia, its accompanying handwriting disorders, and resulting case problems.* Paper presented at the meeting of the American Society of Questioned Document Examiners, Toronto, ON, Canada.

Harris, J. J. & Mills, D. H. (1963). Medical records and the questioned document examiner. *Journal of Forensic Sciences, 8*(3), 453–461.

Harris, J. J. (1953). Disguised handwriting. *Journal of Criminal Law, Criminology and Police Science, 43*(5), 685–689. doi: 10.2307/1139667.

Harris, J. J. (1958). How much do people write alike? A study of signatures. *Journal of Criminal Law, Criminology, and Police Science, 48*(6), 647–651. doi: 10.2307/1140273.

Harris, J. J. (1986). The document evidence and some other observations about the Howard R. Hughes "Mormon Will" contest. *Journal of Forensic Science, 31*(1), 365–375. doi: 10.1520/JFS11896J.

Harris, P.R. (1980). *Disguise, forgeries and look-alike writing.* Paper presented at the meeting of the American Society of Questioned Document Examiners, Vancouver, BC, Canada.

Harris, R. (1911). *Hints on advocacy: Conduct of cases civil and criminal : Classes of witnesses, and suggestions for cross-examining them, etc., etc.* (14th ed.). London: Stevens and Sons.

Harrison, W. R. (1958). *Suspect documents: Their scientific examination.* New York: Praeger.

Harrison, W. R. (1964). *Forgery detection: A practical guide.* New York: Praeger.

Harrison, W. R. (1966). *Suspect documents: Their scientific examination. Second impression with supplement, 1966.* London: Sweet and Maxwell.

Hart, B. O., & Rosenstein, J. (1964). Examining the language behavior of deaf children. *The Volta Review, 66*(9), 679–682.

Hart, L. J. (1985, September). *Illusions of disguise.* Paper presented at the meeting of the American Society of Questioned Document Examiners, Montreal, QC, Canada.

Harvey, O. L. (1934). The measurement of handwriting considered as a form of expressive movement. *Journal of Personality, 2*(4), 310–321. doi: 10.1111/j.1467-6494.1934.tb02107.x.

Harvey, R., & Mitchell, R. M. (1973). The Nicola Brazier murder: The role of handwriting in a large-scale investigation. *Journal of the Forensic Science Society, 13*(3), 157–168. doi: 10.1016/S0015-7368(73)70789-1.

Hayes, J. L. (1987). *Connecting strokes.* Paper presented at the meeting of the American Society of Questioned Document Examiners, Vancouver, BC, Canada.

Haywood, C. L. (1991). *Continuing the search for the black "J" and "W."* Paper presented at the meeting of the American Society of Questioned Document Examiners, Orlando, FL.

Head, H. (1963). *Aphasia and kindred disorders of speech* (Vols. 1–2). New York: Hafner.

Hécaen, H., Penfield, W., Bertrand, C., & Malmo, R. (1956). The syndrome of apractognosia due to lesions of the minor cerebral hemisphere. *AMA Archives of Neurology and Psychiatry, 75*(4), 400–434. doi: 10.1001/archneurpsyc.1956.02330220064007.

Hecker, M. & Eisermann, H. W. (1986). *Forensic identification system of handwriting (FISH).* Paper presented at the meeting of the American Society of Questioned Document Examiners, Savannah, GA.

Hecker, M. R. (1981, June). *The change of handwriting as a process of identification.* Paper presented at the 9th meeting of the International Association of Forensic Sciences, Bergen, Norway.

Hecker, M. R. (1983). *Effects of unusual paper supports on handwriting.* Paper presented at the meeting of the American Society of Questioned Document Examiners, North Lake Tahoe, NV.

Hecker, M. R. (1996). *The scientific examination of sex differences in handwriting.* Paper presented at the meeting of the American Society of Questioned Document Examiners, Washington, DC.

Hensel, E. B., Khan, I. A., & Dizon, J. F. (1973). Forensic examination of peculiar writing systems. *Journal of the Forensic Science Society, 13*(2), 143–152. doi: 10.1016/S0015-7368(73)70782-9.

Hepler, A.B., Saunders, C.P., Davis, L.J., & Buscaglia, J. (2012). Score-based likelihood ratios for handwriting evidence. *Forensic Science International, 219*(1–3), 129–140.

Herkt, A. (1986). Signature disguise or signature forgery? *Journal of the Forensic Science Society, 26*(4), 257–266. doi: 10.1016/s0015-7368(86)72493-6.

Herkt, A., Boot, D., & Walsh, D. (1999). Module 7: Structural and line quality inconsistencies. In B. Found & D. Rogers (Eds.), Documentation of forensic handwriting comparison and identification method: A modular approach. *Journal of Forensic Document Examination, 12*, 37–44.

Herrick, V. E. (1960a). *Comparison of practices in handwriting.* Madison, WI: University of Wisconsin.

Herrick, V. E. (1960b). *Handwriting and related factors: 1890–1960.* Washington, DC: Handwriting Foundation.

Herrick, V. E. (Ed.). (1963). *New horizons for research in handwriting: Report.* Presented at the Invitational Conference on Research in Handwriting (1961: University of Wisconsin), Madison, WI: University of Wisconsin Press.

Herrick, V. E., & Okada, N. (1963). The present scene: Practices in the teaching of handwriting in the United States-1960. In V. E. Harrick (Ed.), *New horizons for research in handwriting* (pp. 17–32). Madison, WI: University of Wisconsin Press.

Herrick, V. E., Reuther, C. A., Bryan, G., Anderson, L., & Okada, N. (1960). *Comparison of practices in handwriting advocated by nineteen commercial systems of handwriting instruction.* Madison, WI: Committee on Research in Basic Skills, University of Wisconsin.

Hicks, A. F. (1996). *Dyslexia: Its effect upon handwriting.* Paper presented at the meeting of the American Society of Questioned Document Examiners, Washington, DC.

Hilton, O. (1941). The collection of writing standards in criminal investigation. *Journal of Criminal Law and Criminology, 32*(2), 241–256. doi: 10.2307/1137033.

Hilton, O. (1956). Education and qualifications of examiners of questioned documents. *Journal of Forensic Sciences, 1*(3), 35–42.

Hilton, O. (1957). Characteristics of the ball point pen and its influence on handwriting identification. *The Journal of Criminal Law, Criminology, and Police Science, 47*(5), 606–613. doi: 10.2307/1139043.

Hilton, O. (1958). The relationship of mathematical probability to the handwriting identification problem. In R. A. Huber (Ed.), *Questioned Documents in Crime Detection: Proceedings of the R.C.M.P. Crime Detection Laboratories Seminar no. 5 held at Ottawa, Oct. 27–Nov. 1, 1958* (pp. 121–130). Ottawa: Queen's Printer.

Hilton, O. (1963). Some basic rules for the identification of hand-writing. *Medicine, Science and the Law, 3*(2), 107–117.

Hilton, O. (1965). A further look at writing standards. *The Journal of Criminal Law, Criminology, and Police Science, 56*(3), 382–389. doi: 10.2307/1141257.

Hilton, O. (1967). *A second look at signature standards.* Paper presented at the meeting of the American Society of Questioned Document Examiners, San Francisco, CA.

Hilton, O. (1969a). Consideration of the writer's health in identifying signatures and detecting forgery. *Journal of Forensic Sciences, 14*(2), 157–166.

Hilton, O. (1969b). A study of the influence of alcohol on handwriting. *Journal of Forensic Sciences, 14*(3), 309–316.

Hilton, O. (1970). Identification of numerals. *International Criminal Police Review, 241*(25), 245–250.

Hilton, O. (1974). *Ethics and the document examiner.* Paper presented at the meeting of the American Society of Questioned Document Examiners, Milwaukee, WI.

Hilton, O. (1975). *Influence of age and illness on handwriting identification problems.* Paper presented at the meeting of the American Society of Questioned Document Examiners, Colorado Springs, CO.

Hilton, O. (1976). Ethics and the document examiner under the adversary system. *Journal of Forensic Science, 21*(4), 779–783. doi: 10.1520/JFS10561J.

Hilton, O. (1979). Is there any place in criminal prosecutions for qualified opinions by document examiners? *Journal of Forensic Sciences, 24*(3), 579–581.

Hilton, O. (1980). *Distinctive qualities of today's pens.* Paper presented at the meeting of the American Society of Questioned Document Examiners, Vancouver, BC, Canada.

Hilton, O. (1982) *Scientific examination of questioned documents* (Rev. ed). New York: Elsevier/North-Holland.

Hilton, O. (1983). How individual are personal writing habits? *Journal of Forensic Sciences, 28*(3), 683–685.

Hilton, O. (1984). Effects of writing instruments on handwriting details. *Journal of Forensic Sciences, 29*(1), 80–86. doi: 10.1520/jfs11637j.

Hilton, O. (1986). *Individual or class characteristics in foreign numbers.* Paper presented at the meeting of the American Society of Questioned Document Examiners, Savannah, GA.

Hilton, O. (1987). Line quality—Historic and contemporary views. *Journal of Forensic Sciences, 32*(1), 118–120.

Hilton, O. (1988). *Document examination and the ASQDE Code of ethics.* Paper presented at the meeting of the American Society of Questioned Document Examiners, Aurora, CO.

Hilton, O. (1993). *Scientific examination of questioned documents.* (Rev. Ed.). Boca Raton, FL: CRC Press.

Hilton, O. (1995). Relationship of mathematical probability to the handwriting identification problem. *International Journal of Forensic Document Examiners, 1*(3), 224–229.

Hirsch, M. W., Jarvik, M. E., & Abramson, H. A. (1956). Lysergic acid diethylamide (LSD-25): XVIII effects of LSD-25 and six related drugs upon handwriting. *Journal of Psychology, 41*(1), 11–22. doi: 10.1080/00223980.1956.9916201.

Hladij, H. (1999). Similarities in handwriting of closely related people. *International Journal of Forensic Document Examination, 5*, 221–232.

Hodgins, J. H. (1967, March). Request specimen writing for comparison purposes. *Royal Canadian Mounted Police Gazette,* 15–16.

Hodgins, J. H. (1971). Determination of sex from handwriting. *Canadian Society of Forensic Science Journal, 4*(4), 124–132. doi: 10.1080/00085030.1971.10757284.

Hodgins, J. H. (1973). *A resume of some recent research.* Paper presented at the meeting of the American Society of Questioned Document Examiners, Washington, DC.

Hooten, A. B. (1992). A case study of dating multiple sclerosis onset by handwriting. *Journal of Forensic Document Examination, 5*, 55–63.

Horan, J. J. (1985). *The size of forged signatures.* Paper presented at the meeting of the American Society of Questioned Document Examiners, Chicago, IL.

Horan, J. J., & Horan, G. J. (1984, September). *A study of numbers.* Paper presented at the meeting of the International Association of Forensic Sciences, Oxford, UK.

Horton, R. A. (1992). *A study of the occurrence of certain handwriting characteristics in a random population.* Paper presented at the meeting of the American Society of Questioned Document Examiners, Milwaukee, WI.

Hotimsky, S. (1972, September). *Anonymous letters written by left-hand.* Paper presented at the meeting of the International Association of Forensic Sciences, Edinburgh, UK.

Houp, K. W., & Pearsall, T. E. (1984). *Reporting technical information.* New York: Macmillan.

Howard, L. B. (1986). The dichotomy of the expert witness. *Journal of Forensic Science, 31*(1), 337–341. doi: 10.1520/jfs11893j.

Huber, R. A. (1955). *The identification of Eskimo writing.* Ivugivik, Quebec: unpublished report in the case of Eskimo SEEGOALOOK, Writing Threatening Letters.

Huber, R. A. (1959). Expert witnesses: In defence of expert witnesses in general and of document examiners in particular. *Criminal Law Quarterly, 2*(3), 276–295.

Huber, R. A. (1960). On looking over Shakespeare's 'secretarie'. *Stratford Papers on Shakespeare,* 51–70.

Huber, R. A. (1963). *Interpolating first principles of handwriting identification.* Paper presented at the 1st International Meeting in Questioned Documents, i.e., the 3rd meeting of the International Association of Forensic Sciences, London, England.

Huber, R. A. (1972). The philosophy of identification. *Royal Canadian Mounted Police Gazette, 34*(7/8), 8–14.

Huber, R. A. (1980). The quandary of "Qualified" Opinions. *Canadian Society of Forensic Science Journal, 13*(3), 7. doi: 10.1080/00085030.1980.10757344.

Huber, R. A. (1982). *Handwriting identification: Facts and fundamentals. A potpourri of comments intended to educate, consolidate, stimulate, and/or substantiate.* Paper presented at the meeting of the American Society of Questioned Document Examiners, Boston, MA.

Huber, R. A. (1983). *Quarter century search and survey.* Paper presented at the meeting of the American Society of Questioned Document Examiners, Lake Tahoe, NV.

Huber, R. A. (1990). *The uniqueness of writing.* Paper presented at the meeting of the American Society of Questioned Document Examiners, San Jose, CA.

Huber, R. A. (1995). *Handwriting examination as a scientific discipline.* Paper presented at the meeting of the American Society of Questioned Document Examiners, Chicago, IL.

Huber, R. A., & Headrick, A. M. (1987, August). *The identification process.* Paper presented at the meeting of the International Association of Forensic Sciences, Vancouver, BC, Canada.

Huber, R. A., & Headrick, A. M. (1990). Let's do it by numbers. *Forensic Science International, 46*(3), 209–218. doi: 10.1016/0379-0738(90)90307-k.

Hull, J. M. (1993, April). *The relationship between disguised handwriting and years of formal education: final results.* Paper presented at the meeting of the Southwestern Association of Forensic Document Examiners.

Humphreys, H. N. (1855). *The origin and progress of the art of writing ...* London: Day & Son.

Huth, E. J. (1982). *How to write and publish papers in the medical sciences.* Philadelphia, PA: ISI Press.

International Organization for Standardization (ISO). (2012). ISO/IEC 17024:2012 Conformity assessment–General requirements for bodies operating certifications of persons. Retrieved from https://www.iso.org/standard/52993.html (accessed November 15, 2017).

Impedovo, S. & Abbattista, N. (1982). Handwritten numeral recognition; the organization degree measurement. In H. Marko & International Conference on Pattern Recognition (1982). *Proceedings of the 6th internal conference on pattern recognition, Munich, Germany, Oct. 19–22, 1982* (pp. 40–43). Silver Spring, MD: IEEE Computer Society Press.

Imwinkelried, E. J. (1982). *The methods of attacking scientific evidence.* Charlottesville, VA: Michie.

Irwin, K. G. (1967). *The romance of writing, from Egyptian hieroglyphics to modern letters, numbers, and signs.* New York: Viking Press.

Isokoski, P., & Käki. (2002, April). Comparison of two touchpad-based methods for numeric entry. In *Proceedings of the SIGCHI Conference on Human Factors in Computing System* (pp. 25–32). ACM.

Iwasaki, S., Kaiho, T., & Iseki, K. (1995). Handedness trends across age groups in a Japanese sample of 2316. *Perceptual and Motor Skills, 80*(3), 979–994. doi: 10.2466/pms.1995.80.3.979.

Jacquin-Keller, A. M. (1985). *Is it possible to verify a manuscript document written in foreign characters?* Paper presented at the meeting of the American Society of Questioned Document Examiners, Montreal, QC, Canada.

Jamieson, J. A. (1983). Effects of slope change on handwriting. *Canadian Society of Forensic Science Journal, 16*(3), 117–123. doi: 10.1080/00085030.1983.10756927.

Jarvis, M. W. B. (2010). The music-calligraphy of Johann Sebastian and Anna Magdalena Bach. *Journal of Forensic Document Examination, 20*, 49–61.

Jenkins, J. (1813). *The art of writing reduced in seven books*. Andover, MA: Flagg & Gould.

Jones, D. G. (1986). Guided hand or forgery? *Journal of the Forensic Science Society, 26*(3), 169–173. doi: 10.1016/S0015-7368(86)72473-0.

Kalera, M. K., Srihari, S., & Xu, A. (2004). Offline signature verification and identification using distance statistics. *International Journal of Pattern Recognition and Artificial Intelligence, 18*(07), 1339–1360.

Kam, M., Fielding, G., & Conn, R. (1997). Writing identification by professional document examiners. *Journal of Forensic Sciences, 42*(5), 778–786.

Kam, M., Gummadidala, K., Fielding, G., & Conn, R. (2001). Signature authentication by forensic document examiners. *Journal of Forensic Sciences, 46*, 884–888.

Kam, M., & Lin, E. (2003). Writer identification using hand-printed and non-hand-printed questioned documents. *Journal of Forensic Sciences, 48*(6), 1391–1395.

Kam, M., Wetstein, J., & Conn, R. (1994). Proficiency of professional document examiners in writer Identification. *Journal of Forensic Science, 39*(1), 5–14. doi: 10.1520/JFS13565J.

Kapoor, T. S., Kapoor, M., & Sharma, G. P. (1985). Study of the form and extent of natural variation in genuine writings with age. *Journal of the Forensic Science Society, 25*(5), 371–375. doi: 10.1016/s0015-7368(85)72416-4.

Karlsson, J. E. (1987). What is the probability that Jones' signature is genuine? *Canadian Society of Forensic Science Journal, 20*, 114.

Kashi, R. S., Hu, J., Nelson, W. L., & Turin, W. (1997). On line handwritten signature verification using hidden Markov model features. In *Proceedings of the Fourth International Conference on Document Analysis and Recognition*, 18-20 August 1997. (pp. 253–257).

Kaye, D. H. (1994). Commentary on "Proficiency of professional document examiners in writer identification." *Journal of Forensic Sciences, 39*(1), 5–14.

Keckler, J. A. (1988, September). *Felonious disguise*. Paper presented at the meeting of the American Society of Questioned Document Examiners, Aurora, CO.

Keele, S. W. (1968). Movement control in skilled motor performance. *Psychological Bulletin, 70*(6p1), 387–403.

Keeler, K. (1934). A study of documentary evidence in election frauds (Tattle-tale tallies). *Journal of Criminal Law and Criminology, 25*(2), 324–337.

Kelly, J. H. (1975). *Effects of artificial aids and prostheses on signatures*. Paper presented at the meeting of the American Society of Questioned Document Examiners, Colorado Springs, CO.

Kelly, J. S. (1998). *The examination and identification of numbers*. Paper presented at the meeting of the American Academy of Forensic Sciences, San Francisco, CA.

Kerr, L. K. & Taylor, L. R. (1992). Linguistic evidence indicative of authorship by a member of the deaf community. *Journal of Forensic Sciences, 37*(6), 1621–1632. doi: 10.1520/jfs13352j.

Keys v. Keys, 129 S.W.2d 1103, 23 Tenn. App. 188 (1939).

Kind, S. S., Wigmore, R., Whitehead, P. H., & Loxley, D. S. (1979). Terminology in forensic science. *Journal of the Forensic Science Society, 19*(3), 189–191.

Kingston, C. (1989). A perspective on probability and physical evidence. *Journal of Forensic Sciences, 34*(6), 1336–1342.

Kinner, W. S. A. (1925). The Croonian lectures on some disorders of mobility and of muscle tone with special reference to the corpus striatum. *Lancet, 206*(5314), 1–10. doi: 10.1016/s0140-6736(01)20638-2.

Kirk, P. L. (1953). *Crime investigation: Physical evidence and the police laboratory*. New York: Interscience.

Kiser, R. F., & Torres, B. (1975). *"Like" letter substitution—How dependable?* Paper presented at the meeting of the American Society of Questioned Document Examiners, Colorado Springs, CO.

Klages, L. (1910). *Prinzipien der charakterologie.* JA Barth, Leipzig.

Klement, V. (1983). An application system for the computer-assisted identification of handwritings. In R. W. De Vore, J. S. Jackson, & P. de Bruyne (Eds.), *Proceedings: International Carnahan Conference on Security Technology, October 4–6, 1983, Zürich, Switzerland* (pp. 75–79). Lexington, KY: Office of Engineering Services, University of Kentucky.

Klement, V. R., Naske, R.-D., & Steinke, K. (1980, September). The application of image processing and pattern recognition techniques to the forensic analysis of handwriting. In R. W. De Vore, J. S. Jackson, & K. Fellbaum (Eds.), *Proceedings, Third International Conference: Security Through Science and Engineering, September 22–26, 1980, Berlin, Germany* (pp. 5–11). Lexington, KY: Office of Engineering, College of Engineering, University of Kentucky.

Klimoski, R. J., & Rafaeli, A. (1983). Inferring personal qualities through handwriting analysis. *Journal of Occupational Psychology, 56*(3), 191–202.

Klivans, G. S. (2013). *Gang secret codes: Deciphered.* Santa Ana, CA: Police and Fire.

Klonoff, H., Low, M., & Marcus, A. (1973). Neuropsychological effects of marijuana. *Canadian Medical Association Journal, 108*(2), 150–156.

Knight, B. (1989). Ethics and discipline in forensic science. *Journal of the Forensic Science Society, 29*(1), 53–59.

Koehler, J. J., Schweitzer, N. J., Saks, M. J., & McQuiston, D. E. (2016). Science, technology, or the expert witness: What influences jurors' judgments about forensic science testimony? *Psychology, Public Policy, and Law, 22*(4), 401.

Komal, S., Jasuja, O. P., Singla, A. K., & Singh, S. (1999). A study of the handwriting of visually impaired persons. *International Journal of Forensic Document Examiners, 5*, 39–53.

Konstantinidis, S. I. V. (1987). Disguised handwriting. *Journal of the Forensic Science Society, 27*(6), 383–392. doi: 10.1016/s0015-7368(87)72786-8.

Kraemer, J. I. (1979). A new development in graphic transfer material and an illustration of its illegal use. *Journal of Forensic Science, 24*(4), 875–879. doi: 10.1520/jfs10917j.

Kramer, E., & Lauterbach, C. E. (1928). Resemblance in the handwriting of twins and siblings. *The Journal of Educational Research, 18*(2), 149–152.

Kroon-van der Kooij, L. N. (1985). *A master unmasked or the Pergolesi-Ricciotti puzzle solved.* Unpublished manuscript, The Hague, Criminal Investigation Department, The Netherlands.

Kroon-van der Kooij, L. N. (1987). *Differences between handwriting characters in relation to various nationalities.* Paper presented at the meeting of the International Association of Forensic Sciences, Vancouver, BC, Canada.

Kropinak, R. (1965). *Disguised writing—Effective or noneffective.* Unpublished manuscript, RCMP Crime Detection Laboratory, Regina, SK, Canada.

Kuckuck, W., Rieger, B., & Steinke, K. (1979). Automatic writer recognition. In *Proceedings of the 1979 Carnahan Conference on Crime Countermeasures, University of Kentucky, Lexington* (pp. 57–64).

Kukucka, J., & Kassin, S. M. (2014). Do confessions taint perceptions of handwriting evidence? An empirical test of the forensic confirmation bias. *Law and Human Behavior, 38*(3), 256.

Kulvicius, T., Ning, K., Tamosiunaite, M., & Worgötter, F. (2012). Joining movement sequences: Modified dynamic movement primitives for robotics applications exemplified in handwriting. *IEEE Transactions on Robotics, 28*(4), 145–157.

Kumho Tire Co. v. Carmichael, 526 U.S. 137, 119 S. Ct. 1167, 143 L. Ed. 2d 238 (1999).

Langmaid, R. A., Papadopoulos, N., Johnson, B. P., Phillips, J. G., & Rinehart, N. J. (2014). Handwriting in children with ADHD. *Journal of Attention Disorders, 18*(6), 504–510.

Launius, R. D., Sillitoe, L., & Roberts, A. D. (1988). *Salamander: The story of the Mormon forgery murders.* Signature Books, Salt Lake City, UT.

LeBrun, M., McLaughlin, T. F., Derby, K. M., & McKenzie, M. (2012). The effects of using Handwriting Without Tears® to teach thirty-one integrated preschoolers of varying academic ability to write their names. *Academic Research International, 2*(2), 373.

Lee, C. D., & Abbey, R. A. (1922). *Classification and identification of handwriting.* New York: Appleton.

Leedham, G., & Chachra, S. (2003, August). Writer identification using innovative binarised features of handwritten numerals. In *Document Analysis and Recognition, 2003. Proceedings of the Seventh International Conference* (pp. 413–416). IEEE.

Legge, D. (1965). Analysis of visual and proprioceptive components of motor skill by means of a drug. *British Journal of Psychology, 56*(2 & 3), 243–254. doi: 10.1111/j.2044-8295.1965.tb00962.x.

Legge, D., Steinberg, H. & Summerfield, A. (1964). Simple measures of handwriting as indices of drug effects. *Perceptual and Motor Skills, 18*(2), 549–558. doi: 10.2466/pms.1964.18.2.549.

Legień, M. (1984). The handwriting test as a method of diagnosing narcotic dependence. *Psychiatria Polska, 18*(3), 233–240.

Lei, H., & Govindaraju, V. (2005). A comparative study on the consistency of features in on-line signature verification. *Pattern Recognition Letters, 26*(15), 2483–2489.

Lemke, E., & Kirchner, J. (1971). A multivariate study of handwriting, intelligence and personality correlates. *Journal of Personality Assessment, 35*(6), 584–592.

Leson, J. L. (1974). *The education and qualifications of questioned document examiners.* Unpublished master's thesis, George Washington University, Washington, DC.

Lester, D., Werling, N., & Heinle, N. H. (1982). Graphoanalytic differences by sex and handedness. *Journal of Perceptual and Motor Skills, 55*(3), 1190. doi: 10.2466/pms.1982.55.3f.1190.

Lester, D., Werling, N., & Heinle, N. H. (1983). Differences in handwriting as a function of age. *Perceptual and Motor Skills, 57*(3), 738. doi: 10.2466/pms.1983.57.3.738.

Leung, S. C. (1986). *A case of lipstick writing on a body.* Paper presented at the meeting of the American Society of Questioned Document Examiners, Savannah, GA.

Leung, S. C. & Cheung, Y. L. (1988). *On opinion.* Paper presented at the meeting of the American Society of Questioned Document Examiners, Aurora, CO.

Leung, S. C., Cheng, Y. S., Fung, H. T., & Poon, N. L. (1993). Forgery I—Simulation. *Journal of Forensic Science, 38*(2), 402–412. doi: 10.1520/JFS13420J.

Levander, M., & Schalling, D. (1988). Self-assessed and examiner-assessed writing hand posture in Swedish left-handers. *Neuropsychologia, 26*(5), 777–781. doi: 10.1016/0028-3932(88)90016-4.

Levy, J. (1974). Psychobiological implications of lateral bisymmetry. In S. J. Dimond & J. G. Beaumont (Eds.), *Hemisphere function in the human brain.* London: Elek Science.

Lowinson, T. S. (1986). Classic schools of graphology. In B. Nevo (Ed.), *Scientific aspects of graphology* (pp. 5–46). Springfield, IL: Charles C. Thomas.

Lindblom, B. (1983). Identifying characteristics in the handwriting of the visually impaired. *Canadian Society of Forensic Science Journal, 16*(4), 174–191. doi: 10.1080/00085030.1983.10756933.

Lindblom, B. (1991). *The examiner as forensic consultant and expert witness—Professional and ethical considerations.* Paper presented at the meeting of the American Society of Questioned Document Examiners, Orlando, FL.

Linden, J., Marquis, R., & Mazzella, W. (2016). Forensic analysis of digital dynamic signatures: New methods for data treatment and feature evaluation. *Journal of Forensic Sciences, 62*, 382–391.

Lines, S. R. & Franck, F. E. (2003). Triplet and sibling handwriting study to determine degree of individuality and natural variation. *Journal of the American Society of Questioned Document Examiners, 6*(1), 48–55.

Livingston, O. B. (1949). Bogus check file classified by trademarks. *Journal of Criminal Law and Criminology, 39*(6), 782–789.

Livingston, O. B. (1963). Frequency of certain characteristics in handwriting, pen-printing of two hundred people. *Journal of Forensic Sciences, 8*(2), 250–259.

Liwicki, M. (2012). Automatic signature verification: In-depth investigation of novel features and different models. *Journal of Forensic Document Examination, 22*, 25–39.

Liwicki, M., Schlapbach, A., & Bunke, H. (2011). Automatic gender detection using on-line and off-line information. *Pattern Analysis and Applications, 14*(1), 87–92.

Liwicki, M., Schlapbach, A., Loretan, P., & Bunke, H. (2007). Automatic detection of gender and handedness from on-line handwriting. In *Proceedings of the 13th Conference of the Graphonomics Society* (pp. 179–183).

Liwicki, M., van den Heuvel, C. E., Found, B., & Malik, M. I. (2010). Forensic signature verification competition 4NSIGComp2010: Detection of simulated and disguised signatures. In *2010 International Conference on Frontiers in Handwriting Recognition (ICFHR), 16–18 November 2010* (pp. 715–720).

Locard, E. (1951). The inert hand. *International Criminal Police Review, 45*, 45–47.

Lockowandt, O. (1976). *Present status of the investigation of handwriting psychology as a diagnostic method.* Washington, DC: Journal Supplement Abstract Service, American Psychology Association.

Longstaff, M. G., & Heath, R. A. (2003). The influence of motor system degradation on the control of handwriting movements: A dynamical systems analysis. *Human Movement Science*, 22(1), 91–110.

Lorr, M., Lepine, L. T., & Golder, J. V. (1954). A factor analysis of some handwriting characteristics. *Journal of Personality, 22*(3), 348–353.

Lyter, A. H. I., Harris, J. J., & Greenwood, B. R. (1983). *The ball-point pen—Nomenclature, definitions and writing characteristics.* Paper presented at the meeting of the American Society of Questioned Document Examiners, Lake Tahoe, NV.

MacInnis, S. E. (1994). Adolescent handwriting—Native versus nonnative. *Canadian Society of Forensic Science Journal, 27*(1), 5–14. doi: 10.1080/00085030.1994.10757020.

Maguire, K. B. & Moran, T. L. (1996). *Identification of written text writings by the forensic information system for handwriting.* Paper presented at the meeting of the American Society of Questioned Document Examiners, Washington, DC.

Malik, I.M., Liwicki, M., Dengel, A., & Found, B. (2014). Man vs. machine: A comparative analysis for signature verification. *Journal of Forensic Document Examination, 24*, 21–35.

Mally, R. (1956). The ball-point pen. *Kriminalistik, 10*, 56–60.

Mansfield, W. W. (1943). Disguise in handwriting. *Medico-Legal Society Transactions, 11*(1), 23–29.

Marcelli, A., Parziale, A., & De Stefano, C. (2015, August). Quantitative evaluation of features for Forensic Handwriting Examination. In *13th International Conference on Document Analysis and Recognition (ICDAR), 2015* (pp. 1266–1271). IEEE.

Marcie, P., & Hécaen, H. (1979). Agraphia writing disorders associated with unilateral cortical lesions. In K. M. Heilman & E. Valenstein (Eds.), *Clinical neuropsychology* (pp. 92–127). Oxford: Oxford University Press.

Margenau, H., & Bergamini, D. (1964). *The scientist.* New York: Time.

Margolin, D. I. (1984). The neuropsychology of writing and spelling: Semantic, phonological, motor, and perceptual processes. *The Quarterly Journal of Experimental Psychology, 36A*(3), 459–489. doi: 10.1080/14640748408402172.

Margolin, D. I., & Wing, A. M. (1983). Agraphia and micrographia: Clinical manifestations of motor programming and performance disorders. *Acta Psychologica, 54*(1–3), 263–283. doi: 10.1016/0001-6918(83)90039-2.

Marquis, R., Bozza, S., Schmittbuhl, M., & Taroni, F. (2011). Handwriting evidence evaluation based on the shape of characters: Application of multivariate likelihood ratios. *Journal of Forensic Sciences, 56*(1), S238–S242.

Mason, S. (Ed.). (2010). *Electronic evidence* (2nd ed.). London: LexisNexis Butterworths.

Masson, J. (1988). Deciphering the handwriting of the recently blinded. *Forensic Science International, 38*, 161–171.

Masson, J. F. (1985). Felt tip pen writing: Problems of identification. *Journal of Forensic Sciences, 30*(1), 172–177. doi: 10.1520/jfs10978j.

Masson, J. F. (1988). A study of the handwriting of adolescents. *Journal of Forensic Sciences, 33*(1), 167–175. doi: 10.1520/JFS12447J.

Masson, J. F. (1990). *A look at the hand lettering of draftsmen.* Paper presented at the meeting of the American Society of Questioned Document Examiners, San Jose, CA.

Masson, J. F. (1992). The effect of fibre tip pen use on signatures. *Forensic Science International, 53*(2), 157–162. doi: 10.1016/0379-0738(92)90192-Y.

Masson, J. F. (1996). *An evaluation of simulated and traced signatures and consideration of the potential for determination of the writer's identity.* Paper presented at the meeting of the American Academy of Forensic Sciences, Nashville, TN.

Mathyer, J. (1950). Ball pens and the expert appraisal of written documents. *International Criminal Police Review, 43*, 357–360.

Mathyer, J. (1963). *Writing and signatures made by the "guided hand."* Paper presented at the First International Meeting in Questioned Documents, London, UK.

Mathyer, J. (1965). *A few remarks concerning the training of a document expert.* Paper presented at the meeting of the American Society of Questioned Document Examiners and RCMP Crime Detection Laboratories, Ottawa, ON, Canada.

Mathyer, J. (1969). The influence of writing instruments on handwriting and signatures. *Journal of Criminal Law, Criminology and Police Science, 60*(1), 102–112. doi: 10.2307/1141743.

Mathyer, J. (1974). A new dimension in document examination: The scientific study of oil artist paintings and of pencil artist drawings: A recent case. Paper presented at the meeting of the American Society of Questioned Document Examiners, Milwaukee, WI.

McAlexander, T. V. (1997). Assigning weight to handwriting differences for elimination purposes: What constitutes a true significant difference? *International Journal of Forensic Document Examiners, 3*(1), 4–7.

McAlexander, T. V., Beck, J., & Dick, R. M. (1991). The standardization of handwriting opinion terminology. *Journal of Forensic Sciences, 36*(2), 311–318.

McAlexander, T. V., & Maguire, K. B. (1991). Eliminating ill-founded eliminations in handwriting comparison cases. *Journal of the Forensic Science Society, 31*(3), 331–336.

McBride, H. E. A., & Siegel, L. S. (1997). Learning disabilities and adolescent suicide. *Journal of Learning Disabilities, 30*(6), 652–664.

McBride, M., Pelto, M., McLaughlin, T. F., Barretto, A., Robison, M., & Mortenson, S. (2009). The effects of using Handwriting Without Tears® procedures and worksheets to teach two preschool students with severe disabilities to write their first names. *The Open Education Journal, 2*, 21–24.

McCarney, D., Peters, L., Jackson, S., Thomas, M., & Kirby, A. (2013). Does poor handwriting conceal literacy potential in primary school children? *International Journal of Disability, Development and Education, 60*(2), 105–118.

McCarthy, J. (1970). *Excellence in forgeries: A case study.* Paper presented at the meeting of the American Society of Questioned Document Examiners, Houston, TX.

McCarthy, J. F. (1978). *The axioms of handwriting comparisons.* Paper presented at the meeting of the International Association of Forensic Sciences, Wichita, KS.

McCarthy, J. F. (1981). *Were these entries made in the normal course of business?* Paper presented at the meeting of the American Academy of Forensic Sciences, Los Angeles, CA.

McCarthy, J. F. (1984, September). *Two penmen's abilities in simulating signatures.* Paper presented at the meeting of the International Association of Forensic Sciences, Oxford, UK.

McCarthy, J. F. (1988). *Problems involved in eliminating authors.* Paper presented at the meeting of the American Society of Questioned Document Examiners, Aurora, CO.

McCarthy, J. F., & Williams, T. (1987, August). *A second survey of the handwritings of black students in the United States in a study of the black "J" and "W."* Paper presented at the meeting of the International Association of Forensic Sciences, Vancouver, BC, Canada.

McCarthy, J. F., & Winchester, J. (1973). The autopen. *Journal of Forensic Science, 18*(4), 441–447. doi: 10.1520/jfs10051j.

McCarthy, W. F., Jr. (1982). *A collection of modern European handwriting systems.* Paper presented at the meeting of the American Academy of Forensic Sciences, Orlando, FL.

McCarthy, W.F., Jr. (1984). *Dyslexia and its effect on handwriting.* Paper presented at the meeting of the American Society of Questioned Document Examiners, Nashville, TN.

McClary, C. R. (1997). A study of baseline alignment in signatures and handwritten sentences. *International Journal of Forensic Document Examiners, 3*(1), 35–44.

McElrath, G. W., & Bearman, J. E. (1956). Scientific method, statistical inference, and the law. *Science, 124*(3222), 589–590.

McKeever, W. F. (1979). Handwriting posture in left-handers: Sex, familial sinistrality and language laterality correlates. *Neuropsychologia, 17*(5), 429–444. doi: 10.1016/0028-3932(79)90050-2.

McKeever, W. F., & VanDeventer, A. D. (1980). Inverted handwriting position, language laterality, and the Levy-Nagylaki genetic model of handedness and cerebral organization. *Neuropsychologia, 18*(1), 99–102. doi: 10.1016/0028-3932(80)90090-1.

McKeever, W. F., & VanEys, P. P. (1989). Inverted handwriting posture in left handers is related to familial sinistrality incidence. *Cortex, 25*(4), 581–589. doi: 10.1016/s0010-9452(89)80019-x.

McLennan, J. E., Nakano, K., Tyler, H. R., & Schwab, R. S. (1972) Micrographia in Parkinson's disease. *Journal of the Neurological Sciences, 15*(2), 141–152.
McNally, G. A. (1988). Professional ethics in the court room. Paper presented at the meeting of the American Academy of Forensic Sciences, Philadelphia, PA.
McNally, J. P. (1974). *Signatures under stress.* Paper presented at the meeting of the American Academy of Forensic Sciences, Dallas, TX.
McNally, J. P. (1976, February). *The guider is the writer.* Paper presented at the meeting of the American Academy of Forensic Sciences, Washington, DC.
McNally, J. P. (1978). *Certainty or uncertainty.* Paper presented at the meeting of the International Association of Forensic Sciences, Wichita, KS.
Mcneil, E. B., & Blum, G. S. (1952). Handwriting and psychosexual dimensions of personality. *Journal of Projective Techniques, 16*(4), 476–484.
Mercer, S. A. B. (1959). *The origin of writing and our alphabet (a brief account).* London: Luzac.
Merlino, M. L., Springer, V., Kelly, J. S., Hammond, D., Sahota, E., & Haines, L. (2007). Meeting the challenges of the *Daubert* trilogy: Refining and redefining the reliability of forensic evidence. *Tulsa Law Review, 43*(2), 417–445.
Michel, L., & Baier, P. E. (1985). The diaries of Adolf Hitler: Implication for document examination. *Journal of the Forensic Science Society, 25*(3), 167–178. doi: 10.1016/s0015-7368(85)72388-2.
Michon, J. H. (1872). *Sisteme de la graphologie* [A system for graphology]. Paris: Garnier Frees.
Middleton, W. C. (1938). The ability to judge sex from handwriting. *The Scientific Monthly, 46*(2), 170–172.
Miller, J. J., Patterson, R. B., Gantz, D. T., Saunders, C. P., Walch, M. A., & Buscaglia, J. (2017). A set of handwriting features for use in automated writer identification. *Journal of Forensic Sciences, 62*(3), 722–734.
Miller, J. T. (1972a). Departure from handwriting system. *Journal of Forensic Sciences,* 17(1), 107–123. doi: 10.1520/JFS10120J.
Miller, J. T. (1972b). *Training and certification.* Paper presented at the meeting of the American Society of Questioned Document Examiners, Chicago, IL.
Miller, J. T. (1973). Professionalization of document examiners: Problems of certification and training. *Journal of Forensic Sciences, 18*(4), 460–468.
Miller, L. (1985). *The elimination of suspects in criminal cases.* Paper presented at the meeting of the American Academy of Forensic Sciences, Las Vegas, NV.
Miller, L. S. (1984). Bias among forensic document examiners: A need for procedural changes. *Journal of Police Science and Administration, 12*(4), 407–411. doi: 10.1080/00450618.2013.797026.
Miller, L. S. (1987). Forensic examination of arthritic impaired writings. *Journal of Police Science and Administration, 15*(1), 51–55.
Miller, L. S. (1991). Genetic and social influences on handwriting style: A forensic examination of family signatures. *World Association of Document Examiners Journal, 143,* 3–8.
Miller, L. S. (1995). Identification of human figure drawings through questioned document examination techniques. *Forensic Science International, 72*(2), 91–105. doi: 10.1016/0379-0738(94)01680-4.
Miller, L. S., & Harralson, H. (2005). An examination of tremor and distortion caused by extrinsic handwriting conditions. *Journal of Forensic Document Examination, 17,* 65–82.
Mohammed, L. A., Found, B., Caligiuri, M., & Rogers, D. (2011). The dynamic character of disguise behavior for text-based, mixed, and stylized signatures. *Journal of Forensic Sciences, 56*(Suppl 1), S136–S141.
Moody v. Rowell, 17 Pick. 490 (1835).
Moon, H. W. (1977). A survey of handwriting systems by geographic location. *Journal of Forensic Sciences, 22*(4), 827–834. doi: 10.1520/JFS10427J.
Moore, D. S. (1983). The importance of shading habits in handwriting identification. *Journal of Forensic Sciences, 28*(1), 278–287.
Morgan, M., & Zilly, P. (1991). Document examinations of handwriting with a straightedge or a writing guide. *Journal of Forensic Sciences, 36*(2), 470–479. doi: 10.1520/JFS13049J.
Morris, R. N. & Richards, G. B. (2010). What is the basis for a handwriting elimination? *Journal of the American Society of Questioned Document Examiners, 13*(2), 43–64.
Morton, S. E. (1980). How does crowding affect signatures? *Journal of Forensic Sciences, 25*(1), 141–145. doi: 10.1520/JFS10948J.

Muehlberger, R. (1988). *Class characteristics of Hispanic writers in the southeastern United States.* Paper presented at the meeting of the American Academy of Forensic Sciences, Philadelphia, PA.

Muehlberger, R. J. & Vastrick, T. W. (1992). *A traced forgery: Is there a need for handwriting comparisons?* Paper presented at the meeting of the American Society of Questioned Document Examiners, Milwaukee, WI.

Muehlberger, R. J. (1982). *Variation, a measure of genuineness.* Paper presented at the meeting of the American Society of Questioned Document Examiners, Boston, MA.

Muehlberger, R. J. (1984). *The Bulgarian connection: An examination of Cyrillic handwriting.* Paper presented at the meeting of the American Society of Questioned Document Examiners, Nashville, TN.

Muehlberger, R. J. (1990). Identifying simulations: Practical considerations. *Journal of Forensic Science, 35*(2), 368–374. doi: 10.1520/jfs12838j.

Muehlberger, R. J., Newman, K. W., Regent, J., & Wichmann, J. G. (1977). A statistical examination of selected handwriting characteristics. *Journal of Forensic Sciences, 22*(1), 206–215.

Mueller, B. (1939). Zur Frage des Beweiswertes der Schriftgutachten nebst statistischen Untersuchungen über die Häufigkeit einiger Schriftmerkmale. *Archiv fur Kriminologie, 104*(3/4), 105–116.

Münch, A. (1987, August). *The comparison of very similar handwriting—Reflections on the real value of handwriting analysis.* Paper presented at the meeting of the International Association of Forensic Sciences, Vancouver, BC, Canada.

Mutual Benefit Life Ins. Co. v. Brown, 30 N.J. Eq. 193 (1878).

NAS (National Research Council-National Academy of Sciences). (2009). *Strengthening forensic science in the United States: A path forward.* Washington, DC: National Academies Press.

Nash, R. (1959). *American writing masters and copybooks: History and bibliography through colonial times.* Boston, MA: Colonial Society of Massachusetts.

Nash, R. (1969). *American penmanship 1800–1850: A history of writing and a bibliography of copybooks from Jenkins to Spencer.* Worcester, MA: American Antiquarian Society.

Naske, R.-D. (1982). Writer recognition by prototype related deformation of handprinted characters. In H. Marko & International Conference on Pattern Recognition (1982). *Proceedings of the 6th international conference on pattern recognition, Munich, Germany, Oct. 19–22, 1982* (pp. 819–822). Silver Spring, MD: IEEE Computer Society Press.

National Child Development Study. (1966). *First report: 1958 cohort: 11,000 seven-year-olds.* London: Longman.

Nemecek, J. (1974). *Ball point pen oddities.* Paper presented at the meeting of the American Society of Questioned Document Examiners, Milwaukee, WI.

Nemecek, J., & Currie, C. (1972). *Handwriting under hypnosis.* Paper presented at the meeting of the International Association of Forensic Sciences, Edinburgh, UK.

Neudert, G. (1963, April). *The importance of agraphia in expert opinions on handwriting.* Paper presented at the First International Meeting in Questioned Documents, London, England.

Newhall, S. M. (1926). Sex differences in handwriting. *Journal of Applied Psychology, 10*(2), 151. doi: 10.1037/h0067056.

Newman, K. W. (1975). *A study of unaccustomed-hand writing.* Unpublished manuscript, Washington, DC: Georgetown University Forensic Science Laboratory.

Newton, L. H. (1981). Lawgiving for professional life: Reflections on the place of the professional code. *Business & Professional Ethics Journal, 1*(1), 41–53.

Nicholson, P. J. (1984). A system for the classification of block capital handwriting. *Journal of the Forensic Science Society, 24*(4), 415.

Nicholson, P. J. (1987, August). *The relative variability of pen lift and pen path habits in block capital writing.* Paper presented at the meeting of the International Association of Forensic Sciences, Vancouver, BC, Canada.

Nicolaides, K. N. (2012). Using acceleration/deceleration plots in forensic analysis of electronically captured signatures. *Journal of the American Society of Questioned Document Examiners, 15*(2), 29–43.

Niels, R. M. J., & Vuurpijl, L. G. (2005). Using dynamic time warping for intuitive handwriting recognition. In A. Marcelli, & C. de Stefano (Eds.). *Advances in Graphonomics: Proceedings of the 12th Conference of the International Graphonomics Society, 26*–29 June 2005, Salerno, Italy. (pp. 217–221).

Nihei, Y. (1980). Developmental change in motor organization: Covert principles for the organization of strokes in children's drawing. *Tohoku Psychologica Folia, 39*, 17–23.

Nisbett, R. E., & Wilson, T. D. (1977). Telling more than we can know: Verbal reports on mental processes. *Psychological Review, 84*(3), 231. doi: 10.1037//0033-295x.84.3.231.

NIST (National Institute of Standards and Technology). (2009). *FIPS PUB 186-3: Digital signature standards (DSS).* Gaithersburg, MD: Information Technology Laboratory.

NIST (National Institute of Standards and Technology). (2013). *Measurement Science and Standards in Forensic Handwriting Analysis Conference.* Retrieved from https://www.nist.gov/news-events/events/2013/06/measurement-science-and-standards-forensic-handwriting-analysis

NIST (National Institute of Standards and Technology). (2015). *International Symposium on Forensic Science Error Management.* Retrieved from http://www.nist.gov/forensics/forensic_error_mgmt_2015.cfm (accessed January 3, 2016).

NIST Law Enforcement Standards Office (2013). Retrieved from: http://www.nist.gov/oles/forensics/forensic-database-questioned-documents-table.cfm (accessed January 3, 2016).

Noblett, M. G. (1991). *Storage and retrieval of individual writings in large databases of handwriting.* Paper presented at the meeting of the American Society of Questioned Document Examiners, Orlando, FL.

Norinder, Y. (1946). *Twin differences in writing performance: A study of heredity and school training.* Lund: Hakan Ohlssons Bodtryckeri.

Nousianen, H. (1951). Some observations on the factors causing changes in writing style. *Nordisk Kriminalteknisk Tidsskrift, (Northern Criminal Technical Journal) Sweden, 25*(8), 92.

Ogg, O. (1959). *The 26 letters.* New York: Thomas Y. Crowell.

Olkin, I. (1958). *The evaluation of physical evidence and the identity problem by means of statistical probabilities.* Paper presented at the meeting of the American Academy of Forensic Sciences, Cleveland, OH.

Onofri, E., Mercuri, M., Archer, T., Ricciardi, M. R., Massoni, F., & Ricci, S. (2015). Effect of cognitive fluctuation on handwriting in Alzheimer's patient: A case study. *Acta Medica, 31,* 751.

Osborn, A. S. (1910). *Questioned Documents: A study of questioned documents with an outline of methods by which the facts may be discovered and shown.* Eagan, MN: Lawyers' Cooperative Publishing Company.

Osborn, A. S. (1922). *The problem of proof.* New York: Matthew Bender.

Osborn, A. S. (1929). *Questioned documents* (2nd ed.). Albany, NY: Boyd Printing.

Osborn, A. S. (1946). *Questioned document problems* (2nd ed., rev.). Albany, NY: Boyd Printing.

Osborn, J. P. (1984). *Writing instruments' effects on traced signatures.* Paper presented at the meeting of the American Society of Questioned Document Examiners, Nashville, TN.

Oskoui, M., Coutinho, F., Dykeman, J., Jetté, N., & Pringsheim, T. (2013). An update on the prevalence of cerebral palsy: A systematic review and meta-analysis. *Developmental Medicine & Child Neurology, 55*(6), 509–519.

Packard, R. J. (1960). Alcohol and handwriting. *The Criminal Law Quarterly, 3,* 57–59.

Parker, J. L. (1989). *Repeated disguise beats the clone defence.* Paper presented at the meeting of the American Society of Questioned Document Examiners, Crystal City, VA.

Parkinson, J. (2002). An essay on the shaking palsy. *The Journal of Neuropsychiatry and Clinical Neurosciences, 14*(2), 223–236.

Parush, S., Pindak, V., Hahn-Markowitz, J., & Mazor-Karsenty, T. (1998). Does fatigue influence children's handwriting performance? *Work, 11*(3), 307–313.

Parziale, A., Santoro, A., & Marcelli, A. (2016, October). Writer verification in forensic handwriting examination: A pilot study. In *15th International Conference on Frontiers in Handwriting Recognition (ICFHR), 2016* (pp. 447–452). IEEE.

Peck, M., Askov, E., & Fairchild, S. H. (1980). Another decade of research in handwriting: Progress and prospect in the 1970s. *Journal of Educational Research, 73*(5), 283–298.

Peeples, E. E., & Retzlaff, P. D. (1991). A component analysis of handwriting. *The Journal of General Psychology, 118*(4), 369–374.

Pepe, A.L., Rogers, D., & Sita, J. (2012). A consideration of signature complexity using simulators' gaze behaviour. *Journal of Forensic Document Examination, 22,* 5–13.

Peters, B. A., Lewis, E. G., Dustman, R. E., Straight, R. C., & Beck, E. C. (1976). Sensory, perceptual, motor and cognitive functioning and subjective reports following oral administration of δ9-tetrahydrocannabinol. *Psychopharmacology, 47*(2), 141–147. doi: 10.1007/BF00735812.

Peters, M. (1986). Incidence of left-handed writers and the inverted writing position in a sample of 2194 German elementary school children. *Neuropsychologia, 24*(3), 429–433. doi: 10.1016/0028-3932(86)90030-8.

Peters, M., & McGrory, J. (1987). The writing performance of inverted and noninverted right-and left-handers. *Canadian Journal of Psychology/Revue Canadienne de Psychologie, 41*(1), 20. doi: 10.1037/h0084146.

Peters, M., & Pedersen, K. (1978). Incidence of left-handers with inverted writing position in a population of 5910 elementary school children. *Neuropsychologia, 16*(6), 743–746. doi: 10.1016/0028-3932(78)90009-x.

Pettus v. United States. (2012). DCCA 8-CF-1361. Retrieved from http://legaltimes.typepad.com/files/08-cf-1361_mtd.pdf (accessed January 10, 2013).

Phillips, J. G., Rogers, D. K., & Ogeil, R. (2008). Alcohol consumption, dependence and the spatial characteristics of handwriting. *Journal of Forensic Document Examination, 19*, 15–27.

Phillips, J. G., Stelmach, G. E., & Teasdale, N. (1991). What can indices of handwriting quality tell us about Parkinson's handwriting? *Human Movement Science, 10*(2–3), 301–314. doi: 10.1016/0167-9457(91)90009-M.

Pick, A. (1903). Ueber eine eigentumliche Schreibstorung. Mikrographie, in Folge cerebraler Erkrankung. *Prag. med. Wschr.*, 23, 1–4.

Plamondon, R., & Lorette, G. (1989). Automatic signature verification and writer identification: The state of the art. *Pattern Recognition, 22*(2), 107–131. doi: 10.1016/0031-3203(89)90059-9.

Plamondon, R., & Maarse, F. J. (1989). An evaluation of motor models of handwriting. *IEEE Transactions on Systems, Man, and Cybernetics, 19*(5), 1060–1072.

Pophal, R., & Dunker, E. (1960). Zeit lupenstudien des Schreibvorganges (Slow motion studies in handwriting movements). *Zeitschrift Fur Experimentelle Und Angewandte Psychologie, 1*, 76–99.

Popkiss, A., & Moore, J. (1945). Handwriting classification. *Police Journal, 18*, 3955.

Porac, C., Coren, S., & Searleman, A. (1983). Inverted versus straight handwriting posture: A family study. *Behavior Genetics, 13*(3), 311–320. doi: 10.1007/bf01071876.

Poulin, G. (1999). The influence of writing fatigue on handwriting characteristics in a selected population part one: General considerations. *International Journal of Forensic Document Examiners, 5*, 193–220.

Provins, K. A., & Magliaro, J. (1989). Skill, strength, handedness, and fatigue. *Journal of Motor Behavior, 21*(2), 113–121.

Purdy, D. C. (1982). The requirements of effective report writing for document examiners. *Canadian Society of Forensic Science Journal, 15*(3–4), 146–151. doi: 10.1080/00085030.1982.10756909.

Purdy, D. C. (1985). Basic elements of a quality assurance system for forensic document examiners. *Forensic Science International, 29*(1), 11–20. doi: 10.1016/0379-0738(85)90029-5

Purtell, D. J. (1963). Handwriting standard forms. *Journal of Criminal Law, Criminology and Police Science, 54*(4), 523–528. doi: 10.2307/1140788.

Purtell, D. J. (1965). Effects of drugs on handwriting. *Journal of Forensic Sciences, 1*(3), 335–345.

Purtell, D. J. (1969). *Curriculum for a document examiner*. Paper presented at the meeting of the American Society of Questioned Document Examiners, Toronto, Canada.

Purtell, D. J. (1980). Modern handwriting instructions, systems, and techniques. *Journal of Police Science and Administration, 8*(1), 66–68.

Quine, W. V. (1957). The scope and language of science. *The British Journal for the Philosophy of Science, 8*(29), 1–17.

Quirke, A. J. (1930). *Forged, anonymous, and suspect documents*. London: Routledge.

Rabin, A. & Blair, H. (1953). The effects of alcohol on handwriting. *Journal of Clinical Psychology, 9*(3), 284–287. doi: 10.1002/1097-4679(195307)9:3<284::AID-JCLP2270090306>3.0.CO;2-6.

Radley, R. W. (1983). *Stencil forgery? Considerations of a case history*. Paper presented at the meeting of the American Society of Questioned Document Examiners, Lake Tahoe, NV.

Raibert, M. H. (1977). Motor control and learning by the state space model. Unpublished doctoral dissertation, Massachusetts Institute of Technology, Cambridge, MA.

Ravetz, J. R. (1971). *Scientific knowledge and its social problems*. Oxford: Clarendon Press.

Reed, G. F., & Smith, A. C. (1962). A further experimental investigation of the relative speeds of left and right-handed writers. *The Journal of Genetic Psychology*, 100(2), 275–287.

Regent, J. (1977). Changing slant: Is it the only change? *Journal of Forensic Sciences, 22*(1), 216–221. doi: 10.1520/jfs10389j.

Regent, J. (1989). *The significance of characteristic uniformity in the identification process.* Paper presented at the meeting of the American Society of Questioned Document Examiners, Arlington, VA.

Reid v. Warner, 17 Low. Can. 489 (1867).

Reitberger, L. (1941). Zur Frage des Beweiswertes der Schriftgutachten nebst statistischen Untersuchungen über die Häufigkeit einiger Schriftmerkmale. *Archiv fur Kriminologie, 108*, 130–136.

Remillard, J. L. G. (1970, May). *Abnormal cardiac rhythm and handwriting.* Unpublished manuscript, RCMP Crime Detection Laboratories Ottawa, ON, Canada.

Resdon, R. (1959). The graph test. *International Criminal Police Review, 131*, 226–236.

Reynolds, D. (2008). Gaussian mixture models. *Encyclopedia of Biometric Recognition.* Retrieved from http://extwebprod.ll.mit.edu/mission/communications/publications/publication-files/full_papers/0802_Reynolds_Biometrics-GMM.pdf (accessed October 23, 2012).

Rhodes, E. F. (1978). *The implications of kinesthetic factors in forensic handwriting comparisons.* (D.Crim.). University of California, Berkeley, CA. Retrieved from http://search.proquest.com/pqdtglobal/docview/302917932/citation/7E64140CD9774D79PQ/1 (accessed January 3, 2017).

Rhodes, H. T. F. (1963, April). *The principles of identification application to handwriting.* Paper presented at the 1st International Meeting in Questioned Documents, London, UK.

Richardson, J. T. (1978). A factor analysis of self-reported handedness. *Neuropsychologia, 16*(6), 747–748. doi: 10.1016/0028-3932(78)90010-6.

Richiardi, J., Ketabdar, H., & Drygajlo, A. (2005). Local and global feature selection for on-line signature verification. In *International Conference on Document Analysis and Recognition, 2*, 29 August–1 September, 2005 (pp. 625–629).

Risinger, D. M. (2000). Defining the 'Task at Hand': Non-science forensic science after *Kumho Tire v. Carmichael. Washington & Lee Law Review, 57*, 767–800.

Risinger, D. M. (2007). Cases involving the reliability of handwriting identification expertise since the decision in *Daubert. Tulsa Law Review, 43*(2), 477–595.

Risinger, D. M., Denbeaux, M. P., & Saks, M. J. (1989). Exorcism of ignorance as a proxy for rational knowledge: The lessons of handwriting identification "expertise." *University of Pennsylvania Law Review, 137*(3), 731–792. doi: 10.2307/3312276.

Risinger, D. M., & Saks, M. J. (1996). Science and nonscience in the courts: *Daubert* meets handwriting identification expertise. *Iowa Law Review, 82*, 21.

Robertson, J., & Guest, R. (2015). A feature based comparison of pen and swipe based signature characteristics. *Human Movement Science, 43*, 169–182.

Robinson, A. (1995). *The story of writing.* London: Thames & Hudson.

Rogerson, P. A. (1994). On the relationship between handedness and season of birth for men. *Perceptual and Motor Skills, 79*(1), 499–506. doi: 10.2466/pms.1994.79.1.499.

Ronan, C. A., & Needham, J. (1978). *The Shorter 'Science and Civilisation in China'* (Vol. 1). Cambridge: Cambridge University Press.

Rosenblum, S., & Werner, P. (2006). Assessing the handwriting process in healthy elderly persons using a computerized system. *Aging and Clinical Experimental Research, 18*(5), 433–439.

Roulston, M. G. (1959). *The fatigue factor: An essay dealing with the effects of physical fatigue on handwriting habits.* Unpublished manuscript, RCMP Crime Detection Laboratories.

Ruenes, R. F. (1975). *Guided hand signature and forgery.* Paper presented at the meeting of the American Society of Questioned Document Examiners, Colorado Springs, CO.

Saks, M. J., & VanderHaar, H. (2005). On the "general acceptance" of handwriting identification principles. *Journal of Forensic Sciences, 50*(1), 119–126.

Saperstein Associates. (2012). *Handwriting in the 21st century? Research shows why handwriting belongs in today's classroom.* Saperstein Associates. Retrieved from https://www.hw21summit.com/media/zb/hw21/H2948_HW_Summit_White_Paper_eVersion.pdf (accessed June 15, 2012).

Sassoon, R., Nimmo-Smith, I., & Wing, A. M. (1986). An analysis of children's penholds. *Advances in Psychology*, 37, 93–106.

Saudek, R. (1929). *Experiments with handwriting.* New York: William Morrow.

Saudek, R. (1978). *Experiments with handwriting.* Reprint. Sacramento, CA: Books for Professionals.

Savage, G. A. (1978). Handwriting of the deaf and hard of hearing. *Canadian Society of Forensic Science Journal, 11*(1), 1–14. doi: 10.1080/00085030.1978.10756844.

Schenk, T., Walther, E. U., & Mai, N. (2000). Closed-and open-loop handwriting performance in patients with multiple sclerosis. *European Journal of Neurology, 7*(3), 269–279.

Schmidt, R. A. (1975). A schema theory of discrete motor skill learning. *Psychological Review, 82*(4), 225–260.

Schmidt, R. A. (1976). The schema as a solution to some persistent problems in motor learning theory. In G. E. Stelmach (Ed.), *Motor control: Issues and trends*. New York: Academic Press, 41–65.

Schmitz, P. L. (1967). *Should experienced document examiners write inconclusive reports?* Paper presented at the meeting of the American Society of Questioned Document Examiners, San Francisco, CA.

Schomaker, L. (2007, September). Advances in writer identification and verification. In *Ninth International Conference on Document Analysis and Recognition, 2007. ICDAR 2007.* (Vol. 2, pp. 1268–1273). IEEE.

Schroeder, E. H. W. (1971). Checlass: A classification system for fraudulent checks. *Journal of Forensic Sciences, 16*(2), 162–175.

Schroeder, E. H. W. (1974). A revised method of classifying fraudulent checks in a document examination laboratory. *Journal of Forensic Sciences, 19*(3), 618–635.

Schröter, A., Mergl, R., Bürger, K., Hampel, H., Möller, H.-J., & Hegerl, U. (2003). Kinematric analysis of handwriting movements in patients with Alzheimer's disease, mild cognitive impairment, depression and healthy subjects. *Dementia and Geriatric Cognitive Disorders, 15*(3), 132–142.

Schwid, B. L. (1995, August). *Forensic case study: Multiple personality.* Paper presented at the 7th International Graphonomics Society Conference, London, ON, Canada.

Schwid, B. L., & Marks, L. W. (1994). Forensic analysis of handwriting in multiple personality disorder. In C. Faure, P. Keuss, G. Lorette, & A. Vinter (Eds.), *Advances in Handwriting and drawing: A multidisciplinary approach* (pp. 501–513*)*. Paris: Europia Press.

Schwid, B. L. & Teulings, H.-L. (2013). Writings of a person with dissociative identity disorder: A longitudinal and a kinematic study. *Journal of Forensic Document Examination, 23*, 41–61.

Sciacca, E., Langlois-Peters, M., Margot, P., & Velay, J. (2011). Effects of different postural conditions on handwriting variability. *Journal of Forensic Document Examination, 21*, 51–60.

Scott, C. C. (1988) *Inconclusive opinions as viewed by the courts.* Paper presented at the meeting of the American Society of Questioned Document Examiners, Aurora, CO.

Scott, R. C. (1989, Fall). Errata. *American Society of Questioned Document Examiners Newsletter.*

Sellers, C. (1942). *The scientific approach.* Paper presented at the meeting of the American Society of Questioned Document Examiners, Montclair, NJ.

Sellers, C. (1962). Assisted and guided signatures. *The Journal of Criminal Law, Criminology, and Police Science, 53*(2), 245–248. doi: 10.2307/1141089.

Sellers, C. (1966). *The qualifications of an examiner of questioned documents.* Paper presented at the meeting of the American Society of Questioned Document Examiners, New York.

Sellers, C. (1968). *Rights and responsibilities of a questioned document examiner.* Paper presented at the meeting of the American Society of Questioned Document Examiners, Lexington, KY.

Shaneyfelt, L. L. (1974). *The versatile writer.* Paper presented at the meeting of the American Academy of Forensic Sciences, Dallas, TX.

Shanon, B. (1978). Writing positions in Americans and Israelis. *Neuropsychologia, 16*(5), 587–591. doi: 10.1016/0028-3932(78)90086-6.

Shanon, B. (1979). Graphological patterns as a function of handedness and culture. *Neuropsychologia, 17*(5), 457–465. doi: 10.1016/0028-3932(79)90052-6.

Shiver, F. C. (1996). *Case Report: The individuality of handwriting demonstrated through the field screening of 1000 writers.* Paper presented at the meeting of the American Society of Questioned Document Examiners, Washington, DC.

Simpson, G. M. (1970). Controlled studies of Antiparkinsonism agents in the treatment of drug induced extrapyramidal symptoms. *Acta Psychiatrica Scandinavica, 45*(S212), 44–51. doi: 10.1111/j.1600-0447.1970.tb02070.x.

Simsons, D., Spencer, R., & Auer, S. (2011). The effects of constraining signatures. *Journal of the American Society of Questioned Document Examiners, 14*(1), 39–50.

Sita, J., Found, B., & Rogers, D. K. (2002). Forensic handwriting examiners' expertise for signature comparison. *Journal of Forensic Sciences, 47*(5), 1117–1124.

Skelly, J. D. (1987). Guided deathbed signatures. *Canadian Society of Forensic Science Journal, 20*(4), 147–149. doi: 10.1080/00085030.1987.10756953.

Slavin, M. J., Phillips, J. G., Bradshaw, J. L., Hall, K. A., & Presnell, I. (1999). Consistency of handwriting movements in dementia of the Alzheimer's type: A comparison of Huntington's and Parkinson's diseases. *Journal of the International Neuropsychological Society, 5*(1), 20–25.

Slyter, S. A. (1995). *Forensic signature examination*. Springfield, IL: Charles C. Thomas.

Smith, T. L. (1954). Six basic factors in handwriting classification. *The Journal of Criminal Law, Criminology, and Police Science, 44*(6), 810–816.

Smith, T. L. (1964). Determining tendencies: The second half of a classification for handwriting. *Journal of Criminal Law, Criminology and Police Science, 55*(4), 526–528.

Smith, W. A. (1955). *Ancient education*. New York: Philosophical Library.

Snape, K. W. (1980). Determination of the direction of ball-point pen motion from the orientations of burr striations in curved pen strokes. *Journal of Forensic Sciences, 25*(2), 386–389. doi: 10.1520/jfs12142j.

Souder, W. (1934). The merits of scientific evidence. *Journal of the American Institute of Criminal Law and Criminology, 25*, 683–684.

Sperry, G. R. (1990). *Off-handed identification, in aggravation*. Paper presented at the meeting of the American Society of Questioned Document Examiners, San Jose, CA.

Spiegler, B. J., & Yeni-Komshian, G. H. (1983). Incidence of left-handed writing in a college population with reference to family patterns of hand preference. *Neuropsychologia, 21*(6), 651–659. doi: 10.1016/0028-3932(83)90063-5.

Spoerhase, C. (2014). Images and insertions of script: On Johann Caspar Lavater's representations of handwriting in print. *Word & Image, 30*(4), 431–443.

Squire, H. W. (1968). *Graphology as a method of selecting employees*. Unpublished Master's thesis, Ohio State University, Columbus, OH.

Srihari, S. & Leedham, G. (2003). A survey of computer methods in forensic handwritten document examination. In *Proceedings of the Eleventh International Graphonomics Society Conference, Scottsdale, Arizona* (pp. 278–281).

Srihari, S., Huang, C., & Srinivasan, H. (2008). On the discriminability of the handwriting of twins. *Journal of Forensic Sciences, 53*(2), 430–446.

Srihari, S. N. (2013). Determining writership of historical manuscripts using computational methods. *On-line Proceedings Automatic Pattern Recognition and Historical Handwriting Analysis*, Erlangen, Germany.

Srihari, S. N., Cha, S.-H., Arora, H., & Lee, S. (2002). Individuality of handwriting. *Journal of Forensic Sciences*, 47(4), 1–17.

Srihari, S. N., Meng, L., & Hanson, L. (2016). Development of individuality in children's handwriting. *Journal of Forensic Sciences*, 61(5), 1292–1300.

Srihari, S. N., & Singer, K. (2014). Role of automation in the examination of handwritten items. *Pattern Recognition, 47*(3), 1083–1095.

Srihari, S. N., Tomai, C. I., Zhang, B., & Lee, S. (2003). Individuality of numerals. *ICDAR, 3*, 1096–1100.

Stangohr, G. R. (1968). Opposite-hand writing. *Journal of Forensic Sciences, 13*(3), 376–389.

Stangohr, G. R. (1971). Comments on the determination of nationality from handwriting. *Journal of Forensic Sciences, 16*(3), 343–358.

Stangohr, G. R. (1984). *Elusive and indeterminate results*. Paper presented at the meeting of the American Society of Questioned Document Examiners, Nashville, TN.

Starch, D. (1913). The measurement of handwriting. *Journal of Educational Psychology, 4*, 445–464.

Steinke, K. (1981). Recognition of writers by handwriting images. *Pattern Recognition, 14*(1–6), 357–364.

Stellar, S., Mandell, S., Waltz, J. M., & Cooper, I. S. (1970). L-Dopa in the treatment of Parkinsonism: A preliminary appraisal. *Journal of Neurosurgery, 32*(3), 275–280. doi: 10.3171/jns.1970.32.3.0275.

Stevens, V. (1964). *Similarities in the handwriting of members of one family as compared to unrelated groups.* Madison, WI: Wisconsin State Crime Laboratory.

Stevens, V. (1970). Characteristics of 200 awkward-hand signatures. *International Criminal Police Review, 237,* 130–137.

Stinson, M. D. (1997). A validation study of the influence of alcohol on handwriting. *Journal of Forensic Sciences, 42*(3), 411–416.

Stoel, R. D., Berger, C., Kerkhoff, W., Mattijssen, E. J. A. T., Dror, I. E., Hickman, M., & Strom, K. (2014a). Minimizing contextual bias in forensic casework. *Forensic Science and the Administration of Justice: Critical Issues and Directions, 67,* 67–86.

Stoel, R. D., Dror, I. E., & Miller, L. S. (2014b). Bias among forensic document examiners: Still a need for procedural changes. *Australian Journal of Forensic Sciences, 46*(1), 91–97.

Stone, A. M. (1962). *Teacher's guide for basic handwriting.* Indianapolis, IN: Bobbs-Merrill.

Strub, R. L. (1980). Alzheimer's disease—Current perspectives. *Journal of Clinical Psychiatry, 41*(4), 110–112.

Suddath, C. (2009). Mourning the death of handwriting. *Time Magazine, 174*(4) http://dental.buffalo.edu/content/dam/www/news/imported/pdf/July09/TimeThorntonHandwriting.pdf (accessed June 15, 2012).

Sullivan, J. W. N. (1949). *The limitations of science.* New York: New American Library.

Sulner, A. (2014). Handwriting: Cognitive bias. In *Wiley Encyclopedia of Forensic Science.* Eds., A. Jamieson and A. A. Moenssens, Hoboken, NJ: John Wiley and Sons, 1–15.

Swett, G. C. (1959). Science and document examination. Paper presented at the meeting of the American Society of Questioned Document Examiners, Chicago, IL.

SWGDOC (Scientific Working Group for Forensic Document Examination). (2013a). *Published Standards.* Retrieved from http://www.swgdoc.org/index.php/standards/published-standards (accessed March 15, 2017).

SWGDOC (Scientific Working Group for Forensic Document Examination). (2013b). *Standard for scope of work of forensic document examiners.* Retrieved from http://www.swgdoc.org/index.php/standards/published-standards (accessed March 15, 2017).

SWGDOC (Scientific Working Group for Forensic Document Examination). (2013c). *Standard guide for examination of handwritten items.* Retrieved from http://www.swgdoc.org/index.php/standards/published-standards (accessed March 15, 2017).

Talmadge, M. (1958). Expressive graphic movements and their relationship to temperament factors. *Psychological Monographs: General and Applied, 72*(16), 1–30.

Tan, G. X., Viard-Gaudin, C., & Kot, A. C. (2009). Automatic writer identification framework for online handwritten documents using character prototypes. *Pattern Recognition, 42*(12), 3313–3323.

Tang, Y., & Srihari, S. N. (2014). Likelihood ratio estimation in forensic identification using similarity and rarity. *Pattern Recognition, 47*(3), 945–958.

Tannenbaum, S. A. (1930). *The handwriting of the Renaissance, being the development and characteristics of the script of Shakspere's time.* New York: Columbia University Press.

Tappolet, J. A., & Ottinger, E. (1982). Transfer of signatures with transparent pressure tape: Some experiments. *Forensic Science International, 20*(1), 61–69. doi: 10.1016/0379-0738(82)90107-4

Tariq, S., Sarwar, S., & Hussain, W. (2011). Classification of features into strong and weak features for an intelligent online signature verification system. In *Proceedings of the First International Workshop on Automated Forensic Handwriting Analysis (AFHA),* (pp. 17–18). September 2011, Beijing, China.

Taroni, F., Champod, C., & Margot, P. (1998). Forerunners of Bayesianism in early forensic science. *Jurimetrics, 38*(2), 183–200.

Taroni, F., Marquis, R., Schmittbuhl, M., Biedermann, A., Thiéry, A., & Bozza, S. (2012). The use of the likelihood ratio for evaluative and investigative purposes in comparative forensic handwriting examination. *Forensic Science International, 214*(1–3), 189–94.

Taroni, F., Marquis, R., Schmittbuhl, M., Biedermann, A., Thiéry, A., & Bozza, S. (2014). Bayes factor for investigative assessment of selected handwriting features. *Forensic Science International, 242*(1–3), 266–73.

Tarver, J. A. (1988). *Micrographia in the handwriting of Parkinson's disease patients.* Paper Presented at the meeting of the American Society of Questioned Document Examiners, Aurora, CO.

Tarver, J. A. (1989). *Micrographia in the handwriting of Parkinson's disease patients.* Paper Presented at the meeting of the American Academy of Forensic Sciences, Las Vegas, NV.

Taylor, L. L., & Hnilica, V. (1991). Investigation of death through body writing: A case study. *Journal of Forensic Sciences, 36*(5), 1607–1613. doi: 10.1520/JFS13184J.

Taylor, L. R., & Chandler, H. (1987). A system for handwriting classification. *Journal of Forensic Sciences, 32*(6), 1775–1781.

Temple, C. M. (1990). Academic discipline, handedness and immune disorders. *Neuropsychologia, 28*(3), 303–308. doi: 10.1016/0028-3932(90)90023-h.

Tenwolde, H. (1934). More on sex differences in handwriting. *Journal of Applied Psychology, 18*(S), 705–710. doi: 10.1037/h0074973.

Teulings, H. M., & Thomassen, A. J. (1979). Computer-aided analysis of handwriting movements. *Visible Language, 13*(3), 218–231.

Teulings, H.L. (1996). Handwriting movement control. In S.W. Keele and H. Heuer (Eds.), *Handbook of perception and action.* Vol. 2, Motor Skills (pp. 561–613). London: Academic Press.

Teulings, H.-L., & Stelmach, G. E. (1991). Control of stroke size, peak acceleration and stroke duration in Parkinsonian handwriting. *Human Movement Science, 10*(2–3), 315–334. doi: 10.1016/0167-9457(91)90010-U.

Thiéry, A., Marquis, R., & Montani, I. (2013). Statistical evaluation of the influence of writing postures on on-line signatures. Study of the impact of time. *Forensic science international, 230*(1), 107–116.

Thomassen, A. J. W. M., & Teulings, H.-L. H. M. (1979). The development of directional preferences in writing movements. *Visible Language, 13*(3), 299–313.

Thomassen, A. J. W. M., & Teulings, H.-L. H. M. (1983). The development of handwriting. In M. Martlew (Ed.), *The Psychology of written language: Developmental and educational perspectives* (pp. 179–213). New York: Wiley.

Thomassen, A. J. W. M., van Galen, G. P., Keuss, P. J. G., & Grootveld, C. C. (1983). Motor aspects of handwriting—Preface. *Acta Psychologica, 54*(1–3), 1.

Thompson, E. M. (1893). *Handbook of Greek and Latin palaeography.* London: Kegan Paul, Trench, Trubner & Co.

Thorndike, E. L. (1915). The resemblance of young twins in handwriting. *The American Naturalist, 49*(582), 377–379.

Thornton, J. I. (1997, July). The DNA statistical paradigm vs. everything else. [Letter to the Editor]. *Journal of Forensic Sciences, 42*(4), 758.

Thornton, J. I., & Rhodes, E. F. (1986, January). Brief history of questioned document examination. *Identification News, 36*(1), 12.

Thorton, M. (1985). *Royal feud.* New York: Simon & Schuster.

Thuring, J. P. (1960). The influence of LSD on the handwriting pressure curve. *Advances in Psychosomatic Medicine (or Fortschritte der Psychosomatischen Medizin), 1,* 212–216.

Todd, I. (1965, January). Handwriting of the blind. *Identification News, 15,* 4–9.

Tong, W., Lee, J. E., Jin, R., & Jain, A. K. (2011). Gang and moniker identification by graffiti matching. In *Proceedings of the 3rd international ACM workshop on multimedia in forensics and intelligence* (pp. 1–6). ACM.

Torres, B. (1987, February). *A study of Vietnamese class characteristics.* Paper presented at the meeting of the American Academy of Forensic Sciences, San Diego, CA.

Totty, R. N. (1981). A case of handwriting on an unusual surface. *Journal of the Forensic Sciences Society, 21*(4), 349–350. doi: 10.1016/S0015-7368(81)71420-8.

Totty, R. N. (1995). *Skilled copies of signatures.* Paper presented at the meeting of the American Society of Questioned Document Examiners, Chicago, IL.

Totty, R. N., Hall, M. G., Hardcastle, R. A., & Brown, C. (1982). A computer based system for the identification of unknown typestyles. *Journal of the Forensic Science Society, 22*(1), 65–73.

Totty, R. N., & Hardcastle, R. A. (1986). A preliminary assessment of the SIGNCHECK system for signature authentication. *Journal of the Forensic Science Society, 26*(3), 181–195. doi: 0.1016/S0015-7368(86)72476-6.

Totty, R. N., Hardcastle, R. A., & Dempsey, J. (1983). The dependence of slope of handwriting upon the sex and handedness of the writer. *Journal of the Forensic Science Society, 23*(3), 237–240. doi: 10.1016/s0015-7368(83)72249-8.

Towson, C. S. (1971). Low blood sugar levels and handwriting. *Canadian Society of Forensic Science Journal, 4*(4), 133–144. doi: 10.1080/00085030.1971.10757285.

Towson, C. S. (1975). Handwriting instruction in Canada. Private communication.

Trankell, A. (1956). The influence of the choice of writing hand on the handwriting. *British Journal of Educational Psychology, 26*(2), 94–103. doi: 10.1111/j.2044-8279.1956.tb01364.x.

Tripp, C. A., Fluckiger, F. A., & Weinberg, G. H. (1957). Measurement of handwriting variables. *Perceptual and Motor Skills, 7*(3), 279–294. doi: 10.2466/pms.1957.7.3.279.

Tripp, C. A., Fluckiger, F. A., & Weinberg, G. H. (1959). Effects of alcohol on the graphomotor performances of normals and chronic alcoholics. *Perceptual and Motor Skills, 9*, 227–236. doi: 10.2466/pms.1959.9.h.227.

Trizna, L. A., & Wooton, E. X. (1995). *Asian hand printing.* Paper presented at the meeting of the American Academy of Forensic Sciences, Seattle, WA.

Trizna, L. A., & Wooton, E. X. (1996). *Hand printing of the Middle East and the subcontinent.* Paper presented at the meeting of the American Society of Questioned Document Examiners, Washington, DC.

Trueblood, E. (1963). *General philosophy.* New York: Harper & Row.

Trueman, P. (1991, May). When memory disobeys. *Ottawa Magazine*, 13–14.

Tucha, O., & Lange, K. W. (2004). Effects of nicotine chewing gum on a real-life motor task: A kinematic analysis of handwriting movements in smokers and non-smokers. *Psychopharmacology, 173*(1–2), 49–56.

Tucha, O., Tucha, L., & Lange, K. W. (2008). Graphonomics, automaticity and handwriting assessment. *Literacy, 42*(3), 145–155.

Tucha, O., Walitza, S., Mecklinger, L., Stasik, D., Sontag, T. A., & Lange, K. W. (2006). The effect of caffeine on handwriting movements in skilled writers. *Human Movement Science, 25*(4), 523–535.

Turnbull, S.J., Jones, A.E., & Allen, M. (2010). Identification of the class characteristics in the handwriting of Polish people writing in English. *Journal of Forensic Sciences, 55*(5), 1296–1303.

Tweedy, J. S. (1995). *A study of Hmong handwriting.* Paper presented at the meeting of the American Society of Questioned Document Examiners, Chicago, IL.

Twibell, J. M., & Zientek, E. L. (1995). On coincidentally matching signatures. *Science & Justice, 35*(3), 191–195.

Tytell, P. V. (1991). *Defining the terms "class characteristic" and "individual characteristic:" A progress* report. Paper presented at the meeting of the American Society of Questioned Document Examiners, Orlando, FL.

Tytell, P. V. (1995). *Pen pressure as an identifying characteristic of signatures — Verification from the computer.* Paper presented at the meeting of the American Society of Questioned Document Examiners, Chicago, IL.

United States v. King, 532 F. 2d 505 (Court of Appeals, 5th Circuit 1976).

United States v. Starzecpyzel, 880 F. Supp. 1027 (S.D.N.Y. 1995).

United States Bureau of the Chief Postal Inspector. (1954). *A manual for examiners of questioned documents.* Washington, DC: The Department.

Van der Plaats, R. E., & Van Galen, G. P. (1990). Effects of spatial and motor demands in handwriting. *Journal of Motor Behavior, 22*(3), 361–385.

Van der Plaats, R. E., & Van Galen, G. P. (1991). Allographic cariability in adult handwriting. *Human Movement Science, 10*(2–3), 291–300.

Vastrick, T. A. (1993). *1993 ASQDE handwriting systems survey.* Paper presented at the meeting of the American Society of Questioned Document Examiners, Ottawa, ON, Canada.

Vastrick, T. W. (1982). Illusions of tracing. *Journal of Forensic Science, 27*(1), 186–191. doi: 10.1520/jfs11463j.

Vernon, M. (2005). Fifty years of research on the intelligence of deaf and hard-of-hearing children: A review of literature and discussion of implications. *Journal of Deaf Studies and Deaf Education, 10*(3), 225–231. doi: 10.1093/deafed/eni024.

Vida, M.D., Nestor, A., Plaut, D.C., & Behrmann, M. (2016). *Spatiotemporal dynamics of similarly-based neural representations of facial identity.* Proceedings of the National Academy of Sciences. doi: 10.1073/PNAS 1614763114.

Walch, M. A., & Gantz, D. T. (2004). Pictographic-matching: A graph-based approach towards a language independent document exploitation platform. In *Proceedings of the First ACM Workshop on Hardcopy Document Processing*, 8–13 November 2004, Washington, DC. (pp. 53–64).

Wallner, T. (1975). Die relative konstanz der handschrift. *Zeitschrift für Menschenkunde, 39*, 139–147.

Walsh, E., Mehta, M. A., Oakley, D. A., Guilmette, D. N., Gabay, A., Halligan, P. W., & Deeley, Q. (2014). Using suggestion to model different types of automatic writing. *Consciousness and Cognition, 26*, 24–36.

Walters, A., & Flynn, W. J. (1974). The illusion of traced forgery on zinc oxide-coated photocopy paper. *Journal of Police Science and Administration, 2*(4), 376–380.

Walters, A. S., & Hening, W. A. (1992). Noise-induced psychogenic tremor associated with post-traumatic stress disorder. *Movement Disorders*, 7(4), 333–338.

Wann, J. P., & Athenes, S. (1987). *Structural influences in writing script: An analysis of highly skilled footwriting.* Proceedings of the 3rd International Symposium on Handwriting and Computer Applications, Montreal, QC, Canada.

Wann, J., & Nimmo-Smith, I. (1991). The control of pen pressure in handwriting: A subtle point. *Human Movement Science, 10*(2–3), 223–246.

Watkins, R., & Gorajczyk, J. (1996). *The effect of alcohol concentrations on handwriting.* Paper presented at the meeting of the American Academy of Forensic Sciences, Nashville, TN.

Watson, R. S., & Pobgee, P. J. (1979). A computer to check signatures. *Visual Language, 13*(3), 232–238.

Webster's New Encyclopedic Dictionary. (1995). Merriam-Webster Inc.New York: Black Dog & Leventhal Publishers.

Weiderman, K. (2012). *Illicit literacy and legitimate learning: Examining the situated learning experiences of graffiti writers in a small, northern California town.* Doctoral dissertation, Humboldt State University.

Weiss, E. H. (1982). *The writing system for engineers and scientists.* Englewood Cliffs, NJ: Prentice-Hall.

Welch, J. R. (1986). The linking of a counterfeit document to individual sheets of dry-transfer lettering through the transfer of fluorescent glue. *Journal of the Forensic Science Society, 26*(4), 253–256. doi: 10.1016/s0015-7368(86)72492-4.

Welch, J. R. (1996). *A review of handwriting search cases as an indicator of the individuality of handwriting.* Paper presented at the meeting of the American Society of Questioned Document Examiners, Washington, DC.

Wellingham-Jones, P. (1991a). Characteristics of handwriting of subjects with Multiple Sclerosis. *Perceptual and Motor Skills, 73*, 867–879. doi: 10.2466/pms.73.7.867-879.

Wellingham-Jones, P. (1991b). *Drugs and handwriting.* Tehama, CA: PWJ Publishing.

Wellingham-Jones, P. (1991c). Mouth-writing by a quadriplegic. *Perceptual and Motor Skills, 72*, 1324–1326. doi: 10.2466/pms.1991.72.3c.1324.

Wellman, F. L. (1913). *The art of cross-examination.* New York: Macmillan.

Wenderoth, M. (1989, Fall). *Frye test and competency. American Society of Questioned Document Examiners Newsletter.*

Werner, P., Rosenblum, S., Bar-On, G., Heinik, J., & Korczyn, A. (2006). Handwriting process variables discriminating mild Alzheimer's disease and mild cognitive impairment. *The Journals of Gerontology, 61*(4), 228–236.

Wetstein, J., Kam, M., & Conn, R. (1994). Proficiency of professional document examiners in writer identification. *Journal of Forensic Sciences, 39*(1), 5–14.

Whiting, F. (1997). Alternate handwriting styles-One writer or two? *International Journal of Forensic Document Examiners, 3*(2), 167–175.

Whiting, F. I. (1996). The application of reasoning to the evaluation of fundamental differences in handwriting comparisons. *Journal of Forensic Science, 41*(4), 634–640.

Whittaker, E. (1973). The adversary system: Role of the criminalist. *Journal of Forensic Sciences, 18*(3), 184–187. doi: 10.1520/jfs10439j.

Widla, T. (1990). The influence of spontaneous writing on stability of graphic features. *Forensic Science International, 46*(1–2), 63–67.

Wigmore, J. H. (1896). Proof by comparison of handwriting; its history. *American Law Review, 30*, 481.

Wigmore, J. H., Chadbourn, J. H., & McNaughton, J. T. (1940). *A treatise on the Anglo-American system of evidence in trials at common law: Including the statutes and judicial decisions of all jurisdictions of the United States and Canada.* Boston, MA: Little, Brown.

Will, E. J. (2012). Pilot study: Inferring relative speed of handwriting from the static trace. *Journal of Forensic Document Examination, 22*, 55–63.

Williams, R. M. (1985). *The bank robbery note file, an automated approach to document screening.* Paper presented at the meeting of the American Society of Questioned Document Examiners, Montreal, QC, Canada.

Williams, S. G. (1903). *The history of medieval education.* Syracuse, NY: C. W. Bardeen.

Wilson, S. K. (1912). Progressive lenticular degeneration: A familial nervous disease associated with cirrhosis of the liver. *The Lancet, 179*(4626), 1115–1119.

Winchester, J. M., & McCarthy, J. F. (1971). *Data obtained from a survey of the handwriting of black students in grades one through twelve in a study of the letter forms "J" and "W."* Paper presented at the meeting of the American Society of Questioned Document Examiners, Seattle, WA.

Wing, A. M. (1979). Variability in handwritten characters. *Visible Language, 13*(3), 283–296.

Wing, A. M. (1980). The height of handwriting. *Acta Psychologica, 46*(2), 141–151. doi: 10.1016/0001-6918(80)90006-2.

Wing, A. M., & Nimmo-Smith, I. (1987). The variability of cursive handwriting measure defined along a continuum: Letter specificity. *Journal of the Forensic Science Society, 27*(5), 297–306.

Wing, A. M., Nimmo-Smith, I., & Eldridge, M. A. (1983). The consistency of cursive letter formation as a function of position in the word. *Acta Psychologica, 54*(1), 197–204.

Wooton, E. X. (1994). *A preliminary discussion of research and reference materials using the U.S. INS collection of handwriting from other countries.* Paper presented at the meeting of the American Society of Questioned Document Examiners, Long Beach, CA.

Wrenshall, A. F., & Rankin, W. J. T. (1965). *Automation and the cheque file or document searching and the push button age.* Unpublished manuscript, Royal Canadian Mounted Police Fradulent Cheque Section.

Wrottesley, F. J. (1910). *The examination of witnesses in court, incl. examination in chief, cross-examination and re-examination.* Toronto: Carswell.

Yalon, D. (Ed.). (2003). *Graphology across cultures.* UK: British Institute of Graphologists.

Yan, J. H., Rountree, S., Massman, P., Smith Doody, R., & Li, H. (2008). Alzheimer's disease and mild cognitive impairment deteriorate fine movement control. *Journal of Psychiatric Research, 42*(14), 1203–1212.

Yancosek, K. E., & Mullineaux, D. R. (2011). Stability of handwriting performance following injury-induced hand-dominance transfer in adults: A pilot study. *Journal of Rehabilitation Research & Development, 48*(1), 59–68.

Young, P. T. (1931). Sex differences in handwriting. *Journal of Applied Psychology, 15*(5), 486–498. doi: 10.1037/h0072627.

Zhang, B., Srihari, S. N., & Lee, S. (2003). Individuality of handwritten characters. In *Proceedings of the Seventh International Conference on Document Analysis and Recognition-Volume 2* (pp. 1086). IEEE Computer Society.

Ziegler, L. F. (1988, September). *Nigerian handwriting.* Paper presented at the meeting of the American Society of Questioned Document Examiners and the Southwestern Association of Forensic Document Examiners, Aurora, CO.

Ziegler, L. F., & Trizna, L. A. (1994). *African hand printing.* Paper presented at the meeting of the American Society of Questioned Document Examiners, Long Beach, CA.

Zimmerman, J. (1991). *Handwriting identification based on an unaccustomed-hand standard.* Paper presented at the meeting of the American Society of Questioned Document Examiners, Orlando, FL.

Zirkle, G. A., King, P., McAtee, O. B., & Van Dyke, R. (1959). Effects of chlorpromazine and alcohol on coordination and judgment. *Journal of the American Medical Association, 171*(11), 1496–1499. doi: 10.1001/jama.1959.03010290054013.

Zirkle, G. A., McAtee, O, B., King, P. D., & Van Dyke, R, (1960). Meprobamate and small amounts of alcohol: Effects on human ability, coordination, and judgment. *Journal of the American Medical Association, 173*(16), 121–123. doi: 10.1001/jama.1960.03020340041011.

Zitzelsberger, A., The left-handed writer. (1958). In R. A. Huber (Ed.), *Questioned Documents in Crime Detection: Proceedings of the R.C.M.P. Crime Detection Laboratories Seminar No. 5 held at Ottawa, October 27-November 1, 1958.* (pp. 31–40). Ottawa: Queen's Printer.

Index

B

C

D

E

F

G

H

I

J

K

L

R

S

T

U

V

W

Z

For Product Safety Concerns and Information please contact our EU representative GPSR@taylorandfrancis.com Taylor & Francis Verlag GmbH, Kaufingerstraße 24, 80331 München, Germany

Batch number: 10722120

Printed by Printforce, the Netherlands